ZONDERVAN
HANDBOOK
of BIBLICAL
ARCHAEOLOGY

ZONDERVAN HANDBOOK
of BIBLICAL ARCHAEOLOGY

RANDALL PRICE with H. WAYNE HOUSE

ZONDERVAN®

ZONDERVAN

Zondervan Handbook of Biblical Archaeology
Copyright © 2017 by World of the Bible Ministries, Inc. and H. Wayne House

This title is also available as a Zondervan ebook.

Requests for information should be addressed to:
Zondervan, *3900 Sparks Dr. SE, Grand Rapids, Michigan 49546*

ISBN 978-0-310-28691-2

Cover design: Studio Gearbox
Cover imagery: © tunart/www.istock.com, © H. Wayne House, © Mark Connally/www.holyland photos.com, © Oren Gutfeld
Interior design: Kait Lamphere
Part pages imagery: © Markus Pfaff/Shutterstock, © WitR/Shutterstock, © Karel Gallas/ Shutterstock, Image Farm

Printed in the United States of America

17 18 19 20 21 22 23 24 25 26 27 /DCI/ 15 14 13 12 11 10 9 8 7 6 5 4 3 2

Dedication

To my wife Beverlee,
who has shared with me
in the pre-dawn risings,
long days of digging,
and thrilling discoveries.
You are my greatest treasure!
Proverbs 25:2

RANDALL PRICE

To my wife, Irina, whose love for Christ, the Bible, theology,
and archaeology inspires me in my own life and work.
"He who finds a wife finds a good thing,
and obtains favor from the LORD."
Proverbs 18:22 (NRSV)

H. WAYNE HOUSE

Acknowledgments

Without the assistance of many people a handbook of this nature could not be accomplished. The authors first and foremost express deep appreciation to their wives (Beverlee Price and Irina House) for their encouragement and loving support throughout the project. The authors also thank their respective schools (Liberty University, Faith International University, and Faith Seminary) for the use of their research facilities. Dr. Price is grateful for the research and photographic assistance of Ms. Ayelet Shapira, Mrs. Michele Cowell, Mr. David Beauregard, Mr. Britt Paramore, and Mr. Dan Stuart (for assistance in the preparation of several charts). He also expresses appreciation to Mr. Stephen Rost for preparing the indices, Dr. David Graves for assistance in preparing the glossary, and Dr. Oren Gutfeld of the Hebrew University Institute of Archaeology. Dr. House likewise wishes to thank his assistant Mrs. Elizabeth Summers for her help. The authors express sincere gratitude to the museums and institutions in the US, Germany, England, Israel, Jordan, Egypt, Greece, Turkey, and Italy that permitted them to research and photograph their collections. We also express thanks to Mr. Alexander Schick of the bibelausstellung in Sylt, Mr. Martin Severin of Inner-cube Publications for his expertise and use of photographs, Ayelet Shapira, Casey Olson and Alexandra Toy for photographic assistance, and many others as noted in the photo credits. Finally, we thank Zondervan Publisher Dr. Stan Gundry and Mr. Madison Trammel for allowing us to bring this work to the public, Dr. Nancy Erickson for her fine editorial work, Mrs. Kim Tanner for her design skill, and the entire Zondervan production team for their excellent craftsmanship in publishing which has made this handbook both a useful and beautiful complement for students and teachers of the Bible.

Table of Contents

List of Images... 8

Abbreviations... 11

Preface... 15

Introduction to Biblical Archaeology............................ 17

ARCHAEOLOGY AND THE OLD TESTAMENT

1. Introduction to Archaeology and the Old Testament 45
2. The Pentateuch 47
3. The Historical Books.. 106
4. Wisdom Literature 146
5. The Prophets 160
6. Archaeological Discoveries and the Old Testament.................... 194

ARCHAEOLOGY AND THE INTERTESTAMENTAL PERIOD

7. Introduction to the Intertestamental Period 203
8. The Second (Zerubbabel) Temple 205
9. The Second (Herodian) Temple 208
10. The Dead Sea Scrolls 218

ARCHAEOLOGY AND THE NEW TESTAMENT

11. Introduction to Archaeology and the New Testament 233
12. The Gospels and Acts 235
13. The Letters of Paul 308
14. The General Letters and Revelation............................... 322
15. Archaeological Discoveries and the New Testament 328

Maps... 333

Glossary 351

Endnotes... 359

Bibliography 379

Scripture and Extra-Biblical Index.............................. 395

Subject Index.. 404

List of Images

1. Chart, Formation Processes 23
2. Comparison of biblical and archaeological data 25
3. Rosetta Stone.............................. 30
4. Archaeological strata......................... 33
5. Taking level at Tel es-Safi.................... 34
6. Jar with bone deposit........................ 34
7. *lmlk* seal jar handle......................... 36
8. Handle of wine amphora 36
9. Oil lamp ceramic typology 37
10. Chart, Archaeological Periods 41
11. Enuma Elish............................... 48
12. Chart, Enuma Elisha Creation Account 48
13. Comparison of Adapa Story and Genesis 50
14. Chlorite cylinder seal 50
15. Iron Age plaques with griffins 51
16. Göbekli Tepe.............................. 53
17. T-shaped pillars at Göbekli Tepe 53
18. Human figure at Göbekli Tepe 54
19. Chart, Patriarchal Ages 55
20. Sumerian King List 56
21. Eridu Genesis.............................. 57
22. Ark Tablet 58
23. Gilgamesh Epic............................. 58
24. Chart, Gilgamesh Flood Epic 59
25. Atrahasis Epic 59
26. Chart, Atrahasis and Flood.................... 60
27. Ark Construction in biblical and ANE Accounts ..64
28. Babylonian World Map 65
29. Mt. Ararat 66
30. Bust of Sargon 69
31. Model, Eanna temple Ziggurat................. 70
32. Tower of Babel Stele 72
33. Chart, dating the Patriarchs 77
34. Cylinder seal impression...................... 78
35. MB gate at Tel Dan 82
36. Mud brick construction 84
37. Book of the Dead 86
38. Ipuwer Papyrus 89
39. Chart, Ipuwer and Exodus.................... 89
40. Merneptah Stele 90
41. Berlin Statue Pedestal Relief.................... 91
42. Burial chamber shrines........................ 92
43. Tomb of Tutankhamen........................ 92
44. Ark of the Covenant 94
45. Egyptian priests with an ark 94
46. Wooden chest of Tutankhamen................. 95
47. Portable shrine 95
48. Depiction of guardian figures.................. 96
49. 10 commandments............................ 97
50. Ark of Covenant model 97
51. Tomb 25 at Ketef Hinnom 99
52. Silver scroll (unopened) 100
53. Silver scroll (opened) 100
54. Balaam inscription.......................... 100
55. Bronze serpents............................ 102
56. Arnon boundary............................ 103
57. Mesha Inscription 104
58. Suzerain-Vassal treaty 105
59. Hittite suzerain-vassal treaty................. 105
60. Kadesh Agreement.......................... 107
61. Randall Price at Tel Jericho 108
62. Southern end of Tel Jericho 108
63. Reconstruction, Jericho N side................ 109
64. Chart, Bible/Archaeology on Jericho's Fall....... 110
65. Egyptian sickle sword 111
66. Altar on Mt. Ebal.......................... 112
67. Tell Qasile temple.......................... 113
68. Pillars in Tell Qasile temple.................. 114
69. Bulla from City of David 115
70. Incised holes for Tabernacle 115
71. Model of the Tabernacle...................... 116
72. Tel Shiloh 116
73. IA fortification walls........................ 118
74. Tel Dan Stele 119
75. Tel Zayit abecedary 120
76. Ophel Canaanite ostracon.................... 121
77. Ishba'al inscription......................... 122
78. Moon god Sin Stele 124
79. Geshur entrance gate........................ 124
80. Sarcophagus with six fingers 125

81. Polydactylism x-ray 126
82. Terracotta ritual house 128
83. First Temple model 128
84. 'Ain Dara' temple 129
85. Cherubim at 'Ain Dara' temple 130
86. Tel Motza zoomorphic figure 131
87. Solomonic wall 132
88. Shrines similar to First Temple 133
89. Garfinkel and model shrine .... .134
90. Shalmanezzer III obelisk 136
91. Randall Price on Broad Wall 137
92. Siloam Inscription 137
93. Jerusalem Prism 138
94. King Jehoichin Ration Tablet 139
95. Zechariah bowl fragment 140
96. King Uzziah Inscription 141
97. Hagab seal 143
98. Nehemiah's wall 144
99. Xerxes relief 145
100. Chart, Wisdom Literature 148
101. Timna Park shaft 151
102. Deep shaft 151
103. Lachish relief 152
104. Iron Age II seal 153
105. Figure of Baal 154
106. Dead Sea text of Psalm 22:16 155
107. En-Gedi caves 156
108. Mesopotamian school 158
109. Sumerian love poem 159
110. Sargon II 161
111. Royal steward inscription 162
112. Bulla with crucial missing letter 162
113. *Messianic Rule* scroll 163
114. Cyrus cylinder 167
115. Great Isaiah scroll 168
116. Gabriel Revelation 169
117. Lachish Letters with YHWH 170
118. Documents sealed with bullae 171
119. Lamentation over ruin of Ur 173
120. Madaba Map 174
121. Clay temple model 176
122. Fragment of 1QDaniel 178
123. Ashurnasirpal II cylinder seal 181
124. Hittite vassal treaty 182
125. Chart, Nineveh's repentance 184

126. Fall of Ninevah (Babylonian Chronicle) 185
127. Assyrian soldiers on relief 186
128. Ekron inscription 188
129. Sy Gitin and Trude Dothan 188
130. Seven-spouted oil lamp 189
131. Chart, OT Archaeological Discoveries 194–200
132. Papyrus Fouad 266 204
133. Mt. Gerizim 206
134. Herodian Temple 209
135. Second Temple quarry 210
136. Herodian street 211
137. Temple menorah on plaster 212
138. "Pure for God" seal 213
139. Remains of Soreg inscription 214
140. Torah scroll medallion 217
141. Chart, OT books in Dead Sea Scrolls 218
142. Classifying Dead Sea Scrolls 219
143. Muhammad Ubiayt at Cave 1 219
144. Randall Price inside cave 53 220
145. Scroll fragment from cave 53 220
146. Temple Scroll jar 220
147. Temple scroll 221
148. Copper Scroll 221
149. Significance of Dead Sea Scrolls 223
150. Artist conception of Qumran 224
151. Descent to Cave 6 225
152. Qumran Plateau excavation 226–27
153. Price Qumran excavations 228
154. Ovoid store jar with bowl lid 229
155. Animal bone deposit at Qumran 229
156. ICHTHUS, Nativity Church 236
157. Aerial view, Nativity Church 236
158. Star marking Christ's birthplace 236
159. "Property of Herod" ostraca 237
160. Palace of Herod the Great 237
161. Herod's palace, Masada 238
162. Herod's fortress, Masada 239
163. Temple Mount from Mt. Olives 238–39
164. Temple Mount's southern wall 240
165. Temple Mount's western wall 240
166. Synagogue, Herodium 241
167. Site of Herod's tomb 242
168. Herod's tomb model 242
169. Herod's sarcophagus 243
170. Pinnacle of the Temple 244

171. "Our Father" Anagram.........................245
172. Peter's house (uncovered)......................246
173. Peter's house (detail) 247
174. Ruins of Chorazim.............................248
175. Magdala stone table...........................249
176. Mt. Zion ossuaries 250
177. Seat of Moses, Chorazim 251
178. Tomb of Absalom..............................252
179. Tomb of Zechariah 253
180. Randall Price and fallen stones..................254
181. Temple destruction evidence.....................255
182. Crucified man heel bone 257
183. Tomb near Megiddo 258
184. Place holder for plug tomb......................259
185. Rolling-stone tomb 259
186. Diagram, rolling-stone tomb.....................260
187. First-century fishing boat.......................263
188. Theodotus inscription 264
189. Tombstone, Q. Aemiulus Secundus 267
190. Capernaum synagogue..........................268
191. Remains, first-century synagogue 269
192. Kursi cave chapel 270
193. Kursi Byzantine church 270
194. OT and NT Jerichos............................272
195. Herod's Winter Palace, Jericho 272
196. Roman Road to Jericho.........................273
197. Pontius Pilate inscription........................274
198. Chart, Pilate inscription.........................275
199. Site of Bethany 276
200. Burial cave at Bethany..........................277
201. Bethany baptism site 278
202. Sea of Galilee 279
203. Entrance to Bethsaida..........................281
204. Mt. Gerizim...................................285
205. Jacob's well 285
206. Site of Samaritan temple........................286
207. Samaritan Priest and scholar.....................286
208. Pool of Bethesda...............................288
209. Pool of Siloam 289
210. Drawing of first-century Pool....................289
211. Caiaphas' house 291
212. Caiaphas' house ancient steps 291
213. Prison at Caiaphas' house.......................292
214. Chain holes in prison walls 292
215. Caiaphas' Ossuary 293

216. John Ryland Papyrus...........................293
217. Akeldama.....................................294
218. Nicanor Gate..................................295
219. Double Gate today.............................296
220. Drawing of "Beautiful Gate".....................297
221. Caesarea Hippodrome 297
222. Caesarea Theater 298
223. Lintel from Corinth synagogue 301
224. Inscription of Gallio 302
225. Ephesus theater................................303
226. Asiarch inscription.............................305
227. Temple warning stone...........................307
228. Erastus Inscription.............................309
229. Artemis statue.................................313
230. Mural of Paul and Thecla.......................314
231. Philippian jail 315
232. Inside Philippian jail 315
233. Apostle Philip's grave 318
234. Inside Philip's grave 318
235. Plan of Olympia sanctuary.......................320
236. Antikes Olympia stadium 321
237. Ancient Olympic starting line 321
238. Strigil..323
239. Smyrna.......................................324
240. Agora in Smyrna...............................325
241. Graffito.......................................325
242. Altar of Zeus 326
243. Chart, NT Archaeological Discoveries 328–331
244. Map, Ancient world............................333
245. Map, EB IV- MB I 334
246. Map, MB-LB III...............................335
247. Map, Routes of the Exodus 336
248. Map, IA I Sites................................337
249. Map, IA II Sites...............................338
250. Map, Persian Period Israel 339
251. Map, Hellenistic Period 340
252. Map, Hasmonean Period 341
253. Map, Second Temple Period 342
254. Map, First-century Roman Empire................343
255. Map, First-century Asia Minor...................344
256. Map, First Temple Jerusalem.....................345
257. Map, Persian Period Jerusalem...................346
258. Map, Second Temple Jerusalem 347
259. Map, Modern Middle East 348
260. Map, Modern Israel............................349

Abbreviations

AB	Anchor Bible
ABD	*Anchor Bible Dictionary*. Edited by David Noel Freedman. 6 vols. New York: Doubleday, 1992
ABW	*Archaeology in the Biblical World*
ACB	Archaeological Commentary on the Bible
AJSL	*American Journal of Semitic Languages and Literatures*
ANEP	*The Ancient Near East in Pictures Relating to the Old Testament*. 2nd ed. Edited by James B. Pritchard. Princeton: Princeton University Press, 1994
ANET	*Ancient Near Eastern Texts Relating to the Old Testament*. Edited by James B. Pritchard. 3rd ed. Princeton: Princeton University Press, 1969
ANF	Ante-Nicene Fathers
ANT	*Archaeology of the New Testament*. Jack Finegan. Princeton: Princeton University Press, 1992
A&NT	*Archaeology and the New Testament*. John McRay. Grand Rapids: Baker Books, 2003
ARCH	*Archaeology*
AUDS	Andrews University Dissertation Series
AUSS	*Andrews University Seminary Studies*
BA	*Biblical Archaeologist*
BAR	*Biblical Archaeology Review*
BASOR	*Bulletin of the American Schools of Oriental Research*
BASORSUP	Bulletin of the American Schools of Oriental Research Supplement
BBR	*Bulletin for Biblical Research*
BBRSUP	*Bulletin for Biblical Research, Supplements*
BCOTWP	Baker Commentary on the Old Testament Wisdom and Psalms
BDB	Brown, Francis, S. R. Driver, and Charles A. Briggs. *A Hebrew and English Lexicon of the Old Testament*
BEP	Bethsaida Excavation Project
BIB	*Biblica*
BIIW	*The Bible In Its World: The Bible and Archaeology Today*. K. A. Kitchen. Eugene, OR: Wipf and Stock, 2004
BO	Bibliotheca Orientalis
BREV	*Bible Review*
B&S	*Bible and Spade*
BSAC	*Bibliotheca Sacra*
BWL	*Babylonian Wisdom Literature*. Wilfred G. Lambert. Oxford: Claredon, 1960
CAD	*The Assyrian Dictionary of the Oriental Institute of the University of Chicago*. Chicago: The Oriental Institute of the University of Chicago, 1956–2006

CAH	Cambridge Ancient History
CBQ	*Catholic Biblical Quarterly*
CHB	*Cambridge History of the Bible*. Edited by P. R. Ackroyd, et al. New York: Cambridge University Press, 1984
CONBOT	Coniectanea Biblica: Old Testament Series
COS	*Context of Scripture*. Edited by William W. Hallo and K. Lawson Younger. 3 vols. Boston: Brill, 2003
CTM	*Concordia Theological Monthly*
CTR	*Criswell Theological Review*
CUSAS	Cornell University Studies in Assyriology and Sumerology
DCH	*Dictionary of Classical Hebrew*. Edited by David J. A. Clines. 9 vols. Sheffield: Sheffield Phoenix Press, 1993–2014
DDD	*Dictionary of Deities and Demons in the Bible*. Edited by Karel van der Toorn, Bob Becking, and Pieter W. van der Horst. Leiden: Brill, 1995. 2nd rev. ed. Grand Rapids: Eerdmans, 1999
DJD	Discoveries in the Judean Desert
DSD	*Dead Sea Discoveries*
EAEHL	*Encyclopedia of Archaeological Excavations in the Holy Land*. Edited by Michael Avi-Yonah. 4 vols. Jerusalem: Israel Exploration Society and Massada press, 1975
EDSS	*Encyclopedia of the Dead Sea Scrolls*. Edited by Lawrence H. Schiffman and James C. VanderKam. 2 vols. New York: Oxford University Press, 2000
EVQ	*Evangelical Quarterly*
GKC	*Gesenius' Hebrew Grammar*. Edited by Emil Kautzsch. Translated by Arther E. Cowley. 2nd ed. Oxford: Clarendon, 1910
GTJ	*Grace Theological Journal*
HALOT	*The Hebrew and Aramaic Lexicon of the Old Testament*. Ludwig Koehler, Walter Baumgartner, and Johann J. Stamm. 3rd ed. Leiden: Brill, 1995, 2004
HCOT	Historical Commentary on the Old Testament
HSM	Harvard Semitic Mongraphs
HTR	*Harvard Theological Review*
IAA	Israel Antiquities Authority
IB	*Interpreter's Bible*. Edited by George A. Buttrick et al. 12 vols. New York: Abingdon, 1951–1957
IDB	*The Interpreter's Dictionary of the Bible*. Edited by George A. Buttrick. 4vols. New York: Abingdon, 1962
IDBSUP	*Interpreter's Dictionary of the Bible Supplementary Volume*. Edited by Keith Crim. Nashville: Abingdon, 1976
IEJ	*Israel Exploration Journal*
ISBE	*International Standard Bible Encyclopedia*. Edited by Geoffrey W. Bromiley. 4 vols. Grand Rapids: Eerdmans, 1979–1988
JAC	*Jahrbuch für Antike und Christentum*

JAOS	*Journal of the American Oriental Society*
JBL	*Journal of Biblical Literature*
JCS	*Journal of Cuneiform Studies*
JEA	*Journal of Egyptian Archaeology*
JETS	*Journal of the Evangelical Theological Society*
JNES	*Journal of Near Eastern Studies*
JSOT	*Journal for the Study of the Old Testament*
JSOTSUP	Journal for the Study of the Old Testament Supplement Series
JJS	*Journal of Jewish Studies*
JSS	*Journal of Semitic Studies*
LCL	Loeb Classical Library
LPPTS	*The Library of the Palestine Pilgrim's Text Society*
LTB	*Lost Treasures of the Bible.* Clyde E. Fant. Grand Rapids, 2008
NEA	*Near Eastern Archaeology*
NEAEHL	*The New Encyclopedia of Archaeological Excavations in the Holy Land.* Edited by Ephraim Stern. 4 vols. Jerusalem: Israel Exploration Society & Carta; New York: Simon & Schuster, 1993
NPNF	Nicene and Post-Nicene Fathers
NOVT	*Novum Testamentum*
NTS	*New Testament Studies*
OGIS	*Orientis Graeci Inscriptions Selectae.* Edited by Wilhelm Dittenberger. 2 vols. Leipzig: Hirzel, 1903–1905
OIP	Oriental Institute Publications
ORANT	*Oriens Antiquus*
OROT	*On the Reliability of the Old Testament.* Kenneth A. Kitchen. Grand Rapids: Eerdmans, 2003
OTM	Old Testament Message
OTS	Old Testament Studies
PEQ	*Palestine Exploration Quarterly*
RB	*Revue biblique*
REVQ	*Revue de Qumran*
SBLDS	Society of Biblical Literature Dissertation Series
STDJ	Studies on the Texts of the Desert of Judah
TYNBUL	*Tyndale Bulletin*
TDOT	*Theological Dictionary of the Old Testament.* Edited by G. Johannes Botterweck and Helmer Ringgren. Translated by John T. Willis et al. 8 vols. Grand Rapids: Eerdmans, 1974–2006
THEM	*Themelios*
TWOT	*Theological Wordbook of the Old Testament.* Edited by R. Laird Harris, Gleason L. Archer Jr., and Bruce K. Waltke. 2 vols. Chicago: Moody Press, 1980
UF	*Ugarit-Forschungen*
VT	*Vetus Testamentum*

VTSUP	Supplements to Vetus Testamentum
WAW	Writings from the Ancient World
WBC	Word Biblical Commentary
WTJ	*Westminster Theological Journal*
ZAW	*Zeitschrift für die alttestamentliche Wissenschaft*
ZIBBC	*Zondervan Illustrated Bible Backgrounds Commentary*. Edited by John Walton and Clint Arnold. 9 vols. Grand Rapids: Zondervan, 2009
ZPEB	*Zondervan Pictorial Encyclopedia of the Bible*. Edited by Merrill C. Tenney. 5 vols. Grand Rapids: Zondervan, 1975

Preface

You are involved in Bible study and have come across something in the text that relates to ancient persons, places, or events. How can you understand this past context? What is needed is to travel back in time and see the ancient world, what the cities were like that the biblical figures occupied and how its people lived, and then to understand from them the meaning they attached to their religion and customs. In other words, it is necessary to understand the biblical message in its original historical context before we can apply its truths in our own time. If this were possible, you would be able to add deeper meaning and more reality to your experience with the Bible.

Although we cannot return to the past, it can come to us. It is available to us in the form of the historical and archaeological records. The historical record consists of documents (including the Bible) that have been retained or recovered in living societies to preserve evidence of earlier behavior. The archaeological record contains culturally deposited objects that are no longer a part of an ongoing society but, once found, furnish evidence along with the historical record of the past.

The science of archaeology is a modern means of revealing the lost record of the ancient world and, for the student of Scripture, the world of the Bible. While its purpose is not to prove (or disprove) the historicity of the people and events recorded in Scripture, it can help immeasurably to confirm the historical reality and accuracy of the Bible and to demonstrate that faith has a factual foundation. Moreover, it serves to illustrate and illuminate the background and context of Scripture so that the alien world of the past becomes more understandable in the present.

Archaeology is an art as well as a science and therefore requires interpretation. Within the Christian community different positions have been adopted with respect to the understanding of biblical events, especially those that occurred in the earliest historical periods. At this time, the archaeological evidence for the earliest recorded biblical events is sparse or unattainable and offers a challenge for interpreters who seek to reconcile the Genesis account with historical evidence from the material culture. Nevertheless, we know more today about the background of the pre-patriarchal and patriarchal periods than did those who have gone before us. Our approach in this handbook has been to give what information is available from the archaeological record and to allow the reader to draw his or her own conclusions. Having said this, it is our conviction that the archaeological evidence known to date supports an historical and literal interpretation of the biblical events and is expected to continue to do so with future excavations.

It should be noted, however, that while we believe the results of archaeology, properly applied and interpreted with respect to the biblical and extrabiblical texts, can be used in the field of biblical apologetics, a caution must be issued concerning sensationalist claims based on unsupported or unverified archaeological evidence, often called "pseudo-archaeology." Such claims often appear on the internet or in the tabloids (and sometimes in national news), but, as in any field of research, those who are untrained in a specific field, even though academically trained, should not publish their claims until they have done meticulous research and presented it for peer review. Unfortunately, people of faith tend to unquestionably accept such sensational claims without examining the qualifications of those who make them or the sources they use. They cannot necessarily be criticized for this deficiency since the nature of inquiry is usually beyond their grasp, but the result is a misrepresentation of facts and a distortion and diminution of the very truth of the Bible that people believe the claims support.[1] For that reason there is the need for greater discernment with regard to archaeological claims that are said to prove the Bible in one way or another. If a claim seems too good to be true, it often is, and experts in the field should be consulted for confirmation.

Safe sites for accurate archaeological critique and review of controversial discoveries include biblearchaeology.org, the information website of the Associates for Biblical Research (a body of evangelical field archaeologists and professional researchers conducting active excavations and publishing in the field of biblical and archaeological studies); the magazine *Artifacts*, published by the Near East Archaeological Society, an evangelical organization offering the latest news and professional reviews of archaeological discoveries; and *Biblical Archaeology Review*, which often showcases field archaeologists' work in progress long before official reports are published and seeks to give archaeological insight into biblical subjects (though not usually written from the perspective of a biblical worldview). By accessing these popular/academic resources the student of the Bible who wants to integrate archaeological data into biblical research can avoid sensationalist material and make a reasonable evaluation of the evidence.

Our attempt in this handbook of biblical archaeology is to provide a window to the biblical past through the information available from the field of archaeology. There are numerous books and sets of books that accomplish this purpose, but the information they provide is often too voluminous or too technical for the average student of Scripture. In addition, archaeologists have made new discoveries that have not received comment in popular books on archaeology. Without access to the academic journals and field reports, most people's acquaintance with these new discoveries is from media sources that often do not objectively interpret the finds or put them in a proper biblical context. One of the aims of this work has been to give priority to the most recent discoveries and relate them (where possible) to biblical texts. Therefore, while this book has been highly selective in the number of texts and archaeological examples, it has attempted to be as contemporary as possible (while not neglecting the historic archaeological finds most important for biblical studies). The decision to relate the archaeological finds to biblical texts in the canonical order was based on the desire to demonstrate the usefulness of archaeology to biblical studies and to make the work as accessible and practical as possible for those interested in studying the Bible.

The authors have had significant experience in the fields of both archaeology and biblical studies. Both are active professors teaching biblical studies and archaeology at the undergraduate and graduate levels, and both have done graduate studies or had extensive experience in the lands of the Bible. Both have worked at numerous archaeological sites in Israel and one (Randall Price) directed for over a decade the archaeological excavations on the Qumran Plateau, the site of the community that produced the famous Dead Sea Scrolls, as well as one of the Dead Sea area caves. Both have also served in pastoral and apologetic contexts and have an understanding of how archaeological studies can be applied in ministry.

If the past is a key to the present, we hope that this resource will open to readers the real world of the Bible, reassuring our generation of the historicity of the people, places, and events it describes while enhancing their understanding and enjoyment of the Word of God.

Introduction to Biblical Archaeology

Archaeology has only recently emerged as a field of science (about 200 years ago), and as a discipline it is still in a state of flux. The word "archaeology" is formed from the Greek words *archaios* ("ancient") and *logia* ("word, study of"). Therefore, in its most basic meaning the Greek term *archaiologia* ("archaeology") is a word about or a study of ancient history or culture and the places from which they derive. Definitions of archaeology may differ based on the different aims of a particular archaeologist.[1] However, what is common to all types of archaeology is the recovery and study of the material culture of past civilizations. *Biblical* archaeology, as a subset of the general field, may be defined as an application of the science of archaeology to the field of biblical studies. The Bible, as Old Testament, is a selective account of the history of a people and a place in relation to God. As New Testament, this account is furthered, and its history includes other peoples and lands, particularly in relation to God in the person of Jesus Christ. In relation to these concerns, biblical archaeology deals with the tangible remains of the history of the places and the people within, or providing reference to, the biblical context. The Bible has a theological perspective; archaeology has a scientific perspective. Yet when brought together in the service of a greater knowledge that informs both, a new discipline is created, joining archaeological research with biblical interpretation to the benefit of both the academy and the pulpit.

This relationship was instrumental to the advent and advancement of archaeology. In the nineteenth century the lands of the Bible were opened to exploration at about the same time that historical criticism was posing questions regarding the historicity of the Bible.

Bible-believing explorers, sponsored by geographical and historical societies (such as the Palestine Exploration Fund), employed archaeological techniques to uncover ancient sites with the express intent of providing scientific evidence in support of the Bible. In a preface to a work analyzing how biblical interpretation used archaeological evidence in this early period, Professor J. Edward Wright criticizes the attitudes and actions of both academics and popularists of the day:

> Many of the practitioners in the twentieth century were devout people—mostly Christians—who thought that archaeology could provide them with "scientific evidence" to prove the Bible's historicity and concomitantly, its theology. They firmly believed that archaeology could bolster their confessional apologetics and help them defend their religious beliefs in a society that increasingly valued "scientific" evidence. It was only natural that untrained and ill-informed popularizers would seize upon the "scholarly" discoveries, interpret them within their theological matrix, and exploit them shamelessly for their purposes.[2]

A leading voice during this period in support of using archaeology together with the Bible was William Foxwell Albright, the acknowledged dean of American biblical archaeology: "Discovery after discovery has established the accuracy of innumerable details, and has brought increased recognition of the value of the Bible as a source of history."[3] This use of archaeology should not be overly criticized, as many have done, as though it reduced the discipline simply to an apology for the Bible. Those who used archaeology for this purpose respected its methodology and furthered its development. After all, archaeology is a tool for recovering "something" of the ancient past, and that "something" has more importance than the tool itself. It may be suspected that such criticism is rooted more in the priority given to the Bible than in the lack of priority given to the broader use of archaeology. Nevertheless, the majority of publications utilizing biblical archaeology have reflected a positive respect for the contribution it has made to biblical studies. One discovery that has highlighted this importance has been the discovery of the Dead Sea Scrolls. The ongoing study of these documents and of the archaeology of the Qumran community that produced them has revolutionized our understanding of the accuracy of the transmission of the Hebrew text and of the religious perspectives and practices of Jewish sects in late Second Temple Judaism.

A more critical, even skeptical, attitude toward the use of archaeology with the Bible dominated scholarship at the end of the twentieth century and into the twenty-first. In part this was a reaction to overstatements of archaeological and biblical connections made earlier in the twentieth century by leading figures in the field, such as W. F. Albright and his assistant G. Ernest Wright. However, this is attributable primarily to challenges raised by the field of historical criticism that undermined the Bible as a consistently reliable historical document.

The alleged lack of historical confirmation from archaeology for biblical persons and events created a tension between biblical studies and archaeology. In response, some religious leaders and institutions began to distance biblical studies from archaeology (fearful that the field was now controlled by secularists and critics of the Bible) while secular archaeologists working in the lands of the Bible began to distance their practice from reference to the Bible (fearful that they would be labeled as religiously motivated).

The Use of the Term "Palestine" and "Palestinian" in Biblical Archaeology

The commonly accepted term for archaeological research conducted in the southern Levant is Syro-Palestinian or Palestinian archaeology. Although the term is used with reference to ancient Palestine, this was never a name used in the Bible for the place where the ancient Hebrews settled (the land of Canaan). The only use of the term "Palestine" in an English rendering of the Bible is in the KJV's translation of Joel 3:4. Here the verse describes the Philistine coastal plain (Philistia). The KJV translates "Palestine" for the Hebrew term *peleshet*, used some 250 times in the Hebrew Bible to denote Philistia or the Philistines. Similarly, the term "Palestinian" is not used in the Hebrew Bible to designate the ancient people group descended from Abraham (Hebrews, Israelites, Jews, and Ishmaelites).

In the Old Testament, the Hebrew terms used to describe the region that encompassed geographical sites east and west of the river Jordan including lower Syria are ʾEretz-Yisrael ("land of Israel") or just *Yisrael* ("Israel"). This is the same designation that was previously identified as the "land of Canaan," given to Israel as an "everlasting possession" (Gen 17:8; cf. 28:4; 48:4; Exod 6:8; Lev 14:34; Deut 1:8; 2:12; 4:1, 5; 6:11,18; 9:23; 11:31; Josh 1:15 et al.). This "land of promise" was defined geographically in various biblical texts (Gen 15:18; Exod 23:31; Deut 1:7; Josh 1:4; 12:1). Today this region is divided into Israel, the West Bank (biblical Judea & Samaria), the Hashemite Kingdom of Jordan, Lebanon, and parts of Syria.

Although publications make reference to "Palestine in the time of Christ," the New Testament usage follows the Old Testament; the land where Jesus lived is referred to in the Greek New Testament simply as "the land of Israel" (Matt 2:20–21; 10:23).

A derivative of the name "Palestine" first appears in Greek literature in the fifth century BC when the historian Herodotus called the area *Palaistinē*, possibly because this had been a term used by the Egyptians to describe the land to the northeast of Egypt. However, classical use of the term "Palestine" came from Roman sources as a result of the Emperor Hadrian changing the Roman name for the land of Israel ("Judea" and "Galilee") to *Palaestina* and the name of Jerusalem to *Aelia Capitolina* in AD 135. This was meant to minimize Jewish identification with the land of Israel as a punitive measure against the Jews who staged the Second Jewish Revolt. Essentially, Hadrian took the name of the ancient enemies of Israel, the Philistines, latinized it to Palestine, and applied the name to the land of Israel. By this act he had hoped to erase the name Israel from historical memory. This may have also been an act of Hellenization (abhorrent to religious Jews and Jewish nationalists) because the Philistines originated (and had been expelled) from Greece's Aegean islands.

The term "Palestine" entered into Christian parlance through the writings of Eusebius, the favored bishop of the Roman Emperor Constantine (fourth century AD). Eusebius rejected the name *Aelia* for Jerusalem, considered a Christian city, but accepted the name "Palestine" for Israel in compliance with Constantine's anti-Jewish policy. This nomenclature was then assimilated into Christian vocabulary as the Byzantine Empire was being established and continued in later Christian usage, although in the time of the Crusades (AD 1055–1205) the land of Israel was called the Kingdom of Jerusalem.

The next use of the term "Palestine" fell under the Ottoman Empire (1517–1917) when the label became a general designation of the land south of Syria. This does not appear to have been an official designation, as Ottomans and Arabs who lived in Palestine during this time referred to their area as southern Syria. For example, George Habib Antonius, the leading historian of Arab nationalism, considered Palestine to be part of greater Syria. Following the Ottoman period of rule (1917), the term Palestine was used during the British Mandate (1920–1948), but at that time the label referred to both the lands of present-day Israel and Jordan. After Jordan became a separate country (1922), the term "Palestine" was used to denote the places occupied by both Arabs (Palestinian Arabs) and Jews (Palestinian Jews), although prior to the establishment of the state of Israel in 1948 the international press commonly referred to Jews as Palestinians, and not Arabs.

After Israeli independence, those living inside the borders recognized as the state of Israel were known either as Israeli Arabs or Israeli Jews, while those outside this territory either retained a national (Jordanian, Syrian, Egyptian, etc.) or tribal (Bedouin) identity. It was not until the creation of the Palestine Liberation Organization that the term Palestine was used by Arabs, and even then it stood for the land of Israel that they sought to liberate. The term "Palestine" was then adopted by those who were not Israeli citizens living under Israeli rule (West Bank, Golan Heights, Gaza) but has now become the accepted designation for those who consider themselves under occupation, including Israeli citizens (Israeli Arabs). Therefore, the modern use of the term is political rather than historical, and certainly not biblical.

The term "Palestine" with reference to archaeology may be used to avoid the appearance of political bias; however, this is no longer the case since there now exists the distinct entities of the state of Israel with the Israeli Antiquities Authority and the Palestinian Authority with its Palestinian Institute of Archaeology at Bir Zeit University in the West Bank and the Department of Antiquities in Gaza. Moreover, many modern scholars employ the expression biblical archaeology as opposed to Syro-Palestinian and Palestinian archaeology in order to emphasize its relationship with biblical studies. When the focus is on sites within the modern state of Israel (including the disputed territories), the remains of ancient Israelite towns and cities should be identified as Israelite, not Palestinian. This best reflects

historical and archaeological accuracy. Consequently, in this book we have described these regions as biblical Israel (not ancient Palestine or Palestine in the time of Christ) and have employed the phrase archaeology of Israel with reference to archaeological excavations performed in sites identified with the ancient and modern land of Israel.

Biblical Archaeology Today

Further into the twenty-first century, biblical archaeology began migrating back to the field of biblical studies, though not without significant change and challenges. The theories and methods of historical criticism have moved from the realm of scholarship to popular publication and the ever-expanding documentary-entertainment media. The aim has been to enshrine archaeology as real science and to use it to discredit the historical claims of the Bible by demonstrating the absence of supportive data or even contradictory data. Biblically themed films by atheist or agnostic producers have entertained the public while promoting the idea that the Genesis account of the flood and the Exodus account of the Hebrew enslavement and the conquest of Canaan was fiction. Treating biblical accounts in the same manner as Greek mythology, filmmakers have taken creative liberties in altering characters and storylines to fit their imaginative fancy. Some television documentaries, though making use of archaeological research, have used this data to challenge the historicity of Jesus and subsequently declared that no one knows who wrote the New Testament.[4]

In our time, theological shifts, new political realities, and the concern for academic integrity have changed the focus in archaeology from obtaining biblical evidence to a strict scientific approach, a change reflected in new terms for the discipline such as Syro-Palestinian

archaeology or archaeology of the Levant. Therefore, while the science of archaeology has returned to biblical studies, its purpose is sometimes more of a critique of the Bible than a contribution to biblical studies. This viewpoint results not from the approach to the discipline or methodology of archaeology but from the approach to the interpretation of the Bible. If the Bible is viewed as primarily a religious or theological document in contrast to the archaeological data, there will be less inclination to see the Bible as a reliable historical witness to the archaeological sites and the finds that come from them. On the other hand, if the Bible is viewed as both a religious document and an historical document in concert with the archaeological data, it will be given priority in both the selection of archaeological sites and the analysis of their finds. As John Oswalt has observed, "the biblical worldview provides the basis for genuine history writing."[5] These divergent approaches have today crystalized into distinct camps known as "minimalism" and "maximalism."

Minimalists and Maximalists

Simply stated, biblical minimalists are those who minimalize the biblical data in deference to the archaeological data. Biblical maximalists are those who maximize (or prioritize) the biblical data with reference to the archaeological data. Minimalists are critical of past premature interpretations of sites or their finds that make them fit with biblical texts, aware that later excavations have sometimes altered earlier conclusions. However, they are also aware that newer discoveries have also overturned older critical views of the Bible. Minimalists further argue that where the archaeological data has failed to demonstrate the existence of a site or habitation of a site according to biblical chronology, the biblical data should be reevaluated as to its historicity (though not necessarily its theological teaching). For example, the lack of archaeological evidence within a biblical chronology for the patriarchal period through the early monarchy has compelled some minimalists to conclude that the patriarchs did not exist, that the Israelite sojourn and exodus in Egypt did not occur, that the city of Jericho had been destroyed long before the time of Joshua, that the Israelite entrance into Canaan was only by means of a gradual infiltration, and that the figures of David and Solomon (and Jerusalem as their storied capital) is an idyllic etiology or religious propagana invented in the postexilic period. While minimalists do not discount the value of the Bible, they view it primarily as religious or theological stories that may contain bits of historical information rather than as a complete and reliable historical document.

Maximalists critique the more complete documentary evidence of the biblical text and argue that the absence of evidence is not necessarily evidence of absence. Some, like William Dever, charge minimalists of servicing their postmodern historical perspective by a selective use of the archaeological data. His methodology has demonstrated that the remains of the Iron Age I–IIA (1200–925 BC) support the historical accuracy of the Bible in its account of the early monarchy and therefore provides grounds for interpreting historicity in those areas where archaeological evidence is minimal or lacking.[6] In this light, maximalists may remind minimalists of faulty past conclusions based on the lack of archaeological evidence, such as the case of the biblical figure of King David, who was once considered an exaggeration since no archaeological inscription had ever been found bearing a reference to him. However, in 1993 the broken remains of a monumental stele were discovered in secondary usage in the excavations at Tel Dan with an Aramaic inscription containing the dynastic eponym "house of David," the familiar title for Israel used in the Hebrew Bible. If there was a "house" of David, there had to be a David to have a house. Likewise, the criticism against an empire for David and Solomon, because of the paucity of evidence from tenth-century-BC excavations in their capital of Jerusalem, has been answered by the discovery at Khirbet Qeiyafa, a tenth-century fortified Judean town attesting a palace (administrative building), ritual objects, and perhaps an archive. If a small town on the outskirts of Judah could have such impressive evidence of an empire, surely the capital of that empire was even more established. In addition, finds of ritual shrines at Khirbet Qeiyafa predate the Solomonic temple by thirty years but utilize important architectural designs written in the Torah that describe how the temple should be constructed. Add to this the nearly contemporary Syrian temples that bear a similar tri-partite layout and architectural features (including cherubim figures) and it becomes difficult to discount the historicity of the First Temple.

Maximalists believe that the archaeological data should speak for itself before combining it with literary data, whether from the Bible or any other document. They recognize that the Bible has compositional complexities and that care must be taken before attempting to find biblical or other historical parallels or correspondences. However, it is more likely than not that excavation in the sites (or suspected sites) mentioned in the Bible will have a touchpoint with the history it records. Moreover, due to the inherent limitations of archaeology, maximalists believe that the literary texts must be considered (and given priority) as a more complete record if the archaeological data is to tell its story in the full context of history.

The Abbreviations BC and AD

BC ("before Christ") and AD (*anno Domini*, "in the year of our Lord") are abbreviations that have been employed in classical history since the Roman monk Dionysius Exiguus introduced the system in AD 500 (although the first recorded use of the related concept BC is with the Venerable Bede, AD 700). While the use of these terms assumes a Christian worldview, their almost exclusive use in Western literature argues for their use in this publication whose audience is primarily Christian students, pastors,

and educators. However, it should be noted that the archaeological community involved in excavations in Bible lands, which includes those who are secular and Jewish as well as Christian, prefer the more neutral abbreviations BCE ("Before the Common Era") and CE ("Common Era") to designate the same time periods as BC and AD. Those using these latter abbreviations in fields of study informing biblical studies should not be thought of as less biblical, since this is the accepted academic terminology.

The Limitations of Archaeology

As important as archaeology is to biblical studies, it nevertheless has inherent limitations that need to be understood so that archaeological data is not given priority (positively or negatively) over the biblical data. The primary limitation of archaeology is the extremely fragmentary nature of archaeological evidence. Only a fraction of material culture has survived. Most of the great civilizations of the past were destroyed in antiquity through wars, looters, erosion, natural disasters, or simply the ravages of time. To this we may add the hundreds of sites that have been and continue to be destroyed through building projects (ancient and modern), military maneuvers, religious and political uprisings, and pillaged by looters (such as ISIS) who have elevated black market antiquities into an international cartel. Another problem includes the formation processes that affect both the remains and the interpretation of them. These processes include the actions of cultural formation (human behavior) and non-cultural formation (natural environment) that may erode, relocate, and transform the data left at the site, including the removal of layers of history. Such

activity destroys the archaeological record preserved for that time period.

Moreover, of the thousands of known surviving ancient sites, only a fraction have been surveyed, much less excavated. For example, less than 1 percent of ancient Egypt has been discovered and excavated, despite the preeminent attention paid to this site since the beginning of archaeology as a discipline. Of those sites that are eventually excavated, usually only a fraction (somewhere around 5 percent) of the site is actually dug, a process sometimes taking decades. Then, only a percentage of what is excavated is ever published. Of the 500,000 cuneiform texts discovered over the past centuries, only 10 percent have been published. The meticulous work of organizing, analyzing, and interpreting finds in labs and research facilities by multiple professionals assigned materials in their area of expertise (sometimes on several continents) may occupy many years of work. Often these professionals have multiple projects or additional teaching or research responsibilities. These restrictive conditions, as well as the need for accuracy in interpreting the finds and the costs of publication, often result in delays in the publication of final excavation reports. This limits both scholarly and public

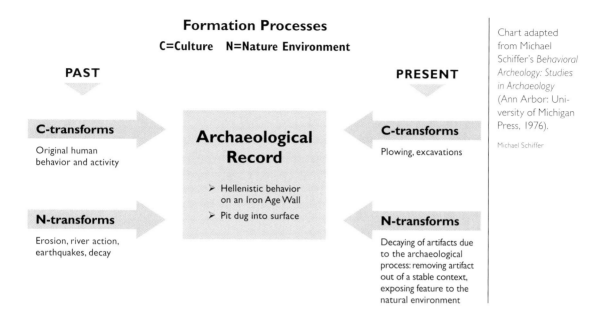

Formation Processes

C=Culture   N=Nature Environment

PAST

C-transforms

Original human
behavior and activity

N-transforms

Erosion, river action,
earthquakes, decay

**Archaeological
Record**

➢ Hellenistic behavior
on an Iron Age Wall
➢ Pit dug into surface

PRESENT

C-transforms

Plowing, excavations

N-transforms

Decaying of artifacts due
to the archaeological
process: removing artifact
out of a stable context,
exposing feature to the
natural environment

Chart adapted
from Michael
Schiffer's *Behavioral
Archeology: Studies
in Archaeology*
(Ann Arbor: Uni-
versity of Michigan
Press, 1976).

Michael Schiffer

access to the results of the excavations and prolongs the process of gaining information on a site. For example, the initial publication of the Ashkelon excavations did not come until after twenty-five years; Kathleen Kenyon's final report from Jericho waited some thirty years; and the Dead Sea Scroll fragments from Cave 4 took over forty years.

Further limitations come from restrictions to sites due to political disputes that make excavation in war zones impossible or restrict excavation to certain nationalities, the high financial costs of excavation, and the difficulty of securing permits from authorities that have political or parochial concerns. Even when data is derived from an archaeological site, the data may be complex and must be accurately interpreted in order to understand its possible relationship to the biblical data. Premature conclusions based on incomplete data may lead an interpreter to delineate an inaccurate relationship, such as sometimes occurred with discoveries related to the Bible in the nineteenth and early twentieth centuries.[7]

These limitations should also caution critics from drawing unwarranted conclusions concerning the historicity or historical accuracy of the Bible based solely on the archaeological remains, and especially on the lack of them—the fallacy of negative proof. However, when archaeology takes into account the historical data provided by a literary source, it has an advantage in interpreting the limited data from the field. For example, a document like the Babylonian Chronicle provides unique correlation of ancient ruling figures and historical events only partially recovered through archaeological excavation. When the Bible is properly regarded as an historical (not simply religious or theological) document, it may provide the needed historical information to identify archaeological sites and assist in the proper interpretation of finds. Therefore, archaeology must not be considered an objective and final statement in the matter of historical or biblical interpretation.[8] On the other hand, even though archaeology has recovered only a fraction of the whole, that fraction has been overwhelmingly successful in providing a positive confirmation of biblical historicity.

The Bible as an Archaeological Document

The incompleteness of the historical data available to us from archaeology should warn against the attempt to use it to critique the more oft complete information available in the literary documents. For this reason it is improper to elevate the archaeological data above the biblical text in order to challenge the latter's integrity. Therefore, the Bible, as a literary document, should be given priority in the final determination of accuracy in the history it records. Moreover, it should be recognized that the Bible is *both* a literary and an archaeological document, and so it represents the best surviving testimony we possess in the archaeological record of biblical times, places, and events. Having said this, it must be admitted that the Bible is a selective record that is theologically oriented. The composition of the Bible and the nature of archaeological data are complex, and care must be taken in making historical connections between them.[9] Just as the biblical text provides information for the archaeologist, the information from archaeology provides assistance in resolving historical, chronological, linguistic, and lexicographical problems, as well as providing an accurate portrayal of the details of ancient sites, structures, and daily life that is lacking or unclear in the biblical text. While the Bible is a completed revelation, it is not an exhaustive one, and though its message can be readily understood in any age, it is still selective in its material. Therefore, archaeology as an interpretive tool can enlarge the scope of the biblical context and make its ancient descriptions and references more understandable.

The Value of Archaeology for Biblical Studies

For the most part, those who recorded the Bible were firsthand witnesses to the peoples, places, and events they described. This has been of particular importance in recent debate concerning the chronological setting of the patriarchs and the exodus and in the question of the authenticity of the Gospels in their oral transmission. Whether or not we accept the testimony of the apostles and Gospel writers, they claim a firsthand experience as evidence of the veracity of their theological claims (Luke 1:1–4; Acts 1:21–22; 1 Cor 15:6; 1 John 1:1–3). In the post-apostolic period, whenever a question concerning the biblical past arose, Scripture was acknowledged as the final testimony to what had actually happened. The testimony of the Bible was simply to be believed as the facts of faith. With the advent of a more critical age, skeptics theorized that the Bible was the late product (postexilic period) of religious Jews seeking to create an origin history to rival those of the great civilizations of the past. Archaeology addresses such theories of textual formation with data from the biblical period that enables interpreters to make a plausible case for most events occurring within the times described. Even so, archaeology should not be expected to answer every question, as though all the remains of history were waiting to be unearthed and all the archaeologist needed to do was find the right place. The relationship of archaeology to the Bible, which records incidents of history, is best understood as an intersection at some, but not all, points (see diagram below). This tangential relationship between the biblical text, history, and archaeology cautions us to observe some basic principles in using these sources to validate one another:

- Archaeology is also a "text" and therefore needs interpretation.
- There should be no conflict between a correctly interpreted archaeological text and a correctly interpreted biblical text (provided consistent methods of interpretation are employed).
- The failure of a model is *not* the failure of the source.[10]

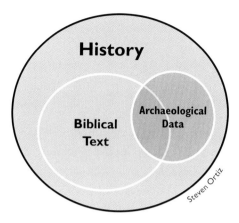

Methodology for the Use of Archaeology in Biblical Teaching

Because of the limitations presented above, as well as the intention of the biblical writers in recording historical information, archaeology is only occasionally able to correlate with the biblical text. It must also be recognized that both the biblical text and the archaeological data are interpretational. Having said this, it should be noted that once hermeneutical concerns are addressed, the occasions where text and artifact intersect usually have been spectacular and supportive for the historicity of the biblical text, bringing information of the material culture directly from the original sites and thereby enhancing biblical studies. With respect to interpretation, William G. Dever has argued for a "common sense" approach, defending the case for historical accuracy by identifying convergences of the archaeological evidence, the extrabiblical textual record, and biblical texts to mark a specific "event" or "datum."[11] The archaeological data alone may not be "self-interpreting," but it may still speak for itself once it is heard in context with other comparative information.[12]

A general methodology for integrating archaeological data into biblical interpretation might be as follows.[13]

1. *Recognize the need for integrating biblical texts and archaeological data.* Just as exegesis is a tool for uncovering the meaning of a text, excavation is a tool for uncovering its historical context and cultural meaning. Since the biblical texts are in an historical context, there exists the possibility of finding a correlation between text and artifact. For example, archaeological data has provided the interpretive elements necessary to understand more thoroughly a culture-bound practice or terminology. The discovery of literary Aramaic papyri from Elephantine and Koine Greek papyri from Egypt have aided in the proper interpretation of Jewish cultural practices and New Testament theological terms.

2. *Develop an understanding of the way archaeology works.* In order to use archaeological data the biblical interpreter needs to be acquainted with archaeological technique and terminology and have access to technical archaeological resources (e.g., field reports, peer-reviewed journals, specialized studies, digital databases, and magazines). A number of popular magazines and online sites are dedicated to showcasing on-going archaeological digs, reporting on news from the field, and publishing interpretive articles showing how archaeology relates to the biblical text.[14]

3. *Identify the ways archaeological data might influence the understanding of the biblical text.* Once the class of text is identified as having content that fits within the context of the Near East, basic interpretive diagnostic questions (who, what, when, where, how, why) are asked of the text to identify historical, cultural, social, and religious problems that may be addressed by analogous archaeological data.

4. *Construct a biblical-archaeological exegesis.* The two sources of data are combined after using critical thinking to discern how the

archaeological data best fits with the biblical data. Priority should be given to the written text while using archaeology as a control for the historical context. This results in a fuller understanding of the text in context.

5. *Teach the resulting exegesis.* In preaching/ teaching there should be an explanation of the selected archaeological data and the way it aids in understanding the biblical text. The benefit for the biblical teacher will be a more confident and credible proclamation of a historically informed text, resulting in a more informed audience that is capable of more accurate application.

Given this understanding of the convergence of the archaeological discipline with biblical studies and a practical methodology for use in teaching, it is important to consider the specific ways that archaeology contributes to biblical studies.

The Contribution of Archaeology to Biblical Studies

Confirming the Word of the Bible

A common misconception is that the purpose of archaeology is to prove the Bible. However, since the Bible describes itself as the "word of truth" (Ps 119:43; 2 Cor 6:7; Col 1:5; 2 Tim 2:15; Jas 1:18), it cannot be proved or disproved by archaeology anymore than can God by the limited evidence of this world (cf. Eccl 3:10–11). What archaeology can do is bring historical confirmation to the historical statements in the text of Scripture. One of the meanings of the word "confirm" is "to give new assurance of the validity of something." Such validation may come in the identification of a biblical site, from inscriptions uncovered at a site, or from artifacts that relate to customs or practices mentioned in the Bible. Amihai Mazar, director of the Hebrew University of Jerusalem's Institute of Archaeology, explains: "In certain cases, we can even throw light on certain events or even on certain buildings which are mentioned in the Bible. We can enumerate many subjects like this where the relationship between the archaeological finds and the biblical narrative can be established."[15]

The Bible commends its confirmation through the historical evidence of the past. In the book of Job, Bildad implored: "Ask the former generation and find out what their ancestors learned" (Job 8:8). The prophet Isaiah also declared that knowledge of the past was essential to understanding the revelation of God in history: "Remember the former things, those of long ago; I am God, and there is no other; I am God, and there is none like me" (Isa 46:9). For this reason commemorative celebrations such as the Passover were commanded to preserve and pass on the experience of the exodus generation to their descendants (Exod 12:14, 27, 42; cf. 2 Kgs 23:21; Deut 32:7). This same imperative was voiced in the New Testament with respect to confirming the events related to the ministry of Jesus: "That which was from the beginning, which we have heard, which we have seen with our eyes, which we have looked at and our hands have touched—this we proclaim concerning the Word of life" (1 John 1:1). Likewise, historical investigation of the available evidence was stated by Luke to be the proper method in reporting past events: "With this in mind, since I myself have carefully investigated everything from the beginning, I too decided to write an orderly account for you, most excellent Theophilus, so that you may know the certainty of the things you have been taught" (Luke 1:3–4). On the basis of such statements it is appropriate for students of Scripture to pursue the archaeological evidence of the past that touches upon the peoples, places, and events of the Bible.

One benefit of a pursuit to uncover the facts of the past is that such facts assist the believer in forming a realistic and rational relationship with God.

Archaeology aids in bringing the theological message of the Bible into a real world context where real faith is possible. William R. Osborne explains the need for this in light of the methodological shifts that have occurred within biblical theology:

> The rise of source and form criticism in the nineteenth century presented a fragmented text that found its meaning primarily in the segmented extrapolations of various compository hands. Consequently, as source criticism and the historical-critical method became more widely accepted, the range of focus within biblical studies continued to narrow. Biblical studies were replaced with anthropologies of the ancient Near East and histories of ancient religion. Others sought to alleviate this tension by unsatisfactorily asserting that the historicity of the text is not of primary importance. Searching for history in the Bible, for these authors, is an inappropriate inquiry of the text. However, disregard for historical veracity leads to an anemic biblical theology, given that the biblical writers themselves viewed the Scriptures as dealing in history.[16]

One example of this confirmation may be seen in a significant detail concerning the route of the exodus. The biblical text states, "When Pharaoh let the people go, God did not lead them on the road through the Philistine country, though that was shorter. For God said, 'If they face war, they might change their minds return to Egypt'" (Exod 13:17). From this passage it is understood that military opposition threatened the Israelites if they escaped by the northern route along the coastal plain. The Egyptian Tale of Sinuhe (ca. 1800 BC) tells of a runaway official who hid from Egyptian soldiers stationed at a military defense installation ("walls of the ruler") in this area (Berlin manuscript 3022, sec. 9, lines 11–20). But as this account is thought by some scholars to be fictional,

verification of the "walls of the ruler" awaited excavations at the Philistine site of Deir el-Balaḥ, where an extensive Egyptian fortification was revealed to have existed along this route. This archaeological evidence brought new confirmation of the historicity of the Exodus account, at least with respect to this important detail concerning its route.

Another example of confirmation has come in the identification of historical figures mentioned in the biblical text. Excavations at Tel Miqne uncovered an inscription that conclusively identified the site as biblical Ekron, a Philistine city mentioned in the Old Testament from the time of the conquest through the postexilic period. This identification had long been uncertain due to conflicting locations given in ancient literature. The inscription also attested a brief list of the rulers of Ekron, ending with the seventh-century-BC King Achish (a Philistine name mentioned in the biblical books of Samuel and Kings). In excavations in Area G of the ancient city of David forty-five bullae were discovered. The bullae were preserved by the fire that had destroyed Jerusalem during the final Babylonian invasion. These bullae contained fifty-three individual names, many of which are recorded in the Old Testament. Such finds confirm the accuracy of incidental historical details in the biblical text and, by extension, argue for the accuracy of the greater historical record.

Correcting our Wording of the Bible

Another contribution of archaeology in the service of the biblical text is in the area of lexicography. One of the first steps in understanding Scripture is the possession of a text that accurately reflects the original text. Since we only have apographs, the ancient copies that have been transmitted through scribal tradition, accuracy often depends on comparing these copies and the versions (translations of these texts) that have been part of their transmission histories. Archaeology has provided many of these from the sands of Egypt to the caves of Qumran, as well as thousands of inscriptions in both the languages of the Bible (Hebrew, Aramaic, and Greek) and its cognate languages (languages related to the biblical languages). The discovery of ancient manuscripts and inscriptions provide the basis for restoring the original form, grammar, and syntax of Hebrew, Aramaic, and Greek words of the Bible as well as clarifying their precise meaning and usage in the time they were written.

In 2007 Richard Steiner revealed that he had deciphered a number of Semitic texts in various Egyptian scripts over the past twenty-five years.[17] These texts had been discovered more than a century ago, inscribed on the subterranean walls of the pyramid of King Unas at Saqqara in Egypt, which dates between the twenty-fifth and thirtieth centuries BC. What these texts show is that Proto-Canaanite, the common ancestor of Phoenician, Moabite, Ammonite, and Hebrew, existed already in the third millennium BC as a language distinct from Aramaic, Ugaritic, and the other Semitic languages. These texts also are important to biblical scholars because they shed light on several rare words in the Bible that will help make future translations more precise.

One of the most significant discoveries in this regard was that at Qumran in the late 1940s of some 1,000 documents, known as the Dead Sea Scrolls. The discovery included the oldest known copies of the Old Testament, with some whole copies of books (such as Isaiah) and fragments of every book except Esther. This discovery demonstrated how well the scribes had preserved the biblical text over time. It also provided variants that helped textual critics resolve textual problems, and it has enhanced our understanding of the biblical text reflected in versions such as the Septuagint (Greek translation of the Old Testament) and the Samaritan Pentateuch. As a result, Harold Scanlin stated that "every major Bible translation since 1950

has claimed to take into account the textual evidence of the Dead Sea Scrolls."[18]

In addition, many archaic terms in the original languages of the Bible that are used only once (*hapax legomena*) have been properly understood from the same or related terms in other texts and inscriptions recovered in archaeological excavations. For example, in older translations of 1 Samuel 13:21 we read: "and the charge for a sharpening was a *pim* for the plowshares, the mattocks, the forks, and the axes, and to set the points of the goads" (NKJV). The Hebrew term *pim* appeared only here, and since its meaning was unknown, it was simply recognized as an obscure unit of measurement. However, archaeologists unearthed stone weights inscribed with the word *pim* and, judging from their weight in relation to the same amount of silver, have determined that a *pim* was about two thirds of a shekel. Since this discovery all modern translations translate the text as "and the charge was two-thirds of a shekel. . . ." Without the aid of archaeology, this term would have remained obscure and our translation ambiguous (though the meaning of the verse was unaffected).

Clarifying the World of the Bible

Just as archaeology can clarify the text of the Bible, it can also offer clarification to the world in which the historical events of the Bible occurred. A cardinal rule in biblical study is that every text must have a context. The better a biblical student is able to understand a text in the original context of the ancient world, the better he will be able to properly interpret the text and apply it in the modern world. Amihai Mazar, again, explains the importance of this. "Archaeology is our only source of information that comes directly from the biblical period itself . . . a whole picture of daily life from this period, which is the only evidence that we have from the biblical period except the Bible itself."[19] Modern interpreters live thousands of years, if not thousands of miles, removed from the time and culture of the places and peoples of the Bible. We will misinterpret and misapply theological truths of the biblical text if we assume that they can be correctly understood from either a Western orientation or a modern cultural perspective. We do not live in the world of the Bible (even if some may geographically live in that region). We cannot anymore correctly reconstruct the customs of the patriarchs from local Bedouin tribes than we can the practices of first-century Judaism from the later traditions of the Jewish rabbis. We must have data directly from the times and places of the biblical world.

Archaeological excavation gives us this clarity. Discoveries across the ancient world have now revealed much of the shape and substance of ancient life. Tomb paintings and reliefs have revealed depictions of ancient Semites similar to the biblical patriarchs. From the high cliffs of Behistun we have a portrait of the Persian monarch Darius the Great, from an Assyrian black obelisk of Salmanezzer III a picture of the Judean King Jehu, and from Israel a painted image of King Hezekiah. The discovery of the Rosetta Stone, a trilingual text, enabled the decipherment of Egyptian hieroglyphics and with it the history and culture of ancient Egypt. The same may be said for other ancient civilizations, such as the Sumerians, Hittites, Assyrians, Babylonians, and Persians, whose history was previously only known from fragmentary literary accounts, many of questionable accuracy. The details of daily life, society, culture, and religion these archaeological discoveries have given us enable biblical students to understand the ancient context with greater clarity than at any previous time in history (since biblical times) and have made possible the accurate recreations of the world of the Bible enjoyed in television documentaries and feature films.

The Rosetta Stone—Key to Egyptian Hieroglyphic

The ancient Egyptian writing called hieroglyphics (from two Greek words: *hieros* "sacred" and *glypho* "engrave")[20] was given a special aura of mystery by the European artists who romanticized the ruins of Giza and Thebes. For Europeans, who took fancy with them, they were regarded as either decorative motifs or as having some mystical meaning known only to the pharaohs. Most scholars agreed they held a mystical meaning for the Egyptians but realized that if they could be deciphered much of that lost culture could be recovered. However, the meaning of the hieroglyphs continued to be elusive.

Then in 1798, soldiers under the command of General Napoleon Bonaparte, who along with a corps of French scientists had invaded Egypt the year before, began amassing large numbers of freshly discovered Egyptian artifacts. As it would turn out, they were destined to be only collectors and not keepers. Just a year later the treasures fell into the hands of the British when they routed the French fleet and drove Bonaparte's army from Egypt. Among this newly won collection of antiquities that the British sent back to their national museum in London was a large slab of black basalt stone inscribed from top to bottom with ancient writing. It had been found by the French army officer Lieutenant P. F. X. Bouchard while reconnoitering near the village of Rosetta on the left bank of the Nile River. Almost 4 feet high, 2 1/2 feet wide, and 1 foot thick, the stone weighed 1,676 pounds! Aptly named the Rosetta Stone, it soon drew particular interest when it was observed that the writing it contained was in different scripts. Further study revealed that the scripts were parallel texts, each recording the same account. The text at the top of the stone was written in the indiscernible hieroglyphs, the middle text in what appeared to be a cursive form of hieroglyphic (called Demotic), and the bottom text in Koine Greek. Because this Greek (the same as that in the New Testament) was easily read by scholars, it was hoped that someone could work from the known to the unknown. By first comparing the easily understood Greek words with the Demotic text (which was thought to be readable), it was assumed that perhaps some light could be shed on the cryptic hieroglyphs (which were thought to be only symbolic). As the Greek text of the Rosetta Stone was translated, it was learned that this was a commemorative stela which had once stood in an Egyptian temple. It recorded a decree issued from Memphis (the ancient Egyptian capital) in 196 BC extolling the triumphs of King Ptolemy V Epiphanes. The inclusion of this name (the only royal name preserved in the hieroglyphic section of the stone) was to become essential to finally cracking the code of the hieroglyphs.

The first successful attempt to read the Egyptian text was made by Thomas Young (best known as the author of the wave theory of light). He correctly identified a recurring group of hieroglyphic signs written within an oval (called a cartouche) with the name of King Ptolemy. It was already known that foreign names were written with these unique hieroglyphs, but still the meaning of the signs themselves escaped the scholars. Then, a young Frenchman by the name of Jean-François Champollion entered this drama of decipherment. A gifted linguist, Champollion energetically applied himself to the task at hand. He compared Young's hieroglyph for "Ptolemy" on the Rosetta Stone with a newly discovered (1819) obelisk from an Egyptian temple near Aswan that contained the names of Ptolemy and Cleopatra in Greek. He was able to further isolate the cartouche for Cleopatra and, working from this decipher, other royal names as well. Finally, in 1822 he announced triumphantly that he had solved the riddle of the

hieroglyphs. To the surprise of many scholars, he demonstrated that hieroglyphics were not merely symbols, but signs with phonetic value—a readable language! Therefore, because of the discovery of the bilingual text of the Rosetta Stone, the hidden secrets of Egyptian language and subsequently ancient Egypt's history, religion, and culture were opened to the world.[21]

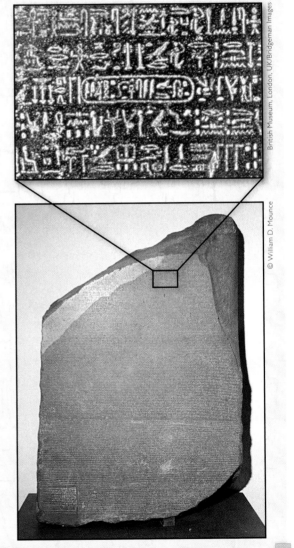

British Museum, London, UK/Bridgeman Images

© William D. Mounce

Complementing the Witness of the Bible

A final contribution that archaeology makes to biblical studies is that it provides complementary or supplemental historical, cultural, and religious information. While a vast and diverse witness to the lands, peoples, and events of ancient history, the Bible is a selective record that necessarily excludes much of historical significance (such as the name of the Pharaoh of the exodus), with the result that in certain accounts critics have questioned the Bible's historicity. Although archaeology also has its limitations in revealing the larger context, excavations in the biblical lands have added a complementary witness to the biblical authors that both enhance the biblical accounts and validate their accuracy. For example, archaeology has given us several parallel accounts of the creation and flood whose similarities complement the biblical account and, at the least, indicate a catastrophic worldview shared by most ancient civilizations. These complementary discoveries also reveal the theological differences between the biblical and extrabiblical accounts and so serve to emphasize the Bible's distinctiveness when compared with other ancient Near Eastern religions.

Another Old Testament example of this complementary witness is the case of the Israelite king Omri, who was one of the most important rulers of his time (885–874 BC) and established Samaria as the capital of the Northern Kingdom. The biblical text, however, allots him only a passing reference (1 Kgs 16:21–28). From the viewpoint of the biblical chronicler, his idolatry and prideful accomplishments did not merit significant recognition. Archaeology has been able to supply Omri's extrabiblical exploits from the recovered records of his foreign foes. These records revealed that the biblical writers were correct in their assessment of his character and actions.

The archaeological recovery of such incidental information has been especially helpful in reconstructing and understanding the interaction between Jesus and his contemporaries in various Jewish religious sects, but none left any written records of their beliefs and practices. The New Testament provided selective information concerning the Pharisees and Sadducees, as did the writings of the first-century Jewish historian Flavius Josephus, who included details on several other sects. The later rabbinic writings also gave some details. When the Dead Sea Scrolls were discovered, they offered complementary descriptions and even dialogue between their Jewish community (believed by the majority of scholars to be Essenic) and these sects. This information generally supported the accuracy of the New Testament accounts (as well as the extrabiblical accounts) and has provided extensive commentary on the messianic perspective that controlled the Dead Sea sect at the time of Jesus and the formation of the early church. The contribution of archaeology in bringing this complementary witness has been well stated by Gonzalo Báez-Camargo: "No longer do we see two different worlds, one the world of 'sacred history' and the other the world of 'profane history.' All of history is one history, and it is God's history, for God is the God of all history."[22]

Identifying an Archaeological Site

The remains of an ancient site are called a tel, "mound" (Hebrew *tel*, Arabic *tell* or *tall*), because it resembles a small hill as a result of successive habitation layers deposited through destruction. This is related to an older Arabic term *khirbet* ("ruin"). These archaeological mounds were formed through time as cities became ruins due to natural and manmade disasters (earthquakes, flooding, enemy assault, demolition, burning, etc.). Usually the following city was built over the previously destroyed site so that over time the site grew in size and in its final phase came to resemble a hill. Archaeologists survey these sites in a number of ways to determine what part of the site should be targeted for initial excavation. This involves fieldwork recording and assessment of the layout of sites and its features (non-portable artifacts like architecture). Various samplings of sherds (pieces of ancient pottery) collected from the topsoil give a rough idea of habitation at the site. Since structures usually contain the best possibility of locating datable artifacts (inscriptions and pottery and coins buried in relation to rooms) and other information needed to properly interpret the site, these need to be located if possible. For this purpose, simple probes or drilling can be used, along with metal detectors. However, archaeologists also use advanced technology such as remote sensing employing satellites, conventional photographs and infrared photographs from aerial reconnaissance, and archaeogeophysical exploration employing geophysical surveys using various subsurface radar such as magnetometers, ground-penetrating radar, and resistivity.[23] These methods can provide an idea of the forms of structures and other objects as well as their locations and approximate depths.

Excavating an Archaeological Site

Within a tel can be found the different levels of ancient civilizations stacked one upon another like the layers of a cake. The goal of the archaeologist is to discover the various contexts (things that have left traces in the archaeological sequence such as walls and pits) present in these layers and to document the context of each find so as to be able to determine its nature and date in relation to the whole site.

When archaeology was in its infancy, the method of excavation was generally to remove whatever earth was covering structures and artifacts so they could then be removed and studied. The advantage to this method was that more of a tel was excavated, but the disadvantage was that the specific spot where the object was found (in relation to other objects) was lost and there was no attention given to the different occupational periods that were originally part of the site. The trench method of excavation was an early correction to this, as it did what its name implies and cut a slice from top to bottom at a part of the tel deemed to have the most important artifacts (such as a palace or temple). This method revealed, and to some extent preserved, the record of strata (distinct layers of earth deposited in different periods of time) but still did not permit archaeologists to locate precisely their finds in relation to one another.

The identification and interpretation of the layers (strata) is known as stratigraphy. The geological and archaeological strata that make up an archaeological tel can be identified and interpreted with respect to the different periods of occupation they contain. Geologist Charles Lyell devised the stratigraphic method based on the observation that sedimentation takes place according to uniform principles. Lyell's Law of Superposition states that natural processes deposit layers in a sequence, so that soils deposited earlier will be older than the later soils deposited on top of them. Sometimes the sequence will have been overturned or interrupted by artificial features such as pits, but these can be understood in light of the larger context. Stratigraphic excavation reveals a temporal sequence and thereby provides the basis for determining a relative chronology of the site based on the relationships created between contexts in time and by comparison with similar sites. An absolute chronology may be determined from datable finds (such as index pieces and coins) found in the contexts.

The procedure in excavation is to completely remove each context in reverse order, the last deposited layer first, and only after full documentation to progress to the next layer until the oldest strata is reached.

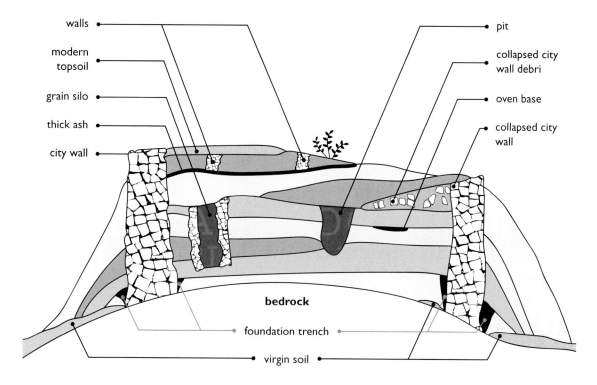

walls
modern topsoil
grain silo
thick ash
city wall

pit
collapsed city wall debri
oven base
collapsed city wall

bedrock

foundation trench

virgin soil

This is necessary because excavation destroys by removal the existing record of history, which is preserved only in the documentation. The aim is to record as much data as possible in each context in order to make the most accurate interpretation possible. Various methods are employed to achieve this goal. The open-area method of excavation (known as the Reisner-Fisher method) stresses the broad exposure of architecture and thus permits the mapping of the entire site as it is progressively revealed. This enables the archaeologist to see the big picture of the site. However, precise documentation of finds in contexts is also necessary, so another method was devised for this purpose by Mortimer Wheeler and developed by Dame Kathleen Kenyon. The Wheeler-Kenyon method lays out the site on a grid pattern. This method allows the archaeologist to interpret the stratification of a site and to control the data associated with stratum and each find in that layer and to then recreate the find spot of artifacts in their original location at the site. This grid divides the site into manageable squares (usually 5 x 5 m or 10 x 10 m) separated by a 1-meter-wide unexcavated section called a balk. This method allows archaeologists to measure accurately each find in the exact place where it was found and keep a record of all finds in relation to each other. Generally, the open-area method in combination with the Wheeler-Kenyon method is used to achieve the widest and most accurate control in the excavation and documentation of a site.

Documenting an Archaeological Site

The task of the archaeologist is to document each stratum in relationship to the other strata, along with their artifacts, in order to understand the site. How well this will be performed depends on how well the site is documented. Usually the permit issued

Using transit to establish benchmark and locus levels (note marked strata in left middle of photo) at Tel es-Safi.

Alexander Schick

to the archaeologist by the antiquities authority in the country of origin obligates the archaeologist to publish the results of their excavation. To this end, every possible means should be employed to capture and record data down to the microscopic level. A transit is used to obtain an eye level and then to record daily measurements in relation to a fixed point (benchmark), or a GPS device may also be used for this purpose. This information is recorded in field notes and stored on a laptop or other storage device.

Beverlee Price uncovering storejar with bone deposit at Qumran.

The data from each and every strata is recorded at the beginning and end of the day, according to its place (locus), in written and electronic form. Such data includes top plans, side drawings (to record changes in strata), drawings, and photographs (2D and 360°) of features and artifacts in situ. Every artifact or soil sample is removed from the site and properly inventoried, labeled, and recorded so each day's work can later be restored layer by layer from the published final report.

A newer trend in archaeology is a multi-disciplinary approach that includes both social and natural sciences. The inclusion of these sciences allows for all the data from the material culture to be collected and studied, including microscopic evidence of plants and seeds and evidence of factors affecting environmental change. Techniques such as wet sifting (to find small objects missed by dry sifting), flotation (soaking soil samples to separate plant fibers and seeds), and chemical tests of the soil from various stratum (to determine salinity and alkalinity) all help piece together the puzzle of life in the various periods of habitation at ancient sites.

Dating an Archaeological Site

The contents of different layers of material culture are unique to definite time periods. In order to determine the time of a layer, archaeologists use a combination of (a) relative and (b) absolute dating methods. Examining artifacts from a site in this way provides a crosscheck that can help narrow the range of dates and arrive at a fixed date for the stratum.

(a) Relative dating establishes a geologic structure or event to a chronological sequence relative to another geologic structure or event associated with it in the same strata (the typological sequence of artifacts or arrangement of artifacts having shared attributes). In this sequence the artifacts found below will usually be older than those found above. Exceptions to this may be the result of soil that has been disturbed or intruded into by either natural or mechanical means. The ancient world, including the events given in the Bible, is relatively dated. While we have specific dates given in the Bible, there is no known ancient calendar that can be used to pinpoint these dates.

For relative dating, pottery, inscribed materials, and coins are the most useful artifacts for determining an approximate time period. Coins may contain a date or be datable based on the images they bear (such as inscriptions, portraits, and other objects). Coins have been found in such quantity and so securely dated that a sizeable database exists for almost every type of coin. However, coins provide only a limited range for dating, as coinage did not begin in the lands of the Bible until the seventh century BC, many coins remained in circulation for centuries, and many coins have degraded to a point where no information can be read. In the case where a date can be obtained, the best one can say is that it gives the earliest date the strata in which it was found could have been deposited.

Pottery (terra cotta) as fired clay is practically indestructible and is the most common artifact used to determine the date for a particular stratum. It does not usually contain datable information in and of itself, although some jar handles bear stamps that record a name, place, or image that dates it to a specific time, such as those classed as *la-melek* ("belonging to the king") stamps, typical of the reign of King Hezekiah in the eighth–seventh centuries BC, or wine amphora stamps revealing their provenance (e.g., Rhodes) and sometimes the name of the recipient (e.g., King Herod). Furthermore, analyzing the form and function of pottery can provide information about ancient households, the standard of living (inclusion of imported wares), community and political organization, and the degree and origin of trade throughout the region and internationally. However, this is only possible once the larger context of the site is identified by comparison with evidence from other regional sites.

(b) Absolute (sometimes called chronometric) dating establishes the specific date of a geologic structure or event to a previously determined calendar. This is done by testing organic (carbon-based) samples through scientific means to provide a range of possible ("absolute") dates. This method attempts to fix a calendar date for events in the ancient world. Although we live our daily lives by this method, celebrating birthdays and remembering death days, this is a modern method. Yet, scholars have developed a chronological timeline for ancient events based on observed synchronisms with other chronologies from Egyptian, Assyrian, Canaanite, and Israelite. Synchronous material includes information gathered from records, artifacts, and even specific documentation regarding astronomical (usually lunar) activity. In addition, comparing the results from nearby (regional) sites that have been excavated allows an archaeologist to determine if certain sites were contemporary with one another and if they shared a local culture or civilization.

Jar handle stamped with *lmlk* (belonging to the king).

Courtesy of Liberty Biblical Museum/photo by Ayelet Shapira

Handle of wine amphora with stamp indicating shipment came from Rhodes.

Courtesy of Liberty Biblical Museum/photo by Ayelet Shapira

Pottery is so common in every occupation level at every site that over time a relative sequence of types has been well documented, producing a ceramic typology. Because the index of all pottery types has been dated in relation to other dated artifacts even broken pieces of pottery (sherds) that have distinctive characteristics (rims, handles, bases) serve as diagnostic sherds or indicatives (index pieces). Even without indicatives, a collection of body sherds from a site can help establish the type of pottery that was present and provide information on the size and influence of the site (e.g., imported pottery). Nevertheless, because styles can be repeated later in time (e.g., Byzantine oil lamps mimicking Iron Age style) and because there are subtle regional differences in pottery types that must be compared by those who are experienced with these sites (often unpublished), excavations employ professionals in ceramic typology to analyze and draw their most significant samples.

A new process called rehydroxylation measures hydroxyl groups (molecules in the clay that react with environmental moisture that changes in temperature over time) to potentially yield fairly precise dates. However, because the rehydroxylation technique is temperature dependent, errors can be introduced by inaccurate temperature estimates of a specimen site over time. Much more testing needs to be done to establish the accuracy of the method. Another process called neutron activation analysis (NAA) does not determine the date of pottery but can determine the geographic location from which the clay was obtained to make the vessel in relation to a database of local soils. This was useful at Qumran, where it was important to determine which pottery was imported (e.g., Motza clay) and which was made at the local kilns. Some theorists of the origin and nature of the Qumran community have used this data to support their case.

Absolute dating is obtainable from scientific methods that produce specific chronological dates for artifacts. It is useful in constructing a more specific sequence of events in relation to other data from the site. Absolute dating requires that something in the artifact change over time for such tests to produce results. Therefore, for archaeology such testing is done on objects that were once alive, such as bone, skin, wood, plant matter, and carbonized seeds (such as olive and date pits). The testing methods include radiometric dating (carbon 14 and accelerated mass spectrometry), fluorine testing, dendrochronology, and soil and pollen analysis.

Carbon 14 (C-14) remains constant in plants so long as they are alive, but upon death the radioactivity of C-14 decreases at a well-established rate and can therefore be measured. This dating method is to be used primarily in materials such as wood and bones.

Israelite oil lamps from various periods establish a ceramic typology (top row, from left): Early Bronze, Intermediate Middle Bronze, Middle Bronze/Late Bronze, Iron Age; (bottom row, from left): Hellenistic, Hasmonean (Maccabean), Early Roman/Herodian styles/Late Roman Byzantine styles

Courtesy of Liberty Biblical Museum/photo by Ayelet Shapira

(Accelerator mass spectrometry [AMS] dating is able to obtain a date from a very small sample.) However, wood in desert regions may remain in its natural state for hundreds of years before used in an archaeological context and dates obtained from C-14 testing may have wide ranges. Therefore, C-14 is only effective for dating when calibrated with other dating techniques such as dendrochronology, a method based on examining the number, width, and density of the annual growth of tree rings. This was particularly useful in determining that some wood beams stored in the Al-Aqsa Mosque on the Temple Mount that had last been used in the Islamic and Byzantine periods actually came from the Second Temple period, and perhaps even the First Temple period.[24] However, it should be observed that radioactive dating methods cannot be calibrated with known dates before 5,000 years ago, and all dates have a plus or minus variance, sometimes in the range of hundreds of years.

Another dating method called thermoluminescence relies indirectly on radioactive decay and overlaps with radiocarbon dating, but unlike carbon 14 or AMS, it can be used to date pottery. However,

it is less accurate, such as in the case of a sample deposited near the subsoil or rock at the bottom of a pit or fill that has a measurably different level of radioactivity. This is because the radioactive elements in the clay of a pot are derived from the ceramic itself and from its environment, and both must be tested (usually on site) in order to get a proper reading. If the pottery is too close to objects from different levels or is not in situ, this method will prove ineffective.

In addition, ancient DNA can sometimes be extracted from trace collagen in bones to determine the specific species, gender, and age of the animal. My (Price) excavation at Qumran used this method on sheep, goat, gazelle, and bovine bones and was able to pinpoint the extinct species of goat that was raised at the site over 2,000 years ago.[25] This method was also employed on manuscripts written on animal skin, like the Dead Sea Scrolls. Because there were tiny fragments that could not be associated by any other means, this method isolated the specific genotype of each animal and was able to match up discordant fragments from the same animals that formed a single scroll.

Fluorine testing can be used on bones of the same

age found in the same deposition layer. It determines the rate of time an object has been buried in the ground based on the amount of fluoride ions it has absorbed from groundwater in the soil. Because the amounts of fluoride in groundwater fluctuate, as do the rates of absorption from object to object, this method is only useful as a crosscheck with artifacts from the same site with established dates.

Archaeological Periods in Relation to the Bible

The chronological data that informs the archaeological periods comes from a comparison of the internal biblical chronology with conventional dating (which assumes an uniformitarian perspective) and extrabiblical chronologies (e.g., Egyptian, Assyrian). Due to debates over the geological periods (which inform the archaeological periods), prioritizing the internal biblical chronology or the extrabiblical chronologies, the supposed problems of chronological gaps, missing genealogies, use of lunar or solar or luni-solar calendars, and the reconciliation of archaeological data with biblical data, published chronologies have numerous differences. These pertain mainly to the earlier archaeological periods (Early Bronze–Iron I), with most scholars agreeing on established dates by Iron II (eighth century BC and on). The controversy over dating has resulted in high and low chronologies with different dates for pivotal events such as the patriarchs, the sojourn/exodus and conquest (early or late), and the settlement/time of the judges (long or short). These differences are noted in the chart below, and although we have revised the conventional chronology based on synchronisms and recent archaeological discoveries, such as those in Egypt by Manfred Bietak,[26] we have not attempted to interact with older revised chronologies that involve more radical shifts in these periods, such as those of David Rohl and John J. Bimson.[27]

The biblical flood must have occurred before the archaeological periods. However, it is not possible to correlate a date for this event consistent with the biblical chronology and the conventional geological/archaeological periods because of differences over the interpretation of the data on which these timetables are based. Given this understanding, we have used the conventional and accepted dates for the archaeological periods beginning with the pre-patriarchal period, which represents the emergence of early civilizations after the flood.

Archaeological Periods and Biblical History

From the outset archaeology as a discipline developed terms to distinguish the different periods of time based on technological achievement. Because ancient societies seemed to have developed the use of certain metals at different times, the age of the society was determined by the time it was thought a metal began to be produced or traded by that culture, primarily for cutting tools and weapons. A three-age system was proposed by Christian Tomsen (1788–1865), with the earliest age indicated by the lack of metal technology, the Stone Age. The next two periods came in order of the appearance of metal technology, the Bronze Age and the Iron Age. After these two periods, the time periods for the biblical world were based on the dominant civilization: Persian, Hellenistic, and Roman. This is a preferable means to distinguish extant peoples groups at the various sites since it is now known that bronze production occurred as early as the Stone Age (e.g., the ritual wands and maces found in the Cave of the Treasure in Israel), and iron was produced in ancient Sumeria ca. 3000 BC (e.g., an iron blade found in a Hattic tomb in Anatolia dated to 2500 BC). On this basis we can understand the general distinctions of these periods:

THE BRONZE AGE (new order of social complexity) is a time of development of urban civilizations, the foundation of city-states, major architectural achievements, proto-writing systems, religion, and educational institutions. The Bronze Age begins in the ancient Near East with the Sumerian civilization (ca. 3500 BC, the date of the earliest written texts) and ends as a result of invasion of Aegean Sea Peoples into the eastern Mediterranean (ca. 1200 BC). The biblical events related to the patriarchs, Moses, Joshua, and the judges take place during the Bronze Age.

THE IRON AGE (unified nationalities) is a time of development of smaller kingdom-states based on their national identity centered around a common god. The biblical events of the kingdom of Israel (united monarchy through the exile) take place during this period. The Iron Age begins with the collapse of the Bronze Age civilizations and the spread of metal-working technology in the region (in some part due to the Sea Peoples) and ends with the fall of the kingdom-states under the Neo-Babylonian and Persian Empires.

THE BABYLONIAN PERIOD (587/6–538 BC) is the period between the fall of the Southern Kingdom of Judah and the rise of the Persian province of Yehud. The usual understanding of this period in Judah during the Neo-Babylonian period is a condition of desolation following the collapse of the elite, mostly urban, sector of Judean society as the result of forced exile. The textual and archaeological evidence is more sparse for this period than others, and while it reveals that major sites and rural areas lost a high percentage of their population, an Israelite material culture continued in areas such as the Negev and survivor settlement activity persisted in certain rural regions such as Benjamin and the Judean Hills and Jerusalem. Even local administrative and ritual activity may have occurred among the ruins of major sites such as Tell en-Naṣbeh and the Temple Mount. Therefore, while devastated, Jewish life continued in Judah until the return of exiles to rebuild and refortify major population areas.

THE PERSIAN PERIOD (539–330 BC) is characterized by the rise of the Archimedean Empire and defeat of the Neo-Babylonian Empire in 539 BC by Cyrus the Great, a conquest that included Judah/Judea, now known as the province of Yehud (Aramaic for Judah). Consequently, an archaeological indicative for this period are the Yehud coins, one of the first coins introduced to ancient Israel (whether by the Persian authorities or a local semi-autonomous authority). Ezra 1:2–4; 5:13–16; 2 Chronicles 36:22–23 (supported by the Cyrus Cylinder) state that foreign captives were returned to their ancestral homes and allowed to rebuild their ruined sanctuaries. The biblical text (Ezra 2; Neh 7:6–7) describes the return of the Babylonian/Persian exiles to Judah, and Assyrian cuneiform texts found in excavations near Jerusalem imply a Jewish population from Assyria was also resettled in the province of Yehud. The Persian domination of the province ended with the conquest of Judah by Alexander the Great (330 BC).

HELLENISTIC PERIOD. The **Early Hellenistic period** (330–323 BC) began with the conquests of Alexander the Great and the defeat of the Persian Empire. The **Late Hellenistic period** (330–149 BC) is characterized by the Hellenization of the region through the division of Alexander's kingdom (Daniel 11:3–4). In Israel this focuses on the time of Jewish persecution under the rule of the Seleucid (Greek) king Antiochus IV

Epiphanes (175–164 BC), who banned Jewish religious observance, and the subsequent Maccabean Revolt (167–142 BC) that ended Greek influence.

HASMONEAN PERIOD (167–37 BC). This is the time of the rule in Israel of the Maccabean (Hasmonean) dynasty that occupied the offices of both priest and king. The defeat of Antiochus IV by Judah Maccabee (164 BC) led to the reconsecration of the Second (Zerubbabel) Temple and an independent Jewish government in 142 BC. During this period a number of Jewish sects arose, including the *Yaḥad* (Qumran Community). The archaeological indicatives for this period include the "slipper-style" Hasmonean oil lamp, the slight changes in the pottery forms of domestic and industrial vessels, and the bronze Hasmonean coins minted by the various rulers (Alexander Jannaeus, Antiochus VII Sidetes, John Hyrcanus I and II, Judah Aristobulus, Mattathias Antiigonus).

ROMAN PERIOD (149 BC–AD 638). The **Early Roman period** (149 BC–AD 135) begins with the Roman destruction of Carthage in the Third Punic War (149–146 BC), making Syria a province, and Pompey the Great's incorporation of the region (including Israel) into the Roman Republic (63 BC). This is also known as the Late Second Temple period with an emphasis on the Herodian dynasty (Herodian period, 63 BC–AD 70). This time also saw the Qumran Community flourish and end (AD 68), the ministry of Jesus of Nazareth (4 BC–AD 33), growth of the early church, and the First Jewish Revolt against Rome (AD 66–70). The **Middle Roman period** includes the Second Jewish Revolt (AD 135–200) and the completion of the Jewish Mishnah (AD 200). This period is also known as the Mishnaic period. The **Late Roman period**, also known in this early part as the Talmudic period, includes the production of the Talmud (AD 200–330) and the Roman adoption of Christianity as a state religion (AD 330), resulting in Byzantine Christian rule in the Holy Land until the Muslim invasion in AD 638. This period is also known as the Byzantine period.

Both the Bronze and Iron Ages can be divided and subdivided into more precise periods of development and social change during which the events recorded in the Old Testament occurred. While there is a margin of error in the earliest dates, these periods may be understood generally according to the following chart.

Archaeological Periods and Biblical History

Archaeological Period	Chronological Date	Historical Events	Biblical Historical Event
Early Bronze I	ca. 3300–2950 BC ±150	Early Dynastic Period in Egypt (ca. 3100 BC); urbanization, city-states, cuneiform and hieroglyphic writing	Period of the patriarchs (ca. 2275–2000 BC); destruction of Sodom and Gomorrah in 2067 BC at end of EB III period; nomadic lifestyle, transient culture
Early Bronze II	ca. 2950–2700 BC ±125	Canaanite settlement, worship centers	
Early Bronze III	ca. 2700–2176 BC ±50	Beginning of Egyptian Old Kingdom	
Early Bronze IV	ca. 2176–1973 BC	Population decrease, cities destroyed in Canaan; end of Egyptian Old Kingdom	
Middle Bronze I (IIA)	ca. 1973–1750 BC ±10		Patriarchs (ca. 2000–1700 BC, Hoffmeier's dating; ca. 1900–1600 BC, Kitchen's dating); Egyptian sojourn (ca. 1876–1446 BC, early date)
Middle Bronze II (IIB)	ca. 1750–1615 BC ±10	Egyptian Middle Kingdom	
Middle Bronze III (IIC)	ca. 1615–1483 BC ±10	Hyksos Egyptian Dynasty (ca. 1663–1555 BC); subjugation of Canaan by Thutmoses III in his 22nd year (ca. 1483 BC)	
Late Bronze I	ca. 1483–1400 BC	Egyptian New Kingdom (1539–1096 BC)	Exodus 1446 BC; wilderness wanderings (ca. 1446–1406 BC); conquest (ca. 1406 BC, early date)
Late Bronze II	ca. 1400–1290 BC	Amarna Period, ca. 1386–1334; campaign of Seti I (ca. 1290 BC)	Period of the judges (ca. 1400–1050 BC, early date); Egyptian sojourn (ca. 1400–1270 BC, late date)
Late Bronze III	ca. 1290–1177 BC	Ramesside Egyptian period (ca. 1292–1069 BC); Philistine invasion in 8th year of Ramesses III (ca. 1177 BC); invasion of Sea Peoples (ca. 1200 BC)	Exodus (ca. 1270 BC); conquest (ca. 1230 BC); judges (ca. 1200–1050 BC, late date)
Iron IA	ca. 1177–1100 BC	Collapse of Bronze Age civilizations	United Israelite Monarchy (ca. 1050–930); Saul (ca. 1050–1010 BC); David (ca. 1010–970 BC); Solomon (ca. 970–930 BC)
Iron IB	ca. 1100–1000 BC	Rise of smaller chiefdoms and kingdom-states	
Iron IC	ca. 1000–925 BC	Invasion of Pharaoh Shishak (ca. 925 BC)	
Iron IIA	ca. 925–800 BC	Neo-Assyrian Empire (ca. 911–612 BC)	Divided Monarchy (ca. 930–587/6*)
Iron IIB	ca. 800–722 BC	Fall of Samaria and exile of Northern Israelite Kingdom to Assyria (ca. 722 BC)	
Iron IIC	ca. 722–587/6 BC	Neo-Babylonian Empire (ca. 911–612 BC)	Judah alone (722–587/6 BC); fall of Jerusalem and destruction of First Temple (587/6 BC)
Babylonian Period	587/6–538 BC	Judean exile in Babylon	Exilic Period (587/6–338 BC); return to Judah (538 BC)
Persian Period (Iron III)	538–330 BC	Persian hegemony over Israel	Second Temple (Zerubbabel) rebuilt (538–515 BC); Nehemiah rebuilds walls (444 BC)
Hellenistic Period	330–149 BC	Alexander conquers Persian Empire; division by generals (Ptolemaic and Seleucid Empires); Antiochus IV desecrates Jewish Temple (168 BC)	Hellenization of Jews; Maccabean Revolt (167–160 BC)
Hasmonean Period	167–37 BC	Second Jewish Revolt ends Greek rule over Israel and establishes Jewish state with rulers and priests from Hasmonean (Maccabean) Dynasty.	Purification of Second (Zerubbabel) Temple; Beginning of Qumran Community (c. 134 BC)
Roman Period (Byzantine Period)	149 BC–AD 637	Roman conquest; General Pompei enters Jerusalem Temple (63 BC); Herod the Great builds Second (Herodian) Temple (20 BC)	Jesus and early church, New Testament; destruction of Second Temple (AD 70); Jewish Diaspora, Byzantine Christian rule (AD 325–637)

*587 BC date is based on chronological data in Roger C. Young, "When Did Jerusalem Fall?" *JETS* 47/1 (March 2004): 21–38 and Andrew E. Steinmann, *From Abraham to Paul: A Biblical Chronology* (St. Louis: Concordia, 2011), 162–78.

PART 1

ARCHAEOLOGY
and the
OLD TESTAMENT

1 | Introduction to Archaeology and the Old Testament

Archaeology supports historical study by the discovery and interpretation of artifacts in situ. This is to say that the focus is on finding things in their original contexts and then explaining them in terms of their functions and roles in antiquity. For the Old Testament, the original context is the ancient Near East—its geography, languages, culture, and customs, not to mention its own accounts of history and the factors (religious and political) that affected how it told and what it preserved of that history. In understanding the difficulties facing modernity and trying to discover and interpret the earliest archaeological history of the Bible, two factors must be taken into account.

First, the further back in history one goes, the less archaeological information one has available. The ravages of time, successive occupation that destroyed the foundations of previous occupations, lack of enduring writing materials or means of preservation, and other causes reduce the chance of recoverability. It is estimated that at least 96 percent of this information from the ancient world is lost to us and can never be recovered. For this reason we should not necessarily expect to find direct archaeological evidence of and correlation with the patriarchs, the exodus, the conquest, or even the early monarchy under Kings David and Solomon. That we *do* find information that can help us in confirming the historicity of these people and the reliability of the recorded events is remarkable and should be treated as such and interpreted as evidence of the larger historical context now unrecoverable. This data permits us to see that the biblical events, which took place within a chronologically conditioned geography, reflect accurately the terminology, places, and customs unique to their time and place in history. This is precisely what we see as we move forward in time with the later periods that are more recoverable. Kenneth Kitchen underscores this point in the conclusion of his magisterial defense of Old Testament historical reliability:

> The periods most in the glare of contemporary documents—the divided monarchy and the exile and return—show a very high level of direct correlation (where adequate data exist) and of reliability. That fact should be graciously accepted by all . . . When we go back (before ca. 1000) to periods when inscriptional mentions of a then-obscure tribal community and its antecedent families (and founding family) simply cannot be expected a priori, then chronologically typological comparisons of the biblical and external phenomena show clearly that the Hebrew founders bear the marks of reality and of a definite period. The same applies to the Hebrews' exodus from Egypt and appearance in Canaan . . . The Sinai covenant (all three versions Deuteronomy included) has to have originated within a close-set period (1400–1200)—likewise other features. The phenomena of the united monarchy fit well into what we know of the period and of ancient royal usages. The primeval protohistory embodies early popular tradition going very far back, and is set in an early format. Thus we have a consistent level of good,

fact-based correlations right through from circa 2000 BC (with earlier roots) down to 400 BC. In terms of general reliability . . . the Old Testament comes out remarkably well, so long as the writings are treated fairly and evenhandedly, in line with independent data, open to all.[1]

Kitchen's closing remarks make a bridge to our second factor: one must recognize that the biblical authors, who lived in the world of the ancient Near East and, though superintended by God, did not approach history (or chronology) as we do, especially in the Western world. We come to history with the goal to establish objectively a complete and precise order of events and to validate them historically (such that any gaps, omissions, or unexplainable inconsistencies are deemed unacceptable). However, the biblical writers were selective of events and their order, and interpretation was subject to their particular perspective and authorial intent.

Moses wrote from his unique perspective and experience as an educated Egyptian, Levitical priest, pastoralist, and national legislator—as the other biblical writers wrote from theirs. This did not affect the historicity or accuracy of their accounts, but it may affect our understanding of them as we try to reconcile them with the limited context gleaned from the archaeological record. Moreover, after the biblical authors wrote to their generation, God used those in later generations (such as Ezra) to collect, order, and sometimes contemporize language and references in their writings, all the while preserving their historical accuracy and theological integrity. For this reason we should not expect to always find a neat fit with archaeological data, even when and where it is available. Still, the Israel presented in the Old Testament did exist, and to the extent it is able,

archaeology can recover it and reveals that it conforms to known history. As William G. Dever has noted:

> Ancient Israel is there, a reality perhaps often hidden in the idealistic portraits of the Hebrew Bible or obscured by its overriding theocratic version of history, and also hidden in the dirt awaiting the discoveries of the archaeologist. It is *archaeology*, and only archaeology, that gives back to all those ordinary, anonymous folk of the past . . . their long-lost voice, allowing them to speak to us today.[2]

We should add to this that archaeological interpretation is also affected by factors (religious and political) and older interpretations of previous data. Its connection, then, with the biblical text needs to be carefully evaluated. Some older interpretations of particular sites and artifacts, especially under pressure from religious sponsors, that once "fit" with the Bible have been amended and even changed in light of new information from later excavations. On the other hand, modern religious and political pressures to disavow any connection with the Bible have in some cases caused neglect or reinterpretation of older data to conform to acceptable standards.[3] This opinion is, of course, controversial but cannot be discounted if an accurate interpretation of all of the available data is the goal. These factors should caution us to not assume that everything in the Bible, especially the earlier chapters of the Bible, can be verified in a scientific manner or that the archaeological data is out there waiting to be discovered. However, as has been repeatedly stated, "The absence of evidence is not evidence of absence." We may have only a little evidence, but a little tells us a lot. What we can and have verified concerning the reliability of the Old Testament should be sufficient to allow us to accept what we cannot verify.

2 | The Pentateuch

GENESIS

Genesis 1–2

Ancient Near Eastern Creation Accounts

> In the beginning God created the heavens and the earth ... This is the account of the heavens and the earth when they were created, when the LORD God made the earth and the heavens. (Gen 1:1; 2:4)

The account of creation in the book of Genesis takes center stage in the Bible and is recorded as a matter of proto-history. Similar accounts of creation, though without the central position given in the Bible, were also recorded by other ancient Near Eastern civilizations. The oldest creation account is the Sumerian Eridu Genesis, discovered in Nippur. Recorded on a single fragmentary tablet, it states that the gods An, Enlil, Enki, and Ninhursanga made black-headed people and created conditions suitable for animals to live and reproduce. Afterward, kingship (government) was lowered from heaven, and the first cities, Eridu, Bad-Tibira, Larsa, Sippar, and Shuruppak, were founded.

A more complete Sumerian creation account is contained in five tablets from the early second millennium BC, also discovered at Nippur and now housed in the Musée du Louvre (Paris). Each tablet contains different details of creation. However, the Sumerian god Enki is the unifying figure in all of the accounts, creating the world and appointing lesser gods over his creative order, with the sun god Utu over the cosmos. Enki as creator brings fertility to the world by filling the Tigris and Euphrates Rivers with his semen, stocking the marshland with fish, bringing forth rain clouds to water the earth, and creating everything necessary for human life (animals, crops, houses, and industry). In other tablets a similar watering of the world is seen, but with a focus on the sexual prowess of Enki and the resulting birth of gods and goddesses. In one particular text there is a more thorough account of the creation of mankind in which the opening lines reflect the opening lines of Genesis: "In those days, in the days when the heaven and earth were [created] ..."[1]

Another Babylonian account of creation is found in the seventeenth-century-BC Epic of Atrahasis, discovered in Sippar (in modern Iraq). It explains the creation of mankind as a response to a revolt by the lower gods, who were forced to do heavy labor for the chief god Enlil and the Anunna-gods (higher gods). The birth goddess Mami/Nintu, with the aid of the god Enki, was called to create mankind as a work force to relieve the lower gods. The stuff of human creation was the blood of the slaughtered god Aw-ilu mixed with clay that was spat upon by the god Igigi. This story is quite unlike the creation of man in Genesis who is considered a representative of God to rule over his creative order (Gen 1:27–28) and to cultivate the garden in which he was placed (Gen 2:8, 16).

Enuma Elish Tablet

© 2013 by Zondervan

An ancient Mesopotamian account called Enuma Elish was recovered in the form of fragmented Akkadian tablets found in the remains of the library of Ashurbanipal at Nineveh. The original date of composition was probably between the fourteenth and eleventh centuries BC. It gives another Babylonian version of creation by the chief god Marduk and, like the Epic of Atrahasis, explains the purpose of creation—that mankind could provide service to the gods. However, this so-called Babylonian Genesis was not written with a focus on a creation story but as a political document praising Marduk in order to promote his chief status in the Babylonian pantheon, which would exalt the city of Babylon and enhance Hammurabi's own position and power. Nevertheless, in its account of creation there are similarities to the biblical account.

- Both accounts view the creation of heaven, earth, and its inhabitants (human and animal) as a divine act.
- Both view mankind's creation from the ground (clay . . . dust) and see the work of humans as tending the land (either as a representative of the creator, as in the biblical account, or by contrast, to work for the creator god in place of the lesser gods, as in the Babylonian account).
- In addition, there are seven tablets in Enuma Elish and seven days in the Genesis account. Furthermore, the creation of mankind is in the sixth tablet of the Babylonian account and takes place on the sixth day of the biblical account.

Genesis 1–2—Ancient Near Eastern Creation Accounts

Enuma Elish Creation Account	Biblical Creation Account
Gods rule the heavens and earth (IV. 20–25; V. 1, 135)	God created the heavens and the earth (Gen 1:1)
Watery chaos separated into heaven & earth (IV. 137–140)	An unformed and unfilled condition (Gen 1:1–2)
Light pre-exists creation of sun, moon, stars (I. 102; V. 1–12)	Light created before the luminaries (Gen 1:3–5)
Number seven frequently used (IV. 46; V. 17)	Seventh day (rest from creation) (Gen 2:2–3)
Man made from clay (mixed with blood) (VI. 33)	Man made of dust from the ground (Gen 2:7)
Tend land (in place of lesser gods) (VI. 8, 34)	Man tasked with tending garden (Gen 2:15)

"Enuma Elish Tablets I–VI," COS 1:390–402.

Most of these similarities are expected for a logical order of creation, except the creation of light before the luminaries, which is an unnatural order of creative events shared only by this text and that in Genesis. The differences between these accounts are pronounced: polytheism in Enuma Elish versus monotheism in Genesis, a theogony (origin of the gods) in Enuma Elish versus a cosmogony (origin of the cosmos) in Genesis, and a complex mythology in Enuma Elish versus a straightforward, simple storyline (even anti-mythical) in Genesis. This can be seen in the Babylonian gods being identified with nature, whereas God in Genesis is the creator distinct from nature (his creation). At best this comparison reveals that this particular order, especially the creation of light before the luminaries, was passed down in the common culture before it was dispersed at Babel and it became embedded in divergent local mythologies over time. The differences eliminate the biblical account (which was recorded later) borrowing from the earlier Babylonian account. This is especially the case for the Sumerian account, in which the creator god and the lesser gods engage in sexual relations as acts of creation and/or fertility, in contrast to the Bible's sovereign creator, who acts alone.

At one time Ebla epigraphist Giovanni Pettinato claimed that there were four parallel creation texts attested on three tablets that contained two similar versions in the cuneiform tablets unearthed at Ebla (modern Tell Mardikh), an important ancient city-state near Aleppo, Syria from the third millennium BC.[2] However, the tablets Pettinato thought contained creation stories are now known to be lexical compilations,[3] and most of the extant Eblaite materials are bilingual lexical lists and incantations. Ebla has not yielded any literary narrative texts like the Sumero-Babylonian creation stories, perhaps because these would be most likely found in scribal school tablets, and only the contents of palace rooms have been recovered from the site. It is important to note this since Pettinato's early translations (1978) and alleged interconnections between Ebla and the Bible (1979–1980) remain in circulation on the Internet.

Genesis 3:1–23

Babylonian Parallel to the Fall

Now the serpent was more crafty than any of the wild animals the LORD God had made. He said to the woman, "Did God really say, 'You must not eat from any tree of the garden'?" … "For God knows that when you eat from it your eyes will be opened, and you will be like God, knowing good and evil." When the woman saw that the fruit of the tree was good for food and pleasing to the eye, and also desirable for gaining wisdom, she took some and ate it. She also gave some to her husband, who was with her, and he ate it. … To Adam he said, "Because you listened to your wife and ate fruit from the tree about which I commanded you, 'You must not eat from it' Cursed is the ground because of you; through painful toil you will eat food from it all the days of your life." (Gen 3:1, 5–6, 17)

The Babylonian story of Adapa (also known as Adapa and the Food of Life) has been preserved in four cuneiform fragments (designated A, B, C, D). The oldest and longest (B) is from the Kassite Babylonian period (fourteenth century BC) from the Egyptian archives at Tell el-Amarna of Pharaohs Amenhotep III and IV. The other three (A, C, D) are from Assur (seventh century BC) from the library of Ashurbanipal at Nineveh. According to the legend, Ea (the god of the subterranean freshwater ocean and of wisdom) created Adapa with wisdom but not immortality. Adapa was the first of the semi-divine sages (*apkallu*) and served as counselor to the first of the antediluvian kings in bringing civilization to mankind. As such, he represents an archetype for humanity. In addition, he served as priest of Ea's temple (Abzu House) at Eridu.

Called to heaven by the sky god Anu for committing an egregious act, he was given preparatory instruction by Ea on how to conduct himself in the court of the gods. He was to show reverence to the gatekeepers of Anu and not to eat or drink what Anu offered him, for this would be "bread of death" and "water of death" (apparently as punishment for incurring the god's wrath). However, in heaven Adapa so pleased Anu's gatekeepers that Anu decided not to punish Adapa but to reward him with the gift of immortality. This was to be obtained through Adapa's eating the "bread of life" and drinking the "water of life." But because of Ea's deception, Adapa refused these gifts and Anu sent him back to earth with the declaration that he had rejected immortality and consequently brought ill upon mankind.

The story of Adapa offers a parallel to the biblical account of the fall of mankind in so far as it relates to an explanation of why man suffers death as a mortal. According to E. Ebeling another syllabary may equate the meaning of the name of Adapa (*a-da-ap*) with "man," like the Hebrew *adam* (Gen 5:2). It has been asserted by some scholars that the similarities with Genesis are superficial and do not form a real comparison with the biblical account. One reason for this objection has been an unwarranted

Late Akkadian or Neo-Sumerian (2200–2100 BC) Chlorite cylinder seal depicting a banqueting scene with a female and a deity on either side of a date palm (sacred tree).

Alexander Schick

concern over critical views that argue the biblical creation stories are sourced in ancient Near Eastern mythology. However, the other differences in these accounts are sufficient to demonstrate that the later biblical authors could not have recast their more historical accounts from their pagan counterparts. Meanwhile, the similarities between the accounts argue for a common historical event.

As the comparison chart reveals, like Adam, Adapa was understood to be the first man and divine representative of the creator. Just as Adam was to care for the garden

Genesis 3:1–23—Comparison of Adapa Story and Genesis 3

Adapa: Story of Adapa	Adam: Genesis
Created by/Son of god Ea (A.5)	Created by/son of God (Elohim) (2:7; cf. Lk. 3:38)
First man (A.5)	First man (5:2)
Representative of mankind (A.5; B.68; D.68)	Representative of mankind (3:17)
Priest of Ea's sanctuary (A.9, 19)	"Priest" of garden "sanctuary" (2:15; 3:8)
"Food of life" (B.59–60)	"Tree of life" (3:22)
Immortality gained through eating (B.68)	Immortality gained through eating (3:22)
Deceived by Ea (B.29–30)	Deceived by serpent (3:13)
Death for disobedience to Anu (D.15)	Death for disobedience to Elohim (3:2, 11, 19)
Exiled to earth to die as mortal (B.71)	Exiled from garden to die as mortal (3:23–24)

(Gen 2:15, the Hebrew verbs "work" and "keep" here imply the duties of a priest in a sanctuary, cf. Num 3:7–8; 8:26; 18:5–6), so Adapa was to care for Ea's sanctuary (by providing fish). Just as there was a "tree of life" in the garden, whose fruit (food) might have bestowed immortal life on Adam and his wife (Gen 3:22), so Adapa was offered the "food of life" to gain immortality like the gods. Deception also played a role in both accounts, as Eve (through the serpent) was deceived, and Adapa (through Ea) was deceived, with both exiled from one place to experience death as mortals on the outside. For Adam (and Eve) it was outside the garden sanctuary (the place of God's presence, Gen 3:8), and for Adapa it was from the heavenly court of Anu to the realm of the earth. While the text is missing in the story of Adapa, it has been assumed that Anu punished Ea for his deception that resulted in mankind not gaining immortality. If so, then there is an additional parallel here to the punishment of the serpent (and the unmentioned non-human figure behind the serpent), Gen 3:14–15.

Genesis 3:24

Representations of Cherubim in the Ancient Near East

After he drove the man out, he placed on the east side of the Garden of Eden cherubim and a flaming sword flashing back and forth to guard the way to the tree of life. (Gen 3:24)

This text includes the first mention of heavenly creatures called *keruvim* (which is transliterated in English as "cherubim"). If the Hebrew meaning is like the Akkadian word *karabu* ("to pray, bless"), then perhaps their role as heavenly intercessors between God and his creation is implied. Therefore, the presence of the cherubim imagery in their sanctuary assured the Israelites that they had angels watching over them and assisting them in their fearful approach to the fiery God of Mount Sinai (cf. Deut 5:23–26). Images of cherubim were ubiquitous in the Israelite sanctuary, embroidered on the veil of the tabernacle (Exod 26:31) and temple (2 Chr 3:14), carved into the tabernacle's walls, doors, paneling, and lavers (1 Kgs 6:27–35; 7:29, 36), and present as the huge olivewood sculptures that overshadowed the ark (1 Kgs 6:23–28; 8:6–7; 2 Chr 3:10–13).

The problem of identifying the appearance of the cherubim has existed at least as far back as the Second Temple period. The Talmud states that the cherubim (of the ark) were one of five things missing from the Second Temple as compared with the First (b. Yoma 21a). Even though it is said that the Second Temple contained images of the cherubim (b. Yoma 54a), Flavius Josephus, who was from a priestly family and offers eyewitness descriptions of the Second Temple, says of the cherubim: "No one can tell what they were like" (*Ant.* 8.3, 3). Despite this, the Talmud offers an opinion:

> Rav Katina said: "When the Jewish people would go up to Jerusalem during the Festivals, the Keepers of the Sanctuary would roll back the curtain covering the Holy Ark, and would reveal to the Jews who came up to Jerusalem, the cherubs, which were in the form of a male and female, embracing each other. And they would say to them, to the Jews: 'See the love which G-d has for you, like the love of a male and female.'" (b. Yoma 54a)

Iron Age terracotta plaques depicting griffins (cherubim figures), from Israel

Courtesy of Liberty Biblical Museum/photo by Ayelet Shapira

CM

This statement, however, may be more pedagogical than historical.

Cherubim-like figures are found in ancient Near East iconography on everything from monumental architecture in temples and palaces to reliefs and seals. They are variously depicted as creatures that are composites of human and animals. In Sumer the figures are of winged humans; in Egypt, Syria, and Israel the figures are of winged humans or a composite of a lion and a human (sphinx); in Assyria and Babylon, a winged bull and a human; and in Greece, a bird and a human (griffin). The composite character may represent attributes of God as displayed in examples of his creation. The human part represented human intellect and emotions, while the winged-animal part represented power and speed. Combined, these traits were manifestly beyond both human and animal and suggested an order above the earthly creation—the angelic.

In Genesis 3:24 the cherubim appear as guardians of God's creation, stationed at the east of Eden to prevent invasion from outside (the place of exile) and thus preserve the sanctity of the garden with its tree of life. Examples of this guardian function have already been noted from Egypt in relation to the pharaoh, but this is implied in the images of such creatures flanking the thrones of kings (such as the relief of Ahiram, king of Byblos, seated on a cherub throne) or placed at the entrances to temples (such as at 'Ain Dara'). The tabernacle and the temple were entered from the east, and the cherubim were placed over the ark of the covenant (Exod 25:18–22), the footstool of the LORD, guarding the divine presence. In Solomon's Temple two fifteen-foot cherubim were also placed as guardians of the ark within the inner sanctuary (1 Kgs 6:23–28). In addition, images of the cherubim decorated the curtains of the tabernacle (Exod 26:31) and the walls of the temple (1 Kgs 6:29).

Similar to the guardian motif from Byblos depicting king Ahiram seated on a throne and flanked by winged lions, the golden throne chair of King Tutankhamen has arms made like winged lions and his burial chamber

is surrounded on four sides by pairs of winged human figures. Excavations in Samaria have produced a number of ivory plaques (ca. tenth–ninth centuries BC) that were probably part of the decoration of the royal palace. These carved reliefs provide the closest geographical and chronological examples to the interior decoration of the Solomonic Temple. One important example portrays cherubim protectively flanking a central figure in a shrine with their wings touching as the wooden cherubim fashioned by Solomon (as well as those on the ark of the covenant) were said to have done (Exod 25:20; 1 Kgs 6:27; 1 Chr 28:18). To what degree the Samaritan images represent the cherubim on the ark is unclear since these images were likely influenced by local pagan mythology.

The function of the cherubim is implied in the verse that describes the cover: "There, above the cover between the two cherubim that are over the ark of the covenant law, I will meet with you and give you all my commands . . ." (Exod 25:22). Based on the words "There . . . I will meet with you," one function of the cherubim was to make possible the representative presence of sinful man before the presence of Yahweh. In the First Temple Solomon constructed two cherubim of olivewood standing ten cubits (15 ft) high, with a wingspan of twenty cubits (30 ft). These cherubim were made to cover (or overshadow) the ark and its poles (1 Kgs 8:7–8; 2 Chr 5:8), implying a guardian function as present in the ancient Near Eastern examples.

Genesis 4:3–4

Archaeological Evidence for Early Ceremonial Practice

> In the course of time Cain brought some of the fruits of the soil as an offering to the LORD. And Abel also brought an offering—fat portions from some of the firstborn of his flock. The LORD looked with favor on Abel and his offering. (Gen 4:3–4)

Wide view of archaeological site of the Göbekli Tepe ceremonial complex

Mike Caba

The first mention of ceremonial practice begins with the first family and the mention of offering being made to the LORD. This assumes an altar and may imply the existence of an early worship center or sanctuary. Scholars such as Gordon Wenham see sanctuary imagery implied in the unique Hebrew terms used in Genesis 2–3 (elsewhere only in Leviticus) to describe the approach of the divine presence, the position of the sacred tree in the garden, the garden's east-west orientation, the priestly position and duties of Adam, and the presence and purpose of the cherubim.[4] This, and the divine action involved in killing animals to clothe the first couple (Gen 3:21), may explain why after the expulsion from the garden ceremonial activity is depicted as an already established practice.

The oldest known ceremonial center is an early Neolithic site in Göbekli Tepe ("Pot Belly Hill") unearthed in a field in the center of the Harran Plain, 17 kilometers east of central Sanliurfa, a town in south-eastern Turkey. Terah and his son Abram also settled for a time in Harran (Gen 11:31; 12:1–5; spelled Haran in English translations). According to conventional dating based on a virtual warehouse of flint tools including knives, choppers, and projectile points, it is ten-thousand–twelve-thousand-years-old and was created between 6000 and 7000 BC. Others would argue that this was a resumption of a Neolithic lifestyle after the flood (Gen 9:20). The site was first discovered in 1986 when a local man found a statuette in his field. Area surveys uncovered rings of standing pillars, and geomagnetic surveys in 2003 revealed at least twenty more rings of pillars piled together under the earth.

T-shaped pillars with carved figure of a fox

Mike Caba

Pillar with stylized human figure

Mike Caba

Subsequent excavation uncovered numerous statuettes adorned with wolf heads, pigs, storks, foxes, fawns, scorpions, snakes, and headless human figures.

Klaus Schnidt, a researcher at the German Archaeological Institute who has worked the site, suggests that the large "T" shaped pillars at the site (the largest are 18 ft tall and weigh sixteen tons) are stylized human figures, based on carved arms that angle from the shoulders of some pillars with hands reaching toward their loincloth-draped bodies. Others depict outstretched arms and may depict priests. In addition, he identified the life-sized Urfa statue, along with a number of broken heads as guardians of the Göbekli Tepe Sanctuary. The ceremonial aspect of the site also suggests that religious motivation helped develop civilization (rather than resulting from it as a need to maintain order) by drawing people together to construct a center such as this. Such a level of cooperation requires hierarchical organization, and the archaeological evidence at the site suggests a patriarchal social system, implied by the exaggerated depiction of male genitals on the human figures. In addition, the ancient inhabitants of Göbekli Tepe subsisted on agriculture along with hunting and gathering, which accords with Genesis's description of the lifestyles of Cain and Abel (Gen 4:2), as well as Noah and his descendants after the flood (Gen 9:20; 10:8–9). At this point, though some have suggested sacrificial practice from the presence of bones at the site, it is too early to make this conclusion. What this archaeological site does reveal is the evidence of worship or ceremonial practice in the earliest record of human activity.

Genesis 5:1–32; 9:29; 11:10–26

Decline in Lifespans and the Archaeological Record

> This is the written account of Adam's family line . . . Altogether, Adam lived a total of 930 years . . . Seth lived a total of 912 years . . . Enosh lived a total of 905 years . . . Kenan lived a total of 910 years . . . Mahalalel lived a total of 895 years . . . Jared lived a total of 962 years . . . Methuselah lived a total of 969 years . . . Lamech lived a total of 777 years . . . Noah lived a total of 950 years . . . This is the account of Shem's family line. . . . (from Gen 5:1–32; 9:29; 11:10)
>
> Shem lived 600 years . . . Arpachshad lived 438 years . . . Shelah lived 433 years . . . Eber lived 464 years . . . Peleg lived 239 years . . . Reu lived 239 years . . . Serug lived 230 years . . . Hahor lived 148 years. (Gen 11:1–26, author's translation)

In the antediluvian genealogy from Adam to Noah, the lifespans given for the majority of the names approach a millennium (excluding Enoch who was taken by God at the age of 365). Such extreme longevity made it possible for Methuselah at 969 years to overlap with Adam and Noah at the beginning and end of the genealogy. From the perspective of oral transmission this is significant, since Noah received information only one generation removed from the original source of human origins. However, after the flood there is a marked, though gradual, decrease to lifespans approaching our modern age limits. This unique contrast between the antediluvian and postdiluvian lifespans finds an archaeological parallel in a four-sided clay prism inscribed in Sumerian cuneiform (dated to the eighteenth century BC).

Ages of the Patriarchs

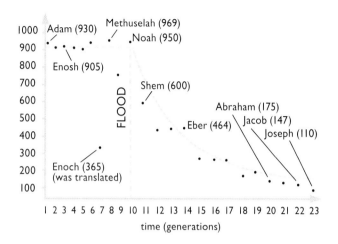

The main subject of the text is a directory of Sumerian and foreign dynasties, and for this reason the document has been called the Sumerian King List. The Sumerians (ca. 3500 BC) were one of the earliest postdiluvian civilizations that settled in the Tigris and Euphrates delta region. Fifteen copies of the Sumerian King List are extant, and these copies vary in some details, such as omitting the list of the pre-flood kings, in the names and number of the kings, and the order of dynasties.[5] These differences reflect the complex compositional and transmission history of the account (probably composed before ca. 2000 BC).

According to the Sumerian inscription, kingship was divinely bestowed ("lowered from heaven"), and the register of ruler's names appears to legitimize their reigns as official. Like the table of ten nations (based on their family heads) in Genesis 5, the Sumerian King List records the names of ten Sumerian kings who ruled before the flood. The unrealistically long lifespans for these kings ranging in the tens of thousands of years (the longest is 43,200 years) might suggest that this is a fictional account, and some Assyriologists hold this opinion. However, some of these names are known from other inscriptions and appear to be historical figures. The earliest named ruler, En-me-barage-si of Kish (ca. 2600 BC), with a lifespan of 900 years, as well as his successor Aga (lifespan of 625 years), is found in the Epic of Gilgamesh. This has led some to conclude that Gilgamesh was also an historical king of Uruk. For this reason, the majority of scholars accept the Sumerian King List as an historical record and explain the extreme reigns as epochs named after dynastic rulers or as intentional literary hyperbole to enhance the prestige of the ruler. However, these may simply be the translator's misinterpretation because the Sumerian numbering system is not fully understood.[6] With respect to this text in Genesis, what is significant is the same pattern in both accounts with longer lifespans for the prediluvian kings and shorter lifespans for the postdiluvian kings, whose number parallels the ten historical kings of Genesis 10. This indicates that the Bible and copies of the Sumerian King List must have had a common historical source.

Genesis 6:13–9:17

Noah's Ark and the Flood: Ancient Near Eastern Comparative Accounts

The first-century Jewish historian Flavius Josephus observed:

> This flood and the ark are mentioned by all who have written histories of the barbarians. Among these is Berosus the Chaldean . . . Hieronymus the Egyptian, author of the ancient history of Phoenicia, by Mnaseas and by many others . . . this might well be the same man of whom Moses the Jewish legislator, wrote. (*Ant.* 1.93–95)

This statement provides us with evidence from antiquity that the story of the flood was not only known in the area of the Fertile Crescent (Mesopotamia to

Egypt) but, as Josephus notes, by "all" who had recorded pagan histories from antiquity. How extensive this list might have been to Josephus is unknown, but we know that the story of the flood has been embedded in many of the world's cultures and beliefs. Josephus's statement that these might concern the same man (Noah), whose story Moses recounts in the book of Genesis, also suggests a comparison of ancient accounts with the Bible. However, except for the partially preserved account of Berosus in the writings of the church fathers, no other accounts from antiquity were known until late in the 1860s, when Assyriologist Henry Rawlinson recruited his student Henry Smith to help catalog the Assyrian-Babylonian section of the British Museum. Its collection of cuneiform tablets had come from excavations at ancient Mesopotamian sites, including those of Austen Henry Layard and Rawlinson at Nineveh. In this collection Smith discovered a Babylonian account of the flood and published it in 1872. Its similarities to the biblical flood account created a public sensation, as have new discoveries of similar pre-biblical flood accounts that

have surfaced among these cuneiform texts since. Based on these Mesopotamian discoveries, the consensus view is that the archetypal account of the flood (including that preserved in Genesis) originated in Mesopotamia.

These comparative flood stories contain details such as the building of an ark, animals in the ark, the landing on a mountain, birds sent out to determine if the waters had receded, and the worship of the gods through sacrifice after the landing. However, while these details compare favorably with the biblical account, they also have pronounced differences, not only with the biblical account but also with each another. This indicates that the various versions of the flood tradition were the result of the same processes that affected the transmission of other ancient stories across time, in which texts are adapted, abridged, and modified according to the distinct cultures and religions. The following archaeological discoveries contain flood accounts.

Sumerian King List (Sumerian Flood Account)

The earliest mention of a flood is an Old Babylonian account dated in its original composition to about 2300

The four sides with cuneiform text of the Weld-Blundell Prism/Sumerian King List, Uruk Exhibit

BC, the end of the classical period and about a thousand years after the Sumerian civilization was at its peak. There are nineteen fragmentary copies of the King List and no two are alike. However, there is enough shared data to understand they were derived from a common account of Sumerian history. The King List is essentially a royal registry of eight Sumerian rulers who lived in the pre- and post-flood eras. After the flood, kings ruling over city-states assumed power over the others. The earliest listed ruler whose historicity has been archaeologically verified is Enmebraragesi of Kish (ca. 2600 BC), so it is plausible that the document contains some historical figures who were later mythicized.

Although not technically a flood account, the flood appears in this account as an epochal event dividing and defining the Sumerian history related to these rulers. This usage of the flood assumes that the writer and his audience knew the details of the flood; otherwise the recorded events on either side of the flood would not have had the significance that is implied. As Kenneth Kitchen has noted, "the Sumerians and Babylonians of ca. 2000/1800 BC believed so firmly in the former historical occurrence of such a Flood that they inserted it into the Sumerian King List."[7]

The termination of antediluvian kingship by the flood implies that something in the outworking of their rule brought this about. If so, it would correspond to Genesis 6:1–7, which gives an explanation for the flood as divine punishment for the corruption of mankind. Although nothing is mentioned about the deliverance of mankind from the flood, this can be assumed from the statement, "after the flood kingship was again lowered from heaven."[8] Had mankind not survived the flood there would be no one upon whom kingship could be conferred. It should also be noted that none of the cities where the King List says kings ruled before the flood were seats of kingship after the flood. This implies a major interruption in civilization! There is also the implication of the extent of the flood, as civilization, embodied in the

concept of kingship, needs to be renewed on the earth after the time of the flood. The Sumerian King List names twenty-three rulers of the city of Kish between the flood and a contemporary of Gilgamesh, though some divide this list into two nonsuccessive parts with only eleven generations of kings in between. Figuring the basis of the average reign of these kings at about two hundred years, the date of the Mesopotamian flood would be around 2900–2800 BC, a date that is in the ballpark of the biblical chronology but has problems correlating with the conventional geological/archaeological timetable.

Eridu Genesis (Sumerian Flood Account)

The oldest ancient Near Eastern flood account is the Ziusudra Epic (named after the principal character) and is often linked to other fragments to produce a theoretical reconstruction known as the Eridu Genesis (named after Eridu, the first city). The single Sumerian tablet that contains this account is quite fragmentary, with only one-third of the original text extant. However, the missing parts can be reconstructed from other sources, such as the text recorded by the Sumerian King List and Berosus. In the account, kingship (human rule) is said to come down from heaven, but later Enlil, the chief of the gods, and An, the sky god, determine to wipe out mankind with a flood.

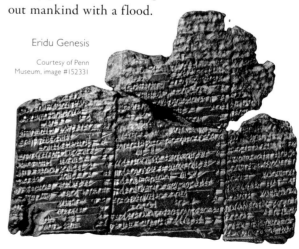

Eridu Genesis

Courtesy of Penn Museum, image #152331

However, Ziusudra, a Sumerian king-priest, is warned by Enki, the god of subterranean waters, through a vision and told to make a boat to escape the deluge. The details of construction are lost, but when the text resumes it describes the ferocity of the floodwaters due to a destructive wind. Surviving the flood, which last seven days and nights, Ziusudra made an opening in the boat so Utu the son god could let in his light. Thereafter, Ziusudra sacrificed oxen, sheep, and barley cakes with other ingredients to Utu. At first Enlil and An are angry to find that there are survivors of their flood, but Enki intercedes and in the end

Ziusudra is rewarded with eternal life for preserving animals and the seed of mankind and dwelt in the land of Dilmun, a place regarded as holy by the Sumerians and described in paradisical terms similar to the garden of Eden.

Simmonds Cuneiform Tablet/Ark Tablet (Old Babylonian Account)

In this Akkadian literary account (ca. 1900–1700 BC), the hero Atrahasis is warned by Enki to escape

a flood that will destroy mankind by building a boat. The selection of Atrahasis by Enki may be implied by his relation to a temple, perhaps Enki's temple, although he is not said in this text to be a priest. The direction he is given is to "draw out the boat that you

Simmonds Cuneiform/ Ark Tablet

will make on a circular plan."[9] This was apparently an adaptation to the story to fit the local convention of the round boat that was in vogue in Mesopotamia for river navigation; however, this craft was 230 feet in diameter with sides (walls) 20 feet high. Like the biblical account, but unique to the Mesopotamian accounts, this text mentions that the animals were brought on the boat "two by two." It also refers only to wild animals (animals of the steppes), but domesticated animals should be assumed, as it would have been thought unnecessary to mention that they were included. In the Atrahasis Epic (below) both wild animals and domesticated animals (cattle and sheep) are mentioned together. In other respects it follows the biblical story line, although the text does not contain the landing place of the boat.

Gilgamesh Epic (Old Babylonian Flood Account)

Another Old Babylonian account of the flood, and the most complete, is contained in a group of tablets known as the Gilgamesh Epic, based on the quest for immortality of its main character, King Gilgamesh, who ruled the Mesopotamian city of Uruk around 2600 BC. Because no copy of the entire text was discovered, scholars had to make a composite text based on fragments from periods separated by over one thousand years

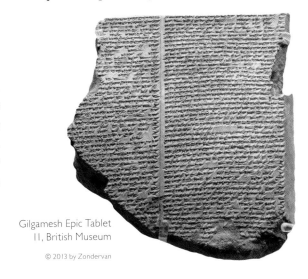

Gilgamesh Epic Tablet II, British Museum

Comparison of Gilgamesh Epic and Biblical Flood Account

Similarities	Differences
Ship was built (Gen 6:14; Lines 26, 28)	Multiple gods made flood with black cloud (Lines 101–110)
Bitumen used on ship (Gen 6:14; Lines 54, 66–67)	The gods had a counselor (Lines 117–18)
Food was stored (Gen 6:21; Lines 43–47)	Noah figure (Utnapishtim) instructed to leave gods (Lines 206–09)
Animals put onto ship (Gen 7:8–9; Lines 84, 86)	Ark was cube-shaped not barge-shaped (Line 30)
Family on ship (Gen 7:1–10; Line 85)	Ark launched and moved into position not lifted (Lines 79–80)
Waters covered the mountains (Gen 7:20–22; Lines 132, 139)	Workmen brought on ark (Line 37)
Ship had a window (Gen 6:8; Line 140)	Seven decks not three decks, interior divided into nine parts; flood at dawn (Lines 63, 100)
Birds sent out (Gen 8:6–12; Line 16)	Utnapishtim closes the ark door vs. God (Lines 91, 97)
Altar used in sacrifice (Gen 8:20–22; Line 164)	The gods helped with removal, food prep; frightened, battle occurred (Lines 88–94, 117–19, 178–201)
God/god pleased with altar sacrifice (Gen 8:20; Lines 167–69)	Storm six days and seven nights vs. forty days and forty nights (Lines 131–34)
Boat landed on a mountain (Gen 8:4; Lines 145–52)	Mount Nimush (Nisir) vs. mountains of Ararat as landing place (Lines 145–52)
Raven (Gen 8:7; Lines 160–61)	Raven vs. raven and dove (Lines 154–61)

"Gilgamesh," COS 1.132:458–60.

(1750 BC–612 BC). The epic as we have it today is recorded on twelve tablets. The flood story, which appears in tablet eleven, seems to have been borrowed directly from the Atrahasis Epic (which is also incomplete). In the story recounted here, Gilgamesh, in his search for immortality, discovered Utnapishtim, king of the Sumerian city state of Shuruppak, who with his wife was the sole survivor of the flood and as a result had been given immortality like the gods as a reward for preserving mankind from the flood. They were living in Dilmun, the same place Ziusudra settled in the Sumerian account. In his account of the flood, he says the creator god Ea

favored him by warning him in a dream of the flood that the god Enlil was sending to destroy mankind and commanding him to build a boat (cf. Gen 6:13–17) in the shape of a cube of 120 cubits squared. Utnapishtim sealed his boat with pitch, tar, and oil and took aboard his treasures and all kinds of animals (cf. Gen 6:18–22; 7:1–16). The sun god Shamash showered down loaves of bread and rained down wheat (apparently as food for the journey). Then came the heaven-sent storm that destroyed the rest of mankind (cf. Gen 7:17–23). By Utnapishtim's reckoning, the storm ended on the seventh day, and the dry land emerged on the twelfth day (cf. Gen 7:24). After the boat landed, Utnapishtim sent out a dove, a swallow, and finally a raven (cf. Gen 8:3–11). When the raven did not return he left the boat and offered a sacrifice to the gods (cf. Gen 8:12–22).

Atrahasis Epic (Old Babylonian Flood Account)

The Atrahasis Epic was discovered in the Library of Ashurbanipal and subsequently published in 1976 by George Smith as *The Chaldean Account of Genesis*.

Epic of Atrahasis (1635 BC, Year 12), King Ammisadqua of Babylon (Sippur?), British Museum (ME 78941)

In 1965 Alan Millard was studying cuneiform texts that had been stored in the British Museum since 1899. Among them he found a text whose wording sounded strangely like the book of Genesis.[10] What he had discovered was a previously unknown fragment of the Atrahasis Epic, which he published with W. G. Lambert. The now almost complete text of 1,245 lines was a significant advance over the 300 lines preserved in the Sumerian account.

The Atrahasis Epic, presented from the theological perspective of the Babylonians, contains information not found in the Gilgamesh Epic, with many details that are similar to the biblical accounts of the creation and flood. The gods, who rule the heavens and earth, make man from the clay of the earth mixed with blood (cf. Gen 2:7, 3:19) to take over the lesser gods' chores of tending the land (see Gen 2:15). When people multiply on the earth and become too noisy, a flood is sent (after a series of plagues) to destroy mankind (cf. Gen 6:13). One man, Atrahasis ("exceedingly wise"), whose name appears in the Sumerian King List as the king of Shuruppak, is given advance warning of the flood by the god Enki and told to build a boat (cf. Gen 6:14). He was apparently chosen due to his relationship to the god, for in the text we read: "Now there was one Atrahasis whose ear was open to his god Enki. He would speak with his god and his god would speak with him" (Column II, Lines 54-55). (Before the Early Dynastic period, kings were subordinate to priests and sometimes lived with them in the temple complex.) Atrahasis builds a boat with a roof, covers it with pitch, and loads it with food and animals and birds. Through this means he is saved while the rest of the world perishes (cf. Gen 6:17–22). Much of the text is destroyed at this point, so there is no record of the landing of the boat. Nevertheless, as in the conclusion of the biblical account, the story ends with Atrahasis offering a sacrifice to the gods and the chief god accepting mankind's existence (cf. Gen 8:20–22).

Similarities Between the Atrahasis and Biblical Flood Accounts

Atrahasis Account	Genesis Account
People multiply and cause trouble (I.i. 353–59; II.i., 2–8)	Wickedness of people brings judgment (Gen 6:13a)
Flood sent to destroy mankind (II.vii., 44–47)	Flood sent to destroy mankind (Gen 6:13b)
One man (Atrahasis) warned of the flood (III.i., 11–23)	One man (Noah) warned of flood (Gen 6:14)
Builds boat; fills with animals, food (III.i., 25–33; ii., 11–42; iv., 24–25; vi., 9–10)	Builds boat; fills with animals, food (Gen 6:17–22)
He is saved while the world perishes (III.iii., 11–18)	He is saved while world perishes (Gen 6:21)
[Damaged text; missing description of the landing]	Boat lands in mountains of Ararat (Gen 8:4)
After departure from vessel makes an offering (III.v., 31–36)	Noah makes sacrifice on an altar (Gen 8:20)
Offering accepted; gods will let mankind continue to live (III.viii., 9–18)	God accepts offering; makes covenant with mankind (Gen 8:21–22)

Based on W. G. Lambert, A. R. Millard, and M. Civil, *Atra-Ḥasīs: the Babylonian Story of the Flood* (Oxford: Clarendon, 1999), 42–105.

Berosus (Babylonian Flood Account in Hellenistic Period Record)

Berosus was a Babylonian court astrologer under the Seleucid ruler Antiochus I (280–261 BC). He had access to ancient Babylonian records, which he published in Greek in three volumes under the title *Babyloniaca* (History of Babylonia). The work as a whole is lost, but fragments survived in the Roman records of Pliny the Elder, Marcus Vitruvius Pollio, Censorinus, and in the writings of Flavius Josephus. In a fragment containing the story of the flood, Berosus says that Cronus, the father of Zeus (= Marduk) appeared to Xisuthrus (= Ziusudra) in a dream and told him that a flood would destroy mankind. He was also told to preserve the accumulated knowledge of mankind by burying in the city of Sippur (in Babylonia) all the tablets that constituted a library of the ancient world. Next, he was to build a boat and take his family, closest friends, and wild animals. As in the Genesis account, after the flood Xisuthrus twice sends out birds that returned to him covered with mud. He sent out birds a third time that did not return. Realizing that the land was drying out, he broke open a seam on a side of the boat and saw it had landed on a mountain in the land of Armenia (ancient Urartu = Ararat). He then set up an altar and sacrificed to the gods. Xisuthrus, his wife, and the steersmen went away and were not seen again, but a voice from heaven told the survivors to honor the gods and explained that Xisuthrus and his company had been honored by the gods and had gone to their abode. The survivors were told to go to the city of Sippur and dig up the tablets and restore knowledge to mankind. Berosus added as confirmation of this history that people had gone to the Gordyenian Mountains in Armenia and scraped off pieces of pitch to make into talismans.

Where Did These Stories Come From?

Modern criticism of the Genesis account, because it does not appear to conform to scientific consensus, has produced attempts by biblical scholars to explain the text in light of ancient Near Eastern literary parallels. Some have argued for the direct dependence by the author of Genesis on these myths, including adoption of their worldview, while others have argued that the biblical author had a polemical purpose to explain Israelite monotheistic origin and early history against the mythological background of their neighbors, whether in Egypt or Mesopotamia.[11]

Concerning the issue of literary dependence, Eric Cline has questions: "Why are so many people looking for Noah's ark, while not a single person is looking for Utnapishtim's ark or Ziusudra's ark or Athrahasis's ark? Why are we so interested in the biblical story and yet almost nobody has heard of the earlier Babylonian and Sumerian versions, which are almost identical?"[12] The search for Noah's ark is based on a belief that the biblical version represents an historical account, while the earlier ancient Near Eastern versions represent a corruption of the original story from a mythological worldview. In other words, there is only one historical ark, and its description and landing spot are best understood from the biblical account. Still, this is to presume that the biblical account should have priority as the most accurate account, even though it is in time the latest. On the contrary, many scholars contend that the biblical account was derived from the earlier known Mesopotamian accounts. This question of literary dependence between the Bible and the comparative flood accounts has been reduced to three options:[13] (1) They were originally Israelite accounts that were borrowed and adapted for the Mesopotamian religion and culture; (2) they were originally Mesopotamian tales that were borrowed and adapted by the Israelites to fit their conception of God; (3) both the Mesopotamian and Israelite (biblical) accounts came from a common ancient source.

With respect to the first option, since the composition of Genesis (as part of the Torah) is ascribed to Moses (Deut 31:24–26), and the Mesopotamian accounts date prior to that time (nineteenth–seventeenth centuries BC), it appears unlikely that the earlier Mesopotamian stories were derived from the later Israelite account. Concerning the second option, it is probable that Moses used sources in compiling his accounts in Genesis. A fragment of the Gilgamesh Epic was discovered in Israel in the 1956 excavations at Megiddo.[14] While this simply could have been part of an administrative archive, it allows for the possibility that pagan flood accounts were in circulation in Israel. Does this mean that there was a literary dependence on the Mesopotamian texts in compiling the biblical accounts? Even if such were the case, the Mesopotamian accounts may have themselves been based on an historical report of the great flood, and the selective use of extrabiblical sources need not conflict with the concept of biblical inspiration.[15]

However, neither the possession of nor occasional use of extrabiblical texts by the biblical writers demand that there was a literary dependence upon them. The biblical writers continually stress that their primary source was divine revelation. Secondary sources may have been used in some cases, but it does not appear that they were in this case.[16]

One explanation for the similarities between the biblical and ancient Near Eastern accounts has been that Moses was aware of them and was responding polemically to the opposing theological concepts they contained. One of the purposes of the Pentateuch is to establish Israel's distinction as God's chosen nation in the midst of the nations. This required Moses to both react to and to interact with competing notions about God, the creation, and the flood that had exerted an influence on Israel in their wider cultural context. While this does not address the question of origin, it does address the use of the older material and the need to provide an accurate (historically and theologically) interpretation of the event by comparison with an uncorrupted version. Moreover, Moses's source of reference was Egyptian (Acts 7:22), and there are only scant resemblances in this literature to a destruction of mankind by a flood. Therefore, while the biblical writers may have used secondary sources in some cases, it does not appear that they did in this case, since much of the biblical account is unique and there are many significant differences and omissions between it and the pagan accounts.

However, could there have been a tradition dependence, that is, could the biblical accounts simply be variations of Mesopotamian myths? Again, this is unlikely. One reason for this is that the biblical account is monotheistic (one God) and its characters ethically moral. By contrast, the Mesopotamian stories are polytheistic (many gods) and its characters ethically capricious (e.g., they are selfish, jealous, lie, and are fearful). This contrast is evident, for example, in the way the two texts treat the account of the post-flood world. In the biblical text God accepts Noah's sacrifice and promises to never again destroy the earth by a flood (Gen 8:20–22). In the Atrahasis Epic the gods discover to their chagrin that they have wiped out their only source for food (people's sacrifices), and so because they are hungry decide to put up with mankind (who can feed them). These gods do not appear to be able to control the consequences of the flood they caused, whereas the God of Genesis controls the flood from beginning to end because he, as Umberto Cassuto states, "is outside nature and above it."[17] Another reason is that important details in the accounts differ (such as the sizes of the boat, the duration of the flood, the sending out of the birds, etc.). Millard summarizes the question of alleged borrowing when he says:

> All who suspect or suggest borrowing by the Hebrews are compelled to admit large-scale revision, alteration, and reinterpretation in a fashion that cannot be substantiated for any other composition from the ancient Near East or in any other Hebrew writing … Granted that the Flood took place, knowledge of it must have survived to form the available accounts; while the Babylonians could only conceive of the event in their own polytheistic language, the Hebrews, or their ancestors, understood the action of God in it. Who can say it was not so?[18]

Moreover, in the development of myth it can be observed that over time history can be made into myth and myth can become more mythical, but myth does not become more simple, believable, and historical. Therefore, the later, more simple, believable, and historical account of the flood in Genesis could not be dependent on earlier mythical Mesopotamian accounts. Rather, the historical event of the flood as documented in the simpler Genesis account was made into myth. Todd Beall has explained that this can be seen in the different genre reflected in these accounts:

The account in all of Genesis 1–11, including the flood account of Genesis 6–9, is told in a straightforward narrative prose. It is not poetry or exalted language: the standard narrative marker, the *waw* consecutive imperfect, is used sixty-five times in Genesis 6:1–9:17. Indeed, if one were to look at the account likely to be more original, it would be the biblical account, which is far simpler and less embellished than its ANE counterparts.[19]

The difference between myth and historical narrative in these comparative accounts can be seen from a comparison of details such as the duration of the flood and the size and shape of the boat that delivered from the flood. In the ancient Near Eastern accounts the flood lasts a short time (six to seven days), but in the Bible it rains for forty days and nights, and the flood waters do not abate until the 378th day. This is more realistic in keeping with the concept of a universal flood that covered the whole earth to a height of 20 feet above the highest mountains. Likewise, in the pagan accounts the boat is not a seaworthy vessel, being described as either round or a cube. The Bible, by contrast, describes a rectangular vessel 450 feet long, 75 feet wide, and 45 feet high, dimensions that can be demonstrated to be seaworthy (similar dimensions have been used to build modern cargo barges). Since myth only becomes more mythical over time and not more historical, it is not possible for the Bible to have gotten its account from these pagan sources. More likely, all of these accounts are based on the preserved knowledge of these common historical events. The biblical author received his data from sources that had remained faithful to the true God as well as from direct divine revelation. The other deviations can be explained as the kind of departures expected from the loss of a shared society after the division of nations in the post-flood ancient Near East

(see Gen 10–11). Having left the source of true revelation and interpretation, those authors adapted their collective memories of the historical events to fit their new cultural mythology.

These factors make it unlikely that the biblical author borrowed from the Mesopotamian accounts. This, then, argues for both the Mesopotamian and Israelite (biblical) accounts being derived independently from a common ancient source. Whether this was an oral tradition or a written account is uncertain, but it is understandable that as time and distance from the original account occurred, along with changes in religious perspective, the account would be modified and adapted to fit with the prevailing culture. This explains some of the substantive differences between the Mesopotamian accounts themselves.

Genesis 6:13–16

The Construction of the Ark

> So God said to Noah, "I am going to put an end to all people, for the earth is filled with violence because of them. I am surely going to destroy both them and the earth. So make yourself an ark of cypress wood; make rooms in it and coat it with pitch inside and out. This is how you are to build it: The ark is to be three hundred cubits long, fifty cubits wide and thirty cubits high. Make a roof for it, leaving below the roof an opening one cubit high all around. Put a door in the side of the ark and make lower, middle and upper decks." (Gen 6:13–16)

The Hebrew term in the biblical account for the ark of Noah is *tebah*, which here denotes a kind of container used as a vessel (Gen. 6:14). The same word is used of the woven papyrus basket that bore the infant Moses safely on the Nile River (Exod 2:3).[20] In the Old Babylonian account titled Ark Tablet, an instruction manual for building an ark, the construction takes the shape of a coracle or gufa, the traditional round, basket-like boat used by the Mesopotamians. These vessels were made out of palm-fiber rope and made watertight with bitumen. Interestingly, this account gives the most extensive description (twenty lines) of ancient caulking yet known. Likewise, the biblical ark was covered inside and out with a sealant called in Hebrew *kopher* ("pitch"), which may be either bitumen or a type of tree resin (also used in ancient ship construction). The crafts constructed in the Atrahasis and Gilgamesh epics were thoroughly sealed with bitumen, including the door (in Atrahasis). The shape of the biblical ark, however, is rectangular and made of an unknown type of wood identified in Hebrew as gopher wood ("cypress," NIV). The shape of Utnapishtim's ark is similar, although its dimensions form a perfect cube. The shape of the boat in Atrahasis is like that of a blimp. The Akkadian term *makurru* implies a large cargo ship shaped like a football or gibbous moon. Atrahasis's boat is of reed construction: "The carpenter carried his axe, the reed worker carried his (flattening) stone, the child carried the pitch. . . ."[21] The size of all the boat constructions are huge, based on their stated dimensions (see chart below), although the vessel of Ziusudra in the Sumerian Eridu Genesis account is simply described as a "big boat."

Genesis 8:4

The Landing of the Ark

> And on the seventeenth day of the seventh month the ark came to rest on the mountains of Ararat. (Gen 8:4)

Many of the Old Babylonian accounts are missing the text that records the grounding of the ark, but in the Epic of Gilgamesh it is stated that Utnapishtim's boat came to rest on Mount Nisir (Nimush) in Kurdistan. Berosus records that "to this day a small part of the ship that came to rest in Armenia remains in the Gordyenian Mountains in Armenia and some people go there and scrape off pieces of pitch to keep them as good luck charms."[22] Flavius Josephus (*Ant.* 1.93) cites this same report but says that the Armenian mountain was also called Baris and was opposite Minyas. This place has been identified as Urartu and equated with the modern sites known as Mount Ararat and Mount

Source	Shape	Size	Structural Material	Water-Proofing Material
Bible	rectangular box	450 x 75 x 45 feet	wood	pitch
Eridu Genesis	unknown	"huge" ("The Eridu Genesis," *COS* 1.158:515)	reed (people used materials from their houses) hull was drilled	unknown
Gilgamesh	cube (120 x 120 x 120 cubits with six decks and seven floors)	120 x 120 x 120 cubits	wood	bitumen
Atrahasis	like a large blimp, completely roofed over with door	(the tablet is damaged where the dimensions of the ark would be stated)	reed	bitumen
Berosus	probably like that of Atrahasis since he appears to have used this source	"five stadia in length, and two in breadth" (3,034 x 1,213 ft)	wood (Josephus [*Ant.* I. iii., 5–6] cites Berosus and mentions "timber" remains)	bitumen (*Ant.* 1.93–95)
"Ark Tablet"	round (with roof)	230 x 20 feet	palm-fiber rope	bitumen

Çudi. Some scholars have argued that there was no landing on a mountain based on their interpretation of a local river flood in some of these sources. In the Atrahasis Epic it is said that Atrahasis "severed the mooring line and set the boat adrift."[23] From this statement it is assumed that there was no mountain landing but a sail down the river into the Persian Gulf. However, it is difficult to interpret this as a river flood since the information in Gilgamesh, with which this account agrees, clearly states that the boat came to rest upon a mountain. The Epic of Ziusudra has also been said to describe a river flood that floats the boat to a distant land rather than a landing on a mountain. However, the metaphorical terminology used in the text to describe dead bodies in relation to insects, a raft, and a riverbank do not make the case that the flood itself was a river flood, especially in view of the fact that the text in the preceding line uses the term "sea" and the clear statement that the intention of the gods was to completely destroy all mankind.[24]

Babylonian Map of the World (BM 92687)

Alexander Schick

The biblical text gives the landing place as "the mountains of Ararat." The Hebrew term 'rrt ("Ararat") is usually thought to designate a region of eastern Turkey that was once dominated by the Urartians,[25] whose name was derived from the term "Ararat." The comparative ancient Near Eastern cuneiform texts have not helped in understanding the precise mountain in view for the landing. However, according to Irving Finkel, the Assistant Keeper of Ancient Mesopotamian script, languages, and cultures at the British Museum, there is a reference in the Simmonds Ark Tablet that can be aligned with the oldest known map, the Babylonian World Map, to offer a geographic location: "The oldest map in the world ... tells us now where the Ark landed after the Flood! After 130 years of silence this crumbly, famous, much-discussed lump of clay divulges an item of information that has been sought after for millennia and still is!"[26] He believes that this location on the Babylonian World Map indicates travel straight through Urartu (indicated on the map) to a mountain that lay in the north at the very end of the Mesopotamian world. He identifies this mountain with modern Mount Ararat: "Ironically, whatever phenomena adventurers may claim to have found, it is Mount Ararat today that is closest in location and spirit to the original conception of the Babylonian poets."[27] Finkel explains that the Assyrian Gilgamesh Epic identified Mount Nisir (modern Pir Omar Gudrun in Iraqi Kurdistan near Suleimaniyah) as the landing place but argues that the Assyrians were reacting against the much older Babylonian tradition that reflected "far beyond Urartu" because they preferred a mountain closer to their home in the Zagros mountain range.

Mount Ararat, called Mount Masis by Armenians and Agri Dagh (Ağrı Dağı) by Kurds and Turks, is identified, according to some Islamic scholars, in Q Nuh 11:44 by the term *al-judi* (Çudi), where the term appears without the word "mountain" and translates literally from Arabic as the "high place" or "the highest." If this term refers to the highest mountain, it would best fit Mount Ararat, which at 16,854 feet is the highest mountain in the region. While geologists debate the status of this volcanic mountain as a late-formed strato volcano versus sedimentary core overlaid by volcanic deposition,[28] there is geologic evidence of pillow lava (formed underwater) as high as 12,000 feet, and there is archaeological evidence from as early as the Late Chalcolithic Age of habitation on and near this mountain.[29]

Mt. Ararat, eastern Turkey 16,854 feet (5,137 m)

Expeditions have sought the landing place elsewhere. One in Dogubeyazit province, some 1.9 miles (3 km) to the southwest from the Turco-Iranian highway near the Telçeker village and at the foot of Mount Ararat, is a formation known as the Durupinar site. Turkish geologists have positively identified it as a natural formation of the Telçeker earthflow or mudflow.[30] Another expedition to Mount Suleiman in the Elborz Mountains in Iran discovered a formation. It was identified by geologists as a blockey remnant of volcanic or metamorphic rock. In 2013 Sirnak University in eastern Turkey held a symposium to discuss the historical and archaeological issues related to the site of Mount Çudi in southeastern Turkey, based on Syrian Christian tradition and some Islamic scholars following Q Nuh 11:44. The German scholar

Friedrich Bender conducted a survey of the mountain in 1953 and did a shallow excavation that recovered small wood chips bound together with an asphalt-like substance. His test yielded a radiocarbon date of 6500 years for the wood sample and 50,000 years for the asphalt sample. However, no further excavation has been done to verify this earlier report. If the older Mesopotamian accounts of Mount Ararat are supported by the oldest map in the world, and the deviations from this tradition can be explained, then modern Mount Ararat appears to be the strongest candidate. And it has only been Mount Ararat where in the past century and a half eyewitness claims to a wooden structure have been made.

Several search teams from the 1950s through the 1990s claimed to have found dark-colored wood beams on the western side of Mount Ararat in Parrot Glacier at elevations ranging from 12,000–14,000 feet. While not all of the samples were radiocarbon dated, most have yielded younger dates than expected. In 2012 small wood chips mixed with a black material were allegedly retrieved through core sampling beneath the glacier on the eastern plateau at an elevation of 16,500 feet. AMS testing yielded a date between the sixteenth and seventeenth centuries AD, and the black material was judged to be volcanic. Despite the lack of material evidence for a structure on the mountain, a local Kurdish shepherd and others insist that they were eyewitness to a large wooden structure on the western side of the mountain, and expeditions continue to be mounted to try and discover the source of these claims.

Genesis 10:8–9

Archaeological Evidence for the Identity of Nimrod

Cush was the father of Nimrod, who became a mighty warrior on the earth. He was a mighty hunter before the LORD; that is why it is said, "Like Nimrod, a mighty hunter before the LORD." (Gen 10:8–9)

Although mentioned by name only four times in the Old Testament, the biography of Nimrod given in Genesis 10:7–12, his later characterization as a "mighty warrior on earth" (1 Chr 1:10), and his depiction as the founder of the Assyrian empire (Mic 5:6) have occupied scholars intent on identifying him with a known historical figure. The Jewish writers Philo and Josephus (*Ant.* 1.4.2) offered their respective suggestions that he was a giant who opposed God (*QG* 2.82) or the tyrant behind the erection of the Tower of Babel (*Ant.* 1.113–114). Genesis 10:10–12 includes within his kingdom the Sumerian cities of "Babylon" (Eridu?), "Uruk," and "Akkad," all in the land of Shinar (southern Mesopotamia/Babylonia), as well as the Assyrian cities of "Nineveh," "Rehoboth-Ir" (Reḥovot City), "Resen," and "Calah" (Kalhu). Since archaeology has uncovered the remains of some of these cities, it may be conjectured that it could provide evidence for identifying the ruler who built up this extensive ancient empire.

One suggestion has been the Egyptian Pharaoh Amenhotep III (1408–1369 BC) because of his prowess as a hunter and his boast that he extended his rule to the Euphrates. Another has been the patron god of Lagash, Ninurta, who was the Sumerian god of war and is described in the Sumerian myths as a great hunter. He was also later worshiped as a principal Assyrian deity. However, the biblical account does not call him a deity, but a man, and the south to north direction of this empire building in Mesopotamia indicates a third-millennium-BC setting. Therefore, a proper candidate must be sought from this geographic area and from among human rulers of the third millennium BC. In this regard, the famous Mesopotamian hero Gilgamesh has been suggested

as a candidate since he acted as a tyrant and opposed deity. However, while fifth ruler of the First Dynasty of Uruk (based on the Sumerian King List), there is no archaeological account of Gilgamesh as a founder or conqueror of any city (Sumerian or otherwise).

One candidate fits the aforementioned criteria and has significant support from the archaeological record is the third-millennium Semitic king of Sumer and Akkad renowned as the first empire builder. Also known as Sargon the Great, "the Great King" (Akkadian *sharrukin*, meaning "the true king" or "the king is legitimate") founded and ruled Akkad in the twenty-third and twenty-second centuries BC and conquered the Sumerian city-states. The following are a summation of arguments by Douglas Petrovich in favor of this identification.

1. *The identification of Nimrod's genealogical origin in Cush with Sargon's geographical origin in Sumerian Kish.* This point requires equating biblical Cush with Sumerian Kish, based on the proposal that many peoples would have descended from and numerous territories would have been named after Cush/Kish, the grandson of Noah. The Sumerian King List names Kish as the first city on which "kingship was [again] lowered from heaven" after the flood and that then became the leading city of Sumer. Archaeological excavation of the once impressive Palace A at Kish dates to this period and support the Sumerian records.

2. *Nimrod and Sargon were both credited with bringing Akkad into prominence.* Although archaeologists have not yet discovered the site of the city of Akkad, the ancient texts discovered by archaeologists give its location in the area of Babylon and Kish, and its history in these ancient records is extensive. The archives at Ebla were contemporary with the First Dynasty of

Kish and suggest that Akkad was not prominent until Sargon restored Kish and subsequently made it his new capital. From there he launched his conquests on Mari and Ebla and the land of Assyria. This fits with the biblical record of Nimrod's location in Sumer. The second city listed in Genesis 10:10 is Uruk, the center of power in Mesopotamia when Sargon came into his rule in Kish and the city he had to conquer to command all of Sumer. The third city listed is Akkad, a city Sargon developed as his capital and the place from which he extended his rule to the north.

3. *Nimrod and Sargon were both involved in initial building projects in Assyria.* Nimrod is said to have been the first to build up the principal cities of Assyria (Gen 10:11–12). The first recorded penetration in the archaeological record from southern Mesopotamia into Assyria is a date formula from Nippur that credits this to Sargon. Honorary inscriptions on the monuments of native governors record Sargon's rule in Assur and Nineveh. Remains of a statue (a head) that dates to the reign of Manishtushu, the second son of Sargon to rule after him, also attest to Sargon's rule. In addition, inscriptional evidence attests to Manishtushu's rule in Nippur and his restoration of the Ishtar temple. Because history records him as a less powerful figure, his attaining this stature strongly implies that his father had earlier seized the power in Assur. The archaeological evidence, though scant, supports Sargon's activity in Assyria. For example, the inscription of a seventeenth-century-BC Hittite king noted that Sargon crossed the upper Euphrates to receive the submission of the city of Hahhum. In addition, the archives of the northern site of Ebla mention Sargon's Kish as one of

only two southern Babylonian cities, implying that commercial trading was conducted via Kish and that Sargon's control therefore extended to the Assyrian lands of northern Mesopotamia.

In addition, archaeological evidence from the sites of Tell Mozan, Tell Leilan, and Tel Brak, all cities opposite northern centers of Assyrian power, argues for Sargon's mastery in Assyria. The evidence at Tell Leilan includes change in settlement patterns and pottery production as a state-level society emerged (Leilan phase IIa, 2400–2300 BC) and altered agricultural life as Mesopotamia united under Sargon and the Akkadian empire (Leilan phase IIb, ca. 2300–2200 BC). Tel Brak was established under the Akkadian empire as an imperial distribution center that exercised control over Tell Leilan and Tell Mozan, and considerable civil improvements were instituted, including canal management that reflects the influence of southern Mesopotamian expertise (since they developed these techniques). Moreover, the Akkadian influence on the material culture (greater than that of the Hurrians) can be seen from a palatial brick building attributed to Sargon's grandson, Naram-Sin, unearthed at Tel Brak. However, at this same time (ca. 2200 BC) Akkadian domination ended (as the occupation phase IIb at Tell Leilan and Tel Brak reveal) and the sites were abandoned. This indicates that Sargon had previously built up these cities in the south and north.

4. *Nimrod and Sargon both had a lasting influence on Assyria.* The biblical account indicates that Nimrod had a lasting influence on the Israelites, especially with his exploits in Assyria, since at the end of the biblical period the prophet Micah equated the "land of Assyria" with Nimrod (Mic 5:6). In like manner, Sargon exerted a

lasting influence on the Assyrian culture with his introduction of the eponymic dating system to his empire. This system, which keeps track of successive years by designating each year with a title of a memorable event from that year, continued in use throughout the history of Assyria.

5. *Nimrod and Sargon both were legendary for their military exploits.* The Hebrew text in Genesis 10:9 calls Nimrod a *tsir* "mighty hunter" (literally "champion of game"). Nimrod appears as the first and foremost of hunters, and it can be assumed he hunted men in the same way he hunted animals. The extension of Nimrod's empire from south to north, though not stated, was certainly by means of military conquest. In later times the hunting exploits and military conquest of Assyrian kings were the dominant themes of palace reliefs discovered at Nineveh. The biblical text says that he did this "before the LORD," a phrase that simply means it was observed by God and not that his actions had divine approval. However, the next words in the text "That is why it is said, 'Like Nimrod, a mighty hunter before the LORD'" indicates that this aspect of his reputation may have been extended to successive generations (similar to the later Assyrian reliefs) through a traditional proverb (cf. 1 Sam 19:24). In like manner, Sargon was renowned for his military conquests and depicted specific acts of brutality in his propagandistic reliefs to instill fear in his subjects and enemies. Sargon's Stele of Ishtar shows seven captured prisoners entangled in a royal figure's cloak while their heads are smashed with a battle mace. The royal figure has been interpreted as Ishtar, the Akkadian dynastic goddess, who acts as a warrior deity on behalf of Sargon. Another Akkadian monument, the Sargonic Victory Stele from Telloh, depicts a military campaign in the slaughter and enslavement of captives. In addition, Sargon's Obelisk, the first known obelisk-like monument from ancient Mesopotamia, depicts an Akkadian battle in which enemy soldiers are shown pierced by a spear, suspended by their arms, and bound with neck stocks while vultures and wild animals devour human carcasses. These steles, which are only a small part of the larger evidence of Akkadian military brutality, are sufficient to show Sargon's reputation in this regard.

Bronze head (Akkadian Period c. 2300–2200 BC) possibly of Sargon, Iraq Museum, Bagdad, Iraq.

De Agostini Picture Library/M. Carrieri/ Bridgeman Images

The inscriptional and material cultural evidence from archaeological excavation in ancient Mesopotamia provides historical evidence for the important comparison of Sargon with biblical Nimrod. If this evidence compiled by Petrovich holds and is strengthened by further discoveries from the field, it may be said that the case for the identity of Nimrod may have been solved.

Genesis 11:4, 9

The Tower of Babel

> Then they said, "Come, let us build ourselves a city, with a tower that reaches to the heavens, so that we may make a name for ourselves; otherwise we will be scattered over the face of the whole earth." . . . That is why it was called Babel—because there the LORD confused the language of the whole world. From there the LORD scattered them over the face of the whole earth. (Gen 11:4, 9)

The tower was constructed in the general vicinity of Shinar (Gen 11:2), southern Mesopotamia/Babylonia, where the city of Babylon would later be founded. Van der Veen and Zerbst argue that Hebrew *shinar* is derived from Akkadian *shumer*, such that the site may be equated with ancient Sumer.[31] The Hebrew term used for the "tower" (v. 4) is *migdal*, a term used elsewhere in the Old Testament for a military tower. However, since the context is Mesopotamia, it was the most appropriate word in the Hebrew vocabulary to describe the ziggurat, a structure in Mesopotamian culture historically fitting the author's description. Even so, the Hebrew root *gdl*

("to be large"), is roughly the equivalent of the Akkadian word *zaqaru* ("to be high") used for "ziqqurat," and, in fact, the form of the ziggurat may be thought of as successive "towers" built one upon the other.

Some thirty Mesopotamian ziggurats have been found from the north (Mari, Tell-Brak, and Dur Sharrukin), the south (Ur and Eridu), and the east (Susa and Chogha Zanbil). Some claim the earliest structures that may be called ziggurat are those discovered at the Ubaid temples at Eridu from the Ubaid period (4300–3500 BC) and at the Sumerian city of Uruk (biblical Erech/modern Warka) dated to the Jamdet Nasr period (3100–2900 BC). However, archaeologists confidently date the origin of the ziggurat to the Early Dynastic period (2900–2350 BC), where good examples exist at Ur, Mari, and Nippur. The remains of these ziggurats, the later structures built on top of the earlier ones for sacred continuity, consist of stages of towers stacked upon another and decreasing in size as they progressed upward (similar to the early form of the step pyramid, such as that of Djoser at Saqqara in Egypt). The side dimensions of these structures range from 66 ft (20 m) to 295 ft (90 m). The attendant priest accessed these platforms by means of steps or ramps. The ziggurat was

Model of ziggurat of the Eanna temple, Uruk.

©artefacts-berlin.de; Material: German Archaeological Institute dedicated to the city's patron deity, and the progressive platforms were usually topped by the figure of a god or goddess. This kind of ziggurat could have been a descendant of the Babylonian tower of Babel.

The importance of the Mesopotamian temple economy has been noted in the Early Dynastic texts from Lagash and Shuruppak. Walton notes that a text associated with the goddess Eanna, the patron deity at Uruk/Erech (Gen 10:10) and mentions that its temple of the ziggurat had both a cultic function and a cosmic function "linking heaven and earth" or "heaven and the netherworld."[32] Based on this text, it might be conjectured that the purpose of the ziggurat was for the deity's access from the realm of mankind to the heavenly realm of the gods. The ziggurat does not figure in cultic rituals associated with these temples (possibly because rituals have their focus on human access to the gods), but the absence of reference in the known texts to the use of the ziggurat makes any conclusion tentative. These texts also associate the sanctuary and its ziggurat with a cosmic mountain, which is typically identified in this mythology with the divine abode. The stairway (Akk. *simmiltu*) supported by the structure of the ziggurat was the access point for the gods to travel between heaven and earth. This term is cognate to the Hebrew *sullam* (series of rising rows of stones, stepped ramp, flight of steps) that appears only in the story of Jacob's dream of a "stairway" stretching between heaven and earth (Gen 28:12). The ziggurat provided the deity with essential services for the journey to the top and the gateway to the heavenly abode. The biblical text mentions that the structural material used for the "tower of Babel" was fired mud "bricks" (Gen 11:3), a practice foreign to Israelite construction. Finegan observes, "kiln-fired bricks are first noted during the late Uruk period and become more common in the Jamdet Nasr period toward the end of the fourth millennium."[33] This verse mentions that bitumen (Heb. *khemer*) was used as mortar to bind the fired bricks (which formed only the outer layer of the ziggurat). The use of this expensive material indicates most likely the city's temple complex that contained the ziggurat.

Given this understanding of the archaeological data, it seems that Moses's account of the building of the city focuses on the erection of a tower structure, the ancestor of a ziggurat, and how its builders related it to the divine abode. In addition, the biblical text states that the purpose of the structure was to prevent the people from being scattered abroad (in contrast to the original divine mandate in Gen 1:28 and its restatement in 9:1, 7). In other words, this verse describes an urbanization project to keep the population together around a single administrative complex with the temple as its center. This would allow them to cooperate in common production that would have benefits far greater than that of segregated ("scattered") societies. Such a purpose can be seen in the Late Uruk period in the precinct of Eanna, where architecture layout and city planning appear to be distinctly dedicated to the goddess and her temple, which towered over the flat-roofed buildings in the city. This urbanization process contributed to the deification of human rulers who maintained control over the temple-state, a form of government described of the gods in Mesopotamian mythology. According to Walton, "the ziggurat and the temple complex provide the link between urbanization, of which they are the central organ, and Mesopotamian religion, which they typify. The ziggurat and the temple complex were representative of the very nature of Mesopotamian religion as it developed its characteristic forms."[34] The problem in this passage is not the construction of a city but the purpose of the city and its cultic center that deified humans and thus degraded the nature of God. Once this concept took hold, mankind would alter its entire relationship with the creator, a thought reflected in the words of Genesis 11:6: "If as one people speaking the same language they have begun to do this, then nothing they plan to do will be impossible for them." The wording is similar to that in Genesis 3:22: "The man has now become like one of us . . . He must not be allowed to reach out his hand and take from the tree . . . and live forever." This act of divine distortion and degradation was formalized later in Babylon, but its roots appear at this beginning in Babel.

The oldest representation of the tower of Babel comes from an unprovenanced black stone stele from the period of Nebuchadnezzar II (604–562 BC). Although from a private collection, it has been authenticated by epigraphists who have worked on the cuneiform inscription on the stela. It has been called the tower of Babel stele because it portrays the tower of Babel and King Nebuchadnezzar II, who ruled Babylon and restored temples all over Babylonia, calling himself the "great restorer and builder of holy places." One of these he reconstructed was Etemenanki, a 300-foot-high ziggurat-temple dedicated to the god Marduk. The stele's inscription describes a related boast: "I made it the wonder of the people of the world, I raised its top to the heaven, made doors for the gates, and I covered it with bitumen and bricks."[35] This language is reminiscent of that in our Genesis text that describes the boast of the builders of the tower of Babel: "let us build . . . a tower that reaches to the heavens" (v. 4). The scholars who published the Tower of Babel stele argue that Nebuchadnezzar II restored the original tower of Babel and repeated the original boast in his inscription.[36]

Tower of Babel Stele; contemporary overlay details Nebuchadnezzar and tower (604–562 BC)

The Schøyen Collection, MS 2063, Oslo and London

A Word About Unprovenanced or Undocumented Antiquities

Unprovenanced or undocumented antiquities are artifacts that have been removed from their original context and are therefore no longer useful to the archaeologist whose goal is to preserve the original information of a site through proper excavation and documentation of finds in situ. This does not mean that unprovenanced antiquities have no value in understanding the archaeological record or with respect to biblical studies. Quite a number of the important artifacts in world museums today came from an earlier time when the significance of provenance was not as well recognized or came into their collections through well-meaning donors who acquired them from local antiquity markets or were appropriated when their government occupied a foreign country. Even most of the famous Dead Sea Scrolls are technically unprovenanced and the cave site designated for them has depended upon the memory and integrity of those who found them or sold them. Unprovenanced antiquities provide general information about the period from which they come (being able to be approximately dated by comparison with similar provenanced examples) and in some cases are the only known example of an artifact.

Antiquity sellers (who illegally dig up objects) do not generally tell antiquity dealers (who may legally sell these objects) about the specific provenance of their artifacts because their activity is prosecutable and they fear an authority may arrest them and close down their site or a competitor might locate it and steal from them. There is a debate today over whether museums should own or display unprovenanced pieces and whether private collectors should purchase such items (even where legal) from antiquity dealers (including auction houses). On one side of the debate are those who say the purchase of unprovenanced artifacts encourages the illegal international antiquity black market, despite stringent attempts to stop its activity. They rightly observe that such antiquities can only come from looting tombs or known but unexcavated sites and are destructive practices that not only ruin the work for archaeologists but rob the world of the unrecoverable information for biblical and other studies. In recent years the Bagdad Museum in Iraq was looted of many of its finest provenanced artifacts as a result of the Gulf War, as were the Egyptian Museum in Central Cairo and the Mallawi Egyptian Museum of Antiquities, which was ransacked and most of its contents stolen or damaged during the protests in that country. Terrorist organizations such as ISIS capture sites and their museums and sell antiquities to finance their military operations. While it may be argued that the existence of a market for antiquities encourages looting and the illegal trade, it is an unfortunate reality that looting has not been stopped by local enforcement (where this seriously exists), and it is unrealistic to believe that the trade can be stopped given the desire of collectors, the high investment value of antiquities, and the political unrest and economic deprivation that exists.

On the other side of the debate are those who argue for the educational value of exhibiting unprovenanced antiquities and for their ownership by those who legally acquire them from licensed dealers and treasure them as witnesses to the history of the lands of the Bible. They would contend that postmodernism has affected society in such a way that there is increasing ignorance, along with decreasing interest, in the places and cultures of the past, especially biblical sites. Having actual archaeological examples of this past to show students is of practical importance in furthering their realistic knowledge of the biblical world and even for influencing some to become archaeologists. To this end many colleges and universities, especially where there is little access to established museums with exhibitions of provenanced finds, have created "biblical museums" to provide their students access to real-world artifacts. In this context, while students are educated from these collections, they should be taught to have proper respect for the remains of the past and informed about the dangers to archaeological sites from illegal activities. Therefore, since the debate is far from settled, most archaeologists discourage any activity that might be detrimental to the preservation of archaeological sites and many oppose any sale of unprovenanced finds.

Genesis 12–50

The Historicity of the Patriarchal Period

The early biblical period, often called the patriarchal period, is attested in the archaeological record of the Middle Bronze Age. The archaeological evidence for this period includes the Code of Hammurabi, Egyptian and Hittite texts, and thousands of clay tablets from the Amorite city of Mari (Tell Hariri), Nuzi (city of the biblical Horites), Tell Leilan, and Alalakh. In addition, the Syrian site of Ebla (Tell Mardikh) has offered some comparative material in the form of law codes, legal and social contracts, and religious and other types of texts.

Comparisons between these texts and the Bible have shown that the proper names recorded there are the same or similar, many having the same theophoric element (addition of words for God, such as *ya* or *el*; see *yaʿakov/*Jacob and *rachel*) as those appearing in the patriarchal narratives. Since names tend to be unique to a given time period, this evidence helps confirm the chronology of the patriarchs. In addition, laws that governed the patriarchs' social behavior were based on the local customs and time period during which the cultures that made them existed. In Genesis 49 Jacob blesses his twelve sons and gives each a share of the inheritance, but in the later Mosaic law the first-born son is to receive a double inheritance (Deut 21:15–17). The reason for this legal contradiction is that the inheritance laws governing the patriarchs find their source in the culture of their contemporaries in the ancient Near East, such as the law code of Lipit-Ishtar (twentieth century BC). By contrast, the Neo-Babylonian laws of the first millennium BC have the sons of a first wife receiving a double portion and secondary sons only a single portion. The changing social customs reflected by these laws indicate that Abraham observed laws that were specific to a certain time and place.

The patriarchal narratives also describe their lifestyle as nomadic and report that they frequently migrated between the lands of Canaan and Egypt. Evidence for this geographical migration pattern can be seen from the tomb mural of Beni Hasan, dating to around 1890 BC (during the patriarchal age). It portrays a parade of thirty-seven Asiatics from the region of Shut (which includes the area of Sinai and southern Canaan) led by Abishai (their chief) coming to trade with the Egyptians. This discovery not only reveals the appearance of people like the biblical patriarchs but confirms that people from the area of Canaan came to Egypt during the time and in the same manner as did Abraham and Sarah (Gen 12:10), Jacob and his sons (Gen 42:5; 43:11; 46:5–7), and Joseph (Gen 37–50). While direct material evidence is generally lacking for specific biblical persons and events, archaeological finds from this period have demonstrated that the biblical details are historically

accurate—facts that could only have been preserved by those who actually experienced the conditions at this time. Even so, the recovery of the arched city gate of Laish (biblical Dan), dating from the time of the patriarchs, is one archaeological find that may correlate with an actual event connected with the biblical Abraham (Gen. 14:14).

Genesis 11:28, 31

The Time of the Patriarchs

> While his father Terah was still alive, Haran died in Ur of the Chaldeans, in the land of his birth ... Terah took his son Abram, his grandson Lot son of Haran, and his daughter-in-law Sarai, the wife of his son Abram, and together they set out from Ur of the Chaldeans to go to Canaan. But when they came to Harran, they settled there. (Gen 11:28, 31)

The biblical account of the patriarchs in Genesis 12–50 (including Joseph) indicates a Middle Bronze date from the late third millennium to mid-second millennium BC (2166–1805). This traditional dating was defended by early-twentieth-century scholars like William F. Albright,[37] Ephraim Speiser,[38] and Cyrus Gordon,[39] employing archaeological data from the fifteenth-century-BC archives of Mari and Nuzi. They cited social and cultural customs that had apparent parallels in the patriarchal narratives and therefore supported the early date for the origin of these stories. Mid-twentieth century scholars such as David Noel Freedman viewed Abraham as a "warrior-chieftain" and "merchant prince," who, if not literate, would have employed professional scribes, whose records and transactions could have been preserved and transmitted to future generations. He argued for an even earlier date based on proposed parallels in the Ebla tablets.[40] However, in the latter part of the twentieth century, scholars judged the ancient Near Eastern parallels as "unconvincing,"[41] and the Ebla material was deemed both controversial and fraught with interpretive difficulties.[42] Next came the advent of the source-critical method and the work of historical critical scholars like Thomas Thompson[43] and John Van Seters,[44] who raised a new challenge to the traditional view. Focusing on alleged anachronisms in the patriarchal narratives, these scholars believed the "traditions" they contained better reflected a mid-first-millennium (Iron Age II) composition date. This was the earlier conclusion of the nineteenth-century form-critical school of Julius Wellhausen that developed the documentary hypothesis theory and placed the redaction of the Pentateuch in the postexilic period.[45]

In response to these charges, conservative scholars have pointed out that the Mari and Nuzi parallels are still valid witnesses to patriarchal practices even if they might not have been the context or influence for them. Victor Matthews has continued to point to the nomadic and pastoral nature of the patriarchs, which, despite some contact with urban centers, remains a characteristic of foreigners in Canaan of the second millennium.[46] Moshe Weinfeld and others have demonstrated that ancient Near Eastern royal grant treaties such as those from Nuzi, Ugarit, and Hattusa formed the pattern for the Abrahamic covenant.[47]

In addition, Egyptian local color plays a role in the setting of these narratives. For example, the Story of Sinuhe (ca. 2000–1800 BC) offers parallels to the type of tribal configuration seen in the patriarchs, of the movement of Semitic groups between Canaan and Egypt and of a religious tolerance toward these groups that fits a second millennium context. There is still the Code of Hammurabi, Egyptian and Hittite texts, and comparative material from Tell Leilan and Alalakh. Kenneth Kitchen has also shown that a specific form of treaties and covenants (Gen 21; 26; 31) and geo-political conditions (Gen 14) reflect an accurate picture of Bronze Age conditions, and he has shown that the price of slaves at twenty shekels, as well as the mention of other commercial products, recorded

in second-millennium texts is accurately stated in the patriarchal accounts (cf. Gen 37:28).[48] Alan Millard has argued that in view of the fragmentary nature of our archaeological and epigraphic evidence it is inaccurate to dismiss elements in these narratives as anachronistic and therefore inauthentic to the period. The contention that these are absent from the archaeological record in the time the Bible places the patriarchs is an argument from silence.

The claim that anachronisms are present in the patriarchal narratives means that while there may be historical elements in accounts, the stories about them recorded much later could be fictional. Kitchen argues against this, noting in light of comparative ancient Near Eastern examples that though the narratives as a whole reflect a form of ancient biography,[49] the accurate transmission of the details in the text should not be questioned. As evidence he cites the example of an Egyptian text known as Tales of the Magician (ca. 1600 BC), which records events occurring a thousand years earlier.[50] In this text a list of seven rulers are mentioned in correct succession, indicating that such historical and chronological data could be carefully preserved. Since less than half this period of time existed between the end of the patriarchs and the recording under Moses, reliability of such ancient transmission should be accepted.

Conservative scholars acknowledge that the eventual editing of the archaic script into Standard Hebrew during the time of the monarchy necessitated some changes. For example, the name of the city of Bronze Age Laish was changed to Dan, its name from the Iron Age, and the Bronze Age site of Ur was clarified as Chaldean. However, Kitchen contends that these narratives were accurately transmitted over time, a fact revealed by the inclusion of names, practices, and other details unique to the Bronze Age.[51] Of these, the onomastic argument is the strongest. Consider the names of Abram's close relations, such as his great-grandfather Serug, grandfather Nahor, and father Terah (and even Abram's own name), names that appear in Old Assyrian and Babylonian texts and Neo-Assyrian texts and furthermore correspond with places in the Euphrates-Habur region of Syro-Mesopotamia. This geographical linkage with Abram and his lineage agree with the biblical accounts that his family came from Ur and settled in Harran (Gen 11:28, 31). Moreover, the names of the patriarchs place them in a cultural setting within the Northwest Semitic language group of the Amorite population of the early second millennium BC. Names with an *i/y* prefix such as *yitsak* ("Isaac"), *ya'akov* ("Jacob"), *yoseph* ("Joseph"), and *yishmael* ("Ishmael") belong to this type of name, whose appearance diminishes significantly in the first millennium and onward.[52] Therefore, the most appropriate time during which men with these names would have lived would have been the pre-Israelite period, in accordance with the biblical text. In like manner, the places mentioned in the patriarchal narratives also reveal a historical consistency when compared to the archaeological evidence from the ruins of Ur, Hebron, Beersheba, and Shechem. In particular, the city of Harran in upper Mesopotamia, which in the biblical text seems to have been a commercial center in the time of Abraham, was abandoned after the patriarchal period and remained unoccupied from about 1800 BC until 800 BC. It is improbable that someone inventing the story later would have chosen Harran as a key location when the town had not existed for hundreds of years.

A late composition in the first millennium BC would have no access to such detailed information. Moreover, archaeological analysis of the alleged anachronisms shows that they fit a Bronze Age context better than that of the Iron Age (see below on the domestication of the camel anachronism). The archaeological evidence also favors a Bronze Age date for other details in the patriarchal narratives, such as

the patriarchal sojourns in Egypt. Genesis 12:10 notes: "Now there was a famine in the land, and Abram went down to Egypt to live there for a while because the famine was severe." The tomb mural of Beni Hasan in Middle Egypt depicts Semites migrating from Canaan to Egypt in the Middle Bronze period (Eighteenth Egyptian Dynasty). Almost all of the statements about life in Egypt are positive, hardly something that could have been said by any Israelite after the time of Egyptian captivity! In the Iron Age Egypt was considered a threat. Therefore, compromise in returning to it (Num 11:18–20; 14:3–4) or making alliances with it were tantamount to treason (1 Kgs 11:40; 14:25; Neh 9:17; Isa 30:2; 31:1), idolatry (1 Kgs 12:28; Isa 19:1; Jer 44:15), or death (2 Kgs 23:29; Jer 42:15–19; 43:2–44:15). Israel is always identified as having come out of Egypt, and in the prophets Egypt is condemned (Isa 19:1–17). However, with respect to an Egyptian context, a hieroglyphic relief on a wall in the temple of Amun at Karnak (Luxor, Egypt) mentions a defensive site in the Negev as "The Fort (or Fortified Town) of Abram." Israeli archeologist and historian Yohanan Aharoni believed that Fort Abram was the term used by the Egyptians for the Israelite city of Beersheba. This was because in the Egyptian list of cities in the Negev, Beersheba was omitted even though it was a prominent site during that time. The most likely explanation for this is that the new defensive site at Beersheba had been given the name of Abram because he was the original founder of the city (Gen 21:32–33). Roland Hendel says of this: "When a government builds fortifications, it is natural to name them for illustrious local or national heroes. Abram of Biblical fame surely fits the bill."[53] While it is true that the archaeological evidence for the patriarchs is not as well attested as it is for biblical people and events in the first millennium, there is sufficient comparative and inferential data from the archaeological record to keep the patriarchs where they belong, in a second millennium context.

Proposed Dating for the Patriarchs

BIBLICAL PERSON/EVENT	PERIOD	DATES(S)	PROPONENTS	STANDARD	FIRST WRITTEN	EVIDENCE
EARLY DATE I—Late 3rd, Early 2nd Millenium BC						
Abraham Entrance into Canaan (Genesis 12:4)	Middle Bronze I Middle Bronze II	2166–1991 2091	Archer Barker Waltke	Internal Biblical Chronology	Moses	Antiquity of Accounts (Genesis 14) Nomadism-migration Personal names, places
Isaac Offered on Mt. Moriah (Genesis 22)	Middle Bronze I Middle Bronze I	2066–1886 2051	J. Davis (Fundamentalist/ Evangelical schools)			Excavations at Ur, Ebla Amorities (20th-18th centuries B.C.) Geopolitical conditions (MB IIA)
Jacob Entrance into Haran (Genesis 28:5)	Middle Bronze IA Middle Bronze IA	2006–1859 1929				Climate of region in MB I
EARLY DATE—Late 2nd Millenium BC						
Patriarchal Events	Middle Bronze II A	2000–1800	Glueck Albright	Archaeology	Monarchy	Pottery in Negev Beni-Hasan mural (1890 BC)
Patriarchal Events	Middle Bronze II A-B	1991–1786	Kitchen Millard	Egyptian Chronology	Moses	Egyptian backgrounds (Middle Kingdom) Geopolitical conditions (Genesis 14)
Patriarchal Events (remembered traditions)	Middle Bronze II B-C	1750–1550	A. Mazar	Archaeology	Court of David & Solomon	Mari/Nuzi archives Prosperous urban culture Hyksos Dynasty
LATE DATE—1st Millenium BC						
Patriarchal Events (remembered in monarchy)	Iron IA	1250–1150 (settlement period)	Aharoni Z. Herzog	Archaeology	United Monarchy	Excavations at Beersheba (no MB) Anachronisms in Genesis accounts
EXTREME DATE—Exilic–Post-Maccabean						
Patriarchal Traditions (created as religious history)	Persian/Greek	400–165	T. L. Thompson Van-Secters	Form Criticism Structural Analysis	Exilic/Post-Exilic	Literary tradition/Oral tradition Use of folklore JEDP theory

The Stones Cry Out, Copyright © 1997 by World of the Bible Ministries, Published by Harvest House Publishers, Eugene, Oregon 97402

Genesis 12:16; 24:10–11, 19, 64

Did the Patriarchs Domesticate the Camel?

He treated Abram well for her sake, and Abram acquired sheep and cattle, male and female donkeys, male and female servants, and camels. . . . Then the servant left, taking with him ten of his master's camels loaded with all kinds of good things from his matter. He set out for Aram Nahariam and made his way to the town of Nahor. He had the camels kneel down near the well outside the town; it was toward evening, the time the women go out to draw water. . . . After she had given him a drink, she said, "I'll draw water for your camels too, until they have had enough to drink." . . . Rebekah also looked up and saw Isaac. She got down from her camel. (Gen 12:16; 24:10–11, 19, 64)

These texts take for granted that the camels, Hebrew *gemalim*, used by the patriarchs were domesticated. In fact, the camel, which appears fifty-four times in the Old Testament, is mentioned prominently in the accounts of Abraham (Gen 12:16), Isaac (Gen 24:10), and Jacob (Gen 31:34). However, the majority of scholarly opinion has shifted away from that of previous scholars,[54] and almost all now concede that the archaeological and epigraphical evidence does not support the domestication of the camel before 1200 BC, a time well after that indicated in the Bible for the patriarchs. The unusual word order of Genesis 12:16[55] and the supposed late domestication of the camel is indicative of late composition to some scholars.[56] This question of camel domestication may seem a trivial matter, but the issue at stake is the historicity of the patriarchs. Since the 1970s, scholars of the patriarchal narratives, such as Thomas Thompson and John Van Seters, have claimed that alleged anachronisms (camels, Chaldean Ur, and Philistines in Palestine) require an Iron Age (first millennium BC) date. In their view the biblical chronology that places the patriarchs traditionally in the Middle or Late Bronze Age is erroneous. This conviction is so secure that Van Seeters has stated, "As for camels . . . most scholars, even those who argue for an early date for the patriarchal traditions, regard the mention of camels as an anachronism."[57]

In response, some conservative scholars have proposed that the idea was added later by a redactor, maybe in the time of Gideon and the Midianite camel-invaders (Judg 6–7). Other conservative scholars have suggested it was an adaptation,[58] or, noting the fragmentary nature of evidence, claim it is a fallacy to dismiss historicity by an argument from silence. However, the evidence both archaeologically and epigraphically is not as lacking as has been supposed. Scattered osteological and iconographic evidence shows that camels, at least on a limited scale, had been domesticated much earlier. M. M. Ripinsky placed the date of the domestication some time in the fourth millennium BC.[59] R. W. Bulliet traced the domestication of the camel in stages, the first occurring in southeastern Arabia in the fourth or third millennium and then in southwestern Arabia.[60] The second stage, some time after 2000 BC, involved the use of camels to transport incense from southwestern Arabia northward. Other evidence offered has included a nineteenth/eighteenth century camel figurine and Sumerian lexical works in the early second millennium BC. However, one of the clearest lines of evidence follows the research that distinguishes between the two species of camel associated with the ancient Near East, the dromedary (long legged with a single hump) and the Bactrian camel (stocky with two humps). This is useful because the archaeological evidence demonstrates an earlier domestication for the Bactrian camel than the dromedary.[61]

Important archaeological sites like the Umm an-Nar island, Tell Abraq, and as-Sufuh have produced a copious amount of dromedary camel bones dating to the third and second millennium BC. Many signs, such as the lack of additional camel remains in the proximate areas and the overall smaller bone size of Iron Age remains than those of the Bronze Age, suggest that these bones point to the wild form of the dromedary and should not be considered as viable evidence for early domestication. Much of the data from Israel, Uruk, Egypt, and comparative sites also point to a later time of domestication, perhaps toward the end of the second millennium BC. Moreover, the mere presence of camel remains is not sufficient proof of domestication. There are many factors that must be considered and evidences to be weighed (time, climate, breeding season, etc.) before a species can be labeled domestic.[62]

Modern impression of a cylinder seal showing figures (on right and left) astride a camel. Syrian, 18th century BC

© Walters Art Museum, Baltimore, USA/ Bridgeman Images

While an early domestication for the dromedary is questionable, there are a few theories of how and why the Bactrian camel could very well have experienced an early domestication. Before these theories are examined, however, it is important to note that the Bactrian camel's natural habitat was typically, if not always, outside the sphere of urbanization. This suggests that the camel's contact with ancient people was sparse. Ancient people did, however, employ camels in the desert on account of their adaptation to the harsh desert environment.[63]

> It has to be kept in mind that the domestication of the camel does not, as in most cases of domestication, imply an adaptation of the animal's ways of life to man, but an adaptation of man to the camel's way of life [. . .] This is especially true for the use of the camel as a beast of burden under hostile desert conditions. While the wild Bactrian camel . . . is a fugitive animal and is known to be very shy . . . there are some factors which are thought to have advanced tameability in the process of domestication . . . The first possibility is related to climatic change. Droughts in the ancient Near East could have forced the camel to seek out well-populated and habitable areas. Second, camels have a propensity to return to the area where they first bred. Third, camels remember good food sources. Factors such as these very well could have led to the domestication of the Bactrian camel, even during the time of the patriarchal period (cf. Gen 24:64; 37:25).[64]

There is sufficient empirical evidence for the domestication of the Bactrian camel pointing back to the patriarchal period. "Some early Bronze Age finds of clay camels attached to miniature clay carts in Southern Turkmenistan [a country in central Asia] suggest that the two-humped camel (also known as Bactrian) was already employed in the area by the early 3rd millennium BCE."[65] In conjunction with additional data, "the cart models provide a history of how wheeled transportation emerged in the area and later developed. By 3000 BCE, the climate became more arid and the people [of Turkmenistan] could no longer trust their cattle-pulled carts to make long journeys. Two-humped camels were more able to handle the drier climate, so that (Bactrian) camel-pulled carts became the new standard for this region in the second half of the 3rd millennium."[66] Additionally, there are third-millennium-BC gold and silver vessels that depict what appear to be Bactrian camels. These vessels were discovered in situ in Gonur Depe of Turkmenistan, a Bronze Age archaeological site.[67]

More evidence is found in a Sumerian love song from the Old Babylonian period. The poetic literature mentions the camel and implies domestication: "Make the milk yellow for me, my bridegroom . . . O my bridegroom, may I drink milk with you, with goat milk from the sheepfold . . . fill the holy butter churn . . . O Dumuzi, make the milk of the camel . . . yellow for me—the camel [am.si.har.ra.an], its milk is sweet . . . Its butter-milk, which is sweet, make yellow for me."[68] In this love song, belonging to the genre of pastoral poetry, am.si.har.ra.an denotes a domesticated animal. In Sumerian mythology Dumuzi is the son of Duttur, the divine mother of sheep. Dumuzi with his surname or title Sipad ("shepherd") appears as the lord of the shepherds and flocks and is the god in charge of domesticated herd animals in the Sumerian pantheon. Inanna requests churned camel's milk as well as goat's milk. Both are described as "pleasant and sweet." To interpret [a camel] in this context as a wild camel puts considerable strain on the interpretation of the poetry.[69] Furthermore, the appearance of the Bactrian camel in animal lexical lists (e.g., the urra lists from the Old Babylonian period and, perhaps, a Sumerian tablet belonging to the Ur III period) suggest that "the people of Mesopotamia gained some acquaintance with the Bactrian camel in the Old Babylonian period, at the end of the 3rd / beginning of the 2nd millennium."[70] It is precisely the Bactrian camel that appears in a cylinder seal from Syria in the eighteenth century BC clearly depicting two figures riding astride (see photo). It is perfectly possible that the camel of Genesis 12:16, et al. could be the Bactrian camel, which experienced an early domestication. Therefore, the presence of camels in the patriarchal stories can be defended, and the story can be treated as primary evidence of camel use.

Genesis 14:1–17

The Antiquity of the Patriarchal Narratives

The historicity and antiquity of the patriarchal narratives has been questioned by the minimalist school in archaeology. However, Genesis 14 provides an example of literary recording of events in the Torah that demonstrates the use of historical sources in its composition. These literary sources can be analyzed with respect to the archaeological sources to judge whether or not they reflect events that fit the time they describe. Genesis 14:1–17 is an account of an invasion of lower Canaan by a coalition of Mesopotamian kings. In the battle Abraham's nephew Lot, who was living in Sodom, is captured with his entire household (Gen 14:12). Abraham then entered the conflict and rescued his nephew and his family. In the account of the battle there appears a detailed and precise listing of names and places (both foreign and local), often explained by more contemporary names, such as "the vale of Siddim" for "the Dead Sea Valley," verse 3, or "the Valley of Shaveh" for "the King's Valley" (the lower Kidron valley), verse 17. These literary clarifications are among the traits that indicate this chapter has the mark of antiquity, especially when viewed in light of the archaeological record. While the specific kings mentioned in the Genesis account are not found in cuneiform accounts, names like theirs appear in the Mesopotamian texts of this period, confirming the individuals in the biblical report fit the time and places ascribed to them.

Consider the names of the four eastern kings given in verse 1. "Amraphel...king of Shinar" is thought to be a typical West Semitic name from Lower Mesopotamia, found in both Akkadian and Amorite sources and possibly connected with the Amorite name *amud-pa-ila*.[71] "Shinar" in Egyptian texts is used for Babylonia.[72] "Arioch king of Ellasar" appears as the *arriyuk(ki)/arriwuk(ki)* in texts from Mari (Amorite) and Nuzi (Hurrian).[73] At Mari this was the name of the fifth son of Zimri-Lim, Mari's king.[74] "Kedor-laomer king of Elam" is clearly an Elamite name, composed of familar Elamite terms: *kudur* ("servant") and *lagamar*, a principal goddess in the Elamite pantheon.[75] It fits the type of Elamite royal names known as a Kutur type and is known from at least three royal examples.[76] "Tidal king of Goyim" is well attested as an early form of the Hittite name *Tudkhalia*, which was used as the name of at least five Hittite rulers.[77] One is said to have served as a "king of peoples/groups," which reflects the political fragmentation that existed in the Hittite empire in Anatolia (Turkey) in the nineteenth and eighteenth centuries BC and permitted the kind of alliance pictured in Genesis 14.[78]

In addition, the political conditions depicted by this alliance and that of the Transjordanian coalition of kings in the Dead Sea basin were possible in only one period of history—the early second millennium BC. Only at this time does the archaeological record reveal that the Elamites were aggressively involved in the affairs of the region (the Levant), and only in this period were Mesopotamian alliances so unstable as to permit such a confederation.[79] The term "Goyim" is a Hebrew translation of the Akkadian word *umman*, a term used to characterize various peoples who came as invaders.[80] Therefore, this king was most likely a vagabond ruler who assembled various tribes and provinces into his army. Given this understanding and the shifting political situation, it is logical that an Elamite king would head a coalition of Mesopotamian city-states and launch a punitive raid on rebel Canaanite kings. After this time, and especially in the first millennium BC, the political map became completely incompatible with the conditions necessary for such a formation.

To these time-bound indicators of historicity we may add the accuracy of the invasion route taken by the Eastern kings, the use of a Hebrew term for "trained men" in verse 14, which is only attested outside this passage in a nineteenth-century-BC Egyptian text and fifteenth-century-BC letter from Ta'anach, and the description of Melchizedek, which accurately depicts a second-millennium setting.[81] These details in Genesis 14, attested in extrabiblical documents of the time, likely could not have been invented and correctly assigned to their respective nations and geographical settings by a Hebrew writer living at a later time. Thus, the antiquity of this account within the larger context of the patriarchal narratives indicates that there is substantial reason to regard the whole as historically accurate.

Genesis 14:14

Abraham and the Middle Bronze Gate at Dan

> When Abram heard that his relative had been taken captive, he called out the 318 trained men born in his household and went in pursuit as far as Dan. (Gen 14:14)

The Israelite site of Tel Dan in the Golan Heights is named after the ancient city of Dan, known from the phrase in the Bible "from Dan to Beersheba." However, before it was called Dan, we read in the Egyptian execration texts that its earlier name was Laish (see Judg 18:7, 14).[82] According to Joshua 19:47 it was also known as Leshem; however, Laish would have been the name of the city in the time of the patriarchs. The archaeological excavations at this site have uncovered a great deal of the city of Laish and revealed a very large Canaanite city with a highly

developed material culture, rich tombs, and massive fortifications of sloping ramparts. Here was discovered a four thousand-year-old mud brick gate in the midst of these ramparts, built with an arch (an architectural achievement supposedly invented by the Romans two thousand years later). The mud brick gate is complete with all its courses to the very top. According to its excavator, Avraham Biran, the reason it was preserved:

> was not because of anything that we did, it appears that the people in antiquity, for some reason or the other, the people of Laish, the Canaanites who lived in Laish, had decided that the gate was of no use so they blocked it and filled it with earth and then they covered it. So all the steps that led into the city were covered with the natural soil of the area so that all that we did was simply to remove the earth and to uncover the construction both of the steps and here's another stone construction which was probably an embankment holding, protecting the gate. Maybe there was something wrong in the structure. We found a crack in the tower and maybe that was reason they decided to abolish the gate and to open up another gate somewhere else.[83]

The gate served as the main gate to Laish. Biran further states:

> Abraham in the book of Genesis proceeded to defeat the kings of the north who took his nephew Lot prisoner. The text says in Genesis 14 that, "Abraham came as far as Dan." Now, of course in those days the name of the city was Laish and not Dan. I imagine that the biblical copyist who found the name Laish, said "who remembers Laish anymore, its been gone, forgotten," so he wrote Dan instead. But to my way of thinking, Abraham, no doubt, was invited to visit the city of Laish and for all I know they had gone through the gate before it was blocked.[84]

Middle Bronze Gate of Laish (Tel Dan), sealed in 2013 for preservation

EXODUS

The books of Exodus, Joshua, Judges, and Ruth tell of massive migration, warfare, and catastrophic conditions that affected the peoples of both Egypt and Canaan. While these are the kind of events that archaeology is usually able to verify, there are factors that reduce this considerably. First, it must be understood that a proud people such as the Egyptians would hardly have recorded a national defeat by foreign slaves. Therefore, it is unlikely that there will be found any inscriptional evidence in Egypt of plagues being linked to the Hebrews. Second, the Hebrew's migration (exodus) from Egypt and sojourn in the Sinai desert would have been archaeologically invisible; that is, everything would have been used and nothing left behind as material evidence. Even if there were remains, the desert environment would have destroyed or covered what little there was. In like manner, when the Hebrews fought with the local Canaanite population, only three cities were actually destroyed (Jericho,

Ai, and Hazor) and the Hebrew settlement among these peoples is difficult to distinguish, as they would have used materials from the indigenous culture (the pottery styles are similar, though the Hebrews' are sometimes more plain). Therefore, we should not be surprised if there is insufficient data in the archaeological record to allow a comprehensive synthesis of the material evidence with the biblical accounts. This is why it has been notoriously difficult to locate on archaeological grounds the date of the exodus as well as the identity of the pharaohs of the oppression and exodus. While the Pharaoh of the exodus is unnamed, scholars have sought to identify him in order to verify the historicity of the biblical account.[85]

It is often stated that it is less important to know *when* the exodus happened than *that* it occurred. However, since there is both literary and archaeological evidence that has possible connections to the exodus from several periods spanning hundreds of years, in making a final case for the historicity of the exodus, the data and a reliable date must be reconciled. The date for the exodus can be argued from the internal chronology given in 1 Kings 6:1 which indicates that the exodus occurred either 480 years (MT) or 440 years (LXX) before Solomon began to build the temple in Jerusalem in 967 BC (1 Kgs 11:42; 2 Chr 9:30 argues this is Solomon's fourth regnal year). Whether one accepts the figures of the MT or the LXX in this matter, taken literally the date would fall within the fifteenth century BC. Proponents of this early date accept an MT priority and argue that Solomon began to build the temple in year 480, month 2, so the elapsed time was 479 years plus fifteen to forty-five days, therefore 479 + 967 = 1446 BC. They find support for this date in the statement of Jephthah (ca. 1100 BC) to the king of Amman in Judges 11:26 that the Israelites had already been in the land for three hundred years (1100 + 300 = 1400, approximately coinciding with the early date for the conquest). Adding another forty years brings us to 1440, which is close to the date obtained from using the 480 years of 1 Kings 6:1. Other support for this date is argued from the genealogy of Heman the musician in 1 Chronicles 6:33–37. From Heman (who lived in the time of David) back to Korah (who lived in the time of Moses) there were eighteen generations. Adding one additional generation brings us to the time of Solomon. If there are twenty-five years per generation (19 x 25 = 475 years) and these are added to the date of Solomon's fourth regnal year (475 + 967=1442) we again arrive at a date close to that derived from the data in 1 Kings 6:1. Further support for the early date has been argued from Ezekiel 40:1 which is said to provide a precise date for a Jubilee year in 574 BC. "According to Jewish sources, this was the 17th Jubilee. The first year of this Jubilee cycle was 622 BC (49 inclusive years). Going back 16 Jubilee cycles, to when the counting began, brings us to 622 + (16 x 49) = 1406 BC, the early date for the Conquest. Adding the 40 years from the departure from Egypt (Dt 1:3; Jos 4:19, 5:10), the date of the exodus can be fixed at 1446 BC."[86] Proponents of the late date (thirteenth century BC) argue for a reinterpretation of the literal 480 years of MT 1 Kings 6:1. They see either that a literary phenomenon was employed to connect a contemporaneous temple construction with the original or that 480 years is "a symbolic number that derives from 12 x 40, 40 years being a symbolic number for a generation."[87] Since an actual generation is around twenty-five years, the real-time interval from Solomon's fourth year to the exodus would be 12 x 25 = 300 years + 967 BC = 1267 BC (the time of the reign of Rameses II). It is then possible to find biblical and archaeological synchronism for this date in the statement of Exodus 1:11 that the Israelites built for Pharaoh the storage cities of Pithom (Pi-Atum = Tell er-Rataba) and Raamses (Pi-Ramesse=Qantir, near the old site of Avaris = Tell el-Dab'a). Both of these cities were identified exclusively with Pharaoh Ramesses II who reigned from 1279 to 1213 BC. Further support for a late date is based on the appearance of "Israel" on the Stele of Merneptah (which requires a date no later than 1250 BC) and the fixed radiocarbon date for the destruction of Hazor of 1320 BC, the time of Joshua's conquest (Josh 11:10). Early date proponents reply that the name "Rameses" in Exodus 1:11 is an editorial updating of an earlier name that went out of use (cf. its use in Gen 47:11) and fits the examples of similar updates of Bethel, Dan, and Hormah in which the later redactor did not include the earlier name. They also contend that the thirteenth-century destruction layer at Hazor is the result of the attack on the city by Deborah and Barak and their allies (Judg 5:14–18) and that if Hazor was destroyed by Joshua in the thirteenth century BC there would be no city for Jabin to rule (Judg 4:2), since the city was not rebuilt until the time of Solomon. They also argue from the Merneptah Stele that Israel was regarded a state which would imply a prior settlement in the land of Canaan and therefore an earlier exodus and conquest (fifteenth century BC).

A case for the historical nature of the exodus can be made from the Egyptian color of the Hebrew narrative

Egyptian tomb painting of making mud bricks, like task of Hebrews slaves

De Agostini Picture Library/S. Vannini/ Bridgeman Images

(such as "delivery stool," Exod 1:16), Egyptian loanwords (such as the name of Moses, Exod 2:10), the description of Canaan as a "land flowing with milk and honey," which appears in the Egyptian Tale of Sinuhe and the Annals of Thutmoses III, the uniform use of the term *pharaoh* ("great house") for the king during the New Kingdom (Eighteenth Dynasty, ca. 1550–1292 BC), the comparative Egyptian accounts of foreign (Semitic) slaves in Egypt (including their harsh treatment, use in building projects, and records of runaway slaves), an account of plagues similar to those mentioned in the Bible, such as in the Ipuwer Papyrus (thirteenth century BC), the importance of magic to the Egyptians (compare Moses's miracle in Exod 7:9–10), and the archaeological discovery of certain places such as Avaris (Tell ed-Dab'a), Ramesses (Pi-Ramesse), Migdol (Tell Defari), Succoth (Tell Masuta), and the Balah and Timsah Lakes (Yam Suph/Re[e]d Sea?; Exod 1:11; 12:37; 14:1–2), mentioned in relation to the Hebrews. Such local color and geographical details affirm the historicity of the Egyptian record in Exodus because they were the product of eyewitnesses living in the time and place and would be unlikely for writers to invent centuries later.

There are also ancient Near Eastern law codes that have many parallels to the Ten Commandments and Mosaic law (Ur-Nammu Code ca. 2000 BC; Laws of Eshunna ca. 1900 BC; Lipit Ishtar Code ca. 1870 BC; Code of Hammurabi ca. 1700 BC; Hittite Laws ca. 1500 BC). In addition, the Egyptian Stela of Merneptah (twelfth century BC) refers to the *'apiru* ("nomads, wanderers") as slaves and makes the first mention of the term "Israel" as a nation-state, indicating that the Hebrews had long since immigrated to Canaan and developed into nation status. In the case of Joshua's conquest, although the history of the archaeology of Jericho (Tell es-Sûltan) has been variously interpreted, it has in the final analysis revealed evidence in support of the details of the biblical text (Josh 6:3–24). This evidence includes fortification walls that collapsed outwardly (Josh 6:20), a layer of burned debris and ash three feet thick (Josh 6:24), and storage jars full of grain indicating a short siege in the spring and unused by the invaders, just as the Bible describes (Josh 2:6, 3:15, 6:17–19).

In addition, according to Brad C. Sparks a total of ninety ancient Egyptian texts with Exodus parallels or Exodus-like motifs or content have been identified by Egyptologists, archaeologists, and Semiticists in the professional literature.[88] We may add to this translations of Proto-Sinaitic inscriptions identified by Douglas Petrovitch that appear to give conditions, names, and details related to the exodus figures.[89] Sparks's list of parallels include people and events such as Moses's mother Jochebed, Moses's flight from Egypt, Moses's contest with the Egyptian priests, the ten plagues and various accounts of individual plagues (including the plague of blood, plague of darkness, and death of the firstborn), the parting of the waters, the drowning of the Egyptian army, the Red Sea crossing, and the pillar of cloud.[90] These parallels are found in various types of Egyptian works such as Primeval Revolt texts, chaos literature, and apocalyptic literature. While the interpretation of these texts with regard to the exodus are controversial, there is a growing concensus among Egyptologists that they reflect historical events that relate to the exodus, either in the form of memory or myth. Conservative Egyptologists find in this material new support for the biblical account as accurately recorded history.[91]

Exodus 4:21

Egyptian Background of the Hardening of the Heart Motif

> The LORD said to Moses, "When you return to Egypt, see that you perform before Pharaoh all the wonders I have given you the power to do. But I will harden his heart so that he will not let the people go. (Exod 4:21)

Why did God tell Moses that he would harden Pharaoh's heart even before he heard Moses's request (as well as afterward, Exod 9:12; 10:20, 27; 11:10; 14:8)? It is also true that the Pharaoh "hardened his [own] heart" (Exod 8:15, 32; cf. 1 Sam 6:6), but, this divine intention

must still be understood. The answer may be found in the archaeological data containing the theological perspective of the New Kingdom, in that divine hardening may have been employed for polemical purposes in light of a similar act in the Egyptian theology of the afterlife. It was a normal practice among Egyptian rulers to claim divine honors for themselves down to Roman times. Paranoiac divinity was ascribed to Egyptian kings in the Eighteenth Dynasty and particularly to the mid-fifteenth century Pharaoh Thutmoses III.[92] The pharaoh was considered to be an incarnation of the Sun god Re and Horus-Osiris, the three most important gods in Egypt.[93] He was the incarnation of the god Horus in life, the incarnation of the god Osiris in the afterlife, and was called "son of Re" and "the god of heaven."

With this theological status, a pharaoh was viewed as the primary god of the world.[94] Consequently, the pharaoh's word was viewed as a "creative force," the word of a god, which controlled history, as well as the natural elements, and could not be reversed or overruled. Given this understanding, God's hardening of the will of Pharaoh and ultimately forcing it to bow to the divine will demonstrated his sovereign power over the Egyptian pantheon, a power the Pharaoh embodied in the theology of Egypt. However, archaeological discoveries in Egypt have provided an additional insight into why God chose to "harden" Pharaoh's heart. The funerary text known as the Book of the Dead reveals the theology of the ancient Egyptian death cult.

After the dead was embalmed and entombed, he had to face a trial in the afterlife. This judgment was a frequent subject for funerary art, especially on papyri and coffins. A painted detail of this scene can be seen on the coffin of the Twenty-First Dynasty Pharaoh Tanakhten-ettahat (1075–945 BC), as well as in mural form in the scroll of the Egyptian Book of the Dead. The "weighing of the heart" scene depicts a hall of judgment where the deceased guilt or innocence was determined. At the center of the scene is a scale holding the deceased's heart (depicted in a canopic jar). The Egyptians considered the heart the seat of intellect and emotion and central to rebirth in the afterlife. The heart was weighed against the standard of truth (signified by the hieroglyphic symbol of a feather), representing Maat, the goddess of truth. Overseeing the judgment was Osiris, jackal-headed god of the underworld, while the scribe Anubis records the judicial process. If judged guilty, the wrongdoer's fate was destruction, depicted by the demon Ammit behind Annubis waiting to devour the wrongdoer and end his hope of an afterlife. However, if the deceased was judged guiltless he received eternal life and its rewards.

In order to pass through this judgment the deceased had to successfully declare his innocence in the form of forty-two negative confessions.[95] However, the heart burdened by collective sins during life would be heavier than an untroubled one, and when weighed on the balance of a scale against the feather of truth (of the goddess Maat) would tip the scales and reveal that the negative confession was false. This resulted in the soul being devoured by Ammit. The devoured soul was then condemned to a continual existence deprived of all comforts and the company of loved ones and tormented by perpetual struggle with the gods and priests.

To prevent this potential threat in the afterlife the Egyptians devised a means to prevent the heart from contradicting a negative confession. For this purpose it was crucial that the heart remain with the body during the mummification process so that it would be present for the judgment. A heart scarab containing an incantation (Spell 30B in the Book of the Coming Forth by Day) ordered the heart to not witness against the deceased's testimony before Osiris.[96] On some New Kingdom heart scarabs a human head replaced that of a beetle, indicating this scarab's role with the deceased. The incantation, in part, read: "Do not contradict me with the judges, do not act against me with the gods … Do not make my name stink to the gods who made mankind."[97] Through the inscribed spell the stony character of the scarab was transferred to the fleshly heart, making it "hard" and therefore unable to speak.[98] These protective amulets were typically wrapped with the mummy or inside the chest cavity, (a fact revealed by X-rays of Egyptian mummies).[99] This ritual act of "hardening of the heart" reversed the natural function of the unhardened heart and resulted in salvation, since the individual was now decreed sinless through silence.[100] So confident were the Egyptians in this preventive technique that the negative outcome of the weighing of the heart is never

Weighing of the heart, Egyptian Book of the Dead Papyrus. Egyptian Museum, Berlin

Alexander Schick

depicted, only the deceased being positively received by Osiris and presented with offerings.

The divine action of God hardening Pharaoh's heart was a polemic against the Pharaoh as a god of Egypt, just as the ten plagues were against various gods of the Egyptian pantheon. Because Pharaoh represented the salvation of all Egypt, God's hardening the heart of Pharaoh reversed this, resulting in destruction. Pharaoh's inability to respond naturally and thereby stop the divinely ordered plagues resulted in not only his but Egypt's destruction.[101] Thus, archaeology has provided new insight into a difficult theological concept by giving us the proper background and setting of the Egyptian beliefs.

Exodus 7:10–12

Egyptian Priests and Snake Spells

> So Moses and Aaron went to Pharaoh and did just as the LORD commanded. Aaron threw his staff down in front of Pharaoh and his officials, and it became a snake. Pharaoh then summoned wise men and sorcerers, and the Egyptian magicians also did the same things by their secret arts: Each one threw down his staff and it became a snake. But Aaron's staff swallowed up their staffs. (Exod 7:10–12)

This text dealing with Egyptian magic, snakes, and spells has an archaeological context that also ties in with the Semitic culture. Richard Steiner provided interpretation for Semitic passages in Egyptian texts that were discovered more than a century ago, inscribed on the subterranean walls of the pyramid of King Unas at Saqqara in Egypt.[102] Steiner has deciphered a number of Semitic texts in various Egyptian scripts over the past twenty-five years. He explained that serpent spells written in hieroglyphic characters had confused scholars who tried to read them as if they were ordinary Egyptian texts, when in fact they were Semitic—no continuous

Semitic texts from this period had ever been deciphered before. The pyramid in which the text appears is dated to the twenty-fourth century BC, although other Egyptologists proposed dates for them ranging from the twenty-fifth to the thirtieth centuries BC.

Steiner was able to decipher the texts because he recognized the Semitic words for "mother snake" and that the surrounding spells, composed in Egyptian rather than Semitic, also spoke of the mother snake. Furthermore, he recognized that the Egyptian and Semitic texts elucidated each other. Though written in Egyptian characters, the texts were composed in a Semitic dialect used by the Canaanites in the third millennium BC. He surmised that the Canaanite priests of the ancient port city of Byblos (modern Lebanon) provided these texts to the kings of Egypt. Just as they imported materials for mummification, it seems they also imported magical spells to protect the royal mummies against poisonous snakes that were thought to understand Canaanite. According to Steiner, even though the Egyptians viewed their culture as superior to that of their neighbors, their fear of snakes made them open to the borrowing of Semitic magic.

Exodus 12:41, 51

Archaeological Evidence and the Exodus

> At the end of the 430 years, to the very day, all the LORD's divisions left Egypt. . . . And on that very day the LORD brought the Israelites out of Egypt by their divisions. (Exod 12:41, 51)

The biblical exodus is at one and the same time the most well-known and celebrated event in history and yet the least attested in the archaeological record. However, it must be recognized from the beginning of such a search for evidence that from the Egyptian side there is no precedent for the recording of defeats, especially with respect to the gods, and from the Israelite side, like all nomads in the desert, they would be archaeologically invisible (although such people do leave traces). It is not without reason that direct evidence could surface in the future, similar to the recent discovery of a mudbrick road in the desert along the supposed exodus route that could have been used by the chariots of Pharaoh pursuing the Hebrew slaves. Nevertheless, at the present time the best approach to this question is to examine the indirect evidence of historical consequence (the existence of the story as a central and defining history in the Bible and the history of Israel) and in the local Egyptian color given in the biblical account and supported by archaeological finds. As with the patriarchal narratives, the information is too precise and too time bound to have been simply invented in another context and time.

As to the first indirect evidence, that of historical consequence, it is evident that 3,500 years of an unbroken tradition with the celebration of the Passover had a historical root and cause: "This event lies so deep in the national consciousness and is referred to so frequently as the starting-point and basis of the national development, that it is impossible to escape the conviction that it was a historical fact, rather than a product of religious imagination."[103] In the case of the Bible, its origin in writing claims to have come from the hand of Moses, the leader of the exodus, and throughout the Bible the event serves as a constant reference point and object lesson to Israel. As Yair Hoffman notes, "The exodus from Egypt is the most frequently mentioned event in the O.T. Apart from the story itself in Ex. i-xv, it is mentioned about 120 times in stories, laws, poems, psalms, historiographical writings and prophecies."[104] In this regard it is necessary to consider how significantly the exodus tradition permeates Israelite historiography. Ronald E. Clements notes this when he says,

> The exodus from Egypt provides a focus for the Old Testament, and has influenced its understanding of God. He had brought Israel, his people, "out of Egypt." Thus the recollection of this event established a basic understanding of the nature and purpose

of Israel's God, which could be used to interpret other events and situations. The use of this "exodus pattern" is very marked in the prophecies of Isaiah 40–55 relating to the forthcoming release of exiles from Babylon in the sixth century BC.[105]

In the same way the exodus event shaped Israel's relationship to history, it also informed Israel's experience in faith. Menahem Haran explains,

> Since the Exodus is perceived in the Bible as a divine event, it serves as one of the most significant symbols of the biblical faith. One of the axioms of this faith is that Yahweh, and not any other deity, brought Israel out from Egypt . . . (Ex. 20:2; Deut. 5:6). The significance of these words is that the deity who brought Israel out of Egypt was the one who now spoke to them and laid on them obligations and commandments.[106]

Egyptologist and archaeologist James Hoffmeier summarizes the type of evidence for this first case well when he writes,

> The biblical evidence for the exodus and wilderness periods . . . so overwhelmingly supports the historicity of these events that the priests, prophets, psalmists, people of Israel, and foreigners believed these events occurred, and consequently they celebrated festivals, sang songs, dated events, and observed laws that assumed that Yahweh's salvation from Egypt was authentic.[107]

Therefore, we cannot explain Israel historically or theologically without an exodus.

A second area of evidence comes from what may be called contextual plausibility. That is, even though we may not have direct historical evidence for any of the persons or events connected with the exodus, or even be able to agree on specific dates, the general outline as presented in the biblical account is true to the times. Therefore, the exodus is far more likely to have occurred than not. For instance, we can show that the details of Egyptian court life and certain peculiarities in the Hebrew language used to describe such activities indicate that the writer had a firsthand knowledge of an Egyptian setting.[108] We have evidence that foreigners from Canaan entered Egypt,[109] lived there[110] and were

Ipuwer Papy-rus, National Museum of Antiquities in Leiden, Netherlands

Erich Lessing/Art Resource, NY

sometimes considered troublemakers,[111] and that Egypt oppressed and enslaved a vast foreign workforce during several dynasties.[112] We also have records that slaves escaped, such as the Tale of Sinuhe,[113] and that Egypt suffered from plague-like conditions.[114] We can prove the presence of people like the Israelites in the Sinai peninsula, at Qadesh-Barnea, and at other places mentioned in the books of the Bible that record this history.[115] We can demonstrate from a comparison with ancient Near Eastern law codes that pre-date the giving of the law at Sinai that its form and structure (following a suzerain-vassal treaty) fit the then-established standard for such texts.[116]

A third area of evidence comes from similarities in Egyptian records that suggest parallels to events described in the biblical account of the exodus. While recognized by Egyptologists, they are generally disputed as having reference to the exodus event.[117] One of these is the Egyptian document known as the Admonitions of an Egyptian Sage: The Ipuwer Papyrus (Papyrus Leiden 344) first translated in 1909.

Comparative Chart of Exodus Account and Ipuwer Papyrus

Exodus Account	Ipuwer Papyrus[118]
[God speaking to Moses]: "Take some water from the Nile and pour it on the dry ground. The water you take from the river will become blood on the ground." (Exod 4:9)	"Behold, Egypt is fallen to the pouring of water. And he who poured water on the ground seizes the mighty in misery." (Ipuwer 7:5)
"And all the water in the Nile was turned to blood. The fish in the Nile died, and the river smelled so bad that the Egyptians could not drink its water." (Exod 7:20–21)	"The river is blood. If you drink of it, you lose your humanity, and thirst for water." (Ipuwer 2:10)
"All the livestock of the Egyptians died. . . . lightning flashed down to the ground. So the LORD rained hail on the land of Egypt. . . . (The flax and barley were destroyed.)" (Exod 9:6, 9:23, 9:31)	"Gone is the barley of abundance. . . . Food supplies are running short. The nobles hunger and suffer. . . . Those who had shelter are in the dark of the storm." (Ipuwer 6:3, 3:3, 7:13)
"[The locusts] covered all the ground until it was black. They devoured all that was left after the hail. . . . Pharaoh's officials said to him, 'How long will this man be a snare to us? Let the people go, so that they may worship the LORD their God. Do you not yet realize that Egypt is ruined?'" (Exod 10:15, 10:7)	"What shall we do about it? All is ruin!" (Ipuwer 3:13)
"Now at midnight the LORD struck every firstborn male in the land of Egypt, from the firstborn of Pharaoh who sat on his throne to the firstborn of the prisoner who was in the dungeon, and every firstborn of livestock." (Exod 12:29)	"Behold, plague sweeps the land, blood is everywhere, with no shortage of the dead. . . . He who buries his brother in the ground is everywhere. . . . Woe is me for the grief of this time." (Ipuwer 2:5, 6:13, 4:3)
"And there was loud wailing in Egypt, for there was not a house without someone dead." (Exod 12:30)	"Wailing is throughout the land, mingled with lamentations." (Ipuwer 3:14)

Its contents were written by a high Egyptian official and describe a lamentation over plague conditions that devastated the country. The extant version dates to the New Kingdom period (1550–1069 BC), although it could have taken place anywhere from the end of the Old Kingdom's Sixth Dynasty (2345–2181 BC) to the Second Intermediate period Middle Kingdom (1650–1550 BC). However, there is nothing in this document that suggests such an early date, and it therefore could have been written in a time period associated with the biblical exodus. Indeed, the hieratic script in which it is written was in use at that time, and its catalog of catastrophic events accord remarkably with those of the exodus plagues.

Another proposed parallel is the use of the Egyptian root *ywy* (*yawi*) with the meaning "I am I" or "I am that I am" in the thirteenth-century-BC Egyptian document called the Destruction of Mankind or the Book of the Cow of Heaven. This is similar to the use of the Hebrew tetragrammaton (YHWH) for the divine name and its explanation to Moses in Exodus 3:14: "I am that I am" or "I will be what I will be." Researcher Brad Sparks has also claimed to identify ninety examples in tomb paintings, reliefs, and other documents that suggest such parallels.[119] While not convincing to most scholars, the nature and form of the proposed parallels are striking and worthy of consideration.

A fourth area of evidence includes archaeological inscriptions of Egyptian origin that appear to identify a nation-state known as Israel. The best known of these is the Stele of Merneptah, which demonstrates from an Egyptian source that there was a nation-state of Israel known to already be in the land of Canaan in the twelfth century BC. There is other evidence from a statue pedestal relief in the Egyptian Museum in Berlin. It bears a hieroglyphic set of cartouches, though the final cartouche is damaged in such a way that scholars dispute its interpretation. The place names on the relief ("Ashkelon," "Canaan") may match those on the Merneptah stela. Supporting this identification is the profile of a bound Asiatic prisoner, which would suggest a West Semitic origin and spelling for the partial inscription of the final name ring, and the fact that no geographical location other than "Israel" is known in association with these other sites that has a name reminiscent of this spelling.[120] In this case, the inscriptional evidence for Israel's existence in an Egyptian source could be pushed back by another two hundred years.

Merneptah Stele, Cairo Museum, with detailing hieroglyphic words: "Israel, Foreign People"

Alexander Schick

A fifth area of evidence is clues from excavation sites. One such site is the palatial district at Avaris (Tell ed-Dab'a), identified in the Eighteenth Dynasty with biblical Ramesses. This site has produced significant evidence for understanding the Nile Delta's history during the Fifteenth and Eighteenth Dynasties.[121] Of interest is the timing of the mid-Eighteenth Dynasty abandonment of Avaris, which Bietak believes occurred after the reign of Amenhotep II (1453–1419 BC) and was followed by an occupational gap. While this gap has not yet been explained, Bietak suggests that the most likely reason for abandonment would be a plague, such as that documented for Avaris in the late Middle Kingdom. Doug Petrovich has offered evidence to support this from the epigraphical record and corroborative data from Theban tomb paintings.[122] Although debated, Petrovich has published a translation of sixteen second-millennium-BC Proto-Sinaitic inscriptions found at Serabit el-Khadim that date from 1842 to 1446 BC. He argues that these Semitic inscriptions are Hebrew and expressly name the biblical figures Asenath, the Egyptian wife of Joseph (Gen 41:45, 50; 46:20), apparently mentioned posthumously, Ahisamach, the father of Oholiab who was one of the two men assigned to construct the Israelite Tabernacle (Exod 31:6; 35:34; 38:23), and Moses.[123] He claims that the Hebrew author of Sinai 361 who complained about the length of their bondage had stated that Moses had provoked astonishment, and that it was

a year of astonishment, due to Baalath (identied in Egypt with Hathor), the goddess (commonly depicted as a cow with horns) thought to be imaged by the golden calf (Exod 32:4). If his argument concerning the proto-consonantal script can be sustained,[124] such evidence would lend support to the historicity of the exodus event.

A sixth area of evidence can be made from the early history of Israel in the land of Canaan. Where did they come from and how did they get there? Israeli archaeologist Amihai Mazar answers these questions:

> During the time of the Judges, the 12th–11th century BC, about 250 sites were founded in the hill country north and south of Jerusalem. This phenomenon of a new wave of settlements in the hill country can be related only to the emergence of Israel, to the appearance of Israel, in this country. Now of course, we can ask ourselves, "Where did they come from?

Berlin Statue Pedestal Relief. Reading the eponymns from left to right: Ashkelon, Canaan, Israel (?). Egyptian Museum, Berlin

Peter Van der Veen

Did they come from Egypt as the Bible tells us or were they local people who settled, as many scholars believe? Or did they come from clans in Jordan, as other scholars believe?" We have a debate concerning the interpretation of the finds. But the finds themselves remain a very important contribution to the phenomenon to the emergence of Israel during that period.[125]

In addition, Bietek has reported the discovery at Medinet Habu, opposite Luxor (ancient Thebes), of reed huts more than three thousand years old having have the same floor plan as ancient Israelite four-room houses. The four-room house is considered by archaeologists as an original Israelite concept since they appear predominantly at Israelite sites during the Iron Age, with their beginning at the time Israel first settled in Canaan and ending with the collapse of the Judean kingdom. The typical four-room house consists of three parallel long rooms (the central room probably serving as a courtyard). These were subdivided and separated by two walls or rows of columns and a broad room across one end. The plan of these huts, which have no Egyptian architectural parallels, is marked in the bedrock. These houses apparently belonged to slave workers and may represent extrabiblical evidence of Israel in Egypt.[126] However, these structures have been dated to the twelfth century BC based on the assumption that the slave workers were employed to demolish the Temple of Ay and Horemheb under Ramesses IV, who reigned ca. 1153 to 1147 BC. Therefore, accepting this as the Israelites (or as Bietak supposes "proto-Israelites") would of necessity challenge both the early and late dates for the exodus.

We stated in our introduction to biblical archaeology that where the archaeological evidence is absent or poorly attested, the literary evidence, that is the Bible, is present and able to provide the proper context for accepting the events it portrays as history. This is the method, given the plausibility of the exodus event from historical consequence and the indirect evidence from archaeology and Israel's history, that we must follow. As Kenneth Kitchen has noted, "Documentary evidence relating to early Israel is rare, so the expectation of finding epigraphic evidence to substantiate the activities of specific individuals, families, or tribes prior to the monarchy is unrealistic."[127] However, when we accept the biblical data and then correctly compare it with what data may be found or inferred from the archaeological record, we are gradually able to build a case that substantiates both the Scriptures and the historical events they record.

Exodus 25:8–9

The Tabernacle

Then have them make a sanctuary for me, and I will dwell among them. Make this tabernacle and all its furnishings exactly like the pattern I will show you. (Exod 25:8–9)

The tabernacle, a prefabricated structure, was similar in form with its wooden parts covered with gold and its posts resting on silver sockets. It was built to house the ark of the covenant within its innermost chamber, the holy of holies. Archaeology has provided a comparative example from the treasures of King Tutankhamen in the Valley of the Kings at Luxor (Egyptian New Kingdom, ca. 1567–1320). Within the tomb there was a large gold-plated shrine consisting of four boxes, fitted one within the other. The innermost gilded wood shrine, adorned by protective cherub-like figures on each side, preserved the embalmed body. It is interesting that rabbinic literature (b. Yoma 72b) interpreted the construction of the ark of the covenant based on an specific understanding of the verb *tsapah* ("overlay") in Exodus 25:11—as thin boxes of gold, placed on both the inside and outside of the acacia wood. If the interpretation is correct, the ark would have been a three-layered box, similar in form to the Egyptian burial shrines just mentioned. Concerning such shrines, Alan Millard notes, "Egypt's craftsmen had been making prefabricated portable pavilions and shrines for many centuries. One lay in the tomb of a queen from the time of its burial, about 2500 BC, until its excavation in 1925. A gold-plated wooden frame provided a curtained shelter for the queen on her journeys."[128]

Gold-plated burial chamber shrines with innermost shrine of gilded wood (resembling tabernacle with holy of holies). Cairo Museum

Tomb of Tutankhamen (c.1370–52 BC) from inside inner chamber. Cairo Museum

In Tutankhamen's tomb, four gold-plated wooden shrines protected the king's body. The largest is 18 feet long, 12 feet 9 inches wide, and 7 feet 6 inches high. A second shrine fitted inside the first, a third inside the second, and a fourth inside that. Each side was made of a wooden frame fitted with carved panels covered with thin sheets of gold. A linen veil decorated with gilt bronze daisies covered the second of these wooden shrines, similar to the coverings of fabric and skins that covered the tabernacle. These are roughly parallel in time and form to the tabernacle, since it, too, was made by the Egyptian-trained craftsmen Oholiab and Bezalel and others (Exod 36:1–4) in the Sinai desert.

Exodus 25:10, 21–22

The Ark of the Covenant

> Have them make an ark of acacia wood—two and a half cubits long, a cubit and a half wide, and a cubit and a half high ... Place the cover on top of the ark and put in the ark the tablets of the covenant law that I will give you. There, above the cover between the two cherubim that are over the ark of the covenant law, I will meet with you and give you all my commands for the Israelites. (Exodus 25:10, 21–22)

The ark of the covenant/testimony was made in the form of a box two and a half cubits long, one and a half cubits wide, and one and a half cubits high. Depending on whether the longer royal cubit or the shorter standard cubit was used, the ark was approximately three to four feet in length and one to two feet in height and width. This design is indicated in the Hebrew word *'aron*, meaning "box" or "chest" (cf. Akkadian *aranu*), and elsewhere describes the temple's money-chest (2 Kgs 12:9; 2 Chr 24:8–11). This description of the ark makes it appear a rather simple construction. However, it becomes more complex when we consider the historical debates in some circles with regard to details of its design. Was the shape of the ark more a rectangle or a square? Were its poles on the long side or the short side? When the cherubim's wings touched one another did they form an arch, or were they straight?

Size:	3 feet 9 inches x 2 feet 3 inches x 2 feet 3 inches (standard cubit) or 5 feet 25 inches x 3 feet 15 inches (royal cubit) (Exod 25:10)
Builder:	Bezalel of the tribe of Judah and Oholiab of the tribe of Dan (Exod 31:2, 6)
Date of Construction:	ca. 1446 BC at Mount Sinai in the Sinai desert
Materials:	shittim wood (inner box) overlaid with gold inside and out; solid gold mercy seat (Exod 25:10, 11–13, 17–19)
How Transported:	permanently installed poles in side of ark; carried only on shoulders of Kohathite Priests (Exod 25:14–15; Num 3:30–31; 4:15; 7:9)
Place Kept:	in holy of holies within tabernacle and temple (Exod 26:34; 1 Kgs 6:19; 8:6)
Date installed in the Temple:	960 BC at the time of temple dedication (1 Kgs 8:4–11; 2 Chron 5:7–10)
Objects in/ with Ark:	tablets of the law, torah, Aaron's rod that budded, golden bowl with last trace of manna (Exod 16:33–34; 25:16; Num 17:10; Deut 31:26; Heb 9:4)
Last Seen:.	ca.622 BC at time of re-installation in temple under Josiah (2 Chron 35:3)

Archaeology provides numerous parallels from the historical and cultural context for understanding these details of the ark and its purpose. Cherubim figures appear in ancient Near Eastern cultures guarding the entrances to palaces and temples, such as those discovered in the palace of the Assyrian governor of Hadatu, at Arslan Tash in northern Syria.[129] The ark was considered a divine touchpoint between heaven and earth: "the ark of the covenant of the LORD Almighty, who is enthroned between the cherubim" (1 Sam 4:4; 2 Sam 6:2; 2 Kgs 19:15; Isa 37:16; Ps 99:1), a placement that gave it the name the "footstool" of God (1 Chr 28:2; Ps 132:7–8). This concept is illustrated in the ancient art of Israel's closest neighbors in Syria and surrounding Canaan.[130]

In Assyrian and Babylonian reliefs the king is usually attended by a representation of the deity that appears as a winged solar disk hovering above his head (see, for example, the relief of King Darius on Mount Behistun). Byblos, Hamath, and Megiddo have attested representations of a king seated on a throne flanked by winged creatures. A tenth-century-BC example of this type depicts King Hiram of Byblos seated on his cherub-throne.[131] Similar images of the Megiddo

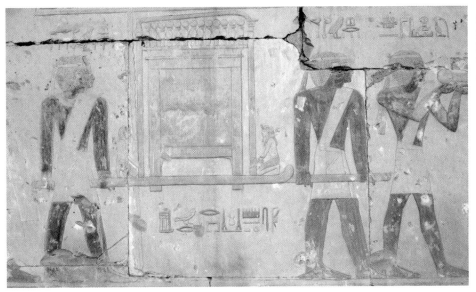

Egyptian wall painting showing priests carrying an ark

© BasPhoto/Shutterstock

ivories are of particular interest because they reflect Phoenician craftsmanship, as employed in building both the First and Second Temples (1 Kgs 5; Ezra 3:7). The craftsmanship on the ivories may give the nearest representation to those on the ark. The purpose for this symbolism was to denote the divine status of the one enthroned, riding upon a heavenly chariot attended by a retinue of celestial beings. Further parallels may be seen in the function of the ark as the repository of a law code.

From ancient Egypt there are examples in processional barques on which statues of the gods were placed. These offer examples of objects similar in form and function to the ark. In addition, the Hebrew word 'aron was used of Egyptian coffins, such as that of Joseph (Gen 50:26), and some Egyptian sarcophagi, such as that of Osiris (adorned with a pair of winged figures), and tomb ware (articles entombed with the mummies) have ark-like appearances. The Egyptian treasures from the tomb of Tutankhamen provide our closest examples to the structure of the ark, since they come from the time of the New Kingdom (ca. 1567–1320), to which the events of the Israelite exodus and wilderness journey belong. Discovered early in the twentieth century within his sealed tomb in the Valley of the Kings at Luxor (ancient Thebes), these treasures are now on display at the Cairo Museum. Within Tutankhamen's tomb were four gilded wooden shrines that protected the Pharaoh's mummified remains. These were designed to fit one inside another (see tabernacle), and the innermost of these was adorned on each side by cherub-like figures. This arrangement is similar to that of the tabernacle and its holy of holies that contained the ark. Moreover, the cherub-like figures on the innermost burial chamber have their wings touching, a position similar to that of the two cherubim on the ark (Exod 25:20; 1 Kgs 8:7; 2 Chr 5:8). This position implies a symbolic guardian role for these creatures in relation to what they surround.

Two other objects in Tutankhamen's tomb have parallels to the ark of the covenant. The first is a finely crafted chest of cedar almost three feet long that may have once held royal robes. It had four wooden transport poles (two on each side) that slid out of view into rings attached underneath. This chest was similar in size to the box-shaped container of acacia wood that held the tablets of the Ten Commandments (Exod 25:10). In like manner, this part of the ark had two carrying poles (Exod 25:13–28) that were used by the Kohathite priests (Num 4:4, 15; 7:9) to transport the ark (1 Chr 15:15). Moreover, the poles for Tutankhamen's chest had collars affixed at the inner ends so they could not be removed. The biblical text explicitly says that the poles for the ark were not to be removed (Exod 25:15) and 1 Kings adds its witness to this fact in recording that these poles protruded through the curtain into the holy place and could be seen by the priests (1 Kgs 8:8; 2 Chr 5:9).

Wooden chest with rings and carrying poles, Cairo Museum

Portable shrine of gold-plated chest topped with Anubis (Egyptian god of the dead), Cairo Museum

Alexander Schick

Guardian figures depicted on Egyptian stone relief

Alexander Schick

A second object, a shrine consisting of a rectangular wooden box overlaid with gold and equipped with carrying poles, resembes the biblical ark; the body of the ark was made of wood overlaid with gold (Exod 25:11). This was for practical protection as well as for religious symbolism and may have been applied as gilding (like gold leaf),[132] an idea perhaps denoted by the language of Hebrews 9:4 indicating the ark was covered on all sides with gold. This method of attaching thin leaves of gold (glued to a fine layer of plaster spread over the wood or applied as hammered sheets to the wood with small nails)[133] was also used on the wooden furniture in Tutankhamen's tomb. It is believed that Solomon later employed this method when he overlaid the entire inside of the temple with gold (1 Kgs 6:21), and especially the two sculptured cherubim that guarded the ark (v. 28).

The lid of the ark, in Hebrew the *kapporet* ("atonement piece") and translated in English Bibles as "mercy seat," was a separate piece of solid gold topped by the cherubim (Exod 25:17–20) that was placed on the ark in the tabernacle (Exod 25:21; 26:34). Here (between the cherubim) the divine presence was manifested (Exod 25:22; Num 7:89). The Egyptian shrine was topped by an image of the god Anubis, which symbolized the presence of this god.

We should not be surprised to find these close parallels to the structure of the ark of the covenant among the Egyptians, since Bezalel (Exod 37:1–9), the craftsman who constructed the ark, probably learned and plied his craft in Egypt. He undoubtedly had experience with chests and shrines similar to those found in the tomb of Tutankhamen.

Exodus 31:18

The Ten Commandments in Archaeological Context

When the LORD finished speaking to Moses on Mount Sinai, he gave him the two tablets of the covenant law, the tablets of stone inscribed by the finger of God. (Exod 31:18)

The ark contained sacred objects associated with God's presence with Israel in the desert. These served as a witness to future generations of the Mosaic covenant. In ancient Near Eastern religions, sacred shrines held images of gods, but since physical representations of God were forbidden in ancient Israel, the divine image was communicated through God's law contained within the ark. This law was comprised of ten words (Ten Commandments), which had been inscribed on a pair of stone tablets. These tablets of the law remained a permanent fixture within the ark (2 Chr 5:10).[134] The Hollywood depiction of these tablets is usually monumental. Whether intentionally or not, the cinemagraphic portrait of an eighty-year-old man hefting huge stone slabs weighing hundreds of pounds down a rugged mountain makes the Bible seem more fantasy than reality.

Archaeology, however, offers a more accurate picture. Based on discoveries of similarly inscribed stone tablets, the Ten Commandments were probably carved on stone flakes not much larger than the size of a man's hand.[135] This size is implied by the relatively small size of the ark itself. In a debate between the two rabbinic sages Rabbi Meir and Rabbi Yehuda, the former says that the stone tablets and the Torah scrolls were placed side by side within the ark. The latter contended that in the fortieth year of the desert sojourn, a shelf was attached to an exterior side of the ark to hold the Torah scroll.[136] Either way, only tablets like those just described could have fit within the ark.

Archaeology also helps us to understand the reason why these tablets were deposited within the ark of the covenant. In ancient Near Eastern cultures during Moses's time, the custom was to put legal documents and agreements between rival kingdoms at the feet of their god in their sanctuary. This god acted as the guardian of treaties and supervised their implementation. Egyptian records provide an example of this in which a pact between Ramesses II and Hattusilis III. Their concord is sealed by depositing a treaty at the feet of both the Hittite king's god Teshup and the Pharaoh's god Ra. The tablets of the law set within the ark were likewise at the "feet" of God, since the ark was his footstool. Another possible example of this custom in the Bible may be seen in the prophet Samuel recording the ordinances of the kingdom and setting them "before the Lord," that is, at the foot of the ark (1 Sam 10:25). King Hezekiah too may have been acting in accordance with this custom when he "spread ... out before the Lord" the threatening letter of the Assyrian Rabshakeh (Isa 37:14).

Ten Commandments (replica) Bible Society, Jerusalem

Randall Price showing size of tablets with ark model

That Israel adopted practices similar to other pagan cultures is no problem to the uniqueness of God's special revelation to them as a chosen people. Ritual practice is evident from the beginning of the Bible (Gen 4:3) and remained a part of the practice after the flood (Gen. 8:20) and in all of the separate cultures that developed after the division of the nations at Babel (Job 1:5; Exod 8:25–26). God accommodated local customs, yet with a distinct theological meaning that magnified his unique relationship with Israel by contrast.

LEVITICUS

Leviticus 16:7–10

Ancient Near Eastern Parallels to the Scapegoat Ritual

> Then he is to take the two goats and present them before the LORD at the entrance to the tent of meeting. He is to cast lots for the two goats—one lot for the LORD and the other for the scapegoat. Aaron shall bring the goat whose lot falls to the LORD and sacrifice it for a sin offering. But the goat chosen by lot as the scapegoat shall be presented alive before the LORD to be used for making atonement by sending it into the wilderness as a scapegoat. (Lev 16:7–10)

This ritual connected with the Yom Kippur (Day of Atonement) ceremony has as its central act the sending away of one of two goats, the scapegoat, to rid Israel of its national guilt. In ancient Near Eastern texts, rites of riddance can be found among the Egyptians and the Canaanites, and the Ugaritic religion also had a scapegoat ritual. The Hittites also had a ritual of removing evil from humans by transferring it to animals (although a woman was used in the case of royalty). In this ritual, performed for the elimination of a plague, a bull was driven to the open country (Ashella, line 8) and a ram was driven to the land of the enemy (Uhhamuwa, lines 4–5), both decorated with colored ribbons. According to early rabbinic tradition, the Israelite practice was to tie a red ribbon to the horns of the scapegoat (m. Yoma 4:2). One of the most striking parallels is in the Babylonian Akitu festival, where the following elements were present:

- Purification of holy space is combined with propitiatory offerings.
- The priestly figures bathe beforehand (some translations add that they wore linen as Aaron did).
- Smoke is used in the sanctuary.
- A slaughtered animal or its blood is used to purify the space.
- The deity is presented with roasted meat after the cleansing.
- The carcasses of the slaughtered animals are disposed of outside the civilized area.
- Those who conduct the temple-purification ritual are made unclean; however, the Babylonian functionaries are temporarily banished, whereas Aaron and the temple functionaries are instructed to bathe.[137]

In addition, the "scapegoat" in Leviticus 16:10 is literally "for Azazel." Most English translations take this term to mean "wilderness," following later rabbinic tradition, which interpreted it as a place name from the root ʿzz, which is cognate to Arabic ʿazâzu, "rough ground." However, laʾazaʾzel, "for Azazel," is parallel to layhwh ("for the LORD"; 16:8–10), which suggests that Azazel is some type of being rather than a place. The Qumran sectarians read ʿzzʾl as a name (11Q26), and this was also the dominant view in midrashic literature from the early postbiblical period (3 En 4:6; Pirqe R. El. 46). In this interpretion Azazel is most commonly thought of as a desert demon. The sins of the community "were carried by the goat and returned to this demon for the purpose of removing them from the community and leaving them at their source in order that their power or effect in the community might be completely broken."[138] The image of a demon in the form of a goat finds archaeological support from the Megiddo Ivories and from the Canaanite god Mot/Motu known from Ugaritic literature.

These archaeological parallels demonstrate a long and ancient tradition of purification rituals in the ancient Near East, and, though also having significant differences from the Yom Kippur ritual, nevertheless provide evidence that the biblical ritual has the antiquity given it in the Pentateuch.

NUMBERS

Numbers 6:24–26

High Priestly Benediction

> The LORD bless you and keep you; the LORD make his face shine on you and be gracious to you; the LORD turn his face toward you and give you peace. (Num 6:24–26)

In 1979 Israeli archaeologist Gabriel Barkay began excavating an archaeological site southwest of Jerusalem's Old City in the Hinnom Valley. This site, called Ketef Hinnom, is adjacent to St. Andrew's Church, now on the grounds of the Menachem Begin Heritage Center. The rock-hewn tomb complex in this area of natural caverns had been mostly destroyed by later quarrying activity, but one tomb, tomb 25, had been preserved intact because the lining of the roof of the cave had collapsed and covered the floor of the cave with a thick deposit that made it appear that the tomb was empty. For this reason its contents had been protected from tomb robbers, and as a result Barkay's team recovered more than 1,000 objects. These included small pottery vessels, artifacts of iron and bronze (including arrowheads), needles and pins, bone and ivory objects, glass bottles, and jewelry.

With such a vast treasure to inventory, the team almost overlooked a couple of tiny objects that looked like discarded cigarette butts. Though this hoard was important, these last objects proved to be the more sensational find when it was discovered that they were silver scrolls with inscriptions scratched into their thin metallic sheets. Once opened, an ancient Hebrew text was found resembling the biblical Aaronic benediction in Numbers 6:24–26. It was this text that the LORD commanded Aaron and descendants to recite in blessing the sons of Israel (v. 23). In this manner, the LORD said, "So they will put my name on the Israelites, and I will bless them" (v. 27). Moreover, these texts appear to include a phrase that reveals a literary dependence on Deuteronomy 7:9: "Know therefore that the LORD your God is God; he is the faithful God, keeping his covenant of love to a thousand generations of those who love him and keep his commandments." Because these texts also included a statement of YHWH as "rebuker of evil," a term found in later apotropaic (incantation) texts, it has been suggested that the scrolls were worn around the neck as a type of talisman.

Excavation Director Gabriel Barkay at Tomb 25, Ketef Hinnom

Unopened silver scroll,
Ketef Hinnom

Alexander Schick

For this reason the scrolls, whose designation is KH1 and KH2, have been popularly referred to as silver amulets. Some scholars refer to them simply as Amulet A and B.

This discovery has been called one of most significant discoveries ever made for biblical studies. This is because of the scrolls' contribution to our knowledge of the development of the Hebrew alphabet and because the scrolls contain the earliest citations of biblical texts, more than 300 years earlier than the Dead Sea Scrolls. This dating was confirmed by the West Semitic Research Project at the University of Southern California employing advanced photographic and computer enhancement techniques. This permitted the script to be read very precisely, rendering a secure date on paleographic grounds immediately prior to the Babylonian destruction of Jerusalem in 587/6 BC. This dating at the end of the First Temple period has issued a challenge to the Documentary Hypothesis view, which contends that the priestly school composed the Torah only in the postexilic period. Advocates of this theory do not accept this early dating as evidence that all of the Torah existed at that time, but they have admitted that some of the material found in the Pentateuch must have existed in the First Temple period.

Opened Scrolls (KH1 and KH2), Ketef Hinnom

Alexander Schick

Some continue to challenge a pre-exilic date, arguing for a Second Temple period date,[139] but this has been successfully answered by Ahituv.[140]

Numbers 22–24; 31:8, 16

Archaeological Evidence for Balaam Son of Beor

[Balak] sent messengers to summon Balaam son of Beor, who was at Pethor, near the Euphrates River, in his native land. Balak said: "A people has come out of Egypt; they cover the face of the land and have settled next to me. Now come and put a curse on these people, because they are too powerful for me. Perhaps then I will be able to defeat them and drive them out of the land. For I know that whoever you bless is blessed, and whoever you curse is cursed." (Num 22:5–6)

In the biblical account the Moabite king Balak hired the diviner/prophet Balaam son of Beor to pronounce a curse on the Isrelites as they passed through their land, but the LORD caused Balaam to bless Israel instead (Num 22:1–24:25). As a result of his act being thwarted, Balaam developed an alternate means of attack on Israel

Deir 'Alla, Balaam, Son of Beor fragment

© Baker Publishing Group and Dr. James C. Martin courtesy of the Jordanian Ministry of Antiquities and the Amman Archaeological Museum, Jordan.

Deir 'Alla Balaam Texts (Combination I)[141]

(1) [VACAT] The sa]ying[s of Bala]am, [son of Be]or, the man who was a seer of the gods. Lo! Gods came to him in the night [and spoke to] him

(2) according to these w[ord]s. Then they said to [Bala]am, son of Beor, thus: "Let someone make a [ ] hereafter, so that [what] you have hea[rd may be se]en!"

(3) And Balaam rose in the morning [ ] right hand [ ] and could not [eat] and wept

(4) aloud. Then his people came in to him [and said] to Balaam, son of Beor, "Do you fast? [ ] Do you weep?" And he

(5) said to them, "Si[t] do]wn! I shall inform you what the Shad[dayin have done]. Now come, see the deeds of the g[o]ds! The g[o]ds have gathered

(6) and the Shaddayin have taken their places in the assembly and said to Sh[, thus:] 'Sew the skies shut with your thick cloud! There let there be darkness and no

(7) perpetual shining and n[o] radiance! For you will put a sea[l upon the thick] cloud of darkness and

(8) you will not remove it forever! For the swift has reproached the eagle, the voice of vultures resounds. The st[ork has] the young of the NHS-bird and ripped up the chicks of the heron. The swallow has belittled

(9) the dove, and the sparrow [ ] and [ ] the staff. Instead of ewes the stick is driven along. Hares have eaten

(10) [ ]. Freemen [] have drunk wine, and hyenas have listened to instruction. The whelps of the

(11) f[ox] laughs at wise men, and the poor woman has mixed myrrh, and the priestess

(12) [ ] to the one who wears a girdle of threads. The esteemed esteems and the esteemer is es[teemed.] and everyone has seen those things that decree offspring and young.

(13) [ ] the deaf will her from afar [

(14)] the eyes of] a fool will see visions. Sheger and Ashtar for [.

(15) [ ] the leopard. The piglet has chased the young

(16) [of] those who are girded and the eye . . . ."

through the use of cult prostitutes to bring some of the Israelites into a context of worship to Baal at Peor (Num 25). (Peor is probably Pitru, a site mentioned in Assyrian sources as situated on the west bank of the Euphrates, about 12 miles south of Carchemish.) This resulted in the LORD sending a plague on Israel and Moses avenging the matter, leading to the Israelites killing Balaam (Num 31:8, 16).

Fragments of an Aramaic text discovered at Deir 'Alla in Jordan are attributed to a seer called Balaam son of Beor. Known as the Deir 'Alla Inscription, or Balaam Son of Beor Inscription, it was discovered in the remains of a building (possibly a temple) on whose plaster walls the inscription had been written in red and black ink (perhaps for emphasis). Remains of plaster sections containing the inscription have been put together in twelve combinations, but only two had enough readable text to translate. While the inscription is written in Aramaic, the language is Ammonite and represents the oldest piece of Aramaic literature. Though dated several centuries after the time of Balaam (ca. 840–760 BC), the text may preserve an extrabiblical oracle of the prophet. If so, it provides information about him previously unknown, such as his title as "a seer of the gods" and his association with Ashtar (the consort of the Moabite god Chemosh) and the fertility deity Shegar (known from Ugaritic and Phoencian texts). If the building was a temple, then it is possible that this was an honorary inscription to these gods who at one time had responded to Balaam's actions as a seer. In the bits of the divination/prophecy preserved it appears that he was cursing the gods and goddesses who had brought about the period of drought, darkness, and death and so seeking the intercession of goddesses Ashtar and Shegar to restore the land to fertility.

Baal at Peor, whom the biblical text says Balaam seduced the Israelites into worshiping, had an association with Ashtar and fertility rites.

Numbers 21:8–9

Archaeological Examples of the Bronze Serpent

> The Lord said to Moses, "Make a snake and put it up on a pole; anyone who is bitten can look at it and live." So Moses made a bronze serpent and put it up on a pole. Then when anyone was bitten by a snake and looked at the bronze snake, they lived. (Num 21:8–9)

The account in verses 6–9 explains that because of Israel's sin the Lord sent poisonous snakes to kill the people. There is a snake in the desert of Israel today call the *seraph* ("fiery") because it has a fatal bite that burns like fire until it brings death. The bronze image of a serpent that Moses made and hung on a pole was a means to focus the Israelites' faith in God who had promised that all who were bitten by such fiery serpents and would look to his promise (symbolized in the serpent that was the cause of their impending death) would live. On account of the significance of this event, the Israelites in the wilderness preserved this object for centuries, but by the time of King Hezekiah (715–687 BC) it had become a cult object called "Nehushtan"

Bronze snakes reflective of the brazen serpent from sacred precincts at Hazor, Megiddo, Tel Mevorakh, Shechem, Gezer, and the Midianite shrine at Timna.

Shlomo Moussaieff Collection, Herzliyya. Courtesy Eretz Israel Museum, Tel-Aviv. Photo by Alexander Schick.

("brazen [thing]"). Lowell Handy argued that the Nehushtan was the symbol of a minor god of snakebite-cure within the temple.[142] Whatever its purpose, it no longer served the original purpose of memorializing the divine deliverance in the wilderness but had attracted its own veneration, so Hezekiah destroyed it (2 Kgs 18:4).

The copper for the original image of the serpent was available to Moses from the hoard of items taken as plunder from Egypt (Exod 3:22). However, copper ore was mined in Timna, about 18 miles north of the Gulf of Eilat, where the Egyptians who operated the mining industry also had cultic installations, including a temple to Hathor for the miners and wayfarers situated at the foot of the natural sandstone formations in this region. Many associate the Hathor cult, whose goddess assumed the image of a cow, with the making of the molten calf as a god (Exod 32:4, 8, 31; cf. 1 Kgs 12:28). With the decline of Egyptian control of the region in the middle of the twelfth century BC, the mines at Timna and the Hathor temple were abandoned. However, the Midianites, who stayed in Timna for a brief period after the Egyptians, restored cultic activities in the Hathor temple. The excavator, Beno Rothenberg, believed the temple was founded during the reign of Pharaoh Seti I (1318–1304 BC) but argued that it may have been shared with the Midianites during the Egyptian phase since *massebot* (in Hebrew, "standing stones") on the western side of the shrine are on the same stratigraphic level as the Hathor altar.[143] Among the archeological finds in this Midianite shrine were a large number of votive gifts brought especially from Midian, including highly decorated Midianite pottery and metal jewelry. Among the cultic objects was a copper snake with a gilded head. It bears similarities to the copper serpent described in Numbers 21:6–9 and has an historical connection to the Israelites in the wilderness, since Jethro a high priest of Midian, was Moses's father-in-law and is described in the biblical text as advising Moses in Israel's organization and worship in the desert (Exod 18:1–24).

Snake cults had already been established in Canaan during the Broze Age prior to the arrival of the Israelites. Excavations have uncovered snake cult objects at the pre-Israelite cities of Megiddo, Gezer, Shechem, Ekron (a ureus, which formed part of the headdress of a statuette of an Egyptian deity associated with its Neo-Assyrian-type palace), and Hazor, where the object was found within the holy of holies in a Canaanite temple (Area H).

Numbers 21:13

The Arnon as a Territorial Border

> They set out from there and camped alongside the Arnon, which is in the wilderness extending into Amorite territory. The Arnon is the border of Moab, between Moab and the Amorites. (Num 21:13)

Wadi Mujib, historically known as Arnon, is a gorge in Jordan that enters the Dead Sea at 410 meters (1,350 ft) below sea level. The Mujib Reserve of Wadi Mujib is located in the mountainous landscape to the east of the Dead Sea, approximately 90 kilometers south (55 miles) of Amman. The 220-square-kilometer (85 sq miles) reserve was created in 1987 by the Royal

Society for the Conservation of Nature and is regionally and internationally important, particularly for the bird life that the reserve supports. It extends to the Kerak and Madaba mountains to the north and south, reaching 900 meters above sea level in some places. This 1,300-meter (4,300 ft) variation in elevation, combined with the valley's year round water flow from seven tributaries, means that Wadi Mujib enjoys a magnificent biodiversity that is still being explored and documented today. Over three hundred species of plants, ten species of carnivores, and numerous species of permanent and migratory birds have been recorded until this date. Some of the remote mountain and valley areas are difficult to reach and thus offer safe havens for rare species of cats, goats and other mountain animals.

The Mujib reserve consists of mountainous, rocky, and sparsely vegetated desert (up to 800 m), with cliffs, gorges, and deep wadis cutting through plateaus. Perennial, spring-fed streams flow down the wadis to the shores of the Dead Sea, which lies 400 meters (1,300 ft) below sea level.

The slopes of the mountainous land are very sparsely vegetated, with steppe-type vegetation on plateaus. Groundwater seepage does occur in places

The ancient border of the Arnon (modern Wadi Mujeb) in Jordan

along the Dead Sea shore, for example at the hot springs of Zara, which supports a luxuriant thicket of Acacia, Tamarix, Phoenix, and Nerium, and a small marsh. The less severe slopes of the reserve are used by pastoralists for the grazing of sheep and goats.

The Arnon has always been an important boundary line. Before the Hebrew period it separated, for a time at least, the Moabites from the Amorites (Num 21:13, 26; Deut 3:8; Judg 11:18). After the Hebrew settlement it divided, theoretically at least, Moab from the tribes of Reuben and Gad (Deut 3:12, 16). But in fact, Moab lay as much to the north as it did to the south of the Arnon. To the north, for example, were Aroer, Dibon, Madaba, and other Moabite towns. Even under Omri and Ahab, who held part of the Moabite territory, Israel did not hold sway farther south than Ataroth, about 10 miles north of the Arnon. The Moabite king Mesha, in his inscription (Moabite Stone, line 10), says that the Gadites (not the Reubenites) formerly occupied Ataroth, from where he expelled the people of Israel. He mentions

(line 26) his having constructed a road along the Arnon. The ancient importance of the river and of the towns in its vicinity is attested by the numerous ruins of bridges, forts, and buildings found upon or near it. Its fords are alluded to by Isaiah (16:2). Its "heights," crowned with the castles of chiefs, were also celebrated in Num 21:28. Military campaigns in the wadis of the Arnon form part of the subject matter of the "Book of the Wars of the LORD" (Num 21:14).

Mesha Inscription

Todd Bolen/www.BiblePlaces.com, taken at the Louvre

DEUTERONOMY

Deuteronomy 29:9–13

Covenant Making in the Ancient Near East

Carefully follow the terms of this covenant, so that you may prosper in everything you do. All of you are standing today in the presence of the LORD your God—your leaders and chief men, your elders and officials, and all the other men of Israel, together with your children and your wives, and the foreigners living in your camps who chop your wood and carry your water. You are standing here in order to enter into a covenant with the LORD your God, a covenant the LORD is making with you this day and sealing with an oath, to confirm you this day as his people, that he may be your God as he promised you and as he swore to your fathers, Abraham, Isaac and Jacob. (Deut 29:9–13)

The covenant that Yahweh made with the sons of Israel at Sinai was not unique. While the demonstration of God's power to confirm the covenant was particular to Israel, the form of the covenant given by God to Moses and through him to the nation had a precedent in established law codes in the ancient Near East. This should be expected, as God, in dealing with his nation in an international context, would accommodate the structure known and practiced in the time so that Israel and the nations could make sense of their expected relationship agreed to at the foot of Mount Sinai:

Suzerain-Vassal Treaty Format

Element	Explanation	Parallel in Deuteronomy
Preamble	The identification of the suzerain by his name and titles.	Moses as covenant mediator (1:1–4)
Historical Prologue	The historical survey of the suzerain's dealings with the vassal. The purpose is to illustrate to the vassal how much the suzerain has done to protect and establish the vassal who therefore owes submission and allegiance to the suzerain	Moses's first sermon: historical review (1:5–4:43)
General Stipulations	The next section of these treaties list the stipulations i.e., what the vassal is required to do and what the suzerain offers in return.	Moses's second sermon, part a: covenant obligations (4:44–11:32)
Specific Stipulations	There may be a requirement that the vassal deposit his copy of the treaty in his temple, where he is to occasionally read and study it to refresh his memory concerning his duties	Moses's second sermon, part b (12–26)
Divine Witnesses	Deities are called as witnesses to the treaty.	Moses calls on "heaven and earth" to witness, since only Yahweh is divine (4:26; 30:19; 31:28; 32:1)
Blessings & Curses	The last section of these treaties contains the blessings (if the vassal obeys) and curses (if the vassal is unfaithful).	Moses's third sermon: blessings & curses (27–28); Moses's fourth sermon: covenant summary (29–30); Succession of covenant mediator from Moses to Joshua (31–34)

When Moses went and told the people all the LORD's words and laws, they responded with one voice, "Everything the LORD has said we will do."…Then he took the Book of the Covenant and read it to the people. They responded, "We will do everything the LORD has said; we will obey." (Exod 24:3, 7)

Throughout the ancient Near East there were many secular documents that followed the same form of covenant making that God performed with Israel. The one that forms the pattern for biblical law is the suzerain-vassal treaty. A suzerain is a lord or king; a vassal is someone inferior who pays tribute to him or fights in his army. These treaties (or covenants) follow a standard form.

The book of Deuteronomy is written in the form of the Hittite suzerain-vassal treaty (ca. 1400–1200 BC) to present to the people of Israel their suzerain's (God as the sovereign king) pledges to his vassals (Israel) and to review their obligations to him. Deuteronomy contains all of the essential elements of these Hittite treaty texts as well as additions that are necessary in the context such as Moses's farewell speech. The chart above shows how Deuteronomy is arranged according to the Hittite treaty format.

Hittite suzerain-vassal treaty on bronze tablet (c. 1235 BC) between Tudhaliya IV (Egyptian) and Kurunta of Tarhuntassa (Hittite), pledging rule of Tarhuntassa to Kurunta and his son

JOSHUA

Joshua 2:1

Reconnaissance Missions in the Archaeological Record

> Then Joshua the son of Nun secretly sent two men from Shittim. "Go, look over the land," he said, "especially Jericho." So they went and entered the house of a prostitute named Rahab and stayed there. (Josh 2:1)

Joshua sent two spies in advance of the Israelite army to assess their military options. Reconnaissance and espionage played a significant role in the military operations of antiquity. In the battle between the Egyptians and the Hittites at Kadesh on the Orontes River (ca.1250 BC), Ramses II reports that as the Egyptian advance guard was about 7 miles from Kadesh, the Hittite king Muwatalli II sent out two Shasu (nomads) spies to deceive him as to the location of the Hittite army. The spies claimed that the Hittite king was so afraid of the Pharaoh that his army was camped at a far distance. This is similar to the biblical spy narrative in which Rahab tells the spies that the men of Jericho were afraid of the Israelites (Josh 2:9–11). The Egyptian relief texts explain that the Shasu statement was a "false report ordered by the Hittites."[1] The Hittite army was actually nearby, just behind the city of Kadesh, and prepared to launch a surprise attack. Ramesses II did not realize this until Egyptian scouts captured two Hittites spies and tortured them into revealing the truth. Accounts of the ensuing battle and the events preceding and following it (known as the "Poem" and the "Bulletin") have been preserved in multiple inscriptions as captions accompanying reliefs in the temples of Abydos, Luxor, Karnack, Abu Simbel, and the Ramesseum. One of these relates the confession of the two Hittite spies:

> When they had been brought before Pharaoh, His Majesty asked, "Who are you?" They replied "We belong to the king of Hatti. He has sent us to spy on you." Then His Majesty said to them, "Where is he, the enemy from Hatti? I had heard that he was in the land of Khaleb, north of Aleppo." They of Tunip replied to His Majesty, "Lo, the king of Hatti has already arrived, together with the many countries who are supporting him . . . They are armed with their infantry and their chariots. They have their weapons of war at the ready. They are more numerous than the grains of sand on the beach. Behold, they stand equipped and ready for battle behind the old city of Kadesh."[2]

Scenes of the Kadesh conflict depict the famous chariot battle, including a depiction of Egyptian officers beating the spies with rods to elicit the above confession. This is what might have happened to the Israelite spies had they been captured by the Canaanites who were sent after them for this purpose (Josh 2:7, 16, 22). Their escape, and its providential means, confirmed to Joshua that the LORD had given Jericho over to the Israelites (Josh 2:24).

Kadesh Agreement, Istanbul Museum

Iocanus/Wikimedia Commons, CC BY 3.0

A copy of the peace treaty established between the Egyptians and the Hittites as a result of the Battle of Kadesh was discovered in excavations at the Hittite capital of Hattusa (modern Boğazköy, Turkey). Written in cuneiform on a clay tablet, it is the earliest extant example of a written international agreement and is today housed in the Istanbul Archaeological Museum.

Joshua 6:20

Archaeology and the Conquest of Jericho

> When the trumpets sounded, the army shouted, and at the sound of the trumpet, when the men gave a loud shout, the wall collapsed; so everyone charged straight in, and they took the city. (Josh 6:20)

The concept of a conquest of the land of Canaan has been disputed by some critics on the grounds that the biblical depiction of a massive military invasion of "the land" (Josh 11:23a) is not supported in the archaeological record. However, the biblical account does not present the conquest in the manner these critics assume. There is no doubt that the conquest was extensive ("the entire land," Josh 11:23a), but this was only a gain of territory sufficient to enable the Israelite tribes to settle into their promised inheritance without further waging war (Josh 11:23b-c 13–17). It was not *total*. Seven tribes remained without their inheritance because they had failed to conquer their land (Josh 18:2–3), and in the time of the judges the tribe of Dan was still unable to possess their land (Judg 18:1). Of the Canaanite cities conquered, only three were burned with fire: Jericho (Josh 6:24), Ai (Josh 8:8, 19–20), and Hazor (Josh 11:13), and at the end of the military campaign the text states that "there are still very large areas of land to be taken over" (Josh 13:1). Even the Jebusites in a key city such as Jerusalem could not be driven out at that time (Josh 15:63). The text reveals that the Israelites had failed to completely drive out the Canaanite inhabitants, so a gradual occupation of Canannite towns occurred with the Israelite tribes settling among the Canaanite population (Josh. 9:21–27; 13:13; Judg. 1:29–33), with Canaanites eventually reinhabiting many of their conquered towns since the Israelites were pastoralists and had no particular need of them. Many distinctive Iron Age examples of Israelite material culture, such as the four-room house, collared-rim jars, and lime-plastered cisterns have Late Bronze (and earlier) Canaanite precedents.[3] This reflects the influence of Canaanite material culture on the Israelites as they lived alongside the resident Canaanites. Therefore, the criticism that there was no conquest because its assumed size and scope does not fit with the archaeological evidence fails because of a misreading of the biblical conquest account. Also, the archaeological evidence that a gradual Israelite settlement occurred in Canaan during this period and into the time of the judges agrees with the picture of daily life found in the historical narratives.

Southern end of Tel Jericho showing retaining wall in Kenyon trench, completed by the Palestinian-Italian excavation

Photo by Henry B. Smith, Jr., Associates for Biblical Research, used by permission.

Therefore, given a proper interpretation of the facts of the conquest, the biblical text and the archaeological data appear to agree.[4]

A second criticism is that the initial attack on the Canaanite city of Jericho, an event attributed in the Bible to divine intervention in bringing down the city walls, cannot be historically supported based on the results of archaeological excavations at the site. Although early excavations by Ernst Sellin and Carl Watzinger (1907–8) and John Garstang (1930–36) produced evidence that the excavators felt was supportive of the biblical account, the later excavation of Kathleen Kenyon (1952–58, but published thirty years later) concluded that an attack had only occurred in the Middle Bronze period and that the city therefore had been destroyed some 150 years before the time that the biblical account puts Joshua in Canaan. One of the reasons for this conclusion was the reported absence of imported Cypriot bichrome pottery, considered a necessary indicative of habitation. Bryant Wood (1985, 1987, 1990) studied her published samples and challenged this assumption. He sought to reassign Kenyon's Middle Bronze pottery dates to the beginning of the Late Bronze Age, a time that fit with the biblical date of the conquest (ca. 1400 BC).[5] However, because of the almost indistinguishable style of this pottery from the final phase of the Middle Bronze to the Late Bronze I periods, and the lack of any Late Bronze pottery sherds found in the subsequent excavations on the tel by an Italian-Palestinian team (1997–2000, 2009–14), Kenyon's dating was reconfirmed.

Although Wood's arguments have not been convincing to most scholars, the Italian-Palestinian team did find some Late Bronze material in tombs from Period V (Late Bronze I, 1550–1200 BC) located northwest of the tel.

Randall Price holding a mudbrick and pointing at destruction level at Jericho in Kenyan trench (same site as trench at back of upper photo)

Casey Olson

This material consisted of Egyptian amulets inscribed with names of pharaohs from 1500 to 1386 BC, indicating that the cemetery was in use during that time. Perhaps some of these amulets were part of the treasures of Egypt (Exod 12:35–36) that the Bible states were given to the departing Hebrews by the Egyptian populace. The excavators also discovered a small, Late Bronze occupation in Area G at the top of Spring Hill, the artificial mound beside Ain es-Sûltan—the spring that provides Jericho with a supply of fresh water. According to the excavators, "a major sustaining wall was identified, presumably terracing the acropolis with public buildings, and at the bottom of which, in Area D, cleaning works brought into light a huge mud-brick wall, just in front of the Spring . . ."[6] Further evidence was found in the area of built tomb D.641 excavated in Area G. This consisted of a square chamber lined with mudbricks in which two individuals were buried. This gave evidence of a Middle Bronze palace on the hill. In the underlying middle terrace, between the limit of the palace and the main terrace-wall, a labyrinthine structure had been interpreted by Garstang as a tomb or cenotaph.[7] In an upper and probably reused level of the building there was found a group of complete Late Bronze I pottery vessels identified as a collection of "funeral equipment."[8]

This evidence demonstrates that there was a Late Bronze habitation at Jericho, even though the remains of this period have not been uncovered on the tel specifically. A primary reason for this is, as the Italian-Palestinian team reported of the Spring Hill and northern plateau, "intensive razing of later periods had removed all strata down to the Middle or even to the early Bronze Age."[9] This assessment was previously made by Amihai Mazar, who stated:

> The finds at Jericho, however, show that there was a settlement there during the Late Bronze Age, though most of its remains were eroded or removed by human activity. Perhaps, as at other sites, the

massive Middle Bronze fortifications were reutilized in the Late Bronze Age. The Late Bronze Age settlement at Jericho was followed by an occupation gap in Iron Age I. Thus, in the case of Jericho, the archaeological data cannot serve as decisive evidence to deny a historical nucleus in the Book of Joshua concerning the conquest of the city.[10]

If, as Mazar suggests, the late Middle Bronze fortifications were continued into the early Late Bronze I period, then, like other evidences of a short siege (see chart below), Kenyon's evidence of the burning of the city *after* the walls had collapsed fits with the biblical data.

In the case of Jericho, then, the details of the literary evidence from the biblical text must take precedence. When these details are viewed in light of the discoveries made at Jericho there is a remarkable correspondence that argues for the historicity of the event. The chart below summarizes the archaeological evidence in relation to the biblical account of the attack on the city.

Reconstruction of the north side of Jericho showing the walls falling while the Israelites are walking around the city, based on the excavations of the Germans in 1907–08. Between the walls, on the sloped rampart, the excavators found houses, some of them built against the lower city wall, as was the case with Rahab's house.

Harmony of the Biblical Account and the Archaeological Evidence for the Fall of Jericho

1. Jericho was a fortified city in 15th century BC (Josh 2:5–7, 15).
During excavation it was clear that there were "remains of the three successive and massive plastered ramparts which surrounded" the city.
2. The city was destroyed by fire (Josh 6:24).
Kathleen Kenyon, during her excavation of the Jericho site in the 1950s, was able to conclude that "walls and floors were blackened or reddened by fire. . . . In most rooms the fallen debris was heavily burnt."[11] While examining the east side, "a layer of burnt ash and debris about one meter thick" was discovered, which indicates a massive fire.
3. The fortification walls collapsed (Josh 6:20).
Some speculate that an earthquake destroyed the walls.
4. The destruction was in the time of harvest due to grain storage (Josh 2:6; 3:15; 5:10).
The destruction of the city appears to have taken place during the spring because that would have been harvest season. When both "Garstang and Kenyon found several storage jars that were buried, they realized that they were storing a large quantity of grain."
5. The grain stored in the city was not consumed indicating a short siege (Josh 6:15, 20).
Typically, within a city of Jericho's size, it would take several months, perhaps years, to consume the amount of grain they were storing. Therefore, the burnt grain found within Jericho indicates that its citizens did not have time to consume it all before the city was destroyed. These observations line up with the description given in the biblical narrative.
6. The grain was never used by the inhabitants or invaders (Josh 6:17–18).
Given the high value of grain during this ancient period, it is quite a unique situation to find such a large quantity of grain in storage jars (let alone burnt grain) after the destruction of a city. Typically, either the inhabitants or invaders would have taken the grain, but they did not. This agrees with God's command to Joshua to burn the grain.
7. The walls were leveled as part of the destruction (Josh 6:20).
The mudbrick walls atop the stone revetment walls were brought completely down. The Palestinian-Italian team verified this in their recent excavations.

Based on the evidence from previous excavations, and especially the Italian-Palestinian finds of collapsed mudbrick walls at the foot of the stone retaining walls on the north side of the tell, Wood has suggested that the walls of Jericho fell outward, creating a ramp upon which the invading Israelites could enter the city. In addition, old photos from the Sellin-Watzinger expedition show a stone revetment wall with a mudbrick parapet on the top of the rampart, with the remains of houses inside the revetment wall. Wood suggests that in one of these surviving houses on the sloping rampart between the revetment wall encircling the bottom of the hill and the city wall that surrounded the top of the tell, Rahab, the harlot might have lived.[12]

Joshua 6:20–21

Weapons of Warfare

> When the trumpets sounded, the army shouted, and at the sound of the trumpet, when the men gave a loud shout, the wall collapsed; so everyone charged straight in, and they took the city. They devoted the city to the LORD and destroyed with the sword every living thing in it—men and women, young and old, cattle, sheep and donkeys. (Josh 6:20–21)

In the account of the battle of Jericho, weapons of war are mentioned. This text describes one of the most common war weapons, the sword. Archaeology has revealed the kind of sword used in the Late Bronze Age (by both the Israelites and Canaanites) as the sickle sword. This sword, which developed from a battle-axe and went through modifications from the Middle Bronze Age (where it had a hooked end to catch the enemy's shields), took the form of the shorter Egyptian sickle sword (*khopesh*) and the longer Canaanite sickle sword. These were made of bronze and took the shape of a scythe with the outer curved side, having the cutting edge on its convex side.

Example of the shorter Egyptian sickle sword used by both the Israelites and the Canaanites

Courtesy of Liberty Biblical Museum/ photo by Ayelet Shapira

These swords had "blood grooves" niched into them, running the length of the blade, to allow blood from battle to flow down the blade and not congeal on the cutting side of the weapon. Some scholars believe that the weapon called in Hebrew the *kidon* (usually translated as "javelin") was also a Near Eastern sickle sword (possibly of Hurrian origin).[13] This weapon appears in Canaanite reliefs as the weapon of the god Baal and was the weapon the Philistine Goliath "slung on his back" (1 Sam. 17:6). The Philistine apparently adopted the use of this weapon from living among the Canaanites.

Another "weapon" mentioned in this text was the trumpet (*shofar*), a "ram's horn." It played a pivotal part in the fall of Jericho, as its sharp horn blasts (accompanied by shouting) served to shock and demoralize the enemy. This same type of psychological warfare was employed to cause confusion and panic among the Midianites (Judg 7:18–22). The archaeological discovery of the Dead Sea Scrolls (in Cave 1) at Qumran contained one Hebrew scroll known as the War Scroll, or War Rule (1Q33), that served as a sort of preparation manual for an eschatological battle between the "sons of light" and the "sons of darkness." In this sectarian document (dated 30–1 BC), one section (2:15–5:2) deals with the rule of the trumpets:

> The Rule of the Trumpets: the trumpets of alarm for all their service for the [. . .] for their commissioned men, by tens of thousands and thousands and hundreds and fifties and tens . . .

On the trumpets of the battle formations they shall write, "Formations of the divisions of God to avenge His anger on all Sons of Darkness" . . . On the trumpets of pursuit they shall write, "God has struck all Sons of Darkness, He shall not abate His anger until they are annihilated." (1Q33 2:15–3:11)

These trumpets are described as being used for signals throughout the battle, for preparation, attack, pursuit, and reassembly, all contributing to the enemy's destruction. In another section describing the function of the priests and Levites in this battle, the Levites are instructed to sound horns in unison to dishearten the enemy:

> Then the priests shall blow on the six trumpets of the slain a sharp staccato note to direct the battle, and the Levites and all the people with rams' horns shall blow a great battle alarm together in order to melt the heart of the enemy. With the sound of the alarm, the battle darts shall fly out to bring down the slain. (1QM 18:3–6)

This tactic of an eschatological war was undoubtedly patterned after the use of the ram's horn in the famous battles of the Bible.

Joshua 8:30–31

Construction of an Altar on Mount Ebal

> Then Joshua built on Mount Ebal an altar to the LORD, the God of Israel, as Moses the servant of the LORD had commanded the Israelites. He built it according to what is written in the Book of the Law of Moses—an altar of uncut stones, on which no iron tool had been used. On it they offered to the LORD burnt offerings and sacrificed fellowship offerings. (Josh 8:30–31)

According to the biblical account, upon entering the promised land an altar was built on Mount Ebal and a ritual offering performed after the pattern prescribed by Moses in Deuteronomy 31:9–13. This was in order to renew the Mosaic covenant with the new generation that had not been part of the experience at Mount Sinai. This covenant ratification was important in the history of ancient Israel, and the site was of religious significance in the national life. For this reason the preservation of such a central site might have been expected.

A Late Bronze Age (ca. 1250 BC) structure was discovered on Mount Ebal in 1980 by Israeli archaeologist Adam Zertal. Excavations by the University of Haifa and the Israel Exploration Society from 1982–1989 revealed that this structure consisted of a circular stone repository with adjacent favissa (an underground area, usually near sacred sites, used to store sacred utensils no longer in use) containing hammerstones and a chalice. Nearby were scattered hearths, potsherds, and large quantities of ash and animal bones. Two scarabs associated with the Late Bronze stratum were of Thutmose II (Eighteenth Dynasty) and Ramses II (Nineteenth Dynasty) and helped fix a mid- to late-thirteenth century date to the establishment of the site. The site had been remodeled in the Iron Age I (ca. 1200–1140 BC), including a structure of unhewn stones (30 x 46 ft / 9 x 14 m) whose interior was filled

Altar on Mt. Ebal

Christof Frank, courtesy of Martin Severin

with layers of animal bones (male bulls, sheep/goat, deer), ash, and Iron I pottery. On the southeastern side of the main structure was a structure at a twenty-two-degree incline that was interpreted as a ramp with paved courtyards adjoining the ramp on each side. Stone installations filled with jars, jugs, juglets, pyxides (cylindrical box with lids), bones, and ashes were found in these courtyards. There were also the remains of an earlier four-room house (a typical Israelite house). Later, the entire site was deliberately covered over with stones, apparently to protect it.

Zertal believed that this evidence pointed to a cultic use of this site in both periods and understood it as a place where sacrifices were offered and ceremonial feasts were held. He argued that this was originally a tribal site in the Late Bronze period and that ceremonial attendants lived in the four-room house, but in the Iron Age I period, when it had developed into a main cult site for Israelites, the residential structures had been removed and an altar had been erected on top of the repository.[14] The central stone structure, then, was for large assembly, and the various installations for the deposit of the offerings of those attending the ceremonies. Zertal identified this structure with the altar of Joshua 8:30–35, which the Israelites were to build in fulfillment of the biblical command in Deuteronomy 27:1–8. Verses 5–6 give the essential details of this command: "Build there an altar to the LORD your God, an altar of stones. Do not use any iron tool on them. Build the altar of the LORD your God with fieldstones and offer burnt offerings on it to the LORD your God." These details are consistent with the archaeological evidence at the site.

Some minimalist archaeologists challenge this identification, especially those who deny an early history to Israel, and subsequently reinterpret the site as a village, a farmhouse, and a watchtower.[15] However, a thorough analysis of the archaeological data by Ralph Hawkins has presented a strong argument in support of Zertal's original assessment and connection to the biblical account. Hawkins's work (2012) critiqued each of the proposals in the excavation reports in light of the Renfrew/Zevit system of behavioral correlates for determining cultic identifications,[16] as well as the historical and sociological position of this structure among the new central hill country settlement sites in the transition from Late Bronze to Iron Age I.[17] Therefore, in light of its central location and Late Bronze date, expanded use during Iron Age I, its established cultic function, and the biblical statements in Deuteronomy and Joshua (cf. 1 Sam 1–10), the archaeological evidence seems to favor this being the altar of Joshua.

JUDGES

Judges 16:23, 25, 29–30

Samson and the Philistine Temple

> Now the rulers of the Philistines assembled to offer a great sacrifice to Dagon their god and to celebrate, saying, "Our god has delivered Samson, our enemy, into our hands." . . . While they were in high spirits, they shouted, "Bring out Samson to entertain us." So they called Samson out of the prison, and he performed for them. . . . Then Samson reached toward the two central pillars on which the temple stood. Bracing himself against them, his right hand on the one and his left hand on the other, Samson said, "Let me die with the Philistines!" Then he pushed with all his might, and down came the temple on the rulers and all the people in it. Thus he killed many more when he died than while he lived. (Judg 16:23, 25, 29–30)

According to the Bible, Samson, one of Israel's judges (military deliverers), was called to a Nazarene vow from birth and given supernatural strength when God's spirit came upon him. In his conflict with the Philistines, Israel's oppressors at that time, Samson was deceived by a Philistine woman and defiled, bringing about the departure of God's spirit. However, in his imprisonment he repented and sought his last revenge against the enemy. Taken to the temple of Dagon to entertain the people, he is placed between two supporting pillars. There he calls upon God for a return of his strength, and he is empowered to collapse the temple, killing him and those inside, as well all who were on the roof (Judg 16:27).

Some scholars have dismissed the historicity of such heroic tales, but as a result of archaeological excavations in Philistine areas, the Samson saga has been given greater plausibility. Excavations at Tell Qasile in northern Tel Aviv and at Tel Miqne (ancient Ekron), 21 miles south of Tel Aviv, have revealed the remains of two Philistine temples. These temples have the same design, an antechamber and main hall with its roof supported by two central pillars made of wood resting on round stone bases and placed along a center axis. More importantly, these pillars are separated by a distance of only 6 1/2 feet (2 m). This construction design makes it quite possible for a tall man to dislodge them from their stone bases and bring the entire structure down,

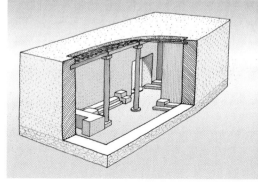

Artist reconstruction of the temple at Tell Qasile

Leen Ritmeyer

Close-up photo showing pillars in the temple at Tell Qasile

© Baker Publishing Group and Dr. James C. Martin. Courtesy of the Eretz Israel Museum, Tel Aviv, Israel.

just as the biblical account records. Unfortunately, the Philistine temple of Dagon in Gaza, brought down by Samson, cannot presently be excavated because it lies under the modern city. However, based on the archaeological examples that have been discovered, there is little doubt that it has the same features.

Archaeologist Aren Maeir of Bar Ilan University has also discovered a Philistine temple and a number of ritual items dating back to the Iron Age (tenth century BC) at Tell es-Safi National Park, near Kiryat Gat (site of the Philistine city of Gath, home of another biblical figure, Goliath). This temple also has pillar bases in the inner sanctum. According to seismologists who examined the site, a major earthquake measuring eight on the Richter scale collapsed the temple.[18]

The date of these temples to the early tenth century BC is consistent with the period of Philistine ascendancy before the Israelite monarchy and its defeat under King David in the late eleventh century BC. The biblical details of Philistine political and religious life, as well as their temple construction, could only have been made by an eyewitness familiar with the events during the time of the settlement and early monarchy (ca. 1200–1000 BC). This supports the historical nature of this biblical account since a later storyteller would probably lack this specific knowledge.

RUTH

Ruth 1:1

Earliest Extra-Biblical Evidence of Bethlehem of Judah

In the days when the judges ruled, there was a famine in the land. So a man from Bethlehem in Judah, together with his wife and two sons, went to live for a while in the country of Moab. (Ruth 1:1)

This verse depicts a famine that sent a certain man (Elimelech) and his Ephrathite family from their home in Bethlehem of Judah to the fields of Moab. Ruth and her mother-in-law Naomi eventually returned to Bethlehem, met Boaz, and became the great-grandparents of King David. A recent archaeological excavation conducted by Ronny Reich and Eli Shukron on behalf of the Israel Antiquities Authority uncovered on the eastern slope of the city of David in Jerusalem a roughly

2,700-year-old clay fiscal bulla (a round stamp affixed to an item)[19] found in conjunction with late Iron Age II pottery sherds. The paleo-Hebrew script on the bulla read: "In the seventh (year). Beit Lehem. For the king."[20] It appears that this bulla sealed a particular shipment sent from Bethlehem for the king of Judah during the seventh year of a Judean king, possibly Josiah or Manasseh. This discovery is significant because it is the first Hebrew inscription so far discovered mentioning the biblical city of Bethlehem. In 2017, the Associates for Biblical Research (ABR), under the direction of Scott Stripling, opened a new excavation on the north side of the site (Field H1) to gain further insight into the critical issue of the location of the cultic shrine.

Fiscal bulla from City of David mentioning Bethlehem

Courtesy Eli Shukron. Used by permission.

I SAMUEL

1 Samuel 1:3

The Tabernacle in Shiloh

> Year after year this man went up from his town to worship and sacrifice to the LORD Almighty at Shiloh, where Hophni and Phinehas, the two sons of Eli, were priests of the LORD. (1 Sam 1:3)

The Bible records that Joshua and the whole congregation of Israel set up the tabernacle at the city of Shiloh (Josh 18:1). Located in the hill country of Ephraim, Shiloh served as the religious capital of Israel during the days of the judges (Judg 21:19; 1 Sam 1:3), and it was there that Samuel was raised by Eli, the high priest (1 Sam 1:24–28; 3:1–21). The tabernacle remained in Shiloh for 369 years until the ark was taken from Shiloh to the battle of Ebenezer (1 Sam 4:1–4), and the Philistines marched on the site (ca. 1104 BC) and destroyed it (1 Sam 4:10–22; Ps 78:60; Jer 7:12–14; 26:6). The remains at Shiloh later served as an object lesson for recalcitrant Israel, as the prophet Jeremiah admonished: "Go now to the place in Shiloh where I first made a dwelling for my Name, and see what I did to it because of the wickedness of my people Israel." (Jer 7:12).

The site of Khirbet Seilun was first identified with the remains of Shiloh in 1838 by American Edward Robinson. The first excavations were carried out from 1926–32 under the direction of W. F. Albright, who discovered that the site had been first settled in the Middle Bronze II period (nineteenth–eighteenth centuries BC). Israel Finkelstein conducted more extensive excavations from 1981–84, uncovering eight strata ranging from Middle Bronze II through the Byzantine period. Large piles of pottery from the Canaanite period (2000–1100 BC) included the remains of animal sacrifices, indicating the site had been a cultic center. An Iron Age I two-story Israelite public building also contained remains of cultic objects, leading to the conclusion that it had adopted

Incised holes in bedrock thought to be for tent poles of the Tabernacle. 2012 excavations at Shiloh by Hananya Hizmi, Staff Officer of the Civil Administration for Judea and Samaria

Photo by Christof Frank. Courtesy Inner-cube, Dusseldorf, Germany earlier Canaanite practice. This may reflect the kind of wickedness condemned in the biblical text that led to Shiloh's destruction being used as a warning to the Israelites of the sixth century BC.

Finkelstein thought the tabernacle would have been set on the top of the tel, but excavations there only revealed a storage complex. A lower placement of the tabernacle may have been in keeping with the later Israelite practice that avoided establishing sanctuaries on high places as was pagan custom (Deut 12:2). However, the tent of meeting was once pitched at the high place at Gibeon (1 Kgs 3:2; 2 Chr 1:3), and the ark of the covenant in the house of Abinadab on a hill (2 Sam 6:3–4).

When the tabernacle was established at Shiloh it became a more permanent installation and was arranged as a compound within an enclosure wall made of fieldstones that had doors (1 Sam 3:15). Such a structure exists in a field on the northern side of the tel, where there are remains of a large, rectangular, walled installation. In 1873 Charles Wilson identified this as a "level court" and took its measurements as 400 feet long and 77 feet wide.[21] This site is much larger than any level space on the summit and is the only level space sufficiently large enough to house a tent the size of the tabernacle. Inside the installation is a subdivided area whose dimensions approximate those for the holy of holies.

Model of the Tabernacle made by the Bibel Center, Breckerfeld, Germany; Timna Park, Israel

Photo by Christof Frank. Courtesy Martin Severin, Inner-cube, Dusseldorf, Germany. Used by permission.

Shiloh excavation of proposed tabernacle site with overlay of biblical tabernacle dimensions

Photo and layout by Christof Frank. Courtesy Martin Severin, Inner-cube, Dusseldorf, Germany.

In 2010–12 Hananya Hizmi conducted excavations within this walled level court. These excavations revealed carved holes along the sides of the enclosure that could have supported wooden poles like those used in the tabernacle (see photo). First Samuel 1:9 speaks specifically of "the doorpost of the LORD's house." Because these holes could have held the beams of a temporary structure it has been suggested that the tent of meeting and the ark of the covenant, which were portable, could have been placed there.[22] Next to these hewn holes were structures dating to the period between the conquest and the beginning of the monarchy. Three large stoves with pottery vessels of a type for commercial use imply this was a central public facility. Bones found in this area dating to the biblical period are thought to be the remains of sacrifices brought to the tabernacle. Moreover, remains found at the southwestern corner of the wall indicate that the entrance gate of the ancient city was nearby, adding to the archaeological evidence that this was indeed the site of the tabernacle.

1 Samuel 17:12

Archaeological Evidence for King David

> Now David was the son of an Ephrathite named Jesse, who was from Bethlehem in Judah. Jesse had eight sons, and in Saul's time he was very old. (1 Sam 17:12)

King David is indisputably one of the most central figures in both the Old and New Testaments, being mentioned some 1,048 times. In the Old Testament he is the primary subject of sixty-two chapters and the author of seventy-three psalms. In the New Testament he figures prominently on both sides of Jesus' genealogy and with reference to the place of Jesus' birth (Matt 1:1, 6, 17, 20; Luke 2:4, 11; 3:31); for "the Messiah is the son of David" (Luke 20:41) and he will be given "the throne of his father David" (Luke 1:32).

In the past, the lack of archaeological evidence, even of the mention of his name, led some scholars to doubt that a historical David had ever existed. In this light, Philip R. Davies wrote, "The figure of King David is about as historical as King Arthur."[23]

Minimalists and historical revisionists had once argued that the "David Myth" was literary creation, drawn from various heroic traditions to explain the formation of Israel's monarchy or that a priestly school surrounding the temple had sought a theological basis for their own concept of divine government. Reasons for the lack of evidence stem from the limited nature of the archaeological evidence, especially as one goes back in time. Also, the Israelites, in contrast to their neighbors, mostly wrote their court documents and other records on papyrus (Jer 36:2, 23), so in the damper climate of Jerusalem, David's royal city, no trace of such perishable material could survive.

Nevertheless, in 1993–94 three fragments of a monumental stela were discovered at the site of Tel Dan in the Golan Heights. Unfortunately, more of the stele was missing than was found, and it seems that the returning Israelite king who had reconquered Dan destroyed his enemies and used the stone as a building block. Most scholars have attributed the text to the ninth-century Aramean usurper Hazael, but Avraham Biran, and George Athas after him, attributed it to Hazael's son Ben-Hadad III, who is reported to have attacked Dan (1 Kgs 15:20), and date the inscription to ca. 796 BC.[24] Other scholars have suggested King Jehu (ca. 845–818 BC)."[25] Hazael's entire reign was characterized by war with Israel, and he went down in biblical history as one of Israel's most brutal enemies (2 Kgs 8:7–15). The biblical record indicates that he decimated Israel's army and turned both it and Philistia into vassal states (2 Kgs 10:32–33; 12:17). Judah also seems to have shared this same fate (2 Kgs 12:17–18). The stele was probably erected as a memorial to these deeds and was likely written in the latter part of Hazael's reign.

The remarkable line in the inscription is one that contains a reference to the king of Israel and the king of the "house of David" (line 9). It appears in the context of the slaying of the Israelite and Judean kings. These lines (7b–9) after reconstruction read: "I killed Jehoram son of Ahab king of Israel and I killed Ahaziahu son of Jehoram king of the House of David."[26] This was the first appearance of the term "David" in an archaeological text and, given the context, could only refer to the historical progenitor of the Davidic line. By deduction, if there was a "house of David" there had to be a "David" to have a house.

As with most controversial inscriptions, epigraphists were divided on whether this was in fact a reference to a person named David. Davies and others argued that there was no word divider, so the term was not meant to be a personal noun but the name of a place. However, epigraphists Anson Rainey and Alan Millard, both experts in ancient Aramaic inscriptions, argued that there were many examples of compound words or names where the word divider is absent.[27] Egyptologist and archaeologist James Hoffmeier further pointed out that *bytdwd* as a place name is completely unattested in the Bible or any cognate literature from the ancient Near East.[28] On the other hand, the reading of "house of David" as a title, dependent on the historic founder of the line, the Judean King David, appears more than twenty times in the Old Testament (see 1 Kgs 12:19; 14:8; Isa 7:2; et al.).

Adding support for the reading from a different direction, epigraphist André LeMaire has argued that the reading of "David" in the Tel Dan Stele has permitted him to read the name "David" in a formerly unreadable line "house of D . . ." on the Mesha Stele (or Moabite Stone).[29] However, even without the name of "David" here, this ninth-century-BC memorial inscription from Moab, like the Tel Dan Stele, also contains other biblical names, such as Omri.

Outer fortification walls of Iron Age (9th century BC) city of Dan, formerly Leshem (Joshua 19:47)

The mention of both Omri and David inside and outside of the biblical text (see Omri in 1 Kgs 16:28) is evidence that they are not literary fictions. In fact, scholars have not doubted the historicity of Omri simply because he is listed in the Mesha inscription. Interestingly, in Assyrian texts the locutions "the land of Omri" and "the house of Omri" appear.[30] If the Assyrians could specify states by the name of a dynasty's founder, regardless of who was currently in power, could not the Arameans? In this regard, the Aramean stele implies that the kingdoms of Israel and Judah during this period were, as the Bible describes, a formidable threat both politically and militarily to the surrounding nations. Revisionists, however, have thought that Israel and Judah were insignificant city-states. Would a dominant foreign power such as Syria have erected a monument commemorating the defeat of unimportant enemies? Again, the archaeological data has demonstrated its value in resolving historical questions, in this case concerning the king (David) and his kingdom.

Tel Dan Stele showing in ancient Hebrew words in red box: "king of Israel," and in black box "house of David." Israel Museum

Kim Walton

2 SAMUEL

2 Samuel 5:10–12

The Kingdom of David, Archaeological Evidence for the Earliest History of Israel

> And he became more and more powerful, because the LORD God Almighty was with him. Now Hiram king of Tyre sent envoys to David, along with cedar logs and carpenters and stonemasons; and they built a palace for David. Then David knew that the LORD had established him as king over Israel had exalted his kingdom for the sake of his people Israel. (2 Sam 5:10–12)

The biblical account of the kingdoms of David and Solomon in the tenth century BC has been largely discounted by minimalists as historical fiction. Archaeologists Garfinkel, Hasel, and Klingbeil describe this shift in thinking:

> In the early years of research, the Biblical narratives of David, Solomon and his son Rehoboam were considered an accurate historical account. Since the 1980's, however, serious doubts have been raised about this tradition. The Bible is merely a literary composition dating from centuries later, it has been argued. According to this approach, these kings were legendary figures. Although the inscription from Tel Dan recovered in 1993 clearly indicates that Savid was indeed a historical figure, it was nevertheless unclear whether he was the ruler of

a large empire or only a local chieftain governing a small territory. As one critic argued, David's kingdom was simply "500 people with sticks in their hands shouting and cursing and spitting."[31]

Minimalist arguments gained support because the evidence for this period is considered sparse and what has existed suggested only a small tribal chiefdom with none of the statements of an empire or a palace and temple complex as given in the narratives in Samuel, Kings, and Chronicles. In this regard, Jamieson-Drake asserted in his dissertation: "There is little evidence that Judah began to function as a state at all prior to the tremendous increases in population, building, production, centralization and specialization which began to appear in the 8th century."[32] In like manner, Israeli archaeologists Israel Finkelstein and Neil Silberman declared: "Not a single trace of tenth-century Judahite literary activity has been found . . . In light of these findings, it is now clear that Iron Age Judah enjoyed no precocious golden age."[33]

However, as noted, new discoveries have begun to provide new support for a tenth-century (even eleventh-century) fortified kingdom as described in Scripture. William Dever offers the archaeological evidence of the Davidic Dynasty from the ninth-century-BC Tel Dan inscription combined with the evidence of a Solomonic kingdom from the building programs in Jerusalem, Gezer, Hazor, and Megiddo, and confirmed by the presence of hand-burnished

ware that predates the destruction levels resulting from the invasion of Shishak.[34] Israeli archaeologists Ronny Reich and Eli Shukron have uncovered walls and fortifications associated with the ancient city of David that were built upon and that utilized the remains of earlier Canaanite and Jebusite fortifications and water systems. Previous excavations under Yigael Shiloh revealed a massive twelve-story high stepped-stone structure from the thirteenth century BC upon which David began to build his city (2 Sam 5:9). This foundational structure may have served as a retaining wall buttressing King David's "Fortress of Zion." Israeli archaeologist Eilat Mazar believes that the monumental buildings she discovered just above this structure are the remains of David's palace, though this conclusion has been questioned on biblical and archaeologal grounds.[35] In excavations near the Temple Mount, Mazar also found the broken rim of a large ceramic jar with an inscription. Dated to the tenth century BC, it predates by 250 years the earliest known alphabetical written text found in Jerusalem. Written in an early Canaanite dialect, it was engraved on the rim of the jar before it was fired. Since the jar predates Israelite rule it was possibly written by the Jebusites, who were also part of the city population in the time of Kings David and Solomon.

The discovery of another inscription at Tel Zayit is even more intriguing. On a large limestone boulder with a bowl-shaped hollow ground into one side, there are two lines of alphabetic writing, known as an abecedary.

Tel Zayit abecedary

Photo courtesy Ron Tappy.
Used by permission.

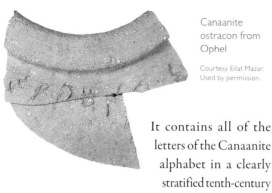

Canaanite ostracon from Ophel

Courtesy Eilat Mazar. Used by permission.

It contains all of the letters of the Canaanite alphabet in a clearly stratified tenth-century context. This provides evidence that there was a literate culture already in existence at the beginning of the first millennium BC. It may further support the existence of Judean-Israelite administrative scribes which indirectly supports a Davidic-Solomonic kingdom. Based on this find David Carr confessed: "The discovery of the Tel Zayit Inscription proves just how dangerous it can be to base arguments about early history on *gaps* in the historical record. Therefore, I believe that other scholars and I were ill advised in reading too much into the relative absence of data for writing in the 10th century BCE."[36]

However, the site that has most defined the archaeological understanding of Judah in the tenth century has been the site of Khirbet Qeiyafa, a one-period Iron Age site built on bedrock with a clear destruction layer and important architectural, artefactual, and inscriptional evidence. This provincial town in the Elah Valley region is located about 18 miles from Jerusalem. Its proximity to and inclusion in a biblical list with the city of Gederah (Josh 15:36) and the discovery of twin gates at the site have identified it as the biblical city of Shaarayim ("two gates"). This is a significant detail in the identification because no other small cities of this period have been found to have had such a gate structure. Its location in the Elah Valley where David defeated Goliath (1 Sam 17:52) and the development of the site as a fortified city during David's time (1 Chr 4:31) also support this identification.

Archaeologists Yosef Garfinkel and Saar Ganor have uncovered impressive fortifications and structures that date the site to the late eleventh to the early tenth centuries BC.[37] The evidence for this date range came from the discovery of a large royal storeroom that contained organic material including seventeen charred olive pits in one storejar. Radiocarbon dating of the pits dated the destruction layer to 1018–948 BC, confirming that the storeroom and adjacent structures were constructed in the time of the reigns of David and Solomon.[38]

The architectural finds at the site include a heavily fortified casemate wall surrounding the city, two gates and two gate piazzas, a group of ten houses adjacent to the wall, a pillared storage building, and a central palatial building. This palace (administration building), covering more than 10,000 square feet, was situated at the center of the acropolis and overlooked the city and countryside. Its walls were 3 feet thick (two to three times the thickness of other walls at the site), suggesting that it supported several stories. All of these constructions are typical of a Judahite city and it is estimated that 100,000 tons of rock were required to build the city. Such a massive project could only be managed by an extensive civil administration, and during this time the only administrative control was that of the Davidic kingdom. Therefore the presence of the palace at Khirbet Qeiyafa, from which the construction was supervised, must be linked to David's rule in the capital city of Jerusalem.

Khirbet Qeiyafa also produced three inscriptions in Canaanite (possibly identified as early Hebrew). Two have been published, one an ostracon with five lines of text (still debated as to its meaning) found in 2008, and another an inscribed pottery store jar found in 2012. This storejar was found in the remains of an open courtyard next to the wall. The skilled hand that produced this incised and very clear inscription points to the existence of trained scribes. The inscription itself is quite significant as it contains the names Beda (*bd'*) and Esh-Baal (*'shb'l*), the latter name appearing in the Bible in a tenth century context (1 Chr 8:33; 9:39; cf. 2 Sam 2:8–15; 3:7 for the name of Saul's son, Ish-Bosheth, a deliberate scribal alteration to avoid using the defamatory name Baal). In the following centuries (ninth–sixth centuries BC) personal names with the element Baal disappear from the biblical text and ancient inscriptions from Judah. This fact helps establish the date of the city during the Davidic kingdom.[39] Moreover, it indicates a scribal culture in the town and the position of the ostracon in one of the buildings suggests the presence of an archive. The presence of these written documents supports the literary compositions ascribed to David and Solomon in the Bible.

Even more startling was the discovery of cultic shrines and objects, such as clay model temples, with architectural features similar to those that would one day adorn the First (Solomonic) Temple in Jerusalem. These were probably votive objects used as a means of local worship, since the tabernacle and tent of meeting were pitched at a distance. These objects reflect active religious practice, and along with the size and scope of the administrative, social, and literary activities in the town, argue for a well-developed state operating at the time.

Therefore, the evidence from this site indicates that if a small outlying city like Khirbet Qeifaya was so developed in the tenth century BC, there can be little doubt that the larger city of Jerusalem existed with the status of a Judean kingdom.

Other evidence in favor of a tenth century Judean kingdom in the epigraphic record for the Levant during Iron Age IIA includes monumental inscriptions, such as the Byblian Shipitbaal Inscription (Phoenician), the Tel Dan Stele (Aramaic), the Mesha Stela (Moabite), and the Tell Fekheriyeh Bilingual Statue (Aramaic and Akkadian). Old Hebrew inscriptions from the ninth century have been found at southern sites such as Arad and northern sites such as Tel Rehov,

Esh-Baal inscription, Khirbet Qeiyafa

Photo by Casey Olson

and the Ahiram Sarcophagus Inscription is from the tenth century.

Another epigraphic example was discovered in 2014 in excavations at Khirbet Summeily, a borderline site (between Judah and Philistia) located about 13.5 miles (22 km) east of Gaza and about 2.4 miles (4 km) west of Tell el-Hesi. Here six anepigraphic (uninscribed) bullae were found in Phase 5 that date from the late eleventh through mid-tenth centuries BC. The context was identified as some sort of office facility, and based on preliminary analysis of pottery and the bullae, these come from the same general period as Tell el-Hesi's three large tripartite buildings from Bliss's City V. One of the bullae preserves the string hole used in attaching it to the papyrus scroll they were intended to seal and indicates the practice of sealing that is regarded as an elite or official activity. As the excavators state:

> We believe that the remains discovered at Summeily demonstrate a level of politico-economic activity that has not been suspected for the late Iron Age I and early Iron Age IIA. This is especially the case if one integrates data from nearby Hesi. Taken together, we contend these reflect greater political complexity and integration across the transitional Iron I/IIA landscape than has been appreciated. Many scholars have tended to dismiss trends toward political complexity (that is, state formation) occurring prior to the arrival of the Assyrians in the region in the later eighth century BCE. However, based on our work in the Hesi region, we believe these processes began much earlier.[40]

These examples demonstrate that political, literary, and archival activity occurred in Judah during the eleventh to tenth centuries and justify an acceptance of the biblical text's description of the Davidic-Solomonic state.

2 Samuel 13:37–38

The Site of Geshur

> Absalom fled and went to Talmai son of Ammihud, the king of Geshur. But King David mourned many days for his son. After Absalom fled and went to Geshur, he stayed there three years. (2 Sam 13:37–38)

The city of Geshur played an important role in the early history of Israel. At the time of the conquest, Geshur was allotted to the half-tribe of Manasseh, although the Geshurites could not be dispossessed and so continued to inhabit Geshur (Josh 13:13). By the time of the Israelite monarchy, Geshur had become an independent kingdom, and a political marriage was arranged between King David and Maakah, the daughter of the king of Geshur (2 Sam 3:3; 1 Chr 3:2). Absalom was the product of their marriage, and when he murdered his half-brother Amnon because he raped Absalom's sister, he fled to Geshur and stayed there for three years (2 Sam 13:37–38). Its power as a political entity at this time can be seen from the fact that the stronger kingdom customarily provided the daughter in a political marriage and that it could harbor Absalom from Israelite justice (2 Sam 14:32). Another statement of this is found in 1 Chronicles 2:23, where Geshur, along with Aram, is said to have captured sixty cities. Absalom's daughter Maakah married Solomon's son Rehoboam and it is recorded that she was his favorite wife (2 Chr 11:21). In 734 BC the city, aligned with Aram, fell to the Assyrian empire under Tiglath-Pileser III, and his successor Shalmaneser IV exiled its population along with Israel's northern kingdom (2 Kgs 15:29–30; 16:7–9). The site was subsequently lost to history.

In 1989, under the direction of archaeologist Rami Arav, excavations began in the lower Golan in search of the New Testament city of Bethsaida.

Basalt stele of moon god Sin set in place in ritual site within gates of ancient Geshur (Bethsaida)

Alexander Schick

Under the remains of a small fishing village he uncovered an impressive Iron Age palace with a vestibule, main room, and throne room surrounded by eight additional rooms. Over the next decade the excavations revealed more of the massive site, with its lower city containing a residential quarter and the upper city containing the public buildings and fortifications, including a ninth-century-BC gatehouse, one of the best preserved in Israel, with a tenth-century-BC gate and bulwarks just beneath. The gate has both an outer and inner entrance, with towers on each side, and is divided by a large paved plaza. All of the architectural work is of local basalt stone, although granaries connected with the gatehouse were made of sun-dried bricks, almost 10 feet (3 m) thick. On the outsides of the inner gate are niches with two steps that led to a

Model of the entrance gate of Geshur (Stratum V.I)

Model and photo by Duane J. Piper (used by permission).

basalt stone basin, where two incense burners were discovered. The apparent use of these structures was for cultic offerings and libations. In this place was found the remains of an Iron Age basalt stele depicting the bull-headed figure of the Mesopotamian moon god Sin brandishing a dagger. The presence of this ancient Near Eastern deity in Israel demonstrates the repeated biblical indictment of the northern kingdom of idolatry, which the cult of such a powerful kingdom would have undoubtedly influenced. That the idol was found smashed may reflect the destruction of the Assyrian conflict or a deliberate act exerted during a time of reform. It has been conjectured that a separate raised platform (*bamah*) to the left of the cultic niche that is approached by a ramp may have been constructed for Israelite worship, since Exodus 20:26 prohibited the use of pagan altars that were equipped with steps.

Excavations in the palace found an eighth-century-BC ostracon bearing the name Akiba (possibly an Aramaic form of *yaʿakov* [Jacob], two jar handles containing the names Zechario ("remembered by the Lord") and a shortened form of Michyahu ("who is like the Lord"), and an Egyptian figurine of the god Pataekos, who was related to Ptah, the god of artists and craftsmen.

Excavations in Jerusalem have revealed the same style of Syrian architecture as found at Bethsaida. King David's Geshurite wife, as any new foreign queen, would have come to Jerusalem with her royal court, including architects to design her own living quarters. This connection with biblical history, as well as the geographic setting and monumental royal architecture at Bethsaida, have convinced archaeologist Arav that he has discovered the city of Geshur.[41]

2 Samuel 21:20

Archaeological Evidence of Polydactylism in the Ancient World

> In still another battle, which took place at Gath, there was a huge man with six fingers on each hand and six toes on each foot—twenty-four in all. He also was descended from Rapha. (2 Sam 21:20)

In this passage the incidental note that the giant slain had extra fingers and toes may be thought to be an exaggeration, but it in fact adds significantly to the accuracy of the account. The interesting observation is the connection between the statement of the extra digits and that he was born to a giant, a detail repeated in 1 Chronicles 20:6: "He also was descended (*nolad*) from Rapha." Extra digits apparently were considered a mark of the Rephaim, a race of giants (2 Sam 21:16, 18, 20, 22; cf. Gen 15:20; Deut 2:11). The condition of polydactylism (extra digits) was not uncommon in the ancient Near East and in other cultures. It is an inherited genetic abnormality, especially in closely interbred communities, and geneticists report it appears in association with the abnormality of gigantism and can be passed on as a hereditary trait. The ancient belief was that polydactylism was characteristic of giants or people with extra strength. In this text and the parallel passage in 1 Chronicles 20:6, a polydactyl giant is slain by King David's nephew Jonathan, while his brother

Shimei killed another. It may be that reporting these details increased the perception of their prowess in defeating such formidable foes. At the same time, it confirms to the modern reader who is acquainted with genetic science that the report is accurate.

The archaeological record provides numerous examples of polydactylism. In a Neolithic temple (ca. sixth millennium BC) at Jericho and at the site of 'Ain Ghazal in Jordan, terracotta statues were found that had six toes.[42] Two examples of polydactylism from the thirteenth century BC appear on clay sarcophagi in quasi-Egyptian style found at Deir el-Balaḥ. One in the Israel Museum portrays a man with six fingers on his left hand, while another excavated by Trude Dothan is indistinct in details but was meant to be polydactylous. There is also a fragmentary portrait statue of an Egyptian of the Thirteenth Dynasty (ca. 1783–1640 BC) discovered near Akko that shows six fingers on his right hand.[43]

In Mesopotamia, priests and sorcerers were consulted concerning the significance of polydactylism. Their advice concerning polydactyl births is recorded in the seventh-century Assyrian collection of teratological omen texts called *šumma izbu* ("If a reject") detailing odd human births.[44]

Anthropoid sarcophagus, Deir-el-Balah, showing six fingers

The formula they followed in this text was that if a child was born with an extra finger(s) on the left hand or foot it was a favorable omen promising prosperity and wealth, but if on the right hand or foot it was a bad omen portending poverty, and if the extra digit was on both it meant the house would be scattered.[45] Eastern Anatolia (or north Syria) attests ninth- or eighth-century-BC bronze composite human and bird figures with six fingers on each hand. These appear in fixed pairs on the rims of bronze cauldrons. Bronzesmiths in Greece also depicted sports figures with six fingers on the right and seven on the left. Polydactylism seems rare today because such abnormalities are removed at birth, but in the world of the Bible they were observed, and this observation, supported by both genetics and archaeological examples, provides an important sense of realism to the biblical accounts.

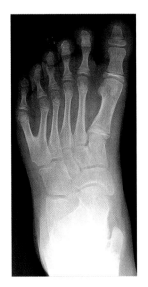
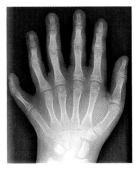

Modern x-rays of hand and foot showing polydactylism. Left hand with mid ray duplication, left foot with postaxial polydactyly of fifth ray

Drgnu23/Wikimedia Commons, CC BY-SA 3.0

I KINGS

1 Kings 4:21; 2 Chronicles 9:26

Evidence of the Kingdom of Solomon

And Solomon ruled over all the kingdoms from the Euphrates River to the land of the Philistines, as far as the border of Egypt. These countries brought tribute and were Solomon's subjects all his life. (1 Kgs 4:21)

These verses indicate that Solomon ruled from the Euphrates River to Philistia and the border of Egypt. Some scholars have contended that the kingdom of Solomon could not have had hegemony over such powerful kingdoms as Egypt to the south and Assyria to the north. Yet, between ca. 1100 and 900 BC both Assyria and Egypt experienced a period of political decline. The Twenty-First Dynasty of Egypt experienced a succession of weak pharaohs who barely held their country together. Assyria suffered a rapid decline in power after the reign of Tiglath-pileser I. Given these factors, it is not unlikely that the smaller country of Israel could have had this influence, especially with its expanded control of neighboring kingdoms through political alliances, including Egypt (1 Kgs 11:1).

As to evidence of the Solomonic kingdom in the capital city of Jerusalem, in 2010 a city wall with a gatehouse dating to the late tenth century BC was discovered in the Ophel. According to Eilat Mazar, the archaeologist that excavated the site, this wall probably connected with the city of David and fits with the biblical description that King Solomon built a fortification line around his new constructions of the temple and the King's palace.[46]

1 Kings 5–8

The Construction of the First Temple and Near Eastern Parallels

> At the king's command they removed from the quarry large blocks of high-grade stone to provide a foundation of dressed stone for the temple. The craftsmen of Solomon and Hiram and workers from Byblos cut and prepared the timber and stone for the building of the temple. . . . King Solomon sent to Tyre and brought Huram, whose mother was a widow from the tribe of Naphtali and whose father was from Tyre and a skilled craftsman in bronze. Huram was filled with wisdom, with understanding and with knowledge to do all kinds of bronze work. He came to King Solomon and did all the work assigned to him. . . . He also made the pots and shovels and sprinkling bowls. So Huram finished all the work he had undertaken for King Solomon in the temple of the LORD. (1 Kgs 5:17–18; 7:13–14, 40)

There is an archaeological debate, based on the Near Eastern architectural parallels, whether the First Temple was constructed in the tenth or ninth centuries BC. The problem is that the biblical chronology (as traditionally understood) places the building in the tenth century, whereas the archaeological examples come from the ninth century. William Mierse in his architectural study of Levantine sanctuaries in the early Iron Age (1200–700 BC) explains:

> [Solomon's Temple] was clearly dependent on older models. From the Middle Bronze Age onward, architectural influences in the region tended to move from Syria down into Palestine. Making the Jerusalem temple a precursor to those at Tell Ta'yinat, Carchemish, and Guzana would clearly break this pattern, but the early Iron Age was a new world with far less continuity than was true of the Middle Bromze and Late Bronze Ages. . . . If the events recorded in the Book of Kings are dated to the ninth-century BCE rather than the tenth, then the building project that engaged Solomon's attention fits into a pattern that was seen in several political centers at the same time."[47]

However, Mierse shows in his work that as the early Iron Age recovered from the cultural collapse of the Late Bronze Age, changes occurred in demographic influences, cultic settings, and political realities. Sanctuary architecture developed in response to meet the new needs of societies. As a result, Solomonic construction, while employing design elements common to regional examples dated a half-century and later and built as an expected statement of kingship, exhibited a structure especially designed to accommodate Israelite worship.

With respect to the common design, the biblical account of the First Temple's construction reveals that from start to finish the work was designed and executed through regional expertise directed by the Tyrian King Hiram. Josephus records that Hiram also built a royal palace and a temple for Melqart, the local deity of the Phoenecian city of Tyre (*Ag. Ap.* i:17). Therefore, while King Solomon employed his own workers, the skill in temple building and furnishing was recognized as a foreign enterprise.

Additional archaeological evidence that forces the date of the First Temple to the tenth century has been the discovery of small ritual objects at Khirbet Qeiyafa. These artifacts take the form of box-shaped ceramic shrines that pre-date the Solomonic construction, yet have a number of architectural design elements that parallel the biblical description. While some twenty architectural terms in this description are no longer known in Hebrew, such as *slaot*, once understood as "columns,"

Terracotta ritual house shrines with twin pillars on the porch and Asherah figure in inner chamber. Similar shrines without pagan deities were uncovered at Khirbet Qeiyafa.

Alexander Schick

and *sequphim*, once understood as "windows," the shrines from Khirbet Qeiyafa revealed the meaning of these two terms. Now it is understood that *slaot* corresponds to triglyphs (ornamental decorations above the columns), and the *sequphim* refer to a triple recessed doorway.[48] This archaeological discovery has changed the way biblical scholars envision the First Temple, not only permitting two out of twenty terms to be identified, but to locate the construction of the First Temple in the time of Solomon's reign, as the Bible states.

This biblical description of the First Temple reveals the similarity in architectural design to Near Eastern tripartite temple design (similar to the Egyptian long-room temple), and its ritual vessels show influences from Egypt, Syro-Phoenicia, and Mesopotamia. However, the Phoenicians (Sidonians), from whom Hiram came, were the closest neighbors of the Israelites, and it was they who controlled the vast reserves of the forest of Lebanon

where the most prized cedar wood existed for such construction. Hiram was King David's material supplier (2 Sam 5:11; 1 Kgs 5:1; 2 Chr 2:3–18). The fourth-century-AD church father Eusebius preserved the record of the Phoenician priest Sanchuniathon, who described how King Hiram had likewise supplied Solomon with materials for the building of the temple.

Alexander Schick

Model of First Temple of Solomon

'Ain Dara' temple, Syria

Jim Monson

Hiram sent his Phoenician architects and craftsmen to advise their Israelite counterparts on building the temple to contemporary specifications. One of these was a half-Hebrew, half-Phoenician artisan named Huramabi (Huram, NIV), who was given oversight of the temple craftsmen. Credit is given to him for the decorative, cast, and overlaid objects in the temple (1 Kgs 7:13–45; 2 Chr 2:13–14). While the imposing limestone sarcophagus of Hiram still exists southeast of Tyre in the village of Hanaway, it is the style of the temples in this region that are of the most interest archaeologically, as they provide the closest parallels to how the biblical First Temple may have appeared.

Although few examples of Phoenician temples exist, a Phoenician temple two centuries older than the First Temple was excavated in Hazor. It was 84 feet x 56 feet and tripartite. At each side of the entrance to the main hall was a round pillar, like those in Solomon's Temple. In addition, ivory panels and sculptures in several Phoenician temples bear pattern decorations similar to the cherubim, palm trees, and open flowers carved in the paneling of the Jerusalem Temple (1 Kgs. 6:35). The best existing examples of the Solomonic style have been found in Syria at Tel Ta'yinat and 'Ain Dara'. Of these examples, the best parallels are those preserved at the 'Ain Dara' temple. Because no known remains of Solomon's Temple exist and the biblical descriptions contain many architectural terms that are uncertain, the archaeological example of the 'Ain Dara' temple may offer the best means of reconstructing the First Temple.

From this example, it is clear that the temple of Solomon was a typical hybrid temple of the long-room Syrian type, with elements that, with a date almost contemporaneous with that of Solomon, allow us to confidently affirm that the construction of the First Temple belongs to the tenth century BC, in harmony with biblical chronology. John Monson has determined that the 'Ain Dara' temple shares thirty-three of the some sixty-five architectural elements mentioned in the Bible in connection with Solomon's Temple.

No other building excavated to date has as many features in common with the Biblical description of the Jerusalem Temple. Both have essentially the same three-division, long-room plan: At 'Ain Dara', it is an entry portico, an antechamber and main chamber with screened-off shrine;

in Solomon's Temple, it is an entry portico (*'ulam*), main hall (*heikhal*) and shrine, or holy of holies (*debir*). The only significant difference between the two is the inclusion of the antechamber in the 'Ain Dara' plan. With this exception the two plans are almost identical. If the royal cubit used to build Solomon's Temple was 52 1/2 centimeters, then the Jerusalem Temple measured approximately 120 feet x 34 feet. The 'Ain Dara' temple is 98 feet long x 65 wide (or 125 x 105 ft including the side chambers) . . . Both temples were built on a platform and had a courtyard in front with a monumental staircase (*ma'aleh*, cf. Ezek 40:22) leading up to the temple. In both cases the portico was narrower and shallower than the rooms of the temple. In both cases the portico was open on one side and had a roof supported by two pillars . . . In both cases spectacular reliefs decorated the walls, and the carvings in both temples share several motifs: The stylized floral designs and lily patterns, palmettes, winged creatures and lions of 'Ain Dara' may be compared with the "bas reliefs and engravings of cherubim, palm trees, and flower patterns, in the inner and outer rooms" of Solomon's Temple (1 Kings 6:29). The elevated podium at the back of the 'Ain Dara' temple, covering a third of the floor area of the main hall and set off from the forepart by a separate screen, is a commanding parallel for the Biblical holy of holies.[49]

These interesting parallels support the biblical claim that Hiram and Phoenician workmen constructed the First Temple on the basic layout and design of the Syro-Phoenecian temples. Perhaps adjustments were made for issues reated to cultic distinctions that had to avoid pagan theological motifs, but for the most part the structures were essentially the same. This should not be a concern, as God often made accommodations to the prevailing culture in order to relate to his people (e.g., Hebrew covenant and law code follow the same format as the Code of Hammurabi and the suzerain-vassal treaty).

Detail of Cherubim at entrance of the 'Ain Dara' temple

© D.serral/Shutterstock

1 Kings 11:4, 8

Evidence of Pagan Cult Centers in the Ninth Century BC

As Solomon grew old, his wives turned his heart after other gods, and his heart was not fully devoted to the LORD his God, as the heart of David his father had been. . . . He did the same for all his foreign wives, who burned incense and offered sacrifices to their gods. (1 Kgs 11:4, 8)

The biblical text records King Solomon's policy in the tenth century of establishing pagan cultic installations for his foreign wives, "who burned incense and offered sacrifices to their gods" (1 Kgs 11:4, 8). According to the text, this practice continued into the ninth century. First Kings 15:13–14 states that "he [Asa] did not remove the high places" and mentions the idolatry of the mother of King Asa (911–870 BC), who erected an image as an Asherah. Likewise, 1 Chronicles 17:3 infers continuing pagan cultic practice in Judah in the time of King Jehoshaphat (870–848 BC).

There are remains of only a few ritual buildings from ninth-century Judah; however, the most significant of these is a 2,750 year-old cultic center discovered at Tel Motza, identified with the biblical town of "Mozah" in the tribal lands of Benjamin bordering Judah (Josh 18:26). It provided evidence of an Iron Age IIA sacred installation in close proximity to Jerusalem, in fact, within walking distance of the capital city. This enclosure, identified as a pagan temple, had massive walls and a wide, east-facing entrance, a form followed by the Jerusalem Temple and other temples in the ancient Near East. Its courtyard contained a ritual platform with a square structure thought to be an altar. Surrounding the altar was a cache of sacred vessels, including ceramic chalices, decorated ritual pedestals, and anthropomorphic and zoomorphic terracotta figurines. These images of human-bearded heads with flat headdresses and curling hair and the animal images of saddled and harnessed horses imply a Philistine influence. Since this worship center was active during the ninth century, it exemplifies the religious problems introduced by King Solomon and faced by the Davidic dynasty during this period. However, with the religious reforms instigated in Judah by King Hezekiah (ca. 715–686 BC), ritual worship was returned exclusively to the legitimate temple in Jerusalem, all foreign worship was abolished, and foreign ritual centers removed.

Zoomorphic figurine used as ritual vessel, excavations at Tel Motza

BAZ RATNER/ Reuters/Newscom

1 Kings 6:1; 2 Chronicles 3:1

Archaeological Evidence for the First (Solomonic) Temple

In the four hundred and eightieth year after the Israelites came out of Egypt, in the fourth year of Solomon's reign over Israel, in the month of Ziv, the second month, he began to build the temple of the LORD … Then Solomon began to build the temple of the LORD in Jerusalem on Mount Moriah, where the LORD had appeared to his father David. It was on the threshing floor of Araunah the Jebusite, the place provided by David. (1 Kgs 6:1; 2 Chr 3:1)

These texts in Kings and Chronicles give explicit information concerning the historical location of the First Temple. On the elevated extension of a ridge above the Ophel where David's palace was built, known as Mount Moriah, the site of the offering of Isaac (Gen 22:2–14) and later of a threshing floor purchased by David at which he erected an altar (2 Sam 24:19–25; 1 Chr 21:18–28), Solomon built the First Temple. Its destruction in 596 BC under the Babylonians supposedly left no trace of the former structures, especially since a Second Temple was built on its foundations by Zerubbabel (Ezra 3:8–11; Hag 1:2–4, 8–9, 14) and then cleared and rebuilt by Herod the Great (John 2:20). Since archaeological access to the site is today restricted due to religious and political sensitivities, it has been impossible to excavate at the place where it is suspected the former temples had been built. In addition, the minimalist school, represented by Israel Finkelstein, discounts the archaeological possibility of the First Temple on grounds that the building accomplishments ascribed to Solomon were a late-eighth century BC invention and that a Jerusalem and temple of the magnitude described in the Bible did not exist.[50] Nevertheless, Israeli excavations in the Ophel have produced finds related to the First Temple and Islamic construction on the Temple Mount has inadvertently produced archaeological data crucial to understanding its structure and location.

In 2010 Israeli archaeologist Eilat Mazar uncovered massive fortifications at the end of the Ophel just south of the Temple Mount. These include a monumental gatehouse and a large section of wall on the fortification line of the ancient city that has been traced to a length of some 210 feet (70 m) winding around the Temple Mount. According to Mazar, her discovery of pottery, bullae, and seal impressions now make it possible to confirm a tenth-century date, including an adjacent royal structure and a tower some 18 feet (6 m) in height.

Portion of the Solomonic wall discovered in Eilat Mazar's excavations in the Ophel.

These structures accord well with the biblical description of King Solomon building a fortification line around his new constructions in Jerusalem, which include the First Temple and his royal palace. Their high level of construction also suggests that they were part of the royal quarter of biblical Jerusalem. This evidence indicates that the Jerusalem of the second millennium BC was home to a strong central government that had the resources and manpower needed to build such massive fortifications such as that constructed by King Solomon during his reign. This is supported by deduction from the site of Khirbet Qeiyafa, a provincial town in the Elah Valley region, where archaeologists have uncovered impressive fortifications, a scribal room, and a palace that date to this period.

This site, though located far from Jerusalem on the

outskirts of Judah, nevertheless has all of the traits of an administrative center (possibly the biblical site of Gederah or Netaim, cf. 1 Chr 4:23). If such a small outlying site was this developed in the tenth century BC, there can be no doubt that the capital city of Jerusalem was well developed, as Scripture attests. A partial inscription in ancient Hebrew found on one of several large storage jars unearthed in the complex at Khirbet Qeiyafa indicates that it belonged to a high-level government official. Seal impressions discovered at the site also argue for a royal context. This accords well with the biblical record of royal construction that employed skilled Phoenician architects and engineers to construct the First Temple (1 Kgs 7:13–14) and may even specifically mention these structures: "until he (Solomon) had completed building his own house, and the house of the LORD, and the wall around Jerusalem" (1 Kgs 3:1). The royal structures, many preserved up to one story in height, are a remarkable find, but even more remarkable is that they were buried slightly more than a foot under topsoil. This indicates that monumental structures from this period were not completely dismantled or destroyed but that later periods simply erected their structures (such as houses in this area of the Ophel) on top of the earlier ones. This leaves the possibility that much more has been preserved from the First Temple period than previously believed. According to Eilat Mazar, this wall probably connected with the city of David and fits with the biblical description that King Solomon built a fortification line around his new constructions of the temple and the king's palace.

In 2006, construction workers for the Islamic Waqf were repairing an electrical cable on the Temple Mount not far from the site where the Muslim Dome of the Rock sits. During the construction they cut numerous long trenches into the fill under the flagstones that are set on the present-day platform. In one of these trenches there was observed (and photographed) an ancient wall.

Eighth-century wall exposed on Temple Mount

Zachi Dvira

From the debris around the wall potsherds were recovered that date the site to the eighth century BC. Among the sherds were the remains of vessels used for ladling oil. The find-spot in relation to a conjectural placement on the site of the First Temple, led Leen Ritmeyer, former architect under Benjamin Mazar of the archaeological excavations below the Temple Mount, to propose that the wall was part of the Chamber of the House of Oil, where the olive oil used in the Temple services was stored.[51]

Other evidence for the First Temple has come from inscriptional material found in excavations. Scores of clay bullae (small seals stamped with the sender's name and attached to documents) were discovered in the Ophel excavations and nearby in a room in Area G of David's City that had been burned in the Babylonian destruction of the First Temple in Jerusalem. Many personal names mentioned in Jeremiah and Chronicles are attested on the bullae, including that of "Azaryahu son of Hilkiyahu," who was a member of the family of high priests who officiated at the end of the First Temple period (1 Chr 9:10). In 2008, an administrative complex from the First Temple period (eighth–ninth centuries BC) was discovered in the northwest part of the Western Wall plaza, which runs adjacent to the Temple Mount. On the floor of these buildings were found inscribed seals and bullae. One of the seals bore the inscription: "[belonging] to Netanyahu ben Yaush." The biblical name "Netanyahu" appears several times in Jeremiah and Chronicles, and the name "Yaush" is found in the Lachish letters (the city destroyed by the Assyrian monarch Sennacherib who threatened to lay siege to Jerusalem; 2 Kgs 19–20; 2 Chr 32, Isa 37).

There are also several inscriptions that refer to the First Temple. An unprovenanced ostraca called the Three Shekels Ostracon is a ninth- to seventh-century-BC receipt for three shekels donated to *bet YHWH* ("house of YHWH"). Another, found at Arad in the Negev from the early sixth century BC and addressed to "Elyashib at Arad" is known as the House of God Inscription because it also mentions "the house of YHWH." While this might refer to the First Temple, there was a rival sanctuary at Arad

that could have been the referent.[52] Another unprovenanced inscription (though claimed to be from the eastern side of the Temple Mount) is a sandstone tablet called the Jehoash Inscription. Dated to the late ninth century BC, it was disputed as a forgery and later exonerated in terms of its ancient patina but is still contested by the Israeli Antiquities Authority on epigraphic grounds (a mixture of early and late words).[53] If genuine, its text corresponds to 1 Kings 12 concerning a renovation made to the First Temple, which it refers to simply as "temple."

There are also clay models of ancient cultic shrines that have parallel features with construction details of the First Temple. An architectural model shrine from Idalion, Cyprus depicts the protective goddess of the house (inside the door) with two columns bearing floral decoration on either side.[54] From Syria comes a terracotta model shrine with twin pillars on the porch that are similar to the bronze columns on Solomon's Temple and an Asherah figure in the gateway, representing divine presence in the temple. Similar features

Khirbet Qeiyafa director, Yosef Garfinkel, with shrine model bearing architectural similarities to Solomon's Temple.

Alexander Schick

are found in terracotta models of shrines from the palace area at Khirbet Qeiyafa. Here a clay temple model has a decorated opening flanked by lions and two columns (again, like the First Temple's twin columns). Each column stands on a lion's head and over the entrance are rows of wooden beams above which appears something like a folded textile similar to the curtain that covered the entrance to the holy of holies. These models date from the early tenth century and from a time before the First Temple was constructed, but Yosef Garfinkel, the director of the Khirbet Qeiyafa excavations, has suggested the columns and the textile evoke similarities with the temple that would later be built in Jerusalem.[55] In addition, diagonal roof beams organized in groups of three (triglyphs) are in the stone model from the site.[56]

2 KINGS

2 Kings 10:34

Assyrian Depiction of the Judean King Jehu

> As for the other events of Jehu's reign, all he did, and all his achievements, are they not written in the Book of the annals of the kings of Israel? (2 Kings 10:34)

The text mentions the acts of King Jehu recorded in the biblical book of Chronicles, but these are selected events and fail to include details of the king's submission to Assyria, which at that time exercised hegemony over Israel. Archaeology can often supply such historical details from extrabiblical inscriptions. One such inscription is found on the Black Obelisk of Shalmaneser III. Austen Henry Layard discovered it in 1846 in his excavations at the central building at Nimrud (ancient Calah, cf. Gen 10:11–12), the royal residence of Shalmaneser III. Shaped like a ziggurat, the 6 foot, 7 1/2 inch tall obelisk contains twenty panels on a four-sided frieze chiseled into its alabaster surface. The inscription records Shalmaneser III's military campaigns (one of which was his plan to subdue the West) and his accession to his thirty-first year which opens with a plea to the Mesopotamian gods and the royal titles of the king. From the list of accomplishments that accompany the king's titles it can be dated to ca. 828–827 BC. Each panel contains a scene showing the payment of tribute by five conquered territories with an inscription identifying those in the scene and its purpose. In one panel the inscription distinctively mentions and depicts King Jehu giving homage and presenting gifts to Shalmaneser, who is seated and holding a tribute vessel. The Israelite king kneels before him while overhead are the sun-god Shamash and the goddess Ishtar. The cuneiform text above this scene reads: "I received the tribute of *Yaw* (*Ia-ú-a*), (the man) of *Bīt-Humrî* (Omri): silver, gold, a golden *saplu* vessel, a golden rhyton, golden goblets, golden beakers, tin, a staff for the king's hand, bud-shaped finials—[these things] I received from him."[57] Historians have identified *Yaw* with King Jehu, whose name was pronounced *Yaw-hu* in ninth-century BC Hebrew. While Jehu was not a descendant of Omri, the Assyrian practice was to identify successive rulers by the name of the ruler of the country from their first contact.

The event illustrated by the Black Obelisk fits into Israel's history during the ninth century BC, when the neo-Assyrian empire began applying pressure against Israel and Syria. The Assyrians sought to expand their territories through war, so Israel joined a coalition with Damascus and local confederacies to oppose Assyria. The coalition failed, but at this time Jehu,

Black Obelisk of
Shalmanezzer
III with detail
depicting King Jehu.
British Museum.

© 2013 by Zondervan

previously a military leader, overthrew the Omride dynasty and usurped the throne (2 Kgs 9:3–6). In 841 BC Shalmaneser invaded Syria and forced Hazael (of Damascus) to pay tribute. Rather than resist Assyria, Jehu submitted to it and gained its protection, especially against Hazael, who already feared further provocation of Shalmaneser III. The payment made by Jehu to the Assyrian monarch depicted on the Black Obelisk is absent from the biblical account of his exploits. Shalmaneser III, too, is not explicitly mentioned in the Bible. Another account of this act was recorded in Shalmaneser's annals: "At that time, I received the tribute of the Tyrians and the Sidonians, and of Jehu (*Ia-ú-a*), (man of) *Bīt-Humrî* (Omri)."[58]

2 Kgs 19:32–36 / 2Chr 32:21–22 / Isa 37:36–37

The Assyrian Siege of Jerusalem

> In the fourteenth year of King Hezekiah's reign, Sennacherib king of Assyria attacked all the fortified cities of Judah and captured them. . . . "Therefore this is what the LORD says concerning

the king of Assyria: 'He will not enter this city or shoot an arrow here. He will not come before it with shield or build a siege ramp against it. By the way that he came he will return; he will not enter this city, declares the LORD.'" (2 Kings 18:13; 19:32–33)

In 701 BC the Assyrian monarch Sennacherib came against Hezekiah king of Judah and against the capital city of Jerusalem. While most of the fortified cities of Judah fell to the Assyrians, both the Bible and ancient historians record that they were unsuccessful in their plan to lay siege to Jerusalem. According to the Bible, God sent death by an angel to the soldiers encamped outside Jerusalem and Sennacherib returned to his palace in Nineveh where he was killed in a political coup (2 Kgs 19:35–37). The historian Herodotus wrote that God struck the Assyrian army with a plague and they returned to Nineveh.[59] The archaeological evidence for this event correlates with and provides additional details for the biblical account.

One evidence for the historicity of this account comes from the remains of Hezekiah's defenses raised against the Assyrian invasion. As the Assyrians approached Jerusalem, Hezekiah hastily fortified the newly expanded, but weaker, western hill of the city. The record of Hezekiah's effort is found in Chronicles: "Then he worked hard repairing all the broken sections of the wall and building towers on it. He built another wall outside that one . . ." (2 Chr 32:5). Part of the fortification structures were uncovered in excavations in the Jewish Quarter.[60] One of the towers and a section of wall were discovered preserved to a height of about 6 feet. The new outside wall that Hezekiah built was discovered by Israeli archaeologist Nahman Avigad during his excavations in the Jewish Quarter (1969–82). This wall is called the "Broad Wall" because of its width of 23 feet. This extreme thickness was necessary to withstand the terrible battering rams of the Assyrian army. Originally this wall stood 27 feet high and ran from the northern area of the western hill south, then westward, toward the present Jaffa Gate. It then continued southward along the edge of the slope above the Hinnom Valley until it swung east to meet the southern tip of David's City at the place where Jerusalem's three main valleys met.[61] The construction of this massive wall reveals the desperation of Jerusalemites to ward off the Assyrian onslaught at all cost and provides archaeological evidence for this historical event.

Randall Price on Broad Wall

Richard Hess

Yet, more evidence has come from archaeology for this event—this time from the Assyrians. In 1830 British Colonel R. Taylor found a hexagonal cylinder at Nineveh that recorded Sennacherib's campaign in Isrsael. The Taylor Prism (other copies in other holdings are known as the Nimrud Prism and the Oriental Institute Prism)[62] gives the Assyrian account of the siege of Jerusalem and King Hezekiah's later tribute payment, but the account significantly omits any mention of conquering Jerusalem.

Siloam Inscription (facsimilie)

Alexander Schick

Sennacherib boasts:

> As for Hezekiah, the Judean who did not submit to my yoke, I surrounded and conquered forty-six of his strong walled towns and innumerable small settlements around them by means of earth ramps and siege-engines and attack by infantry men . . . I brought out from them and counted 200,150 people of all ranks . . . He himself I shut up in Jerusalem, his royal city, like a bird in a cage . . . Fear of my lordly splendor overwhelmed that Hezekiah. The warriors and select troops he had brought in to strengthen his royal city Jerusalem, did not fight . . . He sent his messengers to pay tribute and do obeisance.[63]

The Jerusalem Prism in the Israel Museum, Jerusalem.

Alexander Schick

This statement falls short of declaring that Sennacherib captured Hezekiah or successfully besieged his city. The silence implies a withdrawal and agrees with the biblical account in 2 Kings 19:32–36 that there would be no fighting during the siege.

There is also indirect archaeological evidence from the population growth in Jerusalem and Judah immediately after Sennacherib's campaign. Around 700 BC Jerusalem expanded to three to four times its former size. Such growth cannot be accounted for on the basis of natural population increase. The expansion came from the immigration of Israelites who came to Judah from the northern kingdom after the fall of Samaria in 721 BC and the influx of dispossessed refugees from the territories that Sennacherib took from Judah and gave to the Philistine cities. This adds the testimony that not only was Jerusalem spared but that there was no longer a threat from Assyria at this time. The immigration from northern Israel, which had just suffered devastation from the Assyrians, would hardly have come south to a city that was a target for another invasion. This unprecedented (and to many inexplicable) deliverance argues for the historical plausibility of the miraculous deliverance as recorded in the biblical account (2 Kgs 19:32–37; Isa 37:33–38; cf. 2 Chr 32:20–23).

2 Kings 25:27–30

Babylonian Rations

> In the thirty-seventh year of the exile of Jehoiachin king of Judah, in the year Awel-Marduk became king of Babylon, he released Jehoiachin king of Judah from prison. He did this on the twenty-seventh day of the twelfth month. He spoke kindly to him and gave him a seat of honor higher than those of the other kings who were with him in Babylon. So Jehoiachin put aside his prison clothes and for the rest of his life ate

regularly at the king's table. Day by day the king gave Jehoiachin a regular allowance as long as he lived. (2 Kgs 25:27–30)

Several clay tablets were found by Robert Koldewey in a royal archive room of King Nebuchadnezzar near the Ishtar Gate during his excavation of Babylon in 1899–1917. These tablets, dating from 595 to 570 BC, now known as the Babylonian Chronicles, detail the rations that were given to the Babylonian prisoners. Four of these tablets list rations of oil and barley given to various individuals, including the deposed Judean king Jehoiachin, by Nebuchadnezzar from the royal storehouses, dated five years after Jehoiachin was taken captive. Second Kings 25:27–30 records that Jehoiachin was a prisoner of Babylon, later released and given provisions by the king of Babylon. The clay ration tablets confirm the accuracy of the biblical account. One of these tablets lists the recipients of sesame oil, including Jehoiachin king of Judah, his sons, and his men: "10 (sila of oil) to the king of Judah, Yaukin; 2 1/2 sila (oil) to the offspring of Judah's king; 4 sila to eight men from Judea." Another reads: "1 1/2 sila (oil) for three carpenters from Arvad, 1/2 apiece; 11 1/2 sila for eight wood workers from Byblos . . . 3 1/2 sila for seven Greek craftsman, 1/2 sila apiece; 1/2 sila to the carpenter, Nabuetir; 10 sila to *Ia-ku-u-ki-nu*, the son of Judah's king [1]; 2 1/2 sila for the five sons of the Judean king."[64] The Babylonian Chronicle is housed in the Pergamon Museum in Berlin.

King Jehoichin Ration Tablet. Pergamon Museum, Berlin.

Alexander Schick

2 CHRONICLES

2 Chronicles 20:14–15

Zechariah the Son of Benaiah

> Then the Spirit of the LORD came on Jahaziel son of Zechariah, the son of Benaiah, the son of Jeiel, the son of Mattaniah, a Levite and descendant of Asaph, as he stood in the assembly. He said: "Listen, King Jehoshaphat and all who live in Judah and Jerusalem! This is what the LORD says to you: 'Do not be afraid or discouraged because of this vast army. For the battle is not yours, but God's.'" (2 Chr 20:14–15)

This text describes the prophet Jahaziel's prediction to King Jehoshaphat of a miraculous Israelite victory in a battle with a Transjordan coalition (20:1). The historicity of this battle is assumed by the Chronicler, who refers (20:34) to the testimony of royal archive documents in the book of Kings concerning the military history of Jehoshaphat. Since the compiler of Kings also refers his readers to such documents (1 Kgs 22:45) and the account of this battle of Jehoshaphat is uniquely preserved here (20:1–30), it must be understood to be one of the historical sources referenced in Kings.

Archaeological excavation has also provided historical evidence for the prophet mentioned in this account in an inscription from excavations conducted by the Israel Antiquities Authority in the area of the Gihon Spring in the city of David.

Fragment of ceramic bowl bearing inscription related to Zechariah. Israel Museum.

Z. Radovan.www. BibleLandPictures.com

In remains of walls from the First Temple period at this site, which evidence the destruction of the Babylonian conquest, a fragment of a ceramic bowl was unearthed. The partial inscription in ancient Hebrew gives a defective spelling of the name Benaiah, *ben riyhu*. This resembles the biblical name of the seventh-century-BC figure Zechariah the son of Benaiah, the father of the prophet Jahaziel. The epigraphic date of this inscription (eighth–seventh centuries BC) fits this period. The inscription, engraved on the bowl prior to firing, indicates that it originally adorned the rim of the bowl and was not written on a shard after the vessel was broken. It has been suggested that the bowl was an offertory vessel and bore the name of either the offerer or the one to whom the offering was given for this purpose. According to the account in Chronicles, Zechariah the son of Benaiah was of Levitical descent, being a "a Levite and descendant of Asaph" (20:14).

2 Chronicles 26:23

The Epitaph of Uzziah

> Uzziah rested with his ancestors and was buried near them in a cemetary that belonged to the kings, for the people said, "He had leprosy." And Jotham his son succeeded him as king. (2 Chr 26:23)

King Uzziah or Azariah (790–739 BC) ruled in Judah at a time of decline for Assyria and Egypt, which enabled him to develop his kingdom through extensive building projects, by establishing hegemony over Edom, Philistia, and Arabia, and by reestablishing the southern Red Sea port of Ezion-geber. The prosperity of Judah at this time was the greatest since that of King Solomon. His importance as a ruler is seen in the fact that the Assyrian monarch Tiglath-pileser III, who destroyed the Northern Kingdom and deported most of its citizens, mentioned him four times in his inscriptions as "Azariah the Judean." For most of his reign of fifty-two years he followed God and was influenced by God's prophet Zechariah (2 Chr 26:5). The one mark against this impressive rule was that he usurped the role of the priests, even opposing the high priest (and some eighty priests) by burning incense in the temple and so was punished by God with leprosy (see Exod 30:7–8; Num 16:40; 18:7). This disease forced him to remove himself from public life into co-regency with his son Jotham. Probably in response to his own concern over Israel's future as a result of Uzziah's passing, the prophet Isaiah noted (Isa 6:1) the year of his death (739 BC) as the occasion for his receiving a revelation of the LORD and a recommission to his prophetic mission. According to 2 Chronicles 26:23, his burial was near his ancestors, that is, next to, but not in, the royal tomb of the kings where the Davidic dynasty were buried. Possibly because he was a leper, his internment was in a field designated for special burial that was in association with the royal tombs.

In 1931 in a collection of artifacts at the Russian convent on the Mount of Olives, Hebrew University professor E. L. Sukenik discovered a marble plaque (35 cm high by 34 cm wide by 6 cm deep), inscribed in a Hebrew script that dated it to the period AD 30–70. The artifact known as the Uzziah Tablet reads: "Here were brought the bones of Uzziah, king of Judah. Do not open!" While this marker was too young by seven hundred years to have been attached to the original tomb, the Jewish authorities would not have crafted such a copy unless there was an original that was associated with the royal burial. It is believed that sometime during the Second Temple period Uzziah's bones were moved to another location and that this marker was made in relation to reburial.

King Uzziah Inscription (secondary burial marker for the king). Israel Museum.

Courtesy of Martin Severin, Inner-Cube, Dusseldorf, Germany

2 Chronicles 36/Ezra 1

Parallel texts and Catch-lines in Ancient Near Eastern Texts

Second Chronicles 36:22–23 ends with the proclamation of the Persian monarch Cyrus to permit the exiled Jews to return to Judah:

> In the first year of Cyrus king of Persia, in order to fulfill the word of the LORD spoken by Jeremiah, the LORD moved the heart of Cyrus king of Persia to make a proclamation throughout his realm and also to put it in writing: "This is what Cyrus king of Persia says: 'The LORD, the God of heaven, has given me all the kingdoms of the earth and he has appointed me to build a temple for him at Jerusalem in Judah. Any of his people among you may go up, and may the LORD their God be with them.'" (2 Chr 36:22–23)

The book of Ezra begins at this point and, with the book of Nehemiah, records the rest of the story of the return of a Jewish remnant and the rebuilding of the Jerusalem Temple and the city walls. However, the reader of these verses at the end of 2 Chronicles and the beginning of Ezra (1:1–3a) observes that there is a repetition of the text. This was not a mistake made by a copyist but an intentional technical device employed by ancient scribes in lengthy literary compositions that

required multiple scrolls to contain their work (before it was possible to join separate scrolls together). Apparently, the Chronicles composition had reached the maximum length for a scroll at that time and necessitated an additional scroll to complete the record. Known as catch-lines, these repetitions helped readers correctly connect the end of one scroll to the next and continuing scroll.

Although this is the only example of this in the biblical text, evidence for this same practice can be seen as far back as Mesopotamian cuneiform texts. When a work extended over several tablets, the Mesopotamian scribe inserted catch-lines at the ends of the completed tablet to guide the reader to the next tablet. The appearance of catch-lines in Chronicles and Ezra is evidence of a compositional connection between the two books and therefore of single authorship by a scribe simply designated "the Chronicler." Traditionally, this individual is identified with the postexilic scribe Ezra, who led a group of exiles to Judah in 458 BC and compiled court documents as part of his purpose to unify the nation in their common history and to revive the people's spiritual commitment to their covenant with God.

The recognition of the use of a catch-line in 2 Chronicles and Ezra helps resolve a scholarly debate as to whether the lines mentioning Cyrus and his edict were originally part of one book or the other. As Menahem Haran points out "The answer is neither that the repeated verses belong *only* at the end of Chronicles *nor only* at the beginning of Ezra. The division here is caused by the limits of the size of the scroll. We have here an uninterrupted textual continuity of one work, extending from book to book—that is, from scroll to scroll."[65] In addition, it is clear from the new (introduction of Cyrus) and incomplete thought at the end of 2 Chronicles and the completion of this thought and its fulfillment in history in the beginning of Ezra that the events in one record anticipate continuation in another and that the history they record could not have been adequately understood unless they were intended as a single work. Therefore, this text could not have originally belonged exclusively to one book over the other but was divided only because of the need to inscribe the remaining part of the account on another scroll. While the compiler of this account was forced to make this division at this point, it was only determined by the necessity imposed on him by the limitation of his compositional materials.

EZRA

Ezra 2:1, 46

The Hagab Seal

> Now these are the people of the province who came up from the captivity of the exiles, whom Nebuchadnezzar king of Babylon had taken captive to Babylon (they returned to Jerusalem and Judah, each to their own town . . . Hagab . . . (Ezra 2:1, 46)

The Bible has many lists in the historical books. These are intended as records for national Israel to trace and preserve their genealogical lines. This list, in particular, notes those who, mostly from a new generation born in captivity that had never seen the land of Israel, were willing to trust God and set out as pioneers to return to a ruined city to rebuild. The Jews who took the challenge and made the difficult and dangerous journey to Jerusalem numbered 49,897. One of the many names in this lengthy list was the family of Hagab, a name lost to history except for an archaeological discovery that brought his name to prominence. The discovery was made in excavations under the auspices of the Israel Antiquities Authority at the northwestern part of the Western Wall plaza in Jerusalem. The excavation was a salvage dig being conducted because a new police station was being built over the site and the removal of the previous station had made possible a rare look at this important place near the ancient Upper City near the Temple Mount.

In the course of the excavations, which terminated on the paving stones of the eastern cardo laid by the Roman emperor in the second century AD, one corner of the excavations found that they had dropped from the Byzantine period right into the seventh century BC, the time when the kings Manasseh and Josiah reigned. The excavators discovered that the large paving stones of the Roman street were missing in this place, and they were able to penetrate to the Iron Age material below. Here they found a room with walls to a height of 25 feet. The high quality of its construction and the artifacts that were discovered inside it indicate that the building and especially its inhabitants had a very important status in Jerusalem at the end of the First Temple period. In this room were found ten handles of storage jars for oil and wine that are stamped with royal impressions and on the floor were found a number of Hebrew seals of individuals who held public positions. From this evidence it was determined this was an administrative complex connected to the First Temple. One of the seals that was discovered, a black stone elliptical in shape (1.2 by 1.4 cm), belonged to a private individual and was adorned with the image of an archer shooting a bow and arrow. The name of the archer in ancient Hebrew script next to the image reads *lhgb* meaning "belonging to Hagab."

According to the excavation director, archaeologist Shlomit Weksler-Bdolah, this name is not only in the Ezra text but also appears in the Lachish Letters, also dating to the time of the First Temple.[66] She noted that the image of the archer was influenced by Assyrian wall reliefs in which archers are portrayed in profile in a firing position, each with his right foot in front of his left, like those depicted on the Lachish relief found in the palace of Sennacherib in Nineveh. His attire includes a headband and a skirt that is wrapped around his hips with quiver hanging from his back. His right hand is extended forward holding the bow while his left is pulled back grasping the arrow. This seal represents the first time that a private seal has been discovered bearing a Hebrew name and decorated in the Assyrian style. It testifies to the strong Assyrian influence that existed in Jerusalem at the time. For this reason Hagab, who likely held a high governmental position and had served in a senior military role in Judah, chose to portray himself in the Assyrian style.[67]

First Temple
Seal of Hagab

Courtesy of Israel
Antiquities Author-
ity; Photographer:
Clara Amit

NEHEMIAH

Nehemiah 2:13–15a

Nehemiah's Wall

> By night I went out through the Valley Gate toward the Jackal Well and the Dung Gate, examining the walls of Jerusalem, which had been broken down, and its gates, which had been destroyed by fire. Then I moved on toward the Fountain Gate and the King's Pool, but there was not enough room for my mount to get through; so I went up the valley by night, examining the wall. (Neh 2:13–15a)

Nehemiah was the cupbearer to King Artaexerxes before God commissioned him to Jerusalem to stir the Jewish people to rebuild the demolished walls of their city. Shortly after he arrived he performed a reconnaissance tour by night ride around the city, surveying the damage of its walls. This passage gives us a glimpse into the way the great administrator, Nehemiah, helped his people rebuild the city walls in record time, just fifty-two days.

University of Tel-Aviv archaeologist Israel Finkelstein, however, has contended that "there is no archaeological evidence for the city wall of Nehemiah" and that "archaeologically, Nehemiah's wall is a *mirage*."[68] According to Finkelstein, the Bible's description is not of a wall built by Nehemiah in the Persian Period but of the construction of the Late Hellenistic, Hasmonean city wall. His former colleague David Ussishkin disagrees, noting that unsurmountable difficulty for Finkelstein's view is derived from the biblical account itself. In Nehemiah 3:1–32 there is a detailed description of the course of the wall complimented by the account of his nightly inspection tour mentioned in our text (Neh 2:12–15), as well as a thanksgiving procession upon the completion of the wall in Nehemiah 12:31–40. Ussishkin says that the toponyms mentioned in these texts "relate to Jerusalem of the First Temple Period and not to the later Second-Temple-Period city whose layout differed from that of the earlier city. First and foremost was the situation on the Temple Mount. During the First Temple Period, the royal acropolis of the kings of the House of David, which included the Temple and the royal palace, was situated on the Temple Mount … Other toponyms located outside the Temple Mount also indicate that the biblical text refers to Jerusalem of the First Temple Period."[69] A writer in a later period likely could not have accurately described these past constructions, as they would have been different in the Hellenistic and Hasmonean periods.

Though the evidence is sparse, archaeologists have claimed to find remnants of wall construction in the time of Nehemiah. The "angle of the wall" mentioned in Nehemiah 3:19 was identified on the eastern ridge by French excavator Charles Clermont-Ganneau, R. Weill, and Yigael Shiloh, and a fragment of it is still visible today. Archaeological architects Leen and Kathleen Ritmeyer point to the lowest course of stones with rough bosses in a stretch of the city wall north of the present Golden Gate and identify them as part of the Corner Tower mentioned in Nehemiah 3:31.[70] Hebrew University archaeologist Eilat Mazar, in her excavations in the northern part of the city of David, found part of Nehemiah's wall on the eastern slope in conjunction with some seals inscribed with biblical names, two of which mention the names Gedaliah son of Pashhur and Jucal son of Shelemiah—the two

men who threw the prophet Jeremiah in a pit.[71] While excavating the Northern Tower, one of two towers that sit on the eastern slope near the structure she identifies as King David's palace, two dog graves were discovered. Mazar notes, "dog burials in Israel are characteristic of the Persian period—when the Persian monarch Cyrus the Great permitted the Jews to return from the Babylonian Exile. The largest dog cemetery, with hundreds of burials, was discovered at Ashkelon on the southern coast of Israel. Excavator Lawrence Stager dates theses burials to the first half of the fifth century BC, the early part of the Persian period."[72] Beneath the burials were also found several small potsherds that can be dated to the late sixth and early fifth centuries BC. The date of this find could be further narrowed by the lack of Yehud impressions, seals with the name of Judah in the Persian period that date from the second half of the fifth century BC. The absence of these seals implies that the dog burials were from the first half of the fifth century BC. Therefore, the Northern Tower and its city wall could not have been built before the mid-fifth century but rather around 445 BC, the very time Nehemiah was commissioned to rebuild Jerusalem's walls.[73]

Nehemiah's wall (highlighted) on eastern slope of city of David

Alexander Schick

ESTHER

Esther 1:1

Xerxes Inscription from Persepolis

> This is what happened during the time of Xerxes . . . (Esth 1:1a)

The opening to Esther introduces the reader to the Persian Empire and its monarch Ahasuerus. Details concerning his name and accession to the throne have been provided through archaeological documents and inscriptions. There is a variant reading for Ahasuerus in this opening line of the text. The Septuagint (LXX) translators, Josephus, the Jewish Midrash, and the Peshitta (the Syriac translation of the Bible) all render the name as "Artaxerxes," which is a misinterpretation of the Hebrew, "Ahasuerus."[74] Additional textual witnesses (Syriac and Vulgate)[75] and certain linguistic factors support the Hebrew name.[76] "[Ahasuerus] must be [a transliteration] of the Old Persian *Xsayarsan*, the traditional English form of which is 'Xerxes,' from the Greek."[77] Xerxes (486–465 BC) was the son of the Persian king, Darius I (Darius the Great). While Xerxes finds mention in this verse, the author does not elaborate on how exactly this king of Persia occupied the royal throne at the citadel in Susa. The Gemara (Aramaic for "study"), a section of the Talmud comprising rabbinical analysis of and commentary on the Mishnah, informs us that Xerxes was not the official heir to the Persian throne but went on a quest for the throne and won the crown:[78] "Said Rav: He came to power on his own. Some say this positively; some say it negatively. Those who say this positively [do so] because there was no one as worthy to be the king as he; those who say it negatively [do so] because he was not worthy of the kingship, but he paid out a lot of money and rose [to power] (*Megillah*)."[79] The Greek writings (e.g., Herodotus) and a cuneiform inscription found at Persepolis inscribed by Xerxes himself also affirm his quest for the crown:[80] "Saith Xerxes the king: Other sons of Darius there were, (but)—thus unto Ahuramazda was the desire—Darius my father made me the greatest [. . .] after himself. When my father Darius went away from the throne [died], by the will of Ahuramazda I became king on my father's throne."[81] These archaeological finds have shed more light on an important figure in Jewish history who had a significant role in preserving God's people from Haman's anti-Jewish coup.

Relief of Xerxes with two servants at Persepolis

© Anton_Ivanov/Shutterstock

4 | Wisdom Literature

Comparative Wisdom Literature in the Bible and Ancient Near Eastern Documents

> For gaining wisdom and instruction; for understanding words of insight; for receiving instruction in prudent behavior, doing what is right and just and fair; for giving prudence to those who are simple, knowledge and discretion to the young— let the wise listen and add to their learning, and let the discerning get guidance—for understanding proverbs and parables, the sayings and riddles of the wise. (Prov 1:2–6)

The genre of wisdom literature usually refers to the Hebrew books of Job, Proverbs, and Ecclesiastes, although there are also wisdom psalms. E. I. Gordon proposed that it should be recognized as a generic term broadly embracing the various cultures of the Near East whose literary content is concerned in one way or another with life and nature and man's evaluation of them based upon either his direct observation or insight.[1] In this regard, the wisdom literature of the ancient Near East (including Israel) offers us an international reflection on life, both religious and ethical, that captures the social and political opinions of the time of its respective composition. Yet the literature bears a timeless quality that informs each successful generation, in each unique culture, in much the same fashion.

The concept of wisdom is conveyed by the Semitic root ḥ km, which underlies the basic expression of "wisdom" in Hebrew (ḥokmah), its cognate languages, and the Egyptian concept of maat. The Akkadian language developed the richest terminology for the semantic domain of wisdom within the Semitic languages. The stative verb emēqu(m), "be wise," and its cognates are closest to the range of meanings of the Hebrew ḥkm. The adjective emqu(m) has the meaning of "clever, cunning," as well as "wise" when applied to kings, elders, scribes, mantic experts (e.g., diviners), and above all craftsmen and technicians.[2] The Akkadaian phrase ḥāsis kal šipri (derived from a root that associates understanding with the function of hearing) means "expert in every craft" and refers to the "wisdom" of craftsmen. Similarly, the notion of "skillful making" (epēšu[m]) gave rise to various adjectives meaning "able, experienced." Therefore, the force of the term "wisdom" in Akkadian was upon a skill or experience that brought expertise or enablement in an endeavor.[3] In the Imperial Aramaic of the Babylonian wisdom text Ahikar, the verb appears in line 9 with the meaning "instruct," which is the operation of a figure in line 1 called "a wise and skillful scribe." Again, the idea of technical ability or skill is prominent. In Biblical Hebrew this same basic nuance of "skill" is evident in all derivatives of ḥkm. For example, the term is used of the special ability of artisans in Exodus 28:3; 31:1–11; 35:30–35; 36:1–3, of the technical expertise of stonemasons in 1 Chronicles 22:15, of the trained ability of goldsmiths in Jeremiah 10:9, of the experienced competence of mariners in Psalm 107:27, of the craftsmanship of shipbuilders in Ezekiel 27:8–9, of the artistry of artificers in 1 Kings 7:14, and of the wizardry (unusual art) of magicians in Isaiah 3:3. It also is employed to denote the peculiar prowess enabling the heads of tribes, judges, and kings to perform either special or official tasks (cf. Deut 1:13,15; 16:19; 2 Sam 14:20). Of the 318 uses of the root *ḥkm* in the Old Testament, 196 instances appear in wisdom literature (i.e., Job, Proverbs, Ecclesiastes, and some Psalms).[4] In these contexts it bears an ethical/moral nuance, for just as in the secular realm it had been applied to technical skill, so here it is applied to the ability to cope with life in general. Scott in his study of the term in the wisdom writings concludes: "thus *ḥokmah* gained the sense of 'skill in living,' the trained ability to live in equilibrium with the moral order of the world."[5] The wisdom school of the Israelites viewed the world as an ordered system (under the control of God, cf. Job 1:21; 42:1–2; Prov 16:1–4; 21:1; Eccl 3:1–8; 5:18–19; 12:14), and the responsibility of the *ḥakam* ("wise man") as the instruction of men in the practical affairs of life. This wisdom is, however, neither simply utilitarian or amoral but linked inseparably with the concepts of righteousness and the fear of Yahweh (Prov 9:9–10). Therefore, for the Israelite "wisdom" is related to God's righteous order that has been established ultimately for man's good.

The origin of wisdom literature has been variously explained by scholars. The general assumption of scholarship is that (especially with regard to Israel) oral tradition preserved this body of literature within the community before it took a fixed form. Comparison is often made to those proverbs and sayings scattered in the historical books of the Old Testament (cf. Judg 8:21; 1 Sam 30:24–25; 2 Sam 5:8). The antiquity of proverbial aphorisms has been documented by their inclusion in some of the tablets unearthed in the royal archives at Tell Mardikh (Ebla), which are dated on the basis of the paleography of their literary texts at ca. 2450 BC.[6] This evidence of an early history, coupled with the international scope of wisdom literature, indicates that some transmission of the wisdom tradition took place across the boundaries of time and geography. Modern

scholarship has suggested that this transmission was either by the family (or tribe) or that it was communicated didactically by sages in professional or courtly "wisdom schools." Evidence for the latter is offered from Proverbs 25:1, which describes the "men of [King] Hezekiah" as playing a role in the transmission of the work. Though the association of wisdom with king and court is not to be disputed, no hard evidence for such "schools" as centers of wisdom in Israel exist.[7] Such evidence is usually by extrapolation from comparative texts known from wisdom schools resident in the Egyptian court (e.g., Prov 22:17–24:22 and the *Instruction of Amenemope*). Further, the concept of training a responsible courtier could be construed as part of the wisdom school ideal (cf. Prov 16:10–15; 25:1–5).[8]

Again, the early origins of wisdom literature dictate that such existed long before the formation of the court. It would appear more likely that the source for the wisdom movement was the ethos of the people, a transmission indicated in the father-son sayings of the book of Proverbs (cf. Tobit 4:3, 18–19) and similar types of parental advice in other Near Eastern texts (e.g., Egyptian Ptah-Hotep, *ANET*, p. 414a; Mesopotamian *Ahikar* 2:22, 47). A more vigorous cultivation of wisdom literature was then the product of both wisdom schools (with the probable exception of Israel) and the royal court (e.g., 1 Kgs 4:30; 10:1–8). So, it would seem that the origins of the wisdom movement are to be sought both in society and in the school or court.[9]

Comparative Ancient Near Eastern Wisdom Texts

Biblical wisdom literature shares significant points of comparison with the wisdom literature that existed previously in the ancient Near Eastern context and that God used as a means to communicate to his people. Archaeological discoveries of ancient Near Eastern archives have produced a wealth of cuneiform tablets containing the literary compositions of the civilizations that occupied this region.

The earliest writings are from the Classical Sumerian period (ca. 2500–2400 BC), followed by a period of Semitic influence via the Akkadians, who took control of Sumer in the last quarter of the third millennium (ca. 2300–2000 BC). These latter inscriptions are Akkadian but written in the Sumerian script. This period was followed by a "Sumerian Renaissance" in the Third Dynasty of Ur (ca. 2000–1900 BC). During the Kassite Period (ca. 1500–1200 BC) Babylonian literature developed and Sumerian texts were copied and provided with a Babylonian translation.

Egyptian wisdom literature can be found throughout all periods of ancient Egyptian history, from the Old Kingdom (2700–2160 BC) through the New Kingdom (1550–109 BC). These wisdom texts represent a special category of Egyptian literature dealing with moral codes of behavior and ethical values of the ancient Egyptian society.

Since both Mesopotamia and Egypt influenced and had frequent contact with Israel, it is only to be expected that their wisdom literature would be known and that the Israelites' own wisdom writings would model them and interact theologically with them. Looking at these comparative wisdom writings, delivered to us by archaeology, helps us to better understand the history of these views as well as to be sensitive to the particular nuances in them that may have parallels to those in the ancient Near East.

Archaeology, in providing so many examples of wisdom literature from the ancient Near East, enables us to understand that wisdom schools and wisdom sages in Israel were not isolated from the larger literary context of the civilizations that surrounded them. While the practical observations of human life and relationships are shared experiences and therefore forms the basis for shared style and format in biblical compositions, the discontinuity appears in the theological orientation, which differs with respect to the source of wisdom and its ultimate purpose for mankind, and Israel in particular.

Wisdom Literature of the Ancient Near East

Mesopotamian Wisdom Literature	
Man and His God (2000 BC–1700 BC)	In this Sumerian poetic essay, a dialogue ensues between a man and what is probably his personal god. While a comparison may be made with the biblical book of Job, the theological framework contrasts in a great many details.
Ludlul Bel Nemeqi "The Babylonian Job" (1500 BC–1200 BC)	This was written from the perspective of a man of great wealth and prestige who was faithful to his god, Marduk. While his story is one of personal destruction, it is implied that Marduk is the cause of the various devastating events that take place within the man's life. Eventually the man is restored and gives praise to Marduk.
The Babylonian Theodicy (1400 BC–800 BC)	Also called The Dialogue About Human Misery, this acrostic poem (every line begins with the same sign) consists of a progressive dialogue between a sufferer and his friend.
The Dialogue of Pessimism	Often compared with Ecclesiastes, this text is a conversation between a master and slave about women, piety, and death. The final exchange, in which the master contemplates suicide and the slave apparently quotes a common proverb, points to this being a serious satire on the subject of pessimism.
Sirduri's Advice to Gilgamesh	Gilgamesh, when reaching the garden of the gods, encounters the woman Siduri, who advises him to enjoy his present life because the gods have allotted death to men and immortality only for themselves. This brief text is comparable to Ecclesiastes 9:7–9 in which similar counsel is given.
The Counsels of Wisdom	A collection of Akkadian moral exhortations that describe the counsel of an important court figure to his "son" or pupil. There are ten sections each dealing with a specific subject of moral and ethical conduct, one that includes warnings against female company. The warnings against female company are in many instances parallel to Proverbs 2:16–19 and 6:24–26.

The Story of Ahiqar	This collection of fables and sayings in the wisdom tradition are the words of Ahiqar, a seventh-century seal bearer under Sennacherib and Esarhaddon. The emphasis upon training youth is a feature that is analogous to the book of Proverbs and the personification of wisdom is highly reminiscent of Proverbs 8:1–36.
Advice to a Prince (1000 BC–700 BC)	This sapiental text of Akkadian consists of omen-patterned counsels to a Babylonian ruler concerning the legal privileges guaranteed to citizens of Nippur, Sippar, and Babylon. The author warns the king that retribution will become operative if he abuses his power with respect to taxation, forced labor, and appropriation of personal property.
The Shamash Hymn	Classified as a wisdom psalm, this hymn is a lengthy address to Shamash, the Babylonian god of justice. The motifs that permit classification of this text in the wisdom tradition include Shamash as the overseer of justice and the instruction concerning merchants.
The Instructions of Shuruppak	This Sumerian proverbial text presents the counsel of Shuruppak, the survivor of the flood in Sumerian legend. The formal feature of father as teacher and son as pupil are included, paralleling both Israelite and Egyptian proverbs.

Egyptian Wisdom Literature (2800 BC–100 BC)
The Old Testament makes reference to the "wisdom of Egypt" (1 Kgs 4:30), and it was well known that the "Egyptians were exceedingly fond of aphoristic verses" and "made numerous collections of didactic sayings . . . providing all sorts of rules of wisdom and good manners."[10]

The Old Kingdom (2686–2160 BC)

The Instruction for Ka-gem-ni	This text presents an aged vizier's instruction to his children, especially Ka-gem-ni, his successor as vizier under the next pharaoh. This brief and fragmentary text sets forth rules for life in proverbial fashion.
The Instruction for Prince Hor-dedef	The chief concern of this text is toward preparation for mortuary rituals to ensure participation in the future life. Since the "wise" will respect mortuary religion, practical advice for taking a wife and producing a son to ensure proper entombment is the focus of the text.
The Instruction of Ptah-hotep (2494 BC–2345 BC)	Ostensibly written for his son who would succeed him in office, this instruction reflects the high optimism of this period and the height of Egyptian culture and prosperity. It focuses on problems likely to beset a courtier in royal service including problems with speech, women, pride, and various types of relationships.

The First Intermediate Period (2160–2040 BC)
The optimism and good feeling that characterized the wisdom literature of the Old Kingdom has changed in this period to pessimism and despair. This caused the wisdom writers to question the foundation of their ideological structure, and thus the literature of this period is one of criticism and despondency with conventionalism.

The Dialogue of a Man Tired of Life	The disruption of the tranquility of the Old Kingdom brought about such a dialogue as the one here, between a man and his Ba (roughly equivalent to "soul," but essentially the personification of life forces in which mode one continued to live after death). The man takes the traditional view of mortuary religion. The Ba is a cynic who threatens to abandon the man to the difficulties of his present life with no hope for relief in a future life.
The Song of the Harper	In contrast with most Harper Songs (often accompanied by tomb reliefs, which depict a harper singing a song on the theme of life and death), this song is addressed to the living rather than a deceased pharaoh and betrays a total pessimism about the future life. In its refrain it admonishes its audience to "make holiday, and weary not within!" A similar expression may be found in Ecclesiastes 11:8–10.
The Instruction for King Meri-ka-Re (2160 BC–2040 BC)	This text is in the instructional genre since it includes advice for a son who has now succeeded his father to the throne and requires counsel for the righteous and wise guidance of the kingdom of Maat. In addition to a series of wise admonitions concerning proper policies to follow in administration, there is the inclusion of wisdom theology concerning "the 'Lord of the Hand'" (a title given to a god suggesting his creative power).

The Middle Kingdom (2040–1558 BC)	
With the successful reassertion of authoritarian rule by the twelfth dynasty of the pharaohs at Thebes, the placidity and cynic questioning of the First Intermediate Period was eclipsed by a return to a dogmatic acceptance of divine kingship and mortuary religion. The instructional genre characterizes the texts of this period.	
The Instruction of King Ameh-em-het (1971 BC–1928 BC)	Written by a court scribe under the patronage of Sen-usert I, the instruction is housed as though from the deceased Pharaoh Amen-em-het I upon the ascent of the former to his predecessor's throne. The work appears to be a piece of royal propaganda serving to legitimatize the right of succession of the new pharaoh.
The Instruction of a Man for his Son (1991 BC–1786 BC)	This instruction is also a work of propaganda and an attempt to inculcation within the lesser officials, scribes, and bureaucrats of the kingdom so as to solidify the structure of the kingdom around the cohesive center of the Egyptian throne. The main body of the work is a series of wise admonitions designed to develop the character of these young officials and to make them loyal men of the king.
The New Kingdom (1558–1085 BC)	
Ani, a lower echelon temple scribe, writes concerning the general areas of social, civil, and religious duties, which would become his in the scribal profession. Specifically, these include: obligations to parents, obligations as an honorable man, relation to superiors, friendships, hospitality, and the like.	
The Instruction of Amen-em-opet (19th dynasty/13th century BC)	Most famous of the Egyptian sapiental literature is this composition with many parallels to the biblical book of Proverbs (Prov 22:17; 24:22). The purpose of the instruction is to teach his son to orient himself to the world order overseen by the god of justice by accepting the role of the "silent man" and by avoiding the destructive path of the "passionate man."
The Late Dynastic Period and Hellenistic Rule	
Two works will be considered: The Instruction of Onchsheshonqy, written during the period of Persian domination, and The Instruction of Papyrus Insinger from the Ptolemaic period of Greek influence. While these go beyond the "biblical period" with which we will compare, the works of Ecclesiastes and Ben Sira are considered by most scholars to be from this later period of Hellenistic thought.	
The Instruction of Onchsheshongy	This instruction consists of prosaic communications that set out to make observations in a straightforward and uncomplicated manner and in firm terms on particular topics. The text also contains a group of instructions open to interpretation, leaning toward universality. This combination of concreteness with openness to interpretation is characteristic of the popular proverb.
The Instruction of the Papyrus Insinger (323 BC–30 BC)	According to Perdue, "the key concept of this instruction around which the admonitions and proverbs are centered is the idea of equilibrium, which is the guiding principle of world order, and, therefore, of orderly human activity."[11] There is included in this work the teaching of divine determination and a paradoxical appeal to prepare for burial (according to the prescribed methods of the mortuary cult).

JOB

Job 28:1–11

Copper mining in Timna

There is a mine for silver and a place where gold is refined. Iron is taken from the earth, and copper is smelted from ore. Mortals put an end to the darkness; they search out the farthest recesses for ore in the blackest darkness. Far from human dwellings they cut a shaft, in places untouched by human feet; far from other people they dangle and sway. The earth, from which food comes, is transformed below as by fire; lapis lazuli comes from its rocks, and its dust contains nuggets of gold. No bird of prey knows that hidden path, no falcon's eye has seen it. Proud beasts do not set foot on it, and no lion prowls there. People assault the flinty rock with their hands and lay bare the roots of the mountains. They tunnel through the rock; their eyes see all its treasures. They search the sources of the rivers and bring hidden things to light. (Job 28:1–11)

This text in Job mentions the copper industry that existed from Chalcolithic times. When the Israelites were en route to the land of Israel they were told that it was "a land where the rocks are iron and you can dig copper out of the hills" (Deut 8:9). Even before the Israelites reached their new land, large-scale copper mining in the Timna Valley, located near the site of ancient Ezion-geber (modern Eilat), had already reached a peak (fourteenth–twelfth centuries BC) under the Egyptians, Midianites, and Amalekites. However, there is no evidence of mining or smelting in Timna from the middle of the third millennium BC until the late second millennium BC. The Egyptians appear to be the first to have discovered the rich copper nodules (up to 55 percent copper) in this area of exquisite sandstone formations. During the fourteenth century BC, the time of Egyptian-Midianite copper production at Timna, a new, improved type of smelting furnace was employed, with a bowl-shaped hearth sunk into the ground and lined with clay mortar. In order to increase the temperature of the fire, a clay tube served as a furnace nozzle through which air was forced by bellows.

As the text in Job describes, miners used metal chisels and hoes to dig tubular shafts with footholds in the walls for climbing in and out of the shafts and for underground ventilation. These shafts reached depths of 100 feet and more before reaching copper-rich formations. These shafts widened into underground cavities where the ore nodules were mined. The text depicts these workers hanging from ropes in these cavities, swinging back and forth to work one formation or the other as well as hauling the heavy loads of ore to the surface. When the shafts were abandoned because the ore was used up, they filled up with either mining waste or blowing sand. Thousands of these former mining sites can be identified today as lighter colored, saucer-like plates on the slopes below the cliffs at Timna.

Timna Park mining shaft entrance

© Duby Tal/Albatross/ Alamy Stock Photo

Deep shafts cut in search of copper nodules

Todd Bolen/www .BiblePlaces.com

In the 1930s archaeologist Nelson Glueck was one of the first to do a systematic survey of the copper mines in Timna and date them to the tenth century BC (the time of Solomon); hence they were labeled "King Solomon's Mines." Archaeologists have uncovered the remains of camps used as workshops for copper smelting. One such camp that was excavated contained a number of tools, such as hammers, anvils, and slag heaps and charcoal pits. A central courtyard with a stone-lined storage pit that held the copper ore nodules that were to be crushed on a stone platform was also uncovered.

PSALMS

Psalm 4

Use of stringed instruments

> For the director of music. With stringed instruments. A psalm of David. (Superscription of Ps 4)

"The law laid out the occasions and the ritual for worship, but it was David who prepared the way for the full and glorious praise of God in the worship, not only by organizing the guilds of singers and musicians, but also by writing many psalms that became part of [Israel's] hymnbook."[12] Contained in the superscription of this Davidic psalm is the Hebrew word *neginah*, which denotes a stringed instrument in the psalm titles. The precise nuance of the noun is uncertain, which may be because it can refer generically to all stringed instruments.[13] Perhaps the Hebrew Bible's terse descriptions concerning Israel's musical instruments led to this uncertainty. The Septuagint translators and their trouble rendering some of the Hebrew terminology in the superscriptions may be indicative of this.

It is certainly conceivable that the referent of *neginah* in Psalm 4 may be a musical guild of lyres (*kinor*). "By the beginning of the second millennium, the lyre had established a firm presence in ancient Israel/Palestine. It quickly became the dominant instrument in the region and remained such through the entire Iron Age, enjoying its golden age apparently within the Israelite-Judean monarchy itself as well as in the neighboring areas."[14] There is a copious amount of archaeological evidence for the lyre in ancient art. Much of the art is shown on pottery, reliefs, and seals. Noteworthy are the seals that portray lyre topi. One such seal is the Haifa seal, which "depicts an angular symmetrical lyre of the Tel Batash type and is actually a bronze scaraboid (typical of northern Palestine) [. . .] The Haifa seal portrays a seated lyre player together with what is probably a female dancer playing a drum.

Lachish relief from Sennacherib's palace depicting men playing the lyre

Wikimedia Commons/ Photograph by Mike Peel (www.mikepeel .net)/licensed under CC BY-SA 4.0

This theme is certainly commensurate with the lyre playing group and doubtless derives from the male-female duo of chordophone and membranophone familiar from the orgiastic cults in early Babylon."[15]

This style of music is also illustrated on the reliefs that decorated Sennacherib's palace. "On the south-west corner of the citadel now called Kuyunjik, [Sennacherib] built a splendid residence, which he boldly named 'The Palace Without a Rival,' and which it fell to Layard and his successors to explore over a hundred years ago. Sennacherib's palace was an enormous building containing over seventy halls, chambers, and passages, as far as it was excavated by Layard and his successors, of which almost all contained sculptured walls."[16] The relief/wall detailing Sennacherib's conquest of Lachish depicts three lyrists (perhaps Judeans) being lead into captivity through a wooded area by an Assyrian guard. Apparently the lyre was easy to carry and walk with; a simple plucking of the strings by the lyrist's fingers would play the instrument's range of notes.

Finds such as this help to show that Israel's worship expressed itself in many forms. Worship to Yahweh was not limited to sacrifices and religious feasts; rather, worship in Israel was manifested in every way (Ps 150), even by the notes of musical instruments. "And the [temple] was the most fitting place for God to be praised, for it was where he made his presence known most frequently through the praises of the people. When the people of God were faithful to give him thanks (Ps 122:4), the sanctuary was filled with praise from morning to evening, so much so that David could say that God dwells 'in the praises of Israel' [Ps 22:3]."[17]

Psalm 18:10

Yahweh, Rider of the Clouds

> He mounted the cherubim and flew; he soared
> on the wings of the wind. (Ps 18:10)

Iron Age II seal with lyre player, found at Ashdod

Courtesy of Israel Antiquities Authority; Photographer: Meidad Suchowolski

The theme of this psalm is twofold: "the psalmist, in mortal danger, cries for help, and God appears to deliver him from his danger. But in the amplification, the whole theme has been given cosmic dimension; this cosmic dimension has been achieved by the utilization of language which is rooted in Near Eastern mythology, but which has been transformed to express the Lord's deliverance of his human servant"[18] in polemical fashion. The psalmist's use of poetic language has some similarities to the Akkadian Enuma Elish, but the more likely antecedents are to be found in the Ugaritic Baal Cycle mythology, that is, in the mythology of Israel's more proximate neighbor, the Canaanites.[19] This is not to say that Israelite religion should be perceived as a mere reflection of its surrounding pagan neighbors; rather, God used the known constructs or the matrix of ideas relevant to the ancient Near Eastern world as a medium through which he was best able to communicate new truths to his people at that time period.[20]

One of the major archaeological sites discovered in the Middle East during the twentieth century was at Ras Shamra in Syria. Ras Shamra was the site of the ancient city of Ugarit, capital city of the kingdom of Ugarit that flourished from the fifteenth to the twelfth centuries BCE . . . Excavations of the tell at Ras Shamra began after a farmer accidentally uncovered a tomb at the nearby port of Minet el-Beida in 1928. . . . Among the most important discoveries at Ras Shamra was a collection of six broken tablets that contain myths about the god Baal. These tablets, commonly known as the Myths of the Baal Cycle (or, the Baal-Anat Cycle), were discovered by Claude F. A. Schaffer during the early years of the excavations in the remains of a building on the acropolis that has been labeled the House of the High Priest.[21]

Upon these tablets, Mot and Yam are depicted as the gods of death and the sea, which are often personified as a symbol for chaos in both the literature of the ancient Near East and the Old Testament (Pss 29; 89; Isa 17; 29).[22] The tablets also depict Baal as the storm god who enters into conflict with Yam and Mot, ultimately defeating them in battle (*Chaoskampf*). As a result, Baal creates order out of chaos and, in so doing, is recognized as king. One episode of the myth reads: "Kotaru-wa-Hasisu speaks up: I hereby announce to you, Prince Ba'lu, and I repeat, Cloud-Rider: As for your enemy, O Ba'lu, as for your enemy, you'll smite (him), you'll destroy your adversary. You'll take your eternal kingship, your sovereignty (that endures) from generation to generation" (*CTA* 2.iv 7–27).[23] Here Baal is called "Cloud-Rider," recalling the common image of a storm god equipped with lighting and thunder as his weapons and who rides the clouds in his war chariot. Baal is also depicted as defeating his enemies and thereby earning the right to rule as sovereign king forever. This image of Baal is identifiable, in part, upon "the famous 'Baal with Thunderbolt' stela found near the Temple of Baal in

1932. . . . The primary figure on the stela is clearly Baal, with a war club in his raised right hand and a javelin (lightning bolt) in his left. Below his feet appear to be representations of the sea and the mountains."[24] This iconic symbolism is also attested upon a cylinder seal that dates to the Old Akkadian era. Depicted upon the seal is an offering being presented to a storm god riding upon his war chariot.[25] This was how the storm god was manifested to mankind in ancient Near Eastern literature and art.

These ancient "cloud-rider" or "divine chariot-rider" themes may be the precursors to the imagery applied to Yahweh in Psalm 18, specifically verse 10 (see also Pss 68 and 104); however, its function in the biblical literature seems to be polemical. "The psalmist is caught in the 'cords of death' (*mot*) and torments of Belial (viz. *Yam*), vv 5–6. Next, the Lord comes to deliver him in the theophany characterized by storm and earthquake: vv 7–15.

Baal as warrior riding the clouds with thunderbolt in hand. Louvre, Paris.

Then the Lord rebukes 'ocean' (*yam*) and 'earth' (viz. the underworld, realm of *Mot*) and thus delivers his servant: vv 16–20."[26] The psalmist is not merely portraying Yahweh as a common deliverer; rather, in polemical fashion, Yahweh is pictured as the supreme divine warrior-king who, through his awesome display of power, flies into battle mounted upon his war chariot (the cherubim) to rescue from a flood of enemies. Eugene Merrill states: "The image of Yahweh riding on the heavens and clouds . . . is mythopoeic anthropomorphism adapted, no doubt, from pagan epic sources but with intensely polemic overtones against the depravity of pagan religious conception. The point was that it was not really Baal (or any other god) who rode in triumph in the heavens above, but it was the Lord alone who did so, he who is unique and solitary."[27] Archaeological finds such as this are important because they help contemporary Bible readers discover the fullness of its meaning, build an apologetic for its historicity, and avoid its misinterpretation by imposing modern cultural ideas onto the more cryptic biblical texts.

Psalm 22:16

Clarification from a Dead Sea Scroll Text

> Dogs surround me, a pack of villians encircles me; they pierce my hands and my feet. (Ps 22:16)

The superscription of this psalm ascribes the writing to David, and therefore the suffering and desire for deliverance it describes has been considered to be that experienced historically by the king. Because the Messiah was predicted to come from David's royal seed, Christian interpreters saw David and his experiences as a type of Jesus' experiences, particu-larly in this psalm, which describes rejection by God and men (vv. 1–8), an agonizing torture by enemies (vv. 11–18) that apparently climaxes in death (v. 15), and yet is followed by deliverance (vv. 22–24). The Gospels record the words of this psalm on the lips of Jesus on the cross, so verses 11–18 were understood to be a messianic prediction of Christ's crucifixion. This interpretation was strengthened by the Septuagint's rendering of the last part of verse 16 as "they pierced (*oruxan*, an indicative of *orussō*, "dig, pierce") my hands and my feet." The Syriac Peshitta (a Syriac translation of the Hebrew Bible ca. second century AD) followed this with *bazu* ("pierced"). This reading obviously translated a Hebrew verb, but the MT, the traditional Jewish text, reads *ka'ari* ("like a lion"), understanding a preposition (*ki*, "like") added to a noun (*'ari*, "lion"). Numerous emendations were offered in light of this textual problem, but support for the reading in the versions came with the archaeological discovery of a Hebrew text of this passage in one of the Dead Sea caves at Nahal Hever. This text (5/6 Heb 11.9) clearly read as a verb, *ka'aru* ("they dug at/pierced"). There is no evidence, as some have contended, that Jews or Christians tampered with the text. It is more probable that in one of the manuscripts used by the Masoretes the ink had degraded on consonant *waw* so that it was read by a scribe as a *yod*, resulting in the word being read as a noun rather than a verb.

Dead Sea text of Psalm 22:16 (MT 22:17) showing consonant *waw* (indicting verbal form)

Psalm 62:6–8

David's Petitions and the Caves of 'Ein-Gedi

Truly he is my rock and my salvation; he is my fortress, I will not be shaken. My salvation and my honor depend on God; he is my mighty rock, my refuge. Trust in him at all times, you people; pour out your hearts to him, for God is our refuge. (Ps 62:6–8)

Photo of caves at 'Ein-Gedi

Alexandra Toy

The wilderness psalms contain a series of military metaphors related to David's flight to and refuge at the strongholds of 'Ein-Gedi (see 1 Sam 22–24 for the historical description). The psalms that have this event in the background are Psalms 18, 42, 57, 62, 63, and 142–144. In these psalms different terms are used to describe David's petition for the LORD's deliverance, inspired by his natural rocky surroundings. In this psalm (Ps 62) the word "rock" is *tsor*, which is a flint rock and therefore extremely hard and durable. Unlike the softer limestone cliffs that make up the refuge of 'Ein-Gedi, this rock is a strong refuge and representative of a secure place of deliverance (salvation). In Psalm 18:2 the word used is *sela'*, better understood as a clef in a rock, which denotes:

…places of natural security, in contrast to human made fortresses. However, the idea of fortress is mentioned in the very next word *mezudah*, the very name later applied to the nearby fortress of Masada where Jews fleeing from the Romans in toward the end of the First Jewish Revolt held off the Roman Tenth Legion for a period of three years. Excavations at this site were conducted between 1963–1965 by Yigael Yadin and renewed by others over the next decades. Like Masada, 'Ein-Gedi is a remote and inaccessible site situated in the Judean wilderness yet at a natural spring that provides plentiful game and ideal safe refuge for a man on the run (Psalm 104; 1 Samuel 24:2, 3, 23; Job 39:28).[28]

Another synonym in this text for refuge is the term *misgav*. While these words for "mighty rock," "fortress," and "refuge" have nuances, "the physical object often becomes a symbol of spiritual truths," as here, where they become titles for the LORD himself.[29] Perhaps David, in seeking refuge from Saul during the early monarchial period, interpreted the security that the mountain wilderness of 'Ein-Gedi provided him; thus, David could express that Yahweh was his true *sela'* (Ps 18) and *tsor* (Ps 62).[30]

The ancient site of 'Ein-Gedi, located on the western slope of the Dead Sea (near the caves of Qumran), has seen numerous excavations that have demonstrated that the site was occupied from the earliest periods. The earliest habitation is evidenced in the discovery of a Chalcolithic high place and temple stretching to the end of the period of the Bar Kokhba Revolt (AD 132–135). In the case of this later period, an archaeological survey conducted on behalf of the Institute of Archaeology and the Caves Research Unit in 2001–4, found a group of caves on a cliff facing the Dead Sea that had been used for refuge for these Jewish soldiers. The refuge caves yielded various remains from this period, including coins, pottery, glassware, and weapons. On the basis of the size of the caves and the amount of finds found within them, it can be estimated that dozens of refuges fled to the caves in 135 AD. The nature and variety of the finds suggest that these were families with armed warriors among them who sought safety among these remote and seclusive caves.[31] Such archaeological discoveries reveal how David found security in these caves while his enemies hunted him and why he could call upon the LORD as his rock and salvation in Psalm 62:2 (cf. Ps 18:2).

PROVERBS

Proverbs 22:6

Archaeological Evidence of Child Training

Start children off on the way they should go, and even when they are old they will not turn from it. (Prov 22:6)

This passage instructs on parental methodology with the words "start off" and "children," terms that have a significant background in documents from the ancient Near East. In the Ta'anach letters (Akkadian documents dating from just before the Amarna age [fifteenth century BC]), Albright found a complaint from Amenophis of Egypt that Rewassa of Ta'anach, in the context of mustering troops for war, had not sent his "retainers" (ha-na-ku-u-ka) to greet Amenophis. In the Akkadian Ta'anach letters, the root hnk when applied to people refers to one who is initiated and experienced, having duties commensurate with his status as a military cadet who has completed his training. Similarly, in Genesis 14 these same military cadets (retainers/squires) are called ne'arim ("men," 14:24).[32] The connection of hnk with ne'arim is significant because these are the same roots that appear in Proverbs 22:6, usually translated "train up" and "child." The term hanak acquired the meaning "to train" in a didactic sense (similar to lamad, "teach, instruct"), although it is preferable to view this word as having specific reference to the inauguration process with the bestowal of status and responsibility as a consequence of having completed an initiation process. In short, the word hanak focuses not so much on the process of training as on the resultant responsibility and status of the one initiated.[33] This meaning of hanak in Proverbs 22:6 moves away from a strictly parental admonition for providing the child with good instruction. The na'ar ("child") saw how to be initiated with celebration; status and responsibility have more in view than simply age designation. A study by John MacDonald based on an analysis of hundreds of Ugaritic and Hebrew usages has demonstrated that the age-focused idea of "child" is insufficient for understanding who the na'ar was.[34]

Joseph at the age of thirty is a man, but is called a na'ar, "young Hebrew" (Gen 41:12, 46). The na'ar is frequently active in strictly adult activities (war [1 Sam 17:33, 42; Judg 8:20]; cultic priestly functions [Judg 18:3–6]; special spy missions [Josh 6:21, 23]; personal attendance of a patriarch, prophet, priest, king, or son of a king [Gen 18:7; 2 Kgs 5:1–27; 1 Sam 1:22, 24–25; 2 Sam 9:9; 2 Sam 13:17]; or supervision of the whole Solomonic labor force [1 Kgs 11:28]). Moreover, upper-class role and societal status are consistently ascribed to the na'ar. In the historical books there are no examples of a na'ar of lowly birth.[35] Similarly, the feminine na'arah refers to a highborn young female (Gen 24:16; 34:3; Exod 2:5; Esth 2:4).

Artist's rendering of Mesopotamian school boys writing on clay tablets

Lovell, Tom (1909–97)/National Geographic Creative/ Bridgeman Images

This technical understanding is important in Proverbs, which is addressed to "royal sons." Class distinctions were clearly marked not only in Israel but also at Ugarit, where the only ancient cognate for the term *na'ar* is a term of status used for guild members serving in the domestic sphere and as superior military figures.[36] Based on the ancient Near Eastern usage of the terms as a background for the usage in the Bible, this verse should not be employed as support for early childhood training, since the proverbial *na'ar* was in the process of being apprenticed in wisdom for taking on royal responsibilities consistent with his status.

In the same way, the word *hanak* ("train up") is used almost universally with the dedication or initiation of temples, houses, altars, or walls. Thus, the obligation to a young wisdom "squire" would be to recognize his status as and initiate him into his official capacities or responsibilities with the respect fitting his status. Given this understanding, the phrase "on the way they should go" meant "according to the standard and status" of what would be demanded of the *na'ar* in that culture. Therefore, the acquisition of *hokmah* "wisdom" (a skill in living life) is a duty obligated to the elite whose role in society was to lead, govern, and rule, a training commensurate with its status. While this text has in view a particular class in the ancient world, its understanding should not limit people in modern societies where class distinctions are no longer enforced.

SONG OF SONGS

Ancient Near Eastern Love Poetry

Song of Songs has a complex structure and many poetic devices. An ancient Near Eastern love poem that resembles the biblical love poem between Solomon and his bride in the Song of Songs is the Sumerian Love Poem called "Bridegroom, Spend the Night in Our House till Dawn." This Sumerian love poem was found at Nippur between 1889 and 1900. The tablet was written ca. 2025 BC in cuneiform script[37] and is addressed to King Shu-sin, who ruled the Third Dynasty of Ur.

This love poem, part of the Dumuzi-Inanna love songs, has been found in ancient writings all over the ancient Near East, especially in Egypt, where fertility was a major concern. This poem consists of erotic language expressing the woman's desires for King Shu-sin and may have been sung during ritual ceremonies commemorating the divine marriage between the goddess Inanna and the god Dumuzi.

Both the Sumerian poem and Song of Songs works revolve around a male and female courtship and the concept of love with its allures. Neither attempts to restrain sexual language and vivid erotic imagery. For example, Song of Songs 8:7 states that a flood cannot drown love. The man and woman's love for each other is so strong that a violent flood cannot overpower it. In a similar use of imagery, the Sumerian poem states that the allure of love is as sweet as honey, a substance so strong and binding that love cannot escape.

The Sumerian poem is cultic in nature. While the Song of Songs only mentions the name of the LORD once (Song 8:6) and maintains a high moral standard with its repeated refrain "Do not arouse or awaken love until it so desires" (Song 2:7; 3:5; 8:4), it does not appear to have a ritualistic intent. In this regard it is comparable to secular love poems found in other cultures throughout the ancient Near East. If the Song of Songs is interpreted in this context, it would appear to express the celebration of sexual love between a man and his bride common in other ancient Near Eastern poems. This would argue against the traditional way the Song of Songs has been interpreted in both Judaism and Christianity, as an allegory of divine love (for Israel or the church).

Sumerian love poem, Ur III Period (2037–2029 BC)

© Baker Publishing Group and Dr. James C. Martin courtesy of the Turkish Ministry of Antiquities and the Istanbul Archaeological Museums, Turkey.

The end of the biblical period is well attested in the archaeological record. The attack by the Assyrian king Sennacherib on Judea (including the assault against King Hezekiah of Jerusalem, 2 Kgs 18:13–19:37; 2 Chr 32:1–23; Isa 36–37) has been preserved on official court annals recorded on several six-sided clay prisms inscribed in Assyrian cuneiform: the Taylor Prism, the Nimrud Prism, and the Oriental Institute Prism. These record the name of Hezekiah and give details concerning Senncherib's capture of Judean cities, including the burning of Lachish (2 Chr 32:9), an event preserved in great detail on a ninety-foot-long panel from Sennacherib's palace at Nineveh.

Sennacherib's assassination, as recorded in the Bible (2 Kgs 19:36–37; 2 Chr 32:21; Isa 37:37–38), is also recorded in the Babylonian Chronicle, cuneiform tablets that detail the Babylonian siege of the First Temple. One of these tablets gives a ration list for King Jehoiachin of Judah, who was taken to Babylon during the siege (Jer 52:31–33). A decree of Cyrus the Great (Isa 44:28), similar to that recorded in the Bible concerning the return of the Jews to Jerusalem to rebuild the temple (Isa 41:25; 44:26–45:6; Ezra 1:2, 7–11), was also attested in the Cyrus Cylinder found in the ruins of Babylon (in modern Iraq) in 1879.

ISAIAH

Isaiah 20:1–2

Sargon II, King of Assyria

> In the year that the supreme commander, sent by Sargon king of Assyria, came to Ashdod and attacked and captured it—at that time the LORD spoke through Isaiah the son of Amoz. (Isa 20:1–2)

This text presents a good example of how archaeology can both provide historical verification and additional background and details to the Bible. The reference to the Assyrian ruler Sargon II here is the only mention of him in the Old Testament. Until the University of Chicago's Oriental Institute uncovered his royal palace at Dur Sharrukin ("Fort Sargon"), the site of modern Iraqi village of Khorsabad, from 1928–35, it was the only mention of him in any record of the ancient world. Among the finds from these early excavations of the palace were richly decorated and relief-carved stone slabs, a complete human-headed, winged-bull statue that once guarded an entrance to the throne room, the temples of the major Neo-Assyrian gods, and the Nabu Temple surrounded by residences of Sargon's highest officials.

Sargon II, who took his Assyrian name *Sharrukinu* ("true king") from Sargon of Akkad, the founder of the Babylonian and Assyrian empires (see entry on Nimrod at Gen 10:8–9), figures prominently in the history of Israel, even though not mentioned by name in those biblical texts. Documents from his palace at Khorsabad record that he followed Shalmaneser V, who led the siege on the Israelite northern kingdom (722–721 BC) but died during its capture. In his inscriptions Sargon took credit for the capture of Samaria and the exile of its population. He conquered Gaza and destroyed Rafah, and upon return from other military campaigns rebuilt Samaria, which was settled with people from other countries conquered by the Assyrians. This resulted in a mixed racial population known as the Samaritans who later opposed the Jewish remnant that returned to Jerusalem in 538 BC to rebuild the temple and the city (Ezra 4:1–5). Three fragments of an Assyrian victory stele were discovered at Ashdod in 1963. These record Sargon's suppression of the revolt of the Philistine coastal city of Ashdod (711 BC), which was supported by Judah and others, and how he conquered it and several other cities and made Philistia an Assyrian province. Isaiah's statement records only his capture of Ashdod but reveals its accuracy with respect to history.

Sargon II and dignitary

Wikimedia Commons

Isaiah and some of the royal chronicles then describe the Assyrian capture of Judean cities and siege of Jerusalem (701 BC) under Sargon's son and successor Sennacherib (Isa 36–37; 2 Kgs 18:13–19:37; 2 Chr 32:1–23).

Isaiah 22:15–17

Shebna the Royal Steward

> This is what the Lord, the LORD Almighty, says: "Go, say to this steward, to Shebna the palace administrator: What are you doing here and who gave you permission to cut out a grave for yourself here, hewing your grave on the height and chiseling your resting place in the rock? "Beware, the LORD is about to take firm hold of you and hurl you away, you mighty man." (Isa 22:15–17)

Isaiah's text (Isa 22:15–25) denounces Shebna, an official in King Hezekiah of Judah's court, for building an excessively extravagant tomb for himself apart from his family tomb. Such a building implied a status greater than deserved and therefore was an overt demonstration of prideful arrogance in the sight of God and the nation of Judah.

In 1870 Charles Clermont-Ganneau excavated a partially destroyed tomb that was part of the necropolis in the Silwan Village nested on the western slope of the Kidron Valley and the city of David in Jerusalem. The rock-cut tomb was being used as a residence, but over the door (entrance to the burial chamber) was an inscription later deciphered by Israeli epigraphist Nahman Avigad. According to his work, the text read: "This is [the sepulcher of . . .]-*yahu* who is over the house. There is no silver and gold here but [his bones] and the bones of his slave-wife with him. Cursed be the man who will open this."[1] The description "over the house" indicated a steward, but because part of the crucial name was missing and the part that was in the

Royal steward
inscription from
Silwan

©Baker Publishing Group
and Dr. James C. Martin.
Courtesy of the British
Museum, London, England

inscription was a common ending for many names (*-yahu*), there was only speculation at that time that this was the tomb of the royal steward Shebna. However, because Avigad could narrow the date to the reign of Hezekiah by comparing the style of the lettering to that of the Siloam Inscription discovered in the nearby Hezekiah's Tunnel, his proposed identification was largely accepted.

During Yohanan Aharoni's 1966–68 excavations at the site of Lachish a ceramic juglet containing seventeen bullae was discovered. Many of the bullae attested Hebrew inscriptions that had once sealed documents. One of the seals was inscribed in two lines that read: "Belonging to Shebnayahu" and "the king." These words appearing together signified this "Shebnayahu" as connected to the royal family. Unfortunately, a third of this bulla was missing, so it was impossible to know what relationship this Shebnayahu had to the king. It could have read "son of" or "servant of," but at that time no further identification could be made. However, forty-two years later another bulla stamped with the same seal as the Lachish bulla surfaced in the Jerusalem antiquities market. It was even broken off at the same place. This bulla retained an additional letter that proved that both seals read "servant." Therefore, one can assume that the tomb belonged to "the servant of the king," and most likely to the Shebna mentioned in Isaiah's text.

The evidence that helped confirm that this was the same royal steward came from dating the find by stratigraphy, ceramic typology, and paleography. The juglet and the bullae came from Level II at Lachish, which was a destruction layer attributed to Babylonian king Nebuchadnezzar in 587/6 BC. Below it was Level III, another destruction layer attributed to the Assyrian king Sennacherib in 701 BC.

"Shebnayahu" Bulla
(from Jerusalem an-
tiquity market) with
crucial missing letter

Dr. Robert Deutsch

This period of about a century could be narrowed further by the shape of the juglet and the style of the letters in the inscription to the late eighth or early seventh century BC, a time contemporary with both the Siloam Inscription and the Royal Steward Tomb Inscription.

Because of the careful work of archaeologists and proper documentation (as well as recovery of an unprovenanced find), a positive identification of the Royal Steward Tomb could be made (as well as of the seal). In all likelihood, Shebna, in his royal position as steward, sent a letter from King Hezekiah's court written on papyrus to an official at Lachish. The letter has since decayed and disappeared, but the seal that sealed it has remained and over time provided the necessary archaeological clues to identify the person to whom the prophet devoted eleven lines in the biblical text.

Isaiah 25:6–9

An Archaeological Reference to the Eschatological Banquet

On this mountain the LORD Almighty will prepare a feast of rich food for all peoples, a banquet of aged wine—the best of meats and the finest of wines. On this mountain he will destroy the shroud that enfolds all peoples, the sheet that covers all nations; he will swallow up death forever. The Sovereign LORD will wipe away the tears from all faces; he will remove his people's disgrace from all the earth. The LORD has spoken. In that day they will say, "Surely this is our God; we trusted in him, and he saved us. This is the LORD, we trusted in him; let us rejoice and be glad in his salvation." (Isa 25:6–9)

Parchment copy of Messianic Rule (1QSa) from Cave 1, Qumran

Photograph by Bruce and Kenneth Zuckerman, West Semitic Research, in collaboration with Princeton Theological Seminary. Courtesy Department of Antiquities, Jordan.

The prophet Isaiah here describes a future age of redemption that is formally begun with an inaugural event that scholars have termed the "eschatological banquet." This is a victory banquet attending the time when the LORD of hosts deals decisively with the enemy of humanity (death). The participants will celebrate in the LORD's presence on Mount Zion with food (meaty bones with their marrow/blood and fermented wine) that seems to belong more to the new covenant than the restrictive diet prescribed under the Mosaic legislation. It is understandable that given such conditions there would be an association with the advent of the Messiah and the messianic age. Unless Psalm 23:5–6 (which combines the motif of a shepherd and a banquet) alludes to such a future event, Isaiah 25:6–8 is the earliest reference to this eschatological banquet in the Bible. The archaeological discovery of the Dead Sea Scrolls produced biblical commentary from the Second Temple period. One of the texts that may reflect an early interpretation as well as describe an anticipated application of the eschatological banquet presented in Isaiah is known as the *Messianic Rule* or *Rule of the Community* (1QSa). It was found in Cave 1 at Qumran along with another text known as *The Community Rule* (1QS), a pivotal sectarian document detailing the community's order and lifestyle, to which it may have been appended. *Messianic Rule* is dated to 175–100 BC, and with *The Community Rule* it describes the communal meals of the Qumran sect, and in particular an eschatological meal to be shared as priests with the Messiah. James VanderKam says that the messianic character of these communal meals is unmistakable.[2] Certainly the repeated mention of the Messiah in 1QSa 2.11–22 as a main participant in the eschatological banquet makes this point. That it was understood as eschatological is evident from the opening words of the text: "This is the Rule for all the congregation of Israel in the last days." Moreover, the focus in 1QSa on a "feast" and

the explicit mention of "new wine" (1QSa 2.17–19) strengthens the connection with the Isaianic text. The Qumran text, however, makes a clarification to the biblical text of Isaiah 25 by changing "all peoples" (verse 6) to "men of renown" (1QSa 2.11). This appears to have been done to insure that admission to the banquet was understood to be restricted to those who were ritually pure (such as the members of the Qumran community).

The excavations at the settlement of Qumran under the direction of Roland de Vaux discovered a dining hall stocked with multiple cups, plates, and bowls. It had apparently been abandoned after the earthquake of 31 BC, which seems to have interrupted the sect's habitation at the site. The remains of the communal meals, including the bones, ashes, and pottery vessels used to prepare, cook, and serve the meal, have been found carefully buried on the outside of some of the community buildings and especially on the southern plateau. Such areas were considered clean places that conformed to the biblical laws regulating the ritual disposal of sacrificial remains (Lev 4:12; 6:11; 10:14; Num 19:9). The excavations of the southern plateau under Randall Price, Oren Gutfeld, and Yakov Kalman also uncovered extensive evidence of these deposits and the analysis of the bones and vessels demonstrated both the intentional nature of the burials and the ritual character of the meals.[3]

According to 1QSa 2.22, the communal meal was to be a regular observance and required at least ten men (a *minyan*) to sit together. This may imply that a rehearsal of this anticipated eschatological banquet served as part of the community's preparation for their role in the expected messianic advent that would lead the "sons of light" into a final battle against the "sons of darkness" (as described in the War Scroll found with 1QSa in Cave 1). In 1QSa 2.11–22 instructions are given on the order of sitting and the timing of the elements (bread and new wine) served in the meal.

The Messianic Banquet at Qumran[4]

1QSa (Messianic Rule) 2.11–22

(11) [Th]is [(is the ses]sion of the men of the name [who are invited to] the feast, the men of the name. And they shall sit

(12) [God] leads forth the Messiah (to be) with them: [The Priest] shall enter [at] the head of all the Congregation of Israel and all

(13) [his] br[others, the Sons of] Aaron, the Priests [who are invited to] the feast, the men of the name. And they shall sit

(14) be[fore him each man] according to his glory. And after (them) the [Messi]ah of Israel [shall enter]. And the heads of

(15) the t[housands of Israel] shall sit before him [each m]an according to his glory. (And they shall sit before the two of them, each) according to [his rank] in their camps and their journeys. And all

(16) the heads of the ma[gistrates of the Congrega]tion with [their sage[s and their knowledgable

ones] shall sit before them, each man according to

(17) his glory. And [when they] (solemnly) meet together [at a tab]le of the Community [to set out bread and new w]ine, and to arrange the table of

(18) the Community [to eat and] to dri[nk] ne[w wi]ne, no man [shall stretch out] his hand to the first portion of

(19) the bread or [the new wi]ne before the priest; fo[r he shall] bless the first portion of the bread

(20) and the new wi[ne, and shall stretch out] his hand to the bread first of all. And aft[er (this has occurred)] the Messiah of Israel [shall stret]ch out his hands

(21) to the bread. [And after that] all the Congregation of the Community [shall ble]ss (and partake), each ma[n according to] his glory. And [they] shall act according to this statute

(22) whenever (the meal) [is arr]anged, [when] as many as ten me[n] (solemnly) meet together

In the Price, Gutfeld, and Kalman excavations a large, intact, and sealed ovoid store jar (called Jar 35) was discovered in the context of the animal bone deposits, and its contents initially tested as fermented grape wine.[5] These excavations also have unearthed numerous drinking bowls (matching those in the dining hall found by de Vaux) as part of these deposits. If the bone deposits are part of a communal meal rehearsing the eschatological messianic banquet, these may relate to the "bread" and "new wine" recorded as part of the meal in 1QSa. The research on these connections continues, but what is significant to biblical students is that for the first time we have a biblical text (Isa 25:6–9), the earliest sectarian commentary on that text (1QSa 2.11–22), and possibly the archaeological remains of the meal described in that text available for comparative study.

Isaiah 44:28; 45:1–4, 13

The Cyrus Cylinder

This is what the LORD says to his anointed, to Cyrus, whose right hand I take hold of to subdue nations before him and to strip kings of their armor, to open doors before him so that gates will not be shut: I will go before you and will level the mountains; I will break down gates of bronze and cut through bars of iron. I will give you hidden treasures, riches stored in secret places, so that you may know that I am the LORD, the God of Israel, who summons you by name.... I will raise up Cyrus in my righteousness: I will make all his ways straight. He will rebuild my city and set my exiles free, but not for a price or reward, says the LORD Almighty. (Isa 45:1–3, 13)

The prophet Isaiah gave Israel the divine comfort that the Babylonian exile would one day end and predicted that this would come when the Persian ruler Cyrus, whom the LORD calls *meshiho* ("his anointed/ messiah"), would deliver according to the LORD's purpose. In 539 BC Cyrus conquered Babylon (Dan 5:30–31) and in the next year issued a decree to release the captive Jews (2 Chr 36:22–23; Ezra 1:2–4; 6:2–5), returning them and their looted sacred objects to their land and capital city in Jerusalem (Isa 52:11–12; Jer 27:21–22; Ezra 1:1–11; 5:14–15), and helped them rebuild their ruined temple (2 Chr 36:22–23; Ezra 4:3; 5:13–6:5). Because the decree of Cyrus is recorded in the Bible in two languages (Hebrew and Aramaic) with two distinct emphases, scholars were divided on how well the original decree was reported. However, in 1879 Hormuzd Rassam discovered the Cyrus Cylinder in the remains of the Babylonian temple of Marduk. The barrel-shaped cylinder stone is inscribed in cuneiform and, though incomplete, details the capture of Babylon by Cyrus and his release of the captured people remaining there. The purpose of

the inscription, which is similar in style and content to Mesopotamian building texts, was to commemorate Cyrus's restoration of the temple of Marduk and Dur-Imgur-Enlil, the great wall of Babylon, which his predecessor had built but left unfinished. This is recorded in the last extant lines of the Cyrus Cylinder. While the statement in the Cyrus Cylinder is not the exact same decree as recorded in the Bible, it confirms that the content of that report is accurate. The Cyrus Cylinder shows Persian imperial policy toward its subject peoples as reflected in its description of the restoration of the cult of Marduk in Babylon. In the text of the Cyrus Cylinder Cyrus reviews the history of his rise to kingship in Babylon at the summons of Marduk, who, in response to evil deeds of Nabonidus, acted to save his city. Cyrus renewed the fortunes of the enslaved Babylonians and restored the neglected cult centers of the land and returned their cultic vessels (necessary to revive the cultus). The biblical report of the permission granted by Cyrus to rebuild the temple in Jerusalem is therefore considered another example of this practice.

The Cyrus Cylinder[6]

(lines 20–22a) I am Cyrus, king of the world, great king, mighty king, king of Babylon, king of Sumer and Akkad, king of the four quarters, son of Cambyses, great king, king of Anshan, grandson of Cyrus, great king, king of Anshan, descendant of Teispes, great king, king of Anshan, (of an) eternal line of kingship, whose rule Bel (i.e., Marduk) and Nabu love, whose kingship they desire for their hearts' pleasure.

(lines 28–36) "From [Ninev]eh (?), Assur and Susa, Agade, Eshnunna, Zamban, Meturnu, Der, as far as the region of Gutium, I returned the (images of) the gods to the sacred centers [on the other side of] the Tigris whose sanctuaries had been abandoned for

a long time, and I let them dwell in eternal abodes. I gathered all their inhabitants and returned (to them) their dwellings. In addition, at the command of Marduk, the great lord, I settled in their habitations, in pleasing abodes, the gods of Sumer and Akkad, whom Nabonidus, to the anger of the lord of the gods, had brought into Babylon. May all the gods whom I settled in their sacred centers ask daily of Bel and Nabu that my days be long and may they intercede for my welfare. May they say to Marduk, my lord: "As for Cyrus, the king who reveres you, and Cambyses, his son, [ ] a reign." I settled all the lands in peaceful abodes."

The Cyrus Cylinder, British Museum

© 2013 by Zondervan

Isaiah 53:11

Dead Sea Text Implies Resurrection

> After he has suffered, he will see the light of life and be satisfied; by his knowledge my righteous servant will justify many, and he will bear their iniquities. (Isa 53:11)

Jewish and Christian interpreters alike have long wrestled with the interpretation of the suffering servant of Isaiah 53. The language of the individual in the text is clearly describing a suffering that leads to death, but, if so, it would seem strange to apply this to the prophet Isaiah, since it is written in third person, and the one who suffers and dies intercedes for the nation of Israel, of which the prophet is a part. This, too, has been the difficulty in interpreting the sufferer as Israel, though it elsewhere in Isaiah is given the title of servant, for it would miss the point of the suffering on behalf of the nation if the nation (or a part of the nation) did the suffering. Archaeology can assist in difficult interpretation by providing ancient sources that shed perspective on interpretation, at least with respect to the precedent of antiquity. One such assistance has come from the discovery of the Dead Sea Scrolls, which offer the most ancient version of

the biblical texts, especially the book of Isaiah. The Great Isaiah Scroll (1QIsa), ca. 125 BC, from Cave 1 is the most complete of all the biblical texts found at Qumran. Though it has more than 2,600 variants in its sixty-six chapters, the scroll demonstrates an overall affinity with the MT.

One of the scribal variants between the Qumran text (1QIsa) and the MT can be seen in Isaiah 53:11. The MT reads *yir'eh* ("he will see") against the Septuagint *deixai autō phōs* ("he will see light"). Where did the LXX get such a reading? Was it a later Christian interpolation based on the Christian interpretation of Isaiah 52:13–53:12 as messianic and therefore a prediction of Christ's suffering, death, and resurrection (as implied by "light" being seen after the suffering servant had been killed and buried (vv. 8–9)? 1QIsa 53:11, as well as the other copies of Isaiah found at Qumran, read *yir'eh 'or* ("he will see light") in conformity to the LXX.[7] The variant in the LXX, then, was pre-Christian and could lend support to the idea of a dying and rising messiah.

Some scholars have seen this concept in the *Gabriel Revelation*, an unprovenanced 3 feet by 1 foot inscription called a "Dead Sea scroll on stone," because it has affinities with the form and style of the Dead Sea Scrolls and allegedly was discovered on the eastern side of the Dead Sea.[8] Written in ink, its eighty-seven lines are poorly preserved (both faded and fragmentary). Its text is Hebrew but with Aramaic influence and has been reliably dated to the first century BC. Hebrew University historian Israel Knohl studied the initial reconstruction of the text made by Israeli epigraphist Ada Yardeni and came to a revolutionary conclusion. She interpreted it as an apocalyptic text with a message of catastrophic messianism.[9] The text contains a number of phrases drawn from the biblical prophets but includes terms found previously at Qumran, such as *berit hadashah* ("the new covenant"), and ideas such as the eradication of evil *lesheloshet yamin* ("in three days"), an expression drawn from a combination of biblical texts, most notably with respect to the prophet Jonah's experience (Jon 1:17) and Hosea's prediction

of national Israel's restoration at the time of the messianic advent (Hos 6:2). Knohl saw the messianic figure in the text as leading the fight on behalf of Israel when the nations come against Jerusalem. In the battle he is slain, but Knohl interpreted an unclear word in line 80 as "in three days you will live" and took it to mean that, at the call of the angel Gabriel, he would be resurrected to life after three days. He posited this as a pre-Christian era concept of national redemption by a messiah that included resurrection as part of the redemptive process and that this formed the basis of the later Jewish Gospel writers' story of Jesus' death and resurrection.[10] As could be imagined, many scholars lined up on both sides of the claim, but further study of the text, especially with enhanced photographs made by the West Semitic Research Project,

The Great Isaiah Scroll A (ca. 125 BC) from Cave 1 at Qumran. The oldest complete text of the Book of Isaiah. Shrine of the Book, Israel Museum, Jerusalem.

resulted in new readings. Knohl's crucial word in line 80, reconstructed as *ha'yeh* ("you will *live*"), was reconstructed by others (such as Ronald Hendel) to read *ha'ot* ("the sign"), based on a similar use of the term with "three days" in lines 17 and 19 of this text and in biblical parallels such as Exodus 8:19.[11] While it is acknowledged that the Davidic messiah is presented in this text, the uncertainty over the crucial word has distanced most scholars from the view that there is a reference to resurrection. The new reading was adopted in the English translation of the *Gabriel Revelation* that appeared when the artifact was exhibited at the Israel Museum in 2013. There is no doubt that the *Gabriel Revelation* is an important apocalyptic text that reflects the same eschatological messianism found in the Dead Sea Scrolls and, to an extent, also in the New Testament. However, this relationship would be better understood as both documents find their common concepts in the biblical prophets rather than the latter borrowing from the former. However, the variant reading of resurrection in Isaiah 53:11, *me'amal naphsho yir'eh 'or* ("out of the suffering of his soul [= death] he will see light" [of life]), preserved at Qumran (1QIsaᵃ) as well as in the LXX, might have informed the sect's concept of a messianic resurrection.

Gabriel Revelation, Israel Museum

JEREMIAH

Jeremiah 34:6–7

The Lachish Letters and Nebuchadnezzar's Invasion of Judah

> Then Jeremiah the prophet told all this to Zedekiah king of Judah, in Jerusalem, while the army of the king of Babylon was fighting against Jerusalem and the other cities of Judah that were still holding out—Lachish and Azekah. These were the only fortified cities left in Judah. (Jer 34:6–7)

King Nebuchadnezzar's attack on Judah left few fortified cities, but this text reveals that the city of Lachish continued to resist. However, soon after these words were penned, during the summer of 587/6 BC, Nebuchadnezzar took both Lachish and Jerusalem.

In 1935–36 Starkey excavated Lachish (Tel Lachish) and found eighteen ostraca dating to 600 BC and later (the period of Nebuchadnezzar's incursions into Judah). Three more were found in 1938. The Lachish letters were written in the early sixth century BC on broken pieces of clay pottery. The letters give information about Judah before the Babylonian invasion and the exile. Jeremiah 34:7 speaks of two of the cities mentioned in the letters, Lachish and 'Azeqah. The letters were Hebrew military communiqués from an outpost to the commanding officer at Lachish. One of them reads: "We are waiting (or watching) for the fire signals of Lachish" (it seems to have been written in feverish haste as the Babylonian armies were closing in).

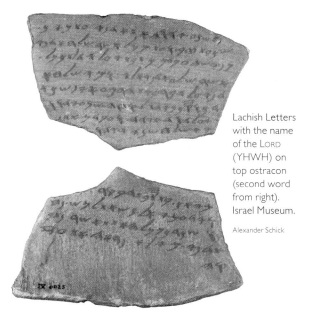

Lachish Letters with the name of the LORD (YHWH) on top ostracon (second word from right). Israel Museum.

Alexander Schick

Jeremiah 32:14

Sealed Jars, Sealed Documents and the Book of Jeremiah

This is what the LORD Almighty, the God of Israel, says: "Take these documents, both the sealed and unsealed copies of the deed of purchase, and put them in a clay jar so they will last a long time." (Jer 32:14)

Archaeological evidence for historical people and events in the book of Jeremiah sometimes comes in small packages. This text mentions the act of preserving sealed documents by storing them in sealed jars. The materials mentioned, once connected with the text through archaeological discovery and interpretation, tell much more than meets the eye. In this text Jeremiah prophesied to his fellow citizens that they would be exiled from the land but also that they would return. In token of God's promise, the LORD commanded Jeremiah to purchase a plot of land and put the sealed deed and an open copy in a jar. The jar would preserve its contents through the time when the Israelites would be removed from the land of Israel and would still be there when they returned. In this way God demonstrated the security of his promise to return the land to Israel in the future. A terracotta jar would protect the contents for a long period of time, depending on local conditions. In the dry region near the Dead Sea, sealed jars containing leather and papyrus documents have been found stored in caves. This arid environment and the negative air flow within the caves helped preserve the scrolls in a pristine condition. A similar state of preservation has been observed in objects from the sealed Pharaonic tombs in the dry sands of Luxor (Upper Egypt). However, the Judean desert scrolls not in jars had either been reduced to fragments or had darkened to such a degree that they could no longer be read by the naked eye. However, even sealed jars could not prevent ultimate decay of the contents stored in the more humid climate of the Judean hills. Such documents on papyrus or leather would suffer decomposition in a relatively short time. For that reason, court documents written on such perishable materials have not survived in capital cities like

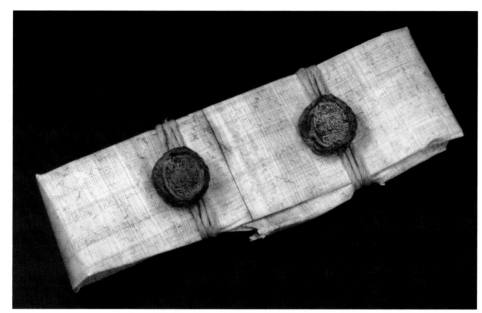

Jerusalem or Memphis (Lower Egypt), where archives certainly existed. However, the seals that were affixed to documents, like the deeds mentioned in this text, are frequently discovered in Jerusalem. These seals, called bullae, bore the name of the owner, sender, or scribe. When an ancient Hebrew letter or deed was written, it was folded and tied. For security a small lump of clay was pressed over the cord. The seal of the sender of the letter or one or more of the parties to the deed was pressed onto the clay to guarantee the document. Large numbers of bullae that were once attached to deeds like Jeremiah's have come to light, although the documents themselves have perished. When a building containing scrolls was burned, the fire quickly consumed the papyri documents but hardened the clay that comprised the bullae. Although these bullae are only half an inch to one inch in length, the hundreds of examples that have been discovered reveal that Jeremiah's action was part of a common process.

In 1982 excavations at Area G of the city of David reached the Babylonian destruction layer. On the lower terrace, just east of the remains of an Israelite four-room

house known as the house of Ahiel, a cache of fifty-one bullae were discovered.[12] For this reason the area has since been dubbed the "Bullae House." Among these inscribed bullae was the name of "Gemaryahu (Gemariah) the son of Shaphan," the scribe in the court of King Jehoiakim (see Jer 36:10–12, 25) who advised him not to burn the scroll of Jeremiah, which contained his prophecies from 627–605 BC (Jer 36:25). Adding to these names were those from other bullae that were part of a hoard of over 250 that surfaced in the Jerusalem antiquities market in 1975.[13] It is believed that they also came from David's City, but not being found in situ they lack the certainty of a find spot that the provenanced bullae enjoy. However, these bullae contain the names of Ishmael, the inter-exilic governor of Judah appointed by the Babylonians after Jerusalem's destruction who assassinated Gedaliah[14] and Berekhyahu ("Baruch") son of Neriyahu ("Neriah") the scribe.[15] This latter name may be a personal scribe of the prophet Jeremiah (Jer 36:4–7) who wrote the words of the prophet and may have had a part in sealing the documents mentioned in this passage.[16]

LAMENTATIONS

Lamentations 1:1–4a

An Archaeological Parallel: Mesopotamian Laments

> How deserted lies the city, once so full of people! How like a widow is she, who once was great among the nations! She who was queen among the provinces has now become a slave. Bitterly she weeps at night, tears are on her cheeks. Among all her lovers there is no one to comfort her. All her friends have betrayed her; they have become her enemies. After affliction and harsh labor, Judah has gone into exile. She dwells among the nations; she finds no resting place. All who pursue her have overtaken her in the midst of her distress. The roads to Zion mourn, for no one comes to her appointed festivals. (Lam 1:1–4a)

The Babylonian king Nebuchadnezzar II burned the city of Jerusalem and the First Temple with fire in 587/6 BC. The prophet Jeremiah, who had previously been taken to Egypt for his own safety, had to mourn its loss from afar. His lamentation (the English term comes from a Greek word meaning to "cry aloud") consists of five poems, the first four written as acrostics (each verse begins and continues in succession with a letter of the Hebrew alphabet). The city lament was a recognized literary form in the ancient Near East. Long before the prophet Jeremiah wrote his mournful words, the Sumerians inscribed similar words of woe on clay tablets in their city of Nippur. Like the book of Lamentations, these dirges contain five Mesopotamian city laments for their ruined cities of Sumer, Ur, Nippur, Eridu, and Uruk. One in particular, the lamentation for the city of Ur, contains words of mourning for the city after it fell to the Elamites (ca. 2000 BC). The

tablets describe the confusion and pain of the people over being abandoned by their gods, who failed to listen to their prayers. These lamentations resemble that of the prophet Jeremiah, not only in its expression of sorrow but also in its hope for eventual restoration. The lamentation over the destruction of Ur is represented by twenty-two fragmentary cuneiform tablets containing multiple copies of the lament. The opening text contains a lament for the various gods who have abandoned the city and the temple: "Ninlil has abandoned that house, the Ki-ur, and has let the breezes haunt her sheepfold. The queen of Kesh has abandoned it and has let the breezes haunt her sheepfold . . ."[17] This is close to Jeremiah's opening words comparing Jerusalem to a lonely widow, abandoned by the LORD: "How deserted lies the city, once so full of people! How like a widow is she, who once was great among the nations!" (Lam 1:1a), and also: "The LORD has rejected his altar and abandoned his sanctuary" (Lam 2:7a). The lamentation for Ur continues with a metaphor of a garden being knocked down, symbolizing the destroyed temple of Ur: "My faithful house . . . like a tent, a pulled-up harvest shed, like a pulled up harvest shed! Ur, my home filled with things, my well-filled house and city that were pulled up, were verily pulled up."[18] Sharing this metaphor, Jeremiah says: "He has laid waste his dwelling like a garden; he has destroyed his place of meeting" (Lam 2:6a). Similarly, the prophet Amos refers to Jerusalem (and the temple) as a "fallen shelter" (Amos 9:11). The lamentation of Ur follows with a sorrowful description of the destruction of its temple: "the good house of the lofty untouchable mountain, *E-kic-nu-jal*, was entirely devoured by large axes. The people of Cimacki and Elam, the destroyers, counted its worth as only thirty shekels. They broke up the good house with pickaxes. They reduced the city to ruin mounds."[19]

Jeremiah's words are similar with reference to the violation of the sanctity of the temple: "The enemy laid hands on all her treasures . . . and [the LORD] did not withhold his hand from destroying. He made ramparts and walls lament . . . their bars he has broken and destroyed . . ." (Lam 1:10; 2:8b, 9b). It is thought that the purpose for the composition of the Mesopotamian city laments was actually to win the favor of their gods and to persuade them not to let the city be destroyed again. If this is the correct interpretation of this literary form, then they were designed for a single purpose and for a single occasion and were retired after the city and temple were restored. It is possible, however, that they may have been revived in the Old Babylonian period for use in the temples to appease the anger of the gods. The biblical purpose, unlike the pagan attempt to placate or influence the gods, was to demonstrate genuine repentance, recognize the justice and sovereign purpose of God in the disaster, and to focus on God's covenant loyalty to Israel and the promise of restoration (see Lam 3:19–42).

Lamentation over the ruin of Ur (ca. 2000 BC)

EZEKIEL

Ezekiel 38:12

Israel's Central Position

> I will plunder and loot and turn my hand against the resettled ruins and the people gathered from the nations, rich in livestock and goods, living at the center of the land. (Ezek 38:12)

This text uses the Hebrew idiomatic phrase *tabbur ha'arets* ("the center of the land") with reference to the unique position of the people of Israel. The words are recorded as those of a coalition of nations who are planning an attack on Israel. However, it appears to reflect a statement that the Israelites used of themselves and that became a source of resentment for these nations. In the biblical text this expression appears in Judges 9:37, often translated "central hill," although the phrase is the same. The Ezekiel text gives the proper concept, and various English translations bring this out as: "center of the world," "center of the land," "navel of the earth," "middle of the land." In light of the Septuagint's translation as "navel" (LXX *omphalos*, cf. Vulgate *umbilicus*), connections have been suggested with the ancient Near Eastern mythological conception of sacred space in which the temple serves as the bond between heaven and earth. Some conjecture that the motif came through Ugaritic literature and passed into biblical literature by absorption from the Canaanite mythology of the cosmic mountain. The Canaanite god El is described as having placed his palace on a cosmic mountain, and in the ancient Near East temples were thought to have been the architectural embodiment of the cosmic mountain. In ancient Near Eastern cosmology the point where heavenly and earthly realms join is sometimes depicted as a garden of god. In Ezekiel 28:13–14 there is mention of "Eden, the garden of God" and "the holy mount of God." In Genesis 2–3 God's presence is in the garden of Eden, which contains a sacred tree and cherubim stationed at its entrance. These motifs were repeated in the decorations of the tabernacle and First Temple's outer curtains and interior paneling, as well its sacred furniture (1 Kgs 6:23, 29, 32; 7:29, 36). This does not mean that the Israelites thought in the same mythological terms as their neighbors but that the original source of God's design for his place on earth informed the common memory, with the Israelites preserving the more accurate concept through divine revelation.

Others argue that the phrase "center of the land" did not have this mythical sense when the Hebrew text was written but that it was attached to the expression during the Hellenistic period when it was translated by the LXX as *omphalos*, with its mythological connotations. However, the divine revelation established Mount Zion in Jerusalem as the "center of the land" with a spiritual orientation, resulting in a truth claim that distinguished it from the other nations. For this reason, talmudic and midrashic literature understood the phrase literally as "navel," with Jerusalem being the point from which the world was created and where the original garden of Eden had its nexus (b. Yoma 54b; Qodashim 10). This text in Ezekiel may have in view Mount Zion, which for the Israelites would represent the earth's [spiritual] "center," where the holy temple stood. This seems to find support in Ezekiel 5:5: "This is what the Sovereign LORD says: This is Jerusalem, which I have set in the center of the nations, with countries all around her." The psalmist's statement adds further support from the divine decision to center God's presence on Mount

Jerusalem at center of Israel on the Madaba Mosaic Map (6th century AD). Madaba, Jordan.

Zion: "For the LORD has chosen Zion, he has desired it for his dwelling, saying, 'This is my resting place for ever and ever; here I will sit enthroned, for I have desired it'" (Ps 132:13–14). This central position made Jerusalem, the capital city, the focus of enemy attack in the past, and according to Ezekiel's prediction for the last days (Ezek 38:16) it will be again in the future.

Ezekiel 43:10–11

Archaeological Examples of Temple Models

> Son of man, describe the temple to the people of Israel, that they may be ashamed of their sins. Let them consider its perfection, and if they are ashamed of all they have done, make known to them the design of the temple—its arrangement, its exits and entrances—its whole design and all its regulations and laws. Write these down before them so that they may be faithful to its design and follow all its regulations. (Ezek 43:10–11)

In preparing the Israelites in exile for their future restoration to their land, Ezekiel was instructed to give them plans for a new temple. This is reminiscent of God's original preparation for Israel's entrance to the land during the exodus, as Moses was instructed to give them plans for the tabernacle (Exod 25:9, 40; 26:30; 27:8; Num 8:4), and the plans for the First Temple under the rules of David and Solomon (1 Chr 28:11–19). In all of these accounts the word used for such plans is the Hebrew term *tabnit* ("model" or "pattern"), which was revealed to those who were to erect these structures. The term *tabnit* itself is somewhat difficult to translate because the intended meaning is less than certain. The Koehler-Baumgartner lexicon, for instance, gives as many as eight separate meanings, including "original, prototype, copy, duplicate, model, image, something like architect's plan."[20] Therefore, the term could denote either the original from which a replica is constructed or the actual replica itself.

According to the Bible, Moses and David were shown the *tabnit* in their respective roles in preparation for the building of the tabernacle and temple and received this information orally and by vision.[21] Five interpretations of the nature of the object designated by this revealed instruction have been offered: (1) an original miniature model; (2) a miniature model that is a copy of the original;[22] (3) an architect's blueprint or plan; (4) an architect's plan that is based on an original; (5) the original itself, i.e., the heavenly sanctuary.[23] The first, an original miniature model, was the view of the rabbis (b. Menahot 29a, Rashi and Ramban to Exod 25:9, 40), who stated that Moses was shown such a miniature model of the tabernacle and its furnishings, maintaining that it was necessary to help Moses understand the complex instructions. Even though the substance of the model conceived of by these commentators was one of miraculous fire, it was still envisaged as a teaching model that Moses, and later David, studied in order to communicate to the "skilled" workers (Exod 35:10; 1 Chr 28:21) the divine design. Hurowitz[24] contends that *tabnit* has in mind an exact copy of the structure to be made based on an analysis of the use of the term and its parallel expression *mar'eh* ("pattern") in several biblical passages (Exod 25:40; Num 8:4). He takes *tabnit* in its basic meaning of "form," "structure," or "shape" to denote a "replica."[25] In 1 Chronicles 28:11, 12, 19, he argues that it means "a (written) model blueprint," while in 1 Chronicles 18:28 it has the meaning of an actual "replica."[26] He also argues from 1 Kings 16:10 that a *tabnit* sent by King Ahaz to Uriah the priest is a depiction of the "original altar" seen by the king on a trip to Damascus and at the same time a "model" for the duplicate altar to be built and installed in the Jerusalem Temple (i.e., the original object that is to be imitated). Davidson thinks it probable "that Moses was given a vision of the heavenly sanctuary and then provided with a miniature model of the heavenly as a pattern to copy in constructing the earthly."[27] This understanding of the term prior to its use in Ezekiel enables us to see that the *tabnit* given by God to Ezekiel and by him to Israel is something the people are to "do" or "make" (Hebrew *'asah*), i.e., build. In other words, there is some detailed plan or model that the Israelites are to follow in their construction of the future temple.

In the ancient Near East the heavenly or cosmic mountain served as the model for temples, cult objects, and laws.[28] In this tradition, F. M. Cross argues that the *tabnit* was a cosmic tabernacle, a concept of the earthly/cosmic dualism that Israel borrowed from the Canaanites.[29] However, there is no warrant for this supposition; rather, Israelite and ancient Near Eastern practices reflect a common source. In archaeological reliefs that depict a ziggurat or temple design, there may be either a sketch of the plans or an actual model. Such is probably the case with a black stone stele that was part of a private collection and published for the first time in 2011. Known as the Tower of Babel stele, it contains a cuneiform inscription and a standing figure of Nebuchadnezzar II portrayed with his royal conical hat, holding a staff in his left hand and a scroll with the rebuilding plans of the tower (though some think it an engraving pen or a foundation nail) in his outstretched right hand.[30] The main image is of the ziggurat-temple design, both in built form and reconstruction plans. If the object in the hand of the king is a copy of the building plans or an engraving pen or stylus for drawing these plans, there is an additional image connected with the biblical concept of *tabnit*.

There are also terracotta models of temples found in the ancient Near East. The site of Khirbet Qeiyafa, a tenth-century-BC site near the valley of Elah, produced clay models of shrines with parallels to the later architectural features in the First Temple. These were probably used as part of cultic rituals because the town was a distance from the worship installations in Gibeon (2 Chr 1:3) and Jerusalem (2 Chr 1:13). Their design, however, may illustrate the concept of *tabnit* that Ezekiel and related texts have in view.

Clay model of a temple. Lourve, Paris.

Alexander Schick

DANIEL

Daniel 1:1, 3, 4

Archaeology and the Date of the Book of Daniel

In the third year of the reign of Jehoiakim king of Judah, Nebuchadnezzar king of Babylon came to Jerusalem and besieged it.... Then the king ordered Ashpenaz, chief of his court officials, to bring into the king's service some of the Israelites from the royal family and the nobility ... to teach them the language and literature of the Babylonians.... Among those who were chosen were some from Judah: Daniel ... (Dan 1:1, 3, 4b, 6a)

Jewish tradition as a whole regarded the book of Daniel to reflect a genuine sixth-century-BC-exilic origin, included the book within the Hebrew canon,[31] and originally ranked its author as a biblical prophet.[32] In the New Testament this position was assumed, with New Testament writers citing Daniel as a prophet and employing the book as an example of predictive prophecy (cf. Dan 9:27; 12:11 in Matt 24:15; Mark 13:14; 2 Thess 2:4; and an allusion in Rev 11:2 and a possible prophetic pattern for Rev 6–19). This is especially the case with Jesus, who does not refer to a book called Daniel but to the agency of Daniel personally (as implied by the use of the Greek preposition *dia*, "by").

However, the majority of modern scholars assume a second-century-BC date for Daniel, understanding its historically accurate predictions of events in the Hellenistic and Maccabean periods to require it to have been composed after this time. While some would trace the first statement of this date for the book to Neoplatonist Porphyry (AD 233–305),[33] the scholarly statements of this view stem from the eighteenth century by J. D. Michaelis and J. C. Eichhorn,[34] both of whom maintained that the final form of Daniel was a pseudonymous product of the late postexilic Maccabean period (168–165 BC). Hebrew lexicographer S. R. Driver also held this opinion.[35] Since Driver's work, the traditional sixth-century date has been regarded by critical scholars as no longer defensible, although it continues to be accepted and defended by some conservative scholars.[36]

While the question of the date of Daniel involves many issues related to the internal evidence of the book, the presence of foreign loanwords (e.g., Persian and Greek), alleged chronological and historical problems, and the nature of predictive prophecy, archaeology can aid in answering the question by offering information on how the book was interpreted in an ancient context and providing manuscript copies whose date helps set a limit for dating theories. In this regard, the discovery of at least ten fragments of Daniel among the Dead Sea Scrolls and the discovery of sectarian documents that cite or allude to the book and reveal ancient interpretation offer significant data for one area of research on this matter.

First, it is important to consider the influence of Daniel on the Qumran community, which began in the second century BC and continued through the first century AD. The earliest record of Daniel's prophetic character is preserved at Qumran, where the book and its predictions played a central role in its apocalyptic community and probably indicated its acceptance on an order approaching canonical status.[37] Its significance as prophecy at Qumran is attested by its frequent citation, especially of Daniel 9–12 (e.g., Dan 11–12 is cited in the eschatological midrash known as the Florilegium [4Q174]) and the many pseudepigraphal imitations that have been discovered (e.g., the Prayer of Nabonidus), as well as the more recent collection of apocalyptic fragments in quasi-prophetic form known as Pseudo-Daniel (4Q243–245). Of special interest to our discussion is the explicit reference in 4Q174 2.3, in which a period of "tribulation" is predicted "as it is written in the book of Daniel the prophet." In weighing this evidence, we must conclude with Koch "that there is no single witness for the exclusion of Daniel from the prophetic corpus in the first half of the first millennium AD. In all the sources of the first century AD—the LXX, Qumran, Josephus, Jesus, and the New Testament writers—Daniel is reckoned among the prophets. In fact the earliest literary evidence of Daniel's inclusion among the third division of the Hebrew Bible, called *ketubim* ("writings") is to be placed somewhere between the fifth and eighth centuries AD."[38]

The book of Daniel was no doubt used as a primary text in the formation of the early movement. As scroll translator and scholar Shemaryahu Talmon states it, "Daniel had, without any doubt, tremendous effects."[39] One of these effects may have come through Daniel's reference to a group of wise men called in Hebrew *maskilim*. This elect company is those of the last days who will understand God's mysterious plan soon to be consummated (Dan 12:4, 9–10). Their eschatological hope is for a rescue of the Jewish remnant in a time of unparalleled tribulation (Dan 12:1–2) and a resurrection of the righteous (Dan 12:3). Their special discernment of the times and influence for righteousness will set them uniquely apart (Dan 12:10). The writers of the Scrolls patterned themselves after these ideals, perhaps even to their custom of wearing linen garments after the fashion of Daniel's "man clothed in linen," who interpreted the chronology of the end time events (Dan 12:6–7). Some have thought that Daniel's prophecy of the seventy weeks (Dan 9:24–27) also may have been adapted for the sect's chronological scheme (see ch. 8).[40] These examples reveal something of Daniel's profound influence on the biblical interpretation of the Qumran sect and appear to confirm that they regarded the composition of Daniel as a genuine prophecy that long preceded their own sect.

Another witness to the influence of Daniel at Qumran is the popularity of the book for the sect. There are some nine copies of Daniel represented by some twenty-two fragments. These fragments came from caves 1, 4, and 6 and have thus been designated as 1QDan[a–b] (1Q71–72), 4QDan[a–e] (4Q112–116), and 6QpapDan (6Q7), and one fragment of Daniel 5 (with a textual variant) allegedly from Cave 4 is now in private hands. Altogether, these fragments attest to chapters 1–11 in Daniel, while chapter 12 is briefly cited in the Florilegium (4Q174): Dan 12:10 in 4Q174 2.3, 4.[41] The Scrolls also contain other witnesses to biblical Daniel such as the Pseudo-Daniel fragments (4Q243–245), Pseudo-Daniel apocalypses (4Q246, 4Q547), related apocryphal documents (4Q550, 4QPrNab), and parallels in other apocalypses (e.g., 4Q174, cf. 4Q180–181). The fragmentary copies of Daniel date from the late second century BC to the middle of the first century AD. On the basis of paleography, they are comparable to the Great Isaiah Scroll A (1QIsa[a]) and the Pesher Habakkuk (1QpHab) and therefore cannot be dated later than 125 BC.[42] This makes a significant point for the limit of dating the book to the second century BC, since such a close date to the

supposed autograph (Maccabean period) presents difficulties because there would be insufficient time for such copies to be produced, distributed, and then received within Judaism. In addition, linguistic comparisons of Qumranic *midrashim* of the third–second centuries BC with the Aramaic and Hebrew chapters of these Daniel fragments have revealed matching traits in vocabulary, style, morphology, and syntax. This same sort of evidence for the dating of Chronicles forced Jacob Meyers to contend: "The discovery of a fragment of Chronicles at Qumran renders a Maccabean date virtually impossible for any part of Chronicles."[43] This has also been the case for the dating of Ecclesiastes based on two Scroll copies found in Cave 4[44] and for many of the Psalms.[45] Frank Cross revised the dates of their autographs on the basis of the new Qumran evidence: "Ecclesiastes, sometimes dated in the second, or even in the first century BC, by older scholars, appears in one exemplar from Cave IV (4QQoha), which dates ca. 175–150 BC. Since the text of the manuscript reveals textual development, it is demonstrably not the autograph, and hence the date of the composition must be pushed back into the third century. A second-century BC copy of the canonical Psalter (4QPsaa), though fragmentary, indicates that the collection of canonical psalms in the Persian period."[46]

Though a Maccabean provenance has been a problem that forced a reassessment of the late date of other books,[47]

Fragment of 1QDaniel[a] (1:10–17; 2:2–6)

this has not been the case with Daniel. Rather, Cross, views Daniel as exceptional, celebrating the fact that the chronological distance from the original was reduced to "no more than a half century younger than the autograph, ca. 168–165."[48] However, given the care exercised by this strict sect in biblical interpretation, its apparent rejection of Maccabean dynastic rule and its priesthood, it is exceptional that the sect would regard the book as Scripture and give it the prominent place it occupied in the sect's prophetic perspective. Scholars have used the Pseudo-Daniel texts and the Prayer of Nabonidus (that has parallels to Dan 4) among the scrolls to argue for a late composition, claiming that material in biblical Daniel was dependent on these intertestamental works. There is simply no precedent of a canonical Jewish book being dependent on an intertestamental noncanonical literary source, while there is abundant evidence that the reverse is true.[49] On the other hand, this evidence of flourishing Danielic pseudepigraphs may attest to a popular trend in copying biblical Daniel, who was recognized as a prophet and whose own apocalyptic composition, the book of Daniel, had already become canonized, or at least a standard reference for apocalyptic chronology. It seems to have served this purpose at Qumran, as it did through a long tradition of later Danielic-style apocalypses that continued down to the Middle Ages.[50]

However, while the early semicursive script of 4QDan[c] (4Q114) has been dated to the late second century BC, the Hebrew of Daniel compared linguistically with that of other Qumran Scrolls makes this impossible. After a comparative analysis by Gleason Archer of the syntax and morphology, the use of postbiblical words, postbiblical pronunciation and spelling, and words used with a postbiblical meaning, he concluded:

> In light of all the data adduced under the four categories just reviewed, it seems abundantly clear that a second-century date for the Hebrew chapters of Daniel is no longer tenable on linguistic grounds.

In view of the markedly later development exhibited by these second-century documents in the areas of syntax, word order, morphology, vocabulary, spelling, and word-usage, there is absolutely no possibility of regarding Daniel as contemporary. On the contrary the indications are that centuries must have intervened between them . . . Otherwise we must surrender linguistic evidence altogether and assert that it is completely devoid of value in the face of subjective theories derived from antisupernaturalistic bias . . . If all of the book was written even as early as the third century (and there really is nothing in the linguistic data to militate against a late sixth-century composition by the ostensible author himself), the supernatural element of fulfilled prediction would still remain.[51]

This conclusion also seems to be supported by a comparative analysis of the Aramaic of Daniel with the Aramaic Elephantine Papyri from Upper Egypt, which are dated to the fifth century BC. British Egyptologist Kenneth Kitchen demonstrated that 90 percent of Daniel's Aramaic vocabulary occurred in documents dated to the fifth century BC or earlier, that Persian loanwords were Old Persian, and that Greek loanwords also could precede the fifth century BC. In addition, some syntactical forms in Daniel were shown to have not survived beyond the fifth century BC, precluding any later date.[52] He thus concluded: "The Aramaic of Daniel (and of Ezra) is simply a part of Imperial (Official) Aramaic—in itself, practically undateable with any conviction within c. 600 to 330 BC."[53] Kitchen's view was supported by University of Liverpool Semiticist Alan Millard,[54] as well as by the leading Aramaist E. Y. Kutscher, who showed from Daniel's Aramaic word order that the provenance was Eastern (Babylon), not Western (Palestine), as the Maccabean date required.[55] Gleason Archer compared the Aramaic of the Genesis Apocryphon (1Q20), dated to the first century BC,[56] with that of Daniel and concluded that the latter was centuries later than the former.[57] When the Aramaic Targum of Job (11QtgJob) was published, scholars agreed that it was younger than the Aramaic of Daniel, but older than the Aramaic of the argumryphon.[58] Working from the assumption of a fixed date for Daniel in the Maccabean period (mid-second century BC), some scholars then attempted to push the date of 11QtgJob to the first century BC and 1Q20 to the first century AD. However, in a comparative study of these texts Robert Vasholz determined that the date of 11QtgJob was late third to early second century BC, a century older than 1Q20.[59] This evidence demands that Daniel, acknowledged as older than 11QtgJob, be pre-Maccabean in origin. In addition, A. York's similar study revealed that 11QtgJob, which corresponds to Job 40:10–11, alludes to Nebuchadnezzar and indisputably reflects the vocabulary of Daniel 3:13, 19; 4:33–34; and 5:20.[60] This, then, would

make the Qumran Targum of Job dependent on some copy of Daniel older than itself. Furthermore, the Daniel fragments, especially 1Q72, show that Daniel was used at Qumran (both in its Hebrew and Aramaic parts) without the expansions found in the Greek. This was apparently the same canonical Hebrew-Aramaic text of Daniel used by the first-century-AD Jewish writer Josephus, since his account of the story of Daniel also lacked any knowledge of these deuterocanonical additions.[61] This suggests that more than one Hebrew recension of Daniel was made prior to the Septuagint translation (ca. 200 BC). As a result of the weight of this evidence, Gerhard Hasel concluded: "The Aramaic documents from Qumran push the date of the composition into a period earlier than the Maccabean date allows. Thus the alternative [early] date for Daniel in the sixth or fifth century BC has more in its favor today from the point of view of language alone than ever before."[62]

HOSEA

Hosea 4:12–13

The Ancient Literature and Iconography of Sacred Trees and Groves

> My people consult a wooden idol, and a diviner's rod speaks to them. A spirit of prostitution leads them astray; they are unfaithful to their God. They sacrifice on the mountaintops and burn offerings on the hills, under oak, poplar and terebinth, where the shade is pleasant. (Hos 4:12–13)

This text depicts the ancient Israelites prostituting themselves by associating with the worship rites of the fertility religions of Canaan. Instead of seeking Yahweh's presence at the temple, Israel sought the mountaintops and gardens or groves—sacred places in antiquity where the gods of antiquity were thought to dwell or manifest their

presence in a special way. "Descriptions of the gardens in Ancient Near Eastern literature mention springs, trees possessing divine attributes, and the overall beauty and fertility of the place. The trees on 'the cedar mountain, the dwelling of the gods' mentioned in the Gilgamesh Epic, are said to be luxuriant."[63] This text states: "They stood still and gazed at the forest, they looked at the height of the cedars, they looked at the entrance of the forest . . . They beheld the cedar mountain, abode of the gods, Throne-seat of Irnini. From the face of the mountain the cedars raise aloft their luxuriance. Good is their shade, full of delight" (Epic of Gilgamesh 5:1–4; see *ANET*, 82). "Throughout the Ancient Near Eastern literature, occasional descriptions of sacred trees with magical powers are known. The kiskanu tree is referred to in Akkadian incantation and magical texts as having some special healing powers. It grows in a pure, abundant place in Eridu. The features of the location remind us of the image of the garden of the gods."[64]

Sacred trees are also attested on ancient Near Eastern artifacts. The Brooklyn Museum houses twelve stone slabs with carved decoration from the Northwest Palace of Ashurnasirpal II. The motif of a stylized tree—the so-called sacred tree—appears on seven of those slabs, which come from (particular rooms of) the ninth-century palace of Nimrud.[65] Carvings of bird-headed creatures with wings, possibly of divine origin, are also seen in conjunction with the sacred tree reliefs from the northwest palace.[66] The use of foreign elements such as these in Israelite worship led to religious apostasy in the forms of outright idolatry (worship of another god in place of the God of Israel), henotheism (worship of the God of Israel under names of other local deities), and syncretism (mixing the worship of the God of Israel with pagan religious practices). All of these practices violated the Mosaic covenant (Exod 20:4, 23; 34:17; Lev 19:4; 26:1) and invited divine judgment (Deut 4:23–24; 28:15). Ultimately, it was because of this kind of idolatry that the northern kingdom went into Assyrian captivity (2 Kgs 17:7–12, 15–18, 23), and a century later idolatry (the sin of King Manasseh) sent Judah into the Babylonian exile (2 Kgs 24:3; 2 Chr 33:2–9).

Trees were also associated with ancient temple sites.[67] Botanic images such as palm trees were part of the interior architecture in Solomon's Temple and its furniture (1 Kgs 6–7).[68] Their purpose was to remind Israel that God was present among them in the same way he had been with Adam and Eve in the garden.[69] The divine ideal was to restore mankind to this pristine relationship between the creator and creature. However, pagan theology had corrupted this original idea and turned wooded groves into sacred shrines of the fertility deities and their cults. The archaeological reliefs depicting these sacred trees illustrate Hosea's struggle against a pervasive motif in his culture despite the command of Deuteronomy 12:2–3: "Destroy completely all the places on the high mountains, on the hills and under every spreading tree, where the nations you are dispossessing worship their gods. Break down their altars, smash their sacred stones and burn their Asherah poles in the fire; cut down the idols of their gods and wipe out their names from those places."

Relief from the Northwest Palace of Ashurnasirpal II depicting bird-headed winged creatures in conjunction with sacred tree

AMOS

Amos 3:2

Analogy with Suzerain-Vassal Relationships

> You only have I chosen of all the families of the earth; therefore I will punish you for all your sins. (Amos 3:2)

The Hebrew term used here for "chosen" is *bahar* and, with respect to the nation Israel, has the idea of divine selection resulting in the notion of a "chosen people" (Deut 7:6; Ezek 20:5). "'But I have been the LORD your God ever since you came out of Egypt. You shall acknowledge no God but me, no Savior except me. I cared for you in the wilderness, in the land of burning heat'" (Hos. 13:4–5). The LORD has a case to make against the inhabitants of the land. "There is no faithfulness, no love, no acknolwedgment of God in the land" (Hos 4:1). These verses support the idea presented here in Amos that God has assumed responsibility for the welfare of Israel based on his covenant with them at Mount Sinai. The background for this can be seen in the relationship defined in the suzerain-vassal treaty.

Archaeological discoveries have unearthed some fifty examples of ancient near Eastern vassal treaties from the middle of the third millennium BC to the middle of the first millennium BC. However, the precise structure of the mid-second-millennium-BC Hittite treaties best define the relations between a suzerain (a superior) and vassal (inferior) in ways that provide literary and conceptual parallels to the covenant God made with Israel at Mount Sinai (the book of the covenant, Exod 20:1–23:33) and renewed on the plains of Moab. It is this latter renewal of the covenant found in the book of Deuteronomy that is modeled on the Bronze Age Hittite vassal treaty format.[70] Examples of the Hittite vassal treaties include the Aleppo Treaty, a tablet written in Akkadian recording a suzerainty treaty made around 1300 BC between Mursili II, king of the Hittites (1339–1306 BC), and Talmi-sharruma of Aleppo in northern Syria. This suzerainty treaty between the powerful king of the Hittites (the suzerain) and the weaker king of Aleppo (the vassal) established Hittite dominance over Aleppo and regulated the relationship between the two kingdoms. Another example is the Treaty of Kadesh (1259 BC), a peace agreement made between the Egyptian Pharaoh Ramesses II and the Hittite King Hattusili III.

In these treaties, if the relationship is familial or friendly, the parties are referred to as "father" and "son." If the relationship is not intimate, the parties are referred to as "lord" and "servant," or "king" and "vassal." In either case the vassal is in the service of the

Hittite vassal (Aleppo) treaty

A. D. Riddle/BiblePlaces.com, taken at the British Musem

suzerain but also under his protection. These suzerain-vassal treaties have a preamble section that identifies the suzerain by his name and titles and demonstrates to the vassal how much he has done to protect the vassal, who owes submission and allegiance. The next section lists the stipulations, or what the vassal is required to do to demonstrate his submission and loyalty to the suzerain. A final section contains the suzerain's blessings (for obedience) and curses (for disobedience). In the preamble the suzerain makes a vassal his own through various acts and, on occasion, promises to know the vassal and to provide security and instructions for loyal behavior, and in turn a vassal responds to the suzerain and on occasion promises to know his overlord when pledging his continuing loyalty and obedience to the great king's stipulations. This understanding from ancient covenant formulation when applied to our passage reveals that the LORD (the suzerain) has

identified himself with Israel (the vassal) as their God and they as his people. Like the Hittite treaties, Israel's obligation as a vassal to their suzerain is in response to his gracious acts on their behalf (Deut 7:6; 14:2; 26:18). He delivered them from the power of Pharaoh and has given them an opportunity to serve him (Exod 19:3–5; 20:2; cf. Jer 11:1–8). This intimate relationship sets them apart from all other nations on earth as those with divine treaty obligations. The LORD is obligated to protect them because he uniquely knows (chose) them as his vassals, and they know (chose) him (cf. Exod 19:8; 24:3, 7) as their suzerain and will obey him. The failure to obey will bring divine punishment, as this verse promises. If, by comparison, Israel appeared to the nations to suffer divine discipline disproportionately, this text assures Israel (and the nations) that it is only because they are the chosen people and that the discipline demonstrates this relationship.

JONAH

Jonah 3:5–8

Events Leading to Nineveh's Repentance in 758 BC

The Ninevites believed God. A fast was proclaimed, and all of them, from the greatest to the least, put on sackcloth. When Jonah's warning reached the king of Nineveh, he rose from his throne, took off his royal robes, covered himself with sackcloth and sat down in the dust. This is the proclamation he issued in Nineveh: "By the decree of the king and his nobles: Do not let people or animals, herds or flocks, taste anything; do not let them eat or drink. But let people and animals be covered with sackcloth. Let everyone call urgently on God. Let them give up their evil ways and their violence." (Jonah 3:5–8)

G. Aalders identifies a common consensus still shared among Old Testament scholars: "In examining the vast literature on the book of Jonah we observe how widespread is the idea that the aim of the author was not to give an account of historical events, but to present a fiction with a moral tendency."[71] The story of Jonah, therefore, is often reduced to mere allegory or parable, with little concern for historical accuracy. Scholars typically point to Jonah's survival in the belly of large fish, Nineveh's mass repentance, and the supernatural growth of the plant as evidence for the book's disinterest in communicating a historically reliable message. However, an equally unexplainable phenomena is the entire city's repentance.

Donald J. Wiseman contends that there is sufficient historical evidence that explains the mass repentance of the Ninevites in response to Jonah's terse prophetic announcement (Jonah 3:4). Wiseman reminds us that the ancient Near East began chronicling astronomic phenomena around the first millennium BC and relating their celestial observations to contemporary and future events. A solar eclipse was considered as one of the more exceptional sightings in antiquity; the event was interpreted in a supernatural way and was always thought to precede a coming calamity.[72] It is important to note that these omens were always directed toward "the country as a whole or at the royal family and nobles and at the overthrow of the dynasty and city."[73] For example, the Assyrian Eponym List recorded a solar eclipse in 763 BC that happened to occur during the reign of Jeroboam II (782–753 BC).[74] In particular, the Enuma Anu Enlil contains a few statements related to these eclipses: "'the king will be deposed and killed and a worthless fellow seize the throne'; 'the king will die, rain from heaven will flood the land. There will be famine'; 'a deity will strike the king and fire consume the land'; 'the city-walls will be destroyed.'"[75] Famines too had a similar supernatural significance to the Assyrians. "It may be no coincidence that among the references to the reign of Assur-dan III of Assyria [eighteen-year reign beginning at 773 BC] in the eponym lists are several to famine (*mutanu*) whether at the beginning and end of, or throughout, a period of seven years."[76] Earthquakes

were also associated with the supernatural sphere: "'When the god Adad is angry the earth trembles'; [. . .] 'When you O god (Ninurta) march, heaven and earth quake.'"[77] Interesting, "[e]arthquakes are recorded at Nineveh in the time of Shalmaneser I [. . .] and for the month Siwan in the reign of Assur-dan (possibly the contemporary of Jeroboam)."[78]

Certainly these events and perhaps additional omens cultivated a particular environment in Nineveh that could have resulted in the mass repentance as recorded in Jonah 3:5–8. In light of these historical events, which occurred in the late eighth century BC, a message of divine wrath from a seer like Jonah in this theologically supercharged and polytheistic context may have confirmed what the Assyrians' omens were already saying.

Events Leading to Nineveh's Repentance in 758 BC	
787	Monotheistic worship of Nabu started
765	Plague throughout Assyria
763	Revolt in the city of Asshur
763	Eclipse of the sun
762	Revolt in the city of Asshur
761	Revolt in the city of Arrapha
760	Revolt in the city of Arrapha
759	Another plague
758	"Peace in the land" (repentance under Jonah?)

NAHUM

Nahum 2:3–7

The Fall of Nineveh in the Babylonian Chronicle

The shields of the soldiers are red; the warriors are clad in scarlet. The metal on the chariots flashes on the day they are made ready; the

spears of juniper are brandished. The chariots storm through the streets, rushing back and forth through the squares. They look like flaming torches; they dart about like lightning. Nineveh summons her picked troops, yet they stumble on their way. They dash to the city wall; the protective shield is put in place. The river gates are thrown open and the palace collapses. It is decreed that Nineveh be exiled and carried away. Her female slaves moan like doves and beat on their breasts. (Nah 2:3–7)

The Babylonian Chronicles, clay tablets that describe the history of the Babylonian kings and their conquests from the eighth–second centuries BC, include a tablet that gives information about the destruction of Nineveh. W. F. Albright contends, "The Babylonian Chronicle and related texts from the eight–sixth centuries BC are generally recognized as the most objective and historically reliable annals that have come down to us from the ancient Orient."[79] The book of Nahum is the prophetic warning to Nineveh that God will allow her to be destroyed. This prophecy was literally fulfilled in 612 BC, when Nabopolassar the Babylonian king and Cyaxares the Median king conquered the city. While Nahum's account is more graphic and telling, his record is congruent with the history in the Babylonian Chronicles.

Coalition between the Media and Babylonian forces brought siege to Nineveh:

The king of Akkad cal[led up] his army and [Cyaxar]es, the king of Mandahordes (*Umman-manda*) marched towards the king of Akkad, [in] … they met each other. The king of Akkad … and [Cyaxar]es … [the …]s he ferried across and they marched (upstream) on the embankment of the Tigris and . . . [pitched camp] against Nineveh." (*ANET* 304)

They stumble on their way. They dash to the city wall; the protective shield is put in place. (Nah 2:5b)

Nineveh is destroyed and plundered while a few Assyrians flee:

From the month Simanu till the month Abu, three ba[ttles were fought, then] they made a great attack against the city. In the month Abu, [the … th day, the city was seized and a great defeat] he inflicted [upon the] entire [population]. On that day, Sinsharishkun, king of Assy[ria fled to] . . . , many prisoners of the city, beyond counting, they carried away. The city [they turned] into ruin-hills and hea[ps (of debris). The king] and the army of Assyria escaped (however) before the king (of Akkad) and [the army] of the king of Akkad. (*ANET* 304–5)

The river gates are thrown open and the palace collapses. It is decreed that Nineveh be exiled and carried away. (Nah 2:6–7)

Babylonian Chronicle (BM 21901) mentioning the fall of Nineveh

© 2013 by Zondervan

HABAKKUK

Habakkuk 1:6–7, 15

Archaeological Evidence of Ancient Near Eastern Cruelty

> I am raising up the Babylonians, that ruthless and impetuous people, who sweep across the whole earth to seize dwellings not their own. They are a feared and dreaded people; they are a law to themselves and promote their own honor. . . . The wicked foe pulls all of them up with hooks, he catches them in his net, he gathers them up in his dragnet; and so he rejoices and is glad. (Hab 1:6–7, 15)

Habakkuk opens this chapter with a complaint to God for the iniquity and wickedness of his people and receives the unexpected reply from the LORD that he was raising up the Chaldeans to discipline Israel. This is followed by a description of the cruelty and brutality of this people who treated their captives like fish caught in a net. Such fearsome tactics employed by ancient Near Eastern armies were bent on intimidating its enemies. Ancient texts refer to military torture and mutilation as a means of both physical and psychological subjugation. An account of the Assyrian King Ashurnasirpal reports: "when a city resisted as long as possible instead of immediately submitting, Ashurnasirpal proudly records his punishment: 'I flayed as many nobles as had rebelled against me [and] draped their skins over the pile [of corpses]; some I spread out within the pile, some I erected on stakes upon the pile . . . I flayed many right through my land [and] draped their skins over the walls.'"[80] Another gruesome account that certainly would have intimidated any enemy reads: "I felled 50 of their fighting men with the sword, burnt 200 captives

Assyrian soldiers recording number of slain prisoners (by head count). British Museum.

from them, [and] defeated in a battle on the plain 332 troops. . . . With their blood I dyed the mountain red like red wool, [and] the rest of them the ravines [and] torrents of the mountain swallowed. I carried off captives [and] possessions from them. I cut off the heads of their fighters [and] built [therewith] a tower before their city. I burnt their adolescent boys [and] girls."[81]

A visual record of such acts of atrocity to prisoners often lined walls and covered the floors of Assyrian and Babylonian palaces and temples.[82] One famous example is the 90-foot long Lachish relief from the palace of Sennacherib in Nineveh. It depicts the Assyrian practice of dismembering enemy bodies by pealing off their skin, decapitating their heads, impaling their bodies on poles, putting hooks in noses, and cutting off the hands of victims. The first actual remains of piles of severed hands were uncovered in excavations at the Hyksos palace at Tell ed-Dab'a (ancient Avaris). In pits in the northern part of the palace (dated to 1600 BC), archaeologists Manfred Bietak and Irene Forstner-Müller found sixteen severed hands.[83] This gruesome practice has not been thought to be native to northern Canaan, from which the Hyksos are thought to have originated, but was an established practice of the Egyptians. If so, the Hyksos of the Fifteenth Dynasty (New Kingdom) may have adopted it to conform to Egyptian military protocol.

Such horrific accounts help explain the astonishment of Habakkuk when informed that these cruel enemies of Israel would be used to perform the spiritual surgery necessary to bring repentance and return the people to pure worship.

ZEPHANIAH

Zephaniah 2:4

The End of Ekron

> Gaza will be abandoned and Ashkelon left in ruins. At midday Ashdod will be emptied and Ekron uprooted. (Zeph 2:4)

The best known enemy of Israel in the Bible was the Philistines. They emerged from a group of Aegean Sea Peoples that invaded the coastal plain of Canaan in the twelfth century BC. During the time of the judges they become Israel's most formidable foe and occupy a large place in the early history of Israel, crossing paths with Samson, Samuel, Saul, and David. King David managed to bring the Philistine territory under Israelite control as a tributary (2 Sam 8:12; 1 Kgs 4:24), and Philistia was forced to pay tribute (2 Chr 27:11), but border conflicts continued between them (1 Kgs 25:27). One of the earliest of the Philistine cities, Ekron, was a border town among the Philistine pentapolis that became one of the leading commercial centers of the eighth century BC because of its quality olive oil production. It was mentioned prominently in the Assyrian annals, and when it came under Neo-Assyrian control (ca. 700 BC) its capture was displayed on a relief in the palace of Sargon II. After this, Ekron re-urbanized, and its olive oil industry flourished. But in 625 BC the prophet Zephaniah announced God's condemnation of Ekron, and in 603 BC the prophecy was fulfilled when the Neo-Babylonian king Nebuchadnezzar II invaded Philistia and destroyed Ekron. With this destruction came the end of the Philistine material culture. The Babylonian uprooting of Ekron was so complete that its very location was unknown until the late twentieth century.

The suspected site of the ancient Philistine city was Tel Miqne, based on its geographical situation at the junction of the coastal plain and the hill country of Judah. From 1983–97 Israeli archaeologist Trude Dotan and American archeologist Sy Gittin did a thorough excavation, but, while the archaeological artifacts emerging from the tel appeared distinctively Philistine, no direct evidence had been found to positively identify it as Ekron. Then on the last day of the fourteenth season of excavation in Field 4, Steve Ortiz overturned a 220-pound rough hewn stone and thought it might be a stela. The archaeologists had seen hundreds of stones like this and had been disappointed each time they had searched the rough scratches that they hoped would form ancient letters. This time, however, was different, and when properly examined an inscription was plainly visible. It was the key to identifying the site as Ekron. The "scratches" formed seventy-two letters in five lines of text in Philistine (Phonecian) script. From the wording and orthography it was identified as

Ekron inscription

Kim Walton. The Israel Museum, Jerusalem.

a dedicatory inscription from a royal Philistine temple. The text reads: "This temple was built by 'Akish, son of Padi, son of Yasid, son of Ada, son of Ya'ir, ruler of Ekron, for *Ptgyh*, his (divine) lady [perhaps referring to Asherah]. May she bless him, and guard him, and prolong his days, and bless his land."[84] The inscription clearly mentions both the name of the king and the name of his city—Ekron. It is extremely rare to find a monumental inscription with the name of a biblical site and its rulers in situ and in a datable destruction level. This not only confirmed the site but allowed every find uncovered over the past fourteen years to be put into a datable historical context.

The finds from the rooms of the multi-storied Philistine palace, built in a Neo-Assyrian style with an Egyptian-style monumental, colonnaded entrance hall to the throne room, included a golden cobra, a uraeus meant to be affixed to a statuette of Egyptian royalty or of a deity, Egyptian-style scarab seals, and a faience amulet of Ptah-patecus, the Egyptian god of craftsmen. These artifacts afford archaeological examples of the pagan influence criticized by this prophet (Zeph 1:4–8). These finds reveal the commercial and cultural links of Ekron with Egypt and as such reflect the political shift that led to its attack by the Babylonians. It also reveals the foreign influence exerted by this Philistine city that affected the Israelites and brought them into idolatry and cultic corruption, leading ultimately to their predicted destruction (Zeph. 2:4–7).

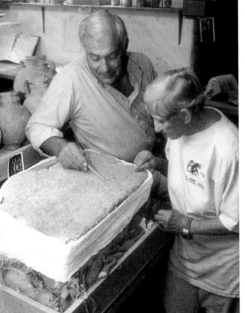

Sy Gitin & Trude Dothan with Ekron Inscription.

© 1995 by Phoenix Data Systems

ZECHARIAH

Zechariah 4:2

The Seven-spouted Lampstand

> He asked me, "What do you see?" I answered, "I see a solid gold lampstand with a bowl at the top and seven lamps on it, with seven channels to the lamps." (Zech 4:2)

In this verse the postexilic prophet Zechariah describes a *menorat zahab* ("golden lampstand") with *shib'a mutsaqot* ("seven spouts") that he saw in one of his visions. Commentators are divided as to whether this description was a unique oil lamp (visionary), the traditional type of lampstand used in the tabernacle and temple, or a special type of lamp used for ritual purposes. While there are disputes over both the MT and the meaning of key terms in the description, most scholars note the features of this lamp as a bowl-like receptacle/reservoir, *gullah* (literally, "curved upper part") resting on top of a cylindrical base or pedestal with the rim of the bowl pinched to form small indentions/spouts, *mutsaqot* (from *tsuq*, literally "narrowness") in which olive oil soaked wicks could lay.[85]

Examples of terracotta seven-spouted oil lamps have been found in archaeological excavations from as early as the Middle and Late Bronze Ages (ca. 2250–1200 BC), but more commonly from the Iron Age (ca. 1200–600 BC).[86] Such ceramic lamps resemble a chalice with flared bottom (for support) and seven spouts formed by pinching the lip of the clay rim together before drying. Most are simple and undecorated and burned olive oil almost exclusively (Exod 25:6), with wicks generally made of twisted flax (Isa 42:3). Archaeology provides numerous examples of cultic stands with this shape, a common form throughout the ancient Near East for two thousand years. Examples from Israel of seven-spouted lamps (with and without pedestals) were found at Taanek (1300 BC), Dothan (1200 BC), Gezer (1000–550 BC), Ain Shems (900 BC), Megiddo I (780–650 BC), Lachish (710 BC) Murabba'at (600 BC), and Tel Dan (ca. 900 BC). The relatively few examples of this lampstand may imply that they were used only for special purposes, such as in cultic ceremonies. The fine example at Tel Dan and its association with the *bama* in the cultic area (Area T, Iron IIB) seems to indicate a ritual use.

Some scholars suggest that this style of lampstand may recall the lighting source used in the Solomonic Temple. Although there are rare examples from the postexilic period of branched lampstands similar to the shape of the menorah that appears in modern Jewish iconography, Zechariah's lampstand appears not to have been branched but had lights emanating from the bowl on top of the stand.

Iron Age I terracotta seven-spouted oil lamp

Courtesy Liberty Biblical Museum. Photo by Ayelet Shapira. Used by permission.

The description of the lighting vessels in the First Temple furnishings (1 Kgs 7:49) make no mention of a lampstand made of branches, let alone seven branches. The traditional menorah is first seen depicted on Maccabean coins struck by Antigonus (40–37 BC) and in connection with the Second (Herodian) Temple in first-century drawings on plaster from the Jewish Quarter, graffiti on stone from an escape tunnel descending to the Pool of Siloam from the southwestern corner of the Temple Mount, and on the famous relief in the Arch of Titus. From this evidence Carol Meyers argues that the kind of lampstand in the First Temple was most likely the kind described by Zechariah: "This kind of lamp is found sporadically in the ruins of Canaanite shrines of the Iron Age and in occasional Bronze Age precursors. Such seven-spouted lamps, set on cylindrical stands, are what would be expected, on archaeological evidence, in a Jerusalem shrine of the Iron II period, which is the period of Solomon's Temple."[87] If, as some commentators believe, Zechariah's vision in 4:2 is related to ritual re-laying or rededicating of the foundation of the Second (Zerubbabel) Temple,[88] this connection of the lampstand with the temple is strengthened.

MALACHI

Malachi 2:2

Archaeological Evidence for Conditions in Judah

"If you do not listen, and if you do not resolve to honor my name," says the LORD Almighty, "I will send a curse on you, and I will curse your blessings. Yes, I have already cursed them, because you have not resolved to honor me." (Mal 2:2)

The consensus of scholarship places Malachi somewhere in the period between the completion of the Second Temple in 515 BC and the work of Ezra and Nehemiah. Social factors mentioned in the book place it between 515 BC and 398 BC. However, due to the lack of distinction between priests and Levites, a date around 500 BC is preferable. Therefore, the time frame for Malachi is postexilic, or during the restoration of Judah when the returned remnant faced the challenge of rebuilding their cities and lifestyles.

Many textbooks in biblical archaeology have treated this period in a cursory fashion,[89] leaving the reader of the Bible with the impression that the Babylonian conquest of Judah had left everything destroyed and that everyone had been exiled. However, an examination of the archaeological evidence reveals that all of Judah did not suffer the same destruction and deportation as Jerusalem and her fortified cities. Excavations at sites in northern Judah and Benjamin show that city life continued to exist after the fall of Jerusalem and throughout the Babylonian period.[90] At sites such as Tel en-Naṣbeh (Mispah), Gibeon, Bethel, and Tell el-Ful (Gibeah), located only 10 miles from Jerusalem, as well as smaller settlements of the central hill country, life continued and even prospered in the late sixth century, with citizens feeling secure enough to build houses outside city walls.[91] The implication of these finds is that in the rural areas daily life continued much as before the destruction. One can guess that after the initial disruption caused by the destruction of Jerusalem and the shift of power entirely to Babylon, the peasant's life returned to semi-normal—a subsistence life with heavy taxes due to the state, only now the state was Babylon and not Judah. And even in Jerusalem, life continued. Houses were rebuilt, and some semblance of city life remained. Even Lamentations at its bleakest does indicate that people still inhabited Jerusalem (see especially Lam 5). Thus, the community in Palestine survived. No evidence exists for a resettlement of foreign populace into Judah of the sort the Assyrians practiced in Israel and elsewhere. Thus the population remained intact and maintained its cultural identity. Furthermore, we should not assume a total absence of contact between those in Babylon and the remaining population in Judah. Jeremiah sent at least two letters to the deportees and received a letter in return (Jer 29). Likewise, at the time of Nehemiah communication between Jews in Persia and those in Palestine took place (Neh 1). No reason exists to doubt a regular contact between the deportees and the Judeans in Palestine throughout this period.

Apparently some form of worship continued among the ruins of the temple (Jer 41:4–5, assuming "the house of the Lord" referred to the temple). Even worshipers from Israelite cities such as Samaria, Shechem, and Shiloh brought offerings and incense to the temple ruins (Jer 41:4–5). Some priests remained, probably of lesser ranks, but the worship patterns and festivals were virtually abandoned (Lam 1:4).

The socio-economic situation in Judah did not change drastically with the restoration. Jerusalem probably saw more rebuilding following the return, as one would expect the families of aristocracy, priests, and skilled craftsman to locate there. In the rural areas life probably continued unchanged. The archaeological evidence indicates a continuity of life in the villages and smaller cities from before the fall of Judah through this period. Some evidence for the economic situation of the early period of restoration can be drawn from Haggai. There are several references to drought, poor harvests, and famine (Hag 1:5–11). These disasters are interpreted as God's response to the people's unfaithfulness (Hag 1:2, 4). Thus, in Haggai's time (520–525 BC) Jerusalem shows evidence of rebuilding and restoration. It was considerably smaller than it had been a century

earlier and certainly not nearly so grand, but it was being rebuilt. Apparently this restored city had no defensive wall until the time of Nehemiah in 444 BC (Neh 2–7). This lack of a defensive wall may not have been the result of economics, nor even of the small size of Jerusalem's population, but more a consequence of its relative unimportance. Judah was apparently governed from Samaria during this time (Neh 4:1–2, 7–8).

Malachi 2:10–16

The Elephantine Aramaic Papyri Marriage Contracts

> You ask, "Why?" It is because the LORD is the witness between you and the wife of your youth. You have been unfaithful to her, though she is your partner, the wife of your marriage covenant. (Mal 2:14)

There is a debate as to whether this context refers to cultic practices and/or social practices. In verse 11, the *hapax legomenon bat ʿel nekar* ("daughter of a foreign god" NRSV) is used with regard to profanation of the temple yet has resulted from an act of "marriage." Some interpreters argue that a pagan goddess is intended, and if the prophet had meant to designate foreign women he would have used the form *nasim nakriyot*. Therefore, "marriage" is taken symbolically of idolatry. Other interpreters point to the fact that the Moabites are called the sons and daughters of Chemosh (Num 21:29), compared to the Israelites, who are called the sons and daughters of Yahweh (Deut 32:19). This is also in a context that refers to idolatrous practice (cf. Deut 17:2; 29:17), but the terms refer distinctly to men and women. Therefore, this passage is best seen as referring to civil unions to foreign (pagan) women, an act that violated the Mosaic legislation and threatened covenant identity. There were laws and protection in effect in Israel against marrying foreign women

(Gen 24:3–4; Exod 34:12–16; Deut 7:3–4; Num 25:1; 1 Kgs 11:1–8). Even the political marriages of Solomon to foreign women, such as pharaoh's daughter, had required a physical separation between them and Israelite places that were to be kept ritually pure (2 Chr 8:11). Such ritual contamination from the presence of a foreign woman could result in profanation of the temple, as Malachi observed.

In verses 14–16 Malachi addresses a second violation of the covenant of marriage, the divorce of legitimate Israelite wives. What provoked this practice in the fifth-century-BC postexilic community may find an answer in the archaeological discovery of an Aramaic papyri archive in Elephantine, an island located in Upper Egypt. A Diaspora Jewish garrison community had settled on the island at the same time period as the postexilic Jewish community addressed by Malachi. These legal documents deal with lawsuits, sales, marriages, loans, gifts, and property rights. Although most of the contracts were written in Aramaic and seem to have been drawn up in either Persian or local Jewish courts, they follow the form of the Egyptian contracts, further evidence of foreign influence on the Jewish community. While some Jews in this settlement observed Jewish customs, many did not. The presence of an illegitimate Israelite temple there is evidence of the ritual apathy that appears to have characterized the community. Moreover, these Jews were living in a pagan environment, which included Arameans, Greeks, Babylonians, and Egyptians, and the Elephantine papyri document cases of intermarriage with this foreign element, just as Malachi described of the Judean community.

This Aramaic archive includes seven marriage texts, three of which are relatively complete.[92] The *Brooklyn Papyrus 7:33f* is of special interest because it contains a marriage contract between Anani and Yehoyishma that reads, "But Yehoyishma shall not have power to marry another man except Anani, and if she does thus, divorce it is, they shall do to her the law of divorce."[93] Reuven Yaron notes that "adultery of the wife (or her entrance upon a second marriage) constitutes divorce . . . but no further punishment is envisaged. This is a radical departure from Jewish law (and oriental law generally), where adultery is always mentioned as a capital crime . . . Old Testament law did not consider adultery as grounds for divorce; rather, texts like Exodus 20:14, Leviticus 20:14, and Deuteronomy 5:18 explain that it is a crime punishable by death . . . there is no suggestion that [a woman] enjoyed such a right in Biblical law."[94] It is possible that a privilege familiar in Egypt entered into Jewish religion and thought at Elephantine because of their proximity, which further illustrates the dangerous syncretism Malachi was addressing.

Additionally, the Elephantine documents "stress the contractual nature of marriage with attention given to the pragmatic legal and economic aspects of the marriage bond [such as] bride-price, dowry, property rights, [children,] and inheritance."[95] This is in contrast to the Old Testament, which presents marriage as a binding covenant, not as a terminable contract. Certainly, these Elephantine marriage and divorce dispositions could have been the antecedents to the more casual Second Temple Jewish marital stipulations. Archaeological finds such as these give insight into the continuity between the influential cultural practices during the Persian period and the socio-religious conditions addressed by Malachi.

Malachi 4:5–6

Allusions to the Return of Elijah in the Dead Sea Scrolls

> See, I will send the prophet Elijah to you before that great and dreadful day of the LORD comes. (Mal 4:5)

This text anticipates a coming messenger like Elijah who will prepare the way for the promised messianic king by reconciling the people of Israel to God before the eschatological judgment. This ninth-century-BC prophet is among the more prominent and mysterious characters in the Bible. He performed miracles and ordered the execution of 850 pagan prophets after the famous confrontation on Mount Carmel (1 Kgs 18:40) and at the close of his ministry was raptured to heaven by a chariot of fire and a whirlwind (2 Kgs 2:11).

The prophet Elijah finds mention in the Qumran sectarian literature dating to the Hasmonean period (152–63 BC). One fragmentary Aramaic text known as Vision B contains an expectation of Elijah as the harbinger to the day of judgment mentioned in Malachi 4:5: "therefore I will send Elijah be[fore . . .]" (4Q558.4).[96] Similarly, in the *Messianic Apocalypse* (4Q521) there may be an allusion to an anointed prophet who speaks of the end of days, either Elijah or a prophet like Elijah: "and the law of your favor. And I will free them with [. . .] it is su[re:]. The fathers will return towards the sons."[97] If one understands God as the speaker, then this passage anticipates the return of an Elijah-type figure that will bring about reconciliation and deliverance in the end of days.[98] Another fragmentary document, which paraphrases the Elijah narratives as recorded in 1 and 2 Kings, is postulated as reflecting the belief in the return of a certain "mighty man," perhaps Elijah, in the last days. The passage reads: "to give them in the hand of each nation [of . . .] [. . .] to the time when a mighty man will rise [. . .] [. . .] [. . .] because for all spirits and . . . [. . .] [. . . the pr]ophets [. . .] (4Q382)."[99]

The allusions and citations of Malachi 4:5 in fragmentary texts reveal the eschatological anticipation of the Qumran community of the literal fulfillment of this prophecy.[100] While the identification of this Elijah-like prophet and the timing of his arrival are often debated, along with the overall cohesiveness of these fragments, the Qumran community, at the very least, expected the eschatological return of Elijah. The New Testament also contains various allusions to an Elijah *redivivus* or to a type of Elijah as the precursor to the Messiah's arrival (Matt 11:14; Luke 1:17; Mark 9:12). Such expectation has been preserved in Jewish tradition and is evidenced in Jewish households at *Pesach* (Passover), as a place at the table is set for Elijah in hope that he will come at this season to announce the arrival of the messiah.

6 | Archaeological Discoveries and the Old Testament

NAME	LANGUAGE	DISCOVERER	LOCATION FOUND	DATE FOUND	SUBJECT	DATE OF ORIGIN	BIBLICAL SIGNIFICANCE
Gedaliah Ben Pashchur bulla	Hebrew	Eilat Mazar	City of David (Jerusalem, Israel)	2017	Clay seal impression of the minister of the Judean King Zedekiah	587/6 BC	This official mentioned in Jer. 38:1 plotted against the prophet Jeremiah and threw him into a pit.
Yehuchal Ben Shelamayahu bulla	Hebrew	Eilat Mazar	City of David (Jerusalem, Israel)	2010	Son of Shelemiah, courtier of Zedekiah who was sent to Jeremiah	587/6 BC	Name of official in Jer 38:1 who joined in plot against Jeremiah
Scroll of Leviticus	Hebrew	Dan Barag, Ehud Netzer, Sefi Porath	Ein Gedi (Israel)	1970 (deciphered in 2015)	Biblical scroll (Lev.1:1–8) found in the holy ark of a Byzantine synagogue (carbonized, but digitally unwrapped)	ca. AD 210–390	This later copy of a Qumran-era scroll represents the earliest evidence of the exact form of the medieval (Masoretic) text
Lachish Gate Cultic Shrine		Sa'ar Ganor	Lachish (Israel)	2016	Six-chambered gate with rival sanctuary horns cut off altar and toilet deposited in holy of holies as a ritual desecration	715 BC	Illustrates Judean King Hezekiah's religious reforms (2 Kgs 18:4, 22; 2 Chr 29:3)
Jerusalem papyrus	Hebrew	Eitan Klein and members of the robbery prevention unit	Judean desert cave (Israel)	2016	Receipt, reading: "From the king's maidservant, from Na'arat, jars of wine, to Jerusalem."	ca. 650 BC	Earliest mention of Jerusalem in a non-biblical text
Gezer palace		Steve Ortiz	Gezer (Israel)	2016	Monumental palace similar to those of same period	Tenth century BC	Tied to reign of King Solomon supporting biblical depiction of early Israelite kingdom.
Gath city gate		Aren Maeir	Tel es-Safi (Israel)	2015	Monumental city gate of the Philistine city of Gath	Tenth–Ninth centuries BC	Site that served as hometown of the biblical figure Goliath (1 Sam 17:4)

NAME	LANGUAGE	DISCOVERER	LOCATION FOUND	DATE FOUND	SUBJECT	DATE OF ORIGIN	BIBLICAL SIGNIFICANCE
Stone Seal		Gabriel Barkay and Temple Mount Sifting Project	Temple Mount (Jerusalem, Israel)	2015	Administrative seal with image of two animals	Tenth century BC	First such seal found in Jerusalem and evidence of biblical description of early kingdom of Judah.
Eshbaal Inscription	Hebrew	Yosef Garfinkel, Saar Ganor	Khirbet Qeiyafa (Shemarayim, Israel)	2012	Jar inscription; one of only four with names from early kingdom of Judah.	Tenth century BC	Bears a name that is the same as that of King Saul's son (1 Chr 8:33).
Lachish Ostracon	Canaanite	Benjamin Sass, Yosef Garfinkel	Lachish (Israel)	2015	3 lines with 9 early Semitic letters	1130 BC	Early witness to the Canaanite alphabet that led to the biblical text
King Hezekiah Royal Seal	Hebrew	Eilat Mazar, Hagai Cohen-Klonymus	Opel (Jerusalem, Israel)	2009	Clay bulla with inscription: "Belonging to Hezekiah [son of] Ahaz king of Judah"	727 BC	Only royal seal of King Hezekiah of Judah (727–698 BC) found by archaeologists in a provenanced context.
Simmons Ark Tablet	Old Babylonian cuneiform	Irving Finkel, Leonard Simmons	Mesopotamia	2014	Clay tablet inscribed with 60 lines of text	1750 BC	First mention in extrabiblical text that animals came on the Ark "two by two"
Canaanite Cultic Site		Itzhaq Shai	Tel Burna (Kiryat Gat, Israel)	2014	Courtyard of the 2,700-square-foot building yielded remains of sacrificial rituals associated with the Canaanite deity Baal.	1300 BC	Temple or palace from the biblical city of Libnah conquered by Joshua (Josh 10:29) and given to Aaron and his sons (Josh 21:13)
Scarab of Sheshonq I	Egyptian hieroglyphic	Thomas E. Levy	Khirbat Hamra Ifdan (Faynan district, Jordan)	2014	Stone seal of Pharaoh Sheshonq who is identified with the biblical Pharaoh Shishak.	931 BC	Provides new evidence for Shishak's raid into Judah (2 Chr 12:2–9).
Khirbet Summeily bullae	Hebrew	Jimmy Hardin, Jeff Blakely	Khirbet Summeily near Gaza, on the ancient border between Judah and Philistia	2014	The judgment seat in Corinth where trials were held.	Tenth century BC	Administrative activity at this remote Judean outpost supports early kingdom of Judah and existence of biblical kings David and Solomon
Khirbet el-Maqatir Egyptian Scarab	Egyptian hieroglyphic	Bryant Wood, Gary Byers, Scott Stripling	Khirbet el-Maqatir (Israel)	2013	Stone scarab of Egyptian 18th Dynasty (reigns of Thutmose III/ Amenhotep II)	1550–1450 BC	Adds support to site being identified with biblical Ai.

NAME	LANGUAGE	DISCOVERER	LOCATION FOUND	DATE FOUND	SUBJECT	DATE OF ORIGIN	BIBLICAL SIGNIFICANCE
Palace from Time of David		Yosef Garfinkel	Khirbet Qeiyafa (Shemarayim, Israel)	2013	Davidic palace with adjacent royal storerooms	Tenth century BC	City planning and royal residences were developed by the time of King David
Matanyahu Seal	Hebrew	Eli Shukron	Jerusalem (Israel)	2012	Stone seal found beneath Robinson's Arch at foot of the Temple Mount with name Matanyahu	ca. 687 BC	Biblical name used in the Kingdom of Judah in latter part of the First Temple period (1 Chr 1:25)
First Temple Water Cistern		Eli Shukron	Jerusalem (Israel)	2012	Discovered beneath Robinson's Arch; Held 66,000 gallons of water	727–698 BC	Attests to public and pilgrim activity at First Temple during the reign of Hezekiah.
Solomonic Wall		Eilat Mazar	Ophel (Jerusalem, Israel)	2010	Gatehouse wall 230 feet long x 19 feet high (another section of this city wall is 115 feet long x 15 feet high)	950 BC	Evidence of Solomonic monumental construction as referenced in 1 Kgs 7:1–12.
Wall of the First Temple		Muslim workers	Temple Mount (Jerusalem, Israel)	2006	Part of wall near Dome of the Rock with pottery and vessel for oil	Eighth century BC	Evidence of location of House of Oil in the First Temple
Seals from Temple Mount Administrative Building	Hebrew	Shlomit Wexler-Bdoulah, Alexander Onn	Temple Mount western area (Jerusalem, Israel)	2008	Seals with name Netanyahu ben Yaush; image of Assyrian-style archer	Eighth–Sixth centuries BC	Reveals name mentioned in the Bible (1 Chr 17; 25; Jer 41) and Lachish Letters
Canaanite Wall		Ronny Reich, Eli Shukron	City of David (Jerusalem, Israel)	2009	Massive wall 26 feet high x 75 feet long protecting a passageway from the fortified city to the eastern slope of the Gihon Spring	1800–1700 BC	Wall from the later patriarchal period giving evidence of pre-Israelite monumental construction in Jerusalem.
Bethlehem Bulla		Hillel Richman, Eli Shukron	City of David (Jerusalem, Israel)	2012	Fiscal (tax-related) seal fond in dirt sifted at Temple Mount Sifting Project	Eighth–Seventh century BC	First mention of the city of Bethlehem outside of the Bible
Cult Shrines from Khirbet Qeiyafa		Yosef Garfinkel	Khirbet Qeiyafa (Shemarayim, Israel)	2011	Clay model ritual shrines in form of temples	Tenth century BC	Revealed meaning of triglyphs in architecture of Solomon's Temple
Ahisamach Inscription (Sania 115)	Egyptian hierpglyphic (with single proto-consonantal Hebrew letter beth)	Deciphered (and interpreted) by Doug Petrovich	Egypt	2012	Stone slab with image of figures and Middle Egyptian caption on display at the Harvard Semitic Museum	1842 BC	Identifies Joseph and his two sons, Ephraim and Manasseh, and is inscribed with the words "6 Levantines: Hebrews of Bethel, the beloved."

NAME	LANGUAGE	DISCOVERER	LOCATION FOUND	DATE FOUND	SUBJECT	DATE OF ORIGIN	BIBLICAL SIGNIFICANCE
Textiles from King David Era		Erez Ben-Yosef	Timna (Arava Valley, Israel)	2015	High quality weaves and colors show important geopolitical presence of the Edomites	Tenth century BC	Provides new information about the Edomites working copper mines under Judean hegemony
World's Oldest Temple		Klaus Schmidt	Göbekli Tepe (southeastern Turkey)	1995	Ancient temple structures with human and animal images	Ca. 10,000 BC	Rewrites the history of civilization and religion
Sacred Marriage Cylinder Seal Impression		Yitzhak Paz, Ianir Milevski, Nimrod Getzov	Bet Ha-'Emeq (Israel)	2015	Musical/cultic scene depicting a sacred marriage	3000 BC	Reveals symbolic-ritualistic world of the Early Bronze Age Canaan
Tel 'Eton Judahite Administrative Center		Avraham Faust	Modern day Turkey	2015	large courtyard with rooms on three sides in typical Israelite 4 room style.	Eighth century BC	New data on biblical Eglon, a Canaanite city conquered by Joshua (Josh 10:34–36; 15:39)
Absalom's Pillar		Ronnie Reich, Eli Shukron	'Ain Joweizeh spring cave (between Jerusalem and Bethlehem)	2011	Only example of a Proto-Aeolic capital (used in monumental royal architecture) connected to a pillar	Tenth–Eighth centuries BC	Absalom copied this type of pillar so that he would be remembered as being connected with royalty (2 Sam 18:18)
Solomon's Copper Mines		Thomas Levy	Southern Jordan	2008	Copper mining tools dated to era of biblical kingdom of Judah	Tenth century BC	Industrial-scale metal production would have been in operation at site during the reigns of Kings David and Solomon
Palace of King David		Eilat Mazar	City of David (Jerusalem)	2008	Monumental royal buildings	Tenth–Ninth centuries BC	Palace of King David or Fortress
Atra-Hasis Epic	Akkadian	G. Smith, A. R. Millard, W. G. Lambert	Babylon, Assyria, Urgarit	1876, 1965	Creation and Flood accounts	1650 BC	Ancient near eastern parallel to Genesis account
Beni-Hasan Tomb Painting	Egyptian Hieroglyphic	Percy Newberry	Beni-Hasan (Egypt)	1902	Tomb painting of Khnumhotep in Middle Kingdom cemetery	1900 BC	Semites from Canaan entering Egypt as in patriarchal period (Gen 12:10; 37:28)
Laws of Hammurabi	Akkadian (Old Babylonian)	Gustave Jéquier Jacques de Morgan	Susa (Iran)	1901	Collection of Babylonian laws	1754 BC	Illustrates ancient Near Eastern law
Merenptah Stele	Egyptian Hieroglyphic	Flinders Petrie	Thebes (Egypt)	1896	Records military accomplishments of Merenptah	1207 BC	First mention of the name "Israel"

NAME	LANGUAGE	DISCOVERER	LOCATION FOUND	DATE FOUND	SUBJECT	DATE OF ORIGIN	BIBLICAL SIGNIFICANCE
Sheshonq Relief (Bubastite Portal)	Middle Egyptian Hieroglyphics	Jean-François Champollion	Karnak Temple of Amun (Egypt)	1825	Military accomplishments of Sheshonq I =Shishak	925 BC	Raid against Solomon's son Rehoboam (1 Kgs 11:40; 14:25; 2 Chr 12:2–9)
"House of David" Inscription	Aramaic	Avraham Biran	Tel Dan (Israel)	1993	Syrian conquest of Israel	Ninth century BC	Earliest mention of David in extrabiblical records
Mesha Stele	Moabite	Frederick Augustus Klein	Dibon (Jordan)	1868	Military accomplishments of Mesha of Moab	850 BC	Moabite-Israelite relations, mentions house of David
Black Obelisk	Akkadian (Neo-Assyrian)	A. H. Layard	Nineveh (Iraq)	1845	Military accomplishments of Shalmaneser III	840 BC	Picture of King Jehu of Judah paying tribute
Balaam Texts	Aramaic	H. J. Franken	Deir alla (Succoth) Jordan	1967	Prophecy of Balaam about the displeasure of the divine council	Eighth century	Famous seer in biblical account (Num 22:5)
Siloam Inscription	Hebrew	Jacob (Eliyahu) Spafford	Jerusalem (Israel)	1880	Commemoration of the completion of Hezekiah's water tunnel	701 BC	Extrabiblical details for biblical account (2 Kgs 20:20)
Sennacherib Cylinder (Taylor Prism)	Akkadian (Neo-Assyrian)	Colonel Robert Taylor	Nineveh (Iraq)	1830	Military accomplishments of Sennacherib	686 BC	Describes siege of Jerusalem (2 Kgs 18:13–19:35)
Lachish Ostraca	Hebrew	James Leslie Starkey	Tell ed-Duweir (Lachish, Israel)	1935, 1938	21 letters from the military captain of Lachish to Yaush (Jerusalem)	588 BC	Conditions during the final Babylonian siege (Jer 34:6–7)
Cyrus Cylinder	Akkadian	Hormuzd Rassam	Babylon (Iraq)	1879	Degree of Cyrus allowing the rebuilding of temples	535 BC	Illustrates the restoration policy of Jerusalem (Ezra 5:13–17)
Amarna Tablets	Akkadian Cuneiform (Canaanite authors)	Egyptian Peasant woman	Tel el-Amarna (Egypt)	1887	Diplomatic correspondence between the Egyptian administration and its representatives in Canaan and Amurru during the New Kingdom	1400 BC	Confirms the Hebrews were established in Mesopotamia by the early second millennium BC
Babylonian Chronicles	Akkadian (Neo-Babylonian)	Donald Wiseman	Babylon (Iraq)	1956	Official reports of Nebuchadnezzar's first decade as king.	626–594 BC	Extrabiblical record of 597 BC capture of Jerusalem and other historical details
Behistun Inscription	Old Persian, Elamite, and Babylonian (Akkadian)	Robert Sherley, Sir Henry Rawlinson	Mount Behistun (Iran)	1835	Multilingual account of Persian victory over Babylon and rise of King Darius	522 BC	Evidence for historicity of Darius the Great

NAME	LANGUAGE	DISCOVERER	LOCATION FOUND	DATE FOUND	SUBJECT	DATE OF ORIGIN	BIBLICAL SIGNIFICANCE
Belshazzar Inscription (Nabonidus Chronicle)	Akkadian Cuneiform	Henry Rawlinson	Ur (Tell el-Muqayyar) Iraq	1854	Belshazzar listed as coregent with King Nabonidus	556–539 BC	Clarification of Daniel as "third ruler in the kingdom" (Dan 5:29)
Code of Hammurabi	Akkadian Cuneiform	Gustave Jequier	Susa (Iran)	1901	282 laws dealing with morality, commerce, and religion (predates Mosaic law by 200 years)	1765–1700 BC	Evidence for 15th century chronology of the Mosaic law and evidence of early writing in Canaan
Ebla Tablets	Eblaite Cuneiform	Paolo Matthiae	Tel-Mardikh (Syria)	1976	Royal Archives containing many types of texts	2350 BC	Provide historical background of Syria in late 3rd millennium
Gilgamesh Epic	Akkadian (Neo-Assyrian)	Hormuzd Rassam	Nineveh (Iraq)	1853	The exploits of Gilgamesh, Enkidu, Utnapishtim and the search for immortality	2000 BC	Extrabiblical parallel to Genesis account of the Flood
Goliath Inscription	Proto-Canaanite	Aren Maeir	Tel es-Safi (Gath) Israel	2005	Oldest Philistine inscription with name similar to the biblical name of Goliath	Ninth century BC	Support for the historicity of the Philistine Goliath of Gath (1 Sam 17:4)
Hattusa (Hittite capital)	Neshite Cuneiform	Hugo Winckler, Theodore Makridi Bey, Kurt Bittel, Peter Neve	Boğazkale (Turkey)	1906, 1907, 1911–13, 1931 1963–94	Royal archives of the Neo-Hittite Empire (30,000 tablets recording laws, legends, covenants, and myths)	1600–1300 BC	Historicity of Hittite kingdom in Anatolia that may be related to biblical Hittites (Gen 15:20).
House of YHWH Ostracon	Hebrew	Ruth Amiran, Yohanan Aharoni	Tel Arad (Israel)	1962–67	Receipt for the donation of silver to the First Temple	800 BC	Earliest piece of evidence referencing the Temple outside of biblical text
Great Karnak Inscription of Merneptah	Egyptian Hieroglyphics	Jean-Francois Champollion, Karl Richard Lepsius	Karnak temple of Amun (Egypt)	1828–29	Records campaigns of Pharaoh Merneptah, including defeat of Israelites in Canaan campaign as in the Merenptah Stele	1212–1202 BC	Earliest-known artistic representation of the Israelites on a relief
Merneptah Stele	Egyptian Hieroglyphics	Flinders Petrie	Thebes (Egypt)	1896	Pharaoh Merneptah's military exploits	1230 BC	Earliest extrabiblical mention of Israel
Nuzi Tablets	Hurrian (dialect of Akkadian) Cuneiform	Chiera and Speiser	Yorghun Tepe (Iraq)	1925–41	Archive containing family records	1500–1400 BC	Source for contemporary customs in mid-2nd millennium
Weld-Blundell Prism (Sumerian King List)	Sumerian Cuneiform	Hermann Hilprecht, Jacobsen, Thorkild	Library at Nippur (Babylonia) Iraq	1900, 1939	Clay prism listing Sumerian Kings who reigned before and after the "Great Flood"	2017–1794 BC	Genesis account (regarding lifespans before Flood)

NAME	LANGUAGE	DISCOVERER	LOCATION FOUND	DATE FOUND	SUBJECT	DATE OF ORIGIN	BIBLICAL SIGNIFICANCE
Mari	Akkadian (Old-Babylonian) Cuneiform	Andre Parrot	Tel al-Hariri (Syria)	1933	Royal archives of Zimri-Lim containing many types of texts (administrative, legal, religious and prophetic oracles)	Eighteenth century BC	Provides parallels to 1st-millennium practices that may reflect on earlier time of the Patriarchs
Enuma Elish	Akkadian (Neo-Assyrian) Cuneiform	A. H. Layard	Nineveh (Iraq)	1848–76	Account of Marduk's ascension to the head of the pantheon	Seventh century BC	Parallels to Genesis creation accounts
Ugarit	Ugaritic	Claude Schaeffer	Ras Shamra (Syria)	1928	Royal archives of Ugarit (Canaanite religion and literature)	Fifteenth century BC	Closest NW Semitic cognate to Biblical Hebrew

PART 2

ARCHAEOLOGY
and the
INTERTESTAMENTAL PERIOD

7 | Introduction to the Intertestamental Period

"Intertestamental" is a popular Christian term used to refer to a period of time between the end of the period of the production of the Old Testament (Persian period) and the beginning of the period related to Jesus and the production of the New Testament (Roman period), a period of time (about 400 years) equivalent to the Second Temple period, although New Testament production continued after the destruction of the temple (e.g., book of Revelation in AD 95). In academic discussion the events of this time are referred to as the Second Temple period, a time that began with the return of exiled Jews to Judah and the laying of the foundation of the Second Temple (538 BC) until its Roman destruction (AD 70). During this period a number of significant events reshaped the world of the Bible and left significant remains in the archaeological record. It began with Persian rule (539–332 BC), with Judah becoming the province of Yehud and the rebuilding of the temple in Jerusalem. Persian rule was then eclipsed by the conquest of Alexander the Great. The colonization that followed imposed Greek culture (Hellenism) on the Jewish people and created a division between Hellenistic Jews (who adopted Greek culture while retaining the Jewish religious tradition though not practice) and non-Hellenistic Jews. Hellenistic lifestyle (with a corresponding ban on the practice of the Jewish religion) was forced on the entire Jewish population under Seleucid rule (most notably under Antiochus Epiphanes IV), resulting in a Jewish revolt (167 BC) led by Judas Maccabeus and his sons, who successfully established independent rule in Israel (165 to 37 BC).

Under the Maccabean, or Hasmonean, dynasty the offices of both kings and priests were drawn from their family. This resulted in increasing tension with groups such as the Pharisees and break-off groups, such as a band of priests from the Zadokite line who formed a sectarian community on a plateau at the northwestern corner of the Dead Sea (Qumran) around 100 BC. The Hasmonean Dynasty ended due to civil war between the sons of Salome Alexandra (Hyrcanus II and Aristobulus II) and appeals made to the Roman authorities, who saw this an opportunity in the region.

The intertestamental period saw the production of the Septuagint, commissioned by Ptolemy II and produced by Jewish scribes in Alexandria, Egypt ca. 250 BC, the production of copies of the Hebrew Bible, commentaries, and other writings (the Dead Sea Scrolls), the production by Jewish writers of apocryphal and pseudepigraphical documents, the rise and development of Jewish religious and political sects (Pharisees, Sadducees, Herodians, Essenes) and others such as the Zealots and Sicarii ("dagger-men") after the imposition of Roman rule over Israel (beginning in 63 BC with the conquest of the Emperor Pompey) and the imperial decrees that images of the emperor and/or empire be placed in the sacred precincts. This led to the Roman establishment of the Herodian dynasty (beginning with Herod the Great in 37 BC), the second rebuilding of the temple in Jerusalem (completed in 20 BC), and the Roman creation of the province of Judea (6 BC). The culture in Israel at this point was a mixture of Roman, Greek, and Jewish, all setting

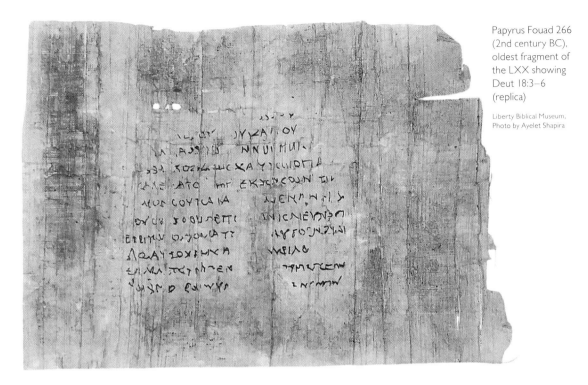

Papyrus Fouad 266 (2nd century BC), oldest fragment of the LXX showing Deut 18:3–6 (replica)

the stage for the religious and political unrest that characterized the time in which Jesus was born and the New Testament was written. Our archaeological focus below will treat briefly the pivotal events of this period that formed the political and religious background for Judaism and its conflicts reflected in the New Testament: (1) the building of the Second (Zerubbabel) Temple; (2) the prevailing influence of Hellenism on the Jewish people as demonstrated by the rule of Antiochus IV; (3) Hasmonean rule (including the priesthood), the establishment of the Qumran Community, and the production of the Dead Sea Scrolls; (4) the Roman invasion leading to political appointments of kings and high priests including the Herodian dynasty its (re)building of the Second Temple and its complex.

8 | The Second (Zerubbabel) Temple

Under the headship of Zerubbabel, who became governor of Judah, and Joshua the high priest (Hag 2:2), the foundation for the first phase of the Second Temple was begun by the people. Following the precedent set in preparation for the First Temple, the people contributed generously to the sacred treasury (Ezra 2:68–69). The first act of restoration was the reconstruction of the altar of burnt offering, which permitted the sacrificial system to be reinstituted and the celebration of the biblical festivals to be restored (Ezra 3:1–5). Like the First Temple, Zerubbabel's Temple was built after the pattern of foreign temples by Phoenician workers (Ezra 3:7–10), in harmony with the decree from the Persian king Darius to rebuild the temple. The Jews who returned from exile were inexperienced and could only build a new temple with the expertise of the Phoenicians. In 538 BC the foundations for the Second Temple were laid; however, the construction of the temple itself met with resistance from Samaritan residents to the north and could not be started again for another fifteen years.

The work was resumed in 520 BC, through the exhortation of the prophets Haggai and Zechariah and a decree from the Persian king Darius, who provided official sanction and support from local taxation to finance the completion of the structure (Ezra 6:1–15). The dedication of this completed structure on March 12, 516/515 BC, some twenty years after the return from exile and exactly seventy years after the desolation of Jerusalem (587/6 BC—a period that had been governed by the state of the temple, see Jer 25:11–12; 29:10; Dan 9:2, 16–17, 24).

The Second Temple was inferior in construction compared to the First Temple, lacking a compound, the two entrance pillars Yachin and Boaz, the two olivewood cherubim that overshadowed the ark, and the ark of the covenant itself. Moreover, while the First Temple had been built at the beginning of Israel's independent rule, the second was constructed under a time of foreign domination. Most importantly, the visible presence of YHWH was absent from the Second Temple. For these reasons the biblical account notes that many of the priests and Levites who were old enough to have seen the First Temple wept at the time this temple's foundations were laid (Ezra 3:12–13).

The Design of the Second (Zerubbabel) Temple

Even though the biblical accounts offer little details of the construction of Zerubbabel's Temple, it seems that it was similar to the First Temple (Hag 2:3) but without an adjacent royal compound. This appears to be verified from the archaeological discovery of the remains of the Samaritan temple on Mount Gerizim (including its 6-ft thick walls and gates and altars) even though it also had two adjacent edifices believed to be a royal residence and administrative building. The temple's northern gate is a replica of the temple described in the Temple Scroll, a Dead Sea Scroll document written when the Second Temple of Zerubbabel was still standing. That the Samaritan temple was modeled after Zerubbabel's Temple is implied by Josephus's account of its origin in which Menachem, a priest in the Jerusalem Temple, marries Nikaso, the daughter of the Samaritan leader Sanballat. This marriage bars Menachem from service in the Jerusalem Temple, so his father-in-law builds him a temple on Mount Gerizim where he can officiate as high priest. Since the Samaritans embraced everything from the Jewish prayers to sacrificial ritual, it is more than probable that the temple they built would have been a replica of the Second Temple of Zerubbabel that was still standing at this time.

The record of Zerubbabel's Temple comes to us from the prophets Haggai (Hag 1:1–8, 12–14; 2:1–9) and Zechariah (Zech 1:7–6:15) and the scribe Ezra (Ezra 1:3–11; 3:13; 4:1–6:22). These texts primarily deal with the temple structure, while the account of the walls of the city and site are found in Nehemiah (Neh 2:11–7:4). He records that there were five external gates, two in the south and one in each of the other walls. Mishnah tractate Middot restates this and notes that these gates were 17 feet (5 m) wide and 34 feet (10 m) high (Mid. 1:3; 2:3). It also names the western gate as the Kiponus Gate (Mid. 1:3).

Aerial view of the remains of the Samaritan temple (under Theodorus Church) on Mt. Gerizim

Bill Schlegel/www.Bible Places.com

Adjoined to the eastern gate were chambers. Middot 1.6 notes these were the Chamber of the Hearth, which had four rooms opening into a reception room, the "Chamber of the Lamb Offerings," and the "Chamber of Shewbread," a place where the Hasmoneans hid defiled altar stones and a chamber led down to a place for priestly ritual purification, the "Chamber of Immersion." Nehemiah also records the ritual acts associated with the temple (Neh 10:32–39; cf. 12:44–47) and the building projects, more than likely connected with the temple precinct (Neh 2:8; 8:1; 12:44; 13:4–7). Nehemiah 3:29 mentions the East Gate within the temple precincts of which Shemaiah was the keeper. Surrounding the temple and the royal compounds was an additional enclosure that had two gates, the Water Gate (Neh 3:26) and the Inspection Gate (Neh 3:31). This latter gate was situated on the east, facing the outer defensive wall of the city. The eastern gate in this defensive wall was called the Horse Gate. It is believed that between the East Gate and the Inspection Gate was the open place where king Hezekiah assembled the priests and Levites (2 Chr 29:4–5) and later Ezra assembled the men of Benjamin and Judah (Ezra 10:9).

Archaeological Evidence

Josephus states that Solomon's Temple was constructed on a square Temple Mount (*Ant.* 15.400). The Jewish sources imply that the Second Temple of Zerubbabel followed the lines of this 500-cubit-square pre-exilic Temple Mount (*Ant.* 8.96; *J.W.* 5.184–85). This 500-cubit-square Temple Mount has been discovered today through an assessment of structures around and on the modern Temple Mount that make known the extensions added to the original in the Hasmonean and Herodian periods. The proof for identifying the sides of the original Temple Mount are as follows:

- the western wall, a now-covered wall preserved as the lowest step of the staircase at the northwest corner of the raised area
- the northern wall, remains of a quarried rockscarp (found in the nineteenth century by Charles Warren) that forms a right angle with the step/wall of the eastern wall
- the eastern wall, the original line of the eastern wall between the sixth century BC offset in the north and the bend in the south equals 861 feet or 500 cubits based on the applied use of the royal cubit of 20.67 inches (525 mm)
- the southern wall, measuring from the southeast corner (indicated by the bend) and corresponding to the northern wall to the intersection with continuation of the step/wall

In addition, when Herod removed the old foundations of the first phase of the Second Temple, he left the old eastern wall with its portico intact. This can be seen today on the outside of the eastern wall, where a seam is visible near the southern corner. This seam separates the Herodian extension (104 ft) to the Temple Mount from the eastern wall (1,405 ft). The pre-Herodian (Hasmonean) masonry that is visible today for 105 feet in the eastern wall can be seen in three courses of large stones with rough projecting bosses (faces) on either side of the present Golden Gate. The southern stretch is visible up to 51 feet south of the Golden Gate, and the northern stretch is visible for 68 feet until it runs into an exposed offset (set back about 2 ft) of Herodian masonry. However, a section of stones of the northern stretch near the Golden Gate are of a style of masonry that may be from the time of Nehemiah. A bend in the eastern wall is visible 240 feet from the southeast corner that in all likelihood indicates the southeast corner of the original 500-cubit-square Temple Mount.

9 | The Second (Herodian) Temple

The Herodian Second Temple occupied Jerusalem's Temple Mount from 20 BC until AD 70. It was the central and most prominent structure in the land of Israel and arguably one of the most impressive structures in the Roman Empire. Herod's construction doubled the size of the previous Temple Mount. This extensive platform, with its huge retaining walls to bear the weight of the fill and of the structures to be built above, was trapezoidal in shape (*Ant.* 8.97; 15.398, 400; 20.221; *War* 5.192). The dimensions of the south wall were 918 feet (280 m), the west wall 1,591 feet (485 m), the north wall 1,033 feet (315 m), and the east wall 1,509 feet (460 m). The total circumference of this sacred precinct was 5,052 feet (1,540 m), and the total area 172,000 square yards (144,000 sq m). This made the Temple Mount the largest site of its kind in the ancient world. Its sacred area was twice as large as the monumental Forum Romanum built by Trajan and three and a half times larger than the combined temples of Jupiter and Astarte-Venus at Baalbek. The surface area of the modern-day Temple Mount, between 35 and 36 acres, reflects a portion of this Herodian enlargement.[1]

The temple faced east according to the biblical precedent, and to pilgrims approaching from the Mount of Olives the temple's white polished limestone and imported marble gave it the appearance of a great snow-clad mountain. Anyone waking in the city saw a glowing golden mountain as its limestone absorbed the morning rays of the sun. Once the sun had fully risen, it reflected off the elevated upper exterior of the structure that was covered with gold. Josephus observed that Herod had applied so much gold that when the sun shone on it, it blinded those who looked at it (*J.W.* 5.5; 6.222). Walking the pedestrian street along the western side of the Temple Mount or striding within the royal stoa, Jews and gentiles alike beheld highly decorated and brightly painted (red, yellow, blue, and purple) architecture. Recording the Jewish reaction to this splendor, the rabbis wrote "whoever has not seen Herod's Temple has not seen a beautiful building in his life" (*Sukkot* 51:2).

This was the magnificent building that Jesus entered for his dedication on the eighth day of his life (Luke 2:21–39), visited three times a year in keeping with the custom for Jewish males living outside Judea (cf. Luke 2:41–49), and in which he completed the last week of his life daily preaching in its courts (Matt 26:55; Luke 21:37). Throughout his lifetime the temple was continually being added to and remodeled, so that each time Jesus visited the structure he was greeted with some new improvement. It is unclear how long the construction of the temple and sacrificial area took, but Josephus records that the construction of the temple took a year and a half and that the stoa and the outer courts took eight years (*Ant.* 15.11.5–6; 420–21). According to the statement of the Jewish authorities recorded in John 2:20, continued work on the temple's structures had taken forty-six years to that point (cf. Sanh. 41.2 and 'Abod Zar. 8.2), and Josephus reports that the temple complex was still receiving further embellishments and repairs until the Jewish Revolt broke out in AD 66 (*Ant.* 20.219). This fact, coupled with the magnificence of the temple just described, helps us understand the Gospel accounts

Herodian Temple (looking east) showing Herodian street along western and southern walls with western staircase (Robinson's Arch) ascending to Royal Stoa in foreground

"Herodian Temple Mount" by Christine Kidd, 20" x 30" oil on canvas (facebook .com/kiddfineart)

recording the disciples' pride in offering Jesus a private tour of the temple (Matt 24:1–2; Mark 13:1–2; Luke 21:5–6) and explains their astonishment at his statement that such an immense structure, so much the focus of Jewish life and faith, was to be completely destroyed (Matt 24:3; Mark 13:3–4; Luke 21:7). Nevertheless, Jesus referred to the temple as his "Father's house" (Luke 2:49; John 2:16), and it is recorded that "zeal for your house [the temple] will consume me" (John 2:17).

Evidence of Herodian Construction

The dilapidated condition of Zerubbabel's Second Temple and Herod's plans to enlarge it on a scale equal to his ambition forced the complete dismantling of the former structure (*Ant.* 15.391). For this reason most archaeologists do not expect any structures from either the First or Second (Zerubbabel) Temples to have survived under the present buildings on the Temple Mount. This, however, does not apply to parts of the retaining walls or the area of the Ophel that lay immediately to the south of the Temple Mount, where remains from previous structures have been discovered. In 2006 a 21-foot (7 m) long wall was found in a trench cut by the Islamic Waqf. This is likely the eastern wall of the Chamber of the Lepers and perhaps also part of the northern gate of the Court of the Women. The latter chamber was one of the four courtyards that belonged to the Court of the Women, with the other three being the Chamber of the Woodshed, the Chamber of the Nazarites, and the Chamber of the House of Oil. Artifacts recovered from the trench seem consistent with this latter identification. As this area has never been built over since the Roman destruction of 70 AD, the wall cannot belong to a post-Herodian construction and therefore is evidence of an Herodian structure.[2]

To build the temple Herod brought in 10,000 skilled workers and employed 1,000 priests to serve as masons and carpenters in order to comply with Jewish law that required the construction of the temple to be the work of the priests (*Ant.* 15.11.2; 389–90). Ancient quarries provide evidence of the source for the materials used for this construction. On the northern side of the Old City is a quarry known as Solomon's Quarry and Zedekiah's Cave that was used during the Herodian period. There is also one dating to the end of the Second Temple period that was found during a construction project in Jerusalem's Shmuel HaNavi Street. The immense size of the stones suggests strongly that they were for use in the construction of Herodian projects in Jerusalem, including the walls of the temple. Across the Hinnom valley from the Temple Mount at a site known as Ketef Hinnom, Gabriel Barkay excavated a First Temple tomb complex that had been used as a quarry in the Roman period (see remarks on Num 6:24–26).

Second Temple quarry at Ramat Shlomo

Several Second Temple period quarries (part of an ancient city of quarries) have also been discovered in the area of northeast Jerusalem's ultra-orthodox neighborhood of Ramat Shlomo. In total, archaeologists uncovered an area of around 11,000 square feet of quarry, as well as ancient pick axes and wedges. Visible at the quarry site are rock masses in various stages of quarrying, including some in a preliminary stage of rock cutting prior to detachment. Most of the quarried

stones weighed some tens to hundreds of tons, and the largest was 26 feet in length. No stones this size had ever been found in an archaeological excavation anywhere in the country except in the walls of the Temple Mount. The large number of outlines of the stone cuts in the white limestone at the quarry showed that this was a massive public program that had employed hundreds of workers at the site, exactly what is described in the sources for an imperial construction project such as Herod's. Further proof came from artifacts found at the site such as iron stakes used to split the stone and datable finds like pottery and coins. These confirmed a date around 19 BC, the time of Herod's expansion of the temple. The use of such immense stones allowed construction without the need for cement or plaster and maintained the stability of the structure of the walls of the Temple Mount for thousands of years. Josephus described the stones used for the temple's construction as "hard and white" (*Ant.* 15.11.3; 392) and of such strength that during the Roman assault on the temple the military's battering rams were unable to cause a breach in the outer wall (*J.W.* 6.4.1; 220–22). The exceptional stones in the quarry gave evidence that this was indeed the site from which the stones for the temple had been taken. Herod used a thousand oxen to transport the stones from the quarry to the construction site and archaeologists also uncovered a part of the ancient main road to Jerusalem used for this transport some 300 feet from the quarry. This road was located only 2 miles (4 km) from the Temple Mount.

Evidence of Temple-Related Structures

On the northwestern side of the Temple Mount, Herod built the Antonia Fortress over the remains of the former Seleucid-period Baris to guard this weaker location and provide a watch and a station for troops to control the crowds on the Temple Mount. To the north of this structure he constructed an open-air reservoir called the Strouthion Pool, originally built as part of an open-air water conduit by the Hasmoneans. On the northeastern side he constructed another reservoir pool known as *Birket Israel* ("the Pool of Israel") to serve as a public cistern and a defense for the northeastern corner of the Temple Mount. The remains of most of these structures have been discovered, and those of the Strouthion Pool can be viewed today near the exit of the Western Wall Tunnel and beneath the Sisters of Zion Convent. From the outside, a portion of the Antonia Fortress is visible within the structure of the building housing an Islamic boys school.

The most visible remains of a structure associated with the Herodian temple are sections of the massive retaining walls still extant today. Herodian ashlars and masonry can be seen in the lower courses of the southern wall and eastern wall on either side of the Islamic period Golden Gate. However, the most impressive example is the exposed section of the Western (or Wailing) Wall (in Hebrew, *Kotel*), which is more than 1,500 feet

in length (north to south) and 900 feet in width (east to west). Its height is approximately 50 feet above the modern plaza with another course of stones continuing down at least another 50 feet (more in the southern end than the northern end). In the 1990s a tunnel was opened alongside the underground course of stones to enable tourists to view the full extent of the Herodian construction. In the course exposed in this tunnel is one of the most massive of the foundation stones yet discovered. Its measurements are 45 feet (13.70 m) x 11.6 feet (3.19 m) x 14–16 feet (4.20–4.90 m) with a weight of nearly 600 tons.

Alongside the Western Wall (and also the southern wall) Israeli archaeologist Benjamin Mazar excavated many structures related to the Herodian Second Temple, including the great western staircase for entrance to the temple known as Robinson's Arch (due to its initial discovery and report in the nineteenth century by British archaeologist Edward Robinson) and a monumental staircase, stretching

Herodian pedestrian street with shops along southern end of the Western Wall showing how street buckled (above sewer channel) when Roman soldiers threw down stones from Temple Mount (see pile of such stone debris from AD 70 at top of photo)

www.HolyLand Photos.org

almost half a mile uphill from the Pool of Siloam to the Huldah Gates at the southern entrance to the temple, carried the Jewish population (including Jesus and his disciples) through the Huldah Gates and onto the Temple Mount. Also, here was found a public building that housed *miqvaot* (ritual immersion pools) that were used by Jews requiring purification to enter the temple precincts. These were mentioned in Acts 2:41 as the place of immersion for Jewish believers in Jesus during the Feast of Pentecost. Traces of gates from Islamic period construction (now sealed) called the Double and Triple Gates marked the sites of the Huldah Gates and the subterranean passages that still lay beyond them. Inside the interior of the Double Gate entrance archaeologists found Herodian columns that had supported portions of the ornate roof design (sections of which were recovered from the debris) and that had given the site the New Testament name "the Beautiful Gate" (Acts 3:2).

Haifa University archaeologist Ronny Reich continued the excavations along the southwestern side of the wall and reached the ancient street 32 feet (10 m) wide and paved with large slabs up to a foot thick. The street was lined with shops (where Jews bought sacrificial animals for the temple), and archaeologists found the remains of merchant activity, such as weights and coins used for transactions. Also found here was the landing for Robinson's Arch, more *miqvaot*, and an inscribed stone that instructed the priests where to stand to blow the trumpets signaling the beginning of the Sabbath. It had originally been located high above on the top corner of the southwestern wall. Within the context of these architectural structures was found a wealth of artifacts that demonstrated Jewish daily life in and around the temple. Also of great significance was the discovery of the lid of a stone sarcophagus bearing the Hebrew inscription: ". . . *ben hacohen hagadol* . . ." ("son of the high priest"). This name is known from the Second Temple literature as the son

of the high priest who had served in the temple. One of the more moving archaeological finds for Jewish people were piles of Herodian stones still lying on this ancient street where they had landed after being thrown down from the western side of the temple complex by Roman soldiers during their destruction of the temple on the ninth of the month of Av, AD 70. Most of the stones weighed two–four tons each but some were in excess of fifteen tons. The force of impact had caved in the flagstones that formed the street, exposing an underground sewer channel, first excavated in 2007 by Reich and his assistant Eli Shukrun, to its exit point deep in the Kidron Valley.

This sewer channel was under an aqueduct that connected the western plaza of the Temple Mount to the city of David, but according to Josephus (*J.W.* 6.9.4) it had been used as an escape tunnel by Jews fleeing from the Romans. Inside this escape tunnel evidence was found of Jewish refugee life, including

Temple menorah etched on plaster from Jewish Quarter (first century AD). Israel Museum.

"Pure for God" seal for temple-related items discovered on the steps leading from the Pool of Siloam to the western pedestrian street

Photo courtesy Eli Shukron. Used by permission.

seal mentioned in the Mishnah (m. Sheqalim. 5:1–5). It is also recorded in the Gemara (m. Shabbat. 2:21) that the only cruse of oil that was discovered in the temple after the victory of the Maccabees over the Greeks, "lay with the seal of the High Priest," a seal that indicated the that oil was pure and acceptable for use in the temple. Such a seal would have been carried by a temple priest to identify items qualified as ritually pure.

Evidence from Temple-Related Artifacts

Artifacts coming from the area of the temple are extremely rare since archaeologists have never been allowed to excavate at this site. Even so, in 1871 French archaeologist Charles Clermont-Ganneau discovered in rubble from the Temple Mount near the Lion's (St. Stephens) Gate a large limestone block with a seven-line Greek inscription. The translation revealed that this was a warning against entering the ritually pure area of the temple courts. In the Jewish sources this stone balustrade (in Hebrew *soreg*) was said to have separated the Court of the Gentiles from the Court of the Women and was the main barrier beyond which gentiles and the ceremonially unclean were forbidden to pass (Kelim 1.8). According to Josephus it stood 5 feet 2 inches (1.57 m) high. To insure that this boundary was not improperly breached, large stone inscriptions in Greek and Latin that threatened death to violators were posted at each entrance to the courts (*Ant.* 15.471). In the New Testament, the apostle Paul is reported to have been accused of violating this prohibition because he had been earlier seen in the company of Trophimus, a non-Jew, and it was assumed he had brought him into the temple (Acts 21:27–31). The riot generated from this accusation resulted in Paul's arrest and subsequent Roman trials (Acts 21:11, 32–28:31). This is the most complete example of this temple warning sign, known as the Soreg inscription, which was taken to Istanbul

cooking pots, oil lamps, a key, First Revolt coins, and the remains of a 60-centimeters-long iron Roman sword inside a decorated leather scabbard. In 2011 archaeologists found here a stone slab with an etching that depicted the menorah that was used in the temple's holy place. It was probably sketched by a priest who had seen the sacred vessel while on duty and had taken refuge in the tunnel with other Jews. This sketch, like a plaster carved image found in the Jewish Quarter from this same period and a Byzantine period pottery sherd found in debris from the Temple Mount by the Temple Mount Sifting Project, depicted menorahs with a tripod base. This archaeological data is significant to the age-old debate regarding the appearance of the menorah that stood in the Second Temple, which in the past was only evidenced by an image of the temple menorah appearing on the relief inside the Arch of Titus's Triumph in the Roman Forum. This image created by a Roman artist depicted the menorah with an octagonal base decorated with various mythological creatures (a hippocamp), a surprising feature since it represented a violation of Jewish law (Exod 20:4).[3] The examples coming from a priestly context would argue strongly for their depiction as genuine.

In Reich's and Shukron's 2011 excavation, soil sifted from the Herodian street beneath Robinson's Arch produced a small stone seal with a two-line Aramaic inscription: *deka'* ("pure") *leyah* ("to/for God"). This seal certifying the ritual purity of an item to be used in the Second Temple is the kind of and today is exhibited in the Museum of the Ancient Orient. A fragmentary example of this inscription was discovered near the Lion's Gate in Jerusalem and is on exhibit in the Israel Museum.

From the Temple Mount, but removed from the original context, are artifacts that have been recovered from construction debris by the Temple Mount Sifting Project. Among the some 6,000 coin finds are the earliest Judean (Yehud) coins from the Persian period, coins of Antiochus IV Epiphanes (175–163 BC), who desecrated the temple, and hundreds of common Jewish coins from the Hasmonean and Second Temple periods. Of special note was the discovery of silver and bronze shekel coins minted by Jews during the First Jewish Revolt (AD 66–70) that contained inscriptions such as "Holy Jerusalem" and "For the Freedom of Zion." Scores of iron arrowheads were also found as evidence of this Jewish war against the Romans. Among the inscribed finds is a clay bullae with an ancient Hebrew inscription, "belonging to Gedaliah, son of Immer *ha-cohen*" (=the priest Pashur; cf. Jer 20:1; 38:1), who may have been a priest or high official, and a potsherd decorated with a menorah such as was used in the temple. During Randall Price's team's work in the project (sifting dirt collected from the valley below the Golden Gate) there was discovered a murex shell, the very shell used by the temple priests to dye parts of their priestly garments, unique tiles (*Opus Sectile*) that created a wave-pattern and came from one of the courts of the temple, and a clay bullae containing an Israelite name written in Egyptian hieroglyphics. Egyptians had influence on Judean kings and officials throughout the First Temple period, beginning with Solomon, who made an alliance with the pharaoh of Egypt and had an Egyptian wife (1 Kgs 9:16; 11:1).

Only intact remains of the Soreg inscription once attached to the separation fence preventing Gentiles from entering the Temple precincts upon pain of death. Istanbul Museum.

Many Egyptian scarabs were also found in the Temple Mount rubble. In addition, pieces of fresco from buildings within the temple precincts, a column of a Doric capital that may have been part of the royal stoa, and a fragment of a sculptured stone engraved with an acanthus leaf (a Herodian style that may have been from the temple itself). All of these artifacts were unearthed on the Temple Mount as a result of non-archaeological excavation (for the construction of the Al-Marwani mosque). Still today lying visible in piles of rubble on the Temple Mount are marble and limestone columns, decorated building stones, and portions of other monumental structures that may have been part of the Second Temple complex. These are inaccessible to archaeologists and remain under the control of the Muslim authorities who, for religious and political reasons, discarded these ancient relics.

Archaeological Excavation in the Shadow of the Temple

In AD 70 the Roman Tenth Legion successively breached the walls of the city of Jerusalem and burned the Second (Herodian) Temple. After the destruction the remains of the Temple proper were pushed over the retaining walls, primarily on the eastern side, though remains have been discovered on the Herodian street running the length of the walls that line the western side of the elevated platform. Many of these remains were reused in buildings in the city through the ages, such as columns from the Royal Stoa used in the Nea Church and ashlar blocks from the Western Wall in an Umayyad Palace (8th century AD) built at the southwestern corner of the Temple Mount. During the second century AD when the Roman Emperor Hadrian punished the Jews for the Bar Kokhba Revolt, he built a temple to the Roman chief god Jupiter on the Temple site and forbade Jews to enter the city upon pain of death. With the Islamic occupation of Jerusalem in AD 638, the Temple Mount was converted to an Islamic mosque and made off limits to non-Muslims. Therefore, despite the abundance of information about the Temple structures provide by Flavius Josephus, the Mishnah (especially tractate Middot) and the Talmud, as well as various other sources, archaeological excavation in the area of the ancient temple on the Temple Mount has never taken place.

Today, archaeological excavation in the eastern section of Jerusalem containing the remains of the ancient Temple Mount remains controversial due to competing religious and political demands over the city and for the site. In AD 691 an Islamic shrine known as the Dome of the Rock was built over the site formerly occupied by the Jewish temple. An Islamic mosque, the Al-Aqsa Mosque (AD 705) was soon built near this structure and for much of the past 1,300 years entry to non-Muslims was strictly forbidden. This prohibition has continued to the present day, with protests mounted by the Islamic Authority for suspected incursions or even the act of tourists making religious gestures at the site. For this reason, in the nineteenth century British explorers conducted limited but extensive excavations in and around the Temple Mount, and their published research has been the primary source of information about ancient subterranean structures, many still off limits to archaeologists. Following 1967 when the area of East Jerusalem returned to Israeli control, excavations were begun at the foot of the Temple Mount, but strictly outside the area of the mosques that remained under the jurisdiction of the Islamic Waqf. These excavations were conducted from 1967 to 1978 below the southwestern and southern walls of the Temple Mount under the direction of

Benjamin Mazar (and his assistant Meir Ben Dov), in the Western Wall tunnels under the direction of Dan Bahat in the 1980s, were renewed below the southwestern and southern walls by Ronny Reich in the 1990s (who with Eli Shukron have continued discoveries related to the temple in the City of David and the tunnels stretching from an area adjacent to the ancient Pool of Bethesda to the Herodian street next to the temple's western retaining wall), and continued in the twenty-first century by Eilat Mazar, the granddaughter of Benjamin Mazar.

While the Islamic authorities do not permit archaeological excavations on the Temple Mount itself, the Islamic Waqf has inadvertently provided archaeologists with abundant data from this site. Beginning in 1996, the Islamic authorities removed more than 20,000 tons of archaeologically rich debris from the southern and eastern portions of the Temple Mount in preparation for the construction of the Al-Marwani mosque. This material was dumped into the Kidron Valley but later recovered by Israeli archaeologists Gabriel Barkay and Zachi Zweig. They established the Temple Mount Sifting Project as a means of searching through this rubble and salvaging what evidence could be found of a Jewish presence on the Temple Mount. Wet sifting in order to separate the smallest artifact from the from the Temple Mount debris, this project has uncovered tons of fragmentary structures and pottery, half of which is dated to the First and Second Temple periods. Thousands of coins, inscriptions, and other items have also been found. Other excavations have taken place at the rear of the Western Wall plaza (Kotel Excavation) and in and around the previous excavations, however, the only ancient remains that have been viewed (or recovered) in situ from the Temple Mount itself have come indirectly from repairs to water lines or electrical cables under the platform conducted by the Islamic Waqf or during the construction activity connected with the building of the Al-Marwani Mosque at the southern end of the platform (at the site of the Solomon's Stables).

There has never been any proper archaeological exploration of the Temple Mount because it is under the jurisdiction of the Waqf, a Muslim religious trust. In order to gain information about this site, early explorers resorted to subterfuge, often at the risk of their lives. In 1911 the ill-fated Parker Expedition, tasked with finding the treasures of Solomon's Temple believed to be located beneath the Temple Mount, attempted, by cover of night, to dig beneath the floor inside the Dome of the Rock. The team barely escaped with their lives when their secret work was discovered. Nevertheless, scientific explorations were conducted during the nineteenth century under the Ottoman administration. These took the form of ordinance surveys and limited excavations around the Temple Mount. As a result, the published works of British explorers Charles Warren, Charles Wilson, and American explorer Edward Robinson have been a primary source of topographical research on the site to modern scholars and archaeologists.

Archaeological excavation outside the Temple Mount was undertaken by the Israel state in 1967 after the Six Day War when the area resumed Israeli control. Major excavations of the southern end of the Western Wall and the southern entrance to the Temple Mount were conducted by Benjamin Mazar and later continued by his granddaughter Eliat Mazar. Excavations by Ronny Reich and Eli Shukron in the City of David and the area of the Gihon Spring at the end of the twentieth century and the first decades of the twenty-first century revealed the continuation of a monumental staircase discovered by Mazar outside the southern wall of the Temple Mount. Under these steps ran a sewer line that drained from the Temple Mount into the Herodian street below. Josephus recorded that this sewer was used as a hiding place for Jews fleeing from the Roman destruction of the Temple in AD 70. In addition, Reuch and Shukron discovered a stone inscribed with a menorah, a golden bell from the robe of a priest, and a purity seal used by a temple priest. Although the Temple Mount has been inaccessible to archaeologists, construction done at the site has inadvertently revealed evidence of the temple. In 2006 a construction project near the Dome of the Rock unearthed eighth-century-BC pottery and the top of a wall (possibly related to the First Temple). From 1996 to 2001, the Waqf, in preparation for the construction of a new mosque on the southern side of the Temple Mount, removed some twenty tons of archaeologically rich debris and dumped some of it in the Kidron Valley. From the debris, Israeli archaeologist Zachi Zweig recovered temple-era artifacts, and with Dr. Gabriel Barkay the two organized the Temple Mount Sifting Project. For over a decade this project, which transferred the Temple Mount debris to the site of Emeq Tzurim (on the Mt. of Olives), has made significant discoveries of artifacts related to the temple and its services. In 2015 a bulla with the words "belonging to Hezekiah, son of Ahaz, King of Judah" was discovered by sifting debris taken from Eilat Mazar's 2012 excavations in the Ophel. This was the first seal ascribed to Hezekiah that was properly identified within an archaeological context. In this instance, the seal was located in an administrative area connected to the First Temple.

Another artifact found in excavations directed by Eilat Mazar outside the southern wall area of the Temple Mount is a gold medallion, 4 inches in diameter with a menorah depicted on it. Though part of a late Byzantine-era (seventh century AD) hoard, which included thirty-six gold coins, this adornment for a Torah scroll (probably for a synagogue located in the area) reflects the Jewish continued reverence to the Temple Mount even though it had been destroyed centuries before.

Torah Scroll Medallion found near the Temple Mount (7th century AD). Evidence of Jewish identification with the site centuries after the Temple's destruction.

Z. Radovan/www.Bible
LandPictures.com

10 | The Dead Sea Scrolls

The Dead Sea Scrolls are a collection of some 1,100 biblical texts[1] written in Hebrew, Aramaic, and Greek. Most were written on parchment (made from goat or sheep skins) and papyrus (an early form of paper). More than 230 of the total manuscripts represent copies of books in the Hebrew Bible. The rest are apocryphal and pseudepigraphal texts, commentaries on biblical texts, and sectarian documents. These later documents were composed during the Hasmonean period (152–63 BC) through the early Roman period (63 BC–AD 68), the time that a Jewish religious sect calling itself the *Yaḥad* ("community") occupied a settlement at the biblical wilderness site of Secacah (Josh 15:61). The modern term for the site is Khirbet Qumran, modern Arabic terms meaning "ruins" and

"moon" (from *qamar*). This, according to local Bedouins, is based on their experience of seeing the moon reflected in a pool at the top of a cliff overlooking the plateau where the settlement existed. The scrolls were discovered hidden in caves in or in the vicinity of the Qumran settlement, located in the Judean desert on the northwest shore of the Dead Sea some 20 miles southwest of Jerusalem. These scrolls were found only in the caves around this site and not in the settlement itself. Similar texts, considered part of the documents from the Judean Desert, came from other sites along the Dead Sea such as Jericho, Masada, Wadi Murabba'at, Nahal Hever, Nahal Se'elim, Nahal Mishmar, and Khirbet Mird. Based on datable artifacts found in the caves, calibrated carbon-14 dating, and

The Biblical Manuscripts Attested in the Dead Sea Scrolls

Canonical Books	Old Testament Book	Number
Torah	Genesis	25
	Exodus	20
	Leviticus	19
	Numbers	11
	Deuteronomy	39
Prophets	Joshua	2
	Judges	3
	1–2 Samuel	4
	1–2 Kings	3
	Isaiah	22
	Jeremiah	7
	Ezekiel	6
	12 Minor Prophets	10

Canonical Books	Old Testament Book	Number
Writings	Psalms	40
	Proverbs	2
	Job	6
	Song of Songs	4
	Lamentations	4
	Ecclesiastes	2
	Ruth	4
	Daniel	10
	Ezra–Nehemiah	1
	1–2 Chronicles	1
Total		**246/238**
No **Esther** but references exist in other scrolls		

Totals adjusted to read **8** less because some scrolls preserve parts of 2–3 books.

paleographic and scribal dating, the Dead Sea Scrolls range from the third century BC to the first century AD. Many of the Judean desert scrolls coming from the region south of Qumran are dated to the time of the Bar Kokhba Revolt (AD 132–136).

Classifying the Dead Sea Scrolls

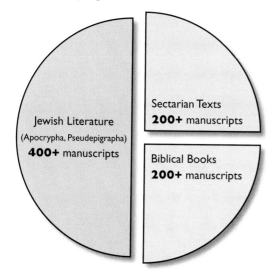

Jewish Literature (Apocrypha, Pseudepigrapha) **400+** manuscripts

Sectarian Texts **200+** manuscripts

Biblical Books **200+** manuscripts

The Discovery of the Dead Sea Scrolls

As the story of their initial discovery of the Dead Sea Scrolls has come to us, in 1946–1947 young shepherd boys of the Ta'amireh Bedouin tribe, Muhammad edh-Dhib, Jum'a Muhammed, Khalil Musa, Muhammad al-Asi, and Muhammad Hammad Ubiayt,[2] discovered a cave in which were stored cylindrical jars covered with bowl lids. Inside these jars were a collection of seven parchment (processed animal skin) scrolls (many wrapped in linen cloths) written in Hebrew and Aramaic. The seven scrolls included biblical manuscripts: two copies of Isaiah (Isaiah A and B), a commentary on Habakkuk, and sectarian scrolls including the Manual of Discipline, War Scroll, Thanksgiving Scroll, and the Genesis Apocryphon. Once the discovery became public with the publication of the Isaiah

Scroll and Habakkuk Commentary in 1950[3] and the scrolls were deemed valuable, the Bedouin (followed by the archaeologists) discovered additional caves, and more scrolls came to light. Once archaeologists began work at Cave 1 (the location of which was initially kept secret by the Bedouins), they discovered the remains of datable pottery such as oil lamps, which placed the earliest use of the cave in the Hasmonean period. The seven initial scrolls eventually found their way through the Bedouin to the antiquities market and to part-time antiquities dealer Khalil Eskander Shahin Kando, and through him four were sold to Syrian Orthodox of Antioch Archbishop Mar Athanasius Yeshue Samuel at St. Mark's Monastery in Jerusalem and three to Hebrew University Professor Eleazer Sukenik. In 1948 the four in the Archbishop's possession were taken to the American Schools of Oriental Research, where John Trever photographed them and sent copies to American archaeologist William Foxwell Albright, who declared them the greatest manuscript discovery of modern times. Eventually, the state of Israel acquired the seven scrolls and a museum known as the Shrine of the Book was constructed to exhibit them as part of the Israel National Museum in Jerusalem.

Sheik Muhammad Hammad Ubiayt in front of entrance to Cave 1. He has been documented to be one of the Tama'arah Bedouins who made the original discovery.

Randall Price uncovers broken scroll jars inside Cave 53 at Qumran.

Photo courtesy Casey Olson and Oren Gutfeld

Leather scroll fragment found inside broken jar in Cave 53 at Qumran.

Photo courtesy Oren Gutfeld

This museum also houses discoveries of artifacts and documents from other caves at Qumran, such as the biblical and sectarian manuscripts from Cave 4 and the Temple Scroll from Cave 11, as well as the various fragments from caves along the western side of the Dead Sea south of Qumran. Other fragments and related artifacts are housed in Jerusalem at the Rockefeller Museum, the École Biblique et Archéologique Française, and the Hebrew University (where conservation and preservation of the scrolls is performed).

Alleged Temple Scroll jar from Cave 11

Photo by Casey Olson; Courtesy William Kando

Between 1947 and 1956 eleven scroll caves were identified, being numbered in the order of their discovery.

Important scroll discoveries include the Copper Scroll (3Q15), found in Cave 3 in 1952, and the Temple Scroll (11Q19), recovered from Kando in 1967 but since proven to have come from Cave 11. In March 2017, further excavation in Cave 11 revealed pieces of textiles connected with the scrolls. The cave of the Copper Scroll contained fragments of fourteen different documents, but the prize find was two copper plates (rolled up in scroll fashion) that were engraved with Hebrew characters (and some Greek ciphers). This unique document contains an inventory of immense treasure (material wealth and ritual items) hidden in sixty-four cryptic locations in and beyond the Judean desert. To date, none of its locations have been positively identified,

Temple Scroll

Z. Radovan/www
.BibleLandPictures
.com

nor have any of the items listed in the inventory been discovered, although several attempts have been made at Qumran, Hyrcania, and Jerusalem.[4] Theories as to the source of the treasure run the gamut from a treasure of the First Temple, the Second Temple, the Qumran community, and the Egyptian pharaoh Akhenaten. The Temple Scroll, at 27 feet, the longest of the Dead Sea Scrolls, was a primary document of the Qumran sect, though it may have preceded the group itself. It is a priestly document written as a revelation from God to Moses giving details for the construction of a properly pure temple and its laws and rituals. A large jar with a conical lid adorned with a small knob, still in the possession of the Kando family, was said to have come from Cave 11 and to have housed the Temple Scroll.

In January 2017, Oren Gutfeld (Hebrew University) and Randall Price (Liberty University) working with the new Operation Scroll made the discovery of scroll Cave 53 southwest of the Qumran Plateau. The cave contained numerous scroll jars hidden in rock-cut niches on the east side and a tunnel at the rear of the cave. At the back of the cave iron picks were found dating to the Second Temple period, apparently used by those who originally hid the scrolls. Although the jars had been broken and robbed by looters in the past, they left behind in the jars scraps of leather, papyrus, linen wrappings, and ties that were once part of the scrolls themselves. This provided evidence that many scroll discoveries are still possible in the Judean desert. In addition, it is now apparent from the discovery of the rock-cut shelves hiding scroll jars and the use of sifting at Cave 53 that additional finds could be made in the scroll caves previously excavated.

Section of the Copper Scroll (cut 15) showing section 8 which describes treasure hidden in the Jerusalem area.

Courtesy of Bruce and Ken Zuckerman, West Semitic Research. Used by permission.

The Dead Sea Scrolls and Biblical Studies

The Dead Sea Scrolls have great significance for biblical studies. Bringing a unique window on the Second Temple period, these documents provide some of our only information on the Jewish sects of the time, such as the Pharisees and Sadducees, who left no writings of their own, as well as the Essenes (if in fact the scrolls are the product of this sect). They refer to Second Temple period rituals, religious views, and social customs, give geographic and topographic information, record historical and political events, reveal Jewish legal interpretations (comparable to later discussions in the Mishnah and Talmud), and contain specialized vocabulary, in some cases paralleling the use in the New Testament such as the Gospel of John and the epistles of Paul. These documents also provide previously unknown information about a Jewish sectarian group who called themselves the *Yaḥad* and of legal practices and social customs only dimly echoed in the much later rabbinic writings (Talmud, Mishnah). In addition, before the discovery of the scrolls the extrabiblical Jewish literature, such as the Apocrypha and Pseudepigrapha, existed only in ancient translations (Greek, Syriac, and Coptic), but the scrolls provided Hebrew and Aramaic versions, allowing scholars for the first time to read these works in their original form. They also reveal that Judaism was hardly monolithic in the Second Temple period and that no one kind can necessarily be assumed as normative for the rest. In other words, the diverse elements that characterized intertestamental Judaism will not permit lumping together their beliefs into a singular Jewish theology. Moreover, the scrolls reveal that Second Temple Judaism, although an heir of biblical Judaism, was no more identical to it than to later rabbinic Judaism. This provides background for understanding the cultural conditions and conflicts that elicited Jesus' parabolic method of teaching and his debates within first-century Judaism.

However, their most important value to biblical studies is for the textual criticism of the Old Testament, helping scholars understand the state of the biblical text in the Second Temple period and its transmission from earlier times and how stable this transmission was until it was fixed with the MT (the traditional text) in the tenth century AD. The chart above reveals the significance of the span of time bridged by the Dead Sea biblical texts (such as that contained in the most complete text, the Great Isaiah Scroll) in relation to the MT (the oldest copy represented by the Leningrad Codex).

Biblical critics had previously believed that an incalculable number of variants must have entered into the biblical manuscripts during its transmission period until it took its final form with the MT. Taking for their point of comparison the Great Isaiah Scroll (1QIsa[a]) dated ca.125 BC, the most complete of the biblical texts and one of the longest books in the Hebrew Bible, it was found that it had a 95 percent agreement with the MT. The 5 percent variation consisted primarily of obvious slips of the pen and spelling alterations. This also proved to be the case for all of the other biblical scrolls among the Dead Sea Scrolls. In fact, about 60 percent of these biblical texts reflect the same text as that in the MT. Although interesting deviations and additions do appear and are of great value in understanding the history of the transmission of the biblical text, on the whole, the scrolls testify to the exceptional scribal preservation of the biblical text through the centuries and validate the traditional text as the closest witness we have to the original. This fact justifies confidence in the Bible's textual transmission and in the modern translations of the Old Testament that are based upon it. Since the discovery of the Dead Sea Scrolls, every new translation of the Bible has taken into account the textual evidence it has provided. Today, all of the Qumran texts have been published (the Discoveries in the Judean Desert series), and the

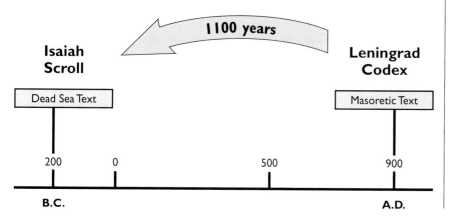

The Dead Sea Scrolls contain the earliest extant copies of the Bible

The scrolls enabled scholars to study the transmission history of the biblical text.

fragments in institutional and private hands are also in the process of publication by Brill as additions to the Dead Sea Scrolls. On the popular level, the biblical texts have been collected and published in a canonical order as *The Dead Sea Scrolls Bible*,[5] and the Leon Levy Dead Sea Scrolls Digital Library and the Dead Sea Scrolls Digital Project (both in partnership with Google) have made available to the public the images of the scrolls and their translation. As to publications on the scrolls, the number is so great that there are publications on the publications of the scrolls and related research.

Excavation at the Site of Qumran

In the late 1940s through the early 1950s, Bedouin and archaeologists found additional fragments of parchment and papyrus scrolls in caves adjacent to Cave 1 and at a site a mile and a half south of these caves. The caves and the scrolls found in them came to be numbered by the order of their discovery. Caves 2, 3, and 11 were located in the vicinity of Cave 1, while Caves 4–10 were located at the southern site. When archaeologists excavated inside Cave 4, they found a large cache of scroll fragments beneath the floor of the cave and additional fragments in the

other man-made caves that, like Cave 4, surrounded a raised marl plateau that contained the remains of ancient buildings. The discovery of scroll fragments in the caves at Qumran led archaeologists to investigate the plateau, theorizing that the remains there might have had a connection with the scrolls. Called by the Arabic name Khirbet Qumran ("ruins of Qumran"), the structures of this settlement were first excavated from 1951–57 by Dominican priest Roland de Vaux, a French biblical scholar in residence at the École biblique in Jerusalem, an academic institute specializing in archaeology and study of the biblical text. A two-story structure on the eastern side of the settlement contained the remains of long plaster-covered benches and inkwells. While the use of the benches is uncertain (they may have been used to stretch out the scrolls and stitch them together), the presence of the inkwells strongly suggests that scribal activity occurred in this building. On the basis of this evidence, de Vaux concluded that this had been a *scriptorium* (room for writing), lending support to the theory that this was the site of the ancient Jewish community who had been involved with the production and preservation of the scrolls, although many of the scrolls came from outside Qumran and were made a part of their library.

Artist reconstruction of the community buildings at Qumran before its destruction in AD 68.

A Ritual Baths
B Potter's Kiln
C Refectory
D Vicinity of Caves 4–10
E Scriptorium
F Stables
G Tower
H Cistern
I Aqueduct
J Storerooms
K Plateau

This connection was further strengthened by the discovery that the jars containing the scrolls had been produced in the kilns at Qumran, that jars and scroll fragments had been hidden in caves cut into the very sides of the plateau that housed the community, and that pottery found at the settlement matched that found in Cave 1 to the north. In the 1990s archaeologists Magen Broshi and Hanan Eshel further strengthened the connection between the plateau and the site of the original discovery by finding an ancient footpath that had once connected the two sites. Yet another connection between the site and the scrolls was de Vaux's discovery of animal bone deposits buried on the outsides of settlement buildings and on the plateau. He interpreted these as ritual meals that had been eaten and disposed of according to the Jewish law concerning the *sancta*. To de Vaux and other scholars at the time, such as Jozef Milik and Eleazar Sukenik, this identified the inhabitants of the settlement as priests. A more specific identification was made with the Essenes, a Jewish sect who claimed descent from the Zadokite priesthood and whom the Roman historian, Pliny the Elder, assigned to an area

of the Dead Sea near En-Gedi (Pliny, *Natural History* 5.17). Based on the ceramic and numismatic evidence, it had been inhabited initially in the Iron Age, but the community's origin under the sect appears to have been in the closing days of the Hasmonean period (second century BC), when pious Jews sought a refuge in the desert due to the abusive policies of the Hasmonean government and the illegitimate status of the temple priesthood. It ended in AD 68 when the Roman army was punishing all Jews in the region for the Jewish Revolt. The buildings at the site were burned, and for the next decade Qumran served as a Roman garrison.

Toward the end of the twentieth century, new theories were raised challenging the view that Qumran was a Jewish, priestly, sectarian settlement. Norman Golb contended that the scrolls were from a library (most likely connected with the temple) in Jerusalem that had been transported to the desert at the onslaught of the Roman response to the Jewish Revolt, between AD 66 and 70.[6] Robert Donceel and Pauline Donceel-Voute argued that Qumran was a Roman villa, based in part on the discovery of luxury item artifacts that did not fit the religious community settlement model.[7]

Randall Price and Eric Ream descend to Cave 6 at Qumran where fragments of thirty-one documents were discovered

Rick Schuler

However, the Roman occupation period could account for such anomalous finds. Lena Cansdale and Alan Crown argued that the settlement was a fortified road station and a port town on the shores of the Dead Sea and therefore a commercial site on a major north-south trade route.[8] Yizhar Hirschfeld amended this proposal and argued that it was a Hasmonean-era fortified manor house that became an agriculturally based fortified trading station during the Herodian period.[9] He based his conclusion on a comparison with his excavations at nearby Ein Feshka (which at one time was joined by a wall to Qumran). However, prior to his death he visited the excavations on the southern plateau directed by Randall Price, where he observed a large collection of animal bone deposits in situ and admitted, "ritual was involved." This admission favored the idea of a religious community rather than his secular model. Another theory was advanced by Yitzhak Magen and Yuval Peleg, who excavated Qumran from 1993–2004, that the site was for pottery production and had nothing to do with a religious settlement.

In 1984–85 Joseph Patrich and Yigael Yadin carried out a systematic survey of some fifty-seven caves north and south of Qumran[10] and subsequently Patrich excavated five caves, concluding their use was for storage by the Qumran sect. In one cave, Patrich discovered a Herodian period juglet wrapped in palm fibers and the residue of a substance thought to be balsam oil (the Romans maintained a prized grove of balsam trees near 'Ein-Gedi) and a store jar containing dried dates. In the mid-1990s Magen Broshi and Hanan Eshel excavated caves immediately north of the Qumran settlement in a ravine. Two of these caves revealed evidence of continued habitation, including hundreds of potsherds. They concluded that these caves were used as summer residences by the families of the Qumran community but were abandoned when the winter rains brought flooding to the site.[11]

In 1994, on the eve of the Palestinian Authority assuming authority over territory in and around Jericho and the fear that Qumran and related areas were to be ceded to Palestinian control, Yitzhak Magen, then

Staff Officer for the Civil Administration for Judea and Samaria, initiated Operation Scroll, an ambitious survey of some 300 cave sites in the Judean desert. The results were a mapping of caves and evidence of habitation based on limited excavation. Magen and Yuval Peleg's excavations inside and outside the Qumran settlement areas to the north and south uncovered four refuse dumps, a paved square, three underground silos (on the plateau) dated to the Iron Age, an overflow channel, and small finds such as ten ostraca, a glass bottle, iron arrowheads, and coins ranging from the second century BC to the first century AD.[12] However, the outstanding find, according to the excavator's preliminary report, was the discovery of a thick layer of clay at the bottom of the re-excavated stepped pool (Pool L-71), which they identified as "high quality potter's clay" and argued was evidence that Qumran

had been primarily a pottery factory servicing the general area and not a religious Jewish settlement as most Qumran scholars had maintained.[13] They also argued that the animal bone deposits were nothing more than discarded meals, buried only to prevent wild dogs and other local animals from getting to the remains, and had nothing to do with ritual practice. These views were in accord with their previously stated belief that Qumran had nothing to do with scroll production and that the scrolls themselves were from Jerusalem and only hidden in the caves at Qumran because it had such caves and was an ideal location in the desert for such a purpose. Scholars reacted to the pottery production theory since no chemical analysis of the clay was released by the excavators to support their contention. Cooper[14] has summarized the evidence against the view, especially the work of

Frederick Zeuner, who conducted a thorough analysis of the clay deposits in the reservoirs at Qumran[15] and performed a chemical analysis of the clay and cistern filling to determine their value as pottery clay. Zeuner collected clay samples from four locations at Qumran, including three potters' basins, Cistern 58, and the Lisan Marl. The clays available at Qumran were primarily composed of limestone and dolomite dust. He concluded: "No experienced potter would think of using this material unleached. Even if leached, half of the sediment in the reservoirs of Qumran consists of carbonates, a composition which would make very bad pottery clay."[16] This means that the clay deposits in the two large Qumran reservoirs proposed by Magen and Peleg as sources for the pottery factory would not have been suitable for use in pottery manufacture.[17]

Further support for a connection between the site and the scrolls came from an investigation of a latrine site mentioned in the War Scroll and Temple Scroll connected with ritual practice. James Tabor observed that the inhabitants of the Qumran community used latrines about 200 feet northwest of the site, a practice conforming to Jewish ritual practice (Deut 23:12–24) and also described as a practice of the Essenes by Josephus.[18] Tabor, Israeli anthropologist Joe Zias, and French archaeologist Stephanie Harter-Lailheugue, believed they could identify this latrine site at Qumran[19] and took soil samples. These samples under microscopic examination revealed desiccated eggs from three distinctly human parasites. However, because of the ritual requirement to cover excrement at the latrines, natural sunlight was not able to neutralize the toxic bacteria in the waste. As a result, those who walked barefoot at the site brought lethal bacteria back

Aerial view of the excavation site of Qumran Community (right) and Randall Price excavations on the Plateau (left).

Photo by Sky View. Courtesy Randall Price.

Randall Price excavating an animal bone deposit on the Qumran Plateau (2006).

Lamar Cooper

to the settlement from the latrines and then spread the contamination when they entered the *miqvaot* (ritual baths). The health problems that were generated by this bacterial infection resulted in a shortened lifespan, with only a 6 percent chance of living to an age of forty.[20] Zias also supported this claim from his experience in studying human remains from the Qumran cemetery, which he said reflected the most unhealthy individuals he had ever seen.

The discovery of this site at Qumran from the War Scroll and the Temple Scroll reveals (1) an observant religious community occupied the Qumran plateau in the first century BC, (2) this community at least produced the scrolls that were used to identify the location of the latrines, and (3) the same ritual practice by Jewish priests and the Essenes indicates them to be the most likely candidates for the identity of inhabitants of the community. Based on this understanding,

the religious inhabitants of the community are also the most likely persons to have hidden the scrolls in the caves at their site and upholds the original theory of de Vaux and others.[21] It should be noted that objections have been raised to this conclusion because it is thought it only works if an Essene hypothesis is assumed and that the details of the case (date and users of the latrine) have not been proven.[22]

Randall Price and Oren Gutfeld, with Yakov Kalman, carried out excavations of the southern plateau in areas not excavated by Magen and Peleg from 2002 to 2012. Structural finds included a round cut reservoir that had been filled in during the Hasmonean period (the fill contained both Iron Age and Hasmonean period sherds), apparently in order to reclaim usable space on the northeastern side of the plateau inside the area where an eastern bounding wall was constructed, a subterranean storage area accessed by cut steps, a portion of an east-west wall running perpendicular and exterior to the eastern wall, and the remains of large cut stones (one with a socket) at the southern end of the plateau that may have been used as a foundation for a wood gate or pen. Unique ceramic finds included a large intact ovoid store jar still sealed with a bowl lid whose contents were partially preserved. Neutron Activation Analysis revealed that the jar had been made of Motza clay from the Jerusalem area, and initial tests on the content residue revealed it was fermented grape wine. This was later disputed, and the identification claimed to be gypsum used to coat plaster. Among the numismatic finds was a wide range of coinage from the second century BC to the fourth century AD. The most significant finds were extensive amounts of the animal bone deposits covered or buried within broken (though sometimes intact) jars, cooking pots, plates, bowls, and cups (all vessels used to prepare and serve a meal). The interpretation of these animal bone deposits is complicated, and scholars have offered a number of different views. In light of the eschatological perspective of the Qumran community (based on a connection with the scrolls), a Qumran text specifically mentioning an eschatological meal eaten in the presence of the messiah (*Messianic Rule*/1QSa 2.11–22)[23] reflects a dependence on the biblical text of Isaiah 25:6–9, which describes an eschatological banquet. The animal bone deposits at Qumran suggests a ritual purpose, like that in the Jerusalem temple with regard to the remains of animal sacrifices, leading a number of scholars to argue for a ritual rehearsal of the anticipated messianic banquet.[24] If this is the case, the existence of so many bone burials indicates participation in a regular communal ceremony, and their coming from the Qumran IB period (103–31 BC), the time of scroll production, adds additional support to the religious settlement interpretation.

Large jars containing animal bones on the southern end of the Qumran Plateau giving evidence of the community's practice of burying the remains of ritual communal meals (2005).

Sealed ovoid store jar (Jar 25) with bowl lid (Hasmonean period) in situ (Qumran)

PART 3

ARCHAEOLOGY
and the
NEW TESTAMENT

11 | Introduction to Archaeology and the New Testament

The archaeology of the New Testament is divided into four distinct areas. First, there are those discoveries that relate to the end of the Hasmonean Period and the coming of the Roman influence in Israel, particularly the rule of Herod the Great. Even though Herod died shortly after the birth of Jesus the Messiah, his accomplishments and his impact on the land in which Jesus would have his ministry, and finally his passion, was enormous. Roman influence in the various portions of Israel, namely Judea, Samaria, and Galilee, may be seen in the buildings, inscriptions, and artifacts that come from that time. We barely encounter Herod himself at the birth of Jesus, but his sons are mentioned at different places in the Gospels and Acts.

The second area of archaeological interest is the life, death, and resurrection of Jesus. He came into conflict with the authorities of his day, whether they be religious or political. Several archaeological discoveries relating to the New Testament relate to people like the priests Caiaphas or Annas, to Herod's sons, or to Roman authorities like Pilate. Also, Jesus' travels and encounters in the Gospels are verified by archaeology, whether it is the temple environs, cities such as Bethany, Capernaum, or Jericho, or the roads and mountains of the land.

The third area relates to the remainder of the New Testament, particularly in the acts of the apostles. The author, Luke, and the apostles or their assistants introduce us to the greater Roman world. Luke was very knowledgeable of his world, including the cities, people, cultural practices, and terminology of the Mediterranean. Scholars have often questioned his conclusions, but the accuracy of his statements has repeatedly been confirmed by archaeological discoveries, such as terms in the apostolic writings that appear in first-century inscriptions and the identification and excavation of cities and provinces of the Roman world to which they make mention. Some critics of the Lucan narratives have questioned the term Asiarch, yet examples of this term for a city-ruler have emerged in such places as Ephesus and Miletus. Further, Luke's use of God-fearers caused some to accuse him of inventing the expression as a term for Gentiles who sought a relationship with the Jewish faith (though not becoming a Jew). However, the expression has been discovered in such sites as Miletus and Aphrodasis. Luke's knowledge and descriptions of the Greco-Roman world are so accurate that scholars such as Mediterranean archaeologist Sir William Ramsay became convinced of Luke's accuracy. The more Ramsay encountered the Greco-Roman world (including archaeological descriptions of cities, customs, terms, and religious practices), the more he started using the New Testament as a guide he could rely on as he did his work.

In addition, new cities are being discovered or confirmed as archaeologists continue to do their work in places like Israel. Magadala, the home of Mary of Magdala (Magdaleum) has been located, while other sites, such as Bethsaida, the home of Peter, Andrew, and Philip, are currently being debated. Not only have we identified numerous New Testament cities but by studying the people of ancient Israel and other countries of the Mediterranean we better understand the biblical texts.

Archaeological work in the lands of the Bible has yielded much understanding of the New Testament period. Cities that we only knew by their mention in the Gospels or the other writings of the New Testament have been found, and many excavated. Difficulties in the New Testament have been clarified, such as the location of Jesus' casting out demons into a herd of swine. Historically this has been identified with one of three sites: Gergesa, Gerasa, and Gadara (Matt 8:28–34; Mark 5:1–13; Luke 8:26–39).[1] Textual variants in the Greek manuscripts have further confused the identification of the place. Two of the sites, namely Gerasa (Jerash) and Gadara (Umm Qeis in northwestern Jordan), are too far from the Sea of Galilee to qualify as the site for the miracle. On the other hand, Gergesa has now been identified with Kursi, on the eastern shore of the Sea of Galilee, and it has a natural slope enabling a herd to run downhill into the sea.

Additional documentary finds in the Judean desert of Israel, especially at Qumran, and the findings of Gnostic documents in the sands of Egypt, at Nag Hammadi, have provided important writings and artifacts that reveal the way in which those who immediately preceded Jesus and followed him understood the nature and work of the Messiah.

Archaeology also helps us to uncover the accuracy of the events in the life of the church, such as the death of an apostle. Only in the last few years have archaeologists found the mausoleum of the apostle Philip, whom church tradition said was martyred in Hierapolis. Now we know that this tradition was accurate.

Last of all, New Testament archaeology has dispelled theories that subjected the biblical narratives to excessive negative criticism, in which the authors were viewed as writing their works in the second century, or, men who fabricated events, miracles, and words of Jesus and the apostles. Certainly, not every event in the text has been confirmed, but pertinent discoveries have mollified the imagination of some critics. Through archaeological discoveries we can learn more about persons who are important characters in the stories told in the Gospels, or at the least, at times, have verification of their existence such as Herod, Pilate, and Caiaphas. Even obscure persons like Erastus, mentioned by Paul in Romans 16:23, have likely been confirmed.[2]

Though one does not do archaeology for the purpose of proving the Bible, since the theology of the Bible is revealed truth, the Bible's revelation of God is within the context of history, and sacred and secular history appear in concert. As Báez-Camargo explains,

> No longer do we see two different worlds, one the world of "sacred history" and the other the world of "profane history." All of history is one history, and it is God's history, for God is the God of all history. This was one of the distinctive messages of the great Hebrew prophets, and in this their universalism consisted. By fitting biblical history into general history, archaeology has demonstrated the validity of many biblical references and data. It has cast light, either implicit or explicit, on many of its allusions to the customs and cultures which prevailed at various periods within biblical history, and it has given us insights into the meaning of a number of passages which otherwise would be not only obscure but also puzzling and even disturbing to the ordinary reader.[3]

12 | The Gospels and Acts

GOSPEL OF MATTHEW

Matthew 2:1

The Site of the Nativity in Bethlehem

> After Jesus was born in Bethlehem in Judea, during the time of King Herod (Matt 2:1a)

Matthew's Gospel recounts that Jesus was born in "Bethlehem in Judea"[1] (Matt 2:1). Bethlehem (Hebrew for "house of bread") is located 6 miles southwest of Jerusalem centered on an "L" shaped ridge, about 2,500 feet in elevation.

Bethlehem is first mentioned in the Bible as the burial place of Rachel in Genesis 35:19 and 48:7.[2] It is also the hometown of Naomi, Ruth's mother-in-law, and of King David. Later, David's grandson Rehoboam is said to have "built up" (fortified) the city (2 Chr 11:6). Nehemiah records that 128 "men of Bethlehem" returned from the exile (Neh 7:26). After this the town largely remains unmentioned until Micah's prophesy, "though you are small among the clans of Judah, out of you shall come for me one who will be ruler over Israel, whose origins are from of old, from ancient times" (Mic 5:2 / MT 5:1). In the New Testament, aside from being Jesus' birthplace, Bethlehem is also the location of Herod's infanticide (Matt 2:16).

Although the city itself has never been fully excavated, archaeological evidence has been found indicating that Bethlehem was occupied from at least the Iron Age (1200–1000 BC). Evidence for this was the discovery of a tomb containing Iron Age II (1000–925 BC) artifacts (found in 1969) and a 2,800-year-old proto-aeolic capital (ninth to eighth centuries BC) discovered by a tour guide under a Palestinian orchard. According to the discoverer, the pillar marks the entrance to a carved water tunnel reaching 250 yards underground. Hebrew University archaeologist Yosef Garfinkel believes a water tunnel of this stature suggests the presence of a large, nearby farm or palace. Such complex construction certainly indicates the work would have been carried out by the central government in Jerusalem.[3] In addition, Roman and Byzantine objects have been found near the Church of the Nativity.

Concerning the birth of Jesus, Luke says that Mary was forced to give birth to Jesus in a manger (an animal feeding trough), "because there was no guest room available for them" (Luke 2:7). Early Christian tradition placed this manger in a cave (or grotto). Justin Martyr, an early second-century native of Shechem (modern Nablus), wrote "But when the Child was born in Bethlehem, since Joseph could not find a lodging in that village, he took up his quarters in a certain cave near the village; and while they were there Mary brought forth the Christ and placed Him in a manger."[4] However, some scholars argue that the birth place took place in the village[5] in the lower level of a house, probably a cave, a place where mangers were built into the floor for animals brought in at night.[6]

In AD 135, after he established a military post at Bethlehem during the Bar Kokhbah Revolt, Hadrian is said to have planted a sacred grove and erected statues of the Greco-Roman deity Adonis (equivalent to Tammuz

Mosaic floor
with ICHTHUS
acronym at the
Church of the
Nativity

Todd Bolen/
BiblePlaces.com

Aerial view
of Manger
Square and the
Church of the
Nativity

© 1995 by Phoenix
Data Systems

Traditional
place of the
manger within
the grotto,
marked by
image of the
silver star
(of Bethlehem)

mentioned in Ezek 8:14) above the grotto "in which Jesus was born." Scholars theorize that this was an effort to thwart Christian use of the grotto by eclipsing their place of veneration with that of Roman worship. In the early third century, Origen wrote, "in conformity with the narrative in the Gospel regarding His birth, there is shown at Bethlehem the cave where He was born, and the manger in the cave where He was wrapped in swaddling-clothes. And this sight is greatly talked of in surrounding places, even among the enemies of the faith, it being said that in this cave was born that Jesus who is worshipped and reverenced by the Christians" (*Cels.* I, LI). This fact supports the identification of the site with Jesus' birth since the myth teaches that Smyrna, daughter of the king of Syria, conceived a child by him through trickery and the gods intervene and turned her into a myrrh tree. Out of this tree nine months later came Adonis.[7] The pagan parallel to virgin birth is obvious. Moreover, Adonis is related to Hebrew Adonai ("my Lord"), one of the titles of God in the Bible, and was recognized as a fertility deity related to death and rebirth. Again, the parallel with Jesus is evident. Hadrian is also said to have erected a temple to Aphrodite over the place of the site of Jesus' death, burial, and resurrection, possibly because of her love connection with Adonis. Testimony to the history and tradition associated with the site was given by Jerome when he came to Bethlehem in the fourth century AD to begin his translation of the Vulgate (Latin Bible) in a grotto next to the birthplace. He wrote that at that time the city was already "the most venerated site in the world" (*Epist.* 58).

The modern Church of the Nativity in Bethlehem is almost universally accepted as being built over this grotto. The current church, while having been greatly modified and expanded, is largely the church built by Justinian in the sixth-century, having avoided destruction during the Persian invasion, unlike the majority of churches of that period, because of images in the church of the three wise men, which hailed from Persia. Excavations carried out inside the church confirm historical records of an octagonal Constantine-era basilica underneath the current church. Mosaic floors have been found, containing the well-known Greek acronym/acrostic ICHTHUS for the Christian confession: *Iēsous Christos, Theou Uios, Sōtēr* ("Jesus Christ, Son of God, Savior"), as well as columns inscribed with crosses by later Crusader-era pilgrims.

Matthew 2:16

Archaeology and Herod the Great[8]

> When Herod realized that he had been outwitted by the Magi, he was furious, and he gave orders to kill all the boys in Bethlehem and its vicinity who were two years old and under, in accordance with the time he had learned from the Magi. (Matt 2:16)

Most Christians are familiar with Herod the Great because he tried to put the child Jesus to death after his birth in Bethlehem. Certainly the attempt to kill the one "born king of the Jews" (Matt 2:2) was a vicious act, but Herod was guilty of many other atrocities. Herod comes down to us in the records of both sacred and secular history as a ruthless and cunning politician, a paranoid ruler, a successful military campaigner, and preeminently, a master builder.[9]

Herod was born ca. 73 BC. His mother Cyprus was the daughter of an Arabian sheik and his father

Ostraca on fragment of wine amphora (19 BC) found at Masada reading "Property of Herod King of Judea"

Used by permission of Ehud Netzer

Antipater was an Idumean (Edomite) and an adherent of Hyrcanus, one of two princes who struggled to become king of Judea and in 47 BC became an *epistropos* ("overseer") of Judea. In time Herod, with the assistance of his father, was appointed governor of Galilee and gained recognition for the subjugation of bandits in Galilee. This gained him the attention of Rome, so that after the murder of his father Herod was made King of Judea, a position he held for thirty-three years (37–4 BC).[10]

He maintained his authority through an effective use of his army and the manner in which he ingratiated himself to various Roman rulers. He seemed to know intuitively to whom to owe allegiance in the changes within the Roman government.[11]

Palace of Herod the Great at Caesarea Maritima

Herod gained the appellation "the Great" because of his skill as an architect and builder. He built cities and temples in honor of Roman emperors and Roman gods. Archaeological excavations have revealed some of his magnificent projects, such as Caesarea Maritima (25–13 BC), named after the emperor Caesar Augustus, including a harbor, hippodromes, theater, and Roman temple;[12] rebuilding Shomron (Samaria) as the Roman city Sebaste (Sebastia), the Greek name for Augustus; rebuilding the Hasmonean palace-fortresses at Jericho (ca. 37 BC) and Machaerus (ca. 30 BC); and building new palace-fortresses at Masada (37–31 BC) and Herodium (23–25 BC). Despised because of his pagan heritage and Roman appointment, in order to curry the favor of the Jews and impress his Roman superiors, he renovated the Second Temple in Jerusalem (ca. 20–19 BC), reconstructing it from scratch but adding architectural elements appealing to the Roman world such as a Roman-style royal stoa (colannaded and roofed porch).

Tiered palace of King Herod, Masada

Todd Bolen/www .BiblePlaces.com

The existence and achievements of Herod the Great are not challenged today. Confirming Herod's existence, Hebrew University archaeologist Ehud Netzer found at Masada a pottery shard bearing a Latin inscription reading "Herod, King of Judea," listing the type of wine that the king imported from Europe.[13] This find can be dated based on a fragment of an inscription bearing the consular date of 19 BC. The fragment was found in the same context as the wine jar fragment and comes from an amphora marked *garum*, a fish sauce. The amphora also attests the name of King Herod and so it is possible that both the wine and the fish sauce were imported at the same time.[14]

However, scholars have questions surrounding his death[15] and burial place. Josephus recorded the king's elaborate burial at the Herodium, but the precise location of Herod's tomb eluded Netzer for almost forty years.[16] Finally, in 2007 the discovery of a tomb complex was made at Herodium[17] on a side of the hill facing Jerusalem. The huge pillared mausoleum and

Fortress of Herod the Great, Masada

© leospek/Shutterstock

Panorama of the Temple Mount from the Mount of Olives

Southern Wall
and Steps, Temple
Mount

Model of Western
Wall, Temple
Mount

Synagogue at Herodium

sarcophagus inside, made of red imported stone and decorated with rosette ornamentation, suggested not only royalty but despised royalty, since it had been deliberately smashed in antiquity. To Netzer this could have only been hated King Herod and members of his royal family. While this identification has not gone unchallenged (see Herod's Tomb, below), it is a good test case for the relationship between ancient documents and archaeological excavation. Nevertheless, the figure of Herod the Great known from the early Gospel accounts has been verified and magnified by the archaeological excavations of his many architectural achievements.

Matthew 2:19–20

Herod's Tomb

> After Herod died, an angel of the Lord appeared in a dream to Joseph in Egypt and said, "Get up, take the child and his mother and go to the land of Israel, for those who were trying to take the child's life are dead." (Matt 2:19–20)

Matthew, the only Gospel writer who mentions the event, simply states in 2:19 that King Herod died. This is remarkable given the fact that Herod was described in such detail by this author as an enemy of Jesus, and extrabiblical writers such as Josephus (*Ant.* 17.6.5) record his gruesome death (thought to be chronic kidney disease complicated by Fournier's gangrene) as a punishment from God for his sins. However, this restraint serves to strengthen the claim of divine inspiration, since the natural impulse of a human author would have been to include these details to enhance his literary account. In addition, in the next verse he notes, "those who were trying to take the child's life are dead" (2:20). The best explanation for the use of the plural is that it includes both Herod and his son Antipater, whom Herod had murdered just five days before his own death because he learned his son had rejoiced when he mistakenly thought his father had died (*Wars* 1.23.7). Antipater was also noted for his cruelty and may have been involved in the plan to murder the innocents in Bethlehem and its environs in an attempt to kill Jesus.

Site of the Tomb of
Herod the Great

Alexandra Toy

Reconstructed
tomb of King
Herod (from
Herodian), Israel
Museum

Israel Museum

The end of Herod's life reveals the essence of his character manifested throughout his life, including the execution of his wives and sons, not to mention the killing of the infants in search of the Messiah in Bethlehem. Josephus reports that as Herod realized his end was imminent, he ordered that upon his death the Jewish elders from all parts of his kingomd, whom he had locked up in the Jericho hippodrome, should be executed, thus ensuring general mourning at the time of his death (*Ant.* 17.174–181)."

Josephus records that Herod received a truly royal burial. His golden bier was studded with gemstones and draped in royal purple. His corpse was dressed in royal finery wearing a gold crown and with a scepter in his right hand. Accompanying his bier were his military in full battle array, his family members, and some five-hundred servants carrying traditional anointing spices. He records the location of the burial as the Herodian, a truncated conical hill that served as one of Herod's winter retreats located 7.5 miles (12 km) south of Jerusalem on the outskirts of Bethlehem (near the modern Palestinian town of Beit Sahour). Here he had partially constructed a hill to surround his palatial residence that included typical Roman luxury features as well as defensive towers built around the top of the hill. The parade of attendants that escorted Herod's body from Jericho, where he died, came some 25 miles to this Judean desert site to bury him in a royal sarcophagus inside a royal mausoleum.

Hebrew University archaeologist Ehud Netzer spent almost forty years searching for Herod's tomb. After following theories that led him to the interior structures of the Upper Herodian, and especially into one of the imposing guard towers, he turned his attention to the Lower Herodian and an area on the lower slopes where a flat terrace about 100-feet wide and nearly 1,200-feet long had been cut into the hillside. Netzer came to believe that it had been built for the parade of Herod's army and attendants assembled during his funeral.

If so, he thought, the tomb must lay nearby, perhaps within a monumental structure below this terrace. However, in 2007, as his excavation team was investigating a newly uncovered set of stairs on the slope of the hillside above the terrace, Yakov Kalman, a senior member of the excavation team, revealed several large structures while using a backhoe. The size and quality of the structures as well as the elaborate ornamentation on the stones told Netzer that he had finally found what he had long been seeking. Its positive identification seems to align with the location given by Josephus over a water system that originated in Jerusalem.[18]

The finds to date include the podium that bore the royal sarcophagus, the sarcophagus of Herod and other family members, remains of the mausoleum, a theater and royal room (viewing box) replete with exquisite wall paintings and frescos, and corner pilasters partially built into the walls that permitted Netzer to calculate the dimensions of the mausoleum as 30 x 30 feet and 80 feet in height. The mausoleum, built of white limestone, fits Roman design and has a conical roof like tombs at Nabatean Petra, a people to whom Herod was related

Sarcophagus from tomb of Herod believed to have held the remains of the king

Israel Museum

through marriage. On top of the corners of the structure were five decorative urns (a motif also used at Petra).

The mausoleum and sarcophagi were found deliberately smashed by hammers, evidence that Herod remained a hated figure even long after his death, as this destruction was perpetrated by Jews of the First and Second Jewish Revolts who utilized Herodian in their defense against the Romans. Even the discovery itself came under attack as archaeologists Joseph Patrich and Benjamin Arubas[19] later challenged the identification of the tomb as Herodian, charges to which Roi Porat, Yakov Kalman, and Rachel Chachy competently responded.[20]

Matthew 4:5

The Pinnacle of the Temple

> Then the devil took him to the holy city and had him stand on the highest point of the temple. (Matt 4:1)

In Matthew's account of the temptation of Jesus, he says, "Then the devil took him to the holy city and had him stand on the highest point of the temple" (4:5). The Greek *pterugion* (usually translated "pinnacle") literally means "little wing" and referred to the tip or extremity of something, hence, "the edge" or "the summit." Josephus, in his account of the temple says:

> But the fourth front of the temple, which was southward, had indeed itself gates in its middle, as also it had the royal cloisters, with three walks, which reached in length from the east valley unto that on the west, for it was impossible it should reach any farther; and this cloister deserves to be mentioned better than any other under the sun; for while the valley was very deep, and its bottom could not be seen, if you looked from above into the depth, this farther vastly high elevation of the cloister stood upon that height, insomuch

that if anyone looked down from the top of the battlements, or down both those altitudes, he would be giddy, while his sight could not reach to such an immense depth. (*Ant.* 15.11.5)

If this was the place where Jesus stood in Matthew's account, it would have been at the southeastern corner of the Temple Mount itself, above the Kidron Valley, on top of the building known as the Royal Portico. Today the ground level has risen due to centuries of destruction and rebuilding, but when Warren dug a shaft down from that corner of the Temple Mount, he had to go down 106 feet below the elevation of the average level of the temple area to get to the bottom of Herod's foundation blocks.

Pinnacle of the temple

Robert Drouhard

Josephus says the Royal Portico that once stood on the Temple Mount at this spot was 50-feet high.[21] This height, combined with the depth of the Kidron Valley, makes it understandable why Josephus says that the view from this spot would make someone "giddy" and why Satan would have chosen this spot to tempt Jesus.

The first-century historian Flavius Josephus wrote of James the Just's execution by stoning (*Ant.* 20.9.1), but the second century church father Hegesippus said that James was martyred by being thrown off of the pinnacle of the temple.[22] He was said to have been buried at the spot where he died. Although now known to belong to the family of Bene Hezir, a monumental tomb (to the far right with a pyramidal top), almost exactly opposite the southeast corner of the Temple Mount, was known in antiquity as the tomb of James. Given this traditional location for the tomb, if James was thrown off this corner, Finegan says ". . . it would not have been difficult to imagine that that tomb was the monument to James."[23]

Matthew 6:9

Archaeological Examples of "the Lord's Prayer"

> This, then, is how you should pray: "Our Father in heaven, hallowed be your name." (Matt 6:9)

Archaeological examples of early anagrams that relate to the *Pater Noster* (Latin: "Lord's Prayer") have been discovered in widely separated locations from Dura-Europos on the Euphrates River in modern Iraq, to the ruins of Pompeii, to Cirencester, England. The Pompeii anagram must date to before AD 79, when the city was destroyed. The Cirencester anagram is thought to be from the second century. The Dura-Europos example can be no later than AD 257, when that city was abandoned. However, anagrams have also been discovered in several medieval examples. All of them are arranged:

```
ROTAS
OPERA
TENET
AREPO
SATOR
```

Scholars have been unable to fully interpret what these letters mean, but one theory is that they are an anagram of the "Our Father" from Matthew 6:9, since the anagram can be rearranged to look like:

```
P
A
T
A E O
R
P A T E R N O S T E R
O
O S A
T
E
R
```

Anagram of Our Father (Sator Square)

© 2003 M. Disdero

The "A" and "O" stand for Jesus' title "Alpha" and "Omega" in John's Apocalypse (Rev 1:8; 21:6; 22:13).

The theory is that the anagram developed as a secret code to help Christians identify fellow Christians during the early persecution of the church, similar to the fish symbol and the acronym/acrostic ICHTHUS.

Matthew 8:14

Peter's House in Capernaum

> When Jesus came into Peter's house, he saw Peter's mother-in-law lying in bed with a fever. He touched her hand and the fever left her, and she got up and began to wait on him. (Matt 8:14–15)

Although work had been done in Capernaum as early as 1865, it was not until 1968 that the town was fully excavated by Italian archaeologist Virgilio Corbo. Among the ruins excavated at the ancient site a complex of around twelve houses were found near the synagogue, toward the Sea of Galilee, dating from the first century BC to the first century AD. The houses were of typical construction for the time, built out of basalt stones with pebble fill and no mortar, and the floors consisted of beaten earth or pebbles. The walls would not have supported heavy roofs, so it is theorized that they would have been constructed of tree branches covered by a mixture of straw and mud. These were the insula (Roman-style dwellings) of lower class laborers. Artifacts recovered from the houses consisted of lamps, jars, pans, and cooking pots.

Of particular interest is the largest house of the complex, measuring 23 x 21 feet (7 x 6 1/2 m). Since the fourth century the house has been identified as the house of the apostle Peter. In AD 385 Aetheria wrote, "In Capernaum, out of the house of the first of the apostles a church was made...."[24] In AD 570 Anonymous of Piacenza states, "We came to Capernaum into the house of St. Peter, which is a basilica."[25]

This has not convinced all archaeologists, as Kenyon says, "Claims that the house of Peter has been found at Capernaum, based on the find in it of a fish-hook, must be regarded with some skepticism."[26] Kenyon states this since in the floor of this house two

The House of Peter in Capernaum (uncovered)

www.HolyLandPhotos.org

The House of Peter in Capernaum (covered) by Byzantine church foundations

fishhooks were found. The presence of fishhooks and the house's proximity to the sea give evidence that the house belonged to a fisherman. Other finds include two almost intact lamps, one Hellenistic, the other Herodian. Unlike the other houses in the insula, this house's original beaten earth floor was covered several times with crushed limestone not long after its construction, as evidenced by fragments of Herodian lamps in between the layers of limestone. Also, in the largest room of the house the rough basalt walls were successively covered with plaster and decorated. These finds convinced the excavators that "according to a very reasonable interpretation . . . this particular room was treated as a venerated hall from the first century onward and was associated with the memory of Peter, i.e., was remembered as the house of the apostle."[27] In the successive centuries the house continued to be venerated, and eventually an octagonal Byzantine basilica was erected over the house, centered on the venerated room. This adds further ancient testimony that early Christian tradition venerated the spot and must have identified it with the house of the apostle in the Gospel account.

Matthew 11:21

New Testament Chorazin

> Woe to you, Chorazin! Woe to you, Bethsaida! For if the miracles that were performed in you had been performed in Tyre and Sidon, they would have repented long ago in sackcloth and ashes. (Matt 11:21)

Although Jesus performed mighty works in Chorazin, they "did not repent," so Jesus pronounces a woe on them in Matthew 11:20–24, along with Bethsaida and Capernaum. Jesus' threat was not empty. Chorazin today is utterly destroyed and abandoned.

Chorazin was located on a rocky bluff above the Sea of Galilee, about 2 miles from Capernaum.[28] Even in Jesus' time the village was small and poor. Archaeological remains, mostly dating from the second through fourth centuries and all made of the local basalt, include some domiciles, a market, a *miqveh*, an olive oil production facility, and a synagogue.[29] The synagogue was of typical basilica arrangement, 65 feet long and 45 feet wide.[30] The synagogue decorations provide important

Ruins of Chorazim

www.HolyLandPhotos.org

evidence of the high degree of Hellenization occurring at this time, as the Chorazin synagogue did not follow the normal injunctions against graven images but includes centaurs fighting lions and a medusa's head.[31] A so-called "Moses' Seat" was also discovered in the synagogue. Dating the synagogue has proven difficult, with dates proposed ranging from the first through fourth centuries. It is likely to have been rebuilt at least once, perhaps after an earthquake.[32]

Matthew 15:39

New Testament Magdala

> And He sent away the multitude, got into the boat, and came to the region of Magdala. (NKJV)

Many manuscripts of Matthew 15:39 read Magdala (L Θ f 1,13 TR syh) or Magdalan (C N W 33 mae bo), rather than Magadan (thus ℵ* B D). The latter reading is adopted by the NIV and other recent translations. The Aramaic name *Magdala Nunayya* ("Magdala of the fishes") appears in the priestly courses in the Talmud (y. Ta'anit. 4:6, 68d) and refers to a site located on the shore of the Sea of Galilee.[33] Similarly, Midrash

HaGadol on Deuteronomy 13:7, although mistakenly connecting the site with Jesus' mother Miriam, makes the geographical connection with the name Mary Magdelene, i.e., Mary from Magdala. On this basis Magdala is thought to be the hometown of the New Testament Mary who was the mother of the sons of Zebedee (Matt 27:56) and one of those who came to anoint the body of Jesus after the crucifixion and to whom the risen Messiah appeared (Mark 16:1, 9). The site is located less than 3 miles from Tiberias and at the junction to the ancient route from Nazareth to the Sea of Galilee at the former Palestinian village Al-Majdal and has been identified with New Testament "Magdala" (Heb. *migdal*, "tower"). The name is also found in the Nazareth inscription at Capernaum and is mentioned by Josephus, who calls it Tarichea, derived from the Greek word *tapichos* ("fish salters"; *J.W.* 2.20.6 §572).[34]

Magdala in the New Testament era is known from archaeological excavations done by Virgilio Corbo from 1971 to 1977. It was laid out in the typical Roman design, with a main cardo maximus and intersecting side streets. Along the main street Corbo discovered a synagogue in the typical basilica style, the only first-century synagogue that has been discovered

Stone Table with
Menorah, Magdala

in Israel, with a central nave divided by two rows of columns and a perpendicular isle across the back. Late Hellenistic and early Herodian pottery found within the building confirmed the date of construction to sometime within those periods. The city was a center of fishing on the Sea of Galilee, as evidenced by the first-century fishing boat, known as the Ancient Boat and displayed at the Kibbutz Nof Ginosaur, being discovered about 1 mile north of Magdala.

Galilean excavations began at Magdala in 2009 with the first systematic work in June/July 2010.[35] The excavations have uncovered a number of Second Temple period structures at the site, including a room with various tanks for different types of fish, a site where fishing boats were tied, a harbor, streets, and a synogague. Of special interest was the discovery of the synagogue with an ornately carved-stone Torah stand or podium at its center. The relief on this structure contains detailed images of the objects related to the priestly service in the Second Temple, including a pair of two-handled jugs, an oil lamp, a golden altar of incense,[36] and a menorah (its earliest known depection). Also depicted atop the relief

is a large, six-petal rosette that was a common design in Jewish funerary art during the Second Temple period (similar to a find at Gamla on a lintel stone flanked by two palm trees.) These images were most likely made by an eyewitness to these vessels within the temple in Jerusalem. The importance of the Magdala synagogue and the Magdala stone is that together they add new support for understanding the synagogue as a sacred space even while the Temple remained standing. Scholarly consensus has long held that synagogues were only places for assembly and study of the Torah and other sacred books but not sacred spaces in their own right. The archaeological excavations at Magdala, in addition to confirming the New Testament site, are challenging this concensus.

Matthew 16:17

Evidence for Simon Bar-Jonah

> Jesus replied, "Blessed are you, Simon son of Jonah, for this was not revealed to you by flesh and blood, but by my Father in heaven." (Matt 16:17)

Cave with ossuaries, Dominus Flevit

At the Franciscan *Dominus Flevit* ("the Lord Wept") church on the Mount of Olives, workmen were building a new wall in 1953. They happened upon a cave filled with burial remains. Among the over five hundred remains were 122 ossuaries (stone bone boxes), and on these boxes they found forty inscriptions, either carved onto the boxes or written in charcoal in Hebrew, Aramaic, and Greek.

One of the ossuaries bears the name *Simeon Bar [Ynh]*. The last word is uncertain but could be "Jonah." Although this ossuary is not Peter the apostle's, it nonetheless gives evidence that the alias Jesus calls him in Matthew 16:17 was used during the time of Peter's life.

The first-century church father Clement wrote his *Letter to the Corinthians* (pre-AD 70) that Peter died where Paul died. Tertullian, in *The Demurrer Against the Heretics* (AD 200) states that Peter, like Paul, came to Rome and died there. Lactantius, in a treatise called *The Death of the Persecutors* (ca. AD 318), wrote that Peter came to Rome under the reign of the Emperor Nero. Christian tradition also identifies

the Mamertine Prison, a dank subterranean complex (today beneath a Renaissance church), as Peter's final lodging before he was crucified. Italian archaeologists have found frescoes and other evidence that indicate that it was associated with St. Peter as early as the seventh century AD.

The site identified by the Roman Church as St. Peter's tomb is at the west end of a complex of mausoleums dating between AD 130 and AD 300 that was partially destroyed to provide for the building of the first St. Peter's Basilica (ca. AD 330). The grave identified with St. Peter is at the base of the aedicula under the floor. Archaeological extraction in 1953 revealed it contained both human and animal bones. However, later, another set of bones was found that had been transferred without the archaeologists' knowledge from a niche in the north side of the graffiti wall that abuts the red wall on the right of the aedicula. Radiocarbon dating determined that these were the bones of a 60–70-year-old man. Despite these finds set within the context of church tradition, Antonio Ferrua, the archaeologist who headed the excavation of St. Peter's Tomb, stated that there was no conclusive evidence that these were the bones of St. Peter.[37] Archaeology in this case cannot necessarily prove a tradition, but it does provide archaeological evidence of the existence of the early veneration of the site in relation to Peter.

Matthew 23:2

The Seat of Moses

> Then Jesus said to the crowds and to his disciples: "The teachers of the law and the Pharisees sit in Moses' seat. So you must be careful to do everything they tell you. But do not do what they do, for they do not practice what they preach." (Matt 23:1–3)

Jesus refers to the *kathedras* ("seat") of Moses in reference to the authority that the scribes and Pharisees had in religious matters. In fact, Jesus told the people to do whatever they told them to do.

This seat was a reserved bench or chair within the synagogue, set aside by the leaders of the synagogue for distinguished members or the ruler of the synagogue. As such, it was a sign of authority. One such seat was discovered in the ruins of Chorazin. These seats were made of stone and often included an inscription bearing the reason for the giving the seat to a particular individual.

Synagogue seat of Moses, Chorazim

www.Holy LandPhotos .org

In the case of the Chorazin synagogue, the Aramaic inscription reads, "Remembered for the good of Judah ben Ishmael who made this platform and its staircase. As his reward may he have a share with the righteous" (b. Hullin 118b).

Matthew 23:29

The Tombs of the Prophets

> Woe to you, teachers of the law and Pharisees, you hypocrites! You build tombs for the prophets and decorate the graves of the righteous. (Matt 23:29)

In Matthew 23 Jesus pronounces a series of woes on the scribes and Pharisees as representatives of Israel's apostasy, climaxing with a historical summary concerning the national religious leadership. As part of this declaration he mentions the hypocrisy of erecting tombs for the prophets and righteous.

In the Kidron Valley, on the eastern slope opposite the Golden Gate, there is a large Jewish cemetery that was used as a burial ground as far back as the end of the Middle Bronze Age. Here, in a complex of Second Temple period burial caves, are four monumental tombs built for Jerusalem's Hasmonean and later Herodian aristocracy (ca. late second century BC to AD 70). All of the tombs are hewn into the solid rock of the valley slope. They are traditionally named for biblical figures: Absalom, Zechariah, and James, but only one of them, the Tomb of James, which is the oldest, bears a Hebrew inscription at its entrance with the occupant's family name *Bene Hezir* ("sons of Hezir") and indicates this was a priestly family. The tomb's inscription also reveals that the cave was used by several generations of the Hezir family.[38] Its location in the Kidron Valley, famous for its royal Iron Age tombs, could only be afforded by the most wealthy and influential. The Bible mentions a Hezir as founder of the seventeenth priestly division (1 Chr 24:15), and another who was

Tomb of
Absalom in
Kidron Valley

it is recorded that Zechariah was stoned "between the altar and the sanctuary" (Luke 11:51), located nearby.

The Tomb of Absalom consists of a rock cube decorated with Ionic columns around the lower part, while the upper part is made of ashlars and has a round drum shape, topped with a conical concave roof. While referred to as a tomb, it is called a *nephesh* or a memorial. It is suggested that the tomb was associated with Absalom because it resembles a pillar and, according to 2 Samuel 18:18, Absalom built himself a memorial in the "Kings Valley" (another name for the Kidron Valley). Medieval Jewish tradition held that it was Absalom's tomb, and on that basis Jews, Christians, and Muslims stoned the monument for centuries to curse King David's miscreant son for the crimes of murdering his half brother Amnon and rebelling against his father. Despite this tradition, the tomb has been dated to the first century AD, a thousand years after the time of Absalom, so it cannot have been his tomb.

However, new light was shed on the history of Absalom's Tomb in 2003, when Joe Zias an Israeli anthropologist and former curator with the Israel Antiquities Authority, and Emile Peuch, chief epigrapher of the Dead Sea Scrolls Project at the École Biblique in Jerusalem, announced the discovery of a highly worn Byzantine Greek inscription at the top of the outer façade of Absalom's tomb. The forty-seven word inscription reads: "This is the tomb of Zechariah, martyr, very pious priest, father of John."[39] The inscription reveals that local Christians venerated the site and believed Zechariah, the father of John the Baptizer (Luke 1:5–26, 57–66), was buried in the tomb.

Zias and Peuch believe other names are on the monument and have been able to read one newly deciphered inscription as "Simeon who was a very just man and a very devoted old (person) and waiting for the consolation of the people."[40] They identify this figure as the devout Jewish man whom the Gospel of Luke records prophesied over the infant Jesus on the steps

among the leaders who ratified the covenant with Nehemiah (Neh 10:20). The Bene Hezir tomb was accessed through two tunnel passages, one lower down on the cliff and the other connecting to the tomb of Zechariah just south. It features a portico with two columns and an inner central chamber surrounded by side chambers. These side chambers each have several *kokhim* (Hebrew) or *arcosolia* (an arched recess featuring a shallow trough or bed on which to place the body). Its traditional association with James comes from a Christian tradition that says it was the spot where Jesus appeared to James and where he was buried, landing there after being thrown from the pinnacle of the temple.

The Tomb of Zechariah is also a *nephesh* (lit. "soul"). It has no opening but is a solid block cut from the hillside, topped by a pyramid shaped roof. The roof has an Egyptian-style cornice held up by Ionic columns. It has been dated to the second half of the first century BC. Some have theorized that it was a monument in connection with the Bene Hezir tomb adjacent to it. It may have been traditionally associated with Zechariah, since

of the temple (Luke 2:25–35). They also believe they may find the name "James, brother of Jesus," because a fourth-century Christian tradition states that Zechariah, Simon, and James were buried together in the Kidron Valley. This tradition, in the case of James (the Just), goes back to the second century in a citation of Hegesippus included by the fourth century historian Eusebius in his *Ecclesiastical History*.

While Byzantine testimony may well reflect ancient history, with the fourth-century-AD campaign under Queen Helena, mother of Constantine the Great, to recover and restore the holy places of Christianity, it also had a compelling reason to connect physical sites to New Testament persons and events. Nevertheless, the mounting archaeological clues confirm Jesus' statement concerning the erection in this place of monuments to the prophets.

Matthew 24:1–2

The Destruction of the Temple Mount

Jesus left the temple and was walking away when his disciples came up to him to call his attention to its buildings. "Do you see all these things?" he asked. "Truly I tell you, not one stone here will be left on another; every one will be thrown down." (Matt 24:1–2)

Jesus' dire warning for Jerusalem was fulfilled a mere forty years after he gave it, during the First Jewish Revolt. In AD 66 the Jews of Judea revolted. They had long resented Roman rule, but when Roman procurators increased taxes and took over assigning the high priests, they had enough. Rome had never understood Jewish religious sensibilities, which were unique among all the peoples they had conquered. They refused pagan images to be erected in their temple, nor would they worship the Caesar. Although many Roman rulers gave deference to the Jews, some, including Caligula and (to a certain extent) Pilate, seemed to almost revel in inciting them. Thus, when Florus, the Roman procurator, confiscated a large amount of silver from the temple, the Jews rioted, massacring the Roman garrison in Jerusalem. Cestius Gallus, the governor of Syria, sent more troops, but these were also defeated. Rome's retribution was swift and massive. Three legions were brought to Israel, totaling 60,000 troops and their supports. Joesphus says these were garrisoned on the Mt. of Olives opposite the Temple Mount (*J.W.* 5:69–70). The Tenth Roman Legion (*Legio X Fretensis*; "Legion of the Sea Straits") was stationed inside Jerusalem to carry out a military siege. Literary tradition suggested their camp was within the present-day Armenian Quarter of the Jewish Quarter, but only a few stamped tiles of the Roman Tenth Legion hve been found in excavations. A Roman column mentioning the Tenth Legion can be found on a narrow street inside Jaffa gate however, it has been dated to AD 200. It provides evidence of the continued presence of the Tenth Legion long after the temple's destruction. Archaeologists have proposed a location in the area of the Holy Sepulchre or on the Ophel (south of the temple). In this area was found a Roman milestone carved by the Roman Tenth Legion with a a Latin inscription mentioning both the Roman emperor Vespasian and his son Titus, commander of the Roman army at the time of the suppression of the Great Revolt. Though defaced, the inscription also appears to mention Flavius Silva, procurator of Judea and commander of the Tenth Legion, who oversaw the destruction of Jerusalem and the conquest of Masada.

While the evidence here, too, only is represented by the stamped tiles, extensive remains should not be expected, as the larger units were stationed on the outskirts of the city at the site of modern Givat Ram.[41]

Rome first swept through Galilee, killing or enslaving an estimated 100,000 people. They then marched south, besieging Jerusalem, which fell in the summer of AD 70. When the Romans broke through the walls, they went on a destructive rampage, tearing down and burning anything they could get their hands on, including the temple with all its treasures. They pushed the huge stones Herod had used to build the walls off the Temple Mount, crushing the street below. Excavators have discovered vivid evidence of this destruction beside the Temple Mount's Western Wall.

The Roman Empire was especially proud of their suppression of the Jewish revolt. G. A. Keddie notes: "[the] Roman emperor Vespasian, and his sons Titus and Domitian, initiated and maintained an empire-wide discourse proclaiming Iudaea capta ("Judaea captured"). By means of coins, monuments, statues, literary propaganda, and the institution of a new Judaean tax, the Flavian emperors magnified their successful suppression of this provincial revolt in order to legitimate their

Randall Price and destruction stones

Richard Hess, used by permission

dynasty."[42] Archaeologists have found that the commemorative Judea capta coinage, with some forty-eight varities, is one of the most prevalent coins from the era. This coinage was originally issued by the Roman Emperor Vespasian to celebrate his son Titus's conquest of Judea and the destruction of the Second Temple, possibly commemorating the event of Titus parading temple treasures and Jewish captives in Rome (famously depicted on the Arch of Titus's Triumph). Several different Judea capta coins were minted, the most popular one having the picture of a Jewish woman (symbolizing Judea) seated, bound, and mourning. This may have been based on the Jewish prophecy of Isaiah 3:8, 25–26: "Jerusalem staggers, Judah is falling . . . Your men will fall by the sword, your warriors in battle. The gates of Zion will lament and mourn; destitute, she will sit on the ground." Sometimes this figure is joined by that of a triumphant emperor holding a spear, with his foot on the helmet of a defeated soldier. Usually a palm tree (a Jewish symbol of freedom) separates the two figures. One rare coin shows the bust of Titus on one side and on the other side a captive Jew, probably Simon Bar Giora, who was carried off to Rome, scourged and executed in the Forum Romanum.

A commonly voiced objection to Jesus' statement that "not one stone will be left on another" (cf. Luke 19:44) is that visible remains of structures still exist. In fact, the Romans deliberately left three towers and their wall on the western side as a reminder of the size and strength of the city they had defeated. The notion that all of the structures of the temple compound would be removed comes from a misreading of the text. Jesus did not refer to the Temple Mount's foundation stones retaining and platform walls when he made the statement, but as the context reveals "these things" refer to the "buildings" of the temple court that his disciples were pointing out to him (v. 1; cf. Mark 13:1; Luke 21:5).

These were newer structures and could not have included the eastern wall, which was an old structure and not rebuilt by Herod, or the Western Wall, the southern end of which had not yet been built (as a coin

Western Wall excavations of destruction of Jerusalem

Todd Bolen/ www.Bible Places.com

later than Herod found at its foundation testifies) and was still under construction at the time of Jesus. This also applies to the southern court, which according to Josephus was the last of Herod's extended courts to the north, west, and south and was only completed in AD 65. Therefore, Jesus was referring to the buildings that belonged to the temple proper, all of which were destroyed in the conflagration and subsequent dismantling by the Roman army. Most of the remains of these buildings were pushed off the temple platform on the eastern side (evident from the mound along the wall now covered by a Muslim cemetery) and thrown down to the Herodian street (evident on the excavated southwestern side). Other, more choice, stones were likely exported for reuse in Roman constructions.

Matthew 27:8

The Field of Blood

> So they decided to use the money to buy the potter's field as a burial place for foreigners. That is why it has been called the Field of Blood to this day. (Matt 27:7–8)

Judas was paid thirty pieces of silver to betray Jesus but had a change of heart and returned the money. Since it was "blood money," the chief priests decided they could not return it to the temple treasury, and instead bought "the potter's field as a burial place for foreigners." Matthew adds that it was called in his day the "Field of Blood" (Aramaic, *hakel dama*, cf. "Akeldama" in Acts 1:19). Luke notes that Judas, when he hung himself in grief, did so at this field, and that is also why it is called the Field of Blood. He also says that Psalm 69:25 referred to this field, predicting it would be desolate and no one would live in it.

The site was known throughout church history, being on the south slope of the Hinnom Valley, close to where the valley comes together with the Kidron Valley

in Jerusalem. True to Luke's word, the site, though visited often by Christian pilgrims and used throughout the centuries as a burial place, remains unoccupied. One reason for this, as scholars Leen and Kathleen Ritmeyer, who have published extensively on the history of Jerusalem and the Temple Mount, point out, is that the burial caves at the site were not used to bury "strangers" but some of Jerusalem's most elite—the high priests, including Annas, father-in-law of Caiaphas and one of an inner circle of high priests who presided over the trial of Jesus (John 18:13, 24). They write: "The inner burial chamber of the Tomb of Annas was highly decorated and had *kokhim* burial niches in the walls. The body of Annas was probably placed in the *kokh* (burial niche) disguised by the fake door in the wall on the right."[43] Therefore, the site would have been preserved as a venerated site by the Jews and later by Christians.

Matthew 27:35

Archaeological Evidence for the Crucifixion

> When they had crucified him, they divided up his clothes by casting lots. And sitting down, they kept watch over him there. (Matt 27:35–36)

Until fairly recent times, no physical archaeological evidence had been found of the practice of crucifixion. In 1968 archaeologists working in Givat ha-Mivtar, a suburb of Jerusalem, discovered a sealed family tomb containing twelve burial niches (*kokhim*). In one they recovered an ossuary with the bones of a twenty-four- to twenty-eight-year-old male mixed with those of a child. Based on the ossuary inscription the man's name was "Yehohanan, the son of Hagakol." Examination of the skeletal remains revealed a right heel bone with an iron nail 4 1/2 inches (11 1/2 cm) long imbedded in it. This find constituted the first physical evidence of a crucified victim in the land of Israel and may shed new light on how crucifixions in antiquity were performed.

Although traditionally it was thought that nails were driven through the hands and both feet (one on top of the other), this was not supported by the bones of Yehohanan. In this case, each leg was affixed laterally to the vertical stake. Therefore, this might present a new concept of crucifixion, one in which the victim's legs straddled the cross held up by ankles nailed from the sides. Initially, the anthropologist Haas concluded that scratch marks on the skeleton's wrists suggested that nails had also been driven through the victim's wrists, but later examination by Israeli anthropologist Joe Zias as well as study by Skeles and Charlesworth reversed this verdict, stating that evidence only supported ropes were used to secure the victim to the horizontal beam of the cross.[44] However, the Gospel accounts indicate that Jesus was nailed in both his hands/wrists and feet (Luke 24:39; John 20:25, 27).

Israeli archaeologist Yigael Yadin proposed that Hagakol was a nickname given posthumously meaning "the one hanged with knees apart."[45] Josephus observed that people were crucified in different positions, and Christian tradition records that the apostle Peter was crucified upside down (at his own request).[46] This later position was also noted by the church historian Eusebius as an alternate method in the fourth century AD.[47] In light of this, if Yadin's interpretation can be supported, it suggests that Yehohanan was crucifixied in an unusual position with respect to the normal practice of crucifixion, and his example would, therefore, not necessarily alter the traditional conception of Jesus' crucifixion. At any rate, Yehohanan's remains are a stark reminder of the brutality of crucifixion as a means of execution and how excruciatingly painful the experience must have been.

This discovery also engages the proposal by members of the Jesus Seminar that in keeping with Roman practice, crucified victims were left on the cross to decompose and be ravaged by birds or thrown in a common grave that was exposed to animals.[48] In either case, the customary Jewish burial was not allowed.

Replica of first-century heel bone of crucified man.

Todd Bolen/www.BiblePlaces.com, taken at the Israel Museum

This made the biblical account of Jesus' burial in a tomb nothing more than a work of fiction. However, while this Roman practice may have been the case for Roman slaves, Josephus testified that the Roman authorities did not enforce Roman custom on Jews, even those punished under Roman law, and would have allowed the Jews to follow their burial practices as required by Jewish law (*Ag. Ap.* 2.73). In the case of Jesus, this was expedited by the fact that the crucifixion was on the eve of the Sabbath of the Passover and ritual law demanded all corpses, and particularly those executed by hanging on a tree (Deut 21:22–23) be properly entombed (John 19:31). It is also known that the Sanhedrin had a designated place for the bodies of executed criminals (m. Sanh. 6:5–6), but since Jesus' execution was Roman, his burial was under their jurisdiction. For that reason Joseph of Arimathea, a member of the Sanhedrin, went to Pilate to request a Jewish burial for Jesus. This is all consistent with the evidence from the discovery of Yehohanan's remains. Despite the infamy and disgrace of crucifixion, as a Jew Yehohanan was given a proper burial within his family tomb. This supports the conclusion that Jesus would have been buried according to Jewish law, as the New Testament records (Matt 27:57–60; Mark 15:43–46; Luke 23:50–55; John 19:38–42; cf. 1 Cor 15:4).[49]

Matthew 27:59–60

Sealing the Tomb of Jesus

> Joseph took the body, wrapped it in a clean linen cloth, and placed it in his own new tomb that he had cut out of the rock. He rolled a big stone in front of the entrance to the tomb and went away. (Matt 27:59–60)

According to Jewish practice the body of the deceased was initially laid to rest in the inner chamber of a tomb. First-century tombs characteristically had a small forecourt that led to the interior features of the tomb, including an inner chamber with benches situated along the walls, often with *arcosolia*, arched recesses in the wall, a lower elevation pit (for standing inside the tomb), and tunnel-like niches called *loculi* (Latin) or *kokhim* (Hebrew). No two tombs are exactly alike, and though they share these common features, as Jerusalem archaeologist Shimon Gibson has noted, "individualism was pronounced."[50] This means we have not found, and should not expect to find, a first-century tomb precisely matching the tomb of Jesus as described in the Gospel accounts.

The body of the deceased was laid out on a stone bench and a heavy stone was set into the small entrance door and sealed to thwart the unwanted entrance of animals and grave robbers. Matthew reports that a "big" (Greek *megan*) stone was rolled against (Greek *proskulisas*) the door of Jesus' tomb. Later, Matthew recounts how an angel "rolled back" (Greek *apekulisen*) this sealing stone from the door (Matt 28:2; cf. Mark 16:3–4; Luke 24:2).

However, the image of a rolling-stone tomb as the tomb of Jesus, while the common conception, has been questioned on the basis of archaeological study of Jerusalem necropoli. In the vicinity of Jerusalem there are 1,000 or more rock-cut tombs. Israeli archaeologist Amos Kloner, who has examined more than 900 such tombs, found only four tombs dating from the late Second Temple period (the time of Jesus) that were closed by a rolling stone: the tomb of the Queen Helena of Adiabene, the family tomb of King Herod of Jerusalem, one nearby Herod's Family Tomb, and another located in the upper Kidron Valley.[51] These had a carved out slotted groove to one side of the entrance of the tomb made to receive a disk-shaped stone. The family could roll the stone forward in the track to cover the entryway of the

Tomb near Megiddo

tomb or roll it back to open it, allowing for new burials. These rolling stones weighed tons and could not have been moved by a single person. Gibson supposes that the stone covering Jesus' tomb must not have been so heavy, since he observes both Matthew (27:60) and Mark (15:46) state that Joseph of Arimethea rolled the stone by himself. However, it should not be assumed that these statements mean that Joseph acted alone in the rolling of the stone any more than in transporting Jesus' body to the tomb and wrapping it in a linen shroud (all of which the text says he did). The natural understanding of this is that Joseph took responsibility for and oversaw these tasks; he did not do them personally but had them done. The women on the third day after the burial who came to anoint Jesus' body said to one another, "Who will roll away the stone from the entrance of the tomb?" (Mark 16:3). These three women, even working together, understood that they were unable to move the stone. Gibson also overlooks the clear statement in the next verse (Mark 16:4) that "the stone, which was very large, had been rolled away" (Greek *megas sphodra*). Even a passage in the apocryphal Gospel of Peter states that Pilate sent Petronius the Centurion with soldiers

Cork-shaped stone used to plug entrance to common tombs

Tom Powers/www. BiblePlaces.com

and they rolled there a great stone and laid it against the entrance to the sepulcher (8:31–33).

The rolling-stone tombs, being very rare, were obviously reserved for royal families or the very wealthy and, therefore, not the type utilized by average Jewish families. Amos Kloner calculates that approximately 98 percent of stones used to close the entrances to tombs in Jesus' day were square block stones.[52] These were simple slabs shaped something like a bolt with one end designed to provide a close fit for the small opening forming the doorway of the tomb. The larger remainder of the stone had

Rolling-stone tomb in Nazareth

Alexander Schick

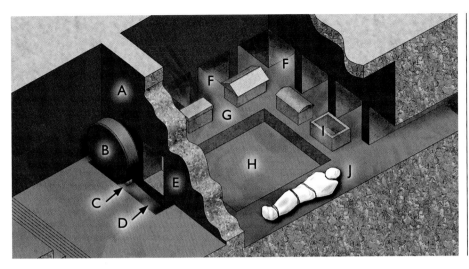

Model of rolling stone
first century tomb

A Front tomb wall
B Rolling stone
C Stopping stone
D Slanted track for
rolling stone
E Entrance
F Niche
G Bench
H Pit
I Ossuary
J Body placed on
bench for burial
preparation

Glenn Klecker

a flange so it would rest against the outside surface of the tomb. These stone "plugs" had the special name *golal* in Hebrew. Often a filling of pebbles or mortar would be added around these to prevent the entrance of small vermin and insects. Therefore, since these are the more common form of sealing tombs and the disk-shaped blocking stones are rare, it would have been exceptional for Jesus' tomb to be so sealed. This led archaeologist Amos Kloner, according to Megan Souter,[53] to argue that the Gospel references to "rolling away" a stone from the entrance to a tomb was a misunderstanding of the normal method of sealing a tomb since square stones do not "roll."[54] This may be true of the average person in Judea and Jerusalem, but Joseph of Arimathea appears to be a wealthy and influential person in the New Testament.

However, Urban C. von Wahlde, in seeking to answer this question, analyzed the use of the Greek verb *kuliō* ("to roll") in the Synoptic Gospels and concluded that the compounds of *kuliō* all have the idea of movement "toward" or "away from."[55] Therefore, in his opinion, the grammar does not fit the idea of moving a square-shaped stone, which would have properly been described as "moved" or "dislodged," although Gibson contends the *golal* could also be "rolled" after a fashion. However, von Wahlde also notes that while the Synoptic Gospels describe the sealing of

the tomb in this manner, the Gospel of John uses a different Greek verb from the root *hairo*, with the meaning that the stone had been "removed" or "taken up" (Greek *ērmenon*) from the tomb (John 20:1). He argues that this description reflects "the Jewish burial practice much more accurately than any of the other gospels. He [John] has given us a detail none of the other gospels have."[56] He further argues that because Jesus' tomb was a borrowed tomb for an ordinary Jewish family, the evidence is in favor of closure by a square stone. He therefore concludes: "It is not that these accounts are necessarily wrong. But they do give the wrong impression. It may very well be that people rolled the 'cork-shaped' stones away from the tomb. Once you see the size of a 'stopper' stone, it is easy to see that, however one gets the stone out of the doorway, chances are you are going to roll it the rest of the way."[57]

Must we conclude that the information in the Gospels gives the "wrong impression?" The grammar of "rolling" (Greek *kuliō* + *pros* "up to" or *apo* "away from") is unambiguous in the Synoptics, and it is an assumption that Joseph of Arimathea was an ordinary man with an ordinary family tomb. The Gospels portray him as a "rich man" (Matt 27:57), a "prominent member" of the Sanhedrin (Mark 15:43), and a man with significant status to be granted a private audience with Pontius Pilate and then given special permission to bury the body of a condemned criminal (not a relation) whose high-profile case had been controversial (John 19:38). This may imply a privileged position, which is reflected in the statement in the apocryphal Gospel of Peter (2:3) that Pilate was Joseph's "friend." This description of an elite in Jerusalem society argues for someone whose family tomb could have fit the category of a rolling-stone tomb.

In addition, the terminology for the tomb as "cut out of the rock" (Matt 27:60; Luke 22:53) is found in the Septuagint of Isaiah 22:16 with reference to a royal tomb. For the poorer lower class a cave was utilized for burial because a rock-cut tomb was too expensive. Joseph of Arimethea was able to afford the most expensive of tombs, the kind used by the upper class and nobility. Christian scholars through the centuries have seen this as a fulfillment of the prediction in Isaiah 53:9 of the Messiah's death: "He was assigned a grave with the wicked, and with the rich, in his death," noting also that as Jesus was a descendant of King David, he was royalty and therefore entitled to an appropriate burial. As to the exceptional grammar of John, commentators have long noticed this particular wording as indeed a detail added by John to the account but have drawn a different conclusion as to the purpose.

One could argue that while the stone had been rolled over the opening, the manner in which it had been rolled away was what was exceptional. The use of the perfect middle/passive participle ("had been moved away") could suggest that the stone had been "thrown" some distance from the tomb, indicating a divine agency. In all accounts angels are mentioned as having entered the tomb, and therefore, must have been responsible for the removal of the stone. Matthew makes this very point: "There was a violent earthquake, for an angel of the Lord came down from heaven and, going to the tomb, rolled back the stone and sat on it" (Matt 28:2). Therefore, in this case, the stone may have been a rolling stone, but it was not technically "rolled away" as was the usual practice, but forcibly moved aside. This, then, was the detail of supernatural intervention witnessed by the women as one evidence of the resurrection that John wished to convey.

While archaeology can provide examples of specific rolling-stone tombs from the period and argue for the more common closure of tombs with square stones, the deciding factor in the case of Jesus' tomb must be the interpretation of the biblical text. The kind of tomb and sealing stone implied in the text fit the archaeological data described above.

GOSPEL OF MARK

Mark 1:1

A Tale of Two Kings

> The beginning of the good news about Jesus the Messiah, the Son of God. (Mark 1:1)

The gospel of Mark begins with a straightforward statement, "The beginning of the good news about Jesus the Messiah, the Son of God." Those who read these words would have been familiar with such a declaration, since this proclamation was also similar to that of the Roman imperial cult, which also spoke of the virgin birth of a child and peace coming from a savior. In 30 BC the emperor Augustus was hailed as a "god and savior of the world, who brings peace on earth." The Myrian Inscription (in Rome) declared ". . . Divine Augustus Caesar, son of a god, imperator of land and sea, the benefactor and savior of the whole world . . . ." After his death Augustus was formerly deified and temples and shrines were dedicated to him by the Emperor Tiberius. The remains of one can be found today at Caesarea Maritima.

This good news of peace (*Pax Romana* or *Pax Augusta*) was proclaimed on coins, inscriptions, and literature of the time, and it was enforced by the Roman power of the sword. It existed for over two hundred years and facilitated the spread of early Christianity throughout the Roman world.

In the city of Priene (in modern southwestern Turkey) archaeological excavation discovered a calendar inscription from the ninth century BC lauding Caesar Augustus's birth as that of a god, prince of peace, and savior of the world. The inscription reads:

> Since Providence, which has ordered all things and is deeply interested in our life, has set in most perfect order by giving us Augustus, whom she filled with virtue that he might benefit humankind, sending him as a savior (*soter*), both for us and for our descendants, that he might end war and arrange all things, and since he, Caesar, by his appearance (excelled even our anticipations), surpassing all previous benefactors, and not even leaving to posterity any hope of surpassing what he has done, and since the birthday of the god Augustus was the beginning of the good tidings for the world that came by reason of him.[58]

The comparison of this inscription with Mark's incipit appears justified. Both make reference to good news, or "gospel," and especially its "beginning," brought by a divine agent called the "savior" and "benefactor" (literally "god"). Moreover, the use in both accounts of the word "appearance" (*epiphanein*), used of a divine manifestation, strengthens this comparison.

Despite this "good news," Roman philosophers such as Epicetus deplored the insufficiency of the *Pax Augusta*: "While the emperor may give peace from war on land and sea, he is unable to give peace from passion, grief, and envy. He cannot give peace of heart, for which man yearns more than even for outward peace."

The Christian immediately sees a comparison of the birth and proclamation of Augustus with that of Jesus the Messiah. However, the good news of Augustus is not the basis of Mark's proclamation. Mark sets forth a counter perspective that was anticipated in the preaching regarding messiah by the prophets of Israel hundreds of years before the birth of Augustus, particularly in Isaiah 9:6–7, in which the messiah's birth is foretold, a son who is God and Prince of Peace.

Augustus Caeasars birthday was celebrated on the first day of the Roman New Year. Of this Paullus Fabius Maximus, proconsul of Asia, wrote: "It is hard to tell whether the birthday of the most divine Caesar is a matter of greater pleasure or benefit. We could justly hold it to be equivalent with the beginning of all things; and he has given a different aspect to the whole world, which blindly would have embraced its own destruction if Caesar had not been born for the common benefit of all."[59] But Mark tells of another birth, more glorious than that of the Caesar, which has been celebrated for 2,000 years, long after Rome fell and the world forgot the great Augustus. Mark further proclaims that this savior of the world, unlike Augustus who brought a temporal peace through the conquest, has brought the hope of everlasting peace through his cross. As a result, whereas Caesar Augustus, Roman ruler of the world, should have been the great king remembered by history, the birth of the King of kings during his reign eclipsed it for all time.

Mark 4:36

The Kinneret "Jesus" Boat

> Leaving the crowd behind, they took him along, just as he was, in the boat. There were also other boats with him. (Mark 4:36)

Until recently, the only evidence available of the construction of first-century fishing boats used on the Sea of Galilee were crude drawings and first-century excavations in the Mediterranean. However, in 1986 a severe drought lowered the water level several meters below normal. Two brothers, Moshe and Yuval Lufan were searching the northwest shoreline for exposed artifacts and discovered the outlines of ancient fishing boats buried in the mud flats.

Shelley Wachsmann, a maritime archaeologist from Texas A&M University, joined by the Israel Antiquities Authority and members of the kibbutz, undertook the difficult excavation of one of the boats, which was in a fragile state and could not be removed by conventional means. He found the mud filling the boat had acted as a natural preservative, and after twelve days of work the team was able to encase the revealed structure in polyurethane and float the boat to a building at the kibbutz where it was submerged in a chemical preservative. After ten years the preservative had replaced the water-soaked wood fibers so that the artifact could be displayed in the open air for public view. It is now on exhibit in the Yigal Alon Center at Kibbutz Nof Ginosar.

Although popularly called the "Jesus boat," there is no evidence Jesus used or had any connection to it. However, it may well have been used at the time of Jesus as radiocarbon dating has given a date ca. 40 BC. The wood used for the boat was not original to it. Rather, it was recycled from other construction and consists of eleven different varieties of trees. At first this was a surprise to scholars who studied the boat, but it has been theorized that numerous repairs had been made to it throughout its life. The boat is approximately 27 feet long, 7 1/2 feet wide and 4 feet deep and built in the typical mortise and tenon construction of the time. It is thought that the boat could have accommodated a crew of fifteen. This analysis compared to ancient descriptions of crews and accounts of naval activities conclude that this was the type of boat the disciples of Jesus would have used to transport him from one side of the Sea of Galilee to the other as the Gospel narratives detail.

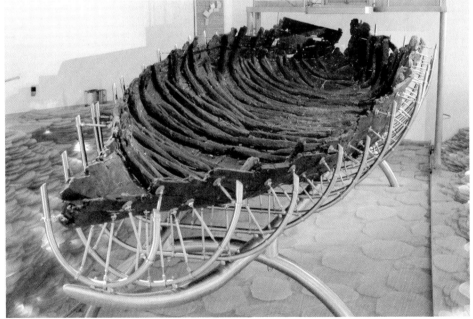

First century
fishing boat

Wikimedia Commons

Mark 5:35

Ruler of the Synagogue (Theodotus Inscription)

> While Jesus was still speaking, some people came from the house of Jairus, the synagogue leader. (Mark 5:35a)

Along with the development of the synagogue as the center of daily and weekly worship for Jews was the rise of the position of the synagogue ruler. The archaeological evidence shows that this position was well established within Judaism. Several examples of the special chair or seat given to the synagogue ruler (often called "Moses's Seat") have been found, including in the synagogue of Chorazin. At Caesarea Maritima the mosaic floor from the synagogue bore the inscription, "Beryllos the head of the synagogue and administrator, the son of Iu[s]tus, made mosaic work of the triclinium from his own means."[60]

There are seven inscriptions in Caesarea and all date between the fourth to sixth centuries.[61] In 1913 Raimond Weill discovered a Greek dedicatory inscription in the Ophel (the area between the City of David and the Temple Mount) commemorating the building of a first-century-AD synagogue (possibly the synagogue of the Freemen in Jerusalem). The Greek inscription reads:

> Theodotus, son of Vettanos, a priest and an archisynagogos, son of an archisynagogos, grandson of an archisynagogos, built the synagogue for the reading of Torah and for teaching the commandments; furthermore, the hostel, and the rooms, and the water installation for lodging needy strangers. Its foundation stone was laid by his ancestors, the elders, and Simonides.

The inscription was named the "Theodotus Inscription" because the first word mentions this priest and calls him an archisynagogos, as well as his descendants. This term means "leader of a synagogue." It appears the ruler's function was presiding over synagogue services, acting as a judge for the community, and serving as a patron of part or most of the synagogue.[62]

Theodotos Synagogue Inscription

GOSPEL OF LUKE

Luke 2:1–20

The Birth of the Messiah

> In those days Caesar Augustus issued a decree that a census should be taken of the entire Roman world. (Luke 2:1)

The historian Luke tells us that Caesar Augustus decreed that "a census should be taken of the entire Roman world" (Luke 2:1). This registration was a standard and regular counting of all the people in the Roman Empire. Emperor Augustus reinstated it after a period of disuse, and was the first emperor to introduce the census in the provinces.

In most of the Roman world the census was for the purposes of taxes and military service. However, the Jews of Judea had gained exception from many civic duties normally compulsory for other citizens of the Roman Empire, military service included. Even this exception did not assuage their resentment at having to register. Many Jews considered the Roman census a violation of Old Testament law, which said the collection of the tax was to go as an atonement offering to God (Deut 30:11–16). Thus, the thought that the taxes collected during the Roman census were going to the emperor, who was considered a god, must have incensed many Jews. Nevertheless, Luke presents Joseph and Mary as obeying the decree, necessitating their journey to Bethlehem to be counted.

Ancient texts have given us insight into the Roman method of counting the population of their empire. Papyri in Egypt have established that the Roman census occurred every fourteen years. One of these papyri, dating from AD 104 (falling on a fourteenth year), is especially interesting concerning Luke's Gospel account. The papyri reads,

> Gaius Vibius, Maximus, Prefect of Egypt. In view of the approaching census, it is necessary for all those residing for any cause away from their own districts, to prepare at once to their own areas of administration, in order that they may meet the family obligation of the enrollment and that the tilled lands may remain in legal possession.[63]

This edict is strikingly similar to Luke's account that Mary and Joseph were obliged to travel to Bethlehem for the census and shows that even almost a century later the procedure of the Roman census had remained unchanged.

We also know what the documents Joseph would have had to file may have looked like. On another Egyptian papyrus, written about AD 48 (another fourteenth year), a woman named Theremoutharion lists the members of those in her household:

> Theremoutharion a freedwoman of the aforesaid Sodates, about 65 years of age, of medium height, with honey-colored complexion, having a long face and a scar on the right knee [. . .] I, the aforesaid Theremoutharion, with my guardian the said Apollonius, swear by Tiberius Claudius Caesar Emperor, that I have assuredly, honestly and truthfully presented the preceding return of those living with me.[64]

Joseph would have listed himself and Mary and, as evidenced in other documents, may have also listed the family he was a part of, in this case the line of David.

There have also been arguments that the timing of the census is off. Historical sources say Quirinius oversaw a census in AD 6. This census was a notorious one, as Josephus relates, ". . . there was one Judas, a Gaulonite, of a city whose name was Gamala, who, taking with him

Sadducee, a Pharisee, became zealous to draw them to a revolt, who both said that this taxation was no better than an introduction to slavery, and exhorted the nation to assert their liberty" (*Ant*. 18.4). He says that this rebellious attitude toward the census and taxation ultimately led to the destruction of the temple in Jerusalem. If this is the census Luke refers to, it is too late for the birth of Jesus. However, there is good reason to believe Luke is not referring to the AD 6 census in his Gospel. In Acts 5:37 Like records the high priest Gamaliel also referring to Judas and the census revolt. It would be unlikely that the otherwise careful historian Luke would have made a chronological mistake in his Gospel despite the fact that he recorded the correct time for the later census in Acts. Further, Luke says the census at the time of Jesus' birth was the "first" census while Quirinius was governing Syria, letting the reader know the specific census he is referring to and that there was more than one. If the date of AD 6 is accepted for the census described by Josephus and Gamaliel, and knowing that Roman censuses took place approximately every fourteen years, there would have been one around approximately 8 BC. We know from Egyptian sources that there was indeed a census between 10 and 9 BC, thus verifying there was indeed a census at that time. Being a frontier province, it is not impossible that a census ordered by the Caesar in Rome would take a period of time to reach Judea. Further, there is evidence that Roman rulers at times attempted to delay a number of imperial edicts due to his fear of inciting the Jews. Josephus's account of the unrest caused by the AD 6 census proved their fears were not unfounded.

Despite the arguments of some, there is good reason to believe Luke's account of a census is accurate. We have documents from the first century indicating that the census of the Roman Empire was held every fourteen years and that people were required to return to the towns of their ancestry to be counted. A document from Egypt (AD 104) records a census requiring all the people were to return to their home cities.[65]

Luke 2:2

Evidence for Quirinius of Syria

(This was the first census that took place while Quirinius was governor of Syria.) (Luke 2:2)

Publius Sulpicius Quirinius was born sometime around 45 BC into a wealthy family from Lanuvium, near Rome. Around 15 BC Augustus appointed him as governor of Crete and Cyrenacia (the eastern half of modern Libya), where he first proved his ability in subjugating people groups under Roman rule. In 12 BC Quirinius was appointed the title of proconsul, and not long after he was sent to the new province of Syria to subdue the Homonadenses. When he had done this he was called back to Rome and appointed the tutor ("rector" in official parlance of Rome) of Augustus's grandson, Gaius. Quirinius was to introduce the heir apparent to the ways of Roman government. The two left Rome on January 29, 1 BC. Around AD 3 Gaius was fatally wounded in a battle in Armenia, and Quintilius was prompted to the governorship of Syria soon after. In AD 6 Judea (the province immediately to the south of Syria) was thrown into disorganization through the failure of Herod Archelaus. Augustus disposed and exiled him and made Judea an autonomous subdivision within the province of Syria. He ordered Quirinius to restore order in Judea, including the imposition of Roman taxes (as opposed to the Roman client-king paying taxes through his own mechanisms). As discussed below, this census caused widespread unrest and ultimately open revolt. Quirinius died in AD 21, wealthy and old, though childless. He must have been well respected in Rome because he was given a public funeral there.

Quirinius's presence in Syria is evidenced by archaeological finds. In the early twentieth century, as Scottish archaeologist and New Testament scholar Sir William M. Ramsay, who pioneered archaeological exploration in Asia Minor, discusses in length, two stone inscriptions that were discovered in and near Pisidian Antioch.[66] The first is a dedicatory stone that formed part of the base of a statue. It reads:

> To Gaius Caristanius
> (son of Gaius, of Sergian tribe)
> Fronto Caesianus Juli[us],
> chief of engineers, pontifex,
> priest, prefect of
> P. Sulpicius Quirinius duumvir,
> prefect of M. Servilius.
> To him first of all men
> at state expense by decree of the decuriones,
>   a statue was erected.

This inscription uses the title Quirinius duumvir, meaning Quirinius was co-ruling with Gaius Caristanius. Ramsay theorized that the two were in charge of different parts of the province, perhaps Caristanus from the north and Quirinius from the south. Another inscription was discovered nearby that gives Quirinius the same title.

One final inscription attesting the name Quirinius is found on the tombstone of Q. Aemilius Secundus, who conducted Quirinius's census in Apamea, just south of Antioch. This inscription is dated to ca. AD 20. The dates of these inscriptions are very important in regard to the reliability of Luke's Gospel.

The passage in Luke 2:2 poses an apparent difficulty to the consistency of the biblical record regarding the birth of Jesus. Luke records that Jesus was born "while Quirinius was governor of Syria." For example, N. F. Gier believes that Quirinius was not the governor of Syria at the time of Jesus' birth but a decade later, and therefore that Luke had made a mistake.[67] However, if the inscription stone above is dated before 4–5 BC, then it is entirely correct that he was governing in Syria. Ramsay dated the inscription to ca. 8 BC. He argued that it would not have been very long after the

establishment of the colony of Syria that the statue would have been put up. Moreover, he argues that the statue may have been occasioned by the victory of Rome over the Homonadenses in 8 BC.[68]

Moreover, Luke uses the participle form of the Greek word *hēgemoneuō* ("ruling," "governing"). Again, if Luke is saying Quirinius was governing in Syria rather than the official governor of Syria, he was correct in his facts. Luke has been proven to be a very careful and thorough historian. It is hard to accept that he would have made such an egregious and easily verifiable mistake. When archaeological evidence is coupled with textual study of his account, the chronology of Luke's Gospel is proven reliable.

Tombstone of Q. Aemiulus Secundus, who conducted Quirinius's census in Apamea in Syria.

Luke 7:5

The Capernaum Synagogue

> This man deserves to have you do this, because
> he loves our nation and has built our synagogue.
> (Luke 7:4b–5)

Luke records that a certain centurion of Capernaum "loved" Israel and built a synagogue. One of his servants becomes sick, and though he calls himself unworthy, he believes Jesus only need say the word and his servant will be healed. Jesus praises the man's faith and heals his servant.

Perhaps one of the most famous sites outside Jerusalem in Israel is the synagogue at Capernaum. Since its excavation from 1905 to 1921 and again in 1969 it has been the site of Christian pilgrimage. However, the synagogue that stands partially restored is from the late second or early third century. It is constructed of an imported white marble. However, when Virgilio Corbo dug trenches along the walls, he discovered the foundations of an earlier building from the first century. The stones of this construction, like those of the ruins of the Roman-period houses surrounding the synagogue, were made of the regional black volcanic basalt. Corbo identified these foundations as part of the earlier synagogue, most likely the one Jesus would have known and taught in.

Although the present synagogue is later, it may have been built in the same style as the earlier one, albeit in marble rather than basalt (such as the Chorazin synagogue). The Capernaum synagogue is built in the basilica style, with a central aisle and two side aisles separated by columns. There was a narrow porch in front of the synagogue and a courtyard to the east of the main hall that featured a covered portico around the edges. The whole building was oriented north-south so that prayers could be directed toward Jerusalem and was located about a hundred yards from the shore of the Sea of Galilee. Excavations also revealed that Romans lived alongside the Jews, as Capernaum was a garrison town housing a detachment of Roman soldiers. This fact explains the presence of the centurion in Luke's account.

Capernaum
Synagogue
(fourth
century AD)

Bill Schlegel/www
.BiblePlaces.com

Luke 8:26

The Country of the Gergesenes[69]

> They sailed to the region of the Gerasenes [Gergesenes], which is across the lake from Galilee. (Luke 8:26)

The exact place of where Jesus allowed demons to leave two men and go into a herd of swine has never been located, mostly due to variations of the name used by the Gospel writers and textual variants within the copies of the Gospels. There are several locations that the church, scholars, and archaeologists have argued is the place of this event.

Part of the issue is where the "region of the Gerasenes" is located. There are three different principle readings in the manuscript copies: Gadarenes, Gerasenes, and Gergesenes. Normally the earliest and most reliable manuscripts are the preferred reading. However, the three readings here in 8:32 and in the parallel passages to this (Mark 5:1 and Luke 8:26) are spread across several important manuscripts. Manuscript "B" has Gaderenes, P75 and one copy of ℵ has Gerasenes, while most copies of ℵ have Gergesenes. P75 is considered one of the best manuscripts, yet it is all but impossible that Gerasa (Jerash) was the area where Jesus performed the miracle because it is over 30 miles from the Sea of Galilee and has no church tradition of being the site. Arguably Gadera is the proper site for the exorcism (located 5 miles southeast of the Sea of Galilee) and it is based on slightly better textual attestation as well as the testimony of Josephus and numismatology. Josephus says that the "villages of Gadara" were "situated on the borders of Tiberias," that is, the Sea of Galilee (*Life*, 9). Coins from Gadera sometimes featured ships.

The oldest and probably best tradition (apart from biblical manuscripts) locates the Gergesenes at a village near the east shore of the Sea, opposite Tiberias. Church fathers identified this place as Gergesa,

First century foundation of synagogue at Capernaum; black basalt stones beneath white marble are first century

today known as Kursi or Kersa. Origen pointed out that sometimes the Greek copies of the Scriptures are incorrect when it comes to proper names. He lists the geographic reasons neither Gerasa or Gadera could be the spot of the miracle of the swine. He concludes, "But Gergesa, from which the name Gergesenes is taken, is an old town in the neighbourhood of the lake now called Tiberias, and on the edge of it there is a steep place abutting on the lake, from which it is pointed out that the swine were cast down by the demons."[70]

Kursi is located at the mouth of the Wadi Samak, also known as the Valley of Kursi, and has excellent grazing areas, especially for swine, which travel easily in the rocky hills. The slopes of the hills in the area run steeply down to the Sea, and it is the only area around the Sea of Galilee that satisfies the geographical criteria of the Gospel account. All three accounts of the miracle say the area where it took place was "on the other side" of the lake (Luke 8:22, Mark 5:1) from the area where Jesus was previously ministering.

The area was excavated and surveyed from 1970 to 1973 and again in 1980 by Vassilios Tzaferis under the Israel Antiquities Authority. Tzaferis, along with Charles Page, returned to the site again from 2001 to 2003. A road construction crew had discovered the site accidentally. In Kursi itself Tzaferis discovered a

Chapel of the miracle of the swine

Church at Kursi

large Byzantine monastery area, probably built in the early sixth century. The ruins of the church contained 8,600 square feet of fine mosaic floors. Small Roman and Byzantine settlements were discovered on the ridge above the site, and many caves were found in the slopes above Kursi. Near the shore a Roman-era fishing village was discovered.

Excavators also discovered a site approximately 650 feet south of the Byzantine monastery and halfway up the slope of a steep hill that was probably constructed at the same time as the monastery. The site appears to have been a chapel constructed around a large boulder and may have commemorated the actual spot where Jesus cast the demons into the swine. The chapel was oriented so that pilgrims could look at the boulder and the sea while sitting on a circular bench under a shelter carved into the rock of the hillside.

The Kursi site appears to have been abandoned during the end of the eighth century after the Muslim conquest and a severe earthquake. Soon sedimentary soil from the wadi covered the site, and it was revealed only after a bulldozer uncovered it more than a thousand years later. As of the time of this writing, nothing has been found identifying the name of this site. It is only through tradition and name preservation that it is known.

Luke 13:4

The Tower in Siloam

> Or those eighteen who died when the tower in Siloam fell on them—do you think they were more guilty than all the others living in Jerusalem? I tell you, no! But unless you repent, you too will all perish. (Luke 13:4)

While teaching on repentance the Lord Jesus uses the example of eighteen men who were apparently killed when the "tower in Siloam" fell on them.

Although archaeologists are not certain, a tower was discovered by Raymond Weill in 1913 at the southern end of the City of David and may be the tower Jesus references in Luke.

The tower was 20 feet in circumference but only the bottom 5 feet were preserved, so its original height is not known. It was made of rough-cut field stones mortared together and plastered on the exterior all the way to its base. No doorway was found in the walls of the tower. Interestingly, it is very close to the newly discovered Pool of Siloam.

Scholars are almost universally convinced it was not a tower designed for defensive purposes. Its location is in a terrible spot for a tower, being only 30 feet from the bottom of the Kidron Valley. If someone walked up the hill a short distance they would have a better view. Instead, the tower is thought to have been a columbarium (a structure used for raising pigeons). The lack of an entrance in the walls of the tower, while odd for a defensive tower, are a hallmark of columbarium. Also, in excavations conducted by Yigal Shiloh, two columbarium towers were discovered less than 70 feet from the Siloam tower. Another argument in favor of the tower's use as a columbarium is its location. While a poor spot for security use, the tower was in the perfect spot for raising sacrificial pigeons for use at the temple. The pigeons or doves would be raised in these towers then brought to the shops along the walls of the temple to be sold to worshipers.

Luke 19:1

New Testament Jericho

> Jesus entered Jericho and was passing through. (Luke 19:1)

Lying about a mile to the south of the ancient tel (Old Testament Jericho), New Testament Jericho, formerly a Hasmonean palace-fortress, was rebuilt by Herod, who had made it his winter capital due to the warm climate. The town featured an amphitheater, a hippodrome, and three royal palaces—in one of which he eventually died. Herod's latest palace was the most opulent, built in two wings spreading across a wadi and connected by a private bridge. The north wing featured a large reception hall and a full Roman style bath complex. The south wing had a large pool and a large façade called an *opus reticulatum* that functioned as a terraced garden. It also had a two-story tower with a commanding view of the area around Jericho. After Herod's death one

Overview of Tell Jericho

© 1995 by Phoenix Data Systems

Excavations of Herod's palace in Jericho

of Herod's servants burned the palace down, but Herod's son Archelaus rebuilt it. Jericho was also known for its date palms, which continue to be grown there today.

Luke records that Jesus stayed with Zaccheus, "chief tax collector." Jericho was on the major highway through the Jordan Rift Valley between Galilee and Jerusalem and as such probably had a toll station, like Capernaum in Galilee. Although it has been suggested that Luke's account of Zaccheus being in a tree when Jesus is passing through Jericho is a contradiction, the suggestion is based on the erroneous idea that there were no trees within the city itself. While this might have been true for the Old Testament city, the Jericho of the New Testament was arranged much like many other Roman cities, with parks, boulevards, and public squares where trees would have been planted.

Luke 23:1

The Pontius Pilate Inscription

> Then the whole assembly rose and led him off to Pilate. (Luke 23:1)

Pontius Pilate is perhaps the best known and infamous of the Roman governors due to his presiding over the trial of Jesus. Although there is some debate, Pilate was probably appointed as governor (prefect) ca. AD 26–27 and was dismissed in AD 37. From secular sources, we know Pilate had a troubled, lackluster career.[71] Although previous Roman government officials in Judea had respected Jewish religious proclivities, Pilate seems to have reveled in agitating them, constantly provoking religious leaders to the point of revolt with seemingly deliberate acts of sacrilege. These include such acts as placing images of

Roman Road to Jericho

the emperor Tiberias in the temple (Philo, *Embassy to Gaius*, 299–305), which led to a major Jewish riot in AD 26 (*Ant.* 18.55–59; *J.W.* 2.169–74), expropriating sacred temple funds to finance the building an aqueduct (*Ant.* 18.60–62; *J.W.* 2.175–77), and the crucifixion of Jesus. Undoubtedly the continued reaction to Jesus' crucifixion, claims of his resurrection, and the growing movement of Jesus followers, especially in Rome, raised questions as to Pilate's ability to control affairs in Judea. The Gospel of Luke makes mention of Pilate's cruelty in an attack on some Galileans (Luke 13:1–2) and records reveal their were several warnings and chastisements from the emperor on this account. When Pilate ordered a bloody attack on a group of prophet-led Samaritans on their sacred Mt. Gerizim, he was recalled to Rome in AD 37 to answer charges. He had hoped to appeal his actions to Tiberias (to whom he had dedicated a *tiberieum*, a temple built to the deified Augustus, at Caesarea Maritima), but the emperor died before he arrived in the city. After his hearing he was not allowed to return

to his post. Philo of Alexandria described Pilate's rule as "ceaseless and supremely grievous cruelty"[72] due to his "vindictiveness and furious temper" (*Legat.* 302).[73]

In church history he has been seen on the one hand as evil for sentencing Jesus to death and later suffering all kinds of maladies as punishments for his deeds, from going insane to decapitation to committing suicide over his guilt, and on the other hand canonized for repenting of his sin, embracing the Christian faith, and suffering a martyr's death.

Pilate is mentioned in all four Gospels as well as other ancient sources such as the writings of Josephus (*Ant.* 18.3–4; *J.W.* 2.9) and Tacitus (*Ann.* 15.44) and in several early church fathers, including Ignatius (*Mang.* 11; *Trall.* 9), Irenaeus (*Haer.*), Tertullian (*Apol.* 21) and Nicene Fathers such as Eusebius (who was the first to report that Pilate committed suicide, *Hist. eccl.* 1.10).

He is also mentioned on coins, minted between AD 26 and 36, which have been discovered in archaeological excavations. The evidence from his coinage reveals that Pilate was trying to promote a form of Roman religion regardless of the offense this brought to the Jews. Unlike his predecessors, Pilate's coinage depicted Roman symbolism connected with the imperial cult (on the reverse side of the coins). These images include the simpulum (a ladle used for Roman priestly libations during sacrifices) and the lituus (the wand of an augur used to interpret natural phenomenon). However, he appears to have attempted to appease Jewish sentiment by substituting agricultural symbolism (three ears of barley or crossed palm branches and a wreathed inscription) on the obverse side of the coins rather than an image the emperor.

However, the most famous mention of Pilate comes from an inscription discovered in Caesarea Maritima in 1961 by Antonio Frova. Frova and his team were excavating the (now) famous theater at Caesarea when they discovered a 2 foot x 3 foot limestone slab with an

Pontius Pilate Inscription

inscription chiseled into it. The inscription, written in three lines on a large stone slab, dates from AD 26–37, placing it during Pilate's rule. The slab is partially broken, and reads (in Latin):

[ ]S TIBERIEUM	(Tiberieum)
[PO]NTIUS PILATUS	(Pontius Pilate)
[PRAEF]ECTUS IUDA[EA]E	(Prefect of Judea)

Though damaged, the first line probably mentions a temple to the divine Augustus, dedicated in honor of the Emperor Tiberias. The second line mentions Pilate, and the third identifies him as the prefect of Judea. The slab is the first and only properly provenanced archaeological evidence of the existence of Pilate. According to John McRay, "Undoubtedly, the stone was first used as part of some important building called a Tiberium, possibly a temple, which was dedicated in honor of the emperor Tiberius."[74] Excavators think it may have been used secondarily as part of a stairway in the theater in Caesarea.

Although Pilate's historical existence has never been seriously challenged, the discovery of this inscription removes all doubt and proves the existence of Pontius Pilate as an historical figure. The inscription also corrected a very common error in Pilate's title. The vast majority of the time Pilate was referred to as the procurator of Judea. That title is now shown to be an anachronism by ancient historians referring to Pilate. Prefects had a more military function than procurators, something that the rough and often rebellious Judean province needed. The slab also vindicates the New Testament's use of *hēgemōn* ("governor"), the Greek equivalent of the Latin *praefecus* for Pilate, rather than *epitpopos* ("procurator"), which later authors (like Tacitus, writing at the end of the first century AD) used to refer to Pilate. The use of *hēgemōn* also points to the early date of the composition of the Gospels, since the title of *epitpopos* began to be used as the title of Roman governors of Judea during the reign of Claudius (ca. AD 41–54).

GOSPEL OF JOHN

John 1:28

Bethany beyond the Jordan

> This all happened at Bethany on the other side of the Jordan, where John was baptizing. (John 1:28)

When John the Baptist was answering the inquiries of the "priests and Levites" from Jerusalem he is said to have been "in Bethany on the other side of the Jordan." There has been debate over this location, which is only mentioned in John's Gospel. One problem is textual as there are two variant readings

in the ancient manuscripts. In some of the oldest and most reliable sources (P66), John 1:28 has *Bēthania* ("Bethany"), although some later manuscripts (C2, K, T, Ψc, 083) read *Bētharaba* ("Betharaba"). Metzger, speaking for the UBS editors, says that while they had difficulty deciding on the correct reading, the UBS reads *Bēthania* "on the basis of age and distribution of evidence" and "the consideration that, if *Bētharaba* were original, there is no adequate reason why it should have been altered."[75] Although the general rules of textual criticism required this conclusion, Metzger adds that Origen thought Betharaba was correct based on personal investigation:

We are aware of the reading which is found in almost all the copies . . . We are convinced, however, that we should not read "Bethany," but "Bethabara." We have visited the places to enquire as to the footsteps of Jesus and His disciples, and of the prophets. Now, Bethany . . . is fifteen stadia from Jerusalem, and the river Jordan is about a hundred and eighty stadia distant from it. Nor is there any other place of the same name in the neighborhood of the Jordan, but they say that Bethabara is pointed out on the banks of the Jordan, and that John is said to have baptized there.[76]

Likewise, Eusebius (the bishop of Caesarea Maritime) thought it should be Bethabara, noting that it was "where John was baptizing (the penitent) across the Jordan. The place is pointed out where many of the brothers even now consider it an honor to wash."[77] The oldest known map of the Holy Land, the sixth-century mosaic Madaba Map discovered in 1884 in the Byzantine floor level of the St. George Greek Orthodox church in the city of Madaba (in modern Jordan),

reads, *Bethabara to tou hagiou Iannōu baptismatos* ("Bethabara, [the place of] Saint John's baptizing"), and places it near Jericho. It has been theorized that the possible discrepancy owes to the place being called Bethany in the first century, but later the name became known as Betharaba[78] and subsequent commentators were unaware of the change.

The Bordeaux Pilgrim (ca. 333) says it was 5 (Roman) miles from the Dead Sea to where "the Lord was baptized by John" in the Jordan, and on the east bank. He also reports that this place was near the hill where "Elijah was caught up into heaven."[79] A hill in this general location has long been known as Jebel Mar Elias. Both tradition and recent archaeological work have confirmed that this hill was probably where John the Baptist lived during his ministry. A little more than two hundred years later (530), Theodosius agrees with the pilgrim, saying that the spot 5 miles up the Jordan from the Dead Sea was marked by a marble column topped with an iron cross and that there was a church there. He also mentions the hill of Elijah nearby.[80] Forty years later (570), Anonymous

Site at Bethany beyond the Jordan

of Piacenza says that there is a well-established tradition that at Epiphany people would come down to the Jordan at the spot described above to be baptized.[81]

In 1997 Jordanian Department of Antiquities excavator Mohammad Waheeb surveyed several sites near Wadi Kharrar, hoping to find the place of Jesus' baptism. One on the east side of the river, at Tell al-Kharrar (the modern name of Jebel Mar Elyas), looked more promising than the others, so Waheeb began an excavation there. He found evidence of occupation at the site from the Hellenistic through Islamic periods, including the remains of heavy stone jars.[82] The presence of stone jars strongly points to a Jewish presence at the site (due to purity laws). Other finds at the site include Roman era pottery and cisterns. He also found a Byzantine-era monastery complex and several churches in and around the site. This complex featured several pools fed by nearby springs. On the west bank of the tel a cave was discovered that was in use during Roman times. A church was built over the cave entrance, and a water channel was constructed that ran from the cave to the nearby wadi.[83] Waheeb posits

that the church remembered the place where John the Baptist resided while he was ministering in the area.[84]

The whole area of Tell al-Kharrar seems to have been an important pilgrimage site. According to the Jordanian Department of Antiquities (who are in charge of the excavations), "The primary evidence for Roman and Byzantine era sacred and secular structures associated with the baptism of Jesus and the mission of John the Baptist now appear to be clustered mostly on the east bank."[85] Thus the site matches the apostle John's description. It is about as far from Jerusalem as Origen says it was, about as far from the Dead Sea as the Bordeaux Pilgrim says it was, and in the same general location as the Madaba Map shows it was. The site is located at a natural ford in the river, which, unlike areas immediately upstream or down, would have provided a convenient spot for entering the water to baptize.

Until another spot provides more evidence, Tell al-Kharrar seems to be the best candidate for Bethany beyond the Jordan, the place where John the Baptist ministered.

Cave by Bethany
beyond the Jordan

Baptismal site at
Bethany beyond
the Jordan

©Alatom/www.istock.com

John 1:44

The Town of Bethsaida

> Philip, like Andrew and Peter, was from the town
> of Bethsaida. (John 1:44)

The town of Bethsaida (lit. "the house of the fisher-man") is mentioned several times in the Gospels. In fact, the area between Bethsaida and Capernaum is where the majority of Jesus' activities in Galilee took place. Here in John's account, Bethsaida is said to be the hometown of Philip, Andrew, and Peter (although it seems that Peter moved to Capernaum at some point). In Mark's Gospel Jesus visits the city and heals a blind man (Mark 8:22–26), while in Matthew and Luke's account Jesus includes Bethsaida in his "woes" (along with Chorazin and Capernaum—Matt 11:21, Luke 10:13).

The location of the city is to this day not known with absolute certainty. The historical record does narrow down the locality somewhat. The Jewish historian Josephus says that Bethsaida was in the territory of Philip the Tetrarch and that he renamed the town "Julias," after the wife of the emperor Augustus (and mother of Tiberias), and raised its status from *kōmē* ("village") to *polis*

("city"). Josephus also says that the Jordan "passes by" Bethsaida-Julius (*Ant.* 18:28). Since Philip's territory was east of the Jordan River, this puts Bethsaida on or near the east bank of the river. Theodosius, writing around AD 530, says that Bethsaida was 6 miles from Capernaum, and that the headwater of the Jordan River was 50 miles from Bethsaida. This suggests that the site of the town was not far from where the Jordan empties into the Sea of Galilee. The proximity of Bethsaida to the lake is also suggested by the name of the city itself, which means "place of the fishers" in Aramaic. Thus two sites are identified as the most likely locations of Bethsaida: Khirbet el-Araj and et-Tell. Roman pottery has been found on the surface at both sites, confirming habitation during Jesus' life, and both are geographically located near where the historical record says they should be.

Khirbet el-Araj is located only about fifty yards from the shore of the Sea of Galilee on the current west bank of the Jordan River. Although it is on the wrong side of the river today, this was not necessarily the case two thousand years ago, as the Jordan at this spot has changed its course many times. In 1889 Gottlieb Schumacher, citing the difficulty of et-Tell's distance from the Sea of Galilee, proposed Khirbet el-Araj as

Sea of Galilee near Bethsaida

the true site of Bethsaida.[86] Although Byzantine-era artifacts have been found at the site, archaeological surveys using ground penetrating radar have shown that there is nothing but sand below the Byzantine layer, strongly suggesting that there was no village here during Jesus' ministry. However, Mendel Nun, an acknowledged expert on the Sea of Galilee, has argued that the level of the Sea of Galilee was lower in ancient times than it is today,[87] and therefore much of the Khirbet el-Araj site is underwater. Another theory holds that there were two Bethsaidas: one, the fishing village at Khirbet el-Araj and the other away from the shore of the lake, at the site called et-Tell.[88] Against the above views are the arguments of Jack Shroder and Moshe Inbar, who assert that el-Araj would have been an "unsuitable" site for a settlement because "its location would have made it subject to periodic seasonal flooding and occasional catastrophic inundation from seismic tsunami waves."[89] Moreover, the site would have been prone to malarial disease from its marshy surroundings, something even Gottlieb realized.

Et-Tell is about 1.2 miles from the lake and about 800 feet from the Jordan River, on a rocky hill on the east side of the Jordan. The hill itself is part of

an alluvial plain known as Beteiha.[90] As its modern name ("the mound") suggests, the site's original name has been lost, even to the locals.[91] Although Edward Robinson identified it as Bethsaida in 1838, it has only been excavated since 1990 by the Consortium of the Bethsaida Excavations Project (BEP).[92] In 1999 Carl F. Savage became Area Supervisor of the dig. The site itself is an oval mound over 1,300-feet long and 650-feet wide, covering twenty acres, making it one of the largest archaeological sites on the Sea of Galilee.[93]

The BEP has identified et-Tell as the ancient capitol of the kingdom of Geshur, perhaps called Zer or Tzed (Josh 19:35). The excavations of the ninth century BC uncovered the palace, a sacrificial area, and a nearly twenty-foot thick wall and monumental gate (one of the largest discovered from this period in Israel) surrounding the city. These finds confirm that the city was one of the most important cities of the Iron Age. Despite these impressive fortifications, the city was destroyed, probably during the Assyrian invasion of the Northern Kingdom. The site was nearly abandoned, with little evidence of occupation and no evidence of construction for the next five hundred years. Archaeologists found evidence of a sudden period of construction and re-occupation during the Hellenistic period in the third century BC. The BEP found the remains of several Hellenistic courtyard-type houses, inside of which they found fishing net weights and needles for repairing nets, iron anchors, and fish hooks.[94] In another house an almost intact wine cellar was discovered. The cellar contained several wine amphorae and vine pruning hooks, leading archaeologists to the conclusion that the house belonged to a vintner.

One of the most interesting finds was a Roman-era temple, which the BEP argues may have been built to commemorate Philip's renaming the city after Julia. The temple follows the typical plan of Roman temples, having a columned porch, a hallway leading to a long, narrow "holy of holies," and a rear porch. An incense shovel and several religious figurines were also found near the temple. Archaeologists also found decorated stones near the temple that are almost identical to stones found in the Chorazin synagogue, leading them to argue that the Chorazin stones were actually taken from the et-Tell site (they are only about 3 miles apart). Other interesting finds are a rare gold coin of Antonius Pious of AD 138, a third-century bronze coin of the emperor Caracalla, and a clay smoking pipe.

Although the BEP did find limestone containers and flint knife blades, suggesting the presence of Jews in the city,[95] some scholars argue that the population of et-Tell was most likely almost totally gentile. Savage disagrees, arguing that in Bethsaida "Gentiles seem to have left only a very modest impact on the archaeological record" and that there was a "marked lack of Gentile presence" in the city.[96] He asserts that the majority of the gentile remains at Bethsaida are from the Hellenistic period and that "a well-defined shift from one cultural orientation [gentile] to another [Jewish] occurs during the transition from Hellenistic to early Roman periods."[97]

A major problem with identifying et-Tell as ancient Bethsaida is et-Tell's distance from the Sea of Galilee.

However, Shroder, a geological expert, examined geological maps of the area and concluded that the current shoreline of the sea is not necessarily the ancient shoreline. Shroder (Chief Geologist BEP) argues that et-Tell sits on a highly active fault line and that the elevation of the entire plain on which et-Tell sits may very well be higher than it was in the first century AD.[98] Moreover, the level of the lake is constantly changing, and the mouth of the northern branch of the Jordan River has built up a delta where it flows into the Sea of Galilee. Thus, the site of et-Tell may very well have been near the shore in Jesus' time. The presence of fishing gear found at et-Tell seems to lend considerable credibility to this theory. Other examples of the phenomenon of a once shore-side town becoming landlocked include Ephesus, once on the shore of the Aegean but now about 6 miles from the sea.

Subsequent geological investigation has given strong evidence to Shroder's argument. At the base of et-Tell, sedimentary clay containing crustacean microorganisms was discovered. Further, large boulders and gravel cover the clay. Carbon-14 tests conducted on organic material underneath this layer of boulders and gravel revealed a date range of AD 68–375. Shroder theorizes that the cataclysmic earthquake of AD 363 caused a large landslide to flow across the plain where et-Tell is located, "cutting Bethsaida off from the shore."[99] After the city was cut off from the shore, it was abandoned by the fourth century.

Based on the above information, et-Tell is now commonly identified as Bethsaida by scholars and archaeologists and has "gained the imprimatur of governmental bodies in Israel."[100] Moreover, it appears Jesus' condemnation of Bethsaida came to pass, as the city was so quickly forgotten that Byzantine pilgrims (who have been shown to be fairly accurate in their identifications of biblical sites) could not find the site, and some of them misidentified the Khirbet el-Araj site as ancient Bethsaida, probably because there may have been a village there at the time and it was close to where Bethsaida should be.

Entrance to
Bethsaida

In 2016, under the supervision of the Kinneret Institute for Galilean Archaeology, the Center for Holy Lands Studies and the NYACK Study Center for Ancient Judaism and Christian Origins, excavations were begun at the site of el-Araj, one of the proposed locations for Bethsaida Julius located at the delta of the River Jordan on the northern shore of the Sea of Galilee. In 2017, evidence was found to strengthen this identification with the discovery of a Byzantine church with walls of gilded glass tesserae for a mosaic, an indication of a wealthy and important church. This matched the description of pilgrim traveler Willibald, the bishop of Eichstätt in Bavaria, who visited the Holy Land in AD 725 and recorded that he visited a church at Bethsaida that had been built over the house of Peter and Andrew. Beneath this Byzantine layer was a layer containing pottery from the first–third centuries AD, remains of an advanced Roman-style bathhouse with a mosaic floor, two coins from the late 2nd century, and a silver denarius featuring the Emperor Nero from the year AD 65–66. This provided evidence that the site was a city, not simply a fishing village, in the Roman period. This agrees with a statement by Josephus that King Herod transformed Bethsaida, which had been a Jewish fishing village, into a Roman polis (*Ant.* 18:28). It was renamed Julias in the early part of the first century.

Formerly, arguments against el-Araj being Julias were based on calculations made by the excavators of Magdala that the level of the Sea of Galilee was 209 meters below sea level during the Roman period, putting the site of el-Araj under water until the Byzantine period.[101] These new discoveries refute that assumption since the Roman layer is 211 meters below sea level. As a result, Dr. Mordechai Aviam of Kinneret College and his team now suggest that el-Araj is the most likely candidate for the location of the lost Roman city of Julias, the home of the apostles Peter, Andrew, and Philip (John 1:44; 12:21). Further seasons of excavation and analysis of finds will confirm or revise this now tentative conclusion.[102]

John 2:1–2

Cana of Galilee

> And on the third day a wedding took place at Cana in Galilee. Jesus' mother was there, and Jesus and his disciples had also been invited to the wedding. (John 2:1–2)

John's Gospel records Jesus' first miracle, turning water into wine, as taking place at "Cana in Galilee" (John 2:1; 4:46). John is the only one to mention Cana and does not give any more specific location other than it is in the region of Galilee. Today there are two sites that may be the Cana of Jesus' miracle. Both are in the hill country above and west of the Sea of Galilee (they are only 6 miles apart). They both have names that seem to preserve the ancient name: Kefr Kenna and Khirbet Qana.[103]

The first site, Kefr Kenna (or Kafr Kanna), is still inhabited and is less than 4 miles northeast of Nazareth and 2.5 miles from Sepphoris, on the road to Tiberias. This site seems to be the one Jerome speaks of as being "not far off" from Nazareth.[104] Later on, the Anonymous of Piacenza (AD 570) says that it was 3 miles from Sepphoris to Cana.[105] This also seems to point to Kefr Kenna. Several more pilgrims describe Cana in similar geographic location to this site, so Finegan believes Kefr Kenna is the Cana of John's Gospel.[106] He argues that at some point the church at Kefr Kenna was converted to a mosque, so that by Crusader times Christian pilgrims had begun visiting Khirbet Qana instead.[107]

Bellarmino Bagatti and Stanislao Loffreda conducted archaeological excavations at Kefr Kenna several times from 1955 to 1969 and found coins dating from the rule of Herod the Great (37–4 BC) to Constantine (AD 326) and ceramics from the Roman and Byzantine periods.[108] They also found what may be the ruins of two synagogues (one at the adjacent site of Karm er-Ras). Finegan postulates this may mean that one was the synagogue for Jews of the village while the other functioned as a synagogue-church for early Jewish-Christians.[109] In 1998 the Franciscans wanted to renovate their shrine at Kefr Kenna and employed Fr. Eugenio Alliata, professor of archaeology at the Studium Biblicum Franciscanum near the Church of the Flagellation in Jerusalem, to explore the area underground at the shrine. Alliata and the Franciscans asserted that they had found the remains of buildings, including an apse with a tomb that dates to the fifth-sixth centuries. Under these remains they believe are "remains of dwellings" including a "small stone cistern" built into a crypt in the floor that dates to the first century. In this cistern

they found stone jars they say date to the first century. The Franciscans claim there is "no doubt that the new data now in our possession confirm the tradition of the shrine of the wedding of Cana."[110] However, other scholars doubt the veracity of these claims and argue, "There is at present no archaeological evidence to demonstrate the antiquity of Kefr Kenna."[111]

The second possible site, Khirbet Qana, is an unoccupied ruin on a 100-meter tall hill overlooking the Beth Netofa Valley, known in ancient times as the Plain of Asochis. This site is 6 miles north of Sepphoris and 9 miles north of Nazareth. It was surveyed by the Israel Archaeology Survey in 1982 and was excavated by a team from the University of Puget Sound, led by Douglas Edwards, from 1997 to 2004.[112] Evidence of occupation spans from the Neolithic to Ottoman periods, with "peaks of settlement" during the early Roman to Byzantine ages.[113] Archaeologists identified streets, plazas, house foundations, and several cisterns, all mostly from the Roman period. At some time in the Byzantine period a cave at the site was "adapted to meet the needs of pilgrims."[114] Josephus says that his "abode was in a village of Galilee, which is named Cana" (*Life*, 8b). The scope of the ruins leads Finegan to argue that this site is the Cana Josephus mentions. In turn, Richardson argues that "The Cana of Josephus is no doubt the same site as New Testament Cana."[115]

Although pilgrims mentioned above are often assumed to be describing Kefr Kenna as biblical Cana, extensive literature from the Byzantine period describing pilgrimages to the Holy Land contains numerous references to Cana, some of which presuppose that Khirbet Qana was the pilgrim site. This remained the case until the early Medieval period. Urban C. Von Wahlde, citing research done by J. Herrojo (who surveyed the "pilgrim cave" described below), agrees with this position, saying that until the "time of the Crusaders there was only a single tradition of Cana's location, and this consistently associated with Khirbet Qana."[116] Laney, contra Finegan, even argues that, "The tradition which supports the identification of Kefr Kenna with Cana of Galilee is quite late, not beginning until the early 17th century when Quaresmius, guardian of the Holy Sepulchre … investigated the two sites and decided in favor of Kefr Kenna."[117] Soon after the Franciscans began to purchase buildings in Kefr Kenna near the village mosque, but "only in 1879 were they able to purchase the mosque itself, where they erected the Franciscan church with its red dome. This is now believed to be the place of Christ's first miracle." Due to this, Laney contends "The evidence of tradition, however, offers only meager support for identifying Cana of Galilee with Kefr Kenna. Until then, all the evidence of tradition points to Khirbet Kana as the correct site for Cana of Galilee."[118] On the other hand, Laney offers convincing evidence that ancient pilgrims visiting Cana were actually describing Khirbet Qana.

Until recently, there was little consensus on which site was the Cana of John's Gospel, however, according to Peter Richardson, "Recent excavations have tipped the scales decisively in favor of Khirbet Qana as the location of Cana."[119] In the cave mentioned above, archaeologists found stone water jars, an altar-like construction with Maltese crosses inscribed into it, and signs of veneration consisting of Greek graffiti on the ceiling and evidence of a church, perhaps with associated monastic structures, all dating to the Byzantine period (sometime during the sixth century AD). The cave itself is actually a complex of connected shafts and rooms that "suggest a deliberate processional way through three of the four caves."[120] This cave complex "corresponds closely to details of the veneration cave in the pilgrim accounts, supporting the identification of Khirbet Qana as pilgrim Cana (and thus the more probable site of Cana of the New Testament and Josephus)."[121]

Edwards offers the following conclusion, based on his findings during archaeological work at the site:

> Constantine gradually converted the Roman Empire to Christianity, and by the fifth or sixth

century some unknown Christian group came to Cana and built what appears to be a large monastery directly over the earlier Jewish town. Numerous coins and very high-quality imported ceramic wares indicate that this group was quite well-to-do (perhaps due to profits from an increasing pilgrim trade of subsidies from the Christian emperor). Arabs then brought Islam to the region and Christianity began to fade.[122]

Due to this, Khirbet Qana was almost forgotten and Kefr Kenna began to attract pilgrims. However, Khirbet Qana was re-established when Crusaders took control of the region for about two centuries starting around AD 1000. On July 4, 1187, the balance of power changed again. People from Cana, with their great view of the valley, no doubt saw a large Crusader army marching to battle at the horns of Hattin (near the Sea of Galilee) against Islamic forces led by the great military general Saladin. The battle resulted in a resounding defeat of the Crusaders from which they never fully recovered. Cana passes out of history shortly thereafter and appears to become a small agricultural village until its abandonment and demise around 1837. As a result of this evidence, nearly all modern scholars agree with this identification of Khirbet Qana as biblical Cana, including Robinson, Albright, Baly, and Aharoni.

John 3:23

Aenon near Salim

> And John also was baptizing in Aenon near Salim, because there was much water, and people were coming and being baptized. (John 3:23)

Aenon is only mentioned once in the Gospels, in John 3:23. There have been a number of attempts to identify the Byzantine site in the Jordan Valley. On the Madaba Map, a mosaic on the floor of the church of Saint George in Madaba, Jordan, two sites are labeled as Aenon, one as Aenon, now Sapsaphas, the other Aenon near Salim. Sapsaphas has long been associated with biblical Bethany beyond the Jordan. It is possible that the designer of the mosaic meant to say that there were some who knew Sapsaphas as Aenon. According to Eusebius, Aenon near Salim was 6 miles south of Scythopolis (Beth Shean), in the Jordan River area (*Onom.* 40.1).[123] Today there is a site nearby called Tel Salim. Another tradition places it 3 miles east of Shechem.

The two latter sites are the obvious choices for the location of Aenon. The second mentioned, near Beth Shean, has the longest tradition and seems to have better geological features than the former. The name Aenon seems to allude to its being near springs (*aenon* is the Aramaic term for "springs"). Tel Salim has several springs in the area, with some as close as 300 meters from the site, lending evidence to Aenon being in the same area. Tel Salim was also near the major north-south highway along the Jordan River, so it is easy to see John ministering to the crowds traveling along this road. Considering this evidence, though circumstantial, the many scholars (including C. Kopp, B. Manzano, B. Pixner, and R. Riesener) opt for this as the location of the Johannine site.

However, two eminent figures, Albright[124] and Murphy-O'Connor,[125] argue for the site near Shechem, mostly based on the modern retention of the name Salim for a village in the area. Koester suggests that John "described the location of Aenon by relating it to the village of Salim, which suggests that he expected some readers to know where Salim was,"[126] a suggestion repeated by J. Ramey Michaels. Michaels says, "the Gospel writer (or his source) assumes some familiarity with these place names—probably more with Salim than with Aenon, or else why would Salim have been mentioned at all?"[127] Koester postulates that since Salim was "best known from the story

of Jacob, who stopped there and bought a piece of land mentioned in John 4:5 and used it as a place of worship," those familiar with that story "may have seen in John's movement to Aenon a foreshadowing of Jesus' ministry in Samaria, where he would tell Jacob's descendants about living water and a new way of worship."[128] The biggest problem with this identification is that the only springs in the area are about 5 kilometers to the west of Salim, probably too great a distance to qualify as being near. Schwartz suggests that Aenon may have been located at Ain el-Biddan, approximately 3 kilometers to the south of Ain Farah, which is near a road between Shechem to Tel Farah (biblical Tirzah, northeast of Nablus) and is an ideal site for baptism of a large group of people. The ease of access and amount of water strengthens the argument, but the primary problem is that it is in the middle of Samaria. It is difficult to believe that a large group of religious Jews would go through Samaria to be baptized by John. Schwartz, however, postulates that if Aenon is in Samaria, then John may have a mission that was oriented to the Samaritans.[129] On the contrary, von Wahlde tentatively holds that Aenon near Salim was simply symbolic and a fiction.[130]

John 4:4–5

New Testament Samaria (Sebastae/Sebastia)

> Now he had to go through Samaria. So he came to a town in Samaria called Sychar, near the plot of ground Jacob had given to his son Joseph. (John 4:4–5)

That the Samaritans worshiped God on Mount Gerizim rather than in Jerusalem is evidenced to this day by a small community of Samaritans who continue to worship there. However, the location of the ancient temple continues to be debated.

Samaritan and Jewish sources both say there was a temple on Mount Gerizim. Josephus, following Herodotus, says the Samaritan temple was built in the days of Alexander the Great (*Ant.* 11.8.2). Abu 'l-Fath, a fourteenth-century Samaritan chronicler, says that there was at one time a temple, but it was destroyed by the Jews.[131]

During Charles Wilson's survey of the Levant in the mid-1870s he found what he described as a fortress and church on Mount Gerizim and thought these were built on top of the Samaritan temple. He also mentioned ruins on top of Tell er-Ras but did not investigate them.[132] In the 1880s F. de Saulcy and V. Guerin identified competing sites as the Samaritan temple, but they did not conduct any excavations.

The site of Tell er-Ras was not excavated until the 1960s, when R. J. Bull conducted work at the site. Bull called the ruins sighted by Wilson "Building A" and continued to dig down.[133] Below Building A he discovered a 135-foot wide courtyard containing a large (60 by 60 x 30 ft) elevated platform of unhewn stone laid on bedrock. He found potsherds in the foundations of the courtyard walls that he dated to the third century BC. Bull called this "Building B" and identified it as the sacrificial altar area of the Samaritan temple.[134]

Mt. Gerizim

Jacob's Well

Site of Samaritan temple

Samaritan priest and Wayne House

Randall Price with Samaritan scholar Benyamin Tzedaka holding a copy of his translation of the Samaritan Pentateuch

However, subsequent excavations have cast doubt on this assertion. Due to the absence of stairs, some have argued that the platform was not a temple itself but served as a podium on which the Samaritans erected a tabernacle. Another theory was that the platform was indeed an altar, and not a temple, and that access ramps or stairs had been removed and possibly used for fill.

However, Israeli archaeologist Yitzhak Magen, working at Tell er-Ras in 1984, placed these theories in serious doubt. He found that there were no Hellenistic buildings on Tell er-Ras, arguing that the Hellenistic pottery Bull found was actually brought to the site as fill by Roman construction workers. However, "Building B" may in fact be the base of a Roman temple to Zeus serving the city of Neapolis and was part of a group of monumental buildings that included a six- to seven-thousand-seat amphitheatre and a hippodrome.

Magen argues that another site on Mount Gerizim, on a high part of the mountain that commands an excellent view of the surrounding territory, is the site of the Samaritan Temple. In uninterrupted excavations on Mt. Gerizim under his direction from 1982 to 2000, he exposed the plan of a sacred precinct with the remains of a tripartite building, an altar in front, and outside, deposits of burned bones and ashes.[135] All of these are indicative of a temple and ritual practice. He also discovered various Samaritan inscriptions dealing with religious customs similar to Judaism. In recognition of the previous cultic site, the later Byzantine Church of Mary Theotokos ("Mother of God") was built over the sacred precinct.[136] Magen dates the initial construction of the sacred precinct and temple to the Persian period followed by a second phase in the Hellenistic period. Of these building's relationships to the Jerusalem Temple, he states: "In the first phase of construction, the precinct and temple were probably copies of those in Jerusalem, but in the second phase, in the Hellenistic period, an independent Samaritan tradition developed that, although influenced by the temple in Jerusalem, no longer exactly imitated it."[137] Magen's excavation report

notes that at Mt. Gerizim "the temple's orientation is similar to that of the Temple in Jerusalem... the temple itself faced east, the altar stood in the eastern part of the precinct, between the temple and the eastern gate, and the Holy of Holies stood near the western wall..."[138] The significance of the Samaritan temple excavations is that it provides a parallel to the first phase of the Second Temple's construction under the priest Zerubbabel (Ezra 3:2–4:3) as well as affirming the Gospel account of Samaritan worship on Mt. Gerizim (John 4:19–21) even after the destruction of the Samaritan temple.

John 5:2

The Pool of Bethesda

> Now there is in Jerusalem near the Sheep Gate a pool, which in Aramaic is called Bethesda and which is surrounded by five covered colonnades. (John 5:2)

The Pool of Bethesda was excavated by the White Fathers, with support of the École Biblique, and by Rouseé and de Vaux from 1957 to 1962. The site was identified as the Pool of Bethesda based on the location's long association with it, and subsequent excavations proved that the tradition was correct. The archaeologists found a pool, divided by a stone dike almost 20-feet wide, just as was described by early church historians and pilgrims. The pool's overall dimensions are large, with an estimated overall area of five thousand square yards. The excavators also found what they identified as a votive offering of a Roman woman named Pompeia, in the shape of a foot. They identified the offering as pagan and perhaps dating as early as the second century AD. Worship of Asclepion, the god of healing, was practiced at the pool and may reflect on the healing tradition connected with the waters of that place mentioned in John 5:4.

The archaeologists found a church built on top of these pools, and based on architectural evidence dated it to sometime in the first two decades of the fifth century.

Pool of
Bethesda

The Persians destroyed this church in the seventh century. It was replaced in the Crusader-era by a small chapel built over the north corner of the Roman pool. They built a stairway down to the pool, presumably to give pilgrims access to the spot of Jesus' miracle. Although the chapel is no longer standing, the stairs down to the pool are still there. Today the Crusader-era Church of St. Anne stands at the site, commemorating the later tradition of the area being the home of Mary's mother, Anne, and the birthplace of Mary.

John 9:7

The Pool of Siloam

"Go," he told him, "wash in the Pool of Siloam" (this word means "Sent"). So the man went and washed, and came home seeing. (John 9:7)

The term Siloam in Greek is the equivalent of the Hebrew *shiloah*, the place connected by the prophet Isaiah with the promise of the birth of the Messiah (Isa 7:3, 14; 8:6). For many years it was believed that the pool at the end of Hezekiah's Tunnel was the Pool of Siloam mentioned in the Gospel of John. This was largely based on tradition from the testimony of early Christian pilgrims. However, this was a later Byzantine pool known as the Virgin's Fountain and is not the ancient Pool of Siloam in which Jesus told the healed blind man to bathe.

Ronnie Reich and Eli Shukron, working on behalf of the Israel Antiquities Authority, discovered the actual biblical pool in 2004. The pool is approximately 300 feet from the Byzantine pool. Archaeologists have uncovered a narrow part of one half of the pool, but the other half lies under an orchard owned by the Greek Orthodox Church, who has not given their permission to excavate the rest of the pool.

Pool of Siloam

Artist reconstruction of Pool of Siloam

What was uncovered revealed a monumental pool, thought to be about 225-feet long and 195-feet wide. It is slightly trapezoidal, with the wide end facing the Tyropoeon Valley. One side had a colonnade, and the steps of the pool were made of dressed stone ashlars. Under the ashlars, Reich and Shukron found plastered steps from an earlier construction. The pool was fed via runoff water carried to the pool under a street that ran from the temple toward the pool and by a channel running from Hezekiah's Tunnel. Coins found embedded in the plaster date the construction of the pool to the mid-first century BC, while the subsequent modifications date to the first century AD. Based on coins found on the stone steps, the archaeologists were able to date the abandonment of the pool at AD 70, during the First Jewish Revolt. The pool quickly filled with silt and was apparently forgotten.

Reich and Shukron argued it was used as a *miqveh* (ritual cleansing bath) or perhaps as a source of fresh water; however, others have asserted that it was a Roman-style public swimming pool.[139] Although the pool fulfils the requirements of a *miqveh*, being fed by a free-running water source, ritual cleansing required the person bathing to be nude. This creates a problem since this pool has no evidence of privacy, and the conservative Jewish society in Jerusalem would not have allowed public nudity, especially in mixed gendered company. While Reich and Shukron propose that wooden poles and mats may have been used to partition the pool (and would not have survived the millennia), Yoel Elitzur disagrees. Due to the problems mentioned above, he argues that Herod built the pool as part of his extensive civic improvement projects, embellishing Jerusalem with many of the opulent features of Roman culture, including a theater, so it is not inconceivable that he would build a swimming pool.[140] In fact, Herod built pools in other cities, including Caesarea, Jericho, Masada, and Herodium (although these pools were all built in his own private palaces).

Of additional significance to the identification of this pool as the Pool of Siloam was the discovery adjacent to the site of a monumental staircase that ascended from the pool to the southern (public) entrance of the Temple Mount where *miqvaot* are plentiful. It would argue that the pool was an important meeting place and therefore required a means of public passage from the lower city to the upper city and the temple area where outside marketplaces were common.

John 18:24

The House of Caiaphas

> Then Annas sent him bound to Caiaphas the high priest. (John 18:24)

One of the most important figures in the life of Jesus was an antagonist, Caiaphas, who, according to Josephus (*Ant.* 18.31) was appointed by the Roman procurator Valerius Gratus as high priest in AD 18 (cf. Matt 26:3, 57; Luke 3:2; John 11:49; 18:13–14, 24, 28; Acts 4:6). It was he who plotted against Jesus and whose action led to his arrest (John 11:48–50) and before whom Jesus stood on trial before the Sanhedrin (John 18:13-24). According to Josephus (*Ant.* 20.206), Caiaphas was the son-in-law of Annas (also called Ananias), the former high priest who was also involved in Jesus' interrogation (John 18:19–23). Josephus speaks frequently of Caiaphas in his accounts (e.g., *J.W.* 2.441; *Ant.* 20.205; *Life* 193) and records that he was removed from office in AD 36 by Vitellius, the Roman governor in Syria, along with Pontius Pilate (*Ant.* 18.4.3).

There are two main proposals for the location of Caiaphas's house. Ancient witnesses locate the high priest's house in the Upper City of Jerusalem. The Bordeaux Pilgrim, visiting Jerusalem in AD 333, spoke of a ruined house said to be that of Caiaphas.[141] By 530, Theodosius says that the site had a church, dedicated to Peter.[142]

The first candidate for the site of Caiaphas's house

House of
Caiaphas,
Armenian St.
Savior Church

Todd Bolen/www
.BiblePlaces.com

is under the present Armenian monastery of St. Savior ("Church of the Redeemer"), across a narrow street from the traditional site of the Upper Room, next to the church of the Dormition Abbey. The Israeli archaeologist Magen Broshi led excavations at the site in 1971–72. He discovered sophisticated and luxurious buildings from the Herodian period, one of which was a magnificent building with frescoes that demonstrated a very good artistic hand. The frescoes feature birds, something Father Bargil Pixner, the late Prior of Dormition Abbey, observed was an astounding find in the house of a Jewish high priest, since there was a Mosaic prohibition on animal illustrations.[143] Other priestly mansions excavated in the Upper City of Jerusalem (in today's Jewish Quarter), while built in the style of Hellenistic or Roman villas, nevertheless complied with the regulations of the Jewish law. Importantly, the mansions in the Upper City contained no human or animal representations, but only geometric patterns. However, Pixner finds it implausible that the Upper Room would have been located so close to the palace of the high priest. This all leads Pixner to conclude that Broshi did not discover Caiaphas's house at this location.

The other contender for Caiaphas's house is under the present-day Church of St. Peter Gallicantu, about

halfway from the Armenian monastery to the Pool of Siloam. The modern church was built in 1931, but there has been a church there since at least the end of the fifth century. Underneath the church there are several rock-cut rooms with upper and lower chambers.

Steps to the
house of
Caiaphas

The upper chambers had galleries cut in the walls, and stairs led down to the lower chambers, but those end abruptly several feet off the floor. High on the walls of the lower rooms are rings that have been suggested to have been used to tie prisoners for whipping. Fourteen crosses have been found, incised and painted on the walls and ceiling of the lower chamber.

Despite this evidence, the identification of the Gallicantu location as Caiaphas's palace has been persistently resisted.[144] After his evaluation of alternatives, Pixner concludes, "If we consider the most ancient local reports, it is clear that today's Church of Saint Peter in Gallicantu, on the eastern slope of Mount Zion, most likely represents the correct location of Caiaphas' house."[145] Despite his conclusion, not everyone is convinced by his argument. For example, Jerome Murphy-O'Connor, while not necessarily arguing for the Armenian monastery location, argues that Caiaphas's house is more likely at the top of the hill (Mt. Zion).[146]

Prison at the house of Caiaphas

Chain holes at Caiaphas prison

The Ossuary of Caiaphas

The historical figure of Caiaphas is not restricted to the New Testament, but is mentioned in the works of Josephus and other extra-canonical sources. The archaeological evidence now adds confirmation to this documentary evidence. In November/December 1990, workmen accidentally discovered a burial cave while making a water park in the Peace Forest in the southern part of Jerusalem on a hill traditionally known as the "Mount of Evil Counsel" (inspired by Caiaphas' words that plotted Jesus' death in John 11:48–50). The burial cave was a single burial chamber with four *loculi* (Heb. *kokhim*), typical of the Second Temple period. Three *kokhim* were on the western wall of the cave (labeled *Kokhim* I, II, and III) and one was on the southern wall (labeled *Kokh* IV). There was a central depression that was filled with debris, including broken ossuaries (bone boxes used in Judaism from 100 BC–AD 70).[147] This family tomb, which contained twelve ossuaries, included an ornate ossuary decorated with traces of bright orange paint and elaborate etchings of rosettes and acanthus leaf design (typical of wealthier Jewish burials). Inside were the bones of two infants, two teenage boys, an adult woman, and a man of about sixty. Aramaic inscriptions were crudely scratched on the ossuary (probably with a nail that was found nearby) reading *Yehosef bar Qayafa* on the long side and *Yehosef bar Qafa* on the narrow side. The Gospels only refer to the high priest as "Caiaphas," but in Josephus references to him also appear as the name "Joseph." Although some scholars have challenged a connection with the high priest due to the unusual spelling of the name and the lack of a title, there has been general agreement among archaeologists that the inscription refers to the high priest Caiaphas.[148] Despite the lack of a title, the opulent nature of the tomb and ossuary indicates a person of high rank. If it is not his bone box, then there is no other person in first-century Israel, known as Caiaphas, who would satisfy the requirements for this ossuary.[149]

Caiaphas
Ossuary

Alexander
Schick

The identification of an individual of rank that was associated with the Jewish trial and execution of Jesus is important for historical Jesus studies and constitutes one of the highpoints in the history of archaeological discovery.[150]

John 18:37–38

John Ryland Papyrus P52

> "The reason I was born and came into the world is to testify to the truth. Everyone on the side of truth listens to me." "What is truth?" retorted Pilate. With this he went out again to the Jews gathered there and said, "I find no basis for a charge against him." (John 18:37–38)

John 18:31–33 and 37–38 are attested by one of the oldest papyrus fragments of the New Testament.[151] It was labeled John Rylands Papyrus P52 because after it was found in Alexandria Egypt in 1920 among the Oxyrhynchus collection and purchased by Bernard P. Grenfell, it was placed with other papyri (P31, P32) in the John Rylands Library in Manchester, England. P52 measures 3.5 by 2.3 inches, "with seven lines of writing on each side": John 18:31–33 on the front (recto) and John 18:37–38 on the back (verso).[152] The

writing is in uncial (capital) letters, and closely relates to papyri written toward the end of the first century and beginning of the second, and probably not later than AD 125.[153] The use of Hadrianic script dates the fragment between ca. AD 117–138[154] and since it came originally from a codex of John, it provides evidence that this form of writing existed already in the first-century AD. Considering that the copies of many great works of ancient literature are dated hundreds of years (sometimes a thousand years) from their original composition, an extant writing within the lifetime of many of the letters' recipients is extraordinary. An important part of this spectacular find is that it was discovered in Egypt, whereas the apostle John, the author of the book, most likely wrote the book from Ephesus in Asia Minor. This piece of information has challenged the long-standing view of textual critics that John was the latest of the New Testament Gospels (ca. AD 160) since this portion of John was in circulation in Egypt by the middle of the second-century AD at the latest. As the transmission of a text takes considerable time, the discovery of P52 has now forced a dating of the Gospel of John to the last decade of the first-century.

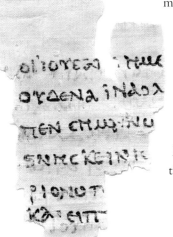

Ryland Papyrus (facsimile)

Alexander Schick

ACTS OF THE APOSTLES

Acts 1:19

Akeldama, The Field of Blood

(With the payment he received for his wicked-ness, Judas bought a field; there he fell headlong, his body burst open and all his intestines spilled out. Everyone in Jerusalem heard about this, so they called that field in their language Akeldama, that is, Field of Blood.) (Acts 1:18–19)

Judas returned the thirty pieces of silver he had been paid by the Sandhedrin and since it was "blood money" the chief priests could not put it in the temple treasury but purchased "the potter's field as a burial place for foreigners" (Matt 17:7). Matthew adds that it was still called the "Field of Blood" in his day (Matt 27:8). Luke further explains this name as arising from the event of Judas hanging himself at this field (Acts 1:18), commenting that the place is called Akeldama in Aramaic (Acts 1:19). He also connects this event with that predicted in Psalm 69:25, arguing that it referred to this field as a place so desolate that no one would live in it (Acts 1:20).

The site has been known throughout church history, located on the south slope of the Valley of Hinnom, close to where the valley comes together with the Kidron Valley in Jerusalem. True to Luke's word, the site, though visited often by Christian pilgrims and used throughout the centuries as a burial place, remains unoccupied. However, Jerusalem scholars Leen and Kathleen Ritmeyer argue the burial caves at the site were not used to bury "foreigners" but some of Jerusalem's most elite—the high priests, including Annas.[155]

Akeldama

© 2013 Robert Drouhard

Acts 3:2

The Beautiful Gate

> Now a man who was lame from birth was being carried to the temple gate called Beautiful, where he was put every day to beg from those going into the temple courts. (Acts 3:2)

While Peter and John were going to the temple, they encountered and healed a "lame" man at the "temple gate called Beautiful." There have been several locations proposed for the Beautiful Gate. The first is the Nicanor Gate of the Mishnah (Mid. 1.4), also referred to as the "Corinthian Gate" by Josephus (*J.W.* 5.5.3). In this account Josephus reports that the Nicanor Gate was "fifty cubits; and its doors were forty cubits; its weight was so great that it took 20 men to move it." He also notes that this gate "opened on the east over against the gate of the holy house itself . . ." The gate gave access from the Court of Women to the Court of Men and was therefore within the temple complex. This gate was undoubtedly destroyed when the Romans besieged the city in AD 70. Its other name, "Corinthian," owes to its base construction in Corinthian bronze (to which were added gold and silver plating). Josephus says as a result of these costly and exquisite materials it "excelled in workmanship and value all the others" (*J.W.* 5.5.3).

The major argument in support of the Nicanor Gate is the Codex Bezae (D), which reads, "But when Peter and John were going out he went with them, and they, astonished, stood in the portico called Solomon's" (Acts 3:11). If this is the case, then the Beautiful Gate must be the Nicanor Gate. Additionally, the Nicanor gate was richly adorned, beautiful, and separated the Court of Women from the Court of Israel, and it was a gate that Peter and John probably went through. These factors may identify the Nicanor Gate as the Beautiful Gate.

A second location proposed for the Beautiful Gate is the Eastern Gate (also known as the Shushan Gate from the Persian period and probably located at the site of the present Golden Gate, called such since the Byzantine period).[156] Jack Finegan suggests that the Greek word for "beautiful," *hōraios*, resembles

Nicanor Gate

www.HolyLandPhotos.org

the Latin *aurea*, meaning golden, giving rise to the gate being called "Porta Aurea," i.e., Golden Gate.[157]

The Golden Gate was in the east wall of the temple complex, directly opposite the Mount of Olives. Because of this, it was associated with Christ's triumphal entry into the city on Palm Sunday. And although the gate existing today was likely built during the Crusader era, there is a persistent legend that Suleiman the Magnificent caused the Golden Gate to be filled in, apparently in an effort to thwart the idea that Jesus would return again through this gate.

Baez-Camargo argues for the Golden Gate being the

gate referred to in Acts because of its early association with the healing of the lame man.[158] Another argument in favor of the Golden Gate is the text of Acts itself. Luke records that Peter and John were going "up to the temple" (Greek, *heiron*) (Acts 3:1). Usually, the term *heiron* refers to the temple complex as opposed to *naos*, which refers to the sanctuary proper. If the apostles had healed the man in the Nicanor Gate, Luke likely would have used the Greek term *naos* instead of *heiron*. Moreover, Luke says that the crowds gathered around the apostles in Solomon's Porch. Aside from Codex Bezae, in order for the chronology of the story to fit together the apostles

Beautiful Gate (Shushan or Golden Gate) on east side facing Mount of Olives

© 2013 Robert Drouhard

Double Gate at southern entrance to Temple Mount

would have healed the man, gone through the Golden Gate, and entered Solomon's Porch.[159] If they would have already entered the temple complex, healed the man at the Nicanor Gate, entered the Court of Men, then come back out to Solomon's Porch, Luke's account would be much more convoluted than is his normal careful style. Moreover, since the reading in Codex Bezae seems to be the variant one, it is likely not the original.

A third proposal for the location of the Beautiful Gate is the site of the Double Gate, now only partially exposed, though built over by a later arched entrance at the top of the monumental staircase on the southern side of the Temple Mount. While the Eastern Gate was used exclusively by the priests, this entrance to the temple was used by the common people. The entrance via the monumental staircase that ascended from the Pool of Siloam passed through two sets of gates called the Huldah Gates after the First Temple period prophetess who held court in this area and whose tomb was nearby. The original Huldah Gates were southern entrances to the 500-cubit-square platform of the pre-Herodian Temple Mount (Mid. 1.3). Even though the name (and location) belonged to the Hasmonean period, it is still appropriate for use in describing these Herodian additions since the Hebrew term means something like "mouse" and aptly describes the tunnels

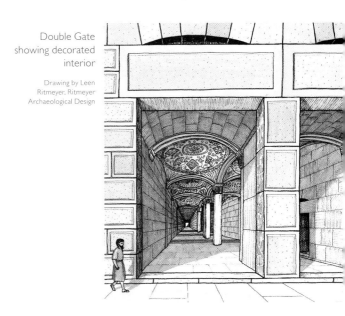

Double Gate showing decorated interior

Drawing by Leen Ritmeyer, Ritmeyer Archaeological Design

behind these gates that resemble the holes used by these animals. The Herodian Double Gate, which led directly onto the temple platform, appears to have corresponded with these original Huldah Gates. Behind the present entrance are remains of Herodian masonry and a lintel from the Double Gate, while inside the passageway most of the original Herodian architecture is intact.

According to Mishnah tractate Middot 2.2 this Double Gate (the western entrance) was used by the people, while the eastern entrance (known as the Triple

Hippodrome at Caesarea Maritima

Gate) was utilized exclusively by the priests. The Double Gate opened into an ornate and richly decorated passageway that led directly up to the royal stoa and to the temple. Portions of this interior decoration were recovered during the excavations of Benjamin Mazar and are now exhibited in the Israel Museum. People in a proper state of ritual purity entered from the right side of the gate and exited from the left. Here those ritually impure, such as the lame, would position themselves in order to beg alms from those entering the temple. This historical detail, coupled with the suggestion that the interior decoration was the reason the gate was called "Beautiful," has been offered as evidence that this was the location mentioned in Acts 3:2, 10.

Acts 10:1

The Archaeology of Caesarea Maritima

> At Caesarea there was a man named Cornelius, a centurion in what was known as the Italian Regiment. (Acts 10:1)

In Acts 10 Luke tells the story of the conversion of Cornelius, a gentile centurion of the Italian Regiment stationed in Caesarea Maritima. Herod the Great, who wanted a good port on the Mediterranean coast of the Levant, built Caesarea Maritima. Previously, Jaffa was the only harbor near Jerusalem, but it was poorly suited for merchant ships. The founding of Caesarea was part of Herod's plan of elevating Judea's standing within the Roman Empire. The city featured a theater, two hippodromes, several pagan temples and Herod's beachside palace. Herod also built a harbor from scratch, constructing a breakwater and wharfs. At the time it was one of the most impressive ports on the Mediterranean.

In AD 6 the Romans disposed Herod's son Archelaus and replaced him with a procurator. They also moved the capitol of Judea from Jerusalem to Caesarea Maritima, leading to even more building in the city.

Caesarea Maritima has been almost continually

excavated since the 1960s. The original excavations were supported by Baron Edmond de Rothschild and led by Hebrew University, the University of Pennsylvania, Cornell University, and other schools. From 1992 to 1998 the Israel Antiquities Authority carried out large-scale excavations of the city.

A temple dedicated to Roma and Augustus, evidencing Herod's efforts to curry favor with Rome, dominated the city center of Caesarea. This temple stood for more than 400 years, after which it fell into disuse. Much of its stone was used for other buildings, and unstable foundations led to the collapse of parts of the building. A church was built on its site in AD 490. One of the hippodromes (the one nearest the ocean and next to Herod's palace) was built in the Roman circus style and used for chariot races. It was about 300 x 50

Theater, Ceasarea Maritima

meters and originally had seats only on two sides, the eastern and southern, giving spectators a spectacular view of the Mediterranean. Later, seats were added to the western side, increasing capacity from 7,500 to 12,500. It was also transformed into an amphitheater used for gladiatorial contests. The western half of the hippodrome was built on sand dug out of the harbor and has subsequently eroded back into the sea. Just south of this circus was the Roman Sepphoris complex, including the governor's palace, a law court, and offices for various governmental officials. The eastern hippodrome was the larger of the two, with a seating capacity of 30,000, but was built long after the time of Herod. It was 440-yards long and almost 100-yards wide. In 1996 Israel Antiquities Authority excavators discovered a large granite obelisk that had once stood in the middle spina of this hippodrome. The obelisk was originally 45-feet tall and weighed over eighty tons. The obelisk was brought from Aswan, Egypt—over 500 miles away.

The most famous remains at Caesarea Maritima is the restored theater. It was excavated from 1959 to 1963 by Italian archaeologist Antonio Frova. The theater was built onto a natural rise southeast of Herod's palace, facing the ocean. It was 200-feet wide, with a central box for distinguished guests. It is estimated that the theater could seat up to four thousand guests. The upper section of the theater has been rebuilt and the rest of the theater restored, including the wooden stage, and performances are held there regularly. During the excavations of the theater the only mention of Pontius Pilate was discovered, written on a stele. It was a public announcement of the dedication of a Tiberium in the city.

Acts 13:6

Pauline Evidence, The Paphos Inscription

> They traveled through the whole island until they came to Paphos. (Acts 13:6a)

In Greco-Roman times Paphos was the capital of Cyprus and today has remains of the Roman governor's palace renowned for its fine mosaics. Paul the Apostle visited the town during the first century AD. When Paul came to Cyprus, Acts 13:6 says he traveled "through the whole island" to Paphos. Here Luke is referring to New Paphos, built in the fourth century BC, which replaced Old Paphos 10 miles away. The Ptolomies made it the capital, and it remained so until the fourth century AD. As the capitol of the island, it would have been the place where the Roman proconsul was stationed, which agrees with Luke's account of the proconsul, Sergius Paulus, summoning Paul and Barnabas.

In 2000 Italian archaeologists led by Filippo Giudice discovered in Paphos fragments of a first- or second-century marble inscription that may refer to Paul. The fragment was found in what is believed to be a first- or second-century Christian church and reads, "…los…osto…." They argue the original read [Pau]los [Ap]osto[los].[160] If this reading is correct, it is early archaeological evidence of Paul's presence on the island.

Acts 13:7

Sergius Paulus

> …who was an attendant of the proconsul, Sergius Paulus. The proconsul, an intelligent man, sent for Barnabas and Saul because he wanted to hear the word of God. (Acts 13:7)

During the apostle Paul's first missionary journey, he visited the Mediterranean island of Cyprus, preaching the Gospel "through the whole island." When he came to the city of Paphos, Paul was summoned by the local proconsul, Sergius Paulus, so that the Roman official could "hear the word of God" (Acts 13:7). Luke described Paulus as "an intelligent man" who believed the Gospel after refusing to be dissuaded by Elymas the Jewish sorcerer.

Within the Roman Empire there were two types of provincial governance. The first (under which Judea fell) were those needing soldiers to keep the peace. These were directly under the emperor's control and were administered by procurators (or governors). The second, under which the island of Cyprus fell (beginning in 22 BC), were those not needing troops because they were more peaceful and "civilized." These provinces were governed by the Roman senate and administered by proconsuls like Sergius Paulus. Prior to the discovery of inscriptions proving there were proconsuls on Cyprus prior to Paul's arrival, some scholars doubted Luke's accuracy in Acts 13. These doubts were overturned early in the twentieth century.

Archaeology has identified several possible inscriptions bearing the name of Sergius Paulus, two from Cyprus and one from Rome. Since Luke did not include Paulus's "first" name (praenomen), there is speculation about who he was and which of the inscriptions actually mentions him (if any).

The earliest inscription found is heavily damaged, and only mentions that one "Paulus" served as a proconsul during the tenth year of an emperor whose name is missing. The inscription was found on Cyprus at Soloi (on the northeast coast of the island), providing at least a Cyprian connection to someone with the name Paulus. However, some (including epigraphy expert T. B. Mitford) have dated the inscription to as late as AD 126, much too late to be associated with Sergius Paulus or the apostle Paul.[161]

Another inscription was found in northern Cyprus, near Kytharia, and is dated to the first century AD. It refers to a man named Quintus Sergius and says he was on the island of Cyprus during the reign of either Caligula or Claudius. The inscription was an imperial decree concerning sacrificial regulations. Initially the name on the inscription was speculated to be Quintus Sergius Paulus, but it has now been determined that the inscription actually names Quintus Sergius Gaius, not the Sergius Paulus of Acts.

The inscription found in Rome, written in Latin, served as a boundary marker (*travertine cippus*) erected by "the river commissioners appointed at the time of Claudius" to "mark out the bank of the Tiber."[162] It mentions someone named Lucius Sergius Paullus (the Latin form of the Greek Paulus) as one of the "curators of the Tiber River under Claudius." These men were assigned to keep tabs on the Tiber, which was prone to catastrophic floods. This evidence appears to be the most helpful in identifying Sergius Paulus.

Although the Tiber inscription has been a subject of discussion for over a hundred years (partly involving the question of Luke's historicity in identifying Sergius Paulus as proconsul on Cyprus), there is nothing in the inscription that would indicate Sergius Paulus could not have served in both capacities during his life. In fact, classical scholars both of previous generations and in recent years have seen less difficulty in accepting the identification than some biblical scholars. The inscription is dated to the 40s AD, but that date doesn't preclude Sergius Paulus from serving as a river "curator" just prior to or after being proconsul on Cyprus. On the contrary, the inscription establishes that "a prominent Sergius Paulus" was "a public official" during the correct time period Luke is describing in Acts, which lends credence to the argument that Luke was "dealing with historical data and situations, not just creating a narrative with historical verisimilitude."[163]

Sometimes a fourth inscription is identified with the Sergius Paulus of Acts. Discovered in Pisidian Antioch, the inscription bears the name of "L. Sergius Paullus the younger, son of L." It is sometimes claimed that the inscription names the son or grandson of the Sergius Paulus of Acts and that his family was from Antioch.[164] It is known that the Sergii Paulii family possessed large landed estates in Galatia near Pisidian Antioch, and they appear to have been the descendants of a Roman veteran who settled in the colony under Augustus. Further, it is also claimed that Paul actually travelled to Antioch because Sergius Paulus convinced him to do so, and even that Paulus wrote letters of support to aid his passage and his stay in Antioch, with the desire for his relatives in Antioch to hear the Gospel.

However, all of this is considerably speculative, and there is no hard evidence that this Antiochene inscription mentions the proconsul spoken of in Acts.

Acts 18:4

The Jewish Synagogue at Corinth

> Every Sabbath he reasoned in the synagogue, trying to persuade Jews and Greeks. (Acts 18:4)

There is some debate concerning the literary and archaeological evidence for a synagogue at Corinth during the first century. The New Testament's internal evidence argues for a Jewish community at Corinth on two accounts: (1) the supposed Jewish origin of Paul's associates at Corinth, including Prisca and Aquila, Lucius, Jason, and Sosipater (Rom 16:21), and Crispus and Sosthenes (Acts 18:2, 8, 17; 1 Cor 1:1, 14; 16:19), and (2) Paul's statement concerning circumcision (1 Cor 7:18–19), which would only make sense if Jews were present. External literary evidence for a Jewish community at Corinth in Paul's time includes the testimony of the Hellenistic Jewish philosopher Philo Judaeus (*Legat.* 281) and the first-century Jewish historian Flavius Josephus, who records that Vespasian transferred six thousand Jews captured during the Jewish Wars to the region to work on the Emperor Nero's project to cut a canal through the isthmus. These Jews would have been sold in the local slave markets and some would have undoubtedly ended up in Corinth.

The archaeological evidence, though sparse, dates back to 1898, when the American School of Classical Studies in Athens found on the Lechaion Road a large limestone block with a Greek inscription that appears to have come from the doorway to a synagogue. The badly damaged inscription read "…GOGE EBR…." This can reasonably be reconstructed as [SYNA]GOGE EBR[AION] ("Synagogue of the Hebrews").[165] There was also found a capital from a half-column with the Jewish symbols of three menorahs, palm branches, and a citron. Although the synagogue itself has not been found and the lintel and capital date between the second through fifth centuries AD, the inscription, joined to the literary evidence, provides cursory confirmation that there was a synagogue in Corinth where, as the New Testament states, the apostle reasoned with the Jews.

Acts 18:12

The Gallio Inscription

> While Gallio was proconsul of Achaia, the Jews of Corinth made a united attack on Paul and brought him to the place of judgment. (Acts 18:12)

Lintel, synagogue at Corinth

When Paul was preaching the gospel in Corinth, "the Jews of Corinth made a united attack on Paul and brought him to the place of judgment. 'This man,' they charged, 'is persuading the people to worship God in ways contrary to the law'" (Acts 18:12–13). The judgment seat, Greek *bēma*, was occupied, Luke reports, by Gallio the proconsul of Achaia. Gallio, even before Paul can mount his defense, issues his verdict: "If you Jews were making a complaint about some misdemeanor or serious crime, it would be reasonable for me to listen to you. But since it involves questions about words and names and your own law—settle the matter yourselves. I will not be a judge of such things" (Acts 18:14–15). Ironically, all the Greeks who had gathered (probably out of curiosity) then "turned on Sosthenes the synagogue leader and beat him in front of the proconsul; and Gallio showed no concern whatever" (Acts 18:17).

Unlike many other historical details in Luke's account, this one helps to confirm Pauline chronology, establishing the overlapping of Paul's ministry in Corinth with that of the Roman governor Gallio, largely accepted by scholars.

Much light was shed on that question beginning in 1905, when a French team working at Delphi unearthed four fragments of a stone slab. The slab is a badly broken inscription of a letter of the emperor Claudius addressing the depressed state into which Delphi had fallen and mentions Gallio as the proconsul of Achaia. In 1910 Emile Bourguet, working with the French team, identified three more fragments, but the German classical philologist and epigraphist Hans Rudolf Pomtow declared that they were not part of the same inscription, so they were ignored in all subsequent discussions of the inscription until 1967, when A. Plassart succeeded

Inscription of Gallio, Proconsul of Achaia

in joining the two groups of fragments and added two more.[166] Although some of his readings of the inscription have since been challenged, the important passages for this discussion are not in question. For our purposes, the relevant parts of the inscription read (brackets indicate missing or illegible text): "Tiber[ius Claudius Cae]sar Augustus . . ." and "[Jun]ius Gallio, my fri[end] an[d procon]sul . . ." The inscription dates the letter to the time when Claudius had been acclaimed imperator for the twenty-sixth time. This must be before August AD 52, when his twenty-seventh acclamation took place. Also, it could not have been prior to November of AD 51, the approximate date of his twenty-fifth acclamation. Moreover, since acclamations were related to military prowess, and normally no major campaigns were undertaken in the winter, Claudius's twenty-sixth acclamation almost certainly took place in the late spring or very early summer of AD 52, probably in April or May. It has been theorized that Gallio arrived in Achaia and after assessing the situation, including Delphi's problems, sent a report to the emperor. Proconsuls normally served for one year (though sometimes they served longer), so this inscription places Gallio in his proconsulship during the most widely accepted time period Paul was staying in Corinth, AD 49–52.

Acts 19:29

Riot at the Theater at Ephesus

> Soon the whole city was in an uproar. The people seized Gaius and Aristarchus, Paul's traveling companions from Macedonia, and all of them rushed into the theater together. (Acts 19:29)

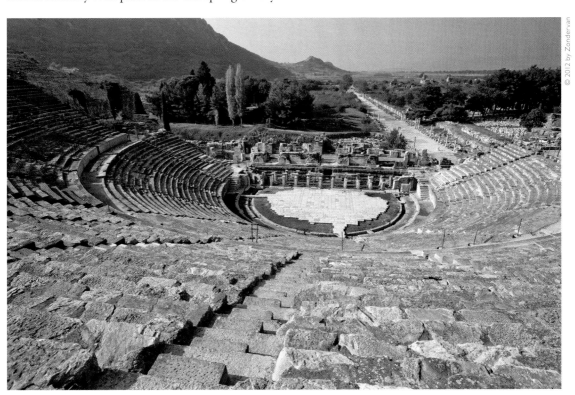

© 2012 by Zondervan

Ephesus Theater

The conflict between Paul and the followers of Artemis (Diana) took place at the Great Theater in Ephesus built into a hill in the middle of Mount Coressus with its façade facing Harbor street. Its seating capacity of up to twenty-five thousand spectators enables the estimation the population of the city at around 300,000. The theater was constructed on a preceding structure from the Hellenistic period (third–first century BC). In the Roman period extensive rebuilding occurred under the Emperors Domitian (AD 81–96) and Trajan (AD 98–117), with a second story added to the stage and the seating increased in the first century AD.

Excavations at the site began in 1895 under Otto Benndorf under a permit from the Ottoman Sultan and continue to this day. Since 1954 the archaeologists of the Ephesus Museum have also participated in excavations. They have revealed that its cavea (the seating sections of Roman theaters) consisted of sixty-six rows of stone seats divided into three horizontal sections by two diazomas. The lowest seats of the cavea had marble backs and were reserved for the city's most important personalities. The skene (the background building to which the platform was connected) consisted of three stories, with the second (first century AD) decorated with pillars, statues, and carvings by the Emperor Nero. The ground floor contained a long eight-roomed corridor with the orchestra constructed in a semi-circle. The façade inside the theatre was decorated with columns bearing niches for statues.

In the year AD 104 a massive inscription was set up on the south retaining wall of the theater detailing a gift made to the city by Salutaris, including a lavish procession that celebrated the Greek and Roman identity of the city. During the Imperial period, gladiatorial games were performed in the theater. This gives evidence supporting the history of spiritual struggle in the Ephesian church and its decline in the second century AD as the Roman character of the city demanded greater conformity to the empire. However, after Christianity became the official religion of the empire, it became a leading city for the councils of the Roman Church.

The Great Theater was destroyed by an earthquake in the fourth century AD, and by the eighth century AD it had been incorporated into the defense system of the city.

Acts 19:31

"Asiarchs" ("officials of Asia")

> Even some of the officials [Asiarchs] of the province, friends of Paul, sent him a message begging him not to venture into the theater. (Acts 19:31)

In Acts 19 the silversmiths of Ephesus, led by a man named Demetrius, were threatening the apostle Paul. The silversmiths' grievance was that Paul's preaching of the gospel, and the subsequent mass conversions, was hurting their business. They incited the city to riot, and a large crowd descended on Ephesus's great theater. The mob seized two of Paul's companions, and when Paul wanted to go to the theater and make a defense, even some local authorities urge him not to do so. In the end the town clerk was able to quiet then disperse the crowd.

In the Greek text of Acts, the officials are called *asiarchōn*, translated as "chief of Asia" (KJV), "Asiarchs" (ESV), "officials of Asia" (NKJV), "provincial officials of Asia" (HCSB), " officials of the province" (NIV), or "provincial authorities" (NET). The word is exceedingly rare in classical ancient literary sources, being mentioned in only a few disparate sources, such as Strabo's *Geography* and a third-century-AD text assigned to Modestinus.[167] It is also only mentioned a few times in the early church fathers, mostly in connection to a letter purported to have been written by the church in Smyrna that mentioned "Philip the Asiarch" in connection with the martyrdom of Polycarp:

Inscription on a pillar on the southeast staircase of the theater of Miletus, 30 miles south of Ephesus, with the name "M(arcus) Antonius Apollodorus, The Asiarch"

This proclamation having been made by the herald, the whole multitude both of the heathen and Jews, who dwelt at Smyrna, cried out with uncontrollable fury, and in a loud voice, "This is the teacher of Asia, the father of the Christians, and the overthrower of our gods, he who has been teaching many not to sacrifice, or to worship the gods." Speaking thus, they cried out, and besought Philip the Asiarch to let loose a lion upon Polycarp.[168]

Asiarchs are also mentioned in a letter written by Augustine to Alypius the Bishop of Thagaste.[169] Augustine was then battling the Circumcellions, a violent group of radicals in North Africa who had destroyed the altar of a church in Hasna. Augustine, attempting to work through official channels, says he had "sent a letter to the Asiarch," presumably attempting to secure his help and protection.[170]

This scant epigraphic evidence caused many scholars of the nineteenth and early twentieth centuries to doubt Luke's historical accuracy in Acts. Some argued that Luke's use of *asiarchēs* was an anachronism that he (or whoever, in their view, wrote Acts) accidentally inserted into his narrative. It is said that the use of the title "lapsed between Strabo's mention in I BC and the epigraphic evidence beginning in late I AD."[171]

However, to date there have been nearly three-hundred references to Asiarchs found on coins and in inscriptions, including over one hundred inscriptions bearing the title unearthed in Ephesus alone. In fact, the term has been discovered in over forty cities in Asia Minor. More significantly, some of the inscriptions found in Ephesus have been dated to within fifty years of the events in Acts 19.[172] Thus, the anachronism argument has been made untenable by archaeological evidence.

Scholars have been divided over the actual function of the *asiarchēs*. Some have viewed them as the highest religious official under the Romans (the majority view being that Asiarchs were priests of the imperial cult), while others argue they were government officials or members of the social elite. Steven Friesen discusses the three examples of "Asiarchs" mentioned in the historical sources.[173] He cites Strabo, who defined Asiarchs as "leaders in the province," Acts 19:31, which doesn't mention anything about their function, and the Modestius text mentioned above, which seems (and indeed many scholars have argued) to connect Asiarchs with provincial high priests. Friesen, citing contextual evidence, doubts the connection and suggests Modestius instead assigned Asiarchs a range of municipal duties that lasted for a specific period and were defined primarily by the city or region in which they were found, which could and often did include priestly activities but were in no way limited to that function.

As mentioned above, there is much numismatic information regarding Asiarchs. This evidence seems to confirm Friesen's assertions. About 90 percent of the coins mention Asiarch with no other identification, including whether they were priests or involved in religion at all. On the other hand, only about 8 percent (a total of twenty-one) specifically mention Asiarch in connection to a religious office. Two refer to specific responsibilities that were not necessarily part of every Asiarch's duties. This evidence seems to support the idea that Asiarchs were simply those with general civic offices or duties.

The inscriptional evidence regarding Asiarchs yields even more credibility to Friesen's argument. Asiarchs are mentioned in connection with everything from organizing public spectacles, including animal fights,[174] gladiatorial contests, and other games, to providing the funds for cities to mint coins, to acting as the secretary of the people. A few of these inscriptions mention the title, Asiarch and priest, but many of them seem to separate specifically the two, in effect saying the person was both an Asiarch and a priest. In fact, Friesen argues that conflating the two terms would create a scenario unknown in the Graeco-Roman world: two distinct and unrelated titles for the same prominent, provincial office.

In regard to Acts 19, the friendly attitude of the Asiarchs toward Paul is troublesome for those who see them as provincial or even local high priests. Alexander Souter, who saw Asiarchs as having to a great extent a religious character, notes, "When we come to study the connexion of the Asiarchs with the Acts narrative, we are puzzled. It seems at first sight so strange that men elected to foster the worship of Rome and the Emperor should be found favouring the ambassador of the Messiah, the Emperor's rival for the lordship of the Empire."[175] He solves the problem by claiming that the imperial cult, of which these Asiarchs were priests, may have been disposed to look with a kindly eye on the new religion because Christianity had an outward respect for civil authority and was the strongest supporter of law and order. Moreover, Souter posits a rivalry between the imperial cult and the cult of Artemis. The Asiarch priests of the imperial cult may have appreciated Paul's negative effect on the Artemis-worship in Ephesus. A more likely scenario is that the Asiarchs in Ephesus were wealthy and influential people of high status who belonged to leading aristocratic families of the city, who also perhaps held some municipal office or civic responsibility and who were kindly disposed to Paul. Such favor from civic leaders was not unprecedented for Paul, who seems to have befriended members of the aristocracy on several occasions.

Acts 21:28–29

The Soreg Inscription

"Fellow Israelites, help us! This is the man who teaches everyone everywhere against our people and our law and this place. And besides, he has brought Greeks into the temple and defiled this holy place." (They had previously seen

Trophimus the Ephesian in the city with Paul and assumed that Paul had brought him into the temple.) (Acts 21:28–29)

Paul was accused by the Jews from Asia of bringing Trophimus, a Greek (non-Jew), into the Jerusalem Temple and thus defiling it. This was a charge that carried a capital offense, as has been proven from inscriptions found near the temple area. Josephus says there were several stone warning inscriptions on the gates (*soreg*) dividing the Court of the Gentiles from the courts reserved exclusively for Jews.[176] These warnings in Greek marked the terminal point for Gentiles who might attempt to enter the Court of the Israelites. Such entrance was prohibited to them under threat of death.

A complete *soreg* inscription was discovered in 1871 by Clermont-Ganneau near the St. Stephen's Gate to the north of the northeastern corner of the Temple Mount. Because it was found during the period of rule by the Ottoman Empire, it was taken to the Istanbul Museum in Turkey, where it is today on display. The inscription reads: "No foreigner [i.e., non-Jew] is to enter within the balustrade and enclosure around the Temple area. Whoever is caught will have himself to blame for his death which will follow." Josephus described such warning inscriptions that were placed around the Jewish entrances to the temple: "Proceeding across this toward the second court of the Temple, one found it surrounded by a stone balustrade, three cubits high and of exquisite workmanship; in this at regular intervals stood slabs giving warning, some in Greek, others in Latin characters, of the law of purification, to wit that no foreigner was permitted to enter the holy place, for so the second enclosure was called" (*J.W.* 5.193–194; cf. *Ant.* 15.417). Another fragment of this inscription was found in December

1935 just outside St. Stephen's Gate and is in the Rockefeller Museum in Jerusalem.

Although Paul had been previously seen in the city with Trophimus, he did not bring him to the temple and therefore was innocent of the Asian Jews' charge of temple desecration. In his defense, Paul stated he had done nothing in violation of the laws of the temple (Acts 25:8) and used the opportunity of his arrest to present his conversion story and the gospel to the crowds who had gathered as a result of the tumult (Acts 26:1–23).

Temple Warning

Israel Museum

13 | The Letters of Paul

ROMANS

Romans 16:23b

The Erastus Inscription

> Gaius, whose hospitality I and the whole church here enjoy, sends you his greetings. Erastus, who is the city's director of public works, and our brother Quartus send you their greetings. (Rom 16:23)

There are three instances of the name Erastus in the New Testament. In Acts 19:22 Erastus is mentioned as going with Timothy to Macedonia while Paul stays behind in Asia. In Romans 16:23 Paul sends Erastus's greetings to the Roman church. Finally, Paul reports that Erastus has stayed in Corinth in 2 Timothy 4:20. Most commentators and scholars assume all three instances mention the same person.

In Acts and 2 Timothy nothing is mentioned about Erastus, but in the Greek text of Romans 16:23 Paul calls him *ho oikonomos tēs poleōs*, which is usually translated as "city treasurer," with the exception of the NIV, which has "director of public works." This title has featured prominently in the ongoing debate over what exactly *oikonomos* means, which in turn determines who Erastus was, and even has an impact on how scholars see the economic stratification represented in the Corinthian church.

Considerable light (and confusion) was thrown onto the discussion with the discovery of a partial first-century inscription in Corinth. It reads, in Latin: ERASTUS PRO AEDILITATE S.P. STRAVIT. The translation of the inscription reads "Erastus in return for his aedileship laid [the pavement] at his own expense." The inscription was originally part of the pavement of a street just east of one of the theaters at Corinth and is missing the left most slab, which may have named Erastus's *praenomen* and *nomen*. The letters are etched into limestone and were probably fitted with bronze letter casts held in place by lead. Andrew Clarke argues that the inscription was a declaration letting the public know that the pavement was laid by an Erastus as part of an election promise. He theorizes that the present information clearly leads to the assumption that an Erastus, possibly a freedman, laid a pavement in the square, east of the stage building of the theater at Corinth, at his own expense and in return for being appointed to the position of *aedile*.[1]

The first issue that must be dealt with is the assertion made by Justin Meggitt that the left side of the inscription is missing and therefore the person mentioned on it might not even be Erastus. He speculates it is just as likely to be "Eperastus," which he contends was a much more common name.[2] This argument has been met with widespread doubt.

Almost immediately the Erastus inscription prompted much speculative discussion as to the likelihood of there being a common identity between the Erasti mentioned in the New Testament and the Erastus of the Corinthian pavement. The main debate centers on two issues: the relative rarity of the name Erastus and the relationship between *aedile* and *oikonomos*. The first issue is fairly easy to decide. The name Erastus is quite rare in ancient archaeological sources. In fact, the inscription found at Corinth is the only mention of it yet found from the first century,[3] and only a few other instances have been uncovered from other locations and time periods. Therefore, the likelihood that the Erastus of the New Testament and the Corinthian inscription are the same is reasonably high.

The principal problem that has dominated the debate over the identification of the Corinthian Erastus and the Erastus of the New Testament is whether *aedile* and *oikonomos* are in any way synonymous. The usual Greek translation of *aedile* is *agoranomos* or *astuvomos*, leading some to question Paul's choice of *oikonomos* for Erastus. However, these terms are not found in use at Corinth until after AD 170, long after Paul wrote to the Romans. Also, *oikonomos* often means someone with a "menial, servile role," while *aedilis* was usually one of the highest offices in a Roman colony's administration and implies someone of high status. However, this was not always the case, and "the title *oikonomos*," L.L. Welborn argues, often refers to a high-ranking position held by a freeborn citizen, as is the case in several cities of western Asia Minor.[4] More specifically, epigraphic examples from Philadelphia, Smyrna, and Hierapolis have conclusively shown that *agoranomos* and *oikonomos* are equivalent expressions and that *oikonomos* could describe a number of positions, including an *aedilis*. Included in the responsibilities of *aediles* were management of the public streets, marketplaces, and buildings, administrating the city treasury, and functioning as judges. Moreover, while an *aedilis* could sometimes be a lowly office, it could also be a position of prestige and considerable economic means. In the context of Corinth, the *aedilis* was most likely a person of substantial means, because he was in charge of and funded the public games, and since the Isthmian Games were much more prominent and extraordinary than in other cities, presiding over them would have imposed an enormous expense on the aedilis, yet being the president of the games was also a highly honoured position. Thus, Goodrich contends that Erastus was a high-ranking municipal official and a member of the economic elite.[5]

Erastus Inscription, Corinth

www.HolyLandPhotos.org

Although many New Testament scholars find reasons to demur, due to the evidence above, Joseph Fitzmeyer concludes the Erastus of the Corinthian inscription is "undoubtedly the same as the one mentioned in the New Testament."[6] On the whole, the evidence and arguments favor identifying the Pauline Erastus and Corinthian Erastus as one and the same.

So why doesn't Paul use the normal Greek equivalents to *aedilis*, aside from the chronological problem mentioned above? It has been suggested that due to Corinth's unusual situation, Paul thought it inappropriate. Perhaps Paul didn't want his readers thinking Erastus was a normal *aedilis/agoranomos*, so he used a term that was more appropriate to Erastus's actual functions in Corinth rather than the technically correct Greek equivalent. Another suggestion is that when Paul mentioned Erastus he was not yet *aedile* but his subordinate, the *quaestor* (which can be an synonym of *oikonomos*) and was later elected as *aedile*.

Another possible line of evidence concerning the identity of Erastus has been offered by John Fotopoulos.[7] If the Erastus of Romans was indeed the *aedile* of Corinth, a very prominent and very public office, he would have been in charge of the marketplace and the public revenue it generated. Almost certainly this involved revenue from the purchase of meat sacrificed to idols and may have generated sensitivity, suspicion, offense, and even animosity against Erastus from some of the Corinthian Christians. This situation may help explain what prompted Paul to write 1 Corinthians 8.

I CORINTHIANS

1 Corinthians 7:22

Freedom from Slavery

> You were bought at a price; do not become slaves of human beings. (1 Cor 7:23)

During Paul's instructions to the Corinthian church regarding accepting their calling in life, Paul mentions the issue of slavery. He explains to those at Corinth that they are the "Lord's freed person" and that they were "bought at a price" so they should not become "slaves of human beings."

Slaves in the Roman Empire could be freed either by their owner releasing them or by someone purchasing their freedom. The Romans saw manumission as the regular reward for their deserving urban slaves, although the majority of slaves, especially those who worked the fields, were never released. However, if freed, slaves were usually granted citizenship. The Greek term used here is *agoradzo*, a word brought to life in its first-century context by its use in the non-literary *koine* papyri, such as those discovered at Oxyrhynchus in Egypt.[8] The word was common in deeds of sale, and its principal idea is that of manumission (the act of freeing a slave),[9] of which there were several methods, both formal and informal. It is this recognition of institutionalized exercise of urban manumission that informs Paul's statements in this Corinthian context. For formal manumissions, a magistrate could grant a slave freedom in his court, a senator could confer freedom on a slave, or a slave could be freed by special instruction in his master's will. For informal manumissions, a slave owner could write a letter of freedom or could pronounce his freedom before friends, who served as a witness that the slave had been liberated. An inscription found on the polygonal wall of the sanctuary at Delphi describes how slaves could be freed in the name of Apollo:

Apollo the Pythian bought from Sosibius of Amphissa, for *freedom* (*eleutheriai*), a female slave (*soma*), whose name is Nicaea, by race a Roman, with a *manumission price* (*timas arguriou*) of three minae of silver and a half-mina. Former seller according to the law: Eumnastus of Amphissa. The *price* (*timan*) he hath received. The *purchase* (*onan*), however, Nicaea hath committed unto Apollo, *for freedom* (*ep' eleutheriai*).[10]

Paul has in view this Graeco-Roman custom of buying-off a slave for freedom by paying a purchase price and it is this motif that forms the concept of redemption throughout the New Testament. This is not surprising, considering the widespread practice of slavery in the Roman Empire, and the relatively common practice of slaves being freed, either through being released by their owners or being "redeemed" by someone else.

EPHESIANS

Ephesians 1:1

The Archaeology of Ephesus

Paul, an apostle of Christ Jesus by the will of God, To God's holy people in Ephesus, the faithful in Christ Jesus. (Eph 1:1)

Excavations began uncovering the remains of Ephesus in the nineteenth century. David George Hogarth discovered that Ephesus had its beginning in the Bronze Age. Excavations have continued intermittently ever since and it is now "the most developed site in Turkey."[11] It was a major metropolis in Asia Minor (now near the town of Selçuk in western Turkey). With 250,000 residents, it was likely the fourth largest city in the Roman Empire. It was an important commercial hub on the major trade highway running from Anatolia to Syria. Unlike many other ancient sites in Turkey, there is no modern city on top of ancient Ephesus, but, according to ancient geographers, it was originally built on the plain at the mouth of the Cayster River on the Aegean coast (Ptolemy V, 2; Strabo XIV, 1, 20ff; Pliny, *Natural History* V, 29, 115). However, silting presented an ongoing challenge, and it was

only through dredging that the harbor was kept open (until 1244). Today, Ephesus has lost its harbor, and the remains of the ancient city that have been uncovered by archaeologists are situated 3 miles inland from the Aegean.[12] Even though the presently excavated site is extensive, much of the city is still buried beneath the silt deposit. Ephesus was also an important administrative center in the Roman Empire. Proconsuls coming to Anatolia often made first landing in Ephesus, and sometime in the first century AD the provincial capital was moved from Pergamon to Ephesus.[13]

Ephesus had a temple dedicated to Isis,[14] but it was known from the seventh century BC as a center of the worship of the goddess Artemis/Diana. The Artemision or temple of Artemis (one of the seven wonders of the world) was destroyed and rebuilt three times before its final destruction in AD 401. The remains of this last temple, and fragments from previous temples, were discovered by excavations conducted by the British Museum in 1869. Although today only one of the 127 columns from the last phase of the temple remains standing, a description of the ancient structure has been preserved by Antipater of Sidon, who compiled the list of the seven wonders of the ancient world:

I have set eyes on the wall of lofty Babylon on which is a road for chariots, and the statue of Zeus by the Alpheus, and the hanging gardens, and the colossus of the Sun, and the huge labour of the high pyramids, and the vast tomb of Mausolus; but when I saw the house of Artemis that mounted to the clouds, those other marvels lost their brilliancy, and I said, "Lo, apart from Olympus, the Sun never looked on aught so grand." (*Greek Anthology* IX.58)

This third phase of the temple described by Antipater commenced in 323 BC and increased the size of the structure. It was recorded as 450 feet (137 m) long x 225 feet (69 m) wide x 60 feet (18 m) high (about four times the size of the Parthenon) and was acknowledged as "the largest religious building in the Hellenistic world."[15] Statues of the goddess Artemis from the temple site recovered in excavations by the British Museum can now be viewed in the Ephesus Room at the Ephesus Museum. There is still debate over the interpretation of some of its features, especially the decoration strung on the cult image's chest. These objects have been seen variously as bee hives, breasts, eggs, or the testicles of sacrificed bulls, all denoting fertility. The Artemesian cult was spread across Asia and the Roman Empire mainly, it is thought, through the "missionary expansion"[16] of Ephesian expatriates.[17] It was also know as a "center for magical practices," particularly the "Ephesian Letters," written magical spells "thought to contain apotropaic power to ward off evil spirits."[18] This emphasis on magic sheds light on the actions of the new Christian converts in Acts 19:19. By the time of Paul Ephesus was the major center of the cult,[19] a fact that helps explain the reaction of the citizens to a supposed threat to the cult by Paul and his companions (Acts 19:23–41). In keeping with this encounter, later

Christians in the city left an inscription that revealed their understanding of the nature of the cult and why so little examples remain:

Destroying the delusive image of the demon Artemis, Demeas has erected this symbol of Truth, the God that drives away idols, and the Cross of priests, deathless and victorious sign of Christ.[20]

Ephesus has an early and long history of Christian presence. The city was a center for early Christianity, being one of the "Pauline cities" (Acts 18–19). Paul stopped there briefly on his way from Corinth to Jerusalem. He reasoned with the Jews at the synagogue. Though the believing Jews in Ephesus urged him to stay, Paul continued on his missionary journey (Acts 18:19–21), but during his third missionary journey he returned and stayed at the city for two to three years (Acts 19:1–9) but was forced to leave after the near riot instigated by Demetrius (Acts 19:23–20:1). Paul's son in the ministry, Timothy, ministered there. Ephesus was also the first of the seven cities addressed by Jesus through John the Revelator (Revelation 1:9; 2:1–2). It also received a letter from the church father Ignatius. Justin Martyr is said to have debated Trypho at the covered colonnade near the harbor of Ephesus around AD 150.[21]

It was popularly held to be the home of the apostle John after his release from exile on the island of Patmos. Although no physical evidence of his residence has been found, early tradition says John lived in Ephesus and died there. Three miles from the city are the remains of a sixth-century basilica in the shape of a crucifix that replaced a fourth-century church built over the traditional site of John's tomb. The emperor Justinian (AD 518–527) took architectural pieces from the Artisimon and Stadium to construct this basilicia,[22] possibly with a supercessionist intent since these were places where Paul and his theology had been confronted. It is thought to have been first built in the second century as a domed, wooden ciborium (canopy) or tegurium (a roofed covering over a sarcophagus)[23] and was replaced by a basilica built by the Byzantine emperor Theodosius in the fourth century.[24] Later traditions recorded that Jesus' mother Mary along with Mary Magdalene died there; ruins of the Church of St. Mary may be found in Ephesus, the site of the ecumenical council of AD 431 that dealt with the Nestorian and Pelagian heresies and where Mary was called *theotokos* (mother of God).

Work has been conducted on and off at the site since 1862, but major excavation began in 1895 by the Austrians, who have been digging at the site until today. Archaeology has revealed that Ephesus experienced a "building boom"[25] in the first century AD, during which a new stadium, a rebuilt and expanded agora, a complex for the Olympic games, and a new theater seating twenty-five thousand were built. A huge temple complex was built, including a large basilica stoa dedicated to the worship of the Roman Caesars.[26] The bouleuterion (council chamber), or odeion (concert hall), has been found next to the Dea Roma stoa that could seat 1,500. Excavators also identified the Varius Bath (or Bath of Scholastica after a Christian woman who restored them), with all the typical Roman features: the apodyterium (changing room), frigidarium (cool pool), caladarium (hot pool), and sudatorium (sweat room).[27] Next to the bath archaeologists found a communal latrine. In a case of ingenious Roman engineering applied to the mundane, clean water ran from the city's aqueducts in a channel at the foot of the seats while grey water flowed through the toilet to flush waste.[28] Along the main thoroughfare of the upper city, archaeologists found the remains of luxurious insulae (apartments),

known as the Terrace Houses, that featured indoor plumbing, baths, heating systems, individual water storage, and "colorfully painted" wall frescoes and mosaic floors.[29] The level of opulence in these houses "clearly shows the comfortable standard of living which Ephesus enjoyed in Late Antiquity."[30] The famous Celsus Library, which at one time contained one of the world's largest collections (12,000 scrolls), would not have been seen by the apostles Paul and John because construction only began in AD 110[31] and was completed around AD 135. The remnants of the gate at the southern end of Ephesus also remain. This gate was built by two freedmen in 3 BC and is dedicated to Caesar Augustus. Inscriptions on it speak of various city ordinances, including one that reads (in Greek), "Whoever urinates here shall be tried in court!"[32]

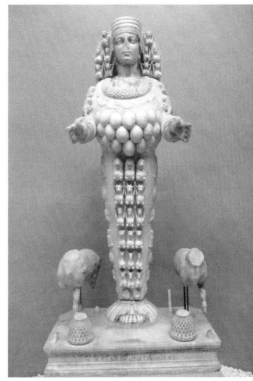

Artemis statue

Paul and Thecla
on wall

So far, no evidence of a synagogue has been found in Ephesus, but a few traces of Jewish presence have been. Excavators found a funerary monument "prepared by the Jews,"[33] and pottery and glass featuring menorahs in the Cemetery of the Seven Sleepers. They also found a menorah carved into a step at the library.[34] This physical evidence supports historical sources that indicate there was a large and influential Jewish population in the city.

High above the city of Ephesus is also located a cave in which the earliest painting of the apostle Paul is found, along with the virgin Mary and an early saint known as Thecla, probably relating to the young woman of a second-century work called The Acts of Paul and Thecla.

Ephesus flourished until AD 262, when an earthquake destroyed much of the city, and Goths sacked it the next year.[35] It was not rebuilt extensively until the mid-fourth century, under Theodosius. Ephesus once again regained importance, culminating in the Third Ecumenical Council in 431. Sometime during the 620s the entire city burned, and in the 800s the harbor silted up. After these events Ephesus was largely abandoned, although it continued to be visited by Christian pilgrims.

PHILIPPIANS

Philippians 1:1

New Testament Philippi

> Paul and Timothy, servants of Christ Jesus, to all God's holy people in Christ Jesus at Philippi, together with the overseers and deacons. (Phil 1:1)

Philippi was founded as a Roman colony in the time of Augustus. It was labeled "little Rome" but its archaeological history began in 5500 BC and attests the oldest Neolithic settlement in Eastern Macedonia and Thrace. A colony was established in 360 BC and was soon conquered by Philip II of Macedon (359–336 BC). The colony was named after him. The Battle of Philippi occurred in 42 BC between the armies of Cassius and Brutus and the supporters of Julius Caesar, Octavian and Mark Antony. In 27 BC the emperor of Rome honored Philippi with the name Colonia Augusta Julia Philippensis.

"Prison" at Philippi

Inside prison at
Philippi

www.HolyLandPhotos.org

The city of Philippi became important to Christianity after the visit of the apostle Paul in AD 49/50. A woman named Lydia (and her family) converted to Christianity after hearing Paul's teaching, and she convinced the apostle to stay with her. After Paul cast a demon out of a fortune-telling slave girl, he was imprisoned there. While Paul and Silas were praying and singing in the prison there was an earthquake and the chains that had bound the apostle were loosed. After Paul convinced the jailer not to kill himself, the jailer also converted (Acts 16:11–34). This church grew, and by the time of Paul's letter to them he praised them for their assistance in his ministry. The city itself prospered until the seventh century, when several severe earthquakes and attacks from Slavic raiders began a long, gradual decline of the city. The area was largely abandoned until the twentieth century, when the new town of Krinides was built nearby.

The French School of Archaeology at Athens excavated Philippi beginning in 1917. One may see a well-preserved Roman road, the Via Egnatia, one of the longest of the roads built by the Romans for military and trading purposes. They also uncovered an agora, built on top of an older market, and also the ruins of a fourth-century church dedicated to Paul and another large fourth-century church just outside the city. They also uncovered a structure popularly thought to be the prison Paul and Silas were held in, but the area was not a prison; rather, it was a complex of religious buildings first erected in the Hellenistic period. Prisons were not built in a religious complex. Nevertheless, frescoes and a small chapel were found in it, leading to the idea that it was the site of Paul's imprisonment.

Additionally, several remains relating to early Christianity may be found at Philippi, which was a major center of Christianity since it was the first Christian community in Europe. At Philippi an episcopal see was established in the mid-fourth century AD. Three early basilicas have been found in that time period, one a basis for the Octagon Church found there.

COLOSSIANS

Colossians 4:13

Evidence of Christianity in Hierapolis

> I vouch for him that he is working hard for you and for those at Laodicea and Hierapolis. (Col 4:13)

Hierapolis lies 6 miles from Laodicea and in the Lycus River Valley. The city was on an elevated plateau 564 feet above the valley floor. It is noted for its white mineral deposits from hot springs. These waters also contributed to very high quality purple dyed wools. Apparently the city had a large Jewish population, and they may have dominated one of the wool-dying guilds in the city. Epaphras is the traditional founder of the church in Hierapolis, and the apostolic father Papias is also said to have lived there.

Unlike the unexcavated site of Colossae, Hierapolis has been extensively excavated since 1957 by an Italian team led first by Paolo Verzone, and since 2003 by Francesco D'Andria. Verzone found extensive Roman ruins, including channels built to direct the spring water to baths in the city. The team also found a large theater (twelve to fifteen thousand seats) and one of the largest necropoli in Turkey. Due to inscriptions found in the necropolis, excavators learned that there must have been gladiatorial games in the city. There was no collosseum in Hierapolis, so scholars theorize that the games may have taken place on the plain near the city.

The necropolis also contains evidence of a large Jewish presence in the city. Excavators found numerous symbol inscriptions, like menorahs, as well as an inscription on an epitaph that reads, "Marcus Aurelius Alexander, also called Asaph, of the people of the Jews." Other evidence of Jewish inhabitants include inscriptions on monuments, such as "the community of the Jews who inhabit Hierapolis." Interestingly, with the arrival of Christianity, all traces of the Jewish presence in the city disappear.

The necropolis also has evidence of Christianity in the city. Beginning in the fourth century, Christian symbols such as crosses and the Greek letters alpha and omega appear on sarcophagi. Some of the inscriptions also shed light on the tumultuous history of the region in relation to battles over theology. Hierapolis is in the region of Phrygia, where the heresy of Encratism (radical asceticism) was particularly strong, especially among the Montanists. Excavators found a sarcophagus inscribed with the Greek word *hydropotes* ("drinker of water"), denoting the deceased affiliated with the Encratites, who abstained from wine—even in the Eucharist.

Hierapolis has had an early and long association with Philip. According to Bovon, as early as the second century, witnesses located Philip's tomb in Hierapolis.[36] Eusebius (quoting second-century sources) placed the apostle Philip's burial place and the apostle's daughters in the city.[37] A fanciful story in the fourth or fifth century apocryphal Acts of Philip says that the apostle, along with his sister Mariamne and Bartholomew, came to Hierapolis preaching the gospel. At this time the city was allegedly called Ophiorhyme (lit. "Snake's Town"), because they worshiped a viper called Echidna. The three evangelists succeed in converting many, including the wife of the local proconsul, sending, it is said, the gloomy tyrant into a rage like an unbroken horse.[38] He has Philip and Bartholomew hung upside down on iron hooks through their ankles, but after Philip called down a curse on the city and a great abyss opened and swallowed up the whole of the place in which the proconsul was sitting, along with seven thousand residents of the city, the people repented and took Bartholomew down. Philip, apparently penitent for what he had done, refused to be rescued, saying "Do not, my children, do not come near me on account of this, for thus shall be my end."[39] Philip died and was buried on the spot and they built the church over that place. Most of the story is richly imaginative, legendary, and symbolic, yet it may be based on an actual account. Hierapolis is located on an active seismic fault, and to this day is known for its hot springs and mineral deposits.[40] Frequent earthquakes that have opened and closed deep fissures rocked the city. It is possible that the author of the Acts of Philip knew this and included it in his story.

There is debate over which Philip is being spoken of in relation to Heirapolis: either the apostle (who had four virgin daughters who, according to tradition, lived in Hierapolis) or Philip the evangelist (who was traditionally martyred). It is probably the case that the two were conflated. That one of the Philips was in Hierapolis and died there is widely accepted, especially in light of the recent archaeological evidence illustrated below.

During his work, Verzone also found a martyrium dedicated to Philip in the city, probably built ca. AD 400.[41] D'Andria continued work there and describes the martyrium as an octagonal structure consisting of eight chapels radiating from a central space enclosed by a rectangular portico consisting of twenty-eight small, square rooms. These rooms were probably used to house pilgrims overnight. The rooms had no floor, leading Francesco D'Andria to argue that the pilgrims must have desired to sleep in direct contact with the holy rock, and rooms were thus designed for incubation rites in which the saint appeared during sleep to announce his prophecies and heal the sick.[42]

The church was probably roofed with a wooden dome covered in lead. The martyrium is notable for its large size, the superior quality of construction and decorative materials, and the elegant, intricate delineation of space within the complex. It allows us an imaginative glimpse at the spectacular structures the early church put so much effort into.

A recent find has provided even more information and seems to confirm not only Philip's presence in Hierapolis but even his death there. In 2010 D'Andria was excavating about forty yards from the martyrium and found a fifth-century basilica-style church with a ciborium (a canopy built over the altar in a church, sometimes used to cover a crypt). While this church dated to approximately the same period as the martyrium, D'Andria found underneath it an older Roman tomb. Further investigation the next year revealed the tomb was accessed by marble stairs worn by the steps of thousands upon thousands of people, which indicated the tomb received extraordinary tribute.

The apostle Philip's grave at Hierapolis

Inside the apostle Philip's grave at Hierapolis

On the face of the tomb are numerous graffiti of crosses and other Christian symbols. Next to the tomb D'Andria found water baths for individual immersions that he theorized were used for healings of sick pilgrims. While all of this certainly confirms that the site was venerated from as far back as the first century, it was an object housed in the Museum of Richmond in the United States that D'Andria argues confirmed the tomb as belonging to Philip.[43] The object is a bread stamp, made of bronze, and is widely thought to have come from Hierapolis. It has an inscription naming Philip and shows him standing between two buildings at the top of a stairway. One has a domed roof like the martyrium, while the other has a roof like the basilica church D'Andria discovered nearby. In the doorway of the basilica is a lamp, which, D'Andria argues, is one of the typical signs that served to indicate a saint's sepulcher. D'Andria thinks the relics of Philip were moved from the tomb to Constantinople toward the end of the sixth century and then may have been taken to Rome later on.

In addition to the two churches, D'Andria identified a great processional road that led through the city to the pilgrimage compound. At the end of the processional road he found a complex he identified as a ritual bathing facility for pilgrims, built in the same style as the martyrium.[44] Unlike the typical Roman gymnasium, this bath complex had individual baths where public nudity, typical of Roman baths, would have been impossible. In the water supply and drainage channels of this building excavators found numerous Christian trinkets, including the usual glass ampules and jars for unguents and *terra cotta eulogia* (small Christian mementos thought to confer blessings and memories of a holy visit) inscribed with crosses and images of Philip. Past the bath was a staircase with a fountain where the pilgrims could slake their thirst. The final forty steps are 40-feet wide, perhaps symbolic of Jesus' desert fast. These are almost certainly the stairs depicted on the bread stamp mentioned above.

A cataclysmic earthquake destroyed the complex along with the rest of Hierapolis in the late seventh century. Smaller churches were erected over the destroyed complex in the ninth and tenth centuries, along with cemeteries. As late as the twelfth century the site was mentioned by Western pilgrims who still came to venerate it.

2 TIMOTHY

2 Timothy 2:5

Athletic Competition in the Greco-Roman World

> Similarly, anyone who competes as an athlete does not receive the victor's crown except by competing according to the rules. (2 Tim 2:5)

Paul's illustration of athletes competing in the games would have been instantly recognized by Timothy and anyone in the early church to whom the letter was read. The games Paul mentions would have been the Olympic games participated in all throughout the Greco-Roman world. Just like the modern games, these were held every four years, but they were always held at Olympia. There were also Olympic-style games held elsewhere, but it was a mark of pride for these foreign games that they adhered to the same rules as the games held in Olympia. The ancient games lasted almost uninterrupted for a thousand years, from 776 BC to AD 395. These games included foot races of various lengths (from 200 m to full marathons), boxing, wrestling, chariot races, discus, javelin, and other throwing competitions. Various archaeological finds have illustrated the popularity of these events, being depicted on all kinds of pottery and inscriptions.

In reference to the rules Paul cites, aside from literary evidence, the remains of pottery and statues of winning athletes provide a glimpse into the rules of the games. All Greco-Roman athletes were expected to adhere to strict rules when competing and often swore oaths to do so and gave sacrifices to Thesius, the patron god of the games. Judges also swore to uphold impartiality and fairness. The punishment for breaking the rules was often harsh. Athletes could be whipped for infractions or given heavy fines for attempting to bribe judges. They could also be fined or banned from the games for trying to fix an event by paying another athlete or accepting payment from a spectator or trainer. Statues of Zeus were erected to memorialize the payment of a fine, some of which have been recovered. Other misconduct could also result in expulsion

and fines. In AD 93 a boxer named Apollonius arrived later than the deadline set for athletes. Although he gave the excuse of being delayed by unfavorable winds, it was discovered he had actually been in Iona fighting for money prizes. He was banned from the games, but he attacked the legitimate winner of the boxing contest and was subsequently fined. Certain cities were even banned from games from time to time.

Athletes who followed the rules and were victorious were crowned with a wreath but were also sometimes immortalized in statue form, the bases of which have been discovered. Some athletes were so famous that they became objects of myth and worship within the Roman Empire. For example, a first-century-AD inscription found at Thasos describes how the failure of the Thasians to honor the memory of Theogones (a third-century-BC Thasian boxing hero said to have 1,300 victories) led to several years of crop failure.

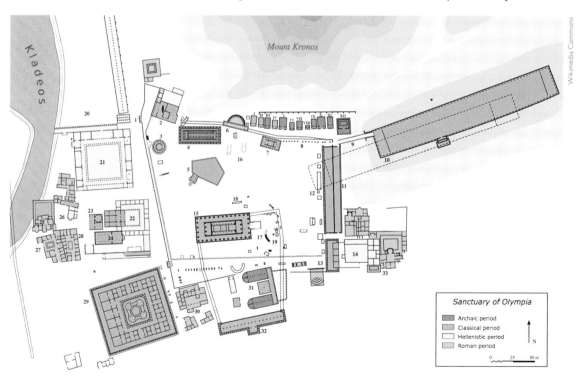

Plan of Olympia sanctuary

Antikes Olympia stadium at Olympia

Wikimedia Commons

Ancient Olympic Starting Line

14 | The General Letters and Revelation

HEBREWS

Hebrews 12:1

Running the Race with Endurance

> Therefore, since we are surrounded by such a great cloud of witnesses, let us throw off everything that hinders and the sin that so easily entangles. And let us run with perseverance the race marked out for us. (Heb 12:1)

The author of Hebrews used the metaphor of an athletic competition in a stadium to illustrate spiritual truth. This was a common practice of moral philosophers in hellenistic cities during the first century as well as in Jewish synagogues of the Greek-speaking Diaspora.[1] The reference to "a cloud of witnesses" seems to describe a city's amphitheater with its ascending rows of seats filled with spectators gathered to watch athletic events. The author uses this general background, based on the "witnesses" in his "hall of heroes" in the previous chapter (11:2–40) offered as examples of constancy in faith, to encourage Christian perseverance as they run their spiritual race toward the heavenly goal and its reward.

The metaphor of running a race is taken from the Greek footrace contests in the pentathlon during the panhellenic games. Bream notes that "at the Olympic Games, the footrace was the only athletic contest for an extended period."[2] This fits well with the charge here to run with "endurance" (Greek *hupomonēs*) since in the marathon the prize is won not simply by how fast one runs, but how far.

In the phrase *ogkon apothemenoi panta* ("throw off everything that hinders") the emphasis is upon the term *ogkon*, "excess weight," probably with reference to the length of a robe, the extra weight of which could interfere with running or to excess body weight. The use of *panta* ("all," "every") reveals that the analogy is not restricted, and could include whatever compromise in conduct might be made in deference to custom or culture and thereby reduce our spiritual progress. Sin is here described as "entangling" or "diverting," another idea drawn from the athletic metaphor where there is the fear of losing ground and being impeded in the race due to shifting the runner's focus from the goal. The writer therefore warns his audience to guard against sin in any form because it will distract them, causing them to look away when they should be fixing their gaze upon Jesus (12:2).

Archaeological discoveries have given us examples of the architecture and elements involved in athletic competition. Stadiums in the form of theaters and amphitheaters appear at sites throughout the Greco-Roman world and images of athletic competitors adorn artifacts from vases to tombs. One object common to both the stadium as well as the bathhouse was the strigil. This curved bronze tool was designed to fit neatly over arms and legs and was employed as a scraper. Archaeological examples of this instrument are plentiful, as they were an essential item in the Greco-Roman bathhouse. Preparation for the race required contestants to remove all clothing before running so that nothing could impede

them progress during the race. The "excess weight" may refer to clothing, but it may also be a reference to the need to resolve a problem faced by every runner on a track. Athletes would also apply olive oil to their unclad bodies to reduce friction when they ran. However, in the act of running they would become coated with a fine layer of dust they kicked up on the track. If they were to participate in other games, they would have to remove the accumulated dirt and debris before continuing.

This practice of "scraping off the excess" may be what the author of Hebrews had in mind when he spoke of "throw[ing] off" or "removing" (Greek *apothemenoi*) that which slows us down in the race of faith. Running through this world the Christian becomes soiled with the things of this world and so must regularly remove these contaminants in order to persevere and reach the goal, that is, conformity to Christ and completed service for him.

REVELATION

Revelation 2:8

Graffiti and the Church in Smyrna

> To the angel of the church in Smyrna write: These are the words of him who is the First and the Last, who died and came to life again. (Rev 2:8)

The church in Smyrna is only mentioned in John's Revelation. It is exhorted not to fear the coming persecution of "those who say they are Jews and are not" (Rev 2:9). Jesus told them they would be thrown in prison as a test. The subsequent history of the city bore these exhortations out.

Smyrna was founded around 1000 BC, declined, and was reestablished 3 miles south of the old city in the fourth century BC. In the second century BC Smyrna became the first city in Asia Minor to host the imperial cult. Coins from Smyrna depict temples to Rome and to the Emperors Tiberius and Hadrian. Statues of Domitian, Trajan, and Hadrian have also been discovered at the city.

New Testament era Smyrna boasted an aqueduct, what may have been the largest grain market in Asia, a stadium, a theater seating perhaps twenty thousand, and the most magnificent gymnasium in Asia. The city itself is estimated to have been the home of over 100,000 people.

Smyrna (Izmir), Turkey

Because modern Smyrna (Izmir) is the third largest city in Turkey, with over 2.6 million residents, much of ancient Smyrna is likely buried under modern buildings. Due to this, all that has been recovered of ancient Smyrna are the remains of the market and a portion of a hill near it, where recently a theater has been discovered.

In the basement of this agora, which collapsed in a severe earthquake in AD 178, hundreds of graffiti were discovered and, according to Professor Cumhur Tanriver, maybe the largest collection in the ancient world.[3] The graffiti reveals daily life during the Hellenistic and Roman periods. The majority of the graffiti are the usual offers of sexual services, political slogans, pagan religious discussion, and statements of civic pride; they are all jumbled together. However, according to Professor Roger Bagnall, who has written on the graffiti, one graffito (little scratch) may be the earliest Christian inscription ever found.[4] The inscription is written in Greek and says, *ho dedōkōs pneuma* ("the one who has given the spirit"). Bagnall argues that this was an encoded message from one Christian to another to let them know there were other believers in the city. Another graffito has an *isopsephism* (*isos*, meaning equal, and *psephos*, meaning

pebble, used for counting), in which one adds the number values of letters to create a single number. The value of *kurios* (Lord) with *omega* (meaning 800) and *pistis* (faith) with *omega* (meaning 800) probably connected these two Christian ideas. The number 8 was used in early Christianity as a special number. Readers of the Bible are familiar with two examples of an *isopsephism* in the New Testament. One example is found in Matthew 1:17, in which the fourteen generations is given three times in the genealogy of Christ (rabbis used the word gematria of this technique) correspond to the value of the Hebrew name David (*daleth* = 4, *waw* = 6, *dalet* = 4). The most famous is the name of the antichrist in Revelation 13:18, where the apostle John says that 666 is the number of a man.

The use of code was necessitated by the fact that Christianity was illegal, considered a heretical cult. The danger to Christians in Smyrna is vividly illustrated by the martyrdom of Polycarp, the city's bishop, in either AD 154 or 166. According to tradition, the proconsul of Smyrna, Quadratus, commanded that Polycarp deny Christ. When he refused, Polycarp, along with ten other Christians, was put to death by being burned at the stake in the city's stadium.

Agora in Smyrna, attesting hundreds of Christian graffiti

Cumhur Tanriver, used by permission

The graffito states: "I love a (woman) whose number is 731." The number is believed to represent the name Anthousa.

Cumhur Tanriver, used by permission

Revelation 2:12

The Church in Pergamon

> To the angel of the church in Pergamum write:
> These are the words of him who has the sharp,
> double-edged sword. I know where you live—
> where Satan has his throne. (Rev 2:12–13a)

Jesus both commends and condemns the church
at Pergamum (Pergamon). He commended them for
holding fast to his name and not denying the faith,
even in the face of one of their own being executed.
But he condemned them for their moral failings,
excoriating some of them for holding the "teaching
of the Nicolaitans" (Rev 2:15). He also says Satan's
throne is in Pergamon.

Called the "most illustrious city in Asia Minor"
by Pliny the Elder (*Natural History* 5, 33), it housed
the Pergamon Library of Attalus, the second most
important in the ancient world after the Library of
Alexandria. Situated on the Caicus River in western modern Turkey, Pergamon became part of the

Roman Empire when the last Attalid king died in
133 BC and willed his kingdom to Rome. It was a
prominent city in the region, behind only Ephesus
and Smyrna in importance, and remained so until the
fourth century AD. It featured an acropolis higher
and steeper than the one in Athens (1,300 ft above
the lower city), which was the cultural, political, and
religious center of the city. The Athenian statesman
Aristides observed that the acropolis could be viewed
from all sides a great distance from the city (*Or* 23.13)
In addition to the acropolis, the city boasted a theater,
water supplied by a twenty-seven-mile-long clay pipe
siphon system, a large barracks, palatial houses on the
acropolis, a spectacular gymnasium, an Askelpeion
(an ancient combination health clinic and medical
school), many temples, and the so-called Great Altar.

Rescue excavations were carried out by the Berlin
Museum between 1878 and 1886. They uncovered the
Great Altar dedicated to Zeus Soter (savior) and Ath-
ena, and likely used for burnt offerings to these deities.
It likely was connected to the Temple of Zeus at the
site. A little beyond it to the north was the Temple

Altar of Zeus,
Pergamon

Pergamon
Museum, Berlin

of Athena (third century BC). The Great Altar was erected in the reign of Eumenes II (197–59 BC) to commemorate a Pergamene victory over the Gauls in 190 BC. Its columned and stair-stepped structure was elaborately decorated with statues and bas-reliefs that depicted the mythological battle between the giants and the Olympian gods known as the *Gigantomachia*. Although it was never finished, the altar was standing when the church was established at Pergamon. The German excavation team transported the altar to Berlin and constructed the Pergamon Museum to house its prize exhibit.

Many scholars have proposed that this altar is the throne of Satan (Rev 2:13a). Second-century apologist Justin Martyr thought the Greek and Roman gods were fallen angels, or demons, so it is not inconceivable that Zeus, as the head of the Greek pantheon, would be associated with Satan (*2 Apol.* 5.4). The location of the Great Altar also evidences its being associated with a throne, being on the top of a high, steep hill. Mountains were often associated with deities in the ancient world, and the Greek gods dwelt on Mt. Olympus. Pergamon was a major center of the imperial cult as well as the cult of Asklepios (which employed serpents in its healing rites).

Archaeological Discoveries and the New Testament

Name	Language	Discoverer	Location found	Date found	Subject	Date of origin	Biblical significance
James Ossuary	Aramaic	Purchased by Oded Golan	Jerusalem	1970s	The 20-inch-long limestone box is believed to be the past repository for the bones of James, brother of Jesus. The side panel of the box contains Aramaic script, which reads "James, son of Joseph, brother of Jesus."	AD 63	If authentic, the ossuary would be the earliest archaeological evidence directly relating to James and Jesus.
Pilate Inscription	Latin	Antonio Frova	Caesarea Maritima	1961	Stone slab with inscription stating "Tiberium Pontius Pilate Prefect of Judea"	First century	This is the only archaeological evidence giving Pilate's name and title.
Gabbatha	Aramaic		Jerusalem		The place in Jerusalem where Pilate had his judicial seat, believed to be the spot where Pilate tried Jesus (Gabbatha in Aramaic; Lithostrotos in Greek)	First century	According to William F. Albright the court location of Jesus' trial that is identified in John 19:13 and Matt 27:27 as "the Pavement" of the Roman Praetorium
Gallio Inscription	Greek		Delphi, Greece	1905	Inscription was found in Delphi identifying "Gallio" as "Proconsul" (AD 51–53)	First century	Corresponds to Luke's record in Acts 18:12–14
Zeus and Hermes	Greek	W. M. Ramsay	Lystra (modern-day Turkey)	1909	Archaeologists unearthed several inscriptions and a temple near Lystra that identified Zeus and Hermes as the two most important gods since they were believed to have visited the earth. These gods were expected to return one day in the future.	First century	Helps scholars understand the reaction of the people when trying to identify Barnabas and Paul as Zeus and Hermes (Acts 14:7–13)
Yohanan Crucifixion	Aramaic	Vassilios Tzaferis	Jerusalem	1968	They discovered that Ben Ha'galgola was crucified with seven-inch spikes driven through the feet and lower arm. In addition, both legs were broken.	First century	Researchers gained vital information about crucifixion practices in the mid-first century that corroborates Christ's crucifixion experience as described in the Gospels (Ps 22; Matt 27; Mark 15; Luke 23; John 19).

Name	Language	Discoverer	Location found	Date found	Subject	Date of origin	Biblical significance
Pool of Bethesda		Conrad Schick	Near the Church of St. Anne	1888	Remains of the Pool of Bethesda mentioned in John 5:2 were discovered.	First century	Previously, this pool had no extrabiblical mention.
Ossuaries	Aramaic and Greek	Construction Workers	Talpiyot, Near Jerusalem	1980	Several burial ossuaries were found with the mark of the cross and various prayers directed to Jesus.	AD 40–50	It indicates early recognition that the followers of Jesus viewed his death on the cross as significant and that Jesus was God.
Dead Sea Scrolls	Hebrew, Aramaic, Greek	Bedouin shepherds	Khirbet Qumran	1947–53	981 scrolls of historical, religious, and linguistic significance	225 BC– AD 68	Messianic concept, sectarian documents of *Yaḥad* sect
John Rylands Papyrus	Greek	Bernard Grenfell	Egyptian Antiquity Market	1920	Papyrus fragments from North Africa and Greece	AD 125	P52 is the oldest known fragment of a canonical Gospel.
Oxyrhyn-chus Papyri	Greek, Latin, and Arabic	Bernard Grenfell, Arthur S. Hunt	Oxyhynchus, Egypt	1897–1900	A group of manuscripts containing thousands of documents on papyrus, vellum, and paper. Many important Greek texts thought to be lost were found at this site.	First–sixth centuries AD	Census parallel to Luke and Acts, Koine Greek was common in the NT
Lysanias inscription			Abila (near Damascus)	Nine-teenth century	An inscription mentioning the salvation of the "August lords" and Lysanias	AD 14–29	Lysanias the tetrarch of Abilene
Kinneret Boat		Moshe and Yuval Lufan of Kibbutz Ginosar	Sea of Galilee	1986	A drought revealed a 2,000-year-old fishing boat in the sediment of the Sea of Galilee.	AD 30–70	Style of fishing boat used by Jesus' disciples
Caiaphas Ossuary	Hebrew	Avi Greenhut	South of Jerusalem	1990	An ornate limestone box believed to contain the bones of Caiaphas, the high priest	AD 42–43	High priest at Jesus' trial
Bema Seat	Greek	Broncer	Corinth, Greece	1935–37	The judgment seat in Corinth where trials were held	ca. 50	Paul's tribunal before Gallio
Capernaum Synagogue	Greek and Aramaic	Charles Wilson	Capernaum, Israel	1866	This synagogue is among the oldest in the world and bears inscriptions in remembrance of its benefactors.	First century, fourth–fifth centuries	Site of Jesus' preaching (Mark 1:21; Luke 4:31; John 6:59)
Peter's House		Father Stanislao Loffreda and colleague Virgilio	Capernaum, Israel	1968	Venerated at Peter the fisherman's house as early as the mid–first century AD	First century, fourth–fifth centuries	Apostle Peter's house located beneath fourth century Byzantine church *domus ecclesiae*
Second Temple Stone Inscription	Hebrew	Benjamin Mazar	Jerusalem	1968	A stone from the southern foot of the Temple Mount bearing the inscription "To the Trumpeting Place"	Second century BC–AD 70	Site at the temple where priest blew trumpet signaling beginning and end of Sabbath

Name	Language	Discoverer	Location found	Date found	Subject	Date of origin	Biblical significance
Tyrannus Inscription	Greek		Ephesus (modern-day Turkey)	1905	A stone pillar found in the ruins of Ephesus; engraved with the name Tyrannus.	First century AD.	Mentions Tyrannus, similar to Luke's account in Acts 19:9
Bronze Sestertius Judaea Capta coin	Greek		Minted in Caesarea and distributed throughout the Roman world		Part of a series of coins minted by the Romans to commemorate the fall of Jerusalem in AD 70	AD 71	Depiction of Jews mourning over the destruction of Jerusalem
Herod the Great ostraca	Latin	Ehud Netzer	Masada	1993	Wine label	AD 73	Evidence of Herod the Great
Arch of Titus	Latin		Southern entrance to the Roman Forum		Column of Tenth Legion	AD 81	Destruction of the temple in AD 70
Mamertine Prison			Rome		Prison and originally part of the Roman Forum	640–616 BC, restored AD 21	Possible prison of Peter and Paul
Temple of Artemis		John T. Wood	Ephesus (modern-day Turkey)	1869	One of the seven wonders of the ancient world, largest temple to Artemis	550 BC	Worshiped all over Asia Minor
Theater of Ephesus		John T. Wood	Ephesus (modern-day Turkey)	1863	The largest theater in Anatolia with 25,000 seats built into the side of a hill	281, 58 BC	Riots against Paul were here.
Altar of Zeus at Pergamon		Carl Hamann	Turkey	1878–86	This altar currently resides in the Pergamon Museum in Berlin. It was originally a terrace to the acropolis of the ancient city.	170–159 BC	Possible Satan's throne where Satan lives (Rev 2:13)
Pompeii Graffiti	Latin	Antonio Sogliano	Pompeii, Italy	1901	Graffiti found scratched on a wall in the ancient city of Pompeii and preserved by a volcanic eruption AD 79	AD 79	Use of Gematria for 666
Coin of Deified Domitian	Greek				Seven stars with Domitian's son sitting on the globe	AD 82–83	Similar to Rev 1:16, where there are seven stars in the hand of the glorified Son of Man
Statue of Ephesian Goddess Artemis		John T. Wood	Ephesus (modern-day Turkey)	ca. 1863	Statue of Artemis covered with multiple fertility symbols	AD 150–200	Image that Paul preached against
St. Philip's Martyrium Hierapolis		Francesco D'Andria	Modern-day Turkey	2011	Philip's tomb discovered but contained no remains	Fourth or fifth centuries AD	Philip was one of the original twelve disciples of Jesus and was martyred.

Name	Language	Discoverer	Location found	Date found	Subject	Date of origin	Biblical significance
Madaba Map	Greek	Monk Ananias, Athanasios Andreakis	Madaba, Jordan	1884	One of the oldest surviving maps of the Middle East, including Jerusalem	AD 542–570	Identification of biblical cities and geography
Basilica of St. John		John T. Wood	Ephesus (modern-day Turkey)	1863	Constructed by Justinian in sixth century AD	First century AD	Tomb of John the Baptist
Tomb of Lazarus			East side of Mount of Olives		Has been considered a possible location of the tomb of Lazarus since the third century AD	First century AD	Confirms John 11:38–44
Jacob's Well			Ancient Samaria, a short distance from Mount Gerizim and the ruins of the Samaritan temple		Jewish, Samaritan, Muslim, and Christian traditions all associate the well with Jacob.	Has been mentioned in various histories for two millennia.	Meeting of Jesus and Samaritan woman (John 4:6–30)
Nazareth Inscription	Greek	Wilhelm Fröhner	Nazareth	1878	Forbids the robbing of tombs	Time of August Caesar and Claudius Caesar	Evidence of early belief in Jesus' resurrection
Pool of Siloam		Eli Shukron	Gihon Spring	2005	Trapezoid pool surrounded by stairs	104 BC–AD 70	Place where Jesus healed the man born blind
Absalom's Tomb Inscription	Byzantine Greek	Emile Puech and Joe Zias	East bank of Kidron Valley	2003	Oldest NT passage carved in stone on Absalom's Tomb	First century AD	Luke 2:25

Ancient World (Early Bronze I–III)

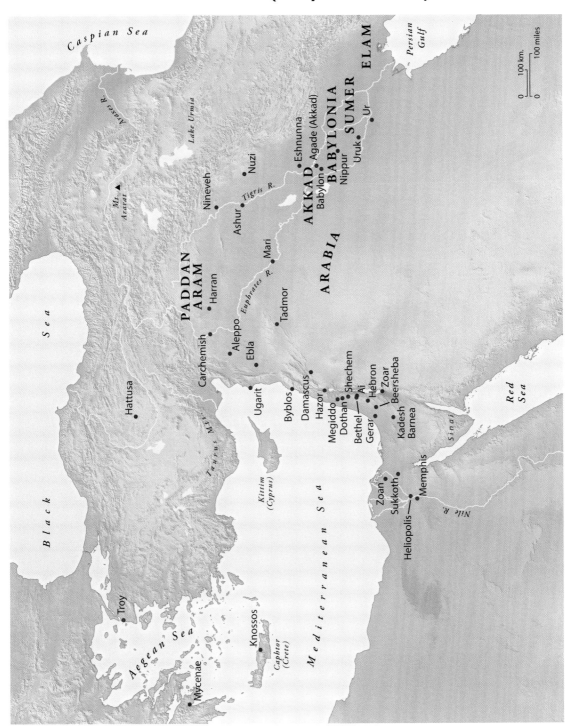

Caspian Sea

Araxes R.

Lake Urmia

Mt. Ararat ▲

Nineveh

Nuzi

Ashur

Tigris R.

Eshnunna

Agade (Akkad)

AKKAD

Babylon

BABYLONIA

Nippur

SUMER

Uruk

Ur

ELAM

Persian Gulf

100 km.

100 miles

Euphrates R.

Mari

PADDAN ARAM

Harran

Tadmor

ARABIA

Carchemish

Aleppo

Ebla

Damascus

Shechem

Ai

Hebron

Zoar

Beersheba

Red Sea

Sea

Hattusa

Ugarit

Byblos

Hazor

Megiddo

Dothan

Bethel

Gerar

Kadesh Barnea

Sinai

Taurus Mts.

Kittim (Cyprus)

Mediterranean Sea

Zoan

Sukkoth

Memphis

Heliopolis

Nile R.

Black Sea

Troy

Knossos

Caphtor (Crete)

Aegean Sea

Mycenae

Early Bronze Age IV–Middle Bronze Age I

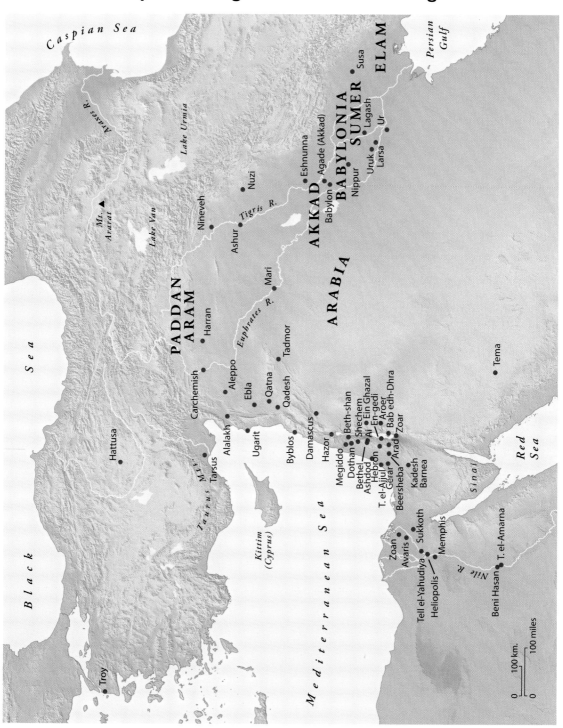

Caspian Sea

Persian Gulf

ELAM

Susa

SUMER

BABYLONIA

Agade (Akkad)

AKKAD

Eshnunna

Lagash

Ur

Nippur

Uruk

Larsa

Babylon

Nuzi

Tigris R.

Nineveh

Ashur

Araxes R.

Lake Urmia

Lake Van

Mt. Ararat

ARABIA

Mari

Euphrates R.

PADDAN ARAM

Harran

Tadmor

Carchemish

Aleppo

Qatna

Ebla

Qadesh

Alalakh

Ugarit

Byblos

Damascus

Beth-shan

Shechem

Ein Ghazal

En-gedi

Bab edh-Dhra

Hazor

Megiddo

Ai

Aroer

Zoar

Dothan

Bethel

Arad

Ashdod

Hebron

Gerar

Kadesh Barnea

T. el-Ajjul

Beersheba

Tema

Kittim (Cyprus)

Red Sea

Sinai

Zoan

Avaris

Sukkoth

Memphis

Tell el-Yahudiya

Heliopolis

Nile R.

T. el-Amarna

Beni Hasan

Taurus Mts.

Tarsus

Hattusa

Black Sea

Sea

Mediterranean Sea

Troy

0   100 km.
0   100 miles

Middle Bronze–Late Bronze III

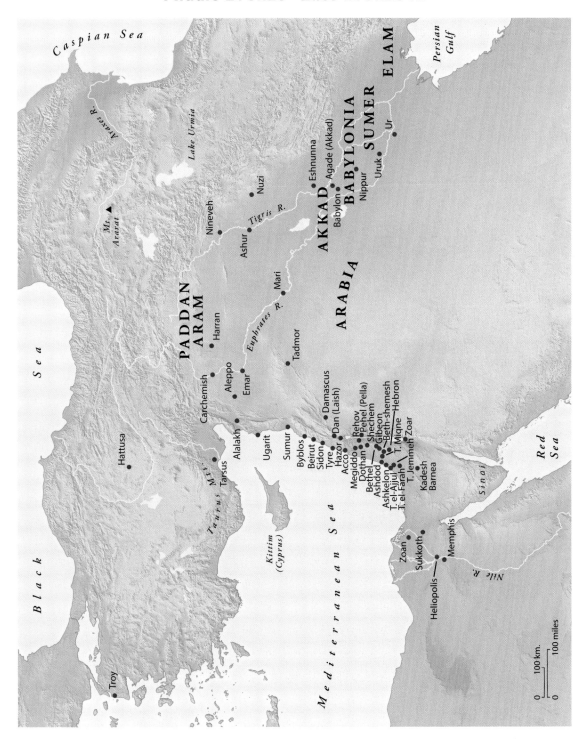

Caspian Sea

Araxes R.

Lake Urmia

Mt. Ararat

Nineveh

Nuzi

Ashur

Tigris R.

Eshnunna

Agade (Akkad)

AKKAD

Babylon

BABYLONIA

Nippur

Uruk

SUMER

Ur

ELAM

Persian Gulf

PADDAN ARAM

Harran

Mari

Euphrates R.

Tadmor

ARABIA

Carchemish

Aleppo

Emar

Damascus

Dan (Laish)

Rehov

Pehel (Pella)

Shechem

Gibeon

Beth-shemesh

Hebron

Alalakh

Ugarit

Sumur

Byblos

Beirut

Sidon

Tyre

Hazor

Acco

Megiddo

Dothan

Bethel

Ashdod

Ashkelon

T. el-Ajjul

T. el-Farah

T. Miqne

T. Jemmeh

Zoar

Kadesh Barnea

Sinai

Red Sea

Black Sea

Hattusa

Taurus Mts.

Tarsus

Kittim (Cyprus)

Mediterranean Sea

Zoan

Sukkoth

Memphis

Heliopolis

Nile R.

Troy

100 km.

100 miles

0

0

Proposed Routes of the Exodus

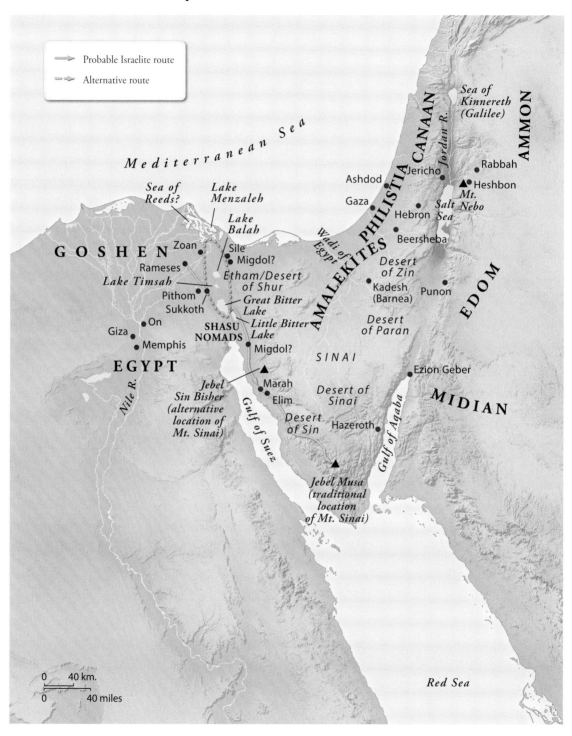

Legend:
→ Probable Israelite route
⇢ Alternative route

Mediterranean Sea

Sea of Reeds?

Lake Menzaleh

Lake Balah

G O S H E N

Zoan

Sile

Migdol?

Rameses

Etham/Desert of Shur

Lake Timsah

Pithom

Sukkoth

Great Bitter Lake

SHASU NOMADS

Little Bitter Lake

Giza

On

Memphis

EGYPT

Migdol?

Nile R.

Jebel Sin Bisher (alternative location of Mt. Sinai)

Marah

Elim

Gulf of Suez

Desert of Sin

Desert of Sinai

Hazeroth

SINAI

Jebel Musa (traditional location of Mt. Sinai)

Gulf of Aqaba

Ezion Geber

MIDIAN

Ashdod

Gaza

Hebron

Beersheba

Jericho

Jordan R.

Rabbah

Heshbon

Mt. Nebo

CANAAN

PHILISTIA

AMALEKITES

Wadi of Egypt

Salt Sea

AMMON

Sea of Kinnereth (Galilee)

Desert of Zin

Kadesh (Barnea)

Punon

Desert of Paran

EDOM

Red Sea

0   40 km.
0   40 miles

336

Iron Age I Sites

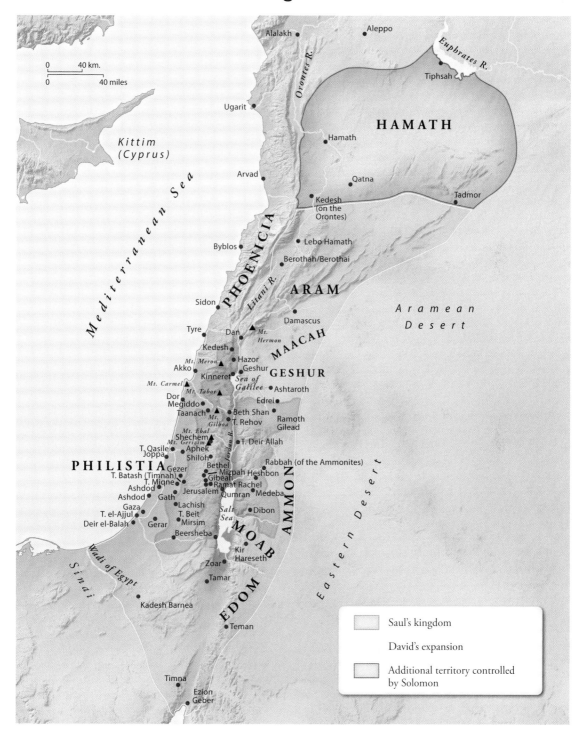

Alalakh
Aleppo
Orontes R.
Euphrates R.
Tiphsah

Ugarit

Kittim (Cyprus)

HAMATH

Hamath

Qatna
Tadmor

Arvad

Kedesh (on the Orontes)

Mediterranean Sea

Byblos

PHOENICIA

Lebo Hamath
Berothah/Berothai

Sidon

Litani R.

ARAM

Damascus

Aramean Desert

Tyre
Dan
Mt. Hermon

Kedesh
Hazor
Geshur

MAACAH

Akko
Mt. Meron
Kinneret
Sea of Galilee

GESHUR

Ashtaroth

Mt. Carmel
Mt. Tabor
Dor
Megiddo
Taanach
Mt. Gilboa
Beth Shan
T. Rehov
Edrei

Ramoth Gilead

Mt. Ebal
Mt. Gerizim
Shechem
T. Deir Allah

T. Qasile
Joppa
Aphek
Shiloh

PHILISTIA

Gezer
Bethel
Mizpah
Heshbon
Gibeah
Ramat Rachel

Rabbah (of the Ammonites)

T. Batash (Timnah)
T. Miqne
Ashdod
Ashdod
Gath
Jerusalem
Qumran
Medeba

Jordan R.

Gaza
Lachish
T. el-Ajjul
T. Beit Mirsim
Gerar
Dibon

AMMON

Salt Sea

Deir el-Balah
Beersheba

MOAB

Kir Hareseth

Zoar

Tamar

Eastern Desert

EDOM

Wadi of Egypt

Sinai

Kadesh Barnea

Teman

Timna

Ezion Geber

Saul's kingdom

David's expansion

Additional territory controlled by Solomon

337

Iron Age II Sites

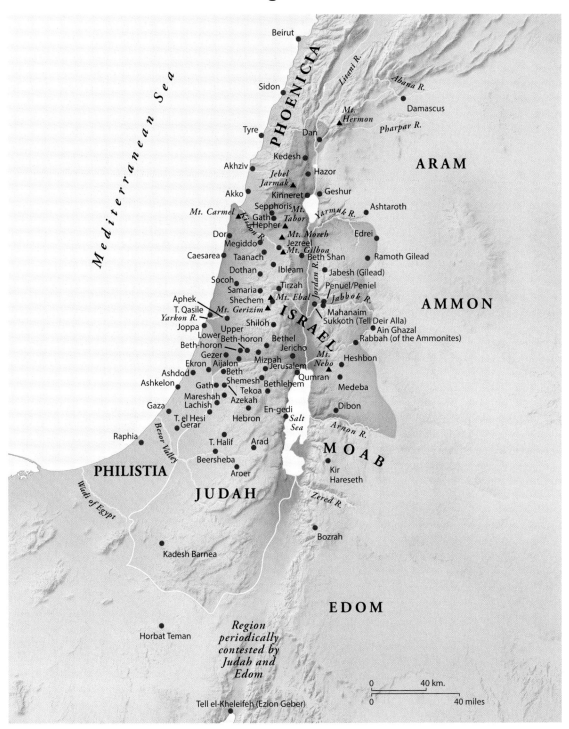

Beirut

Sidon

Tyre

PHOENICIA

Litani R.

Abana R.

Damascus

Mt. Hermon

ARAM

Pharpar R.

Dan

Kedesh

Akhziv

Hazor

Jebel Jarmak

Akko

Kinneret

Geshur

Ashtaroth

Sepphoris

Mt. Carmel

Gath

Hepher

Mt. Tabor

Yarmuk R.

Kishon R.

Mt. Moreh

Edrei

Dor

Megiddo

Jezreel

Mt. Gilboa

Beth Shan

Ramoth Gilead

Caesarea

Taanach

Ibleam

Jabesh (Gilead)

Dothan

Jordan R.

Penuel/Peniel

Socoh

Tirzah

Jabbok R.

Samaria

Shechem

Mt. Ebal

AMMON

Aphek

Mt. Gerizim

ISRAEL

Mahanaim

T. Qasile

Shiloh

Sukkoth (Tell Deir Alla)

Yarkon R.

Ain Ghazal

Joppa

Upper Beth-horon

Bethel

Rabbah (of the Ammonites)

Lower Beth-horon

Jericho

Gezer

Mizpah

Mt. Nebo

Heshbon

Ekron

Aijalon

Jerusalem

Ashdod

Beth Shemesh

Bethlehem

Qumran

Ashkelon

Gath

Medeba

Mareshah

Tekoa

Lachish

Azekah

Gaza

En-gedi

Dibon

T. el Hesi

Hebron

Salt Sea

Gerar

Arnon R.

Raphia

T. Halif

Arad

M O A B

Besor Valley

Beersheba

Kir Hareseth

Wadi of Egypt

PHILISTIA

Aroer

JUDAH

Zered R.

Kadesh Barnea

Bozrah

E D O M

Mediterranean Sea

Horbat Teman

Region periodically contested by Judah and Edom

| 0 | 40 km. |
| 0 | 40 miles |

Tell el-Kheleifeh (Ezion Geber)

Israel in the Persian Period

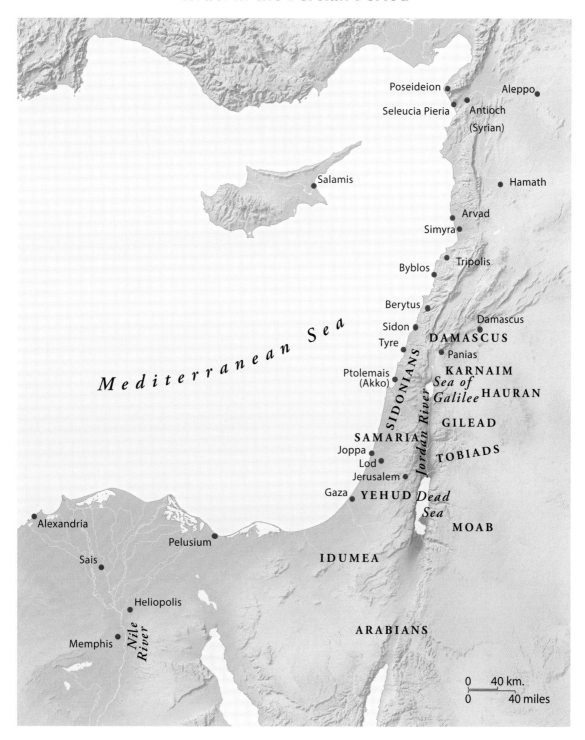

Poseideion
Aleppo
Seleucia Pieria
Antioch
(Syrian)
Hamath
Salamis
Arvad
Simyra
Tripolis
Byblos
Berytus
Damascus
Sidon
Tyre
DAMASCUS
Panias
Ptolemais
(Akko)
KARNAIM
*Sea of
Galilee*
HAURAN
SIDONIANS
Jordan River
GILEAD
SAMARIA
Joppa
TOBIADS
Lod
Jerusalem
Gaza
YEHUD
*Dead
Sea*
MOAB
Alexandria
IDUMEA
Pelusium
Sais
Heliopolis
*Nile
River*
Memphis

Mediterranean Sea

ARABIANS

0   40 km.
0   40 miles

Ancient Near East in the Hellenistic Period

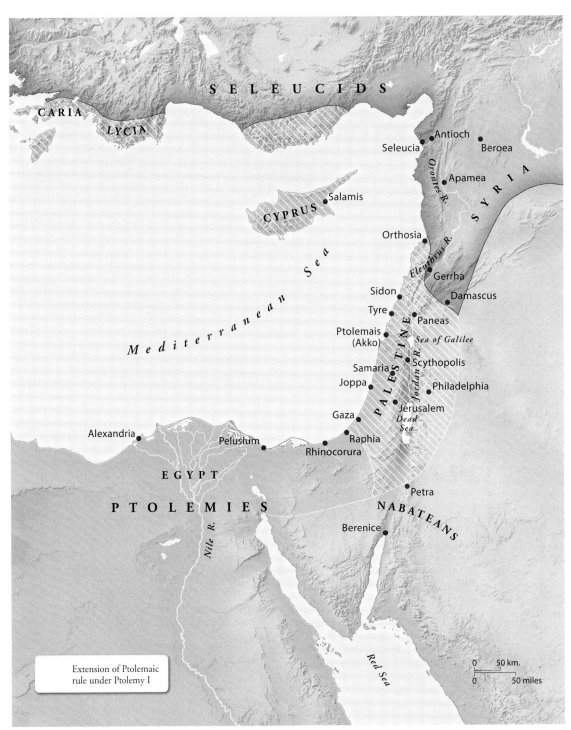

Israel in the Hasmonean Period

Judea before Alexander Jannaeus

Additions of Alexander Jannaeus, 103–76 BC

— Kingdom of Alexander Jannaeus

COELE-SYRIA

Sidon

Damascus

PHOENICIA

Tyre

Dan
(Antiochia)   Paneas

Cadasa

Seleucia

Hazor   Bascama
Bethsaida   Gamala
Gennesaret   Dathema
Taricheae
Arbela   *Sea of*   Hippus
Galilee
GALILEE   Philoteria
Sepphoris

Ptolemais
(Akko)

Mt. Carmel

Dora

GALAADITIS

Jezreel Valley

Strato's Tower

Scythopolis   Pella

SAMARIA   Gerasa

Samaria   Ammathus
Mt.   Shechem
Gerizim
Acrabeta

Jordan R.   PEREA

Apollonia

Alexandrium   Gadora

Joppa   Arimathea   Philadelphia
Lydda   Apherema
Docus
Jamnia   Jericho
Gazara   JUDEA   Esbus   Samaga
Azotus   Jerusalem   Hyrcania   Medeba
Accaron
Herodium   Machaerus
Ascalon
Marisa   Beth Zur   *Dead*   MOABITIS
Anthedon   Adora   Hebron   *Sea*
Gaza   En Gedi
Orda   Gerar
IDUMEA   Masada   NABATEANS

Mediterranean Sea

PHILISTIA

Raphia
Beersheba

Rhinocorura   Malatha

Wadi el-Arish

Petra

0   10 km.
0   10 miles

Israel in the Second Temple (Roman) Period

Sidon

Damascus

Tyre

TYRE

ULATHA

Caesarea Philippi

Gischala

Thella

Raphana

UPPER GALILEE

GAULANITIS

Ptolemais (Akko)

Baca

Bersabe

Gamala

BATANEA

TRACONITIS

Chabulon

Gabara

Bethsaida

Taricheae

Gergesa (Kursi)

Jotapata

LOWER GALILEE

Hippus

Dion

Canatha

Sepphoris

Kafr Kana

Tiberias

AURANITIS

Nazareth

▲ Mt. Tabor

Dora

Japhia

Gadara

Abila

Mediterranean Sea

Esdraelon Valley

DECAPOLIS

Edrei

Scythopolis

Caesarea

Ginae (Jenin)

Pella

Bostra

Jordan R.

Sebaste

Gerasa

Apollonia

Neapolis (Shechem)

Ammathus

PEREA

Mt. Gerizim ▲

SAMARIA

Joppa

Antipatris

Lydda

Gadora

Philadelphia

JUDEA

Archelais

Neara

Jamnia

Jericho

Cypros

Abila

Emmaus (Nicopolis)

Jerusalem

Beth-ramatha

Azotus

Mesad Hasidim (Qumran)

Esbus(Heshbon)

Ascalon

Hyrcania

Medeba

IDUMEA

Betogabris (Beth-guvrin)

Hebron

Machaerus

Dead Sea

Gaza

NABATEANS

Masada

Beersheba

0   10 km.

0   10 miles

◆ Cities of the Decapolis (Pliny)

Territory under Antipas

Territory under Philip

Territory under Procurator of Judea

Territory under the Proconsul of Syria

Extent of the Roman Empire in the First Century

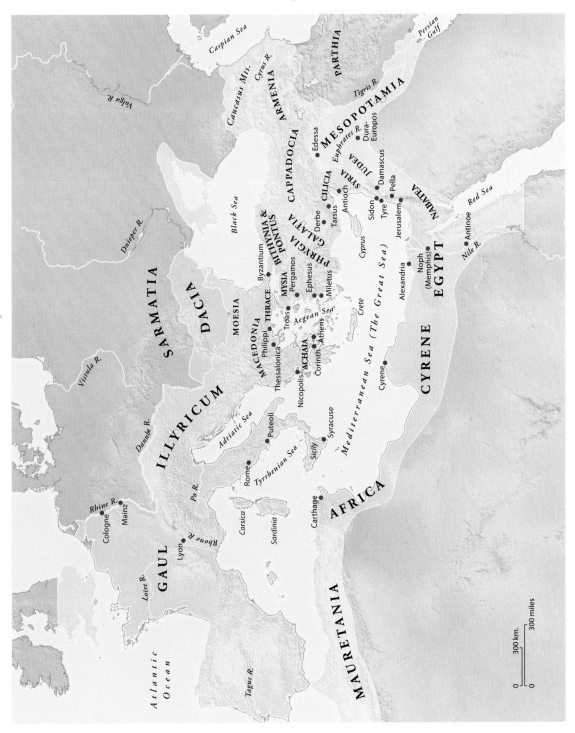

Asia Minor in the First Century

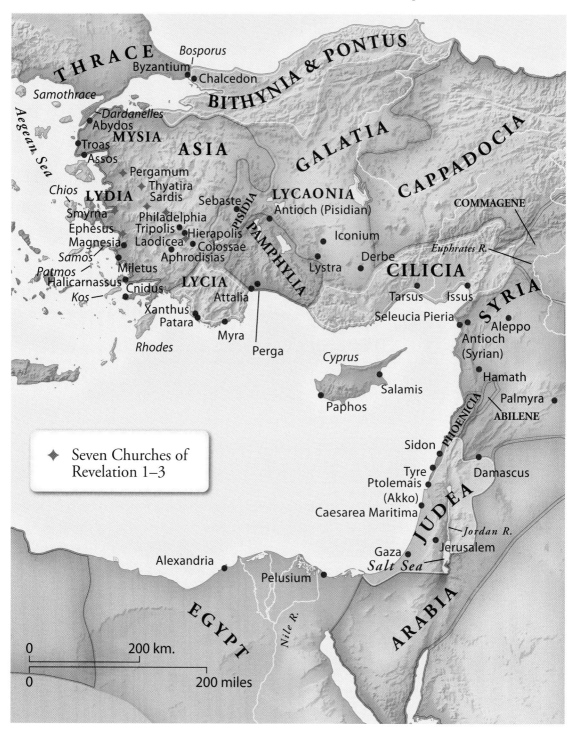

✦ Seven Churches of
Revelation 1–3

0   200 km.

0   200 miles

Jerusalem in the First Temple Period (Iron Age I-II)

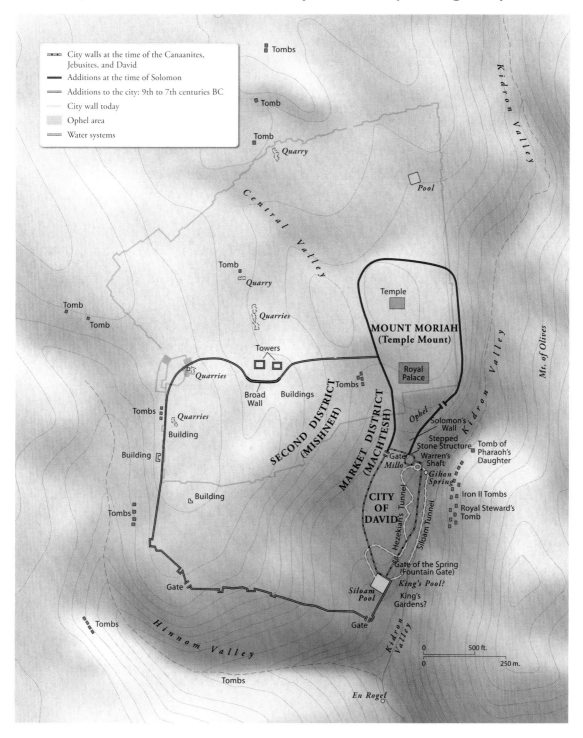

Legend:
- City walls at the time of the Canaanites, Jebusites, and David
- Additions at the time of Solomon
- Additions to the city: 9th to 7th centuries BC
- City wall today
- Ophel area
- Water systems

Tombs

Tomb

Tomb

Quarry

Pool

Kidron Valley

Central Valley

Tomb

Quarry

Temple

Tomb

Quarries

**MOUNT MORIAH
(Temple Mount)**

Tomb

Tomb

Towers

Royal
Palace

Mt. of Olives

Quarries

Tombs

Broad
Wall

Buildings

Ophel

Solomon's
Wall

Kidron Valley

Tombs

Quarries

**SECOND DISTRICT
(MISHNEH)**

Stepped
Stone Structure

Tomb of
Pharaoh's
Daughter

Building

Building

Gate
Millo

Warren's
Shaft

Gihon
Spring

Iron II Tombs

Building

**MARKET DISTRICT
(MACHTESH)**

Royal Steward's
Tomb

Tombs

**CITY
OF
DAVID**

Hezekiah's Tunnel

Siloam Tunnel

Gate

Gate of the Spring
(Fountain Gate)

King's Pool?

Siloam
Pool

King's
Gardens?

Gate

Hinnom Valley

Kidron Valley

Tombs

Tombs

En Rogel

| 0 | | 500 ft. |
| 0 | | 250 m. |

Jerusalem in the Persian Period (Iron Age III)

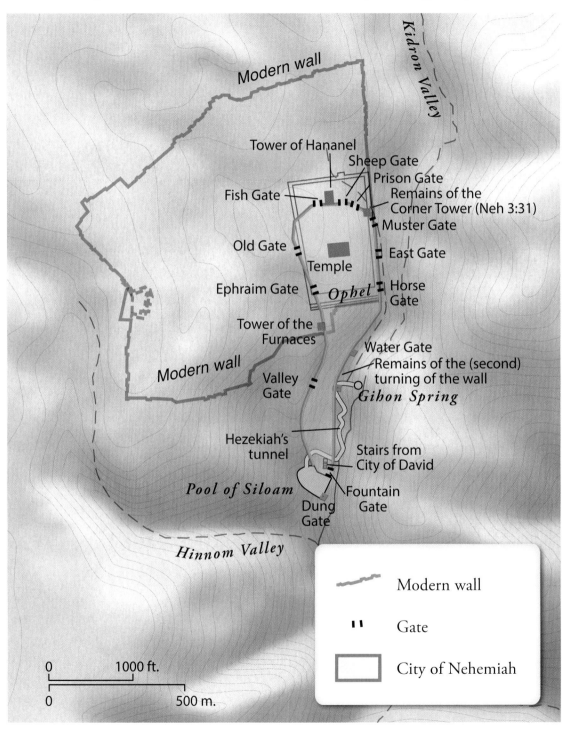

Kidron Valley

Modern wall

Tower of Hananel

Sheep Gate

Prison Gate

Remains of the
Corner Tower (Neh 3:31)

Fish Gate

Muster Gate

Old Gate

East Gate

Temple

Ephraim Gate

Ophel

Horse
Gate

Tower of the
Furnaces

Water Gate

Remains of the (second)
turning of the wall

Modern wall

Valley
Gate

Gihon Spring

Hezekiah's
tunnel

Stairs from
City of David

Pool of Siloam

Fountain
Gate

Dung
Gate

Hinnom Valley

	Modern wall
I I	Gate
	City of Nehemiah

0   1000 ft.

0   500 m.

Jerusalem in the Second Temple (Roman) Period

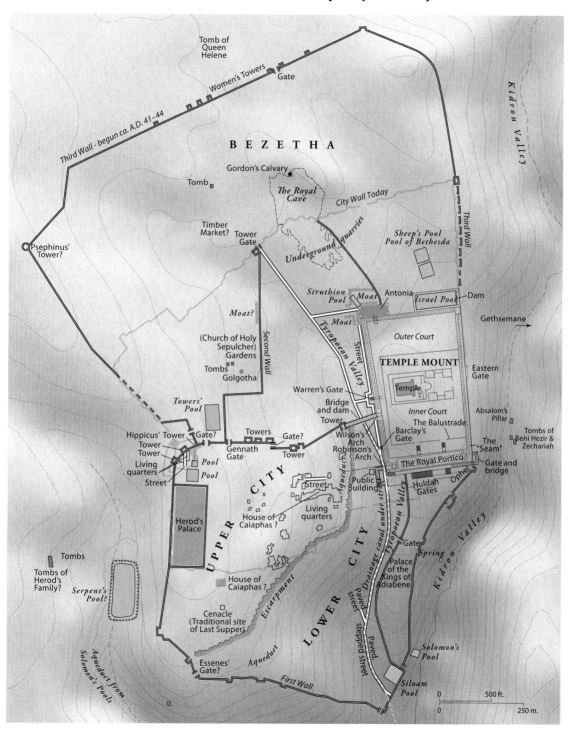

Tomb of Queen Helene

Women's Towers

Gate

Third Wall - begun ca. A.D. 41-44

BEZETHA

Gordon's Calvary

Tomb

The Royal Cave

City Wall Today

Timber Market?

Tower Gate

Underground quarries

Sheep's Pool Pool of Bethesda

Third Wall

Psephinus' Tower?

Struthion Pool

Moat

Antonia

Israel Pool

Dam

Gethsemane

Moat?

Moat

(Church of Holy Sepulcher) Gardens

Second Wall

Tyropoeon Valley Street

Outer Court

Eastern Gate

Tombs

Golgotha

TEMPLE MOUNT

Temple

Warren's Gate

Inner Court

Absalom's Pillar

Towers' Pool

Bridge and dam Tower

The Balustrade

Tombs of Beni Hezir & Zechariah

Hippicus' Tower

Gate?

Towers

Gate?

Wilson's Arch

Barclay's Gate

The "Seam"

Tower Tower

Gennath Gate

Tower

Robinson's Arch

The Royal Portica

Gate and bridge

Living quarters

Pool

Aqueduct

Public Building

Huldah Gates

Ophel

Street

Pool

UPPER CITY

Street

Living quarters

Herod's Palace

House of Caiaphas ?

Drainage canal under street

Tyropoeon Valley

Gate

Tombs

Spring

Kidron Valley

Tombs of Herod's Family?

House of Caiaphas ?

LOWER CITY

Palace of the Kings of Adiabene

Serpent's Pool?

Escarpment

Paved stepped street

Cenacle (Traditional site of Last Supper)

Solomon's Pool

Aqueduct from Solomon's Pools

Essenes' Gate?

Aqueduct

First Wall

Paved

Siloam Pool

Kidron Valley

0   500 ft.
0   250 m.

Modern Middle East

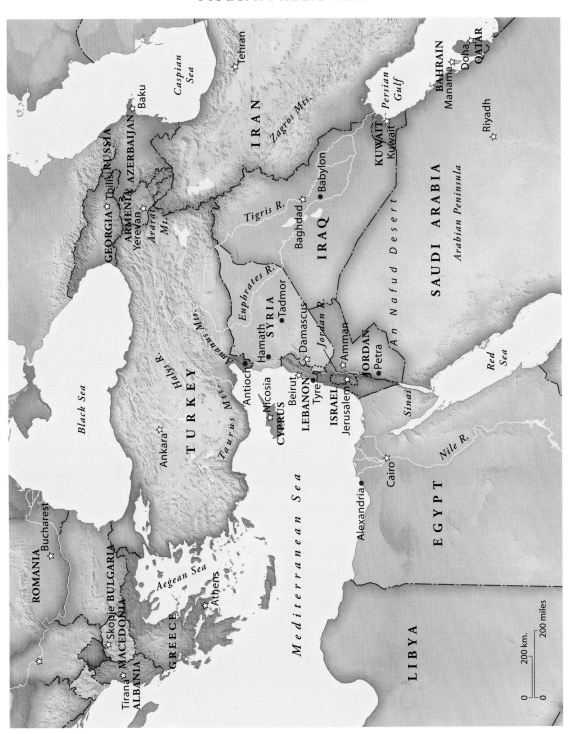

Modern Israel

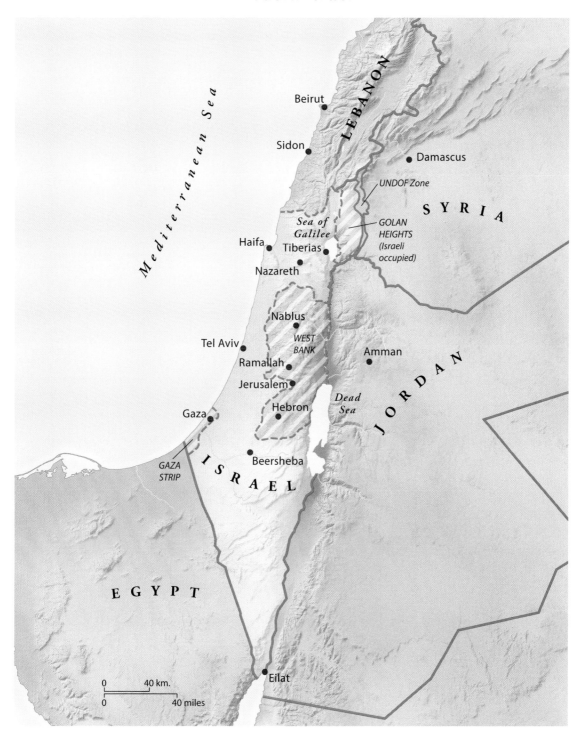

Glossary

Abecedary An inscription consisting of the letters of an alphabet that is generally used to teach students the alphabet.

Absolute dating Dating that establishes the specific date of a geologic structure or event to a previously determined calendar (also called chronometric dating).

Accelerator mass spectrometry A type of radiocarbon dating that makes possible the detection of naturally occurring, long-lived radio-isotopes and therefore can outperform the competing technique of decay counting for all isotopes where the half-life is long enough.

Acropolis The highest elevation of a city where often the most important public structures, fortifications, and especially temples and palaces are built.

Agora The central market place of a city where administrative, commercial, and cultic activities were performed.

Amphora(e) Large store jar with two handles and a pointed bottom, usually used for the transport and storage of wine or other liquids.

Amphitheater (Gk. "theater on both sides" or "around") A two-sided open-air venue used for entertainment, performances, and sports common to the Greco-Roman world. This is distinct from a theater, which consists of half of the same structure.

Anachronism (Gk. *ana* "against" + *chronos* "time") A chronological inconsistency that juxtaposes persons, events, objects, or customs from different periods of time.

Anagram A direct wordplay resulting from the rearrangement of the letters of a word or phrase to produce a new word or phrase using all the original letters exactly once.

Antediluvian The period prior to the flood.

Anthropomorphic Something described or designed in human form, such as the anthropoid sarcophagi of the Philistines.

Apocrypha (Gk. *apokryphos*, "hidden, obscure, or spurious") Non-canonical books that contain figures from Scripture. Some writings found a place in the Septuagint and the Latin Vulgate versions of the OT but not in the Jewish or Protestant Bibles.

Aqueduct Water channel usually associated with high arches to traverse a ravine, though they can also run along the ground.

Archaeogeophysical exploration Ground-based remote sensing technique used for archaeological imaging or mapping.

Archisynagogos (Gk. *arche* "head/leader" + *synagogos* "assembly" = Heb. *rosh ha-keneset*) Title used in classical times referring to the head of the synagogue who served as the leader of the Jewish community.

Artifact A man-made object made from stone, metal, clay or other substance (e.g., coins, flint, figurines, pottery).

Asherah A cultic object in female form (e.g., pillar-base figurines) representing fertility. In the ancient Near East Asherah functioned as a goddess (different goddesses in different religions), but in ancient Israel she was recognized as the consort of the Canaanite deity Baal. The Asherah is often depicted as a carved tree (Asherah pole) set in a high place. In the OT the Asherah was denounced as a false god and idol that corrupted Israel.

Ashlar Large, finely dressed, square-cut stone masonry used as a facing on walls.

Assemblage A group of artifacts of different types found near one another and in the same stratum.

Apotropaic Statues or other images believed to have the power to avert evil influences or bad luck.

Babylonian Chronicle A series of Babylonian historiographical cuneiform tablets chronicling the early years of the Babylonian ruler Nebuchadnezzar II and his capture of Jerusalem in 597/6 BC.

Bamah (Heb. *bamah* "high place") An architectural complex for cultic purposes.

Bar-Kokhba Revolt The second Jewish resistance to Roman rule by the Jews of the Roman province of Judea led by Simon bar Kokhba (AD 132–36).

Basalt A hard common grey/black igneous volcanic rock common in the region of Galilee and Jordan.

Basilica A rectangular building or hall with a central nave and two side aisles. The Romans used them for administrative buildings while the Christians converted them for churches.

Balk The vertical wall of a square left to preserve and read strata. This includes a one meter strip of unexcavated earth left in place on the north and east sides between squares.

Bedouin A member of a nomadic Arab tribe that still inhabits the desert regions of much of the Middle East.

Bema (Gk. *bema* "step") A raised platform or podium from which orators addressed people in the market; often associated with a place of judgment (cf. 2 Cor 5:10).

Berosus (Gk. from Akk. *Bēl-rē'u-šu*, "Bel is his shepherd") A Hellenistic-era Babylonian priest of Bel Marduk and astronomer who wrote books on Babylonian history in Koine Greek from 290 to 278 BC.

Bichromc Ware Two-colored (red and black) pottery found during the MB 2, LB 1 (Cypriot and Syro/Canaanite), and IA (Phoenician) with geometric designs.

Book of the Dead An ancient Egyptian funerary text, originally titled The Book of Coming Forth by Day, that was used from the beginning of the New Kingdom (ca. 1550 BC) to ca. 50 BC.

Boss A chiseled architectural feature on dressed stones, especially in monumental structures, that creates a frame-like effect. In Herodian architecture, huge rectangular building blocks laid in horizontal courses feature flat, projecting central portions (bosses) surrounded by narrow, shallow dressed margins.

Bullae (pl. bulla) Small clay seals stamped with the sender's name and attached to documents.

Chalcolithic (Gk. *chalcos* "copper" + *lithos* "stone") The first archaeological period to use copper.

Capital The top decorative section of a column (or pilaster). In classical architecture there are three types: Doric, Ionic, and Corinthian.

Casemate A thick, defensive (double) wall with rooms or compartments between the walls for storage, defense, or dwelling.

Ceramic typology The careful observation of changing pottery (ceramic) forms to determine a chronological dating sequence.

Cistern A natural or man-made opening used for the storage of water.

Copper Scroll Two scrolls of pure copper (originally joined to form a plaque) from the Second Temple period discovered on a ledge in Cave 3 at Qumran. The scroll contains a list of sixty-six hiding places of treasure thought to be in various locations in the Judean desert and the Jerusalem area.

Covenant A legal contract between two parties. In the ancient Near East and the OT it refers to binding parties through an intensified oath, sometimes ratified by a sacrifice (cf. Gen 15:9–11, 17–18). In the NT the term may carry the same meaning (e.g., new covenant) and signify an agreement, testament, or will.

Cuneiform Cursive wedge-shaped writing created by using a cut reed or stylus on set clay, dating to 3000 BC. The method is attested in Sumerian, Hittite, Ugaritic, Elamite, and Akkadian texts.

Cyrus Cylinder A barrel-shaped baked clay cylinder written in Babylonian cuneiform concerning the conquest of Babylon by the Persian monarch Cyrus in 539 BC and his royal edicts (539–530 BC).

Dendrochronology A method based on examining the number, width, and density of the annual growth of tree rings.

Destruction layer The ash layer between strata that is indicative of a historical destruction and is important for dating the site in relation to documented history.

Destruction of Mankind Ancient Egyptian text from 1323 BC, also known as The Book of the Cow of Heaven, that describes the reasons for the imperfect state of the world in terms of humankind's rebellion against the supreme sun god Ra and the divine punishment inflicted on mankind through the goddess Hathor.

Diagnostic sherds Pieces of pottery, such as rims, handles, bases and painted body sherds that identify the structure of the whole vessel (see Indicatives).

Documentary hypothesis A hypothesis of biblical textual composition proposed by Julius Wellhausen that the Torah was derived from originally independent, parallel, and complete narratives, which were subsequently combined into the current form by a series of redactors.

Elephantine papyri A collection of ancient Jewish documents from a Jewish community at Elephantine (an Egyptian border fortress) in the fifth century BC that includes letters and legal contracts from family.

Epigraphy (Gk. *epi* "on" + *graphein* "to write") The study of ancient languages based on their written forms.

Eschatology (Gk. *eschatos*, "last things") A theological term for the study of the end of the age (the eschaton) and the consummation of world history.

Essenes A Jewish sect identified by Josephus and Pliny as residing around the Dead Sea. There were different groups of Essenes over time and many scholars identify the inhabitants of the Qumran community as Essenes, or "Essenic," despite the fact that sectarian documents among the Dead Sea Scrolls refer to the community as the *Yaḥad*.

Execration Texts Egyptian texts (MB II) inscribed with curses upon cities, towns, and people from Palestine and Syria.

Flavius Josephus First-century Jewish historian who wrote for the Romans an account of Jewish history including the Roman assault and conquest of Jerusalem and the Temple Mount.

Fertile Crescent The crescent shaped region from Canaan to Mesopotamia (sometimes including parts of Egypt) that distinguishes the more fertile area from the desert regions.

Fill A mixed matrix of soil, gravel, rubbish, and pottery used to level an area such as a floor or wall.

First Jewish Revolt The Jewish resistance to Roman rule from AD 66–70, especially in the city of Jerusalem.

First Temple period The period from the building of Solomon's Temple to its destruction by the Babylonians (ca. 966–587/6 BC).

Flagstone Paving stones that are flat and evenly spaced.

Fresco Color painting on plastered walls.

Floatation A method of separating small archaeologically significant materials (plant matter, seeds, etc.) from a soil sample by means of soaking in water in which particles will float to the surface.

Forum romanum (Lat. for "Roman Forum") The main center of a Roman city usually located near the physical center of a Roman town that served as a public area for commercial, religious, economic, political, legal, and social activities.

Genre A category of literary composition characterized by similarities in form, style, or subject matter (e.g., history, poetry, wisdom, apocalyptic literature).

Genesis Apocryphon (designated 1QapGen^{ar}) One of the seven Dead Sea Scrolls discovered in Cave 1 near Qumran. Composed in Aramaic between the third century BC and first Century AD, it records a pseudepigraphal conversation between Lamech, son of Methuselah, and his son, Noah.

Glacis (French for "freeze, slip") A natural or artificial slope found in ancient fortified cities, usually employed for defensive purposes.

Gnostic (Gk. *gnosis*) A sect that infiltrated the early church and believed that the cosmos emanated from a transcendent god and that salvation was achieved through acquiring secret knowledge.

Hermeneutics (Gk. *hermeneuein*, "to interpret") The science of interpreting the Bible utilizing historical, grammatical, and literary principles to help understand the meaning of the text.

Herodian The time period or architectural structures connected with Herod the Great and his family (Herodian dynasty).

Hieroglyphic (Gk. *hierogyphikos*, from *hieros*, "sacred" + *graphein*, "to carve or write"). Ancient Egyptian script (fourth millennium BC) using the form of over 600 pictures or symbols that represent sounds, syllables, and words. Nearly all Egyptian state and ceremonial documents that were to be seen by the public were written in this script. Also, funerary and religious texts were copied using the script.

Hippodrome (Gk. *hippos* "horse" + *dromos* "course") A large racecourse for horses and chariots, like the Roman circus, that appears in Roman-designed cities throughout Israel and Asia Minor.

Hoard A group of coins or other small artifacts discovered together.

Hyksos An ethnically mixed group of Western Asiatic Semitic people who overthrew the Egyptian Thirteenth Dynasty and formed the Fifteenth to Sixteenth Dynasties in Egypt (ca. 1674–1548 BC).

Iconography The study of traditional or conventional images or symbols associated with a subject, especially a religious or legendary subject.

Indicative Diagnostic sherds that have distinct forms at different times in history and assist in dating the stratum in which they are found.

Installation An archaeological structure that served a special function.

Islamic Waqf A charitable trust that maintains jurisdiction over holy sites in Israel and areas under Palestinian authority, including the Temple Mount in Jerusalem. Construction work carried out by the Waqf on the Temple Mount resulted in a large amount of archaeologically rich debris, some of which was collected by Israeli archaeologists connected with the Temple Mount Sifting Project.

In situ (Lat. for "in position" or "on site") The precise location of an artifact in its original location. This is critical for the dating and interpretation of the strata and important for the provenance and interpretation of the artifact or structure itself.

Khirbet Arabic equivalent of the Hebrew tel ("mound").

Koine (Gk. *he koinē dialektos*, "the common dialect") The Greek language of the Septuagint, New Testament, and other commercial and private documents.

Krater A large bowl, often with multiple handles, used for mixing wine and food.

Lapis lazuli A blue stone prized by the ancients for use in artistic creations, such as settings for eyes of idols.

Leningrad Codex (*Codex Leningradensis*) The oldest complete manuscript of the Hebrew Bible (ca. AD 1008) including the Masoretic Text and Tiberian vocalization.

Levant The eastern Mediterranean countries of Israel, Jordan, Syria, Lebanon, Turkey, Cyprus, Egypt, and Greece.

Level A surveyor term to indicate the height above sea level and used to designate a layer or stratum. It can also be used to indicate a locus.

Libations Liquid form of offerings.

Lisan (Arabic for "tongue") The small peninsula on the eastern side of the Dead Sea which separates the north and the south basins (Josh 15:2).

Locus (pl. loci) The feature in an archaeological square, such as a wall, pit, or installation that is different from a previous feature. It can be as minute as the difference in soil or as large as a room.

Madaba Map Sixth-century-AD mosaic map of the Holy Land discovered on the floor of a Greek Orthodox church from the Byzantine period in the town of Madaba, Jordan. This is considered the oldest map of the Holy Land and has been significant in locating ancient sites and features depicted on the map.

Manual of Discipline (1QS, Community Rule) An important sectarian document of the Qumran Community that is definitive for classifying other compositions as sectarian or non-sectarian and describes the unique rules and practices of the community including the communal meal.

Manumission Formal (legal) release of a slave from the condition of slavery.

Martyrium Early churches with a specific architectural form centered on a central element and built on a central plan, circular, octagonal, or cruciform shape.

Masoretic Text The traditional (accepted) Hebrew text of the Bible (ca. AD 1000) composed by the Massoretes, a group of scribes in Tiberias who developed a vowel system so the text could read with confidence.

Maximalists Those who maximize (or prioritize) the biblical data with respect to the archaeological data.

Menorah (Heb., pl. *menorot*) A distinctive seven-branched candelabra or lamp such as that designed for the tabernacle and temple.

Mesha Inscription (also Moabite Inscription) An inscribed stone (stele) of King Mesha of Moab (ca. 840 BC) describing how the Moabite god Chemosh allowed the Moabites to be subjugated to Omri, King of Israel, but later restored the lands of Moab.

Messianic Apocalypse (4Q521) A fragmentary apocalyptic text from Cave 4 at Qumran that makes connection to the healing ministry of the messiah and parallels the language used in Luke 7:22 concerning Jesus' ministry.

Messianic Banquet (also Eschatological Banquet) A sacred communal meal commemorating or celebrating the end of Israel's desolation and signaling the advent of the messianic age of redemption. Such a meal was proleptically enjoyed at Qumran in preparation for the arrival of the messiah (see Rule of the Congregation).

Minimalists Those who minimalize the biblical data in deference to the archaeological data.

Miqveh (pl. *miqvaot*) Stepped immersion pool for Jews to perform their ritual cleansing (immersion) either at home or in public. Most *miqvaot* have a rock cut division (small wall) down the center of the steps to separate pre- and post-ritual immersion.

Mishnah (Heb. *mishnah*, "study by repetition") The first major written redaction of Jewish oral traditions (oral law) and the first work of rabbinic literature.

Monolith (Gk. *monolithus* from *monos* "one" + *lithos* "stone") A large, single-cut stone.

Monotheism (Gk. *mono* "one" + *theos* "god") The belief that there is only one God.

Monumental inscription A stone inscription on a grave marker, cenotaph, or memorial plaque intended as a monument or memorial.

Mount Gerizim A historic sacred site located on the south side of Shechem (Nablus) that housed a Samaritan temple built in the Persian and Hellenistic periods that was destroyed by the Hasmoneans.

Mosaic Pictures or inscriptions made from small cut pieces of colored stone.

Neolithic (Gk. neios "new" + *fithos* "stone"). The new Stone Age period.

Numismatics (Gk. *nomisma*). The science and study of coins, particularly ancient coinage.

Nazarite vow (Heb. *nazir* "consecrated, separated") A voluntary vow that required abstinence from touching or eating unclean foods, drinking wine, and cutting the hair.

Necropolis (Gk. *nekropolis*, "city of the dead," pl. necropoli) A large ancient cemetery with tomb monuments located outside a city.

Neutron Activation Analysis (NAA) A nuclear process used for determining the concentrations of elements in a vast amount of materials. The process allows discrete sampling of elements as it disregards the chemical form of a sample and focuses solely on its nucleus. In archaeology, NAA is used to determine the local soil (origin) of pottery that is helpful for determining patterns of production and trade at archaeological sites.

Nimrud Prism The Nimrud Prism (ca. 720 BC) attests fragments of a cuneiform prism found in the excavations at Nimrud. The prism commemorates the rule of Sargon II and reports his deportation and resettlement of Israelites in the midst of Assyria.

Northwest Semitic A division of the Semitic language family comprising the indigenous languages of the Levant from the Bronze Age through the Iron Age (i.e., Amorite, Ugaritic, Old Aramaic, and Canaanite languages, including Phoenician and Hebrew).

Numismatics (Gk. *nomisma*, "current coin, money, usage", Lat. *numismatis*). The science and study of coins.

Obelisk A four-sided stone pillar with a tapered pyramidal point.

Onomasticon An alphabetical list of geographical sites mentioned in the Bible, most often identified with the one written by Eusebius and translated by Jerome.

Ophel Denotes a fortified hill and describes a prominent feature of Jerusalem's topography, the extended portion of the City of David (the oldest part of Jerusalem) up to the foot of the Temple Mount (See 2 Chron 27:3; 33:14; Neh 3:26; 11:21).

Oriental Institute Prism A hexagonal clay prism in Assyrian cuneiform recording the annals of the Assyrian king Sennacherib, including his attack on the cities of Judah and his attempted siege of Jerusalem. Three versions have survived (all with the same text): the Oriental Institute Prism in the Oriental Institute of Chicago, the Taylor Prism in the British Museum, and the Jerusalem Prism in the Israel Museum in Jerusalem.

Ossuary A limestone box used to store the bones of the dead (secondary burial) after the flesh has decayed from the bones.

Ostracon (pl. ostraca; Gk. *ostrakon*, "a sherd of pottery") A piece of pottery or other substance with an inscription on it.

Ovoid store jar A large baggy-style ceramic jar used in industry as well as in the home for the storage of liquids.

Paleoethnobotany The study of ancient plants and cultures.

Paleography (Gk. *palaios* "old" + *graphein* "to write") The study of ancient writing and texts.

Parchment (Gk. *pergamenon* "of Pergamon'") Writing material made from animal skins (vellum) that originated in the city of Pergamon, Asia Minor.

Parthenon A Greek temple built on the Athenian acropolis from 447 to 432 BC and dedicated to the goddess Athena, the city's patron, whose huge statue filled the interior of the building.

Patriarchs (Gk. *patna* "lineage, progeny") The term refers to the three biblical patriarchs of the people of Israel: Abraham, Isaac, and Jacob.

Papyrus (pl. papyri) A type of paper made from the Egyptian papyrus reed which grows along the Nile River. Papyri was used as writing material during the Old and New Testament periods and the early church.

Pentateuch The first five books of the OT: Genesis, Exodus, Leviticus, Numbers, and Deuteronomy.

Period A time of occupation in the history of a site or stratum.

Phase A subdivision of a period or stratum of occupation.

Pithos (pl. pithoi) An exceptionally large storage jar.

Pilgrim flask A small metal, glass, or ceramic vial shaped like a flattened canteen with one or two small handles on the side and a small spout. It was used by pilgrims in antiquity to carry water or oil.

Polemic (Gk. *polemos*, "war") An argument intended to support a specific position via attacks on a contrary position, usually in religion or politics.

Potsherd (sherd) Broken pieces of pottery that may be used to date archaeological strata.

Polydactylism (Gk. *polys*, "many" + *daktylos* "finger") A congenital physical anomaly in which a person is born with extra digits on the hands and/or feet.

Polytheism (Gk. *polys*, "many" + *theos*, "god[s]") The belief and worship of multiple deities, usually assembled into a pantheon of gods and goddesses.

Probe An exploratory trench or square dug to determine the extent or nature of a locus for future excavation.

Proto-aeolic capital An architectural feature of the ashlar masonry construction system decorated in high relief on both faces and with volutes springing from both sides of a central triangle, a schematization of a palm tree. The form originated in early Israel (tenth century BC) and is a characteristic feature of royal centers in the Iron Age.

Provenance The place of origin or earliest known history of something. In archaeology, it is crucial that provenance is known for an artifact to be useful as a diagnostic tool or in the interpretation of a site's history. Unprovenanced artifacts, usually coming from secondary sources outside a licensed excavation, such as the antiquity market, have limited value as educational examples of the material culture during the archaeological periods.

Pseudepigrapha (Gk. *pseudis* "false" + *epigraphein* "to inscribe or write") commonly refers to works of Jewish religious literature written between 200 BC and AD 200.

Qumran An archaeological site located on a plateau northwest of the Dead Sea that hosted a Jewish community from the Iron Age II through the end of the Second Temple Period (until its destruction by the Romans in AD 68). The Jewish community of the Second Temple period produced and preserved the Dead Sea Scrolls.

Radiocarbon dating (also carbon dating or carbon-14 dating) A method for determining the age of an object containing organic material by using the properties of radiocarbon (C-14), a radioactive isotope of carbon.

Relative dating The science of determining the relative order of past events (the age of an object in comparison to another) as opposed to absolute dating (determining the estimated age).

Reventment A structure (dirt, stone, or mudbrick) placed against a wall to provide strength and prevent erosion.

Roman imperial cult An element of Roman state religion in which emperors and members of their families were regarded as gods.

Sancta (pl. sanctum, Lat. *sanctus* "holy") Holy or sacred places and the vessels and utensils associated with them and their rituals.

Sanhedrin (Heb. *sanhedrin*, Gk. *synhedrion* "sitting together," hence "assembly, council") A term designating the Jewish political assembly at Jerusalem that represented the highest magistracy of the country.

Scarab (Gk. *karabos* "beetle") An Egyptian seal made in the shape of a sacred scarab beetle.

Scriptorium (pl. scriptoria) A formal facility used by scribes to produce and copy documents.

Sarcophagus (pl. sarcophagi) Literally "flesh-eater," a stone coffin with inscriptions and decorations.

Second Jewish Revolt (Bar Kokhba Revolt) Jewish resistance to Roman rule in the Roman province of Judea led by Simon bar Kosiba (also known as Bar Kokhba, "son of a star") from AD 132–136.

Second Temple Period (536 BC–AD 70) The period from the return of the Babylonian exiles to rebuild the temple to its destruction by the Romans.

Septuagint (abbr. LXX, Gk./Lat. *septuginta* "the seventy") The Koine Greek translation of the Hebraic textual tradition that included certain texts which were later included in the canonical Hebrew Bible (Old Testament) made in Alexandria, Egypt by Jewish scholars (ca. 280–150 BC).

Shaft tomb A type of vertical underground burial chamber dug down into a deep rectangular burial structure. Such tombs were often built with a stone floor and lined with mudbrick, masonry, or wood.

Sherd (also shard) A fragment of pottery or other artifact collected to determine the pottery assemblage present at a site.

Shuruppak (from Sumerian "the healing place") An ancient Sumerian city dedicated to Ninlil (the goddess of grain and the air) situated about 35 miles south of Nippur on the banks of the Euphrates and identified with the modern site of Tell Fara.

Sifting The process of filtering soil samples through wire mesh with mounted or hand-held screens to separate out small artifacts such as coins, beads, bits of glass, and metal. Dry sifting involves using only the screens while wet sifting includes the addition of water to separate lighter organic material from heavier non-organic material.

Slip The thin clay coating applied to pottery by dipping the pot into a thick clay liquid then firing it.

Square The basic area of excavation developed for precise documentation of the location of artifacts within a numbered grid system. The standard size is 5 meters x 5 meters, leaving a 1 meter unexcavated balk on the north and east side.

Strabo A Greek geographer, philosopher, and historian who lived in Asia Minor during the transitional period of the Roman Republic into the Roman Empire (44 BC – AD 18). He wrote *Historical Sketches* comprising the history of the known world beginning from the conquest of Greece by the Romans and *Geography* in which he recounts ancient sites.

Stratigraphy The study of soil layers (strata) and layering (stratification) with a focus on the order and relative position of strata and their relationship to one another (relative dating) and the analysis of the layers with archaeological remains to understand the history of occupation at a given site.

Stele or stela (pl. *stelai* or *stelae*, Gk. *stile* "pillar") An upright stone pillar often containing an inscription to commemorate a military victory, boundary, or tombstone.

Stoa (Gk. *stoa*, Lat. *porlicus* "porch") A long, covered hallway to protect the public from the elements, supported with a colonnade of pillars, often with a portico and wall on one side.

Stratification The layers (strata) of a tel created by successive destructions. Consists of archaeological deposits identified as periods of occupation containing artifacts.

Strigil A curved bronze instrument designed to scrape oil and dirt from the arms and legs of athletes and for use in the Roman bathhouse.

Stratum (Lat. *stratum*, "a spread for a bed, quilt, or blanket," pl. strata) A horizontal layer of soil containing artifacts and debris representing a particular time period and dated by using pottery and coins.

Suzerain-vassal treaty A form of an ancient Near Eastern legal document that includes a preamble identifying the parties involved in the treaty: the king or dominant party, the subjugated people, and a prologue that lists the deeds already performed by the suzerain on behalf of the vassal.

Tacitus Roman senator and historian of the Roman Empire. His major works include *Annals* and *Histories*, which examine the Roman emperors beginning with the death of Augustus (AD 14) through the reigns Tiberius, Claudius, and Nero to the first years of the Jewish Revolt against Rome (AD 66–69).

Talmud (Heb. *talmud* "instruction") The collection of rabbinic writings that form the authoritative body of Jewish tradition comprising Jewish civil and ceremonial law, including the Mishnah. There are two versions of the Talmud: the Babylonian Talmud (which dates from the fifth century AD but includes earlier material) and the earlier Palestinian or Jerusalem Talmud.

Targum (Heb. for "translation, or interpretation") Aramaic translation of the Hebrew Bible (Tanach). Collected over a five hundred year period, it is difficult to date individual passages. Fragments were found at Qumran among the Dead Sea Scrolls.

Tel (Heb. *tel* "mound or hill") An unnatural mound created by the repeated destruction and rebuilding of ancient cities on the same site.

Temple Mount Sifting Project An archaeological project undertaken by the Israeli Antiquities Authority to sift and reclaim artifacts from some 20,000 tons of soil and debris dumped in the Kidron Valley by the Islamic Waqf as a result of their construction of the Al-Marwani Mosque in the area of Solomon's Stables.

Temple Scroll (11Q19) A Dead Sea scroll originally discovered in Cave 11 near Qumran but only recovered decades later from the home of an antiquities merchant. The longest of the Dead Sea Scrolls (27 ft), it is written as a revelation from God to Moses and describes the building of an ideal Jewish temple with extensive regulations about temple ritual and priestly practice as well as other Jewish laws.

Terracotta Reddish clay or unglazed ceramic pottery.

Tessera (pl. tesserae, Gk. *tessares* "four") Small, individual square stones used to create a picture or a mosaic.

Tetragrammaton (Gk. *tetragrammaton* "having four letters") It has become a technical term for the name YHWH in the Bible.

Tetrarch (Lat. *tetrarches*) A governor of the fourth part of a provence in ancient Rome, first instituted by Diocletian (AD 292).

Thanksgiving Scroll (1QHa; Heb. *hodayot* "thanks, thanksgiving") One of the first seven Dead Sea Scrolls discovered in 1947 that repeats the phrase "I thank you" in its record of extrabiblical psalms or hymns.

Theophany (Gk. *theophaneia* "appearance of a god") A term that refers to the appearance of a deity to a human.

Tosefta (Heb. "supplement") A large collection of writings, written in Mishnaic Hebrew, that are similar to the Mishnah but not as authoritative for religious Jews.

Triglyphs Ornamental decorations above columns.

Tri-partite A structure constructed with three separate, but connected, buildings, such as a temple with an entrance porch (*ulam*), center room (*debir*), and inner room (*hekel*).

Typology The study and comparison of the various shapes of artifacts for their classification.

Tyropoeon Valley (Heb. *ha gay*) The name for Jerusalem's transverse valley between the Hinnom Valley and Kidron Valley. Also called the Cheesemaker's Valley.

Ugaritic The Northwest Semitic language of Ugarit, spoken by the people of Ugarit (Ras Shamra).

Umayyad The first Arab dynasty of caliphs who ruled the Jerusalem Empire (AD 661–750) and whose capital was Damascus.

Uncial A style of manuscript writing that used capital letters and was common in Greek and Latin manuscripts from the fourth to eighth centuries AD.

Uniformitarianism The theory that the same natural laws and processes that operate in the universe now have always operated in the universe in the past and apply everywhere in the universe, as opposed to the view of catastrophism that argues history has been punctuated by world-changing events.

Uruk The leading city of its day in ancient Mesopotamia founded by King Enmerkar ca. 4500 BC. Located in the southern region of Sumer, it was most famous for its king, Gilgamesh, and the epic tale of his quest for immortality recorded in the Gilgamesh Epic.

Vellum (French *velin* from *vel*, "veal") A fine parchment prepared from the skin of a young calf or lamb and used by scribes to write documents such as biblical manuscripts.

Votive (Lat. *votivus* from *votum*, "vow") A object dedicated in fulfillment of a vow for a religious purpose.

Vulgate (Lat. *versio vulgate*, "edition in vernacular language") The Latin translation of the Bible by St. Jerome (fourth century AD) and the official Bible used by the Roman Catholic Church.

Wadi A dried up waterbed or gully which only flows during the rainy season.

War Scroll (1QM, 4Q491-496, War Rule) Also known as The War of the Sons of Light against the Sons of Darkness, it is one of the seven original Dead Sea Scrolls discovered in Qumran in 1947. It gives marching orders to faithful Jewish fighters for a final war at the end of days.

Yehud Name for Judah beginning in the Persia period.

Zadokite priests (Heb. *bene tsadok* "sons of Zadok") A family of Jewish priests descended from Zadok, the first high priest in Solomon's Temple, and that remained in service until the Hasmonean period.

Zealots A rebellious Jewish sect who opposed Roman domination during the intertestamental period. A sect of the Zealots was founded by Judas the Galilean, who led the Jewish revolt against Rome in AD 6. Other notable Zealots include the Maccabean leaders, Mattathias and his sons and followers, Menahem, who attempted to seize the leadership of the anti-Roman revolt in AD 66, and Eleazar ben Yar, leader of the Jewish revolt at Masada (AD 66–73). Simon, one of the twelve apostles, was also a Zealot, along with the apostle Paul.

Ziggurat (Akkadian *ziqqurratu*, from *zaqāru*, "to build high") A Mesopotamian pyramid-like mound of mud brick constructed with a temple on top.

Zoomorphic Something described or designed in the form of an animal.

Notes

Preface

1. On this point, see the critiques of pseudo-science and archaeological fraud by Robert R. Cargill and others at http://www.bibleinterp.com/articles/frauds.shtml and those of Eric Cline, *From Eden to Exile: Unraveling the Mysteries of the Bible* (Washington, DC: National Geographic Society, 2008). Although we do not agree with all of the conclusions made by these scholars, we agree in general with their guidelines for academic research and insistence upon such researchers having experience in the field of archaeology. See also Randall Price and Gordon Franz, *Setting the Record Straight: Answering Archaeology's Curious Claims* (Lampion Press), forthcoming.

Introduction

1. Guy Gibbon, *Critically Reading the Theory and Methods of Archaeology* (Lanham: Altamira Press, 2014), 7–9.
2. J. Edward Wright "Commendatory Preface" to Mark Elliot, *Biblical Interpretation Using Archaeological Evidence 1900–1930* (Lewiston: Mellen, 2002), ii.
3. W. F. Albright, *The Archaeology of Palestine*, rev. ed. (Harmondswort, Middlesex: Penguin Books, 1960), 128.
4. Statement made in "Bible Secrets Revealed: Lost in Translation," *History Channel*, November 13, 2013, http://www.history.com/shows/bible-secrets-revealed/videos/bible-secrets-revealed-lost-in-translation.
5. John N. Oswalt, *The Bible among the Myths: Unique Revelation or Just Ancient Literature* (Grand Rapids: Zondervan, 2009), 138.
6. See William Dever, *What Did the Biblical Writers Know and When Did They Know It?: What Archaeology Can Tell Us about the Reality of Ancient Israel* (Grand Rapids: Eerdmans, 2001).
7. See Mark Elliot, *Biblical Interpretation Using Archaeological Evidence 1900–1930* (Lewiston: Mellen, 2002).
8. Frederic R. Brandfon, "The Limits of Evidence: Archaeology and Objectivity," *Maarav* 4 (1987): 5–43.
9. This is best accomplished by studying the biblical text and the archaeological data each according to their own interpretive processes before seeking to relate them to one another.
10. Thanks for this insight is expressed to Tom Davis, Tandy Institute for Archaeology, Southwestern Baptist Theological Seminary.
11. This method is defended and employed in Dever's books, *What Did the Biblical Writers Know and When Did They Know It?* and *Who Were the Early Isrelites and Where Did They Come From?* (Grand Rapids: Eerdmans, 2003).
12. F. Brandfon, "The Limits of Evidence: Archaeology and Objectivity," has challenged whether archaeological data can be objectively interpreted. He contends that the textual source's historical memory, including biblical memory, is unreliable, especially as transmitted over time. However, if there is no means of arriving at an objective interpretation of archaeological data, then nothing of the past can be known with any certainty. It is for for this reason that methods of critical interpretation were developed by scholars to identify historical "errors" in ancient texts and develop a reliable corpus of material for comparative research.
13. The methodology has been adapted from Chet Roden, "A Hermeneutic of Convergence: Moving Beyond the Intersection of Archaeology and the Bible" (paper presented to the Near East Archaeological Society at the Evangelical Theological Society, San Diego, CA, November, 2014): 7–19. Roden developed his methodology based on the discussion in John C. Laughlin, "On the Convergence of Texts and Artifacts: Using Archaeology to Teach the Hebrew Bible," in *Between Text and Artifact: Integrating Archaeology in Biblical Studies*, ed. Milton C. Moreland (Atlanta: Society of Biblical Literature, 2003): 115–132.
14. Magazines designed for a popular (non-technical) audience include *Biblical Archaeology Review, Bible and Spade, Artifax, Archaeology, Archaeological Diggings*. Web-based resources include biblicalarchaeology.org (Biblical Archaeology Society; BAS Library, Bible History Daily), biblearchaeology.org (Associates for Biblical Research), lifeandland.org, christiananswers.net/archaeology/home.html.
15. Interview with Amihai Mazar, Institute of Archaeology at The Hebrew University of Jerusalem, Jerusalem, October 1996.
16. William R. Osborne, "Abraham and History (Part 1)," October 23, 2011, http://lawprophetsandwritings.com/author/rusty_osborne/.
17. The Hebrew University of Jerusalem, "Earliest Semitic Text Revealed In Egyptian Pyramid Inscription" *Science Daily*, January 29, 2007, http://www.sciencedaily.com/releases/2007/01/070129100250.htm.
18. Harold Scanlin, *The Dead Sea Scrolls and Modern Translations of the Old Testament* (Carol Stream: Tyndale House, 1993), 27.
19. Interview with Amihai Mazar, Institute of Archaeology at The Hebrew University of Jerusalem, Jerusalem, October 1996.
20. Two excellent sources for further study on hieroglyphics include: W. Vivian Davies, *Egyptian Hieroglyphics*, Reading the Past Series 6 (Berkeley: University of California Press, 1987), and Karl-Theodor Zauzich, *Hieroglyphs without Mystery*, trans. and adapted by Ann Macy Roth (Austin: University of Texas Press, 1992).
21. For more information on the Rosetta Stone see the booklet, *The Rosetta Stone* (London: Department of Assyrian and Egyptian Antiquities of the British Museum) and P. Kyle McCarter, Jr. *Ancient Inscriptions* (Washington: Biblical Archaeology Society, 1997), 35–39.
22. Gonzalo Báez-Camargo, *ACB* (New York: Doubleday, 1984), xxii.
23. See Norman Herz and Ervan G. Garrison, *Geological Methods for Archaeology* (Oxford: Oxford University Press, 1998), 147–180.

24. Peretz Reuven, "Wooden Beams from Herod's Temple Mount: Do They Still Exist? *BAR* 39:3 (May/June 2013): 40–47.

25. Gila Kahila Bar-Gal, Tzviki Rosenerg, and Charles Greenblatt, "Animal Remains from Khirbet Qumran: A Case Study of Two Bones (QUM 392 and 393) from Two Bone Burials" in *Holistic Qumran: Trans-Disciplinary Research of Qumran and the Dead Sea Scrolls*, STDJ Series 87, ed. Jan Gunneweg, Annemie Adriaens, Joris Dik (Leiden: Brill, 2010), 67–78.

26. Early Bronze Age dates are based on synchronisms in Amihai Mazar, *Archaeology of the Land of the Bible 10,000–586 BCE*, AYBRL 1 (New Haven: Yale University Press, 1992); K. A. Kitchen, "Egyptian Chronology in the Historical Chronology of Ancient Egypt, A Current Assessment," *Acta Archaeologica* 67 (1996): 1–13; K. A. Kitchen, "The Basis of Egyptian Chronology in Relation to the Bronze Age," *High, Middle Or Low?: Acts of an International Colloquium on Absolute Chronology Held at the University of Gothenburg 20–22 August, 1987*, ed. Paul Astrom, 1:37–55. The maragin for error in the Egyptian dates in the Early Bronze as well as the uncertainty of synchronisms between Egypt and Israel are based on K. A. Kitchen, "The Chronology of Ancient Egypt," *World Archaeology* 23:2 (October 1991): 201–8 (Table 1). Dates for the Middle Bronze Age are based on William G. Dever, *BA* 50:3 (1987): 148–77, and Manfred Bietak, "Egypt and Canaan during the Middle Bronze Age," *BASOR* 281 (1991); 27–72. Egyptian dates are those of Wente and Van Siclen, *Studies in Honor of George R. Hughes*, Studies in Ancient Oriental Civilization 39 (Chicago: University of Chicago Press, 1977), Table 1.

27. David Rohl, *Exodus: Myth or History* (St. Louis Park, MN: Thinking Man Media, 2015), John J. Bimson, *Redating the Exodus and Conquest*, JSOT (1978). These views have been popularized in the documentary film Exodus: Patterns of Evidence, produced by Timothy Mahoney, 2014. However, in his book, 331, Rohl appears to settle on the early date of 1550 BC for the Exodus.

Chapter 1

1. Kenneth A. Kitchen, *OROT* (Grand Rapids: Eerdmans, 2003), 500.

2. William, G. Dever, *What Did the Biblical Writers Know and When Did They Know It?*, 298.

3. See "Archaeology, Politics, and Local Communities" in *Archaeology, Politics, and the Media. Proceedings of the Duke University Conference, April 23–24, 2009*, ed. Eric Meyers and Carol Meyers (Winona Lake: Eisenbrauns, 2012), 139–219.

Chapter 2

1. *COS* 1.159:516.

2. Giovanni Pettinato, "Ebla and the Bible," *BA* 43 (1960): 208.

3. Mark Chavalas, "Assyriology and Biblical Studies" in *Mesopotamia and the Bible*, eds. Mark Chavalas and Lawson Younger (Grand Rapids: Baker, 2002), 41; and with reference to Alfonso Archi, "The Epigraphic Evidence from Ebla and the Old Testament," *Bib* 60 (1979): 356–66.

4. See Gordon J. Wenham, "Sanctuary Symbolism in the Garden of Eden Story," *Proceedings of the Ninth World Congress of Jewish Studies, Jerusalem, August 4–12, 1985. Division A: The Period of the Bible* (Jerusalem: World Union of Jewish Studies, 1986), 23; Randall Price, *The Desecration and Restoration of the Temple as an Eschatological Motif in the Tanach, Jewish Apocalyptic Literature and the New Testament* (Michigan: UMI, 1994), 182–211; and idem, *The Temple in Bible Prophecy: A Definitive Look at Its Past, Present and Future* (Eugene, OR: Harvest House Publishers, 2005), 196–200.

5. One copy that contains the full list is the Weld-Blundell Prism housed today in the Asmolean Museum of Art and Archaeology at the University of Oxford. For details see Clyde E. Fant and Mitchell G. Reddish, *Lost Treasures of the Bible: Understanding the Bible through Archaeological Artifacts in World Museums* (Grand Rapids: Eerdmans, 2008), 22–26.

6. Raúl Erlando López, "The Antediluvian Patriarchs and the Sumerian King List," *Journal of Creation* 12:3 (1998): 347–57, has suggested that the Sumerian scribe that composed the original antediluvian list had available a document containing numerical information on the ages of eight of the patriarchs, similar to that of the Genesis record. The lives of the biblical patriarchs have a precision of one year. Not including Adam and Noah, following the style of the King List, and rounding the lives of the patriarchs to two digits, the sum of the lives includes six 10^3 signs, six 10^2 signs, and six 10 signs. If the Sumerian scribe mistakenly interpreted the biblical account as being written in the sexagesimal numerical system all durations except two are expressed as multiples of 60^2. A simple tally of the ciphers used yields six 10 x 60^2 signs, six 60^2 signs, and six 60 signs.

7. Kenneth Kitchen, *The Bible In Its World* (Downers Grove: InterVarsity Press, 1978), 30.

8. Thorkild Jacobsen, *The Sumerian King List*. Assyriological Studies 11 (Chicago: University of Chicago Press, 1939), 77. For further information, see Raul E. Lopez, "The Antediluvian Patriarchs and the Sumerian King List," *CEN Technical Journal* 12 (1998): 347–57.

9. Lines 6–7 of "The Ark Tablet," translated by Irving Finkel, *The Ark Before Noah: Decoding the Story of the Flood* (New York: Doubleday, 2014), 125.

10. For more details on this discovery and its content see W. G. Lambert and A. R. Millard, *Atra-Hasis: The Babylonian Story of the Flood* (Oxford: Oxford University Press, 1969) and A. R. Millard, "A New Babylonian 'Genesis' Story," *TB* 18 (1967): 3–18.

11. For these views and discussion see John H. Walton, *The Lost World of Genesis One: Ancient Cosmology and the Origins Debate* (Downers Grove: IVP Academic, 2009) and John N. Oswalt, *The Bible among the Myths*.

12. Eric H. Cline, *From Eden to Exile: Unraveling the Mysteries of the Bible* (Washington, DC: National Geographic Society, 2007), 36–37.

13. For a thorough treatment of the ancient Near Eastern parallels from an evangelical perspective see John H. Walton, *Ancient Israelite Literature in Its Cultural Setting: A Survey of Parallels*

Between Biblical and Ancient Near Eastern Texts (Grand Rapids: Zondervan, 1989).

14. See Tikva Frymer-Kensky, "What the Babylonian Flood Stories Can and Cannot Teach Us About the Genesis Flood," *BAR* (November/December 1978): 32–35.

15. There are numerous instances of non-canonical works cited in both the Old and New Testaments. See Josh 10:13; 1 Sam 24:13; 2 Sam 1:18; Luke 4:23; Acts 17:28; Titus 1:12; Jude 14.

16. Even if the structure of these Mesopotamian narratives is similar to that in Gen 1–11, the congruence could be the result of using an accepted literary convention of the time.

17. Umberto Cassuto, *Commentary on Genesis: From Adam to Noah*, part 1 (Jerusalem: Magnes Press, 1961), 2:20.

18. A. R. Millard, "A New Babylonian 'Genesis' Story," 17–18.

19. Todd S. Beall, "Noah's Flood: Just Another Pagan Myth?" *B&S* 28:4 (Fall 2015): 102.

20. The word means "box" or "container" but context determines its specific connotation as "vessel," such as in the two examples given in the text.

21. "Atra-hasis" *COS*, 1.130:452.

22. Syncellus, *Chronological Excerpts*, 55.

23. "Atra-hasis," *COS*, 1.130:452.

24. The use of comparable metaphor in the Gilgamesh Epic suggests that the reference to "dragonflies [filling] the river" is simply an evocative image of death rather than a literal description of the flood.

25. This is not the only conclusion that the use of the plural requires. Traditional Mt. Ararat is characterized as a double mountain: "Greater Ararat" and "Lesser Ararat." In reality there are two mountains side by side on a vast plain with no mountain ranges in the immediate vicinity. If traditional Mt. Ararat (*Ağrı Dağı*) was the site, the use of the plural might be intended to identify these specific "mountains," rather than a general reference to regional mountains.

26. Irving Finkel, *The Ark Before Noah: Decoding the Story of the Flood* (New York: Doubleday, 2014), 275.

27. Ibid., 295.

28. Igdir University (eastern Turkey) geologist Memet Salih Bayraktutan discovered a sedimentary bed (deep marine deposit) in the Ahora Valley (of Mt. Ararat). He took samples of an erratic rock piece of this settled sedimentary basement and argues this formed the basement of Mt. Ararat during an early stage of volcanic eruption. This would provide evidence countering the late-forming volcano theory that would disqualify Mt. Ararat as the biblical landing site.

29. See Rex Geissler, "Mount Ararat Archaeological Research Reports" (*Proceedings of the International Noah and Judi Mountain Symposium hosted by University of Şirnak*, July 2013), 1–59; Cevat Başaran, Vedat Keleş, and Rex Geissler, "Mount Ararat Archaeological Survey," *B&S* 21:3 (2008): 70–96.

30. Yilmaz Güner, "Is Noah's Ark on Mount Ararat? Geomorphological Development of the Dogubeyazit-Telçeker Landslide Which is Assumed to be Related to Noah's Ark," *Bulletin of Geomorphology* 14 (1986): 27–37.

31. Peter Van der Veen and Uwe Zerbst, "Nimrod the Mighty Hunter" *Journal of the Ancient Chronology Forum* 9 (2004): 35.

32. John Walton, "The Mesopotamian background of the Tower of Babel Account and Its Implications," *BBR* 5 (1995): 155–75. The cited phrase is from *Inanna's Descent to the Netherworld*. See Falkenstein, "The Exaltation of Inanna" *AfO* 14 (1942) 115:14–15; W. W. Hallo and J. van Dijk, *The Exaltation of Inanna* (New Haven: Yale University Press, 1968), lines 5–8.

33. Jack Finegan, *Archaeological History of the Ancient Near East* (Boulder, CO: Westview, 1979): 8.

34. Walton, "The Mesopotamian background of the Tower of Babel Account and Its Implications," 168.

35. A. R. George, trans. and ed., *Cuneiform Royal Inscriptions and Related Texts in the Schøyen Collection*, Cornell University Studies in Assyriology and Sumerology 17 (CDL Press, 2011).

36. The scholars collaborating on the publication of this inscription and one hundred more cuneiform texts in the *Schøyen Collection* include A. R. George, M. Civil, F. Frame, P. Steinkeller, F. Vallat, K. Volk, M. Weeden, and C. Wilcke.

37. W. F. Albright, *Yahweh and the Gods of Canaan* (Garden City: Doubleday, 1968): 51, 62–73.

38. E. A. Speiser, *Genesis*, AB 1 (Garden City: Doubleday, 1964), 85–94.

39. Cyrus Gordon, "Abraham and the Merchants of Ura," *JNES* (January 1958): 28–30.

40. David Noel Freedman, "The Real Story of the Ebla Tablets," *BA* (December 1978): 147–58.

41. M. J. Selman, "The Social Environment of the Patriarchs," *TB* 119 (1976): 119.

42. Alfred J. Hoerth, *Archaeology and the Old Testament* (Grand Rapids: Baker, 1998), 73–4.

43. Thomas L. Thompson, *Early History of the Israelite People: From the Written and Archaeological Sources* (Leiden: Brill, 2000), 121.

44. John Van Seters, *Abraham in History and Tradition* (New Haven: Yale University Press, 1975), 121.

45. Mark S. Gignillat, *A Brief History of Old Testament Criticism* (Grand Rapids: Zondervan, 2012), 57–76.

46. Victor H. Matthews, "Pastoralists and Patriarchs," *BA* 44 (1981): 217.

47. M. Weinfeld, "The Covenant of Grant in the Old Testament and in the Ancient Near East," *JAOS* 90 (1970): 202. See also Tim Hegg, "The Covenant of Grant and the Abrahamic Covenant" (paper read at the Evangelical Theological Society, 1989), http://www.torahresource.com/EnglishArticles/Grant%20Treaty.pdf.

48. K. A. Kitchen, "The Patriarchal Age: Myth or History?" *BAR* 21 (1995): 48.

49. Kitchen, *OROT*, 364–368.

50. Kitchen, "The Patriarchal Age: Myth or History," 57.

51. K. A. Kitchen, *On the Reliability of the Old Testament* (Grand Rapids: Eerdmans, 2003), 313–72.

52. See Kitchen, "The Patriarchal Age: Myth or History?," 90, 92. Ronald Hendel argued against Kitchen that this type of name is perfectly normal through all periods of Northwest Semitic. See "Finding Historical Memories in the Patriarchal Narratives," *BAR* 21:4 (July/August 1995): 57.

53. Roland Hendel, "Finding Historical Memories in the Patriarchal Narratives," 58.

54. A previous generation of ancient Near Eastern scholars such as Cyrus H Gordon, Ephraim Speiser, and William F. Albright cited parallels from the Mari and Nuzi archives as evidence of either a Middle Bronze or a Late Bronze date for the origin of these stories. However, these parallels have since been recognized as realistic only in the Iron Age and have been largely discounted as evidence for the patriarchs.

55. The "unusual" word order is a textual variant that occurs only in the Samaritan Pentateuch, which reverses the order of "male donkeys" and "female servants." However, several other textual witnesses, such as the Septuagint, Targum, Latin Vulgate, and Peshitta, all preserve the more difficult reading. This is not surprising as the Samaritan Pentateuch is known for amending grammatical difficulties (see Emanuel Tov, *Textual Criticism of the Hebrew Bible*, 2nd ed. [Leiden: Brill, 2011], 82–83). This scribal tendency recalls a general principle for discovering the autographic reading: the more difficult reading is usually preferred unless meaningful factors suggest otherwise. Moreover, a careful look at the other various lists of the Patriarch's possessions does not reveal any special motive for inserting or adding anything to Genesis 12:6. From a pure linguistic perspective these observations can hardly be seen as clear-cut evidence of a later elaboration.

56. Claus Westermann, *Genesis 12–36* (Minneapolis: Fortress, 1994), 165; E. A. Speiser, *Genesis*, 90.

57. John Van Seeters, *Abraham in History and Tradition* (New Haven: Yale University Press, 1975):18.

58. Edwin Yamauchi, "Abraham and Archaeology: Anachronisms or Adaptations" *BAR* 39:3 (May/June 2013): 15–32.

59. M. Ripinsky, "The Camel in Dynastic Egypt." *JEA* 17 (1985): 131–41.

60. R. W. Bulliet and Randall Yonker, *The Camel and the Wheel* (New York: Columbia University Press, 1997), 36.

61. M. Heide, "The Domestication of the Camel: Biological, Archaeological and Inscriptional Evidence from Mesopotamia, Egypt and Arabia, and Literary Evidence from the Hebrew Bible," *Ugarit-Forschungen* 42 (2010): 337.

62. Ibid., 338–43.

63. Ibid., 337–38.

64. Ibid., 338.

65. Ibid., 344.

66. Ibid., 345.

67. Ibid; Wiktor Sarianidi, *Gonurdepe. City of Kings and Gods*, figures 94–97; 252.

68. *CAD* I/J, 2; Yitschak Sefati, *Love Songs in Sumerian Literature: Critical Editions of the Dumuzi-Inanna Songs* (Ramat Gan: Bar-Ilan University Press, 1998), 221–22 and W. Horowitz, "'The Ship of the Desert, the Donkey of the Sea': The Camel in Early Mesopotamia Revisited" in *Studies in the Bible, Ancient Near Eastern Literature, and Postbiblical Judaism presented to Shalom M. Paul on the Occasion of His Seventieth Birthday*, Birkat Shalom, edited by Chaim Cohen

et al. (Winona Lake, IN: Eisenbrauns, 2008), 2:604 based on the tablet Ni 9602, as cited in M. Heide, "The Domestication of the Camel: Biological, Archaeological and Inscriptional Evidence from Mesopotamia, Egypt and Arabia, and Literary Evidence from the Hebrew Bible," *UF* 42 (2010): 356.

69. Heide, 356. The primary source can be found in *The Assyrian Dictionary of the Oriental Institute of the University of Chicago* I/J, 2 (lines 18–27).

70. Heide, "The Domestication of the Camel," 358.

71. H. B. Huffmon, *Amorite Personal Names in the Mari Texts* (Chicago: University of Chicago Press, 1965), 128–29.

72. Gerhard von Rad, *Genesis: A Commentary*, trans. John H. Marks (Philadelphia: Westminster, 1961), 171.

73. See Kitchen, "The Patriarchal Age: Myth or History?," 56.

74. See R. K. Harrison, "Arioch" in *The International Standard Bible Encyclopedia* ed. names (Grand Rapids: Eerdmans, 1982), 290. Gerhard von Rad, *Genesis: A Commentary*, 171, believes that this is the same person.

75. K. A. Kitchen, *Ancient Orient and the Old Testament* (Downers Grove: InterVarsity Press, 1966), 44.

76. For these examples see *Cambridge Ancient History*, ed. J. Boardman, I.E.S. Edwards, et al., 3rd ed. (Cambridge: Cambridge University Press), II/1 (1973), 272, 820–821; II/2 (1975), 1041; and III/2 (1991), 748.

77. von Rad, *Genesis*, 171.

78. See John C. Studenroth, "Archaeology and the Higher Criticism of Genesis 14," in *Evidence for Faith: Deciding the God Question*, ed. John Warwick Montgomery (Dallas: Probe, 1991), 159, 162.

79. See Kitchen, *Ancient Orient and the Old Testament*, 46, 73; "The Patriarchal Age: Myth or History?," 57.

80. See Bruce Vawter, *On Genesis: A New Reading* (New York: Doubleday, 1977), 188; Speiser, *Genesis*, AB, 107–8.

81. For details supporting these conclusions see Gordon J. Wenham, *Genesis 1–15*, WBC 1 (Waco, Texas: Word Books, 1987), 318–320.

82. According to Josh 19:47 the site was also known as Leshem.

83. Interview at Hebrew Union College Skirball Museum, Jerusalem (October 12, 1996).

84. Ibid.

85. Gérard Gertoux, *The Pharaoh of the Exodus. Fairy Tale or Real History?* The Crying Stones, No. 4 (Maison de l'Orient Université Lyon 2: LULU, 2017), 1–230; Douglas Petrovich, "Amenhotep II and the Historicity of the Exodus-Pharaoh," TMSJ 17/1 (Spring 2006) 81–110.

86. See Bryant G. Wood, "Recent Research on the Date and Setting of the Exodus" (October 9, 2009), http://www.biblearchaeology.org/post/2009/10/19/Recent-Research-on-the-Date-and-Setting-of-the-Exodus.aspx.

87. James K. Hoffmeier, "What is the Biblical Date for the Exodus?," *JETS* 50 (2007):225–47; and James K. Hoffmeier, "Why a Historical Exodus is Essential for Theology" in *Do Historical Matters Matter to Faith?* eds. James K. Hoffmeier and Dennis R. Magary (Wheaton, IL: Crossway, 2012), 129–30.

88. Brad C. Sparks, "Egyptian Texts relating to the Exodus: Discussions of Exodus Parallels in the Egyptology Literature," in

Israel's Exodus in Transdisciplinary Perspective: Text, Archaeology, Culture, and Geoscience, ed. Thomas E. Levy, Thomas Schneider, William H. C. Propp (Switzerland: Springer International Publishing, 2015), 259.

89. Douglas Petrovitch, *The World's Oldest Alphabet: Hebrew as the Language of the Proto-Consonantal Script* (Jerusalem: Carta, 2016), 28, 115–17, 151–53, 168–72, 180–82, 186–88, 191–200.

90. For a table listing the Egyptologists, archaeologists, and Semiticists publishing Exodus parallels, see Sparks, 263–66.

91. James K. Hoffmeier, "Egyptologists and the Israelite Exodus from Egypt" and Brad C. Sparks, "Egyptian Texts relating to the Exodus: Discussions of Exodus Parallels in the Egyptology Literature," in *Israel's Exodus in Transdisciplinary Perspective: Text, Archaeology, Culture, and Geoscience*, eds. Thomas E. Levy, Thomas Schneider, William H.C. Propp, Quantitative Methods in the Humanities and Social Sciences (Switzerland: Springer International Publishing, 2015), 197–208, 259–81.

92. See "The Divine Nomination of Thutmose III," *ANET*, 446–47.

93. This relationship was especially connected with Pharaohs Thutmose III and his son Amenhotep II. Egyptian theology, enhanced by their military accomplishments, gave them the status of "the sovereign god(s) of heaven and earth."

94. See H. Frankfort, *Kingship and the Gods* (Chicago: University of Chicago Press, 1948), 5; idem, *Ancient Egyptian Religion* (New York: Columbia University Press, 1948), 30; I. Engnell, *Studies in Divine Kingship in the Ancient Near East* (Oxford: Basil Blackwell, 1967), 4–15.

95. See F. W. Read, *Egyptian Religion and Ethics* (London: Watts & Co., 1925), 110–11.

96. For the full documentation of this ritual see A. Hermann, "Das steinhartes Herz," *Jahrbuch für Antike und Christentum* 4 (Munster: Aschendorffsche Verlagsbuchandlung, 1961), 102–3.

97. Christine El Mahdy, *Mummies, Myth and Magic in Ancient Egypt* (London: Thames and Hudson, 1998), 153–54.

98. For other incantations see J. Zandee, *Death as an Enemy* (Leiden: Brill, 1960), 259–62.

99. See James E. Harris and Kent R. Weeks, *X-Raying the Pharaohs* (New York: Scribner's Sons, 1973), 49.

100. See further, E. A. W. Budge, *Egyptian Magic* (London: K. Paul, Trench, Tribner & Co., 1899), 35–37.

101. For a complete analysis and defense of this position in the Exodus plague narratives see Gregory K. Beale, "The Exodus Hardening Motif of YHWH as a Polemic," ThM thesis, Dallas Theological Seminary (Dallas, 1976), especially 46–52.

102. Richard Steiner, lecture entitled "Proto-Canaanite Spells in the Pyramid Texts: a First Look at the History of Hebrew in the Third Millennium BCE."

103. John Merlin Powis Smith, William Hayes Ward, and Julius A. Bewer, *Micah, Zephaniah, Nahum, Habakkuk, Obadiah and Joel*, ICC (New York: Scribner's Sons, 1911), 121.

104. Yair Hoffman, "A North Israelite Typological Myth and a Judean Historical Tradition: The Exodus in Hosea and Amos," *VT* 39/2 (1989): 170.

105. Ronald E. Clements "The Book of Exodus," *IDBSup*, 310.

106. Menahem Haran, "The Exodus," *IDBSup*, 304.

107. James K. Hoffmeier, "These Things Happened: Why a Historical Exodus is Essential for Theology" in *Do Historical Matters Matter to Faith?: A Critical Appraisal of Modern and Postmodern Approaches to Scripture*, ed. James K. Hoffmeier and Dennia R. Magary (Wheaton, IL: Crossway, 2012), 133.

108. In this regard I remember the statement made by an Egyptology teacher at the Hebrew University in Jerusalem that "whoever wrote the Torah must have known Egyptian" because many unusual forms and expressions in the Hebrew text make better sense when an original Egyptian word was assumed. One example was the account of Pharaoh's daughter "bathing" in the Nile. The Hebrew word translated "bathe" is strange and compares better with the Egyptian word for "wash." With this understanding Pharaoh's daughter went to wash her clothes at the Nile rather than take a bath (Exod 2:5).

109. E.g., the painting in Beni Hasan of asiatics entering Egypt in the tomb of Khnumhotep (early nineteenth century BC) and the report of a border guard in the eighth year of Merneptah that shasu were allowed entrance to save them and their flocks. See *ANET*, 259, 416f.

110. Hershel Shanks, "An Israelite House in Egypt?" *BAR* 19:4 (July/August 1993): 44–45.

111. See "The Instruction of Merikare," The Admonitions of Ipuwer," and "The Prophecy of Neferti" in *ANET*, 416f, 441ff, 444ff.

112. For example, on the outer western wall of the Cour de la Cachette at the Karnak temple in Luxor, Egypt, Egyptologist Frank Yurco discovered a register of hieroglyphic inscriptions that portrayed a captive people called the shasu that resemble the Israelites, see Frank Yurco, "3,200-Year Old Pictures of Israelites Found in Egypt," *BAR* 16:5 (September/October 1990): 20–38. For other examples see K. A. Kitchen, "From the Brick-fields of Egypt," *B&S* 10:2 (Spring 1981): 43–50.

113. Aside from the classic tale of Sinuhe, there are various texts that detail the escape of slaves.

114. See, e.g., the Tell el-Amarna texts and the Ipuwer papyrus, which provides an account of plagues of blood, cattle disease, fire phenomena, and strange darkness, similar to those described in the exodus narrative.

115. This can be substantiated from both archaeological sources and infrared satellite photos, which reveal the ancient movements of people from Egypt to Canaan.

116. See John Walton, *Ancient Israelite Literature in Its Cultural Context*, 95–107; K. A. Kitchen, *BIIW*, 79–85.

117. The reason for rejection of these parallels stems from a lack of consensus on interpretation of texts as actual history or religious storytelling and from chronological problems. For a discussion of some of these problems see Timothy P. Mahoney, *Exodus: Patterns of Research—A Filmmaker's Journey Exploring the Bible* (Minneapolis, MN: Thinking Man Films, 2015), ch. 7, viii.

118. This translation is a composite of those by Alan H. Gardiner, *The Admonitions of an Egyptian Sage from a Hieratic Papyrus in Leiden* (Leipzig: Hinrichs, 1909); R. Faulkner, "The Admonitions of an Ancient Egyptian Sage" in *The Literature of Ancient Egypt*,

eds. W. K. Simpson and R. Enmarch (Yale: Yale University Press, 1973), 210–29; and *The Dialogue of Ipuwer and the Lord of All* (Oxford: Griffith Institute Publications/Alden Press, 2009).

119. Brad C. Sparks, "Egyptian Text Parallels to the Exodus: The Egyptology Literature," in *Out of Egypt: Israel's Exodus Between Text and Memory, History and Imagination Conference*, ed. Thomas E. Levy (presented at the Qualcomm Institute, University of California, San Diego, 2013), https://www.youtube.com/watch?v=F-Aomm4O794.

120. See Manfred Görg, Peter van der Veen, and Christoffer Theis, "Israel in Canaan (Long) Before Pharaoh Merenptah? A Fresh Look at Berlin Statue Pedestal Relief 21687," *Journal of Ancient Egyptian Interconnections* 2:4 (2010): 15–25, especially 20.

121. Doug Petrovich, "Evidence for the Exodus from Egypt" June 7, 2013, http://www.biblearchaeology.org/post/2013/06/07/Evidence-for-the-Exodus-from-Egypt.aspx#id_470ee6c0-babe-48d2-ad17-e79885dfff6e.

122. Douglas Petrovitch, *The World's Oldest Alphabet: Hebrew as the Language of the Proto-Consonantal Script* (Jerusalem: Carta, 2016).

123. Douglas Petrovitch, *The World's Oldest Alphabet: Hebrew as the Language of the Proto-Consonantal Script* (Jerusalem: Carta, 2016).

124. See Alan Millard, "A Response to Douglas Petrovich's 'Hebrew as the Language behind the World's First Alphabet?'" *The Ancient Near East Today* 5:4 (2017) and counter-response: Douglas Petrovich, "A Reply to Alan Millard's Response to My 'Hebrew as the Language behind the World's First Alphabet?'" academia.edu (April 17, 2017).

125. Interview with Mazar, Institute of Archaeology, Jerusalem, 1996.

126. Manfred Bietak, "Israelites Found in Egypt: Four-Room House Identified in Medinet Habu," *BAR* 29:05 (September/October 2003), http://www.bib-arch.org/bswb BAR/bswbba2905f2.html. See also Bietak, "An Iron Age Four-Room House in Ramesside Egypt," *Eretz Israel* 23 (1991): 10–12.

127. K. A. Kitchen, "The Patriarchs Revisited: A Reply to Dr. Ronald S. Hendel," *Near Eastern Archaeology Society Bulletin* 43 (1998): 55–56.

128. Alan R. Millard, "Tutankhamun, The Tabernacle and the Ark of the Covenant," *B&S* 7:2 (Spring 1994): 50.

129. See Elie Borowski, "Cherubim: God's Throne?" *BAR* 21:4 (July/August 1995): 36–41.

130. Cf. for a discussion of these evidences, Roland de Vaux, "Les chérubins et l'arche d'alliance, les sphinx gardiens et les trônes divins dans l'Ancien Orient," *Mélanges de l'Université Saint-Joseph* 37 (1960–1961): 91–124 and in English, *Ancient Israel* 1: 298–301.

131. See W. F. Albright, "What were the Cherubim?" in *The Biblical Archaeologist Reader*, 1 (Scholars Press, 1975), 95–97.

132. Jerusalem Talmud Sheqalim, 6:1. Some sources say that this "layer" was only as thick as a gold *dinar* coin (Eruvin, 19a; Mikdash Aharon; Kreiti u'Fleiti, Yoreh De'ah, 43) while others say either a handbreadth (3"; Yoma, 72b; Rabbi Chananel; Abarbanel, Maaseh Choshev, 8:2); one half handbreadth (1.5"); or a fingerbreadth (.75"; Bava Batra, 14a; Bareitha Melekheth HaMishkan, 6). While 3" would require far too much gold for the

133. See the description and references in Umberto Cassuto, *Commentary on Exodus* (Jerusalem: Magnes Press, 1967), 329.

134. The Old Testament, Josephus, and Philo are all unanimous in their verdict that the only items in the ark were the tablets. The other two standard items—the jar of manna and Aaron's rod—were said to have been kept in front of the ark (1 Kgs 8:9; 2 Chron 5:10; Num 17:10; Exod 16:33–34; cf. Philo, *On the Life of Moses* 2.97; Josephus, *Antiquities* 3.6.5 #138; 8.4.1 # 104).

135. Cf. Alan R. Millard, "Re-Creating the Tablets of the Law," *BR* 10:1 (February 1994): 49–53.

136. Cf. Baba Batra 14a for this debate.

137. Christopher B. Hays, *Hidden Riches: A Sourcebook for the Comparative Study of the Hebrew Bible and Ancient Near East* (Louisville: Westminster John Knox, 2014), 158.

138. John E. Hartley, *Leviticus*, WBC 4 (Waco: Word, 1992), 238.

139. Angelika Berlejung, "Ein Program fürs Leben. Theologisches Wort und anthropologischer Ort der Silberamulette von Ketef Hinnom," *ZAW* 120 (2008a): 204–30 and Nadav Na'aman, "A New Appraisal of the Silver Amulets from Ketef Hinnom," *IEJ* 61 (2011): 184–95.

140. Shmuel Ahituv, "A Rejoinder to Nadav Naaman's 'A New Appraisal of the Silver Amulets from Ketef Hinnom,'" *IEJ* 62:2 (2012): 223–32. See also his *Echoes from the Past: Hebrew and Cognate Inscriptions from the Biblical Period* (Jerusalem: Carta, 2008), 49–55.

141. Translation by André Lemaire, *BAR* 11:5 (1985).

142. Lowell K. Handy, "The Appearance of Pantheon in Judah" in *The Triumph of Elohim*, ed. Diana Vikander Edelman, (Grand Rapids: Eerdmans, 1996), 41.

143. Benno Rothenberg, *The Egyptian Mining Temple at Timna*. Institute for Archaeo-Metallurgical Studies; Institute of Archaeology (University College, London: Thames and Hudson, 1988).

Chapter 3

1. John A. Wilson, "The Texts of the Battle of Kadesh," *The American Journal of Semitic Languages and Literatures* 34:4 (July 1927): 278.

2. As cited in Joyce Tyldesley, *Ramesses II: Egypt's Greatest Pharaoh* (Penguin, 2000): 70–71.

3. Paul J. Ray, Jr. "Classical Models for the Appearance of Israel in Palestine," in *Critical Issues in Early Israelite History*, Bulletin for Biblical Research Supplement 3, ed. Richard S. Hess, Gerald A. Klingbeil, and Paul J. Ray Jr. (Winona Lake: Eisenbrauns, 2008), 79–93, especially 92–93.

4. See the complete refutation of this criticism in David S. Merling, *The Book of Joshua: Its Theme and Role in Archaeological Discussions*, Andrews University Dissertation Series (Andrews University Press), 1997.

5. Bryant G. Wood, "Palestinian Pottery of the Late Bronze Age: An Investigation of the Terminal LB IIB Phase" (PhD thesis, University of Toronto, 1985); "A Comparison of the Archaeological and Biblical History of Jericho in the Late Bronze Age," Near East Archaeological Society Paper (South

Hamilton, MA: Gordon-Conwell Theological Seminary, 1987); "Jericho Revisited: The Archaeology and History of Jericho in the Late Bronze Age," American Schools of Oriental Research Paper (Boston, 1987); and "Did the Israelites Conquer Jericho?" *BAR* 16.2 (1990): 44–58.

6. Lorenzo Nigro and Hamdan Taha, eds. *Tell Es-Sultan/ Jericho in the Context of the Jordan Valley: Site Management, Construction, and Sustainable Development*, Studies on the Archaeology of Palestine & Transjordan 2 (Rome: University of Rome, "La Sapienza," 2006), 25.

7. John Garstang, "Jericho: City and Necropolis," *University of Liverpool Annals of Archaeology and Anthropology* 19 (1932): 3–22, 35–54.

8. Lorenzo Nigro, "The Built Tombs on the Spring Hill and the Palace of the Lords of Jericho (*'DMR RH'*) in the Middle Bronze Age" in *Exploring the Longue Durée: Essays in Honor of Lawrence E. Stager*, ed. J. David Schloen (Winona Lake: Eisenbrauns, 2009), 362 n. 6. Because the excavators interpreted the find spot as "an upper and probably reused" part of the main structure, they argued that the finds could not be used to date the structure to the Late Broze period, as had Garstang.

9. Ibid., 365.

10. Mazar, *Archaeology of the Land of the Bible*, 331.

11. Kathleen Kenyon, *Excavations at Jericho, Volume 3: The Architecture and Stratigraphy of the Tell*, ed. Thomas A. Holland (London: BSAJ, 1981), 370.

12. Bryant Wood, "Did the Israelites Conquer Jericho? A New Look at the Archaeological Evidence," May 1, 2008, http://www.bible archaeology.org/post/2008/05/01/Did-the-Israelites-Conquer -Jericho-A-New-Look-at-the-Archaeological-Evidence.aspx.

13. Jeffrey R. Zorn, "Reconsidering Goliath: An Iron Age I Philistine Chariot Warrior," *BASOR* 360 (November 2010): 9–14.

14. Adam Zertal, "A Cultic Center with a Burnt-Offering Altar from Early Iron Age I Period at Mt. Ebal," in *"Wunschet Jerusalem Frieden": Collected Communications to the XIIth Congress of the International Organization for the Study of the Old Testament*, eds. Mathias Augustin Klaus and Dietrich Schunck (Frankfurt am Main: Peter Lang, 1998), 137–54.

15. Minimalists have argued for the structure's interpretation as the remains of a village, a farmstead, a house or domestic space, and a watchtower. The main political and religious objections and objectors to Zertal's position are outlined in Milt Machlin, *Joshua's Altar: The Dig at Mount Ebal* (New York: Morrow, 1991), 44–76.

16. The template for cultic identification of sites was made by Colin Renfrew, *The Archaeology of Cult: The Sanctuary at Phylakopi* (London: British School of Archaeology at Athens/ Thames and Hudson, 1985), 19–20, and modified for Israelite sites by Ziony Zevit, *Religion of Ancient Israel: A Synthesis of Parallactic Approaches* (London: Continuum, 2001), 82.

17. See Ralph K. Hawkins, *The Iron Age I Structure on Mt. Ebal: Excavations and Interpretation*, BASORSup 6 (Winona Lake: Eisenbrauns, 2012), 219–28.

18. Professor Aren Maeir of BIU's Martin (Szusz) Department of Land of Israel Studies and Archaeology reported his team "found impressive evidence of an earthquake in the 8th century BCE, reminiscent of the earthquake mentioned in the Book of Amos 1:1. The team uncovered walls that were moved from their place and collapsed like a deck of cards as a result of the powerful earthquake – assessed at a magnitude of 8 on the Richter scale." See Hana Levi Julian, "Philistine Temple Ruins Uncovered in Goliath's Hometown," *Arutz Sheva* (July 29, 2010).

19. For a discussion of the only other provenanced bulla from Jerusalem see N. Avigad, 'Two Hebrew 'Fiscal' Bullae, *IEJ* 40: 262–66.

20. Ronny Reich, "A Fiscal Bulla from the City of David, Jerusalem," *IEJ* 62:2 (2012): 201.

21. Charles Wilson, "Shiloh," *Palestinian Exploration Fund: Quarterly Statement* 5–6 (1873): 38.

22. Pekka Pitkänen, *Central Sanctuary and Centralization of Worship in Ancient Israel: From the Settlement to the Building of Solomon's Temple* (Piscataway, NJ: Gorgias, 2004), 140–41.

23. Philip R. Davies, "'House of David' Built on Sand," *BAR* 20:4 (July/August 1994): 55.

24. Joseph Naveh, "An Aramaic Stele Fragment from Tel Dan," *IEJ* 43 (1993): 81–98 and Biran, *Biblical Dan* (Jerusalem: Israel Exploration Society, 1994), 277–78; George Athas, *The Tel Dan Inscription: A Reappraisal and New Interpretation* (New York: T&T Clark, 2005), 255–57.

25. J-W Wesselius, "The First Royal Inscription from Ancient Israel: The Tel Dan Inscription Reconsidered," *SJOT* 12 (1999): 175–76.

26. This is the translation by Avraham Biran, director of the Tel Dan excavations, and epigraphist Joseph Naveh from "The Tel Dan Inscription: A New Fragment," *IEJ* 45 (1995): 1–18.

27. One such example is in the Tell Qasile ostracon where the letters *bythrn* without a divider must mean Beyt Horon. See Anson Rainey, "The 'House of David' and the House of the Deconstructionists," *BAR* 20:6 (1994): 47, 68–69.

28. James K. Hoffmeier, "Current Issues in Archaeology: The Recently Discovered Tell Dan Inscription: Controversy & Confirmation," *Archaeology in the Biblical World* 3:1 (Summer 1995): 14.

29. See E. Ben-Zvi, "On the Reading '*bytdwd*' in the Aramaic Stele from Tel Dan," *JSOT* 64 (1994): 29–32, who cautions accepting LeMaire's conclusion without further investigation.

30. See N. Na'aman, "Beth-David in the Aramaic Stela from Tel Dan," *Biblische Notizen* 79 (1995): 19–20.

31. Yosef Garfinkel, Michael Hasel, and Martin Klingbeil, "An Ending and a Beginning: Why We're Leaving Qeiyafa and Going to Lachish," *BAR* 39:6 (November/December 2013): 44. The citation in their statement is by Israel Finkelstein in Robert Draper, "Kings of Controversy," *National Geographic* (December 2010), 67–91.

32. D. W. Jamieson-Drake, *Scribes and Schools in Monarchic Judah: A Socio-Archaeological Approach*, JSOTSup 109 (Sheffield: Almond, 1991), 139–40.

33. Israel Finkelstein and Neil Silberman, *The Bible Unearthed: Archaeology's New Vision of Ancient Israel and the Origin of Its Sacred Texts* (New York: Free Press, 2001), 235, 238.

34. Mark S. Smith, "In Solomon's Temple (1 Kings 6–7): Between

Text and Archaeology" in *Confronting the Past: Archaeological and Historical Essays on Ancient Israel in Honor of William G. Dever*, ed. Seymour Gitin, J. Edward Wright, and J. P. Dessel (Winona Lake: Eisenbrauns, 2006): 275.

35. See Todd Bolen, "Identifying King David's Palace: Mazar's Flawed Reading of the Biblical Text," http://www.bibleinterp .com/opeds/ident357928.shtml and Margreet L. Steiner, "The 'Palace of David' Reconsidered in the Light of Earlier Excavations," http://www.bibleinterp.com/articles/palace_2468.shtml.

36. David M. Carr, "The Tel Zayit Abecedary in (Social) Context" in *Literate Culture and Tenth-Century Canaan: The Tel Zayit Abecedary in Context*, ed. Ron E. Tappy and P. Kyle McCarter, Jr. (Winona Lake: Eisenbrauns, 2008): 125.

37. Shanks, Hershel, "Newly Discovered: A Fortified City from King David's Time," *BA* 35:1 (2009): 38–43.

38. Yosef Garfinkel, Mitka R. Golub, Haggai Misgav, and Saar Ganor, "The 'Ishb'al Inscription from Khirbet Qeiyafa," *BASOR* 373 (2015): 220.

39. Ibid., 230–31.

40. James W. Hardin, Christopher A. Rollston, and Jeffrey A. Blakely, "Iron Age Bullae from Officialdom's Periphery: Khirbet Summeily in Broader Context," Associated Press report, December 20, 2014, http://blog.gulflive.com/mississippi -press-news/2014/12/mississippi_state_archaeologis.html.

41. Rami Arav, "Toward a Comprehensive History of Geshur" in *Bethsaida: A City by the North Shore of the Sea of Galilee*, eds. Rami Arav and Richard A. Freund (Kirksville, MO: Truman State University Press, 2004), 3:1–48.

42. For details and photographs of the statues see K. W. Tubb, "Preliminary Report on the 'Ain Ghazal Statues" *Mitteilungen der Deutschen Orient Gesellschaft zu Berlin* 117 (1985): 117–34; K. W. Tubb, "Conservation of the Lime Plaster Statues of 'Ain Ghazal," in *Recent Advances in the Conservation and Analysis of Artifacts*, ed. J. Black (London: Summer School Press), 387–91 and K. W. Tubb & C. A. Grissom, "Ayn Ghazal: A Comparative Study of the 1983 and 1985 Statuary Caches," in *Studies in the History and Archaeology of Jordan* (Amman: Department of Antiquities, 1995) 5:437–47.

43. Trude Dothan, "Excavations at the Cemetery of Deir el-Balah," Monographs of the Institute of Archaeology 10, *Qedem* (The Hebrew University of Jerusalem, 1978), 134–45.

44. See Erle Leichty, *The Omen Series Šumma Izbu* (Locust Valley, NY: J. J. Augustin, 1970).

45. See *Šumma Izbu* Tablets 6–17 and details in Richard D. Barnett, "Polydactylism in the Ancient World," *Bulletin of the Anglo-Israel Archaeological Society* 6 (1986–1987): 2–3.

46. Maayana Miskin, "Dig Supports Biblical Account of King Solomon's Construction," IsraelNN.com (February 2010).

47. William E. Mierse, *Temples and Sanctuaries from the Early Iron Age Levant: Recovery after Collapse*, History, Archaeology, and Culture of the Levant 4, ed. Jeffrey A. Blakely and K. Lawson Younger (Winona Lake: Eisenbrauns, 2012), 306.

48. For architectural details on Solomon's building construction in light of the Khirbet Qeiyafa model finds see Bruce Hall, "Known

49. John Monson, "The New 'Ain Dara' Temple: Closest Solomonic Parallel" *BAR* 26:3 (May/June 2000): 29–33.

50. Israel Finkelstein, "Jerusalem in the Iron Age: Archaeology and Text; Reality and Myth" in *Unearthing Jerusalem: 150 Years of Archaeological Research in the Holy City*, eds. Galor, K. and Avni, G. (Winona Lake: Eisenbrauns, 2011), 196.

51. For the report with overlay map see Leen Ritmeyer, "Understanding the Destruction on the Temple Mount," http://www.ritmeyer.com/2007/08/31/understanding-the -destruction-of-the-temple-mount-cont/.

52. W. G. Dever, *What Did the Biblical Writers Know and When Did They Know It?*, 212.

53. On this debate see Neil Asher Silberman and Yuval Goren, "Faking Biblical History," *Archeology* (September/October 2003): 20–29 and Victor Sasson, *King Jehoash and the Mystery of the Temple of Solomon Inscription* (iUniverse, 2008).

54. Location: Louvre, Departement des Antiquites Orientales, Paris, France. Description: Cypriot Archaic I, 7th BC. Terracotta, H: 20 cm N 3294.

55. Yosef Garfinkel and Madeleine Mumcuoglu, *Solomon's Temple and Palace: New Archaeological Discoveries* (Jerusalem: Koren Publishers, 2015), 37–60.

56. For details concerning these models in reconstructing Solomon's temple see Yosef Garfinkel and Madeleine Mumcuoglu, *Solomon's Temple and Palace: New Archaeological Discoveries* (Jerusalem: Bible Lands Museum/Biblical Archaeology Society, 2016), 58–98, 172–190.

57. Trans. P. Kyle McCarter Jr. *Ancient Inscriptions: Voices from the Biblical World*. (Washington: Biblical Archaeology Society, 1996), 22.

58. "Annals: Calah Bulls," trans. K. Lawson Younger, *COS* 2.113C:267.

59. *The History of Herodotus*, ed. George Rawlinson, trans. Manuel Komroff (New York: Tudor Publishing, 1956), 2:131.

60. For a detailed account see Yigael Shiloh, "Jerusalem: Eighth to Sixth Centuries BCE," in *The New Encyclopedia of Archaeological Excavations in the Holy Land* (Jerusalem: Israel Exploration Society, 1993), 2:704–712.

61. The first-century historian Flavius Josephus's statements about the walls of Jerusalem, especially the first wall, helped make this determination. See *Wars of the Jews* 5:143.

62. These copies are respectively housed in the British Museum in London, the Museum of Grollenburg, and in the Museum of the Oriental Institute at the University of Chicago.

63. Column 3, lines 18–24, 27, 38–40, 49 of The British Museum Prism (ME 91032). Translation by Mordechai Cogan, *COS* 2.119B:303 (with addition from The Oriental Institute Prism: "who did not submit to my yoke").

64. Benjamin Studevant-Hickman, Sarah C. Melville, and Scott Noegel, "Neo-Babylonian Period Texts from Babylonia and Syro-Palestine," in *The Ancient Near East: Historical Sources in Translation*, ed. Mark W. Chavalas (Malden, MA: Blackwell, 2006), 386.

65. Haran, Menaham, "Explaining the Identical Lines at the End of Chronicles and the Beginning of Ezra" *BR* (Summer 1986): 19.

66. Randall Price interview with Shlomit Weksler-Bdolah at site of Kotel Excavations, June 2010.

67. Much of this information came from Randall Price's personal discussions with Shlomit Wexler-Bdolah when he and his team participated in the June 2011 excavations.

68. Israel Finkelstein, "Jerusalem in the Persian (and Early Hellenistic) Period and the Wall of Nehemiah," *JSOT* 32 (2008): 509.

69. David Ussishkin, "On Nehemiah's City Wall and the Size of Jerusalem during the Persian Period: An Archaeologists View," in *New Perspectives on Ezra-Nehemiah: History and Historigraphy, Text, Literature and Interpretation*, ed. Isaac Kalimi (Winona Lake: Eisenbrauns, 2012), 119–20.

70. Leen and Kathleen Ritmeyer, *Jerusalem in the Time of Nehemiah* (Jerusalem: Carta, 2005), 67.

71. Eilat Mazar, "The Wall that Nehemiah Built," *BAR* 35:2 (March/April 2009): 24–33, 66.

72. Mazar, "The Wall that Nehemiah Built," 28.

73. Ibid., 30.

74. Edwin M. Yamauchi, *Persia and the Bible* (Grand Rapids: Baker, 1990), 187.

75. Frederic Bush, *Ruth/Esther*, WBC 9 (Waco, TX: Nelson, 1996), 340.

76. Ibid., 345.

77. Ibid.

78. Yehuda Landy, *Purim and the Persian Empire*, trans. Rabbi Binyamin S. Moore (Jerusalem: Feldheim Publishers, 1999), 43.

79. Jacob Neusner, ed. and trans. *The Babylonian Talmud: A Translation and Commentary*, vol. 7 (Peabody: Hendrickson, 2011), 53.

80. Yehud Landy, *Purim and the Persian Empire*, 43–44.

81. Perre Briant, *From Cyrus to Alexander*, trans. Peter T. Daniels (Winona Lake: Eisenbrauns, 2002), 519.

Chapter 4

1. E. I. Gordon, "A New Look at the Wisdom of Sumer and Akkad," *BO* 17 (1960): 123.

2. H. P. Muller, "ḥkm," *TDOT* 4: 367.

3. W. G. Lambert, *Babylonian Wisdom Literature* (Oxford: Clarendon, 1960): 1.

4. Leonidas Kalugila, *The Wise King: Studies in Royal Wisdom as Divine Revelation in the Old Testament and Its Envirohment*, ConBOT 15 (Uppsala. CWK Gieerup, 1980): 69.

5. R. B. Y. Scott, *Proverbs; Ecclesiastes*, AB 18 (New York: Doubleday, 1965), xvii.

6. Giovanni Pettinato, "The Royal Archives of Tell Mardikh Ebla," *BA* 39 (May 1976): 45. However, it is now disputed whether the Eblaite material contains a literary corpus.

7. Norman Porteous, "Royal Wisdom," in *Wisdom in Israel and in the Ancient Near East*, Supplements to *VT* 3 (Leiden: Brill, 1955), 247–61.

8. R. K. Harrison, *Introduction to the Old Testament* (Grand Rapids: Eerdmans, 1969), 1011, states that the basic purpose of wisdom literature is "to furnish instruction for a particular class of young men." While it cannot be conclusively demonstrated that this was the *sitz im leben* for Israel, the evidence of courtly or scribal schools in Egypt and Babylon points to this being a most probable setting for the ancient Near East. Cf. schools of upper-class boys trained for scribal positions in Roger N. Whybray, *Wisdom Literature* (Illinois: A. R. Allenson Inc., 1965), 16.

9. Roland E. Murphy, "The Concept of Wisdom Literature," *The Bible in Current Catholic Thouqht* (New York: Herder & Herder, 1962), 48, argues for the validity of the role of the royal court based on the similarities between the forms of international wisdom literature. On the other hand, William McKane, op. cit., 1–9, contends for "broadly-based instruction for the community." Note also that Ecclesiasticus, or the *Wisdom of Jesus Ben Sirach/Sira* (190–180 BC), and the *Wisdom of Solomon* (first century BC) were composed when there was no longer any king or court. Cf. Dianne Bergant, op. cit., 19. Therefore, at least for Israel, the community played a larger role in the history of the wisdom tradition. Cf. further, James Crenshaw, *Studies in Ancient Israelite Wisdom*, Library of Biblical Studies (New York: KTAV, 1976), 7–8.

10. George Steindorff and Keith C. Seele, *When Egypt Ruled the East* (Chicago: University of Chicago Press, 1957), 126.

11. Leo G. Perdue, *Wisdom and Cult: A Critical Analysis of Cult in the Wisdom Literatures of Israel and the Ancient Near East*, SBLDS 30 (Missoula, MT: Scholars Press, 1977), 81.

12. Allen P. Ross, *Recalling the Hope of Glory* (Grand Rapids: Kregel, 2006), 253.

13. *BDB, DCH,* and *GKC.*

14. Joachim Braun, *Music in Ancient Israel/Palestine: Archaeological, Written and Comparative Sources* (Grand Rapids: Eerdmans, 2002), 156.

15. Ibid., 157.

16. R. D. Barnett, *Assyrian Palace Reliefs in the British Museum* (Oxford: Oxford University Press, 1970), 23.

17. Ross, *Recalling the Hope of Glory*, 261.

18. Peter C. Craigie and Marvin E. Tate, *Psalms 1–50*, 2nd ed., WBC 19 (Waco, TX: Nelson, 2004), 173.

19. Ibid. 173.

20. See John N. Oswalt, *The Bible Among the Myths* and Jeffrey J. Niehaus, *Ancient Near Eastern Themes in Biblical Theology*, for excellent discussions on the Bible's relationship to the mythology of antiquity.

21. Clyde E. Fant and Mitchell G. Reddish, *Lost Treasures of the Bible* (Grand Rapids: Eerdmans, 2008), 88–89.

22. F. J. Mabie, "Chaos and Death" in *Dictionary of the Old Testament: Wisdom, Poetry, and Writings*, eds. Tremper Longman III and Peter Enns (Downers Grove: IVP Academic, 2008), 44.

23. William W. Hallo and K. Lawson Younger, eds. *COS* (Boston: Brill, 2003), 1:248.

24. Mark S. Smith and Wayne T. Pitard, *The Ugaritic Baal Cycle*, vol. 2 (Leiden/Boston: Brill, 2009), 21. See James B. Pritchard, *ANEP*, 2nd ed. (Princeton: Princeton University Press, 1969), 689, for another cylinder seal depicting a similar scene.

25. John W. Hilber, "Psalms," in *ZIBBC*, vol. 5 (Grand Rapids: Zondervan, 2009), 333.

26. Craigie and Tate, *Psalms 1–50*, 173.

27. Eugene H. Merrill, *Deuteronomy* (Nashville: Holman Reference, 1994), 447.

28. John Goldingay, *Psalms Vol. 1: Psalms 1–41*, BCOTWP (Grand Rapids: Baker, 2006), 257.

29. R. D. Patterson, "*sela*'," *Theological Wordbook of the Old Testament*, 2:627.

30. Goldingay, *Psalms*, 257.

31. Porat, Roi, Hanan Eshel, and Amos Frumkin, "The 'Caves of the Spear': Refuge Caves from the Bar-Kokhba Revolt North of 'En-Gedi," *IEJ* 59:1 (2009): 21–42.

32. Albright, "A Prince of Ta'anach in the Fifteenth Century BC," *BASOR* 94 (April 1944) 24–25. Cf. *CAD* 6:76.

33. Ted Sturat, "Proverbs 22:6a: Train Up a Child?" *GTJ* (Spring 1988): 10. Much of the data in this entry has been adapted from this article.

34. John McDonald, "The Status and Role of the Naar in Israelite Society," *JNES* 35.3 (1976): 147–70. This article has been summarized briefly also as "The 'Naar' in Israelite Society," *B&S* (Winter 1977) 16–22.

35. McDonald, "The Status and Role of the Naar in Israelite Society," 149.

36. Ibid., 150. A. F. Rainey, "The Military Personnel of Ugarit," *JNES* 24 (1965) 17–27. The Merneptah Inscription and a fourth-century-AD Samaritan Chronicle also distinguish between regular soldiers and the "Na'ar" (See McDonald, 152).

37. Cylde E. Fant and Mitchell G. Reddish, *Lost Treasures of the Bible* (Grand Rapids: Eerdmans, 2008), 247.

Chapter 5

1. Nahman Avigad, "The Epitaph of a Royal Steward from Siloam Village," *IEJ* 3:3 (1953): 143.

2. James VanderKam, *The Dead Sea Scrolls Today* (Grand Rapids: Eerdmans, 2010), 175.

3. See Lamar Cooper, "Qumran and the Messianic Hope," *CTR* 7:1 (Fall 2009): 63–80, and his further comments in "Qumran Pottery Factory Revisited" (paper delivered to the Near East Archaeological Society, Baltimore, MD, Nov 19, 2013).

4. Princeton Theological Seminary Dead Sea Scrolls Project, vol. 1.

5. The initial analysis in Barcelona, Spain, of the contents of the jar identified tartaric acid in the deposit, which has been used as a chemical marker for amphora used for wine storage. The conclusion of this study was that the jar had contained fermented grape wine. See Salvador Butí, Salvadó Nati, Núria Lope, Emilia Papiol, Elena Heras, and Jan Gunneweg, "Determination of Wine Residues in Qumran Amphora-35" in *Bio-and Material Cultures at Qumran: Papers from a COST Action G8 Working Group Meeting Held in Jerusalem, Israel on 22–23 May 2005*, ed. Jan Gunneweg, Charles Greenblatt and Annemie Adriaens (Stuttgart: Frauhofer Verlag, 2006). A subsequent test by other researchers in a different lab did not find the presence of tartrate and concluded the substance was gypsum and the jar

used to store gypsum, probably for plaster production. See K. L. Rasmussen, J. Gunneweg, J. van der Plicht, I. Kralj Cigić, A. D. Bond, B. Svensmark, M. Balla, M. Strlic and G. Doudna, "On the Age and Content of Jar-35—A Sealed and Intact Jar Found on the Southern Plateau of Qumran," *Archaeoletry* 53:4 (August 2011): 791–808. This divergence in test results has not been explained and it is our opinion that it relates to the samples tested, especially after removed from the jar.

6. *COS* 2.124: 315.

7. Eugene Ulrich and Peter W Flint, *Qumran Cave 1: The Isaiah Scrolls: Part 2: Introductions, Commentary, and Textual Variants*, Discoveries in the Judean Desert 32 (Oxford: Clarendon, 2010): 93, 176.

8. Scholars who have discussed this point are Israel Knohl, *Messiahs and the Resurrection in 'The Gabriel Revelation'*, The Kogod Library of Judaic Studies 6 (New York: Continuum, 2009), 85–99; Adela Yarbro Collins, "Response to Israel Knohl, *Messiahs and Resurrection in the 'Gabriel Revelation'*" in *Hazon Gabriel: New Readings of the Gabriel Revelation*, ed. Matthias Henze, SBL 29 (Atlanta: Society of Biblical Literature, 2011), 93–98; Richard Hess, "Messiahs Here and There" in *Israel's Messiah in the Bible and the Dead Sea Scrolls*, eds. R. S. Hess and M. D. Carroll R. (Grand Rapids: Baker, 2003), 103–08; Torleif Elgvin, "Eschatology and Messianism in the Gabriel Inscription," *Journal of the Jesus Movement in Its Jewish Setting* 1:1 (2014): 5–25.

9. Israel Knohl, *Messiahs and Resurrection in 'The Gabriel Revelation'*, The Robert and Arlene Kogod Library of Judaic Studies 6 (New York: Continuum, 2009).

10. Israel Knohl, *Messiahs and Resurrection in "The Gabriel Revelation,"* The Kogod Library of Judaic Studies. (New York: Continuum, 2009), 85–93.

11. Ronald Hendel, "Note to 'Vision of Gabriel,'" *BAR* 35:1 (2009): 8.

12. See Jane M. Cahill and David Tarler, "Excavations Directed by Yigael Shiloh at the City of David, 1978–1985," in *Ancient Jerusalem Revealed*, ed. Hillel Geva (Jerusalem: Israel Exploration Society, 1994), 39–40.

13. For complete details of these bullae see Nahman Avigad, *Hebrew Bullae from the Time of Jeremiah* (Washington: Biblical Archaeology Society, 1987).

14. See Gabriel Barkay, "A Bulla of Ishmael, the King's Son," *BASOR* 290/291 (1993): 109–14.

15. See Hershel Shanks, "Jeremiah's Scribe and Confidant Speaks from a Hoard of Clay Bullae," *BAR* 13:5 (September/October 1987): 58–65.

16. In 1996 a second clay bulla with an identical inscription came to light in a private collection, presumably stamped with the same seal. This bulla contained the traces of a fingerprint, also presumably of Baruch himself. Since the initial publication of these bullae there has been dispute over its authenticity.

17. J. A. Black, G. Cunningham, E. Robson, and G. Zolyomi, "The Lament for Ur" in *The Electronic Text Corpus of Sumerian Literature* (Oxford, 1998), http://etcsl.orinst.ox.ac.uk/.

18. J. Harold Ellens, Deborah L. Ellens, Rolf P. Knierim, and Isaac

Kalimi, *God's Word for Our World: Biblical Studies in Honor of Simon John De Vries* (New York: Continuum, 2004), 287.

19. Black, Cunningham, Robson, and Zolyomi, "The Lament for Ur," http://etcsl.orinst.ox.ac.uk/.

20. "*tabnît*," *KB* 1018.

21. Revelation of temples and cultic objects in dreams or visions is a well-known phenomenon. For biblical and extrabiblical sources, J. Lindbolm, *Prophecy in Ancient Israel* (Philadelphia: Fortress, 1962), 173–82. Victor Hurowitz, *I Have Built You An Exalted House: Temple Buildings in the Bible in Light of Mesopotamian and Northwest Semitic Writings*, JSOTSup 115 (Sheffield: University of Sheffield, 1992), 168, says that another way of revealing a plan of a cult object to its potential fashioner is by revealing a prototype.

22. This view combines the idea of a replica with that of the actual heavenly sanctuary and was suggested by Umberto Cassuto in his commentary on Exodus.

23. For a more detailed discussion of these interpretations see Richard M. Davidson, *Typology in Scripture* (Berrien Springs, MI: Andrews University Press, 1981), 372–74.

24. Hurowitz, 168–70.

25. He cites as references Josh 12:28; 1 Chron 28:18. Cf. Ezek 8:3, 10; 10:10; Deut 4:16, 17, 18; Pss 106:20; 144:12; Isa 44.13.

26. Hurowitz sees two meanings for the term in Chronicles according to the context of its appearance. In verses 11, 12, and 19 it is the "blueprint" for what Solomon is to build, while in verse 18 it is the (earthly, yet to be constructed) "replica." However, he also finds the word bears the same two meanings in 2 Kgs 16:10.

27. Richard Davidson, *Typology in Scripture*, 385.

28. Cf. J. Coert Rylaarsdam, "The Book of Exodus," *IB*, ed. George Buttrick (Nashville: Abingdon, 1962) 1:1021. The primary source for the presentation of the ancient Near Eastern parallels to this is Richard Clifford, *The Cosmic Mountain in Canaan and in the Old Testament*, HSM 4 (Cambridge: Harvard University Press, 1972). For a discussion of the image of the god in Babylonian religion see A. Leo Oppenheim, *Ancient Mesopotamia: Portrait of a Dead Civilization* (Chicago: University Press, 1964), 184–187. Hurowitz, 169–70, cites various Babylonian inscriptions that give examples of revelations of models involving cult objects. He includes a Hittite text in which a dreamer sees a god in a dream and is commanded to make a statue exactly according to what he has seen and dedicate it to the deity. One of the finest collections of ancient Sumerian and Assyrian texts concerning the dedication of temples, temple dedicatory prayers, and cosmic temple typology is the study of Moshe Weinfield, *Deuteronomy and the Deuteronomic School* (Oxford: University of Oxford Press, 1972).

29. Frank Moore Cross, "The Priestly Tabernacle in the Light of Recent Research," in *Temples and High Places in Biblical Times: Proceedings of the Colloquium in Honor of the Centennial of Hebrew Union College-Jewish Institute of Religion March 14–16, 1977*, ed. Avraham Biran (Jerusalem: The Nelson Glueck School of Biblical Archaeology of Hebrew Union College-Jewish Institute of Religion, 1981), 170.

30. Rosella Lorenzi, "Ancient Texts Part of Earliest Known Documents," *Discovery News*, December 27, 2011, http://news.discovery.com/history/archaeology/tower-of-babel-111227.htm.

31. Although today Daniel is included in the Hebrew Bible in the division of the Writings, which might indicate a late origin and inclusion after the first century AD, Josephus, *Contra Apion* 1.8, wrote evidently included it as part of his canon. He describes twenty-two books (five books of Moses + thirteen books of the prophets who succeeded Moses + four hymns and practical precepts), all "justly believed in," and written "of events that occurred in their own time." Daniel must have originally been included in the thirteen books, a fact also attested by the early church fathers Origen (AD 250) and Jerome (AD 400), both of whom were instructed by rabbis, and all the Greek uncials, in the placement of Daniel with the Prophets, separate from the historical books.

32. This followed upon recognition that the Daniel of Ezek 14:20 (cf. 28:3) ranked with Job and Noah and was held up as a model of righteousness and wisdom to the exilic community. While neither Job nor Noah were technically prophets in the later sense of the word, they both functioned in the prophetic role as intercessors to their people (Job 1:5; 42:8–9; Gen 6:8–9, 14; cf. 2 Pet 2:5). The arguments that this "Daniel" was not the biblical character but the much distant figure of Dan'el, the ancient mythical ruler who practiced magical wisdom in the Ugaritic Aqhat epic (*ANET* 153–54a; cf. J. Day, "The Daniel of Ugarit and Ezekiel and the Hero of the Book of Daniel," *VT* 30 [1980]: 174–84) are not convincing. The literary links between the accounts are unclear and verbal parallels are missing. Cf. John E. Goldingay, *Daniel*, WBC 30 (Waco, TX: Word, 1989), 7, 274, who notes the intercessory role of Daniel for "his people," "his city," and "his sanctuary" (Dan 9:15–20) corresponds with Daniel's portrayal in Ezek 14:20.

33. For a complete survey and critique of these critical arguments cf. Robert Dick Wilson, *Studies in the Book of Daniel* (repr. Grand Rapids: Baker, 1972), 2:9–280 and Josh McDowell, *Daniel in the Critics' Den: Historical Evidence for the Authenticity of the Book of Daniel* (San Bernardino, CA: Here's Life Publishers, 1979), 33–128.

34. S. R. Driver, *An Introduction to the Literature of the Old Testament* (Edinburgh: T&T Clark, 1898), 497–516.

35. Driver states, "the age and authorship of the books of the Old Testament can be determined (as far as this is possible) only upon the basis of the internal evidence supplied by the books themselves ... no external evidence worthy of credit exists," xi. For a critique of Driver's position see Stephen M. Clinton, "S. R. Driver and the Date of Daniel," *The Journal of Church and Society* 5:2 (Fall, 1969): 30–41.

36. Cf. e.g., Gordon J. Wenham, "Daniel: The Basic Issues," *Themelios* 2 (1977): 49–52; Edwin M. Yamauchi, "Daniel and Contacts Between the Aegean and the Near East Before Alexander," *EvQ* 53 (1981): 37–47; Arthur Ferch, "The Book of Daniel and the Maccabean Thesis," *AUSS* 21 (1983): 129–141; Eugene E. Carpenter, "The Eschatology of Daniel

Compared with the Eschatology of Selected Intertestamental Documents" (PhD dissertation, Fuller Theological Seminary, 1978), 97–109; Donald J. Wiseman, et. al., *Notes on Some Problems in the Book of Daniel* (London: Tyndale, 1970); Bruce K. Waltke, "The Date of the Book of Daniel," *BSac* 133 (October-December, 1976): 319–29; Gleason Archer, "The Aramaic of the 'Genesis Apocryphon' Compared with the Aramaic of Daniel" in *New Perspectives on the Old Testament*, ed. J. Barton Payne (Waco, TX: Word, 1970), 160–69.

37. Cf. G. W. Anderson, "Daniel," *CHB*, ed. P. R. Ackroyd, et al. (New York: Cambridge University Press, 1984) 1:151.

38. Koch, 123.

39. Interview with Shemaryahu Talmon, Jerusalem, November 12, 1995.

40. Cf. F. F. Bruce, *Biblical Exegesis in the Qumran Texts* (London: Tyndale, 1960), 68–71; Annette Steudel, "[The End of the Days] in the Texts from Qumran," *RevQ* 62 (December 1993): 238.

41. Cf. Eugene Ulrich, "Daniel Manuscripts from Qumran. Part 1: A Preliminary Edition of 4QDana," *BASOR* 268 (November 1987): 18.

42. On the discovery of the fragments themselves, see Dupont-Sommer's announcement in *Apercus preliminaires* as cited by H. H. Rowley, *The Zadokite Fragments and the Dead Sea Scrolls* (Oxford: Basil Blackwell, 1956), 7.

43. Jacob M. Myers, *I Chronicles*, AB 12 (New York: Doubleday, 1965), 165.

44. Cf. J. Muilenburg, "A Qoheleth Scroll from Qumrân," *BASOR* 135 (October 1954): 20–28.

45. See also the statement by William H. Brownlee, *The Meaning of the Qumran Scrolls for the Bible* (New York: Oxford University Press, 1964), 29–30: ". . . one of the Psalms manuscripts from Cave 4 attests so-called Maccabean psalms at a period which is roughly contemporary with their supposed composition. If this is true, it would seem that we should abandon the idea of any of the canonical psalms being of Maccabean date, for each song had to win its way into the esteem of the people before it could be included in the sacred compilation of the Psalter. Immediate entree for any of them is highly improbable."

46. Frank M. Cross, Jr., *The Ancient Library of Qumran and Modern Biblical Studies*, rev. ed. (Grand Rapids: Baker, 1980), 165.

47. Ibid, 36.

48. Cross, *The Ancient Library of Qumran and Modern Biblical Studies*, 43.

49. Robert I. Vasholz, "Qumran and the Dating of Daniel," *JETS* 21:4 (December 1978): 321.

50. Cf. F. Macler, "Les Apocalypses Apocryphes de Daniel," *Revue de l'histoire des religions* 33 (1896): 37–53, 163–76, 288–319; P. J. Alexander, "Medieval Apocalypses as Historical Sources," *Ancient History Review* 73 (1968): 997–1018.

51. Gleason L. Archer, "The Hebrew of Daniel Compared with the Qumran Sectarian Documents" in *The Law and the Prophets: Old Testament Essays in Honor of Oswalt T. Allis*, ed. John H. Skilton (Philadelphia: Presbyterian and Reformed Publishing, 1974), 470–81.

52. Examples include the preposition *le* before a king's name in dates and the word order of the Assur ostracon (seventh century BC), which agrees with Daniel. Cf. Robert I. Vasholz, "Qumran and the Dating of Daniel," *JETS* 21:4 (December 1978): 318–19.

53. K. A. Kitchen, "The Aramaic of Daniel" in *Notes on Some Problems in the Book of Daniel*, ed. P. J. Wiseman, et al. (London: Tyndale, 1965), 75. Kitchen reasserts this conclusion in *BIIW*, 152, n. 10.

54. A. R. Millard, "Daniel 1–6 and History," *EQ* 49:2 (1977): 67–73.

55. E. Y. Kutscher, "HaAramit HaMigrait-Aramit Mizrahit hi o Maaravit?," *First World Congress of Jewish Studies* I (Jerusalem: Magnes Press, 1952), 123–27.

56. The carbon-14 date for 1Q20 yielded the range of 73 BC–AD 14, which accorded roughly with the paleographic dating of the late first century BC. Cf. the chart in *BAR* 17 (November/December 1991), 72.

57. Gleason L. Archer, Jr. "The Aramaic of the 'Genesis Apocyrphon' Compared With the Aramaic of Daniel," in *New Perspectives on the Old Testament*, ed. J. Barton Payne (Waco, TX: Word, 1970), 160–169; "Aramaic," *ZPEB* 1:255.

58. Cf. J. M. P. van der Ploeg and A. S. van der Woude, eds. *Le Targum de Job de la grotte XI de Qumrân* (Leiden: Brill, 1971), 3–5; T. Muraoka, "The Aramaic of the Old Targum of Job From Qumran Cave XI," *JJS* 25 (1974): 442; Stephen A. Kaufman, "The Job Targum From Qumran," *JAOS* 93 (1973): 327.

59. Robert Vasholz, "A Philogical Comparison of the Qumran Job Targum and Its Implications for the Dating of Daniel" (PhD dissertation, University of Stellenbosch, 1976); cf. T. Muraoka, "The Aramaic of the Old Targum of Job from Qumran Cave XI," 425–33.

60. A. York, "A Philological and Textual Analysis of the Qumran Job Targum (11QtgJob)" (PhD dissertation, Cornell University, 1973), 306–32.

61. Cf. F. F. Bruce, "Josephus and Daniel," in *Annual of the Swedish Theological Institute*, ed. Hans Kosmala (Leiden: Brill), 4: 148–62.

62. Gerhard Hasel, "Is the Aramaic of Daniel Early or Late?," *Ministry* (January 1980), 13.

63. Howard N. Wallace, "garden of God," *ABD* (New York: Doubleday, 1992), 2: 906.

64. Ibid., 6: 658.

65. Pauline Albenda, "Assyrian Trees in the Brooklyn Museum," in *British Institute for the Study of Iraq*, vol. 56 (1994): 123–24.

66. Barbara Nevling Porter, "Sacred Trees, Date Palms, and the Royal Persona of Ashurnasirpal II," *JNES* 52:2 (April 1993): 129–39.

67. See M. W. Green, "The Eridu Lament," *Journal of Cuneiform Studies* 30:3 (July 1978): 149.

68. G. K. Beale, *The Temple and the Mission of God: A Biblical Theology of the Dwelling Place of God* (Downers Grove: InverVarsity Press, 2004), 71–72.

69. See Joshua Berman, *The Temple: Its Symbolism and Meaning Then and Now* (Northvale, NJ: J. Aaronson, 1995), 27. See also Donald W. Parry, *Garden of Eden: Prototype Sanctuary* (Salt Lake City, Utah: Desert Book Company, 1994), 126–51.

70. Advocates of a late date for the composition of the Book of Deuteronomy argue for parallels with the Neo-Assyrian vassal

treaty format such as the one attested in the Vassal Treaty of Esarhaddon (672 BC), but they are incomplete parallels because they lack the preamble and blessing/cursing sections. See R. Frankena (1965) "The Vassal Treaties of Esarhaddon and the dating of Deuteronomy," *OTS* 14: 122–54.

71. G. Aalders, "The Problem of the Book of Jonah," *The Tyndale New Testament Lecture* (1948): 8, www.biblicalstudies.org.uk/pdf/tp/jonah_aalders.pdf.

72. Donald J. Wiseman, "Jonah's Nineveh," *The Tyndale Biblical Archaeology Lecture* (1977): 45.

73. Ibid., 45.

74. Ibid., 45–46.

75. Ibid., 46.

76. Ibid., 50.

77. Ibid., 47.

78. Ibid., 48.

79. W. F. Albright, "The Nebuchadnezzar and Neriglissar Chronicles," *BASOR* 143 (1956): 28.

80. Ibid., 4.

81. Ibid., 4–5.

82. Erika Belibtreu, "Grisly Assyrian Record of Torture and Death," *BAR* 17:1 (January/February 1991): 3.

83. Robin Ngo, "Severed Hands: Trophies of War in New Kingdom Egypt" *BAR* 40:2 (March/April 2014): 12.

84. Seymour Gitin, Trude Dothan, and Joseph Naveh, "A Royal Dedicatory Inscription from Ekron," *IEJ* 47:1/2 (1997): 9.

85. For arguments on the interpretation of this vessel see Al Wolters, *Zechariah*, HCOT (Leuven: Peeters, 2014), 115–16; George L. Klein, *Zechariah*, NAC 21B (Nashville: B&H, 2008), 155–56; Eugene Merrill, *Haggai, Zechariah, Malachi*, An Exegetical Commentary (Chicago: Moody Press, 1994), 147–49.

86. For drawings of these examples see Robert North, "Zechariah's Seven-Spout Lampstand" *Biblica* 51:2 (1970): 189, 195, 201 and photos on 193.

87. Carol L. Meyers "Was There a Seven-Branched Lampstand in Solomon's Temple?" *BAR* 5:5 (Sep/Oct. 1979): 47–57.

88. Diana Edelman, *The Origins of the "Second" Temple: Persian Imperial Policy and the Rebuilding of Jerusalem* (London: Equinox, 2005), 136.

89. Older texts in this regard include Yohanan Aharoni, *The Archaeology of the Land of Israel*, trans. Anson F. Rainey (Philadelphia: Westminster, 1982); Kathleen Kenyon, *Archaeology in the Holy Land*, 5th ed. (Nashville: Thomas Nelson, 1985). Later texts have corrected this, see Jodi Magness, *The Archaeology of the Holy Land: From the Destruction of Solomon's Temple to the Muslim Conquest* (Cambridge: Cambridge University Press, 2012) and Ephraim Stern, *Material Culture of the Land of the Bible in the Persian Period 538–332 BC* (Warminster: Aris and Phillips, 1982).

90. Ephraim Stern, *Material Culture of the Land of the Bible in the Persian Period 538–332 BC*, 48.

91. Paul Lapp, "Tell el-Ful," *BA* 28 (1965), 6.

92. Bezalel Porten, "Elephantine Papyri," *ABD* (New York: Doubleday, 1992), 2: 452.

93. Reuven Yaron, "Aramaic Marriage Contracts from Elephantine," *JSS* 3, no. 1 (January 1958): 26, 38–39.

94. Ibid., 39.

95. Andrew E. Hill, "Malachi," in *ZIBBC* (Grand Rapids: Zondervan, 2009), 5:237–38.

96. Puech, Émile, ed. *Discoveries in the Judean Desert XXXVII: Qumran Grotte 4.XXVII Textes En Araméen, Deuxième Partie* (Leiden: Brill, 2009), 179–258.

97. Julio Trebolle Barrera, "Elijah," in *Encyclopedia of the Dead Sea Scrolls* (New York: Oxford University Press, 2000), 246.

98. John J. Collins, *The Scepter and the Star: the Messiahs of the Dead Sea Scrolls and Other Ancient Literature* (New York, 1995), 121. Collins provides a discussion of the eschatological prophet of 4Q521 on pages 117–23.

99. Michael O. Wise, Martin G. Abegg Jr., and Edward M. Cook, *The Dead Sea Scrolls: A New Translation* (San Francisco: HarperCollins, 1996), 347–48.

100. Géza G. Xeravits, *King, Priest, Prophet: Positive Eschatological Protagonists of the Qumran Library* (Boston: Brill, 2003), 110, 187, 190–91.

Chapter 9

1. For visual reconstructions of the Herodian Temple see Randall Price, *Rose Guide to the Temple* (Glendale, CA: Rose Publishing, 2012) and Leen Ritmeyer, *The Quest: Revealing the Temple Mount in Jerusalem* (Jerusalem: Carta, 2006).

2. Leen Ritmeyer, "Understanding the destruction of the Temple Mount," August 31, 2007, http://www.ritmeyer.com/2007/08/31/understanding-the-destruction-of-the-temple-mount/.

3. For a discussion on the different bases see Steven Fine's sidebar, "The Unique Base on the Menorah of the Arch of Titus" in "True Colors: Digital Reconstruction Restores Original Brilliance to the Arch of Titus, *BAR* 43:3 (May/June 2017): 32.

Chapter 10

1. This number is based on the scrolls and fragments of scrolls in the Israeli inventories as well as those owned by private institutions (collectively more than twenty) and individuals (including the Kando family whose total holdings are unknown). For example, the Norweigen collection of Martin Skøyen contains some 135 fragments, that of the Green Collection (estimated at fifteen, though the number may be higher), and that of New Zealand collector David Sutherland at about twelve.

2. These last new names are based on personal and film interviews, verification from the son of the chief of the Tam'ara Bedouin tribe (to which they belonged); confirmation from an Israeli antiquities merchant who first identified Muhammad al-Asi and a member of the Dead Sea Scrolls Foundation who also interviewed Muhammad al-Asi; and a Jordanian newspaper report on Muhammad Hammad Ubiayt's involvement in the original scroll discoveries (caves 1, 4, 11). Randall Price interviewed both men and went with Muhammad al-Asi to caves 1 and 4 along with Israeli archaeologist Yaakov Kalman. Price also accompanied

Muhammad Hammad Ubiayt to the caves and other previously unknown sites to confirm the accuracy of their knowledge.

3. Millar Burrows, ed. *The Dead Sea Scrolls of St. Mark's Monastery*, vol. 1 (New Haven: The American Schools of Oriental Research), 1950.

4. See Hershel Shanks, *The Copper Scroll and the Search for the Temple Treasure* (Washington: Biblical Archaeology Society, 2007).

5. Martin Abegg, Jr., Peter Flint, and Eugene Ulrich, eds., *The Dead Sea Scrolls Bible* (San Francisco: HarperSanFrancisco, 1999).

6. Norman Golb, *Who Wrote the Dead Sea Scrolls? The Search for the Secret of Qumran* (New York: Scribner, 1995).

7. Robert Donceel and Pauline Donceel-Voute, "The Archaeology of Khirbet Qumran," in *Methods of Investigation of the Dead Sea Scrolls and the Khirbet Qumran Site: Present Realities and Future Prospects*, ed. M. O. Wise, et al. (New York: Academy of Sciences, 1998).

8. Lena Cansdale and Alan Crown, "Qumran, Was It an Essene Settlement?" *BAR* 20:5 (1995): 24–35, 73–78. See also Lena Cansdale, *Qumran and the Essenes: A Re-Evaluation of the Evidence*, TSAJ 60 (Tübingen: Mohr Siebeck, 1997).

9. Yizhar Hirschfeld, *Qumran in Context: Reassessing the Archaeological Evidence* (Peabody, MA: Hendrickson, 2004).

10. Patrich, Joseph, "Khirbet Qumran in the Light of New Archaeological Explorations in the Qumran Caves," in *Methods of Investigation of the Dead Sea Scrolls and the Khirbet Qumran Site: Present Realities and Future Prospects*, ed. Michael O. Wise, Norman Golb, John J. Collins, and Dennis G. Pardee, Annals of the New York Academy of Sciences 722 (New York: New York Academy of Sciences, 1994), 73–95.

11. Magen Broshi and Hanan Eshel, "Residential Caves at Qumran," *DSD* 6 (1999): 328–48.

12. Yizhak Magen and Yuval Peleg, "Back to Qumran: Ten Years of Excavation and Research, 1993–2004," in *Qumran, Site of the Dead Sea Scrolls: Archaeological Interpretations and Debates*, ed. Katherina Galor, Jean-Baptiste Humbert, and Jurgen Zangenberg, Studies on the Texts of the Desert of Judah 57 (Boston: Brill, 2006); Yitzhak Magen and Yuval Peleg, "The Qumran Excavations 1993–2004: Preliminary Report," *Judea and Samaria Researches and Discoveries* (Jerusalem: Judea and Samaria Publications 2008), 353–426.

13. For a popular summary of this position see Hershel Shanks, "Qumran—The Pottery Factory," *BAR* 32:5 (September/October 2006): 26–32.

14. Lamar Cooper, "Qumran Pottery Factory Revisited," unpublished paper delivered to the Near East Archaeological Society, Evangelical Theological Society Meeting. Baltimore, MD, Nov 19, 2013.

15. Frederick E. Zeuner, "Notes on Qumran," *PEQ* 92 (1960): 27–36.

16. Ibid, 31.

17. Magen and Peleg, "Back to Qumran," 92–94.

18. James Tabor and Joe Zias, "Biblical Latrine: Ancient Parasites Show That Cleanliness May Have Been Next To Sickliness," *ScienceDaily* (November 14, 2006), http://sciencedaily.com/releases/2006/11/061113180523.htm.

19. Joe E. Zias, James D. Tabor, and Stephanie Harter-Lailheugue, "Toilets at Qumran, The Essenes, and The Scrolls: New Anthropological Data and Old Theories," *RevQ* 22:4 (2006): 631–40.

20. Judy Siegel, "Fatal Cleanliness and Godliness," *The International Jerusalem Post*, Nov 24–30, 2006.

21. I am grateful to Lamar Cooper for drawing these succinct connections, "Qumran Pottery Factory Revisited."

22. Katharina Galor and Jürgen Zangenberg, "Led Astray By a Dead Sea Latrine" *The Jewish Daily Forward*, February 16, 2007, http://forward.com/articles/10107/led-astray-by-a-dead-sea-latrine/#ixzz2ssQIpPZj.

23. For the most recent study of this text see L. H. Schiffman, "Communal Meals at Qumran," *RQ* 10 (1979): 45–56.

24. Jodi Magness, *The Archaeology of Qumran and the Dead Sea Scrolls* (Grand Rapids: Eerdmans, 2002), 113–26; Jodi Magness, "Communal Meals and Sacred Space at Qumran," in *Debating Qumran* (Leuven: Peeters, 2004), 81–112; Phillip J. Long, *Jesus the Bridegroom: The Origin of the Eschatological Feast as a Wedding Banquet in the Synoptic Gospels* (Eugene, OR: Pickwick, 2013): 158–66; Lamar E. Cooper, Sr., "Qumran and the Messianic Hope," *CTR* 7 (2009): 67–68, 78–79.

Chapter 11

1. Gerasa (modern Jerash) is not a serious contender for the location of the story of the demonanic and the pigs, but Gadara (modern Umm Qeis) and Gergesa (modern Kursi) have support. Scholars favoring Gadara include Merrill F. Unger, *Archaeology and the New Testament* (Grand Rapids: Zondervan, 1962), 139–42, and John T. Fitzgerald, "Gadara: Philodemus' Native City," in *Philodemus and the New Testament World*, ed. John T. Fitzgerald, Dirk Obbink, and Glenn S. Holland (Leiden: Brill, 2004), 343–51. Scholars favoring Gergesa include John McRay, *Archaeology and the New Testament* (Grand Rapids: Baker, 1991), 166–68, and Jack Finegan, *The Archaeology of the New Testament* (Princeton: Princeton University Press, 1992), 115–17.

2. I wish to express my appreciation to John McRay's book, *Archaeology and the New Testament*, 17–19, for suggestions on the value of archaeology.

3. Gonzalo Báez-Camargo, *Archaeological Commentary on the Bible* (New York: Doubleday, 1984), xxii.

Chapter 12

1. As opposed to the other Bethlehem, which is in Galilee. See Josh 19:15.

2. Jews continue to venerate the traditional site of Rachel's tomb, near the entrance to the modern city. Although it is considered the third holiest site in Judaism and has a very ancient tradition, the modern tomb is almost certainly not the original tomb of Rachel since the current site is 5 miles south of the southern border of the territory of Benjamin, where Rachel's tomb is said to have been (1 Sam 10:2).

3. Matti Fredman, "Despite Secrecy, Interest Builds around Mysterious First Temple Find outside Bethlehem," *Times of*

Israel, May 19, 2013, http://www.timesofisrael.com/bible-era
-find-intrigues-scholars-despite-attempts-to-hush-it-up/.

4. Justin Martyr, *Dialogue with Trypho*, 78.

5. Kenneth Bailey, "The Manger and the Inn," Associates for
Biblical Research, http://www.biblearchaeology.org/post/
2008/11/08/The-Manger-and-the-Inn.aspx#Article.

6. William Thomson, *The Land and the Book*, Vol. II (New York:
Harper and Brothers, c. 1858, 1871), 503; E. F. F. Bishop, *Jesus
of Palestine* (London: Lutterworth, 1955), 42.

7. Karl Kerényi, *The Gods of the Greeks* (London: Thames &
Hudson, 1980), 75–76.

8. Based on an article by H. Wayne House, 2011, http://www
.hwhouse.com/images/5.HEROD_THE_GREAT.pdf.

9. See the article by L. I. Levine, "Herod the Great," *ABD* 3: 160–69.

10. See the interesting study by Steinmann, where he argues that
Herod reigned from 39–1 BC. Andrew Steinmann, "When
Did Herod the Great Reign?" *NT* 51 (2009) 1–29.

11. "He was such a warrior as could not be withstood . . . fortune
was also very favourable to him" (Josephus, *Bel Jud I*, xxi, 13).
See also "Herod," newadvent.org.

12. Josephus, *Ant.* 15.8.1; *Ant.* 16.5.1; *Bel Jud I*, xxi, 1, 5.

13. Part of the wine jug bearing the inscription is missing and so
it not clear whether the Latin reads "Herod, King of Judea" or
"Herod, King of the Jews." This inscription is one in a series
marked sequentially from No. 804 to 816. The rest of the
series was discovered in different locations at Masada. The
inscriptions indicate that all the jars contained wine from the
Italian producer L. Lenius. See H. Cotton, O. Lernau, and Y.
Goren, "Fish sauces from Herodian Masada," *Journal of Roman
Archaeology* 9 (1996): 236.

14. Piotr Berdowski, "Garum of Herod the Great (Latin-Greek
Inscription on the Amphora from Masada)," *The Qumran
Chronicle* 16:3–4 (December 2008):107–22.

15. Judy Siegel, "US Physician Unlocks Mystery of King Herod's
Death," *The Jerusalem Post*, Jan 27, 2002.

16. News Release of The Hebrew University of Jerusalem, "Tomb
of King Herod discovered at Herodium by Hebrew University
archaeologist" (Jerusalem, May 8, 2007).

17. See Ehud Nezer, "Herodium," *ABD* (New York: Doubleday, 1996).

18. Josephus, *Ant.* 15.325; *J.W.*, 1.420. See D. Amit, "What Was
the Source of Herodion's Water?," http://www.christusrex.org/
www1/ofm/sbf/Books/LA44/44561DA.pdf.

19. Joseph Patrich and Benjamin Arubas, "'Herod's Tomb'
Reexamined: Guidelines for a Discussion and Conclusions,"
in *New Studies in the Archaeology of Jerusalem and Its Region*,
eds. Guy D. Stiebel, Orit Peleg-Barkat, Doron Ben-Ami,
Shlomit Weksler-Bdolah, and Yuval Gadot (Jerusalem: Israel
Antiquities Authority, 2013), 287–300.

20. Roi Porat, Yakov Kalman, and Rachal Chachy, "Herod's Tomb
and the Memorial Complex at Herodium," in *New Studies in
the Archaeology of Jerusalem and Its Region*, eds. Guy D. Stiebel,
Orit Peleg-Barkat, Doron Ben-Ami, Shlomit Weksler-Bdolah,
and Yuval Gadot (Jerusalem: Israel Antiquities Authority, 2013),
257–86.

21. Jack Finegan, *The Archaeology of the New Testament*, rev. ed.
(New Jersey: Princeton University Press, 1992), 204.

22. Eusebius, *Ecclesiastical History* 2.23.

23. Finegan, 308.

24. Quoted in Gonzalo Baez-Camargo, ACB, 202.

25. Ibid.

26. Ibid.

27. Jack Finegan, *The Archaeology of the New Testament: The Life
of Jesus and the Beginning of the Early Church* (Princeton:
Princeton University Press, 1992), 109.

28. Unger, *Archaeology and the New Testament*, 128–29.

29. Finegan, 94–97.

30. Finegan, 96.

31. Ibid.

32. Ibid.

33. For a discussion of this connection see Rachel Hachlili, *Ancient
Synagogues- Archaeology and Art: New Discoveries and Current
Research*, Handbook of Oriental Studies, Section 1, Ancient
Near East 105 (Leiden: Brill, 2013), 527–30.

34. For a complete description of the linguistic and archaeological
evidence for the site see Stefano De Luca and Anna Lena,
"Magdala/Taricheae" in *Galilee in the Late Second Temple
and Mishnaic Periods: The Archaeological Record from Cities,
Towns, and Villages*, eds. D. A. Fiensy and J. R. Strange
(Minneapolis: Fortress, 2015), 2: 280–342.

35. S. De Luca, "Urban Development of the City of Magdala /
Taricheae in the Light of the New Excavations. Remains,
Problems and Perspectives," paper presented at Greco-Roman
Galilee colloquium at Kinneret College on the Sea of Galilee
and Tel Hai Academic College, June 2009, 21–23.

36. See Mordechai Aviam, "The Decorated Stone from the
Synagogue at Migdal: A Holistic Interpretation and a Glimpse
into the Life of Galilean Jews at the Time of Jesus," *NT* 55
(2013): 20.

37. "Antonio Ferrua, [Age] 102; Archeologist Credited as Finding
St. Peter's Tomb." *Los Angeles Times* (May 29, 2003).

38. Katharina Galor and Hanswulf Bloedhorn, *The Archaeology of
Jerusalem: From the Origins to the Ottomans* (New Haven: Yale
University Press, 2015): 98–99.

39. Émile Puech and Joe Zias, "Le tombeau de Zacharie et Siméon
au monument funéraire dit d'Absalom dans la vallée de
Josaphat" *RB* 110:14 (Jan/Oct, 2003): 321–35.

40. Joe Zias and Emile Puech, "The Tomb of Absalom
Reconsidered," *NEA* 68:4 (Dec, 2005): 157.

41. Galor and Bloedhorn, 115–6.

42. George Anthony Keddie, "Iudaea Capta, Iudaea Invicta: The
Subversion of Flavian Ideology in Fourth Ezra," (MA Thesis,
University of Texas at Austin, 2013), vi.

43. Leen Ritmeyer, "The Tomb of the Shroud in Jerusalem,"
http://www.ritmeyer.com/2013/01/13/the-tomb-of-the
-shroud-in-jerusalem/.

44. Joe Zias and Sekeles, "The Crucified Man from Givat
ha-Mivtar: A Reappraisal," *IEJ* 35 (1985): 22–27, and Zias
and J. Charlesworth, "Crucifixion: Archaeology, Jesus, and

the Dead Sea Scrolls" in *Jesus and the Dead Sea Scrolls*, ed. Charlesworth (New York: Doubleday, 192), 273–89.

45. Yigael Yadin, "Epigraphy and Crucifixion," *IEJ* 23 (1973): 18–22.

46. In his discussion of crucifixion of Jewish rebels, Josephus says, "The soldiers out of rage and hatred amused themselves by nailing their prisoners in different postures; and so great was their number, that space could not be found for the crosses nor crosses for the bodies" (*J.W.* 5.451). See Josephus, *The Jewish War: Books 1–7*, ed. Jeffrey Henderson, T. E. Page, et al., trans. Thackeray, vol. 3, Loeb Classical Library (Cambridge, MA: Harvard University Press, 1927–1928), 341.

47. Eusebius, *Ecclesiastical History*, 8:8.

48. J. D. Crossan, *Who Killed Jesus? Exposing the Roots of Anti-Semitism in the Gospel Story of the Death of Jesus* (San Francisco: HarperCollins, 1995) 160–88. See a restatement of this position with some revision in J. D. Crossan and J. L. Reed, *Excavating Jesus: Beneath the Stones, Behind the Texts* (San Francisco: HarperCollins, 2001) 230–70.

49. For further details see Craig A. Evans, "Jewish Burial Traditions and the Resurrection of Jesus," http://craigaevans.com/Burial_Traditions.pdf.

50. Shimon Gibson, *The Final Days of Jesus: The Archaeological Evidence* (New York: HarperCollins, 2009), 156.

51. A Byzantine period report on the tomb of the Holy Sepulchre church (traditional site of Jesus' tomb) says it had a rolling stone. Citation of report or heresay. I have been told a fragment of this original stone is still extant today.

52. Amos Kloner, "Did a Rolling Stone Close Jesus' Tomb?" *BAR* 25.5 (Sept/Oct 1999): 23.

53. Megan Sauter, "How Was Jesus' Tomb Sealed?" *BAR* (2015), https://www.biblicalarchaeology.org/daily/biblical-sites-places/jerusalem/how-was-jesus-tomb-sealed/. Finegan notes that in Nazareth several tombs were sealed with rolling stone, "a type of closure typical of the late Jewish period up to A.D. 70." See Jack Finegan, *The Archaeology of the New Testament: The Life of Jesus and the Beginning of the Early Church* (Princeton: Princeton University Press, 1993), 46.

54. Ibid.

55. See Urban C. von Wahlde, "A Rolling Stone That Was Hard to Roll," *BAR* 41:02 (March/April 2015), page.

56. Ibid.

57. Ibid.

58. As cited in Craig A. Evans, "Mark's Incipit and the Priene Calendar Inscription: From Jewish Gospel to Greco-Roman Gospel," *Journal of Greco-Roman Christianity and Judaism* 1 (2000) 67–81.

59. S. R. F. Price, *Rituals and Power: The Roman Imperial Cult in Asia Minor* (city: publisher, date), 55.

60. Jack Finegan, *The Archaeology of the New Testament: The Life of Jesus and the Beginning of the Early Church* (Princeton: Princeton University Press, 1992), 142.

61. Lee I. Levine, "Synagogue Officials: The Evidence from Caesarea and Its Implications for Palestine and the Diaspora,"

in *Caesarea Maritima: A Retrospective After Two Millennia*, eds. Avner Rabban and Kenneth G. Holum (Leiden: Brill, 1996), 392.

62. For fuller discussion of the Theodotus Synagogue Inscription, see Craig A. Evans, "Theodotus Synagogue Inscription — 1913," *Jesus and the Ossuaries* (Waco, TX: Baylor University Press, 2003), 38–43.

63. BL Papyrus 904 as translated by T. C. Mitchell, *The Bible in the British Museum: Interpreting the Evidence* (London: British Museum, 1988).

64. James Rendel Harris, "The Present State of the Controversy Over the Place and Time of the Birth of Christ," ed. W. Robertson Nicoll, *The Expositor* 5:3 (March 1908): 216.

65. The text may be found in Loeb, Select Papyri 2.108, and a photo of the original is in T. C. Mitchell, *Biblical Archaeology: Documents from the British Museum* (New York: University of Cambridge Press, 1988) 95.

66. W. M. Ramsay, *The Bearing of Recent Discovery on the Trustworthiness of the New Testament*, 2nd ed. (London: Hodder and Stoughton, 1915), 285.

67. N. F. Gier, "Serious Problems with Luke's Census," *God, Reason, and the Evangelicals*. Lanham, Maryland: University Press of America, 1987), 145–49.

68. W. M. Ramsay, *Was Christ Born at Bethlehem? A Study on the Credibility of St. Luke* (London: Hodder and Stoughton, 1898), 236–38.

69. I have included Gergesenes as the preferred reading even though the NIV renders Gerasenes, which I think does not reflect the best understanding of the text.

70. Origen, *Commentary on the Gospel of John*, 6.24 (*ANF* 10.371).

71. "Pontius Pilate, Governor of Judaea," *Encyclopedia Britannica*, https://britannica.com/biography/Pontius-Pilate.

72. Mireille Hadas-Lebel, *Philo of Alexandria: A Thinker in the Jewish Diaspora* (Leiden: Brill, 2012), 70.

73. Giorgio Agamben, *Pilate and Jesus*, trans. Adam Kotsko (Stanford, CA: Stanford University Press, 2015), 9.

74. McRay, *Archaeology and the New Testament*, 204.

75. Bruce M. Metzger and the United Bible Societies, *A Textual Commentary on the Greek New Testament*, 2nd ed. companion volume to the *United Bible Societies' Greek New Testament*, 4th rev. ed. (London; New York: United Bible Societies, 1994), 171.

76. Origen, *Commentary on John*, 6.24 in *ANF* 10.370.

77. Eusebuis, *Onomasticon* D.32.

78. Jordanian Department of Antiquities, "The Baptismal Site (Bethany beyond the Jordan)," http://whc.unesco.org/en/tentativelists/1556/.

79. LPPTS 1-b, 26; P. Geyer and O. Cuntz, eds. *Itinera Hierosolymitana Saeculi III-VIII*, Corpus Scriptorium Ecclesiasticorum Latinorum 39 (Turnhout: Brepols, 1965), 24.

80. LPPTS 2-b, 14–15; Geyer, 145–46.

81. LPPTS 2-d, 10–12; Geyer, 166–68.

82. Rami G. Khouri, "Have Jordanian Archaeologists Found the Place Where Jesus Was Baptized?" *The Daily Star*, May 23, 2005.

83. Katia Cytryn-Silverman, "Kharrar, Wadi," in *EAEHL* 5:1861.

84. Khouri, "Have Jordanian Archaeologists Found the Place Where Jesus Was Baptized?"

85. "The Baptismal Site (Bethany beyond the Jordan)" http://whc.unesco.org/en/tentativelists/1556/.

86. Due to drought, growing population, and increased irrigation, many claim the Sea of Galilee's water levels are at or near their lowest level on record.

87. Gottlieb Schumacher, with additions by Laurence Oliphant and Guy LeStrange, *Across the Jordan* (London: Richard Bentley and Son, 1886), 244.

88. Jack F. Shroder and Moshe Inbar, "Geologic and Geographic Background to the Bethsaida Excavations," in *The Bethsaida Excavations Project Reports and Contextual Studies*, ed. Rami Arav (Kirksville, MO: Thomas Jefferson University Press, 1995), 67.

89. Rami Arav and Carl E. Savage, "Bethsaida: Location and Importance," in *Galilee in the Late Second Temple and Mishnaic Periods: The Archaeological Record from Cities, Towns, and Village*, eds. D. A. Fiensy and J. R. Strange (Minneapolis: Fortress, 2015), 2: 258–60. See also, Bargil Pixner, "Auf der Suche nach Bethsaida," in *Wege des Messias und Stätten der Urkirche: Jesus un das Judenchristendum im Licht neuer archäologischer Erkenntnisse*, ed. Rainer Riesner, 3rd enl. ed. Studien zur biblischen Archäologie und Zeitgeschichte 2 (Giessen: Brunnen, 1996), 127–41; and Bargil Pixner, "Searching for the New Testament Sit of Bethsaida," *BA* 48:4 (1985): 207–16.

90. The evidence indicates that ancient Bethesda was at least in the area.

91. Archaeologists historically have used local knowledge of the land as a guide to finding sites. Often, their ancient names are preserved.

92. Mendel Nun (*Ancient Stone Anchors and Net Sinkers from the Sea of Galilee*, [Kibbutz Ein Gev, 1993]) has challenged the identification of these artefacts as fishing implements. While the BEP admits that some of the initial artefacts were misidentified, many more fishing artefacts have subsequently been unearthed.

93. J. Harold Ellens, ed. *Bethsaida in Archaeology, History and Ancient Culture: A Festscrift in Honor of John T. Greene* (Newcastle upon Tyne: Cambridge Scholars Publishing, 2014), 39.

94. James H. Charlesworth, ed. *Jesus and Archaeology* (Grand Rapids: Eerdmans, 2006), 7–8.

95. Limestone was used exclusively by Jews for food storage due to the stone's ability to remain ritually pure (as opposed to clay pottery). Flint was used to perform circumcisions (Josh 5:2–3).

96. Carl E. Savage, *Et-Tell (Bethsaida): A Study of the First Century CE in the Galilee* (Ann Arbor: ProQuest, 2008), 18.

97. Ibid.

98. Laura Banker, John F. Shroder, Jr., and Moshe Inbar, "Sedimentologic and Paleogeomorphologic Character of the Bethsaida (Beteiha) Plain of the Sea of Galilee," in *Bethsaida: A City by the North Shore of the Sea of Galilee*, eds. Rami Arav and R. A. Freund, Bethsaida Excavations Project 4 (Kirksville, MO: Truman State University Press, 2009), 310–26.

99. The BEP argues that the "dominant trend over many centuries has been for it [the shore of the Sea of Galilee] to move south," away from et-Tell/Bethsaida. John F. Shrer, Jr., Michael P. Bishop, Kevin J. Cornwell, Moshe Inbar, "Catastrophic Geomorphic Processes and Betsaida Archaeology, Israel," in *Bethsaida—A City by the North Shore of the Sea of Galilee*, eds. Romi Arav and Richard a. Freund, BEP (Truman State University Press, 1999), 2:116.

100. According to Steven Feldman, "official maps place Bethsaida at et-Tell and the IAA has erected signs for visitors there. . . ." Steven Feldman, "The Case for el-Araj" *BAR* 26:1 (Jan/Feb 2000): 52.

101. John F. Shroder, Jr., Harry D. Jol, and Philip P. Reeder, "El Araj as Bethsaida: Spatial and Temporal Improbabilities," in *Bethsaida: A City by the North Shore of the Sea of Galilee*, eds. Rami Arav and R. A. Freund, Bethsaida Excavations Project 4 (Kirksville, MO: Truman State University Press, 2009), 293–309.

102. Noa Shpigel and Ruth Schuster, "The Lost Home of Jesus' Apostles Has Just Been Found, Archaeologists Say," *Haaretz* (August 8, 2017), http://www.haaretz.com/archaeology/1.805402.

103. Finegan, *The Archaeology of the New Testament*, 62–63.

104. Jerome, *Letter* 46 (*NPNF* 2.6.60).

105. Finegan, *The Archaeology of the New Testament*, 63.

106. Ibid., 64.

107. Ibid.

108. Bellarmio Bagatti, "Le antichita' di Kh. Qana e di Kefr Kenna in Galilee" *Liber Annus* 15 (1964–65): 251–92.

109. Finegan, *The Archaeology of the New Testament*, 65.

110. Ignazio Mancini, "Excavations Have Confirmed that a Village Existed in the First Century on the Site Where the Shrine of Cana has been Built." *L'Osservatore Romano*, Weekly Edition in English, August 26, 1998, 4, http://www.ewtn.com/library/SCRIPTUR/CANAEXCA.HTM.

111. Ibid.

112. Unfortunately, as of 2012, the findings of this expedition have not been published, probably due to the sad death of Douglas Edwards in 2008.

113. Peter Richardson, *Building Jewish in the Roman East* (Waco, TX: Baylor University Press, 2004), 55.

114. James H. Charlesworth, ed. *Jesus and Archaeology* (Grand Rapids: Eerdmans, 2006), 120.

115. Peter Richardson, "Khirbet Qana (and Other Villages) as a Context for Jesus," *Jesus and Archaeology*, ed. James H. Charlesworth (Grand Rapids: Eerdmans, 2006), 120.

116. James H. Charlesworth, ed. *Jesus and Archaeology* (Grand Rapids: Eerdmans, 2006), 541.

117. J. Carl Laney, "The Identification of Cana of Galilee" in *Selective Geographical Problems in the Life of Christ* (PhD diss., Dallas Seminary, 1977), 107.

118. Ibid., 98.

119. Peter Richardson, "Khirbet Qana (and Other Villages) as a Context for Jesus" in *Jesus and Archaeology*, ed. James H. Charlesworth (Grand Rapids: Eerdmans, 2000), 144.

120. James H. Charlesworth, ed. *Jesus and Archaeology* (Grand Rapids: Eerdmans, 2006), 139.

121. Peter Richardson, *Building Jewish in the Roman East* (Waco, TX: Baylor University Press, 2004), 105.

122. Douglas R. Edwards, "Khirbet Qana: From Jewish Village to Christian Pilgrimage Site" in *The Roman and Byzantine Near East*, ed. John H. Humphrey (Portsmith, RI: Journal of Roman Archaeology, 2002), 3:132.

123. Flavius Josephus and William Whiston, *The Works of Josephus: Complete and Unabridged* (Peabody, MA: Hendrickson, 1987), 6.

124. W. F. Albright, "Aenon," *The Zondervan Encyclopedia of the Bible*, vol. 1-A-C, ed. Merrill C. Tenney (Grand Rapids: Zondervan, 2010).

125. Jerome Murphy-O'Connor, "Nablus (Shechem)," *The Holy Land: An Oxford Archaeological Guide from Earliest Times to 1700* (New York: Oxford University Press, 2008).

126. Craig R. Koester, *Symbolism in the Fourth Gospel: Meaning, Mystery, Community*, 2nd ed. (Minneapolis: Augsburg Fortress, 2003), 186.

127. J. Ramsey Michaels, *John* (San Francisco: Harper, 1984), 46.

128. Koester, *Symbolism in the Fourth Gospel*, 186.

129. Joshua Schwartz, "John the Baptist, the Wilderness and the Samaritan Mission," in *Studies in Historical Geography and Biblical Historiography: Presented to Zecharia Kallai*, eds. Gershom Galil and Moshe Weinfeld (Leiden: Brill, 2000), 104–20.

130. Urban C. von Wahlde, "Archaeology and John's Gospel," in *Jesus Research and Archaeology: A New Perspective*, ed. James H Charlesworth (Grand Rapids: Eerdmans, 2006), 555–56.

131. Abu 'l-Fath, "Nablus (Shechem)," *Samaritan Documents: Relating To Their History, Religion and Life*, trans. and ed. John Bowman (Eugene, OR: Pickwick, 1977), 119–20; Timothy Wardle, *The Jerusalem Temple and Early Christian Identity* (Mohr Siebeck, 2010), 99.

132. C. R. Conder, *Palestine* (New York: Dodd, Mead, & Company, n.d.), 107.

133. Michael Meerson, "One God Supreme: A Case Study of Religious Tolerance and Survival," *JGRChJ* 7 (2010): 45.

134. Magnar Karveit, *The Origin of the Samaritans* (Leiden: Brill, 2009), 206–09; Alan David Crown, ed., *The Samaritans* (Tübingen, Mohr Siebeck, 1989), 167–69.

135. Yitzhak Magen, "The Dating of the First Phrase of the Samaritan Temple on Mount Gerizim in Light of the Archaeological Evidence" in *Judah and the Judeans in the Fourth Century B.C.E.*, eds., Oded Lipschits, Gary N. Knoppers, and Rainer Albertz (Winona Lake, IN: Eisenbrauns, 2007), 157; Reinhard Pummer, *The Samaritans: A Profile* (Grand Rapids: Eerdmans, 2006), 81–84.

136. Yitzhak Magen, "The Church of Mary Theotokos on Mt. Gerazim," in *Christian Archaeology in the Holy Land: Eassys in Honor of Virgilio C. Corbo* (Jerusalem: Franciscan Printing Press, 1990): 333–42.

137. Yitzak Magen, *Mount Gerazim Excavations Volume II: A Temple City* (Jerusalem: Judea & Samaria Publications, 2008): 98.

138. Ibid., 100.

139. Ronny Reich, Eli Shukron, and Omri Lernau, "Recent Discoveries in the City of David, Jerusalem" *IEJ* 57:153–68.

140. Jon C. Laansma, Grant R. Osborne, and Ray F. Van Neste, eds., *New Testament Theology in Light of the Church's Mission: Essays in Honor of I. Howard Marshall* (Eugene, OR: Cascade, 2011), 125; Paul N. Anderson, Felix Just, and Tom Thatcher, *John, Jesus, and History*, vol. 3 in *Glimpses of Jesus through the Johannine Lens* (Atlanta: SBL Press, 2016), 261.

141. David Christian Clausen, *The History, Art and Archaeology of the Cenacle on Mount Zion* (Jefferson, NC: McFarland, 2016), n.p.

142. W. Harold Mare, *The Archaeology of the Jerusalem Area* (Eugene, OR: Wipf & Stock, 1987), 170.

143. Bargil Pixner, *Paths of the Messiah and Sites of the Early Church from Galilee to Jerusalem: Jesus and Jewish Christianity in Light of Archaeological Discoveries*, eds. Rainer Riesner, Keith Myrick, and Sam and Miriam Randall, eds. (San Francisco: Ignatius, 1991), 257. He says, "It is hardly conceivable that the Last Supper, the Pentecost experience and the regular meeting of the original community could have been located close to the palace of the high priest. Therefore, all reasons speak again the late tradition for the site of Caiaphas' house at the Armenian Church of the Savior" (257).

144. Gallicantu is rejected by several scholars as the site of Caiaphas' house. See Hannah M. Cotton, et al., *Corpus Inscriptionum Iudaeae/Palaestinae*, Part 1 Jerusalem, 1–704 (New York: de Gruyter, 2010), 34–35.

145. Bargil Pixner, *Paths of the Messiah and Sites of the Early Church from Galilee to Jerusalem: Jesus and Jewish Christianity in Light of Archaeological Discoveries*, eds. Rainer Riesner, Keith Myrick, and Sam and Miriam Randall (San Francisco: Ignatius, 1991), 257.

146. Jerome Murphy-O'Connor, *The Holy Land: An Oxford Archaeological Guide from Earliest Times to 1700,* 5th ed. (Oxford: Oxford University Press, 2009), 119; see also, Hannah M. Cotton, et al., *Corpus Inscriptionum Iudaeae/Palaestinae*, vol 1: Jerusalem, part 1:1–704 (New York: de Gruyter, 2010), 34–35.

147. Zvi Greenhut, "Discovery of the Caiaphas Family Tomb," *Jerusalem Perspective* 4/4–5: 6–12; Jerusalem, East Talpiyot (*Ya'ar Hashalom*), *Excavations and Surveys in Israel 1991.* 10:140-141; "The 'Caiaphas' Tomb in North Talpiyot, Jerusalem," *'Atiqot* 21: 63–71; "Discovered in Jerusalem: Burial Cave of the Caiaphas Family," *BAR* 18/5: 28–36, 76; "The Caiaphas Tomb in North Talpiyot, Jerusalem" in *Ancient Jerusalem Revealed*, ed. by Hillel Geva (Jerusalem: Israel Exploration Societ,1994): 219–22.

148. See the caution of W. Horbury, "The 'Caiaphas' Ossuaries and Joseph Caiaphas," *PEQ* 126 (1994): 32–48; W. D. Davies and Dale C. Allison, *A Critical and Exegetical Commentary on the Gospel According to Saint Matthew* (London; New York: T&T Clark, 2004), 438–39.

149. Helen K. Bond, *Caiaphas: Friend of Rome and Judge of Jesus?* (Louisville: Westminster John Knox, 2004), 4–8, argues that most of the objections have been met and that the box is most likely the tomb of Caiaphas; See also Z. Greenhut, "Burial

Cave of the Caiaphas Family," *BAR* 18:5 (1992): 28–36, 76 and Ronny Reich, "Caiaphas Name Inscribed on Bone Boxes," *BAR* 18:5 (1922): 38–44, 76.

150. James C. VanderKam, *From Joshua to Caiaphas: High Priests After the Exile* (Philadelphia: Fortress, 2004), 435–36.

151. This papyrus was once considered the oldest, but recently an earlier papyrus fragment of the Gospel of Mark was found as part of Egyptian cartonnage and now is part of the collection of the Museum of the Bible, Washington, DC. For an early report of this see Daniel B. Wallace, "Dr. Wallace: Earliest Manuscript of the New Testament Discovered?" Dallas Theological Seminary, February 9, 2102, http://dts.edu/read/wallace-newtestament-manuscript-first-century/.

152. Jack Finegan, *Encountering New Testament Manuscripts: A Working Introduction to Textual Criticism* (Grand Rapids: Eerdmans, 1974), 85.

153. Finegan, 85–90.

154. K. Aland and B. Aland, *The Text of the New Testament: An Introduction to the Critical Editions and to the Theory and Practice of Modern Textual Criticism*, trans. Erroll F. Rhodes, 2nd ed. (Grand Rapids: Eerdmans, 1995), 99.

155. Leen and Kathleen Ritmeyer, "'Akeldama' and the Hinnom Valley" in *Jerusalem in the year 30 A.D.*, eds. Leen and Kathleen Ritmeyer (Jerusalem: Carta, 2004), 22–23.

156. Finegan notes that the Golden Gate had a depiction of the Persian palace of Shushan to "commemorate the permission granted by the kings of Persia for the rebuilding of the Temple." Jack Finegan, *The Archaeology of the New Testament: The Life of Jesus and the Beginning of the Early Church*, rev. ed. (New Jersey: Princeton University Press, 1992), 209.

157. Jack Finegan, *The Archaeology of the New Testament: The Life of Jesus and the Beginning of the Early Church* (Princeton: Princeton University Press, 1993), 209–10.

158. Gonzalo Baez-Camargo, *Archaeological Commentary on the Bible* (New York: Doubleday, 1984), 239.

159. This is not to say the reading is definitive. Metzger notes this is the "least unacceptable" text. Metzger, *Textual Commentary on the Greek New Testament*, 269.

160. Judith Harris, "Putting Paul on the Map: Apostle's Name Found on Cyprus Inscription," *BAR* 26:1 (January 2000): 14.

161. Ben Witherington III, *The Acts of the Apostles: A Socio-Rhetorical Commentary* (Grand Rapids: Eerdmans, 1998), 400; and see entire discussion at 399–402.

162. David W. J. Gill and Conrad Gempf, *The Book of Acts in Its First Century Setting, Vol 2: The Book of Acts in Its Graeco-Roman Setting* (Grand Rapids: Eerdmans, 1994), 284.

163. George Edmundson, *The Church in Rome in the First Century* (New York: Longmans), 78.

164. Jerome Murphy-O'Connor, *St. Paul's Corinth: Texts and Archaeology*, 3rd ed. (Collegeville, MN: Liturgical Press, 1983, 2002), 161.

165. Clyde, *LTB*, 361.

166. Hans Rudolf Pomtow, "Delphoi" in *Pauly's Encyclopedia of Classical Antiquity*. Supplement Band IV (Stuttgart, 1924), 1189–1432.

167. Steven J. Friesen, *Twice Neokoros: Ephesus, Asia, and the Cult of the Flavian Imperial Family* (Leiden: Brill, 1993) 93–94.

168. "The Encyclical Epistle of the Church At Smyrna, Concerning the Martydom of the Holy Polycarp," 12 in *ANF* 1:41.

169. *NPNF* 1.1:257.

170. Augustine, "Letter to Alypius the Bishop of Thagaste, Concerning the Anniversary of the Birth of Leontis, Formerly Bishop of Hippo" 12 (*NPNF* 1.1:257).

171. R. A. Kearsley, "New Testament Context," in *New Documents Illustrating Early Christianity*, ed. G. H. R. Horsley, (Sydney, Australia: Maquarie University Press, 1987) 55.

172. John McRay, "Archaeology and the Book of Acts," *CTR* 5 (1990): 69–82, 77.

173. Friesen, *Twice Neokoros*, 94–94.

174. This echoes the story of Polycarp's martyrdom mentioned above.

175. A. Souter, "Asiarch" in *Dictionary of the Apostolic Church*, ed. James Hastings (New York: Charles Scribner's Sons, 1916–1918), 103.

176. Louis H. Feldman, *Josephus and Modern Scholarship (1937-1980)* (New York: de Gruyter, 1984), 446.

Chapter 13

1. Andrew D. Clarke, *Secular and Christian Leadership in Corinth: A Socio-Historical and Exegetical Study of 1 Corinthians 1-6* (Leiden: Brill, 1993), 46–57; Robert S. Dutch, *The Educated Elite in 1 Corinthians: Education and Community Conflict in Graeco-Roman Context* (London: T&T Clark, 2005), 81–82.

2. Justin Meggitt, "Paul, Poverty and Survival," *Studies of the New Testament and Its World* (Bloomsbury: T&T Clark, 2000), 139–40; see response by Timothy A. Brookins, "Corinthians Wisdom, Stoic Philosophy, and the Ancient Economy," *Society for New Testament Studies Monograph Series* 159 (Cambridge: Cambridge University Press, 2014), 113–14.

3. However, while Meggitt claims to have "discovered fifty-five examples of the use of the Latin cognomen Erastus and twenty-three of the Greek Erastos . . ." none of these are physical inscriptions uncovered in situ. Justin J. Meggitt, *Paul, Poverty and Survival*, Studies of the New Testament and Its World (Edinburgh: T&T Clark, 1998), 139–40, n. 345.

4. L. L. Welborn, *An End to Enmity: Paul and the "Wrongdoer" of Second Corinthians* (Berlin: de Gruyter, 2011), 270f.

5. John K. Goodrich, "Erastus, *Quaestor* of Corinth: The Administrative Rank of ὁ οἰκονόμος τῆς πόλεως (Rom 16.23) in an Achaean Colony," *NTS* 56 (2010): 90.

6. Jospeh A. Fitzmeyer, *First Corinthians*, AB 32 (New Haven, CT: Yale University Press, 2008), 32.

7. John Fotopoulos, *The Blackwell Companion to the New Testament*, ed. David E. Aune (Malden, MA: Wiley-Blackwell, 2010), 418.

8. See James Hope Moulton and George Milligan, *The Vocabulary of the Greek New Testament Illustrated from the Papyri and Other Non-Literary Sources* (Grand Rapids: Eerdmans, 1930), 6.

9. The seminal study on this is Adolf Deissman, *Light from the Ancient Near East: The New Testament Illustrated by Recently*

Discovered Texts of the Graeco-Roman World, trans. Lionel Strachan (London: Hodder and Stroughton, 1910), 326–33.

10. Translation based on Deissman, *Light from the Ancient Near East,* 327.

11. Mark Wilson, *Biblical Turkey: A Guide to the Jewish and Christian Sites of Asia Minor* (Istambul: Ege Yayinlari, 2010) 203.

12. Ibid., 199.

13. Ibid., 200.

14. Ibid., 209.

15. Ibid., 206.

16. Richard E. Oster, "Ephesus as a Religious Center under the Principate, I. Paganism before Constantine" in *Aufstieg und Niedergang der römischen Welt: Geschichte und Kultur Roms im Spiegel der neuren Forschung,* eds. Hildegard Temporini and Wolfgang Haase (Berlin: de Gruyter, 1990), 1703.

17. Clinton E. Arnold, *Ephesians, Power and Magic: The Concept of Power in Ephesians in Light of Its Historical Setting,* Society for New Testament Studies Monograph Series 63 (New York: Cambridge University Press, 1989) 20.

18. Mark Wilson, *Biblical Turkey,* 202.

19. Oster, "Ephesus as a Religious Center under the Principate," 1703.

20. Ramsay MacMullen, *Christianizing the Roman Empire AD 100–400* (New Haven: Yale University Press, 1984), 18.

21. Wilson, 203.

22. Mark R. Fairchild, *Christian Origins in Ephesus and Asia Minor* (Istanbul: Arkeoloji ve Sanat Yayinari, 2015), 40.

23. Wilson, 224.

24. Edwin Yamauchi, *The Archaeology of New Testament Cities* (Grand Rapids: Baker, 1980) 111.

25. Peter Scherrer,."Ephesus Uncovered," *Archaeology Odyssey* 4, no. 2 (Mar/Apr 2001): 26–37, http://members.bib-arch.org/publication.asp?PubID=BSAO&Volume=4&Issue=2&ArticleID=13.

26. Scherrer,."Ephesus Uncovered," 26–37.

27. Wilson, 213.

28. Ibid.

29. Ibid.

30. Clive Foss, *Ephesus After Antiquity: A Late Antique, Byzantine and Turkish City* (New York: Cambridge University Press, 1979), 74.

31. Wilson, 214.

32. Ibid., 218.

33. Yamauchi, *The Archaeology of New Testament Cities,* 110.

34. Ibid.

35. E. M. Blaiklock, *The Archaeology of the New Testament,* rev. ed. (Grand Rapids: Zondervan, 1984, c. 1970) 125.

36. François Bovon, "Women Priestesses in the Apocryphal Acts of Philip" in *Walk in the Ways of Wisdom: Essays in Honor of Elisabeth Schüssler Fiorenza,* ed. Shelly Matthews, Cythia Briggs Kittredge, and Melanie Johnson-DeBaufre (Harrisburg: Trinity Press International, 2003), 109–21.

37. Paul L. Maier, *Eusebius: The Church History* (Grand Rapids: Kregel, 1999), 104–05.

38. John A. Kelhoffer, *Miracle and Mission: The Authentication of Missionaries and Their Message in the Longer Ending of Mark* (Tübingen: Mohr Siebeck, 2000), 405–06.

39. François Bovon and Christopher Matthews, *The Acts of Philip: A New Translation* (Waco, TX: Baylor University Press, 2012).

40. It is known today as "Pamukkale," Turkish for "castle of cotton," after what has been called the "world's most lavish travertine formation."

41. Edwin M. Yamauchi, *New Testament Cities in Western Asia Minor: Light from Archaeology on Cities of Paul and the Seven Churches of Revelation* (Eugene, OR: Wipf and Stock, 1980).

42. Francesco D'Andria, "The Sanctuary of St. Philip in Hierapolis and the tombs of saints in Anatolian cities" in *Life & Death in Asia Minor in Hellenistic, Roman & Byzantine Times,* ed. J. Rasmus Brandt et al. (Oxford: Oxbow, 2017), n. p.

43. Renzo Allegri, "How I Discovered the Tomb of the Apostle Philip: Interview with Archaeologist Francesco D'Andria," *ZENIT* (2012), http://www.zenit.org/article-34705?1=english.

44. Francesco D'Andria, "Conversion, Crucifixion, and Celebration," BAR 37 (2011): 34–46, 70.

Chapter 14

1. H. A. Harris, *Greek Athletics and the Jews* (Cardiff: University of Wales Press, 1976): 24–95.

2. N. Bream, "More on Hebrews xii. 1," *Expository Times* 80 (1968–69): 150–51.

3. Roger Bagnall, R. Casagrande-Kim, A. Ersoy, and C. Tanriver, eds., *Graffiti from the Basilica in the Agora of Smyrna.* Institute for the Study of the Ancient World (New York: NYU Press, 2016).

4. Ibid.

Bibliography

Introduction to Biblical Archaeology

Albright, W. F. *The Archaeology of Palestine*. Rev. ed. Harmondsworth, London: Penguin, 1960.

Báez-Camargo, Gonzalo. *ACB*. New York: Doubleday, 1984.

"Bible Secrets Revealed: Lost in Translation." http://www.history .com/shows/bible-secrets-revealed/videos/bible-secrets-revealed -lost-in-translation.

Brandfon, Frederic R. "The Limits of Evidence: Archaeology and Objectivity." *Maarav* 4 (1987): 5–43.

Dever, William, G. *What Did the Biblical Writers Know and When Did They Know It?: What Archaeology Can Tell Us about the Reality of Ancient Israel*. Grand Rapids: Eerdmans, 2001.

Elliot, Mark. *Biblical Interpretation Using Archaeological Evidence 1900–1930*. Lewiston, NY: Edwin Mellen, 2002.

Gibbon, Guy. *Critically Reading the Theory and Methods of Archaeology: An Introductory Guide*. Lanham: Altamira Press, 2014.

Kahila Bar-Gal, Gila, Tzviki Rosenerg, and Charles Greenblatt. "Animal Remains from Khirbet Qumran: A Case Study of Two Bones (QUM 392 and 393) from Two Bone Burials." Pages 67–78 in *Holistic Qumran: Trans-Disciplinary Research of Qumran and the Dead Sea Scrolls. Proceedings of the NIAS-Lorenz Center Qumran Workshop 21–25 April 2008*. Edited by Jan Gunneweg, Annemie Adriaens, and Joris Dik. STDJ 87. Leiden: Brill, 2010.

Osborn, William R. "Abraham and History (Part 1)." http://law prophetsandwritings.com/author/rusty_osborne.

Oswalt, John. *The Bible among the Myths: Unique Revelation or Just Ancient Literature?* Grand Rapids: Zondervan, 2009.

Reuven, Peretz, "Wooden Beams from Herod's Temple Mount: Do They Still Exist?" *BAR* 39.3 (2013): 40–47.

Scanlin, Harold. *The Dead Sea Scrolls and Modern Translations of the Old Testament*. Carol Stream, IL: Tyndale House, 1993.

Roden, Chet, "A Hermeneutic of Convergence: Moving Beyond the Intersection of Archaeology and the Bible." Paper presented to the Near East Archaeological Society at the Evangelical Theological Society. San Diego, CA, November 2014. Dr. Roden developed his methodology based on the discussion in John C. Laughlin, "On the Convergence of Texts and Artifacts: Using Archaeology to Teach the Hebrew Bible." Pages 115—132 in *Between Text and Artifact: Integrating Archaeology in Biblical Studies*. Edited by Milton C. Moreland. Atlanta: Society of Biblical Literature, 2003.

Archaeology and the Old Testament

"2,750-year-old temple found near Jerusalem." http://www.foxnews .com/science/2012/12/27/2750-year-old-temple-found-near -jerusalem.

Aalders, G. "The Problem of the Book of Jonah." The Tyndale New Testament Lecture (1948): 8.

Adams, David L. "Between Socoh and Azekah: The Biblical Identity of Khirbet Qeiyafa." Paper presented at the American Schools of Oriental Research Annual Meeting. New Orleans, LA, 18–21 November 2009.

Aharoni, Yohanan, *The Archaeology of the Land of Israel*. Translated by Anson F. Rainey. Philadelphia: Westminster, 1982.

Ahituv, Shmuel. "A Rejoinder to Nadav Na'aman's New Appraisal of the Silver Amulets from Ketef Hinnom." *IEJ* 62 (2012): 223–32.

Albenda, Pauline. "Assyrian Trees in the Brooklyn Museum." British Institute for the Study of Iraq 56, 1994.

Albright, W.F. "A Prince of Ta'anach in the Fifteenth Century BC." *BASOR* 94 (1944): 24–25.

———. "The Nebuchadnezzar and Neriglissar Chronicles." *BASOR* 143 (1956): 28.

———. "What Were the Cherubim?" *Biblical Archaeologist Reader* (Scholars Press): 95–97. 1975

Alexander, P.J. "Medieval Apocalypses as Historical Sources." *Ancient History Review* 73 (1968).

"Ancient Judean Temple Found near Jerusalem." http://rt.com/art -and-culture/ancient-judaean-temple-discovered–861.

"Ancient Texts Part of Earliest Known Documents." Rosella Lorenzi. *Discovery News*. http://news.discovery.com/history/archaeol-ogy/tower-of-babel–111227.htm.

Anderson, G. W. *Daniel*. CHB 1:151. New York: Cambridge University Press, 1984.

Arav, Rami and Richard Freund, eds. *Bethsaida: A City by the North Shore of the Sea of Galilee*. Vol. 1 of *Bethsaida: A City by the North Shore of the Sea of Galilee*. Kirksville, MO: Truman State University Press, 1995.

Archer, Gleason. "The Aramaic of the 'Genesis Apocryphon' Compared with the Aramaic of Daniel." Pages 160–69 in *New Perspectives on the Old Testament*. Edited by J. Barton Payne. Waco: Word Publishers, 1970.

———. "The Hebrew of Daniel Compared with the Qumran Sectarian Documents," in *The Law and the Prophets: Old Testament Essays in Honor of Oswalt T. Allis*. Edited by John H. Skilton. Philadelphia: Presbyterian and Reformed Publishing Co., 1974.

Archi, Alfonso. "The Epigraphic Evidence from Ebla and the Old Testament." *Bib* 60 (1979): 556–66.

Athas, George. *The Tel Dan Inscription: A Reappraisal and a New Interpretation*. New York: Continuum International Publishing Group, 2005.

Averbeck, Richard. "Factors in Reading the Patriarchal Narratives: Literary, Historical, and Theological Dimensions." Pages 115—37 in *Giving the Sense: Understanding and Using Old Testament Historical Texts*. Edited by David M. Howard, Jr. and Michael A. Grisanti. Grand Rapids: Kregel, 2003.

Avigad, Nahman. "The Epitaph of a Royal Steward from Siloam Village." *IEJ* 3 (1953): 137–52.

_____ *Hebrew Bullae from the Time of Jeremiah.* Washington, D.C.: Biblical Archaeology Society, 1987.

_____ "Two Hebrew 'Fiscal' Bullae," *IEJ* 40.4 (1990):262–66.

Banning, E.B. (2011). "So Fair a House. Göbekli Tepe and the Identification of Temples in the Pre-Pottery Neolithic of the Near East." *Current Anthropology* 52.5 (2011): 619–60.

Barkay, Gabriel. "A Bulla of Ishmael, the King's Son," *BASOR* 290/291 (1993): 109–14.

_____ "The Riches of Ketef Hinnom: Jerusalem Tomb Yields Biblical Text Four Centuries Older Than Dead Sea Scrolls." *BAR* 35.4 (2009): 22–35, 122, 124, 126.

Barkay, Gabriel, Marilyn J. Lundberg, Andrew G. Vaughn, Bruce Zuckerman, and Kenneth Zuckerman. "The Challenges of Ketef Hinnom: Using Advanced Technologies to Reclaim the Earliest Biblical Texts and Their Contexts." *NEA* 66.4 (2003): 162–71.

Barkay, Gabriel, Marilyn J. Lundberg, Andrew G. Vaughn, and Bruce Zuckerman. "The Amulets from Ketef Hinnom: A New Edition and Evaluation." *BASOR* 334 (2004): 41–70.

Barnett, Richard D. *Assyrian Palace Reliefs in the British Museum.* Oxford: Oxford University Press, 1970.

_____ "Polydactylism in the Ancient World." *BAR* 16.3 (1990): 46–51.

Barrera, Julio Trebolle. "Elijah." *EDSS* 1:246.

Beale, G. K. "The Exodus Hardening Motif of YHWH as a Polemic." ThM thesis, Dallas Theological Seminary, 1976.

_____ *The Temple and the Mission of God: A Biblical Theology of the Dwelling Place of God.* Downers Grove, IL: InverVarsity Press, 2004.

Belibtreu, Erika. "Grisly Assyrian Record of Torture and Death." *BAR* 17.1 (1991): 52–61, 75.

Ben-Shlomo, David. "Petrographic Analysis of Iron Age Pottery from Khirbet Qeiyafa." Paper presented at the American Schools of Oriental Research Annual Meeting. New Orleans, LA, 18–21 November 2009.

Ben-Yosef, Erez, Ron Shaar, Lisa Tauxe, and Ron Hagai. "A New Chronological Framework for Iron Age Copper Production at Timna (Israel)." *BASOR* 367 (2012): 31–71.

Ben-Zvi, E., "On the Reading 'bytdwd in the Aramaic Stele from Tel Dan." *JSOT* 64 (1994): 29–32.

Berlejung, Angelika. "Ein Program fürs Leben. Theologisches Wort und anthropologischer Ort der Silberamulette von Ketef Hinnom." *ZAW* 120 (2008): 204–30.

Berman, Joshua. *The Temple: Its Symbolism and Meaning Then and Now.* Northvale, NJ: J. Aaronson, 1995.

Best, Robert, M. *Noah's Ark and the Ziusudra Epic.* Winona Lake, IN: Eisenbrauns,1999.

Biesecker L.G. "Polydactyly: How Many Disorders and How Many Genes." *American Journal of Medical Genetics* 12.3 (2002): 279–83.

Biran, Avraham. *Biblical Dan.* Jerusalem: Israel Exploration Society, Hebrew Union College-Jewish Institute of Religion, 1994.

_____ "The Discovery of the Middle Bronze Age Gate at Tel Dan." *BA* 44 (1981): 139—144.

Biran, Avraham, and Joseph Naveh. "An Aramaic Stele Fragment from Tel Dan." *IEJ* 43.2/3 (1993): 81–98.

Black, J. A., G. Cunningham, E. Robson, and G. Zolyomi. "The Lament for Ur." Oxford: The Electronic Text Corpus of Sumerian Literature, 1998.

Blakely, J. A. "Reconciling Two Maps: Archaeological Evidence for the Kingdoms of David and Solomon." *BASOR* 327 (2002): 49–54.

Blakely, J. A. and J. W. Hardin. "Southwestern Judah in the Late Eighth Century BCE." *BASOR* 326 (2002), 11–64.

Boardman, J., I. E. S. Edwards, et al., eds. *CAH.* 3rd ed. 3 vols. Cambridge: Cambridge University Press, 1973–1991.

Bodie, Hodge. *Tower of Babel.* Green Forest, AR: Master Books, 2013.

Bornstein, M. "The Jerusalem Ostracon אלקארץ Reconsidered." *IEJ* 63.1 (2013): 26–38.

Borowski, Elie. "Cherubim: God's Throne?" *BAR* 21.4 (1955): 36–41.

Boyd, Bob. "Assyrian Brutality." *B&S* 3.2 (1990): 61–64.

Boyd, Steven W. and Andrew A. Snelling, eds. *Grappling with the Chronology of the Genesis Flood: Navigating the Flow of Time in Biblical Narrative.* Green Forest, AR: Master Books, 2014.

Braun, Joachim. *Music in Ancient Israel/Palestine: Archaeological, Written and Comparative Sources.* Grand Rapids: Eerdmans, 2002.

_____ "Music in the Ancient Land of Israel: Archaeological and Written Sources." Pages 11–23 in *Sounds of Ancient Music.* Edited by Joan Goodnick Westenholz. Jerusalem: Bible Land Museum, 2007.

Brettler, Marc Zvi. *God is King: Understanding an Israelite Metaphor.* JSOT Press, 1989.

Briant, Pierre. *From Cyrus to Alexander.* Translated by Peter T. Daniels. Winona Lake, IN: Eisenbrauns, 2002.

Broshi M. "The Expansion of Jerusalem in the Reigns of Hezekiah and Manasseh." *IEJ* 24.1 (1974): 21–26.

Brownlee, William H. *The Meaning of the Qumran Scrolls for the Bible.* New York: Oxford University Press, 1964.

Bruce, F. F. *Biblical Exegesis in the Qumran Texts.* London: Tyndale, 1960.

_____ "Josephus and Daniel." Pages 148–62 in *Annual of the Swedish Theological Institute* 4. Edited by Hans Kosmala. Leiden: Brill, 1965.

Brugsch-Bey, Henrich. *Egypt Under the Pharaohs.* New York: Charles Scribner's Sons, 1891.

Budge, E.A.W. *Egyptian Ideas of the Future Life.* Books on Egypt and Chaldea. London: K. Paul, Trench, Trubner and Co., Ltd., 1899.

_____ *Egyptian Magic.* London: K. Paul, Trench, Trubner & Co., Ltd., 1899.

Buhl, Marie-Louise, and Svend Holm-Nielsen. *Shiloh—The Danish Excavations at Tall Sailum, Palestine, in 1926, 1929, 1932 AND 1962: The Pre-Hellenistic Remains.* Copenhagen: The National Museum of Denmark, 1969.

Bulliet, Richard W. *The Camel and the Wheel.* New York: Columbia University Press, 1997.

Burrows, E. "Some Cosmological Patterns in Babylonian Religion." Pages 43–70 in *The Labyrinth.* Edited by S. Hooke. London: SPCK, 1935.

Bush, Frederic. *Ruth/Esther.* WBC 9. Dallas: Thomas Nelson, 1996.

Buti, S., S. Nati, N. Lope, E. Papiol, E. Heras, and J. Gunneweg. "Determination of Wine Residues in Qumran Amphora–35." Pages 71–80 in *Bio-and Material Cultures at Qumran: Papers from a COST Action G8 Working Group Meeting Held in Jerusalem, Israel on 22–23 May 2005*. Edited by Jan Gunneweg, Charles Greenblatt and Annemie Adriaens. Stuttgart: Frauhofer Verlag, 2006.

Cahill, Jane M., and David Tarler. "Excavations Directed by Yigael Shiloh at the City of David, 1978–1985." Pages 39–40 in *Ancient Jerusalem Revealed*. Edited by Hillel Geva. Jerusalem: Israel Exploration Society, 1994.

Carpenter, Eugene E. "The Eschatology of Daniel Compared with the Eschatology of Selected Intertestamental Documents." PhD diss., Fuller Theological Seminary, 1978.

Carr, David M. "The Tel Zayit Abecedary in (Social) Context." Pages 113–29 in *Literate Culture and Tenth-Century Canaan: The Tel Zayit Abecedary in Context*. Edited by Ron E. Tappy and P. Kyle McCarter, Jr. Winona Lake, IN: Eisenbrauns, 2008.

Cassuto, Umberto. *Commentary on Exodus*. Jerusalem: Magnes, 1967.

Chavalas, Mark. "Assyriology and Biblical Studies." Pages 21–67 in *Mesopotamia and the Bible*. Edited by Mark Chavalas and Lawson Younger. Grand Rapids: Baker, 2002.

Chavalas, Mark W., ed. "Sumerian King List." Page 82 in *The Ancient Near East: Historical Sources in Translation*. Translated by Piotr Michalowski. Malden, MA: Blackwell Publishing, 2006.

Clements, Ronald. "The Book of Exodus." *IDBSup* 5:304–12.

Clifford, Richard J. *The Cosmic Mountain in Canaan and in the Old Testament*. HSM 4. Cambridge: Harvard University Press, 1972.

_____ "Creation Accounts in the Ancient Near East and in the Bible." CBQ Monograph Series 26. Washington, DC: Catholic Biblical Association, 1994, 42–49.

Cline, Eric. *From Eden to Exile: Unraveling the Mysteries of the Bible*. Washington, D.C.: National Geographic Society, 2007.

Cline, Eric H. and Graham, Mark W. *Ancient Empires: From Mesopotamia to the Rise of Islam*. Cambridge: Cambridge University Press, 2011.

Clines, David, J.A. "The Tree of Knowledge and the Law of Yahweh," *VT* 24 (1974): 8–14.

Clinton, Stephen M. "S.R. Driver and the Date of Daniel." *The Journal of Church and Society* 5.2 (1969): 30–41.

Collins, John J. *The Scepter and the Star: the Messiahs of the Dead Sea Scrolls and Other Ancient Literature*. New York: Anchor Bible, 1995.

Cooper, Lamar. "Qumran and the Messianic Hope." *CTR* 7:1 (2009): 63–80.

_____ "Qumran Pottery Factory Revisited" Paper Presented to the Near East Archaeological Society at the Evangelical Theological Society Meeting. Baltimore, MD, 19 November 2013.

Cornfeld, Gaalyah. *Archaeology of the Bible: Book by Book*. New York: Harper & Row, 1976.

Cotterell, Arthur. *Oxford Dictionary of World Mythology*. Oxford: Oxford University Press, 1997.

Cox, Dermot. *Proverbs with an Introduction to Sapiential Books*. OTM 17. Wilmington, DE: Michael Glazier, Inc., 1982.

Craigie, Peter C. and Marvin E. Tate. *Psalms 1–50*. 2nd ed. WBC 19. Dallas, TX: Thomas Nelson, 2004.

Crenshaw, James. *Old Testament Wisdom: An Introduction*. Atlanta: John Knox Press, 1981.

Crenshaw, James. *Studies in Ancient Israelite Wisdom*. Library of Biblical Studies. New York: KTAV, 1976.

Cross, Frank Moore. *The Ancient Library of Qumran and Modern Biblical Studies*. Rev. ed. Grand Rapids: Baker, 1980.

_____ "The Priestly Tabernacle in the Light of Recent Research." Pages 109–80 in *Temples and High Places in Biblical Times: Proceedings of the Colloquium in Honor of the Centennial of Hebrew Union College—Jewish Institute of Religion March 14–16, 1977*. Edited by Avraham Biran. Jerusalem: The Nelson Glueck School of Biblical Archaeology of Hebrew Union College, 1981.

Crouse, Bill and Gordon Franz. "Mount Çudi-True Mountain of Noah's Ark." *B&S* 19.4 (2006): 99–111.

Dalley, Stephanie. *Myths from Mesopotamia: Creation, the Flood, Gilgamesh, and Others*. Oxford World's Classics. New York: W. W. Norton & Co., 2008.

Davidson, Richard M. *Typology in Scripture*. Berrien Springs, MI: Andrews University Press, 1981.

Davies, Philip R. "'House of David' Built on Sand." *BAR* 20.4 (1994): 55.

Day, J. "The Daniel of Ugarit and Ezekiel and the Hero of the Book of Daniel." *VT* 30 (1980): 174–84.

Demsky, Aaron. "Discovering a Goddess: A New Look at the Ekron Inscription Identifies Mysterious Deity." *BAR* 24.5 (1998): 53–58.

Deutsch, Robert. "Tracking Down Shebnayahu, Servant of the King." *BAR* 35:3 (2009): 45–49.

de Vaux, Roland. *Ancient Israel: Social Institutions*. New York: McGraw-Hill, 1965, 279–302.

Dever, William G. *Who Were the Early Israelites and Where Did They Come From?* Grand Rapids: Eerdmans, 2003.

Dijkstra, Meindert. "Is Balaam Also Among the Prophets?" *JBL* 114.1 (1995): 43–64.

Dothan, Trude, and Seymour Gitin. "Ekron of the Philistines: How They Lived, Worked and Worshiped for Five Hundred Years." *BAR* 18.1 (1990): 20–25.

Drinkard, Joel F. Jr. "The Socio-Historical Setting of Malachi." *RevExp* 84.3 (1987): 383–89.

Driver, S. R. *An Introduction to the Literature of the Old Testament*. Edinburgh: T & T Clark, 1898.

Duhaime, Jean. *The War Texts: 1QM and Related Manuscripts*. London: T & T Clark, 2004.

Edelman, Diana Vikander. *The Origins of the "Second" Temple: Persian Imperial Policy and the Rebuilding of Jerusalem*. London: Equinox, 2005.

Ellens, J. Harold, Deborah L. Ellens, Rolf P. Knierim, and Isaac Kalimi. *God's Word for Our World: Biblical Studies in Honor of Simon John De Vries*. New York: Continuum, 2004.

El Mahdy, Christine. *Mummies, Myth and Magic in Ancient Egypt*. London: Thames and Hudson, 1998.

Engnell, I. *Studies in Divine Kingship in the Ancient Near East*. Oxford: Basil Blackwell, 1967.

Epstein, H. *The Origin of the Domestic Animals of Africa*. 9 vols. London: Africana, 1971.

"Excavations at Khorsabad." (revised June 17, 2010) Oriental Institute of the University of Chicago. http://oi.uchicago.edu/research/projects/kho/.

Fairman, H.W. "The Kingship Rituals of Egypt." Pages 75–98 in *Myth, Ritual and Kingship*. Edited by S. H. Hooke. Oxford: Clarendon, 1958.

Falkenstein, Adam. *The Sumerian Temple City*. Los Angeles: Undena, 1974.

Fant, Clyde E., and Mitchell G. Reddish. *Lost Treasures of the Bible*. Grand Rapids: Eerdmans, 2008.

Faucett, Lawrence W. *Seeking the Wisdom Writings of Ancient Egypt*. San Diego, CA: Self-published, 1975.

Feldman, Rachel. "Khirbet Qeiyafa Identified as Biblical "Neta'im." University of Haifa, 2010, http://newmedia-eng.haifa.ac.il/?p=2654.2010.

Ferch, Arthur. "The Book of Daniel and the Maccabean Thesis." *AUSS* 21 (1983): 129–141.

Finegan, Jack. *Archaeological History of the Ancient Near East*. Boulder, CO: Westview, 1979.

Finkel, Irving. *The Ark before Noah: Decoding the Story of the Flood*. New York: Random House, 2014.

Finkelstein, Israel, et al. *Shiloh: The Archaeology of a Biblical Site*. Tel Aviv: Tel Aviv University Press, 1993.

Finkelstein, Israel and Neil Silberman. *The Bible Unearthed: Archaeology's New Vision of Ancient Israel and the Origin of Its Sacred Texts*. New York: Free Press, 2001.

Finkelstein, Israel. "Jerusalem in the Persian (and Early Hellenistic) Period and the Wall of Nehemiah." *JSOT* 32.4 (2008): 501–20.

_____ "Jerusalem in the Iron Age: Archaeology and Text; Reality and Myth." Pages 189–201 in *Unearthing Jerusalem: 150 Years of Archaeological Research in the Holy City*. Edited by K. Galor and G. Avni. Winona Lake, IN: Eisenbrauns, 2011.

"First Temple Era Artifacts Discovered near West Jerusalem." http://destination-yisrael.biblesearchers.com/destination-yisrael/2013/01/first-temple-era-artifacts-discovered-near-west-jerusalem.html.

Foster, Benjamin R. "A New Look at the Sumerian Temple State." *Journal of the Economic and Social History of the Orient* 24 (1981): 225–41.

_____ "The Sargonic Victory Stele from Telloh" *Iraq* 47 (1985): 15–25.

Frankena, Thus R. "The Vassal Treaties of Esarhaddon and the Dating of Deuteronomy." *OTS* 14 (1965): 122–54.

Frankfort, H. *Kingship and the Gods*. Chicago: University of Chicago Press, 1948.

_____ *Ancient Egyptian Religion*. New York: Columbia University Press, 1948.

Freedman, David Noel. *Anchor Bible Dictionary*. 6 vols. New York: Doubleday, 1992.

Fretheim, Terence. "The Cultic Use of the Ark of the Covenant in the Monarchial Period." PhD diss., Princeton Theological Seminary, 1967.

Friberg, Jöran. "The Beginning and End of the Sumerian King List." Pages 231–40 in *A Remarkable Collection of Babylonian Mathematical Texts: Manuscripts in the Schøyen Collection Cuneiform Texts I*. New York: Springer, 2007.

Frymer-Kensky, Tikva. "What the Babylonian Flood Stories Can and Cannot Teach Us About the Genesis Flood." *BAR* 4.4 (1978): 32–35.

Geisler, Rex. "Mount Ararat Archaeological Survey." *B&S* 21.3 (2008): 70–96.

Gemser, U.B. *The Instruction of Onchsheshonqy and Biblical Wisdom Literature*. VTSup 7. Leiden: Brill, 1960.

George, A. R. *The Babylonian Gilgamesh Epic: Introduction, Critical Edition and Cuneiform Texts*. Oxford: Oxford University Press, 2003.

George, Andrew, R., ed. *Cuneiform Royal Inscriptions and Related Texts in the Schøyen Collection*. CUSAS 17. Bethesda, MD: CDL Press, 2011.

Geva, Hillel, ed. *The Finds from Areas A, W and X*. Vol. 2 of *Jewish Quarter Excavations in the Old City of Jerusalem Conducted by Nahman Avigad, 1969–1982*. Jerusalem: Israel Exploration Society, 2000.

Gitin, Seymour. "Cultic Inscriptions Found in Ekron." *BA* 53 (1990): 232.

_____ "Ekron of the Philistines: Olive Oil Suppliers to the World." *BAR* 18.1 (1990): 20–25.

_____ "The Rise and Fall of Ekron of the Philistines: Recent Excavations at an Urban Border Site." *BA* 50 (1990): 197–222.

_____ "Last Days of the Philistines." *Arch* 45.3 (1992): 26–31.

_____ "New Philistine Finds at Tel Miqne-Ekron." *BA* 59 (1996): 70.

_____ "Royal Philistine Temple Inscription Found at Ekron." *BA* 59 (1996): 101–2.

Gitin, Seymour, Trude Dothan, and Joseph Naveh. (1997) "A Royal Dedicatory Inscription from Ekron." *IEJ* 48 (1997): 1–18.

Gitin, Seymour, Trude Dothan, and Joseph Naveh. "Ekron Identity Confirmed." *Arch* 51.1 (1998): 30–31.

Glanville, S.R.K. *The Instructions of Onchsheshonqy*. Vol. 2 of *Catalogue of Demotic Papri in the British Museum*. London: British Museum Publications, 1955.

Glassner, J. J. *Mesopotamian Chronicles*. WAW 19. Leiden: Brill, 2004.

Glock, A. E. "Early Israel as the Kingdom of Yahweh." *CTM* 41 (1970): 558–605.

Goldingay, John E. Daniel. WBC 30. Waco: Word Books, 1989.

_____ *Psalms Vol. 1: Psalms 1–41*. BCOTWP. Grand Rapids: Baker, 2006.

Gorali, M. *Music in Ancient Israel*. 3rd and enl. ed. Haifa: The Haifa Music Museum & AMLI Library, 1977.

Gordon, E.I. "A New Look at the Wisdom of Sumer and Akkad" *BO* 17 (1960): 122–52.

Green, Alberto R.W. *The Storm-God in the Ancient Near East*. Winona Lake, IN: Eisenbrauns, 2003.

Green, M. W. "The Eridu Lament." *JCS* 30.3 (1978): 149.

Grigson, C., J. A. J. Gowlett, and J. Zarins. "Late Bronze Age Camel Petroglyphs in the Wadi Nasib, Sinai." *Near East Archaeological Society Bulletin* 42 (1989): 47–54.

Hackett, Jo Ann. *The Balaam Text from Deir 'Alla*. HSM 31. Chico, CA: Scholars, 1984.

Hallo, William W. and K. Lawson Younger, eds. *Canonical Compositions from the Biblical World*. Vol. 1 of *COS*. Leiden: Brill, 1997.

_____ *Monumental Inscriptions from the Biblical World*. Vol. 2 of *COS*. Leiden: Brill, 2000.

_____ *Archival Documents from the Biblical World*. Vol. 3 of *COS*. Leiden: Brill, 2002.

Hallvard, Hagelia. "Philological Issues in the Tel Dan Inscription." Pages 232–56 in *Current Issues in the Analysis of Semitic Grammar and Lexicon II*. Edited by Lutz Edzard and Jan Retso. Wiesbaden: Otto Harrassowitz Verlag, 2005.

Hamblin, William, J. *Warfare in the Ancient Near East*. London: Routledge, 2006.

Handy, Lowell K. "The Appearance of Pantheon in Judah." Pages 27–43 in *The Triumph of Elohim*. Edited by Diana Vikander Edelman. Grand Rapids: Eerdmans, 1996.

Haran, Menahem. "The Exodus." *IDBSup*, 304–10.

_____ *Temples and Temple Services in Ancient Israel*. Oxford: Oxford University Press, 1978.

_____ "Explaining the Identical Lines at the End of Chronicles and the Beginning of Ezra." *BRev* 2.3 (1986): 18–20.

Harris, James E. and Kent R. Weeks. *X-Raying the Pharaohs*. New York: Charles Scribner's Sons, 1973.

Harrison, R.K. *Introduction to the Old Testament*. Grand Rapids: Eerdmans, 1969.

_____ "Arioch," *ISBE*, 290.

Hartley John E., *Leviticus*. WBC 4. Accordance/Thomas Nelson electronic ed. Waco: Word Books, 1992.

Hartman, Ben. "Temple Found in Philistine City, Home of Bbiblical Goliath: Discovery Sheds Light on Samson's Temple." *The Jerusalem Post Christian Edition* (September 2010): 6.

Hasel, Gerhard. "Is the Aramaic of Daniel Early or Late?" *Ministry* (January 1980): 13–14.

Hasel, Michael G. "Israel in the Merneptah Stela." *BASOR* 296 (1994): 45–61.

Hawkins, Ralph K. *The Iron Age I Structure on Mt. Ebal: Excavation and Interpretation*. BBRSup 6. Winona Lake, IN: Eisenbrauns, 2012.

Hays, Christopher. *Hidden Riches: A Sourcebook for the Comparative Study of the Hebrew Bible and Ancient Near East*. Louisville: Westminster John Knox, 2014.

Heide, M. "The Domestication of the Camel: Biological, Archaeological and Inscriptional Evidence from Mesopotamia, Egypt and Arabia, and Literary Evidence from the Hebrew Bible." *UF* 42 (2010): 331384.

Hendel, Roland. "Finding Historical Memories in the Patriarchal Narratives," *BAR* 21.4 (1995): 58.

Hendel, Ronald, "Note to 'Vision of Gabriel.'" *BAR* 35:1 (2009): 8.

Henze, Matthias, ed. *Hazon Gabriel: New Readings of the Gabriel Revelation*. Early Judaism and Its Literature 29. Atlanta: Society of Biblical Literature, 2011.

Hermann, A. "Das steinhartes Herz," *JAC* 4 (1961): 102–3.

_____ "An Exegetical and Theological Consideration of the Hardening of Pharaoh's Heart in Exodus 4–14 and Romans 9." *TrinJ* 5 (1984): 129–54.

Hill, Andrew, E. "*Malachi*." ZIBBC 5. Grand Rapids: Zondervan, 2009.

Hoffman, Yair. "A North Israelite Typological Myth and a Judean Historical Tradition: The Exodus in Hosea and Amos." *VT* 39.2 (1989): 170.

Hoffmeier, James K. "Current Issues in Archaeology: The Recently Discovered Tell Dan Inscription: Controversy & Confirmation." *ABW* 3:1 (1995): 14.

_____ "These Things Happened: Why a Historical Exodus is Essential for Theology." Pages 99–134 in *Do Historical Matters Matter to Faith?: A Critical Appraisal of Modern and Postmodern Approaches to Scripture*. Edited by James K. Hoffmeier and Dennia R. Magary. Wheaton, IL: Crossway, 2012.

Hoffmeier, James K. and Dennis R. Magary, eds. *Do Historical Matters Matter to Faith?: A Critical Appraisal of Modern and Postmodern Approaches to Scripture*. Wheaton, IL: Crossway, 2012.

Hoftijzer, J. "The Prophet Balaam in a 6th Century Aramaic Inscription." *BA* 39 (March 1976): 11–17.

_____ "Prophecy of Balaam Found in Jordan." *B&S* 6 (Autumn 1977): 121—24.

Hoftijzer, J. and G. van der Kooij. *Aramaic Texts from Deir 'Alla*. Leiden: Brill, 1976.

Howard, David M., Jr. and Michael A. Grisanti, eds. *Giving the Sense: Understanding and Using Old Testament Historical Texts*. Grand Rapids: Kregel, 2003.

Huffmon, H.B. *Amorite Personal Names in the Mari Texts*. Chicago: University of Chicago Press, 1965.

Hurowitz, Victor Avigdor. *I Have Built You An Exalted House: Temple Buildings in the Bible in Light of Mesopotamian and Northwest Semitic Writings*. JSOTSup 115. Sheffield: University of Sheffield, 1992.

_____ "'Shutting Up' the Enemy: Literary Gleanings from Sargon's Eighth Campaign." Pages 104–20 in Treasures on Camels' Humps: Historical and Literary Studies from the Ancient Near East Presented to Israel Eph'al. Edited by Mordechai Cogan and Dan'el Kahn. Jerusalem: Magnes Press, 2008.

"In Shiloh, an Intriguing Discovery Alludes to the Tabernacle." *Israel Hayom*, February 16, 2014. http://www.israelhayom.com/site/newsletter_article.php?id=10391.

Izre'el, Shlomo. *Adapa and the South Wind: Language Has the Power of Life and Death*. Mesopotamian Civilizations 10. Winona Lake, IN: Eisenbrauns, 2001.

Jamieson-Drake, D.W. *Scribes and Schools in Monarchic Judah: A Socio-Archeological Approach*. JSOTSup 109. Sheffield: Sheffield Academic, 1991.

Joines, Karen Randolph. "The Bronze Serpent in the Israelite Cult." *JBL* 87.3 (1968): 245–56.

Josephus. Translated by Henry St. J. Thackeray et al. 10 vols. LCL. Cambridge: Harvard University Press, 1937.

Kalugila, Leonidas. *The Wise King: Studies in Royal Wisdom as Divine Revelation in the Old Testament and Its Environment*. ConBOT 15. Uppsala: Gleerup, 1980.

Kang, Hoo-Goo, and Yosef Garfinkel. "The Pottery Assemblage of Khirbet Qeiyafa in the Early Iron Age IIA." Paper presented at the American Schools of Oriental Research Annual Meeting. New Orleans, LA, 18–21 November 2009.

Kaufman, Stephen A. "The Job Targum From Qumran." *JAOS* 93 (1973): 327.

Kenyon, Kathleen. *Archaeology in the Holy Land*. 5th ed. Nashville: Thomas Nelson, 1985.

Kidner, Derek. *An Introduction to Wisdom Literature: The Wisdom of Proverbs, Job and Ecclesiastes*. Downers Grove, IL: InterVarsity Press, 1958.

King, Philip J. *Amos, Hosea, Micah: An Archaeological Companion*. Louisville: Westminster/John Knox, 1988.

———— *Jeremiah: An Archaeological Companion*. Louisville: Westminster/John Knox, 1993.

Kitchen, K. A. "The Aramaic of Daniel." Pages 31–79 in *Notes on Some Problems in the Book of Daniel*. Edited by Donald J. Wiseman et. al. London: Tyndale, 1970.

Kitchen, Kenneth A. *Ancient Orient and the Old Testament*. Downers Grove, IL: InterVarsity Press, 1966.

———— *The Bible In Its World: The Bible & Archaeology Today*. Downers Grove, IL: InterVarsity Press, 1977.

———— "From the Brickfields of Egypt." *B&S* 10.2 (1981), 43–47.

———— "The Patriarchal Age: Myth or History?" *BAR* 21.2 (1995): 48–57, 88, 90–92, 94–95.

———— *Ramesside Inscriptions Volume II*. Oxford: Blackwell, 1996.

———— *OROT*. Grand Rapids: Eerdmans, 2003.

Klein, George L. *Zechariah*. NAC 21B. Nashville: B&H Publishing, 2008.

Kline, Meredith G. "Primal Parousia" *WTJ* 40 (1978): 249–50.

———— *The Structure of Biblical Authority*. Eugene, OR: Wipf and Stock, 1997.

Knohl, Israel. *Messiahs and Resurrection in "The Gabriel Revelation."* The Kogod Library of Judaic Studies. New York: Continuum, 2009.

Kochavi, Moshe, Timothy Renner, Ira Spar, and Esther Yadin. "Rediscovered! The Land of Geshur." *BAR* 18.4 (1992): 30–44, 84–85.

Kramer, Samuel Noah. "'Man and His God,' A Sumerian Variation on the 'Job' Motif." VTSup 3 (1955): 170–82.

———— "Reflections on the Mesopotamian Flood." *Expedition* 9. 4 (1967): 12–18.

———— "The 'Babel of Tongues': A Sumerian Version." *JAOS* 88 Jan/Mar (1968): 108–11.

———— *Sumerian Mythology: A Study of Spiritual and Literary Achievement in the Third Millennium BC*. Rev. ed. Philadelphia: University of Pennsylvania Press, 1972.

Kramer, Samuel Noah and John Maier. *Myths of Enki, the Crafty God*. New York: Oxford University Press, 1989.

Kutscher, E. Y. "HaAramit HaMigrait-Aramit Mizrahit hi o Maaravit?" First World Congress of Jewish Studies I. Jerusalem: Magnes Press, 1952.

Lambert, W. G. *Babylonian Wisdom Literature*. Oxford: Clarendon, 1960.

Lambert, W.G. and A.R. Millard. *Atra-Hasis: The Babylonian Story of the Flood*. Oxford: Oxford University Press, 1969.

———— *Atra-Hasis: The Babylonian Story of the Flood*. Winona Lake, IN: Eisenbrauns, 1999.

Landy, Yehuda. *Purim and the Persian Empire*. Translated by Rabbi Binyamin S. Moore. Jerusalem: Feldheim, 1999.

Lapp, Paul. "Tell el-Ful." *BA* 28 (1965): 6.

Lichtheim, Miriam. *Ancient Egyptian Literature Volume II: The New Kingdom*. Berkeley: University of California Press, 1976.

Lindbolm, J. *Prophecy in Ancient Israel*. Philadelphia: Fortress, 1962.

Ling-Israel, P. "The Sennacherib Prism in the Israel Museum—Jerusalem." Pages 213–47 in *Bar-Ilan: Studies in Assyriology Dedicated to Pinhas Artzi*. Edited by J. Klein and A. Skaist. Ramat-Gan: Bar-Ilan University Press, 1990.

Long, Phillip J. *Jesus the Bridegroom: The Origin of the Eschatological Feast as a Wedding Banquet in the Synoptic Gospels*. Eugene, OR: Pickwick, 2013.

López, Raul Erlando. "The antediluvian patriarchs and the Sumerian king list." *Journal of Creation* 12.3 (1998): 347–57.

Mabie, F. J., "Chaos and Death." In *Dictionary of the Old Testament: Wisdom, Poetry, and Writings*. Edited by Tremper Longman III and Peter Enns. Downers Grove, IL: IVP Academic, 2008.

MacDonald, David. "The Flood: Mesopotamian Archaeological Evidence," *Creation Evolution Journal* 8.2 (1988): 14–20.

MacDonald, John. "The Status and Role of the 'Na'ar in Israelite Society," *JNES* 35:3 (July 1976): 147–70.

Machlin, Milt. *Joshua's Altar: The Dig at Mount Ebal*. New York: William Morrow & Company, 1991.

Macler, F. "Les Apocalypses Apocryphes de Daniel." *Revue de l'histoire des religions* 33 (1896): 37–53, 163–76, 288–319.

Magness, Jodi. "Communal Meals and Sacred Space at Qumran." Pages 81–112 in *Debating Qumran*. Interdisciplinary Studies in Ancient Culture and Religion 4. Leuven: Peeters, 2004.

———— *The Archaeology of the Holy Land: From the Destruction of Solomon's Temple to the Muslim Conquest*. Cambridge: Cambridge University Press, 2012.

Mann, Charles C. "The Birth of Religion." *National Geographic* (June 2011): 35–59.

Marchetti, Nicolò. "A Century of Excavations on the Spring Hill at Tell Es-Sultan, Ancient Jericho: A Reconstruction of Its Stratigraphy," Pages 295–321 in *The Synchronisation of Civilisations in the Eastern Mediterranean in the Second Millennium BC II*. Edited by Manfred Bietak. Vienna: Österreichischen Akademie der Wissenschaftren, 2003.

May, H. G. "The Ark-A Miniature Temple." *AJSL* 52.4 (1936): 215–34.

Mazar, Amihai. *Archaeology of the Land of the Bible 10,000–586 BCE*. New York: Doubleday, 1990.

Mazar, Eilat. *The Complete Guide to the Temple Mount Excavations*. Jerusalem: Shoham Academic Research and Publication, 2002.

———— "The Wall That Nehemiah Built." *BAR* 35.2 (2009): 28–30.

———— *Discovering the Solomonic Wall in Jerusalem: A Remarkable Archaeological Adventure*. Jerusalem: Shoham Academic Research and Publication, 2011.

———— "Excavations at the City of David (2006–2007)." Pages 7–26 in New Studies on Jerusalem 13. Edited by E. Baruch, E. Levy-Reifer, and A. Faust. Ramat Gan: Bar-Ilan University Press, 2007. [Hebrew] 2009.

McCarter, P. Kyle. "'Yaw, Son of Omri': A Philological Note on Israelite Chronology." *BASOR* 216 (Dec., 1974): 5–7.

McCarter, P. Kyle Jr. "The Balaam Texts from Deir 'Alla: The First Combination." *BASOR* 237 (1980): 49–60.

_____ *Ancient Inscriptions: Voices from the Biblical World.* Washington, DC: Biblical Archaeology Society, 1996.

McDowell, Josh. *Daniel in the Critics' Den: Historical Evidence for the Authenticity of the Book of Daniel.* San Bernardino, CA: Here's Life Publishers, 1979.

Mendenhall, G.E. *Law and Covenant in Israel and the Ancient Near East.* Pittsburg: The Biblical Colloquium, 1954.

Merling, David S. *The Book of Joshua: Its Theme and Role in Archaeological Discussions.* AUDS. Berrien Springs, MI: Andrews University Press, 1997.

Mercer, Samuel A.B. *Horus, Royal God of Egypt.* Grafton: Society of Oriental Research 1942.

Merrill, Eugene. *Haggai, Zechariah, Malachi: An Exegetical Commentary.* Chicago: Moody Press, 1994.

Meyerowitz, E.L.A. *Divine Kingship in Ghana and Ancient Egypt.* London: Faber and Faber, 1960.

Meyers, Carol, L. *The Tabernacle Menorah.* Missoula, MT: Scholars Press, 1976.

_____ "Was There a Seven-Branched Lampstand in Solomon's Temple?" *BAR* 5.5 (1979): 46–57.

Meyers, Carol, and Eric M. Meyers. *Haggai, Zechariah 1–8.* AB 25B. Garden City, NY: Doubleday, 1987.

Myers, Jacob M. *I Chronicles 1–9.* AB 12. Garden City, NY: Doubleday, 1965.

Michalowski, Piotr. "History as Charter: Some Observations on the Sumerian King List." *JAOS* 103.1 (1983): 237–248.

Milgrom, Jacob. *Leviticus 1–16.* AB 3. New York: Doubleday, 1991.

Millard, A.R. "A New Babylonian 'Genesis' Story." *TynBul* 18 (1967): 17–18.

_____ "Daniel 1–6 and History." *EvQ* 49.2 (1977):

_____ "Re-Creating the Tablets of the Law." *BRev* 10.1 (1994): 49–53.

_____ "Tutankhamen, the Tabernacle, and the Ark of the Covenant." *B&S* 7.2 (1994): 49–51.

_____ "Earliest Hebrew Inscription Found?" *Tyndale House Newsletter,* February 5, 2010.

Miller, J. M., and G. M. Tucker. *The Book of Joshua.* CBC. Cambridge: Cambridge University Press, 1974.

Miller, James E. "The Etiology of the Tabernacle/Temple in Genesis." *Proceedings: Eastern Great Lakes and Midwest Biblical Societies* 4 (1986), 153–154.

Misgav, Haggai. "The Ostracon from Khirbet Qeiyafa: Paleographical and Historical Implications." Paper presented at the American Schools of Oriental Research Annual Meeting. New Orleans, LA, 18–21 November 2009.

Miskin, Maayana. "Dig Supports Biblical Account of King Solomon's Construction." IsraelNN.com (February 2010).

Mitchell, T.C. *The Bible in the British Museum: Interpreting the Evidence.* British Museum Press, 1988.

Monson, John. "The New 'Ain Dara' Temple: Closest Solomonic Parallel." *BAR* 26:3 (2000): 20–35, 67.

Morales, Michael. *The Tabernacle Pre-Figured: Cosmic Mountain Ideology in Genesis-Exodus.* Belgium: Peeters, 2012.

Muilenburg, J. "A Qoheleth Scroll from Qumrân," *BASOR* 135 (1954): 20–28.

Muller, H.P. "hkm." TDOT 4: 267–70.

Muraoka, T. "The Aramaic of the Old Targum of Job from Qumran Cave XI." *JJS* 25 (1974): 425–33.

Murphy, Roland E. "The Concept of Wisdom Literature." Pages 46–54 in *The Bible in Current Catholic Thought.* Edited by John L. McKenzie. New York: Herder & Herder, 1962.

Na'aman, Nadav. "Beth-David in the Aramaic Stela from Tel Dan." *BN* 79 (1995): 19–20.

_____ "A New Appraisal of the Silver Amulets from Ketef Hinnom." *IEJ* 61 (2011): 184–95.

Naveh, J. "The Date of the Deir 'Alla Inscription in Aramaic Script." *IEJ* 17 (1967): 236–38.

Naville, Edward. *The Old Egyptian Faith.* Translated by Colin Campbell. New York: G. P. Putman's Sons, 1909.

Neusner, Jacob, ed. *The Babylonian Talmud: A Translation and Commentary.* Vol. 7 Peabody, MA: Hendrickson, 2011.

Ngo, Robin. "Severed Hands: Trophies of War in New Kingdom Egypt." *BAR* 40.2 (2014): 12.

Niehaus, Jeffrey J. *Ancient Near Eastern Themes in Biblical Theology.* Grand Rapids: Kregel, 2008.

Nigro, Lorenzo, and Hamdan Taha, eds. *Tell Es-Sultan/Jericho in the Context of the Jordan Valley: Site Management, Construction, and Sustainable Development.* Studies on the Archaeology of Palestine & Transjordan 2. Rome: University of Rome, "La Sapienza," 2006.

Nigro, Lorenzo. "Palestinian Pottery of the Late Bronze Age: An Investigation of the Terminal LB IIB Phase." PhD thesis, University of Toronto, 1985.

_____ *A Comparison of the Archaeological and Biblical History of Jericho in the Late Bronze Age.* Near East Archaeological Society, Gordon-Conwell Theological Seminary, South Hamilton MA. 1987a.

_____ *Jericho Revisited: The Archaeology and History of Jericho in the Late Bronze Age.* American Schools of Oriental Research, Boston, 1987b.

_____ *Jericho Revisited: The Archaeology and History of Jericho in the Late Bronze Age.* Who Was the Pharaoh of the Exodus Symposium, 1987c.

Nigro, Lorenzo. "The Two Steles of Sargon: Iconology and Visual Propaganda at the Beginning of Royal Akkadian Relief." *Iraq* 60 (1998): 85–98.

North, Robert. "Zechariah's Seven-Spout Lampstand" *Bib* 51.2 (1970): 183–206.

Olmstead, A. T. *History of Assyria.* Chicago: University of Chicago Press, 1923.

Oppenheim, Leo. *Ancient Mesopotamia: Portrait of a Dead Civilization.* Chicago: University of Chicago Press, 1964.

Osanai, Nozomi. "A Comparative Study of the Flood Accounts in the Gilgamesh Epic and Genesis." MA thesis, Wesley Biblical Seminary, 2004.

Otzen, Benedikt. "Beliyya'al." *TDOT* 2:1975.

Parker, Richard and Waldo Dubberstein. *Babylonian Chronology 626 BC–AD 75*. Providence RI: Brown University Press, 1956.

Parrot, Andre. *Ziggurats et Tour de Babel*. London: SCM, 1955.

Parry, Donald W. *Garden of Eden: Prototype Sanctuary*. Salt Lake City, UT: Desert Book Company, 1994.

Patterson, R. D. "sela'." *TWOT* 2:627.

Patterson, Richard. "The Imagery of Clouds in the Scriptures." *BSac* 165 (2008): 13–27.

Perdue, Leo G. *Wisdom and Cult: A Critical Analysis of Cult in the Wisdom Literatures of Israel and the Ancient Near East*. SBLDS 30. Missoula, MT: Scholars Press, 1977.

Petrovich, Douglas. "Identifying Nimrod of Genesis 10 with Sargon of Akkad by Exegetical and Archaeological Means," *JETS* 56.2 (2013): 273–305.

_____ "Toward Pinpointing the Timing of the Egyptian Abandonment of Avaris during the Middle of the 18th Dynasty." *The Journal of Ancient Egyptian Interconnections* 5.2 (2014): 9–28.

Pettinato, Giovanni, "Ebla e la Bibbia," *OrAnt* 19 (1980): 49–72. Repr., "Ebla and the Bible," *BA* 43 (1960): 208.

_____ "The Royal Archives of Tell Mardikh Ebla." *BA* 39 (1976): 44–52.

Pitkänen, Pekka. *Central Sanctuary and Centralization of Worship in Ancient Israel: From the Settlement to the Building of Solomon's Temple*. Piscataway, NJ: Gorgias, 2004.

Porat, Roi, Hanan Eshel, and Amos Frumkin. "More Cave Excavations at En-gedi: Finds from the Bar Kokhba Revolt from Two Caves at En Gedi." *PEQ*, 139.1 (2007): 35–53.

Porat, Roi, Hanan Eshel, and Amos Frumkin. "The 'Caves of the Spear': Refuge Caves from the Bar-Kokhba Revolt North of 'En-Gedi." *IEJ* 59.1 (2009): 21–42.

Porten, Bezalel. "Elephantine Papyri." *ABD* 2:452–453.

Porteous, Norman. "Royal Wisdom." Pages 274–61 in *Wisdom in Israel and in the Ancient Near East*. VTSup 3. Leiden: Brill, 1955.

Porter, Barbara Nevling. "Sacred Trees, Date Palms, and the Royal Persona of Ashurnasirpal II." *JNES* 52.2 (1993): 129–39.

Price, J. Randall. *The Desecration and Restoration of the Temple as an Eschatological Motif in the Tanach, Jewish Apocalyptic Literature and the New Testament*. Ann Arbor, MI: University Microfilms International, 1993.

_____ "King David: Mythical Figure or Famous Monarch?" Pages 161–74 in *Stones Cry Out: What Archaeology Reveals about the Truth of the Bible*. Eugene, OR: Harvest House, 1997.

_____ *Searching for the Ark of the Covenant*. Eugene, OR: Harvest House, 2005.

_____ *Rose Guide to the Temple*. Torrance, CA: Rose Publishing, 2012.

Pritchard, James B., ed. *ANET*. 3rd ed. Princeton: Princeton University Press, 1969.

Puech, Émile, ed. *Discoveries in the Judean Desert Xxxvii: Qumran Grotte 4.xxvii Textes En Araméen, Deuxième Partie*. Bilingual ed. New York: Oxford University Press, 2009.

Rad, Gerhard von. *Genesis: A Commentary*. Translated by John H. Marks. Philadelphia: Westminster, 1961.

Ragavan, Deena, ed. *Heaven on Earth: Temples, Ritual, and Cosmic Symbolism in the Ancient World*. OIP 9. Chicago: University of Chicago Press, 2013.

Rainey, Anson F. "The Military Personnel of Ugarit." *JNES* 24 (1965): 17–27.

_____ "The 'House of David' and the House of the Deconstructionists." *BAR* 20:6 (1994): 47, 68–69.

"Rare Hebrew Seal From First Temple Period Discovered In Archaeological Excavations in Jerusalem's Western Wall Plaza." http://www.sciencedaily.com/releases/2008/11/081110174056.htm.

Rasmussen, K. L., J. Gunneweg, J. van der Plicht, I. Kralj Cigić, A. D. Bond, B. Svensmark, M. Balla, M. Strlic, and G. Doudna. "On the Age and Content of Jar–35—A Sealed and Intact Jar Found on the Southern Plateau of Qumran." *Arch* 53.4 (2011): 791–808.

Rawlinson, George, ed. *The History of Herodotus Book II*. Translated by Manuel Komroff. New York: Tudor, 1956.

Read, F. W. *Egyptian Religion and Ethics*. London: Watts & Co., 1925.

Reich, Ronny. "A Fiscal Bulla from the City of David, Jerusalem." *IEJ* 62.2 (2012): 200–5.

Renfrew, Colin. *The Archaeology of Cult: The Sanctuary at Phylakopi*. London: British School of Archaeology at Athens/Thames and Hudson, 1985.

Ripinsky, M. "The Camel in Dynastic Egypt." *JEA* 17 (1985): 131–41.

Ritmeyer, Leen and Kathleen Ritmeyer. *Jerusalem in the Time of Nehemiah*. Jerusalem: Carta, 2005.

Rooker, Mark F. "Dating the Patriarchal Age: The Contribution of Ancient Near Eastern Texts." Pages 217–35 in *Giving the Sense: Understanding and Using Old Testament Historical Texts*. Edited by David M. Howard, Jr. and Michael A. Grisanti. Grand Rapids: Kregel, 2003.

Roskoski, John. "Between the Pillars: Revisiting Samson and the House of Dagon." *B&S* (Winter 2005): 14–18.

Ross, Allen P. *Recalling the Hope of Glory*. Grand Rapids: Kregel, 2006.

Rowley-Gonwy, P. "The Camel in the Nile Valley: New Radiocarbon Accelerator (AMS) Dates from Qasr Ibrim." *JEA* 74 (1988): 245–48.

Rowley, H. H. "Zadok and Nehushtan" *JBL* 58.2 (1939): 113–41.

_____ *The Zadokite Fragments and the Dead Sea Scrolls*. Oxford: Basil Blackwell, 1956.

Rowton, M. B. "The Date of the Sumerian King List." *JNES* 19.2 (1960): 156–62.

Rylaarsdam, J. Coert. *The Book of Exodus*. IB 2. Nashville: Abingdon, 1962.

Saber, A. S. "The Camel in Ancient Egypt." *Proceedings of the Third Annual Meeting for Animal Production Under Arid Conditions*. 1 (1998): 208–15.

Samet, Nili. "The Lamentation over the Destruction of Ur: A Revised Edition." PhD thesis, Bar-Ilan University, 2009.

Sasson, Victor. *King Jehoash and the Mystery of the Temple of Solomon Inscription*. New York: iUniverse, 2008.

Schiffman, L.H. "Communal Meals at Qumran." *RevQ* 10 (1979): 45–56.

Schley, Donald G. *Shiloh: A Biblical City in Tradition and History*. Sheffield: Journal for the Study of the Old Testament Press, 1989, 2009.

Schmidt, Klaus. "Göbekli Tepe, Southeastern Turkey. A Preliminary Report on the 1995–1999 Excavations." *Paléorient* 26.1 (2000): 45–54.

————— "Göbekli Tepe—The Stone Age Sanctuaries. New Results of Ongoing Excavations with a Special Focus on Sculptures and High Reliefs." Documenta Praehistorica XXXVII, 239–256, 2010.

Schomp, Virginia. *Ancient Mesopotamia*. London: Franklin Watts, 2005.

Scott, R. B. Y. *Proverbs; Ecclesiastes*. AB 18. Garden City, NY: Doubleday & Co., 1965.

Selman, M. J. "The Social Environment of the Patriarchs." *TynBul* 27 (1976): 114–36.

Shanks, Hershel. "Jeremiah's Scribe and Confidant Speaks from a Hoard of Clay Bullae." *BAR* 13.5 (1987): 58–65.

————— "An Israelite House in Egypt?" *BAR* 19.4 (1993): 44–45.

————— "Carbon-14 Tests Substantiate Scroll Dates." *BAR* 17 (November/December 1991): 72.

————— "The Mystery of the Nechushtan" *BAR* 33:2 (2007): 58–63.

————— "Newly Discovered: A Fortified City from King David's Time." *BA* 35.1 (2009): 38–43.

————— "Prize Find: Oldest Hebrew Inscription Discovered in Israelite Fort on Philistine Border." *BAR* 36.2 (2010): 51–54.

Shiloh, Yigael. "Jerusalem: Eighth to Sixth Centuries BCE." *NEAEHL* 2:704–12.

Silberman, Neil Asher, and Yuval Goren, "Faking Biblical History." *Arch* 56.5 (2003): 20–29.

Silberman, Neil Asher. "The Solomonic Wall in Jerusalem." Pages 775–85 in *I Will Speak the Riddles of Ancient Times: Archaeological and Historical Studies in Honor of Amihai Mazar*. Edited by Aren M. Maier and Pierre de Miroschedji. Winona Lake, IN: Eisenbrauns, 2006.

Silberman, Neil Asher, W. Horowitz, T. Oshima, and Y Goren. "A Cuneiform Tablet from the Ophel in Jerusalem." *IEJ* 60.1 (2010): 4–21.

Smith, John Merlin Powis, William Hayes Ward, and Julius A. Bewer. *Micah, Zephaniah, Nahum, Habakkuk, Obadiah and Joel*. ICC. New York: Charles Scribner's Sons, 1911.

Speiser, A.E. *Genesis*. AB 1. Garden City, NY: Doubleday, 1983.

Steindorff, G. and K. C. Steele. *When Egypt Ruled the East*. Chicago: University of Chicago Press, 1972.

Steiner, Richard. "Earliest Semitic Text Revealed in Egyptian Pyramid Inscription." http://www.sciencedaily.com/releases/2007/01/070129100250.htm.

Stern, Ephraim. *Material Culture of the Land of the Bible in the Persian Period 538–332 BC*. Warminster: Aris and Phillips, 1982.

Steudel, Annette. "[The End of the Days] in the Texts from Qumran." *RevQ* 62:16:2 (1993): 225–46.

Strawn, Brent A. "Psalm 22:17b: More Guessing." *JBL* 119.3 (2000): 439–51.

Stuart, Douglas. *Hosea-Jonah*. WBC 31. Dallas: Thomas Nelson, 1987.

Stuart, Ted. "Proverbs 22:6a: Train Up a Child?" *GTJ* Spring 9:1 (1988): 3–19.

Studenroth, John C. "Archaeology and the Higher Criticism of Genesis 14." Pages 155–71 in *Evidence for Faith: Deciding the God Question*. Edited by John Warwick Montgomery. Dallas: Probe, 1991.

Suriano, Matthew J. "The Apology of Hazael: A Literary and Historical Analysis of the Tel Dan Inscription." *JNES* 66.3 (2007): 163–76.

Tappy, Ron and McCarter, P. Kyle, Jr. eds. *Literate Culture and Tenth-Century Canaan: The Tel Zayit Abecedary in Context*. Winona Lake, IN: Eisenbrauns, 2008.

Tebes, J.M. "A Land Whose Stones are Iron, and out of Whose Hills You Can Dig Copper: The Exploitation and Circulation of Copper in the Iron Age Negev and Edom." *DavarLogos* 6/1 (2007): 21–47.

"Temple and Rare Cache of Sacred Vessels from Biblical Times Discovered at Tel Motza," Israel Antiquity Authority online news site posting, December 2012.

Tenney, M. C., ed. *ZPEB* Vol. 1, A-C. Grand Rapids: Zondervan, 1975.

Terrien, S. "The Omphalos Myth and Hebrew Religion." *VT* 20 (1970): 315–38.

Thiele, Edwin R. "An Additional Chronological Note on 'Yaw, Son of Omri.'" *BASOR* 222 (1976): 19–23.

Torczyner, Harry, Lankester Harding, Alkin Lewis, and J. L. Starkey. *Lachish I: The Lachish Letters*. London: Oxford University Press, 1938.

Tyldesley, Joyce. *Ramesses II: Egypt's Greatest Pharaoh*. Harmondsworth: Penguin, 2000.

Ulrich, Eugene. "Daniel Manuscripts from Qumran. Part 1: A Preliminary Edition of 4QDana." *BASOR* 268 (1987): 17–37.

Ulrich, Eugene and Peter W Flint. *Qumran Cave 1: The Isaiah Scrolls: Part 2: Introductions, Commentary, and Textual Variants*. DJD 32. Oxford: Clarendon, 2010.

Ussishkin, David. "On Nehemiah's City Wall and the Size of Jerusalem during the Persian Period: An Archaeologists View." Pages 101–30 in *New Perspectives on Ezra-Nehemiah: History and Historiography, Text, Literature and Interpretation*. Edited by Isaac Kalimi. Winona Lake, IN: Eisenbrauns, 2012.

Vall, Gregory. "Psalm 22:17b: The Old Guess." *JBL* 116.1 (1997): 45–56.

VanderKam, James C. *The Dead Sea Scrolls Today*. Grand Rapids: Eerdmans, 2010.

Van der Ploeg, J.M.P. and A.S. van der Woude, eds. *Le Targum de Job de la grotte XI de Qumrán*. Leiden: Brill, 1971.

Van der Toorn, Karel and P.W. van der Horst. "Nimrod before and after the Bible." *HTR* 83 (1990): 1–29.

Van der Toorn, Karel, Bob Becking, Pieter Willem van der Horst. *DDD*. 2nd rev.ed. Grand Rapids: Eerdmans, 1999.

Van der Veen, Peter, Christoffer Theis, and Manfred Görg. "Israel in Canaan (Long) Before Pharaoh Merneptah? A Fresh Look at Berlin Statue Pedestal Relief 21687." *Journal of Ancient Egyptian Interconnections* 2.4 (2010): 15–25.

Vasholz, Robert. "A Philological Comparison of the Qumran Job Targum and Its Implications for the Dating of Daniel." PhD diss., University of Stellenbosch, 1976.

_____ "Qumran and the Dating of Daniel." *JETS* 21.4 (1978): 315–21.

Vawter, Bruce. *On Genesis: A New Reading*. Garden City, NY: Doubleday, 1977.

Waaler, Erik. "A Revised Date for Pentateuchal Texts? Evidence from Ketef Hinnom." *TynBul* 53.1 (2002): 29–50.

Waltke, Bruce K. "The Date of the Book of Daniel." *BSac* 133.532 (1976): 319–29.

Walton, John H. *Jonah*. Bible Study Commentary. Grand Rapids: Zondervan, 1982.

_____ *Ancient Israelite Literature in Its Cultural Setting: A Survey of Parallels Between Biblical and Ancient Near Eastern Texts*. Grand Rapids: Zondervan 1989.

_____ "The Mesopotamian Background of the Tower of Babel Account and Its Implications." *BBR* 5 (1995): 155–75.

Walton, John H. Victor H. Matthews, and Mark W. Chavalas. *The IVP Bible Background Commentary Old Testament*. Downers Grove, IL: InterVarsity Press, 2000.

Wapnish, Paula. "Camel Caravans and Camel Pastoralists at Tell Jemmeh," *JNES* 13 (1981): 104–5.

Weinfeld, Moshe. *Deuteronomy and the Deuteronomic School*. Oxford: Oxford University Press, 1972.

Weippert, Manfred. "The Balaam Text from Deir 'Alla and the Study of the Old Testament." Pages 151–84 in *The Balaam Text from Deir 'Alla Re-evaluated: Proceedings of the International Symposium Held at Leiden, 21–24 August 1989*. Leiden: Brill, 1991.

Wenham, Gordon J. "Daniel: The Basic Issues." *Them* 2 (1977): 49–52.

_____ *Genesis 1–15*. WBC 1. Waco, TX: Word, 1987.

Wensinck, A. J. "The Ideas of the Western Semites concerning the Navel of the Earth." Pages 43–70 in *Studies of A.J. Wensinck: Mythology Collection*. New York: Ayer Co., 1978.

Whybray, Roger N. *Wisdom Literature*. Naperville, IL: A.R. Allenson Inc., 1965.

Williams, R.J. "The Alleged Semitic Original of the Wisdom of Amenope." *JEA* 47 (1961): 100–6.

Wilson, John A. "The Texts of the Battle of Kadesh." *AJSL* 34.4 (1927): 166–67.

Wilson, Robert Dick. *Studies in the Book of Daniel*. Grand Rapids: Baker, 1972.

Wise, Michael O., Martin G. Abegg Jr., and Edward M. Cook. *The Dead Sea Scrolls: A New Translation*. San Francisco: HarperCollins, 1996.

Wiseman, Donald J. *Chronicles of Chaldean Kings in the British Museum*. London: Trustees of the British Museum, 1956.

_____ "Jonah's Nineveh." The Tyndale Biblical Archaeology Lecture (1977): 45.

Wiseman, Donald J., et. al. *Notes on Some Problems in the Book of Daniel*. London: Tyndale, 1970.

Witherington, Ben III. "In the Beginning: Religion at the Dawn of Civilization." *BAR* 39.1 (2013): 57–60.

Wolters, Al. *Zechariah*. HCOT. Leuven: Peeters, 2014.

Wood, Bryant G. "From Ramesses to Shiloh: Archaeological Discoveries Bearing on the Exodus-Judges Period." Pages 256–82

in *Giving the Sense: Understanding and Using Old Testament Historical Texts*. Edited by David M. Howard, Jr. and Michael A. Grisanti. Grand Rapids: Kregel, 2003.

_____ "Did the Israelites Conquer Jericho? A New Look at the Archaeological Evidence." http://www.biblearchaeology.org/post/2008/05/01/Did-the-Israelites-Conquer-Jericho-A-New-Look-at-the-Archaeological-Evidence.aspx.

Wood, James. *Wisdom Literature: An Introduction*. London: Gerald Duckworth & Co., 1967.

Xeravits, Géza G. *King, Priest, Prophet: Positive Eschatological Protagonists of the Qumran Library*. Boston: Brill Academic, 2003.

Yadin, Yigael. *The Scroll of the War of the Sons of Light against the Sons of Darkness*. Translated by B. Rabin and C. Rabin. Oxford: Oxford University Press, 1962.

Yamauchi, Edwin M. "Daniel and Contacts between the Aegean and the Near East before Alexander." *EvQ* 53 (1981): 37–47.

_____ *Persia and the Bible*. Grand Rapids: Baker, 1990.

Yardeni, Ada. "Remarks on the Priestly Blessing on Two Ancient Amulets from Jerusalem." *VT* 41.2 (1991): 176–85.

Yaron, Reuven. "Aramaic Marriage Contracts from Elephantine." *JSS* 3.1 (1958): 1–39.

York, A. "A Philological and Textual Analysis of the Qumran Job Targum (11QtgJob)." PhD diss., Cornell University, 1973.

Young, Dwight W. "The Incredible Regnal Spans of Kish I in the Sumerian Kings List." *JNES* 50.1 (1991): 23–35.

Yurco, Frank. "3,200-Year Old Pictures of Israelites Found in Egypt." *BAR* 16.5 (1990): 20–38.

Yurco, Frank. "Pharaoh Merneptah Meets Israel." *B&S* 18 (2005): 65–82.

Zandee, J. *Death as an Enemy*. Leiden: Brill, 1960.

Zeder, M. A., E. Emshwiller, B.D. Smith, and D.G. Bradley. "The Camel in Arabia: A Direct Radiocarbon Date, Calibrated to about 7000 BC." *Journal of Archaeological Science* 16 (2006): 355–62.

_____ "Documenting Domestication: The Intersection of Genetics and Archaeology." *Trends in Genetics* 22.3 (2006): 139–55.

Zertal, Adam. "Has Joshua's Altar Been Found on Mt. Ebal?" *BAR* 11.1 (1985): 26–43.

Zevit, Ziony. *Religion of Ancient Israel: A Synthesis of Parallactic Approaches*. London: Continuum, 2001.

Archaeology and the Intertestamental Period

Abegg, Martin Jr., Peter Flint, and Eugene Ulrich, eds. *The Dead Sea Scrolls Bible*. San Francisco: HarperSanFrancisco, 1999.

Ben-Dov, Meir. *In the Shadow of the Temple: The Discovery of Ancient Jerusalem*. Translated by Ina Friedman. New York: Harper & Row, 1985.

Brooke, George, J. *The Dead Sea Scrolls and the New Testament*. Minneapolis, MN: Fortress, 2005.

Broshi, Magen, and Hanan Eshel. "Residential Caves at Qumran." *DSD* 6 (1999): 328–48.

Burrows, Millar, ed. *The Dead Sea Scrolls of St. Mark's Monastery*. Volume 1. New Haven: The American Schools of Oriental Research, 1950.

Cooper, Lamar E. Sr., "Qumran and the Messianic Hope." *CTR* 7 (2009): 67–68, 78–79.

_____ "Qumran Pottery Factory Revisited." Paper presented delivered to the Near East Archaeological Society at the Evangelical Theological Society Meeting, Baltimore, MD, 19 November 2013.

de Vaux, Roland. *Archaeology and the Dead Sea Scrolls.* London: Oxford University Press, 1973.

Donceel, Robert, and Pauline Donceel-Voute. "The Archaeology of Khirbet Qumran." Pages 51–72 in *Methods of Investigation of the Dead Sea Scrolls and the Khirbet Qumran Site: Present Realities and Future Prospects.* Edited by M. O. Wise, et al. New York: Academy of Sciences, 1998.

Edelman, Diana. *The Origins of the Second Temple: Persian Imperial Policy and the Rebuilding of Jerusalem.* Oakville, CT: Equinox, 2005.

Fields, Weston, W. *The Dead Sea Scrolls, A Full History.* Vol. 1. Boston: Brill, 2009.

Fiensy, David A. and James Riley Strange, eds. *Galilee in the Late Second Temple and Mishnaic Periods.* Volume 2, *The Archaeological Record from Cities, Towns, and Villages.* Minneapolis: Fortress, 2015.

Fitzmyer, Joseph. *The Dead Sea Scrolls and Christian Origins: Studies in the Dead Sea Scrolls and Related Literature.* Grand Rapids: Eerdmans, 2000.

Flint, Peter W., ed. *The Bible at Qumran.* Studies in the Dead Sea Scrolls and Related Literature. Grand Rapids: Eerdmans, 2001.

Galor, Katharina, and Jürgen Zangenberg. "Led Astray By a Dead Sea Latrine." *The Jewish Daily Forward.* February 16, 2007. http://forward.com/articles/10107/led-astray-by-a-dead-sea-latrine/#ixzz2ssQIpPZj.

Golb, Norman. *Who Wrote the Dead Sea Scrolls? The Search for the Secret of Qumran.* New York: Scribner, 1995.

Haran, Menahem. *Temples and Temple Service in Ancient Israel.* Oxford: Clarendon, 1978.

Hirschfeld, Yizhar. *Qumran in Context: Reassessing the Archaeological Evidence.* Peabody, MA: Hendrickson, 2004.

Josephus. Translated by Henry St. J. Thackeray et al. 10 vols. LCL. Cambridge: Harvard University Press, 1937.

Lefkovits, Judah, K. *The Copper Scroll (3Q15): A Reevaluation, A New Reading, Translation, and Commentary.* Boston: Brill, 2000.

Long, Phillip J. *Jesus the Bridegroom: The Origin of the Eschatological Feast as a Wedding Banquet in the Synoptic Gospels.* Eugene, OR: Pickwick, 2013.

Magen, Yizhak, and Yuval Peleg, "Back to Qumran: Ten Years of Excavation and Research, 1993–2004." Pages 55–113 in *Qumran, Site of the Dead Sea Scrolls: Archaeological Interpretations and Debates.* STDJ 57. Boston: Brill, 2006.

_____ "The Qumran Excavations 1993–2004: Preliminary Report," Pages 353–426 in *Judea and Samaria Researches and Discoveries.* Jerusalem: Judea and Samaria, 2008.

Magness, Jodi. *The Archaeology of Qumran and the Dead Sea Scrolls.* Grand Rapids: Eerdmans, 2002.

_____ "Communal Meals and Sacred Space at Qumran." Pages 81–112 in *Debating Qumran.* Leuven: Peeters, 2004.

Mazar, Eilat. *The Complete Guide to the Temple Mount Excavations.* Jerusalem: The Old City Press, 2002.

Patrich, Joseph. "Khirbet Qumran in the Light of New Archaeological Explorations in the Qumran Caves." Pages 73–95 in *Methods of Investigation of the Dead Sea Scrolls and the Khirbet Qumran Site: Present Realities and Future Prospects.* Edited by Michael O. Wise, Norman Golb, John J. Collins, and Dennis G. Pardee. Annals of the New York Academy of Sciences 722. New York: New York Academy of Sciences, 1994.

Price, Randall. *Secrets of the Dead Sea Scrolls.* Eugene, OR: Harvest House, 1996.

_____ *Rose Guide to the Temple.* Glendale, CA: Rose, 2012.

Ritmeyer, Kathleen and Leen Ritmeyer. *Reconstructing Herod's Temple Mount in Jerusalem.* New York: Biblical Archaeology Society, 1991.

Ritmeyer, Leen. *The Quest: Revealing the Temple Mount in Jerusalem.* Jerusalem: Carta, 2006.

_____ "Understanding the Destruction of the Temple Mount." http://www.ritmeyer.com/2007/08/31/understanding-the-destruction-of-the-temple-mount.

Roitman, Adolfo. *Envisioning the Temple: Scrolls, Stones, and Symbols.* Jerusalem: The Israel Museum, 2003.

Schiffman, L. H. "Communal Meals at Qumran." *RevQ* 10 (1979): 45–56.

Schwartz, Max. *The Biblical Engineer: How the Temple in Jerusalem was Built.* Hoboken, NJ: KTAV, 2002.

Shanks, Hershel. *The Copper Scroll and the Search for the Temple Treasure.* Washington, DC: Biblical Archaeology Society, 2007.

Shanks, Hershel. "Qumran—The Pottery Factory." *BAR* 32.5 (2006): 26–32.

Siegel, Judy. "Fatal Cleanliness and Godliness." *The International Jerusalem Post.* November 24–30, 2006.

Trever, John C. *The Untold Story of Qumran.* Grand Rapids: Fleming H. Revell, 1965.

Ulrich, Eugene. *The Dead Sea Scrolls and the Origins of the Bible: Studies in the Dead Sea Scrolls and Related Literature.* Grand Rapids: Eerdmans, 1999.

VanderKam, James C. *The Dead Sea Scrolls Today.* Grand Rapids: Eerdmans, 2010.

VanderKam, James and Peter Flint. *The Meaning of the Dead Sea Scrolls.* New York: HarperSanFrancisco, 2002.

Werrett, Ian C. *Ritual Purity and the Dead Sea Scrolls.* STDJ 72. Edited by Florentino Garcia Martinez. Boston: Brill, 2007.

Yadin, Yigael. *The Temple Scroll: The Hidden Law of the Dead Sea Sect.* New York: Random House, 1985.

Zeuner, Frederick E. "Notes on Qumran." *PEQ* 92 (1960): 27–36.

Zias, Joe E., James D. Tabor, and Stephanie Harter-Lailheugue. "Toilets at Qumran, The Essenes, and The Scrolls: New Anthropological Data and Old Theories." *RevQ* 22.4 (2006): 631–40.

Archaeology and the New Testament

Allegri, Renzo. "How I Discovered the Tomb of the Apostle Philip: Interview with Archaeologist Francesco D'Andria." *ZENIT* (2012). http://www.zenit.org/article-34705?l=english.

Alleyne, Richard. "Sea of Galilee Water Level at Lowest on Record." *The Telegraph*, August 29, 2008.

Amit, D. "What Was the Source of Herodion's Water?" http://www.christusrex.org/www1/ofm/sbf/Books/LA44/44561DA.pdf.

ANF. Edited by Alexander Roberts and James Donaldson. 1885–1887. 10 vols. Repr., Peabody, MA: Hendrickson, 1994.

Appold, Mark. "Peter in Profile: From Bethsaida to Rome." Pages 133–48 in *Bethsaida: A City By the North Shore of the Sea of Galilee*. Edited by Rami Arav and Richard A. Freund. Kirksville, MO: Truman State University Press, 2004.

Arav, Rami, Richard A. Freund, and John F. Shroder, Jr. "Bethsaida Rediscovered." *BAR* 26.1 (2000): 44–51, 53–56.

Arav, Rami. "Toward a Comprehensive History of Geshur," Pages 1–48 in *Bethsaida: A City By the North Shore of the Sea of Galilee*. Edited by Rami Arav and Richard A. Freund. Kirksville, MO: Truman State University Press, 2004.

"Archeologists Find Evidence of St. Perter's Prison." http://www.telegraph.co.uk/news/worldnews/7852507/Archeologists-find-evidence-of-St-Peters-prison.html.

Atkinson, K. "Synagogues in Judea." *NTS* 43 (1997): 491–502.

Augustine. "Letter to Alypius the Bishop of Thagaste, Concerning the Anniversary of the Birth of Leontis, Formerly Bishop of Hippo." 12 (*NPNF* 1.1:257).

Avni, Gideon. "On Archaeology, Forgeries and Public Awareness: The 'James Brother of Jesus' Ossuary in Retrospect." http://www.bibleinterp.com/articles/archfor358014.shtml.

Báez-Camargo, Gonzalo. *ACB*. Garden City, NY: Doubleday, 1984.

Bagatti, Bellarmino. "Gli antichi sacri de Betlemme in seguito agli scavi e restauri praticati dalla Custodia di Terra Santi." *Publications of the Studium Biblicum Franciscanum,* Vol. 9. Jerusalem: Franciscan, 1952.

Bagnall, Roger S., Roberta Casagrande-Kim, Akin Ersov, and Cumhur Tanriver, eds. *Graffiti from the Basilica in the Agora of Smyrna*. City: NYU Press, 2016.

Barrett, C. K. *A Critical and Exegetical Commentary on the Acts of the Apostles: Acts 15–28*. New York: T & T Clark, 1998.

Barnett, Paul. *Jesus and the Rise of Early Christianity: A History of New Testament Times*. Downers Grove, IL: InterVarsity Press, 1999.

Binder, Donald D. *Into the Temple Courts: The Place of the Synagogues in the Second Temple Period*. SBL Dissertation Series 169. Atlanta: Society of Biblical Literature, 1999.

Blaiklock, E.M. *The Archaeology of the New Testament*. Rev. ed. Grand Rapids: Zondervan, 1984, c. 1970, 1972.

Bolen, Todd. "The Top 5 of 2004." *BiblePlaces Newsletter* 3 (2004). http://www.bibleplaces.com/newsletter/2004dec.htm.

Bond, Helen Katherine. "Caiaphas: Friend of Rome and Judge of Jesus?" Journal. Journal number (Year): 39.

_____ *Pontius Pilate in History and Interpretation*. New York: Cambridge University Press, 1998.

Bovon, François. "Women Priestesses in the Apocryphal Acts of Philip." Pages 109–21 in *Walk in the Ways of Wisdom: Essays in Honor of Elisabeth Schüssler Fiorenza*. Edited by Shelly Matthews, Cynthia Briggs Kittredge, and Melanie Johnson-DeBaufre. Harrisburg: Trinity Press International, 2003.

Brin, Howard B. *Catalog of Judaea Capta Coinage*. Minneapolis: Emmett, 1986.

Burns, Ross. *Damascus: A History*. New York: Routledge, 2005.

Byne, Ryan and Bernadette McNary-Zak, eds. *Resurrecting the Brother of Jesus: The James Ossuary Controversy*. Chapel Hill: University of North Carolina Press, 2009.

Carter, Warren. *Pontius Pilate: Portraits of a Roman Governor*. Collegeville, MN: Liturgical Press, 1989.

Charlesworth, James H. "Jesus Research and Archaeology: A New Perspective." Pages 34–35 in *Jesus Research and Archaeology: A New Perspective*. Edited by James H. Charlesworth. Grand Rapids: Eerdmans, 2006.

Clarke, Andrew D. *Secular and Christian Leadership in Corinth: A Socio-Historical and Exegetical Study of 1 Corinthians 1–6*. Leiden: Brill, 1993.

Collins, Adela Yarbro. "Satan's Throne." *BAR* 32 (2006): 26–39. http://members.bib-arch.org/publication.asp?PubID=BSBA&Volume=32&Issue=3&ArticleID=7.

Corbo, Virgilio. *House of Saint Peter*. Jerusalem: Franciscan, 1968.

_____ *New Memoirs of Saint Peter by the Sea*. Jerusalem: Franciscan, 1968.

Cornfield, Gaalyah. *Archaeology of the Bible: Book by Book*. Edited by David Noel Freedman. New York: Harper and Row, 1976.

Cytryn-Silverman, Katia. "Kharrar, Wadi." *EAEHL* 5:1861.

D'Andria, Francesco. "Conversion, Crucifixion and Celebration." *BAR* 37 (2011): 34–46, 70.

Deissmann, Adolf. "Appendix V: The Synagogue Inscription of Theodotus at Jerusalem." Pages 439–41 in *Light from the Ancient East: The New Testament Illustrated by Recently Discovered Texts of the Graeco-Roman World*. Translated by L. R. M. Strachan. New York: Harper & Row, 1928. Repr., Grand Rapids: Eerdmans, 1965.

Deutsch, Robert. "Roman Coins Boast 'Judaea Capta'" *BAR* 36.1 (2010): 51–53. http://members.bib-arch.org/publication.asp?PubID=BSBA&Volume=36&Issue=1&ArticleID=27.

Dittenberger, W., ed. *Orientis Graeci Inscriptiones Selectae*. Leipzig (1903–1905) 2: 654, 48–60.

Dods, Marcus, Robert A. Watson and William Farrar. *The Exposition of the Bible: A Series of Expositions Covering All the Books of the Old and New Testament, St. Luke-Galatians*. Hartford, CT: S. S. Scranton Co., 1907.

Edwards, Douglas R. "Sifting Through the Past: the Geospatial Future of Archaeology." *Journal of Geographic Information System* 10 (2000): 26.

Ehrenberg, V. and A. H. M. Jones. *Documents Illustrating the Reigns of Augustus and Tiberius*. 2nd ed. Oxford: Clarendon, 1955.

Elitzur, Yoel. "The Siloam Pool: 'Solomon's Pool' Was a Swimming Pool." *PEQ* 140 (2008): 17–25.

Evans, Craig A. *Jesus and the Ossuaries: What Jewish Burial Practices Reveal about the Beginning of Christianity*. Waco: Baylor University Press, 2003.

Fant, Clyde E. *Lost Treasures of the Bible: Understanding the Bible Through Archaeological Artifacts in World Museums*. Grand Rapids: Eerdmans, 2008.

Fant, Clyde E., and Mitchell Glenn Reddish. *A Guide to Biblical Sites in Greece and Turkey*. New York: Oxford University Press, 2003.

Feldman, Steven. "The Case for el-Araj." *BAR* 26.1 (2000): 52.

Fiensy, David A. and James Riley Strange, eds. *Galilee in the Late Second Temple and Mishnaic Periods*. Volume 1, *Life, Culture, and Society*. Minneapolis: Fortress, 2014.

Finegan, Jack. *The Archaeology of the New Testament: The Life of Jesus and the Beginning of the Early Church*. Princeton: Princeton University Press, 1992.

Fitzgerald, John T. "Gadara: Philodemus' Native City." Pages 343–97 in *Philodemus and the New Testament World*. Edited by John T. Fitzgerald, Dirk Obbink, and Glenn S. Holland. Leiden: Brill, 2004.

Fitzmeyer, Joseph A. *First Corinthians*. AB 32. New Haven: Yale University Press, 2008.

Fotopoulos, John. *Food Offered to Idols in Roman Corinth: A Social-Rhetorical Reconsideration*. Tübingen: Mohr Siebeck, 2003.

Freedman, David Noel. *The Anchor Yale Bible Dictionary*. Volume 2. New York: Doubleday, 1996.

Freund, Richard A. "Ereimos: Was Bethsaida a 'Lonely Place' in First Century CE?" Pages 183–212 in *Bethsaida: A City by the North Shore of the Sea of Galilee*. Edited by Rami Arav and Richard A. Freund. Kirksville, MO: Truman State University Press, 2004), 183–212.

Friesen, Steven J. *Twice Neokoros: Ephesus, Asia, and the Cult of the Flavian Imperial Family*. Leiden: Brill, 1993.

Gates, Charles. *Ancient Cities: The Archaeology of Urban Life in the Ancient Near East*. New York: Routledge, 2003.

Gibson, Shimon. "A Lost Cause." *BAR* 30 (2004): 52–59. http://members.bib-arch.org/publication.asp?PubID=BSBA&Volume=30&Issue=6&ArticleID=15.

Giles, Terry, "The Samaritans" in *Near Eastern Archaeology: A Reader*, ed. Suzanne Richard (Winona Lake, IN: Eisenbrauns, 2003), 413–17.

Gill, David W.J. "Acts and the Urban Élites." Pages 105–18 in *The Book of Acts in its First Century Setting: Graeco-Roman Setting*. Edited by David W.J. Gill and Conrad Gempf. Grand Rapids: Eerdmans, 1994.

Golan, Oded. "The Authenticity of the James Ossuary and the Jehoash Inscriptions—Summary of Expert Trial Witnesses." http://www.bib-arch.org/scholars-study/the-authenticity-of-the-james-ossuary.pdf.

Goodrich, John K. "Eastus, Quaestor of Corinth: The Administrative Rank of ὁ οἰκονόμος τῆς πόλεως (Rom 16.23) in an Achaean Colony." *NTS* 56 (2010): 90–115.

Grabbe, Lester. "Synagogues in Pre-70 Palestine: A Re-Assessment." *JTS* 39 (1988): 401–10.

Gutman, S. and A. Berman. "Communication." *RB* 77 (1970): 583–85.

Hachlili, Rachel. *Jewish Funerary Customs, Practices and Rites in the Second Temple Period*. Lieden: Brill, 2005.

Harrill, James A. "Ossuary Update: Final Blow to Israel Antiquities Authority Report." *BAR* 30 (2004): 38–41. http://members.bib-arch.org/publication.asp?PubID=BSBA&Volume=30&Issue=1&ArticleID=10.

_____ *The Manumission of Slaves in Early Christianity*. City: Publisher, Year.

Harris, Judith. "Putting Paul on the Map: Apostle's Name found on Cyprus Inscription." *BAR* 26.1 (2000): 12–14. http://members.bib-arch.org/publication.asp?PubID=BSBA&Volume=26&Issue=1&ArticleID=7.

Hasson, Nir. "Archaeological Stunner: Not Herod's Tomb after All?" *Haaretz,* October 11, 2013.

Herod's Palace at Jericho. http://www.mycrandall.ca/courses/ntintro/images/Jericho.htm.

"Het vroegste christelijke artefact: een graffito" in Smyrna (The Earliest Christian Artifact: a Graffiti in Smyrna), https://gegrammena.wordpress.com/2012/04/03/het-vroegste-christelijke-artefact-een-graffito-in-smyrna/.

Holum, Kenneth G. and Avner Raban, "Caesarea," *NEAEHL* 1:270–91.

Horsley, G. H. R. "An Archisynagogos of Corinth?" Pages 213–20 in *New Documents Illustrating Early Christianity*. Volume 4. Macquarie University (Australia): The Ancient History Documentary Research Centre, 1987, 213–20.

House, H. Wayne, and Joseph M. Holden. *Charts of Apologetics and Christian Evidences*. Grand Rapids: Zondervan, 2006.

_____ "Herod the Great." http://www.hwhouse.com/images/5.HEROD_THE_GREAT, © 2011 H. Wayne House.pdf. This article relies in part on the copyrighted article.

_____ http://www.hwhouse.com/images/5.HEROD_THE_GREAT.pdf.

_____ "Pontius Pilate Inscription." hwhouse.com/images/2.PONTIUS_PILATE_INSCRIPTION, © 2011 H. Wayne House.pdf. This article relies in part on the copyrighted article.

_____ http://www.hwhouse.com/images/5.GALLIO.pdf, © 2011 H. Wayne House. This article relies in part on the copyrighted article.

_____ http://www.hwhouse.com/images/1.CITY_OFFICIALS_IN_THE_ACTS_OF_THE_APOSTLES,© 2011 H. Wayne House.pdf. This article relies in part on the copyrighted article.

_____ http://www.hwhouse.com/images/ 6.ERASTUS_INSCRIPTION, © 2011 H. Wayne House.pdf. This article relies in part on the copyrighted article.

_____ http://www.hwhouse.com/images/ 11.Ossuary of James, son of Joseph and brother of Jesus, © 2011 H. Wayne House.pdf.

Hurtado, Larry. "The Earliest Christian Graffito?" https://larryhurtado.wordpress.com/2012/04/02/the-earliest-christian-graffito.

Israel Ministry of Foreign Affairs. "Bethsaida: An Ancient Fishing Village on the Shore of the Sea of Galilee." http://www.mfa.gov.il/MFA/History/Early%20History%20-%20Archaeology/Bethsaida-%20An%20Ancient%20Fishing%20Village%20on%20the%20shore.

Jeffers, James S., *The Greco-Roman World of the New Testament Era: Exploring the Background of Early Christianity*. Downers Grove, IL: InterVarsity Press, 1999.

Jordanian Department of Antiquities. "The Baptismal Site (Bethany beyond the Jordan)." http://whc.unesco.org/en/tentativelists/1556.

Josephus, Flavius. *The Works of Josephus: Complete and Unabridged*. Translated by William Whiston. Peabody: Hendrickson, 1996, c1987.

Keall, Edward J. "Brother of Jesus Ossuary: New Tests Bolster Case for Authenticity." *BAR* 29 (2003): 52–55, 70. http://members.bib-arch.org/publication.asp?PubID=BSBA&Volume=29&Issue=4&ArticleID=8.

Kearsley, R.A. "The Asiarchs." Pages 363–76 in *The Book of Acts in Its First Century Setting: Graeco-Roman Setting.* Edited by David W. J. Gill and Conrad Gempf Grand Rapids: Eerdmans, 1994.

_____ "New Testament Context." Pages 419–31 in *New Documents Illustrating Early Christianity: A Review of the Greek Inscriptions and Papyri Published in 1979.* Volume 4. Edited by G. H. R. Horsley. Sydney: Maquarie University Press, 1987.

Khouri, Rami G. "Have Jordanian Archaeologists Found the Place Where Jesus Was Baptized?" *The Daily Star.* May 23, 2005.

Kloner, Amos. "A Tomb with Inscribed Ossuaries in East Talpiyot, Jerusalem." *Atiqot* 29 (1996): 15–22.

_____ "Did a Rolling Stone Close Jesus' Tomb?" *BAR* 25:5 (1999): 23–28.

Kloner, Amos and Boaz Zissu. *The Necropolis of Jerusalem in the Second Temple Period.* Interdisciplinary Studies in Ancient Church and Religion 8. Leuven: Peeters, 2007.

Koester, Craig R. *Symbolism in the Fourth Gospel: Meaning, Mystery, Community,* 2nd ed. Minneapolis: Augsburg Fortress, 2003.

Kogan-Zehavi, Elena. "Jerusalem." *NEAEHL* 5:1801–37.

Kuhn, Heinz-Wolfgang. "Bethsaida in the Gospel of Mark." Page 120 in *Bethsaida: A City by the North Shore of the Sea of Galilee.* Edited by Rami Arav and Richard A. Freund. Kirksville, MO: Truman State University Press, 2004.

Laney, Carl F. "Selective Geographical Problems in the Life of Christ." PhD diss., Dallas Theological Seminary, 1977.

Lemaire, André. "Burial Box of James the Brother of Jesus." *BAR* 28.6 (2002): 24–28, 30–31, 33, 70. http://members.bib-archorg/publication.asp?PubID=BSBA&Volume=28&Issue=6&ArticleID=1.

_____ "Ossuary Update: Israel Antiquities Authority's Report Deeply Flawed." *BAR* 29 (2003): 50–58, 67, 70. http://members.bib-arch.org/publication.asp?PubID=BSBA&Volume=29&Issue=6&ArticleID=1.

Lendering, Jona. "P. Sulpicius Quirinius." *Livius: Articles on Ancient History.* n.d. http://www.livius.org/su-sz/sulpicius/quirinius.html.

Liddell, Henry George, Robert Scott, Henry Stuart Jones. *A Greek-English Lexicon.* 9th ed. With revised supplement. Oxford: Clarendon, 1996.

Limberis, Vasiliki. *Architects of Piety: The Cappadocian Fathers and the Cult of the Martyrs.* New York: Oxford University Press, 2011.

Magness, Jodi. "What Did Jesus' Tomb Look Like?" *BAR* 32 (2006): 38–43.

Maier, Paul L. *In the Fullness of Time: A Historian Looks at Christmas, Easter, and the Early Church.* Grand Rapids: Kregel, 1991, 1996.

Mancini, Ignazio. "Excavations Have Confirmed That a Village Existed in the First Century on the Site Where the Shrine of Cana Has Been Built." *L'Osservatore Romano Weekly Edition in English* (1998). http://www.ewtn.com/library/SCRIPTUR/CANAEXCA.HTM.

Matthews, Christopher R. *Philip, Apostle and Evangelist: Configurations of Traditions.* Leiden: Brill, 2002.

Matthews, Victor. "Olympic Losers: Why Athletes Who Did Not Win at Olympia Are Remembered." Pages 81–94 in *Onward to the Olympics: Historical Perspectives on the Olympic Games.* Edited by Gerald P. Schaus and Stephen R. Wenn. Waterloo: Wilfrid Laurier University Press, 2007.

McRay, John. *Archaeology and the New Testament.* Grand Rapids: Baker, 1991.

_____ "Archaeology and the Book of Acts." *CTR* 5 (1990): 69–82, 77.

Meeks, Wayne A. *The First Urban Christians: The Social World of the Apostle Paul.* New Haven: Yale University Press, 1983.

Meggitt, Justin J. *Paul, Poverty and Survival.* Edinburgh: T & T Clark, 1998.

_____ "The Social Status of Erastus: Rom. 16:23." Pages 219–26 in *Christianity at Corinth: The Quest for the Pauline Church.* Edited by Edward Adams and David G. Horrell. Louisville: Westminster John Knox, 2004.

Metzger, Bruce et al., eds. *A Textual Commentary of the New Testament.* 2nd ed. New York: United Bible Societies, 1994.

Metzger, Bruce. *A Textual Commentary on the Greek New Testament.* New York: United Bible Societies, 2002, c. 1971.

Michaels, J. Ramsey. *John.* Grand Rapids: Eerdmans, c1984, 2011.

Millard, Alan. "The Knowledge of Writing in Iron Age Palestine." *TynBul* 46. (1995): 214.

Miller, Stephen G. *Ancient Greek Athletics.* Cambridge: Yale University Press, 2006.

_____ *Anatolia: Land, Men, and Gods in Asia Minor. Vol II: The Rise of the Church.* Oxford: Clarendon, 1993.

Meyers, Eric "Q & A with Mark Goodacre and Eric Meyers." *The Duke University Chronicle,* April 22, 2012.

Mueller, Tom. "King Herod Revealed." *National Geographic,* http://ngm.nationalgeographic.com/print/2008/12/herod/mueller-text.

Murphy-O'Connor, Jerome. *The Holy Land: An Oxford Archaeological Guide from Earliest Times to 1700.* 5th ed. New York: Oxford University Press, c1980, 2008.

_____ *St. Paul's Corinth: Text and Archaeology.* Collegeville, MN: Liturgical Press, c1983, 2002.

_____ *St. Paul's Ephesus: Texts and Archeology.* Collegeville, MN: Liturgical Press 2008.

_____ *Keys to First Corinthians: Revisiting the Major Issues.* New York: Oxford University Press, 2009.

Netzer, Ehud. "Herod's Family Tomb in Jerusalem." *BAR* 9 (1983): 52–58.

Nobbs, Alanna. "Cyprus" Pages 279–89 in *The Book of Acts in its First Century Setting, Graeco-Roman Setting.* Edited by David W. J. Gill and Conrad Gempf. Grand Rapids: Eerdmans, 1994.

Notley, R. Steven. "Et-Tell Is Not Bethsaida." *NEA* 70 (2007): 220–230.

Novak, Ralph Martin. *Christianity and the Roman Empire: Background Texts.* Harrisburg: Trinity Press International, 2001.

NPNF. Edited by Philip Schaff. 1886–1889. 14 vols. Repr., Peabody, MA: Hendrickson, 1994.

O'Callaghan, Roger T. "Vatican Excavations and the Tomb of Peter." *BA* 16.4 (1953): 71.

Oliphant, Laurence. "A Trip to the North-East of Lake Tiberias in Jaulan." Pages 243–67 in *Across the Jordan: Being An Exploration and Survey of Part of Hauran and Jaulan.* Edited by Gottlieb Schumacher, Laurence Oliphant and Guy LeStrange. London: Alexander P Watt, 1889.

Pixner, Bargil. *Paths of Messiah: Messianic Studies in Galilee and Jerusalem.* San Francisco: Ignatius, c1991, 2010.

Price, Randall. *The Stones Cry Out: What Archaeology Reveals About the Truth of the Bible.* Eugene, OR: Harvest House, 1997.

Pummer, Reinhard. "Samaritan Material Remains." Pages 135–195 in *The Samaritans.* Edited by Alan David Crown. Tübingen: Mohr Seibeck, 1989.

Rahmani, L. Y. *A Catalogue of Jewish Ossuaries in the Collections of the State of Israel.* Jerusalem: The Israel Antiquities Authority, 1994.

Ramsay, William M. *The Bearing of Recent Discovery on the Trustworthiness of the New Testament.* New York: Hodder and Stoughton, 1915.
_____ *Letters to the Seven Churches.* Grand Rapids: Baker, 1979.

"Rich Greek graffiti Found in Smyrna's Agora." http://archaeology-newsnetwork.blogspot.com/2013/07/rich-greek-graffiti-found-in-smyrnas.html#.VxxOzWOL7nw.

Richardson, Kristopher Carl. *Early Christian Care for the Poor: An Alternative Subsistence Strategy Under Roman Imperial Rule.* Ann Arbor: ProQuest, 2009.

Richardson, Peter. *Building Jewish in the Roman East.* Waco: Baylor University Press, 2004.

Riesner, Rainer. *Paul's Early Period: Chronology, Mission Strategy, Theology.* Grand Rapids: Eerdmans, 1998.

Ritmeyer, Leen. "Akeldama Tomb of Annas." *Ritmeyer Archaeological Design.* http://store.ritmeyer.com/node/128.

Ritmeyer, Leen and Kathleen Ritmeyer. "Akeldama: Potter's Field or High Priest's Tomb?" *BAR* 20 (1994): 23–35, 76, 78.

Riesner, Rainer. "Synagogues in Jerusalem." Pages 179–211 in *The Book of Acts in its First Century Setting.* Vol. 4, *Palestinian Setting.* Edited by R. Baukham. Grand Rapids: Eerdmans, 1995.

Rothaus, Richard M. *Corinth, the First City of Greece: An Urban History of Late Antique Cult and Religion.* Leiden: Brill, 2000.

Rozenberg, Silvia and Mevorah, David, eds. *Herod the Great: The King's Final Journey.* Jerusalem: The Israel Museum, 2013.

Runesson, Anders, Donald D. Binder and Birger Olsson. *The Ancient Synagogue from Its Origins to 200 C.E.: A Source Book.* AJEC 72. Leiden: Brill, 2008.

Saddington, D. B. "Roman Military and Administrative Personnel in the New Testament." Pages 2409–35 in *Aufsteig Und Niedergang Der Römischen Welt, Religion.* Edited by Hildegard Temporini and Wolfgang Hass. Berlin: de Gruyter, 1996.

Sauter, Megan. "How Was Jesus' Tomb Sealed? Examining the Tomb of Jesus in Light of Second Temple-Period Jerusalem Tombs." *Bible History Daily.* April, 2017. http://www.biblicalarchaeology.org/daily/biblical-sites-places/jerusalem/how-was-jesus-tomb-sealed/.

Savage, Carl. *et-Tell (Bethsaida): A Study of the First Century CE in the Galilee.* Ann Arbor, MI: ProQuest.
_____ *Biblical Bethsaida: An Archaeological Study of the First Century.* Lanham, MD: Lexington, 2011.

Scherrer, Peter. "Ephesus Uncovered." *Archaeology Odyssey* 4 (Mar/Apr 2001): 26–37. http://members.bib-arch.org/publication.asp?PubID=BSAO&Volume=4&Issue=2&ArticleID=13.

Schnabel, Eckhard J. *Paul the Missionary: Realities, Strategies and Methods.* Downers Grove, IL: InterVarsity Press, 2008.

Schwartz, Joshua. "John the Baptist, the Wilderness and the Samaritan Mission." Pages 104–120 in *Studies in Historical Geography and Biblical Historiography: Presented to Zecharia Kallai.* Edited by Gershom Galil and Moshe Weinfeld. Leiden: Brill, 2000.

Schwartz, Shai. "Bethsaida 2011 Season." http://bethsaidaexcavation.com/Bethsaida_2011/index.htm.

Segal, Arthur. *Theaters in Roman Palestine and Provincia Arabia.* Leiden: Brill, 1995.

Shanks, Hershel. *Brother of Jesus: The Dramatic Story and Meaning of the First Archaeological Link to Jesus and His Family.* New York: Continuum, 2003.
_____ "Issue 200: Ten Top Discoveries." *BAR* 35 (2009): 74–96. http://members.bib-arch.org/publication.asp?PubID=BSBA&Volume=35&Issue=4&ArticleID=15.
_____ "Strata: Ritual Bath or Swimming Pool?" *BAR* 34.3 (2008): 24–36. http://members.bib-arch.org/publication.asp?PubID=BSBA&Volume=34&Issue=3&ArticleID=4.
_____ "The Theodotus Inscription." *BAR* 29.4 (2003): 24–36. http://members.bib-arch.org/publication.asp?PubID=BSBA&Volume=29&Issue=4&ArticleID=14.

Sharon, Moshe. *Corpus Inscriptionum Arabicarum Palaestinae.* Vol. 2. Leiden: Brill, 1999.

Siegel, Judy. "US Physician Unlocks Mystery of King Herod's Death," *The Jerusalem Post,* January 27, 2002.

Singer, Suzanne F. "Herod the Great—The King's Final Journey," http://www.biblicalarchaeology.org/daily/people-cultures-in-the-bible/people-in-the-bible/herod-the-great-the-kings-final-journey.

Sloyan, Gerard Stephen. *Jesus on Trial: A Study of the Gospels.* Minneapolis: Augsburg Fortress, 2006.

Smith, Robert Houston. "The Tomb of Jesus." *BA* 30:3 (1967): 74–89.

Souter, A., "Asiarch." Page 103 in *Dictionary of the Apostolic Church.* Edited by James Hastings. New York: Charles Scribner's Sons, 1916–1918.

Staff of BAS. "The House of Peter: The Home of Jesus in Capernaum?" http://www.biblicalarchaeology.org/daily/biblical-sites-places/biblical-archaeology-sites/the-house-of-peter-the-home-of-jesus-in-capernaum.

Strange, James F. and Hershel Shanks. "St. Peter's House. Has the House Where Jesus Stayed in Capernaum Been Found?" Pages 68–85 in *Ten Top Biblical Archaeological Discoveries.* Washington D.C.: Biblical Archaeological Society, 2011.

"Strata: Leading Scholar Lambastes Israel Antiquities Authority Committee." *BAR* 33 (2007): 16. http://members.bib-arch.org/publication.asp?PubID=BSBA&Volume=33&Issue=6&ArticleID=22.

"Strata: Philip's Tomb Discovered—But Not Where Expected." *BAR* 38 (2012): 18.

Swaddling, Judith. *The Ancient Olympic Games.* Austin: University of Texas Press, 2002.

Taylor, Lilly Ross. *The Divinity of the Roman Emperor.* Philological Monographs, Vol. 1. Middletown, Connecticut: American Philological Association, 1931. Reprint, Chicago: Scholars Press, 1975, 273.

Theodosius. *De Situ Terrae Sancte,* 8 Edited by Paul Geyer. CCSL 175. Turnholt: Brepols, 1965.

_____ "On the Topography of the Holy Land." Pages 35–36 in *Library of the Palestine Pilgrims' Text Society.* Volume 1. London: Palestine Pilgrims' Text Society, 1890–97, 10.

"Tomb of King Herod discovered at Herodium by Hebrew University archaeologist." The Hebrew University of Jerusalem, May 8, 2007. " http://members.bib-arch.org/publication.asp?PubID=BSBA&Volume=28&Issue=2&UserID=0&" http://members.bib-arch.org/publication.asp?PubID=BSBA&Volume=28&Issue=2&UserID=0&.

Tzaferis, Vassilios. The Excavations of Kursi-Geresa. 'Atiquot, English Series, Vol. 16 (Jerusalem: 1983).

Treblinco, Paul. *Early Christians in Ephesus from Paul to Ignatius.* Tübingen: Mohr Siebeck, 2004.

Tzaferis, Vassilios. "The Excavations of Kersi-Gergesa." *'Atiqot* 16 (1983). English Series. Jerusalem: Israel Antiquities Authority, 49–51.

Unger, Merrill F. *Archaeology and the New Testament.* Grand Rapids: Zondervan, 1962.

VanderKam, James C. *From Joshua to Caiaphas: High Priests after the Exile.* Minneapolis: Augsburg Fortress, 2004.

von Wahlde, Urban C. "Archaeology and John's Gospel." Pages 522–86 in *Jesus Research and Archaeology: A New Perspective.* Edited by James H. Charlesworth. Grand Rapids: Eerdmans, 2006.

_____ "A Rolling Stone That Was Hard to Roll." *BAR* 41:2 (2015): Pages.

Wachsrmann, Shelly. *The Sea of Galilee Boat: A 2000 Year Old Discovery From the Sea of Legends.* College Station, TX: Texas A & M University Press, 2009.

Walsh, John E. *The Bones of St. Peter.* New York: Doubleday, 1982.

Welborn, L.L. *An End to Enmity: Paul and the "Wrongdoer" of Second Corinthians.* Boston: de Gruyter, 2011.

Wiener, Noah. "Herodium: The Tomb of King Herod Revisited," http://www.biblicalarchaeology.org/daily/biblical-sites-places/biblical-archaeology-sites/herodium-the-tomb-of-king-herod-revisited.

Wilson, Charles William and Charles Warren. *The Recovery of Jerusalem.* London: Richard Bently, 1871.

Witherington III, Ben. "Biblical Views: The Writing on the Wall." *BAR* 35 (2009): 26. http://members.bib-arch.org/publication.asp?PubID=BSBA&Volume=35&Issue=3&ArticleID=5.

_____ *Conflict and Community in Corinth: A Socio-Rhetorical Commentary on 1 and 2 Corinthians.* Grand Rapids: Eerdmans, 1995.

_____ "Graffiti at the SBL." http://benwitherington.blogspot.com/2008/12/graffiti-at-sbl.html.

_____ "Graffiti and Gematria in Early Christianity," http://www.patheos.com/blogs/bibleandculture/2012/04/22/graffiti-and-gematria-in-early-christianity.

_____ *The Acts of the Apostles: A Socio-Rhetorical Commentary.* Grand Rapids: Eerdmans, 1998.

_____ *What Have They Done With Jesus?: Beyond Strange Theories and Bad History—Why We Can Trust the Bible.* New York: Harper, 2006.

Yamauchi, Edwin. *The Archaeology of New Testament Cities.* Grand Rapids: Baker, 1980.

Young, David C. *A Brief History of the Olympic Games.* Malden: Wiley-Blackwell, 2004.

Zangenberg, Jurgen. "Between Jerusalem and the Galilee: Samaria in the Time of Jesus." Pages 393–432 in *Jesus and Archaeology: A New Perspective.* Edited by James H. Charlesworth. Grand Rapids: Eerdmans, 2006.

Zissu, Boaz. "This Place Is for the Birds." *BAR* 35.3 (2009): 30–37, 66–67. http://members.bibarch.org/publication.asp?PubID=BSBA&Volume=35&Issue=3&ArticleID=7.

Scripture and Extra-Biblical Index

Genesis

1–2	48
1–11	63, 361
1:1–2	48
1:1	47, 48
1:3–5	48
1:27–28	47
1:28	71
2–3	53, 174
2:2–3	48
2:4	47
2:7	48, 50, 60
2:8	47
2:15	48, 50, 60
2:16	47
3	50
3:1–23	49, 50
3:1	49
3:2	50
3:5–6	49
3:8	50
3:11	50
3:13	50
3:17	49, 50
3:14–15	50
3:19	50, 60
3:21	53
3:22	50, 72
3:23–24	50
3:24	50, 52
4:2	54
4:3–4	52
4:3	98
5	55
5:1–32	54
5:2	50
6–9	63
6:1–9:17	63
6:1–7	57
6:8–9	368
6:8	59
6:13–9:17	55
6:13–17	59
6:13–16	63
6:13	60
6:13a	60
6:13b	60
6:14	59, 60, 63, 368
6:17–22	60
6:18–22	59
6:21	59, 60
7:1–16	59
7:1–10	59
7:8–9	59
7:17–23	59
7:20–22	59
7:24	59
8:3–11	59
8:4	59, 60, 63
8:6–12	59
8:7	59
8:12–22	59
8:20–22	59, 60, 62
8:20	59, 60, 98
8:21–22	60
9:1, 7	71
9:20	53, 54
9:29	54
10–11	63
10	55
10:7–12	67
10:8–9	54, 66, 160
10:9	69
10:10–12	67
10:10	68, 71
10:11–12	68, 135
11:2	70
11:4, 9	70
11:6	71
11:10–26	54
11:28	74, 76
11:31	53, 74, 76
12–50	73, 74
12:1–5	53
12:4	77
12:6	362
12:10	74, 76, 197
12:16	77, 80
14	75, 80, 81, 157
14:1–17	80
14:1	80
14:3	80
14:12	80
14:14	74, 81
14:17	80
14:24	157
15:18	18,
15:20	125, 199
17:8	18
18:7	157
21	75
21:32–33	76
22	77
22:2–14	132
24:3–4	192
24:10–11	77
24:10	77
24:16	157
24:19	77
24:64	77, 79
26	75
28:4	18
28:5	77
28:12	71
31	75
31:34	77
34:3	157
35:19	235
37–50	74
37:25	79
37:28	75, 197
41:12	157
41:45	91
41:46	157
41:50	91
42:5	74
43:11	74
46:5–7	74
46:20	91
48:4	18
48:7	235
49	74
50:26	95

Exodus

1:11	83, 84
1:16	84
2:3	63

2:5. . . . . 157, 363
2:10 84
3:14 90
3:22 102
4:9. 89
4:21 85
6:8. 18
7:9–10. 84
7:10–12. 87
7:20–21. 89
8:15 85
8:25–26. 98
8:32 85
9:6. 89
9:12 85
9:23, 31 89
10:7 89
10:15 89
10:20, 27. 85
11:10 85
12:14, 27. 26
12:29 89
12:30 89
12:35–36 109
12:37 84
12:41, 51. 87
13:17 27
14:1–2. 84
14:8 85
16:33–34 . . . . 94, 364
18:1–24. 102
19:3–5. 183
19:8 183
20:1–23:33. 182
20:2 . . . . 88, 183
20:4 . . . . 181, 213
20:14 192
20:23 181
23:31 18
24:3, 7 . . . . 105, 183
25:6 189
25:8–9. 92
25:9 175
25:10 . . . . 93, 94, 95
25:11–13 94
25:11 . . . . .92, 96
25:13–28 95
25:14–15 94
25:15 95
25:16 94
25:17–20 96
25:17–19 93
25:18–22 52
25:20 . . . . .52, 95

25:21–22 93
25:21 96
25:22 . . . . .52, 96
25:40 175
26:30 175
26:31 . . . . .51, 52
26:34 . . . . .94, 96
27:8 175
28:3 146
30:7–8. 140
31:1–11. 146
31:2 94
31:6 . . . . .91, 94
31:18 96
32:4 . . . . 91, 102
32:8, 31 102
34:12–16 192
34:17 181
35:10 175
35:30–35 146
35:34 91
36:1–4. 93
36:1–3. 146
37:1–9. 96
38:23 91

Leviticus

1:1–8. 194
4:12 164
6:11 164
10:14 164
14:34 18
16:7–10. 98
16:8–10. 98
16:10 98
19:4 181
20:14 192
26:1 181

Numbers

3:7–8. 50
3:30–31. 94
4:4. 95
4:15 . . . . .94, 95
6:23 99
6:24–26. . . . . 99, 210
6:27 99
7:9. . . . . .94, 95
7:89 96
8:4. 175
8:26 50
11:18–20 76
14:3–4. 76
16:40 140

17:10 . . . . 94, 364
18:5–6. 50
18:7 140
19:9 164
21:6–9. 102
21:8–9. 102
21:13 103
21:13, 26. 104
21:28 104
21:29 191
22–24 100
22:1–24:25. 100
22:5 198
22:5–6. 100
25:1 192
31:8, 16 . . . . 100, 101

Deuteronomy

1:1–4. 105
1:3. 83
1:5–4:43. 105
1:7. 18
1:8. 18
1:13, 15 147
2:11 125
2:12 18
3:8. 104
3:12, 16 104
4:1, 5 18
4:16, 17, 18 368
4:23–24. 181
4:26 105
4:44–11:32. 105
5:6. 88
5:18 192
5:23–26. 51
6:11, 18 18
7:3–4. 192
7:6. . . . . 182, 183
7:9. 99
8:9. 151
9:23 18
11:31 18
12–26 105
12:2–3. 181
12:2 116
14:2 183
16:19 147
17:2 191
21:15–17 74
23:12 228
26:18 183
27–28 105
27:1–8. 112

28:15 181
29–30 105
29:9–13. 104
29:17 191
30:11–16 265
30:19 105
31–34 105
31:9–13. 112
31:24–26 61
31:26 94
31:28 105
32:1 105
32:7 26
32:19 191

Joshua

1:4, 15 18
2:1. 106
2:5–7 110
2:6. . . . . 84, 110
2:7. 106
2:9–11. 106
2:15 110
2:16, 222, 24 106
3:15 . . . . 84, 110
4:19 83
5:10 . . . . 83, 110
6:3–24. 84
6:15 110
6:17–18. 110
6:17–19. 84
6:20 . . . . .84, 107, 110
6:20–21. 110
6:21, 23 157
6:24 . . . . .84, 107, 110
8:8, 19–20 107
8:30–35. 112
8:30–31. 111
9:21–27. 107
10:13 360
10:29 195
10:34–36 197
11:10 83
11:13 107
11:23a 107
11:23b-c 107
12:1 18
12:28 368
13–17 107
13:1 107
13:13 . . . . .107, 123
15:36 121
15:39 197
15:61 218

15:63 107
18:1 . . . . .107, 115
18:2–3. 107
18:26 131
19:15 371
19:47 362
21:13 195

Judges

1:29–33. 107
4:2. 83
6–7. 78
7:18–22. 111
8:20 157
8:21 147
9:37 173
11:18 104
11:26 83
16:23, 25. 113
16:27 113
16:29–30 113
18:3–6. 157
18:7 81
18:14 81
21:19 115

Ruth

1:1. 114

1 Samuel

1–10. 113
1:3. 115
1:9. 117
1:22, 24–25 157
1:24–28. 115
3:1–21. 115
3:15 116
4:1–4. 115
4:4. 94
4:10–22. 115
6:6. 85
10:2 371
10:25 97
13:21 28
17:4 . . . . .194, 199
17:6 111
17:12 117
17:33, 42. 157
17:52 121
19:24 69
22–24 156
24:13 360
24:23 156
30:24–25 147

2 Samuel

1:18 360
2:8–15. 122
3:3. 123
3:7. 122
5:8. 147
5:9. 120
5:10–12. 119
5:11 128
6:2. 94
6:3–4. 116
8:12 187
9:9. 157
13:17 157
13:37–38 123
14:20 147
14:32 123
18:18 . . . . .197, 252
21:16, 18, 20 125
21:20 125
21:22 125
24:19–25 132

1 Kings

3:1. 133
3:2. 116
4:21 126
4:24 187
4:30 . . . . .147, 149
5–8 127
5 95
5:1. 128
5:17–18. 127
6–7 181
6:1. . . . . 83, 131
6:19 94
6:21 96
6:23–28. . . . . .51, 52, 174
6:23, 29, 32 174
6:27–35. 51
6:27 52
6:28 96
6:29 52
6:35 129
7:1–12. 196
7:13–45. 129
7:13–14. . . . . .127, 133
7:14 146
7:29, 36 . . . . .51, 174
7:40 127
7:49 190
8:4–11. 94
8:6–7. 51
8:6. 94

8:7–8 52
8:7 95
8:8 95
8:9 364
9:16 214
10:1–8 147
11:1–8 192
11:4, 8 131
11:28 157
11:40 . . . . 76, 198
11:42 83
12:9 118
12:28 . . . . 76, 102
14:8 118
14:25 . . . . 76, 198
15:13–14 131
16:10 175
16:21–28 31
16:28 119
18:40 193
22:45 139
25:27 187

2 Kings

2:11 193
5:1–27 157
8:7–15 117
9:3–6 136
10:32–33 117
10:34 135
12:9 93
12:17–18 117
12:17 117
15:29–30 123
16:7–9 123
16:10 368
17:7–12, 15–18, 23 181
18:4 . . . . 102, 194
18:13–19:37 . . . . 160, 161
18:13–19:35 198
18:13 136
18:22 194
19:15 94
19–20 134
19:32–37 138
19:32–36 . . . . 136, 138
19:32–33 136
19:35–37 136
19:36–37 160
20:20 198
23:21 26
23:29 76
24:3 181
25:27–30 . . . . 138, 139

1 Chronicles

1:25 196
2:23 123
3:2 123
4:23 133
4:31 121
6:33–37 83
8:33 . . . . 122, 195
9:10 133
9:39 122
15:15 95
17 196
17:3 131
18:28 175
20:6 125
21:18–28 132
22:15 146
24:15 252
25 196
28:2 94
28:11, 12 . . . . 175, 368
28:18 . . . . 52, 368
28:19 . . . . 175, 368
28:21 175

2 Chronicles

1:3 . . . . 116, 176
1:13 176
2:3–18 128
2:13–14 129
3:1 131
3:10–13 51
3:14 51
5:7–10 94
5:8 . . . . 52, 95
5:9 95
5:10 . . . . 97, 364
8:11 192
9:26 126
9:30 83
11:6 235
11:21 123
12:2–9 . . . . 194, 198
20:14–15 139
20:14 140
20:1–30 139
20:1 139
20:34 139
24:8–11 93
26:5 140
26:23 140
27:11 187
29:3 194
29:4–5 206

32

32 134
32:1–23 . . . . 160, 161
32:5 137
32:9 160
32:20–23 138
32:21–22 136
32:21 160
33:2–9 181
35:3 94
36 141
36:22–23 . . . . 39, 141, 166

Ezra

1 141
1:1–11 166
1:1–3a 141
1:2–4 . . . . 39, 166
1:2, 7–11 160
1:3–11 206
2 39
2:1, 46 142
2:68–69 205
3:1–5 205
3:2–4:3 287
3:7–10 205
3:7 95
3:8–11 132
3:12–13 205
3:13 206
4:1–6:22 206
4:1–5 161
4:3 166
5:13–6:5 166
5:13–17 198
5:13–16 39
5:14–15 166
6:1–15 205
6:2–5 166
10:9 206

Nehemiah

1 191
2–7 191
2:8 206
2:11–7:4 206
2:12–15 143
2:13–15a 143
3:1–32 143
3:19 144
3:26 206
3:29 206
3:31 . . . . 144, 206
4:1–2, 7–8 191
7:6–7 39

7:26 235
8:1 206
9:17 76
10:20 252
10:32–39 206
12:31–40 143
12:44–47 206
12:44 206
13:4–7 206

Esther

1:1 145
1:1a 145
2:4 157

Job

1:5 . . . . 98, 368
1:21 147
8:8 26
28:1–11 150
39:28 156
40:10–11 180
42:1–2 147
42:8–9 368

Psalms

4 152
18 156
18:2 . . . . 156, 157
18:10 153
22 328
22:1–8 155
22:3 153
22:11–18 155
22:15 155
22:16 155
22:22–24 155
23:5–6 164
29 154
42 156
57 156
62 156
62:2 157
62:6–8 156
63 156
69:25 . . . . 256, 294
78:60 115
89 154
99:1 94
104 156
106:20 368
107:27 146
119:43 26
122:4 153

132:7–8 94
132:13–14 175
142–144 156
144:12 368
150 153

Proverbs

1:2–6 146
2:16–19 148
6:24–26 148
8:1–36 149
9:9–10 147
16:1–4 147
16:10–15 147
21:1 147
22:6 157
22:17 150
22:17–24:22 147
24:22 150
25:1–5 147

Ecclesiastes

3:1–8 147
3:10–11 26
5:18–19 147
9:7–9 148
11:8–10 149
12:14 147

Song of Songs

2:7 159
3:5 159
8:4 159
8:6 159
8:7 158

Isaiah

3:3 146
3:8, 25–26 255
7:2 118
7:3, 14 288
8:6 288
16:2 104
17 154
19:1 76
19:1–17 76
20:1–2 160
222:15–25 161
22:16 261
25:6–9 . . . . 163, 229
25:6–8 164
29 154
30:2 76
31:1 76

36–37 . . . . 160, 161
37 134
37:14 97
37:16 94
37:33–38 138
37:36–37 136
37:37–38 160
41:25 160
42:3 189
44:13 368
44:26–45:6 160
44:28 . . . . 160, 165
45:1–4, 13 165
46:9 26
52:11–12 166
52:13–53:12 167
53 167
53:8–9 167
53:9 261
53:11 . . . . 167, 169

Jeremiah

7:12–14 115
10:9 146
11:1–8 183
25:11–12 205
26:6 115
27:21–22 166
29 191
29:10 205
32:14 170
34:6–7 . . . . 169, 198
36:2 117
36:4–7 171
36:10–12 171
36:23 117
36:25 171
38:1 194
41 196
41:4–5 191
42:15–19 76
43:2–44:15 76
44:15 76
52:31–33 160

Lamentations

1:1–4a 172
1:1a 172
1:4 191
1:10 173
2:6a, 7a 172
2:8b, 9b 173
3:13,19 180
3:19–42 173

4:33–34 180
5 191
5:20 180

Ezekiel
8:3 368
8:10 368
8:14 236
10:10 368
14:20 368
20:5 182
27:8–9 146
28:3 368
28:13–14 174
38:12 173
38:16 175
40:1 83
43:10–11 175

Daniel
1–11 178
1:1, 3, 4 176
1:1, 3, 4b, 6a .176
4 179
5:29 199
5:30–31 166
9–12 177
9:2 205
9:15–20 368
9:16–17, 24 205
9:24–27 177
9:27 177
11–12 177
11:3–4 39
12 178
12:1–2 178
12:3 178
12:4, 9–10 178
12:6–7 178
12:10 178
12:11 177

Hosea
4:1 182
4:12–13 180
6:2 168
13:4–5 182

Joel
3:4 18
3:18 18

Amos
1:1 114

3:2 182
9:11 172

Jonah
1:17 168
3:4 184
3:5–8 . . . . .183, 184

Micah
5:2 235
5:6 . . . . .67, 68

Nahum
2:3–7 . . . . .184, 185
2:5b 185
2:6–7 185

Habakkuk
1:6–7, 15 186

Zephaniah
1:4–8 188
2:4 187

Haggai
1:1–8 206
1:2–4 132
1:2, 4 191
1:5–11 191
1:8–9 132
1:12–14 206
1:14 132
2:1–9 206
2:2, 3 205
2:4–7 188

Zechariah
1:7–6:15 206
4:2 . . . . .189, 190

Malachi
2:2 190
2:10–16 191
2:14–16 192
2:14 191
4:5–6 192
4:5 . . . . .192, 193

Matthew
1:1, 6 117
1:17 . . . . .117, 324
1:20 117
2:1 235

2:1a 235
2:2 237
2:16 . . . . .235, 237
2:19–20 241
2:20–21 19
4:1 244
4:5 244
6:9 245
8:14–15 246
8:28–34 233
10:23 19
11:14 193
11:20–24 247
11:21 . . . . .247, 278
15:39 248
16:17 249
17:7 294
20:29–34 251
23 251
23:1–3 251
23:2 251
23:29 251
24:1–2 . . . . .209, 253
24:1 255
24:3 209
24:15 177
26:55 208
27 328
27:7–8 256
27:8 . . . . .256, 294
27:27 328
27:35–36 256
27:56 248
27:57–60 257
27:57 260
27:59–60 258
27:60 . . . . .259, 261
28:2 . . . . .258, 261

Mark
1:1 261
1:21 329
4:36 262
5:1–13 233
5:1 . . . . .269, 270
5:35 264
8:22–26 278
9:12 193
13:1–2 209
13:1 255
13:3–4 209
13:14 177
15 328

15:43–46 257
15:43 260
15:46 259
16:1 248
16:3–4 258
16:3 259
16:4 259
16:9 248

Luke

1:1–4 24
1:3–4 26
1:5–26 252
1:17 193
1:32 117
1:57–66 252
2:1–20 265
2:1 265
2:2 . . . . 266, 267
2:7 235
2:4 117
2:7 235
2.11 117
2:21–39 208
2:25–35 253
2:25 331
2:41–49 208
2:49 209
3:31 117
3:38 50
4:23 360
4:31 329
7:4b–5 268
7:5 268
8:22 270
8:26–39 233
8:26 269
8:32 269
10:13 278
11:51 252
13:4 271
19:1 271
19:44 255
20:41 117
21:5 255
21:5–6 209
21:7 209
21:37 208
22:53 261
23 328
23:1 273
23:50–55 257
24:2 258
24:39 257

John

1:28 275
1:44 281
2:1 281
2:1–2 281
2:16 209
2:17 209
2:20 . . . . 132, 208
3:23 283
4:4–5 284
4:5 284
4:6–30 331
4:19–21 287
4:46 281
5:2 . . . . 287, 329
5:4 287
6:59 329
9:7 288
11:38–44 331
11:48–50 . . . . 290, 292
12:21 281
18:13–24 290
18:13, 24 256
18:19–23 290
18:31–33 293
18:37–38 293
18:24 290
19 328
19:13 328
19:31 257
19:38–42 257
19:38 . . . . 257, 261
20:1 260
20:25, 27 257

Acts

1:18–19 294
1:18 294
1:19 294
1:20 294
1:21–22 24
3:1 296
3:2 . . . . 212, 295
3:2, 10 297
5:37 266
7:22 62
10:1 298
13 300
13:6 299
13:6a 299
13:7 299
14:7–13 328
17:28 360
18–19 312
18:2 301

18:4 301
18:8 301
18:12–14 328
18:12–13 302
18:12 301
18:17 . . . . 301, 302
18:19–21 312
19 . . . . .304, 305, 306
19:1–9 312
19:9 330
19:19 312
19:22 308
19:23–20:1 312
19:23–41 312
19:29 303
19:31 304
21:11 213
21:27–31 213
21:29–29 306
21:32–28:31 213
25:8 307
26:1–23 307

Romans

16:21 301
16:23 . . . . 234, 308
16:23b 308

1 Corinthians

1:1 301
1:14 301
7:18–19 301
7:22 310
7:23 310
8 310
15:4 257
15:6 24
16:19 301

2 Corinthians

6:7 26

Ephesians

1:1 311

Philippians

1:1 314

Colossians

1:5 26
4:13 316

2 Thessalonians

2:4 177

2 Timothy

2:5 319
2:15 26
4:20 308

Titus

1:12 360

Hebrews

9:4 . . . . .94, 96
11:2–40 322
11:9 155
12:1 322
12:2 322

James

1:18 26

2 Peter

2:5 368

1 John

1:1–3 24
1:1 26

Jude

14 360

Revelation

1:8 246
1:16 330
2:8 323
2:9 323
2:12 326
2:12–13a 326
2:13 330
2:13a 327
2:15 326
6–19 177
11:2 177
13:18 324
21:6 246
22:13 246

Ancient Near Eastern Texts

Ahikar 2:22, 47 147
Ahikar 9 . . . . 146, 147
Epic of Gilgamesh 5:1–4 181
Gabriel Revelation 167, 169
Instruction of Amenemope 147
Ptah-Hotep 147

Manuscripts

Brooklyn Papyrus 733f 192

Manuscript "B" 269
P52 . . . . 293, 329
P75 269
א 269

Qur'an

Q Nuh 11:44 66

Dead Sea Scrolls and Related Texts

11Q19, Temple Scroll 220
11Q26 98
11QtgJob, Targum of Job 180
1Q20, Genesis Apocryphon 180
1Q33 2:15–3:11 111
1Q72 180
1QDan^{a-b} (1Q71–72) 178
1QIsa^a, Great Isaiah Scroll 167, 178, 222
1QpHab, Pesher Habakkuk 178
1QQoh^a, Ecclesiastes 178
1QS, Community Rule 164
1QSa 2.11–22, Messianic Rule 164, 165, 229
3Q15, Copper Scroll 220
4Q174, 2.3,4 .178
4Q180–181 178
4Q243–245, Pseudo-Daniel 177, 178
4Q246, Aramaic Apocalypse 178
4Q521, Messianic Apocalypse 193
4Q547, Vision of Amram 178
4Q550, Aramaic Texts (Proto-Esther) . .178
4Q558.4, 4QpapVision^b ar 193
4QDan^{a-e} (4Q112–116) 178
4QDan^c (4Q114) 179
4Q174, 4QFlor[ilegium] 177, 178
4QPrNab 178
4QPsa^a, Psalter 178
6Q7, papDan .178

Philo

Legat. 281 301
QG 2.82 67

Josephus

Ag. Ap. 2.73 257
Ag. Ap. i:17 127
Ant. 1.93 55
Ant. 1.113–114 67
Ant. 1.3.6 64
Ant. 1.4.2 67
Ant. 8.3, 3 51
Ant. 8.96 207
Ant. 8.97 208
Ant. 11.8.2 385

Ant. 15.11.2 .210
Ant. 15.11.3 .210
Ant. 15.11.5–6 208
Ant. 15.44 274
Ant. 15.391 .209
Ant. 15.392 .210
Ant. 15.398, 400 208
Ant. 15.400 .207
Ant. 15.417 .307
Ant. 15.420–21 208
Ant. 15.471 .213
Ant. 17.6 241
Ant. 17.174–181 243
Ant. 18.2 278
Ant. 18.3–4 .274
Ant. 18.4 265
Ant. 18.4.3 290
Ant. 18.28 281
Ant. 18.31 290
Ant. 18.55–59 274
Ant. 18.60–62 274
Ant. 20.205 .290
Ant. 20.206 .290
Ant. 20.221 .208
Ant. 20.219 .208
Ant. 20.9.1 245
J.W. 1.23.7 241
J.W. 2.20.6.572 248
J.W. 2.169–74 274
J.W. 2.175–77 274
J.W. 2.441 290
J.W. 5.5 208
J.W. 5.5.3 295
J.W. 5:184–185 207
J.W. 5.192 208
J.W. 5.193–194 307
J.W. 6.220–222 210
J.W. 6.222 208
J.W. 6.4.1 210
J.W. 6.9.4 212
Life 8b 282
Life 9 269
Life 193 290

Mishnah, Talmud, and Related Literature

Kelim 1.8 213
Middot 1.4 295
Pirqe R. El. 46 98
Qodashim 10 174
m. Shabbat 2.21 213
m. Sheqalim. 5.1–5 213
Sukkot 51:2 .208

y. Ta'anit 4:6, 68d .248
b. Yoma 21a 51
b. Yoma 54a 51
b. Yoma 54a 51
b. Yoma 54b 174
b. Yoma 72b 364

Apostolic Fathers

Clement, *Letter to the Corinthians* 250
Eusebius, *Hist. eccl.* 1.10 274
Eusebius, *Onomasticon* 40.1 283

Ignatius, *Mang.* 11 274
Ignatius, *Trall.* 9 274
Irenaeus, *Haer.* 274
Justin Martyr,
    Dialogue with Trypho 78, 235
Justin Martyr *2 Apol.* 5.4 327
Lactantius,
    The Death of the Persecutors 250
Tertullian, *Apol.* 21 274
Tertullian, *The Demurrer
    Against the Heretics* 250

Greco-Roman Literature

Embassy to Gaius, 299–305 274
Greek Anthology IX.58 312
Pliny the Elder, *Natural History* 5.17 216
Pliny the Elder, *Natural History* 5, 33 . . .326
Pliny the Elder, *Natural History*
    5, 29, 115 311
Ptolemy V, 2 311
Syncellus, *Chronological Excerpts* 55
Strabo XIV, 1, 20ff 311
Strabo, *Geography* 304

Subject Index

absolute (chronometric) dating, 35–36
AD (*anno Domini*), 22
'Ain Ghazal, 125
Abinadab, 116
Abraham, 74, 75, 76, 77, 80, 81, 104
Abrahamic covenant, 75
Agri Dagh, 65
Aharoni, Yohanan, 76, 162, 283
Ahisamach, 91
Ain es-Sultan, 109
Akkadian, 50, 58, 64, 67, 68, 69, 70, 80, 93, 122, 148, 182
Akkadian terms
  makurru, 64
  aranu, 93
  hasis kal sipri, 146
  umman, 80
  zaqaru, 70
  sharrukin, 67, 160
  shumer, 70
  simmiltu, 71
Alalakh, 73
Albright, W. F., 17, 18, 115, 157, 185, 219, 283–84
Amenhotep II, 91
Ammonite, 28, 101
Amorite terms
  amud-pa-ila, 80
  arriwuk(ki), 80
  arriyuk(ki), 80
  kudur, 80
  lagamar, 80
amulets, 86, 100, 109
Antiochus I, 60
Arabic terms
  'azdzu, 98
  al-judi, 65
  gamar, 218
  karabu, 50
  khirbet, 31
  la'aza'zel, 98
  tell/tall, 31
Aramaic, 25, 28, 39, 101, 118, 122, 124, 145, 146, 166, 168, 179, 180, 218, 219, 222
Aramaic terms
  bytdwd, 118
  deka', 213

hakel dama, 256
leyah, 213
Arav, Rami, 125
archaeology
  and the Old Testament, 45–46
  contributions biblical studies, 24–31
  definition of, 17–18, 20–21
  excavation procedures, 32–38
  methodology, use in biblical studies, 25–26
  overview of, 15–16
ark of the covenant, 52, 92, 93–96, 97, 117
Armenia, 61, 64, 65
Artemis, 311–12, 13
artifacts
  ark tablet, 58
  Artemis statue, 313
  Babylonian Chronicle, 185
  Babylonian map, 65
  black obelisk, 136
  Bene Hezir tomb, 252
  Berlin Topographical Relief, 90–91
  Caiaphas ossuary, 293
  Canaanite ostracon, 121
  ceramic bowl, 140
  cylinder seal, 78
  Cyrus Cylinder, 167
  Dead Sea text of Psalm 22:16, 155
  Egyptian sickle sword, 111
  Egyptian tomb painting, 84
  Ekron inscription, 188
  Enuma Elish Tablet, 48
  Epic of Atrahatsis tablet, 59
  Eridu Genesis Tablet, 57
  figurine, 131
  fiscal bulla, 115
  fishing boat (first century), 263
  Gabriel Revelation, 169
  Gallio inscription, 302
  Gilgamesh Epic Tablet, 58
  Great Isaiah Scroll, 168
  heal bone of crucified man, 257
  Hasmonean period jar, 171
  Herod the Great sarcophagus, 243
  Herod the Great inscriptions, 237–39
  Hittite treaty on bronze tablet, 105
  Ipuwer papyrus, 89
  Iron Age II seal, 153

Jar 35, 165
Jerusalem Prism, 138
John Rylands Papyrus (P52), 293
Kadesh Agreement, 107
King Uzziah inscription, 141
Lachish relief from Sennacherib's palace, 152
Lamentation over the Ruin of Ur Inscription, 173
Merneptah Stele, 90
Mesha Inscription, 104
Messianic Rule Parchment, 163
Paphos inscription, 299
Pilate inscription, 274
ration tablet, of Jehoichin, 139
Sargon II relief, 161
Sinaitic inscriptions, 85
Soreg inscription, 214
strigil, 323
Sumerian King List, 56
Sumerian love poem, 159
Caesarea Synagogue Officials Inscriptions 264
Tel Dan Stele, 119
Temple Scroll, 220, 221
terracotta plaques, 51
terracotta shrines, 134
Theodotus Inscription, 386
Torah Scroll Medallion, 217
Tower of Babel Stele, 72
undocumented antiquities, 72–73
Asenath (Egyptian wife of Joseph), 91
Ashkelon, 23, 90, 91, 144
Ashurbanipal, 48, 49, 59
Assyria, 29, 35, 38, 39, 52, 65, 67–69, 76, 94, 97, 123, 126, 135, 136, 142
Assyrian terms
  mutanu, 184
  summa izbu, 125
athletics, 313, 319–20, 322–23
Atrahasis Epic, 58, 59–60, 62, 65
Avigad, Nahman, 137, 161, 162,
Avraham Biran, 81
Avaris (Tell ed-Dab'a), 83, 84, 91
Baal, 101, 102, 111, 122, 153, 154, 155, 351
Babylon (Babylonian), 23, 39, 67, 68, 70, 72, 74, 80, 100, 166
Babylonian Chronicles, 23, 139, 160, 184–85
Babylonian Genesis, 48

Babylonian period, 39
Babylonian terms
  a-da-ap, 50
  apkallu, 49
  Ummanmanda, 185
Balaam, 100, 101, 102
Barkay, Gabriel, 99, 210, 216, 217,
BC (before Christ), 22
Beersheba, 61, 76
Berosus, 55
Bethlehem, 114, 115, 235–37, 243
Bethsaida, 123, 125, 278–80
Bezalel, 93, 96
black obelisk, 29, 135, 136
boats, 262–63
book of Daniel, dating, 176–80
Book of the Cow Heaven (see Destruction
    of Mankind)
Book of the Dead (Egyptian), 85, 352
Bronze Age, 38, 39, 75, 76, 79
bronze serpent, 102–03
Broshi, Magen, 224, 226, 291
Byzantine Empire, 19
Caiaphas, 290–91
camel (Bactrian), 76, 77–80, 361n45, 46
Cana of Galilee, 281–83
Canaan, 18, 20, 21, 45, 74, 75, 76, 80, 81,
    82, 83, 90, 98, 103, 107, 108
Canaanite terms
  'shb'l, 122
  bd', 122
Carbon-14 (see also radiocarbon), 36–37, 356
Carchemish, 101, 127
census (see Quirinius)
centurion, 268
Charlesworth, James, 257
cherub, cherubim 21, 50, 51, 52, 53, 93, 94
Code of Hammurabi, 73, 75, 83
coinage, 274
Colossae, 316–19
covenant, 99, 104–05, 130, 141, 183
crusades, 19, 75, 283
crucifixion, 256–57
Cyrus Cylinder, 39, 165–66
Dagon, temple of, 113, 114
Damascus, 135
Dan, 74, 81, 107, 117
Day of Atonement, 98
Dead Sea Scrolls, 16, 18 28, 31, 37, 72,
    100, 111, 164, 167, 177, 192–93, 204,
    218–29,
Deir el-Balah, 27, 125
Destruction of Mankind, 90
DNA, ancient, 37

Documentary Hypothesis, 75, 100
Douglas Petrovitch, 85
Early Bronze Age, 109
Earthquake (Tel-es-Safi), 114
Ebla, 49, 67, 68, 73, 74
Egypt, 21, 22, 28, 29, 74, 76, 82 83, 84, 85,
    86, 87, 126
Egyptian New Kingdom, 92
Eighteenth Dynasty, 84, 85, 91, 112
El-Araj, as location of Bethsaida, 280
Enuma Elish (Mesopotamian flood story), 48
Ephesian letters, 312
Ephesus, 303–04, 311–14
Epic of Atrahasis (Babylonian flood
    account), 47, 48
Epic of Ziusudra, 65
Erastus inscription, 308–10
Eridu Genesis (Sumerian Flood Account),
    47, 57, 65
Eshel, Hanan, 224, 226
Essenes, 203
exodus
  date of, 82–84, 92, 76, 362n75
  departure from Egypt, 21, 24, 27, 87–89,
    99, 104, 363n95
  Egyptian sorcerers, 87
  hardening of Pharaoh's heart, 84–86
  plagues, 84, 363n88
  significance of, 87–92
fall of man, accounts of, 49–50
Finegan, Jack, 71, 245, 248, 281, 282, 295
Finkelstein, Israel, 115, 116, 120, 132, 143,
First Jewish Revolt, 290
First Temple Period, 100, 133, 140, 142,
    143, 144
flotation, 34
flood, various accounts of, 55–63
Galilee, 233, 237, 254, 281–83
Garfinkel, Yosef, 119, 121, 135
Garstang, John, 109
garum (fish sauce), 239
Gath, 114, 125
Gaza, 19, 114
Gedaliah, son of Immer, 214
Gergesenes (Gadarenes, Gerasenes), 269–71
Gibeon, 116
Gilgamesh, 55, 57, 58
Gilgamesh Epic, 58–59, 55, 60, 61, 64, 65,
    67, 361n18
Gobekli Tepe, 53
Golan Heights, 19, 81, 117
golden calf, 91
Goliath, 111, 114, 121
Gordyenian Mountains, 61, 64

Gospel of John, date of, 293
Greece,
Greek terms
  aedile, 308, 309, 310
  aedilis, 309, 310
  aenon, 283
  agoranomos, 309, 310
  apekulisen, 258
  apothemenoi, 323
  archaiologia, 17
  archaios, 17
  arcosolia, 258
  asiarches, 305
  asiarchon, 304
  astuvomos, 309
  bema, 302
  deixai auto phos, 167
  logia, 17
  manumission price, 311
  megan, 258
  megas sphora, 259
  naos, 296
  nomen, 308
  ogkon apothemenoi panta, 319
  oikonomos, 308, 309, 310
  omega, 324
  omphalos, 173, 174
  onan, 311
  orusso, 155
  oruxan, 155
  panta, 319
  pistus, 324
  polis, 278
  praenomen, 308
  price, 311
  proskulisas, 258
  psephos, 324
  pterguion, 244
  purchase, 311
  quaestor, 310
  eleutheriai, 311
  ep'eleutheriai, 311
  epiphanein, 262
  epistropos, 237
  ermenon, 260
  Gigantomachia, 327
  glypho, 29
  hairo, 260
  hapax legomena, 28, 191
  hegemoneuo, 267
  heiron, 296
  hieros, 29
  ho dedokos, 324
  horaios, 295

hupomones, 322
isopsephism, 324
isos, 324
kathedras, 251
koine, 310
kome, 278
kulio, 260
kurios, 324
soma, 311
theotokos, 313
timan, 311
timas arguriou, 311
Gutfeld, Oren, 164, 165, 221, 229
Guzana, 127
Hagab Seal, 142–43
Harran, 53, 76
Hashmite Kingdom of Jordan, 18
Hasmonean Period, 39–40, 203
Hathor, 91
Hazael, 117, 136
Hebrew language, 28, 89, 100, 121
Hebrew terms
  'apiru, 84
  'ari, 155
  'aron, 93, 95
  'asah, 176
  'zz'l, 98
  adam, 50
  bama, 189
  bamah, 124
  ben hacohen hagadol, 212
  ben riyhu, 140
  Bene Hezir, 251
  berit hadashah, 168
  bet YHWH, 134
  Birket Israel, 211
  Bit-Humri, 135, 136
  Chaoskampf, 154
  E-kic-nu-jal, 172
  El, 74
  emequ(m), 146
  epesu[m], 146
  erez-yisrael, 18
  gdl, 70
  gemalim, 77
  golal, 260
  gullah, 189
  ha-na-ku-u-ka, 157
  ha'ot, 169
  ha'yeh, 169
  hahar, 181
  hakam, 147
  hanak, 157, 158
  hkm, 146

  hnk, 157
  hokmah, 146, 147, 158
  hydropotes, 317
  Ia-ku-u-ki-nu, 139
  Ia-u-a, 136
  ka'ari, 155
  ka'aru, 155
  kapporet, 96
  keruvim, 50
  ketubim, 177
  khemer, 71
  khopesh, 110
  kidon, 111
  kinor, 152
  Kokh, 256
  kokhim, 252, 256, 258, 292
  kopher, 64
  Kotel, 211
  la-melek, 35
  layhwh, 98
  lesheloshet yamin, 168
  lhgb, 142
  ma'aleh, 130
  maat, 146
  mar'eh, 175
  maskilim, 177
  massebot, 102
  Megillah, 145
  menorat zahab, 189
  meshiho, 166
  mezudah, 156
  midrashim, 178
  migdal, 70
  minyan, 164
  miqvaot, 212, 228, 290
  miqveh, 247, 290
  mirage, 143
  misgav, 156
  mot, 154, 155
  mutsaqot, 189
  na'ar, 157, 158
  na'arah, 157
  nasim nakriyot, 191
  ne'arim, 157
  neginah, 152
  nephesh, 252
  nolad, 125
  'or, 167
  peleshet, 18
  Pesach, 193
  pharaoh, 84
  pim, 28
  Ptgyh, 188
  rachel, 74

  'rrt ('ararat), 65
  sela', 156
  sequphim, 128
  seraph, 102
  shib'a mutsaqot, 189
  shinar, 70
  shofar, 111
  Simeon Bar [Ynh], 250
  sla'ot, 128
  soreg, 213, 307
  tabnit, 175, 176
  tabur ha'arets, 173
  tebah, 63
  tel, 31
  tsapah, 92
  tsir, 69
  tsor, 156
  tsuq, 189
  waw, 155
  ya-, 74
  Ya'akov, 74, 76, 124
  Yahad, 39, 218, 222
  yahu, 161, 162
  yam, 154, 155
  Yaw (Ia-u-a), 135
  Yaw-hu, 135
  yir'eh, 167
  yishmael, 76
  yisrael, 18
  yitsak, 76
  yod, 155
  yoseph, 76
  ywy (yawi), 90
Hellenistic Period, 39, 143, 144
Herod the Great, 203, 207, 298
Herodians, 203
Hezekiah, 29, 35, 97, 131, 136, 137, 138
hieroglyphics, 29–30
Hittite terms
  Tud-khalia, 80
Hittites, 29, 98, 106, 107
Hoffmeier, James, 88, 118
Horemheb, 92
intertestamental period, 203–05
Ipuwer Papyrus, 83, 89
Iron Age, 38, 39, 107, 114, 120
Iron Age I, 21, 109, 113
Iron Age I-IIA, 21, 75, 76
Ishtar Gate, 139
ISIS, looting by, 22
Islamic Waqf, 133, 209, 215, 216, 217, 353, 357
jar handle, as indicative, 36
Jehoiachin, 139

Jehoshaphat, 139
Jehu, Assyrian depiction of, 135–36
Jericho, conquest of, 107–10
Jerusalem, 19, 126, 132, 136–38, 254
Jesus Christ
    birth, 235–37, 265–66
    burial, 258–61
    crucifixion, 257
    Herod's attempt to kill, 241
    miracles in Chorazin, 247–48
    seat of Moses, 251
    temptation of, 244–45
Jethro, 102
Jochebed, 85
Jordan, 18, 19
Joseph, 74, 76, 91, 95, 157
Josephus, 31, 51, 55, 56, 60, 67, 127, 145,
    239, 243, 244, 245, 257, 266, 274
Josiah, 115, 142
Judah, 39, 117, 119, 120, 121, 122, 131,
    132, 138, 141
Judaism, 204, 264, 287
Judas Maccabeus, 203
Judea, 18, 19, 39, 92, 120, 121, 122, 144
Julius Wellhausen, 75
Kenyon, Kathleen, 23, 33, 108, 109, 110
Khirbet Qeiyafa, 21, 121, 122, 128, 132, 135
King David, 21, 117–19, 21, 120, 144,
King Hezekiah, 29, 35, 97, 102, 131, 136,
    137, 138
King List (Sumerian), 54, 55, 56–57, 60, 67
King Unas, 28 36
Kish, 55, 57, 67–68
Kitchen K.A., 45, 46, 57, 75, 77, 92, 179
Kloner, Amos, 258–260
Kopher, 64
Kurdistan, 64, 65
Kurds, 65
Laish, 74, 75, 81
Late Bronze, 78, 107, 108 109, 110, 112, 127
Latin terms
    Aelia Capitolina, 19
    anno Domini, 22
    Bethania, 275
    Betharaba, 275
    Dominus Flevit, 249
    epitpopos, 275
    hegemon, 275
    loculi, 258
    opus reticulatum, 272
    Opus Sectile, 214
    Palaestina, 19
    Pater Noster, 245
    Pax Augusta, 262

Pax Romana, 262
    sancta, 224
    scriptorium, 223
    terra cotta eulogia, 319
    travertine cippus, 300
    umbilicus, 173
Layard, A. H., 56, 135
Lebanon, 87, 128
Leshem, 81
Levant, 18, 20, 122
Levantine sanctuaries, 127
Legion X Fretensis, 254
library, 313
lifespans (antediluvian), 54–55
Luxor, 92, 95
Lyell, Charles, 32
Magdala, 248–49
Magen, Yitzhak, 224–227, 229, 287
magic, 312
Manasseh, 115, 123, 142
Marduk, 48, 60, 72
Mari, 68, 70, 73, 74, 75, 80
maximalists, 20–21
Mazar, Amihai, 26, 28, 91, 109
Mazar, Benjamin, 133, 211, 216, 298
Mazar, Eilat, 120, 126, 132, 133, 144, 216, 217
Medinet Habu, 92
Melchizedek, 81
Mesopotamia, 56, 58, 67, 68, 70, 76, 79,
    125, 128
Messiah, 243, 261, 262, 265–66, 288
Middle Bronze, 109
Middle Kingdom, 90
Millard, Alan, 60, 62, 75, 93, 118, 179
minimalists, 20–21
Minyas, 64
Moabite, 28, 100, 101, 104, 118
Mosaic Covenant, 97, 112
Moses, 39, 46, 56, 61, 62, 63, 75, 83, 87,
    104, 112
Mount Ararat, 59, 60, 61, 65–66, 361n19
Mount Cudi, 64, 65
Mount Ebal, 66, 111–12
Mount Masis, 65
Mount Nisir/ Nimush, 59, 64, 65
Mount Sinai, 112
Murphy-O'Connor, Jerome, 284, 292
Nebuchadnezzar, 72, 139
Neolithic, 53, 125, 282, 314
Nestorian heresy, 313
Netzer, Ehud, 237, 239, 241, 243
New Covenant, 164, 168, 352
New Kingdom, 84, 85, 86, 92, 95
Nile Delta, 91

Nimrud, 135, 137
Nineteenth Dynasty, 112
Nineveh, 48, 49, 67, 69, 136, 137, 143
Noah's ark, 63–66
Northern Kingdom, 31, 123, 124, 138, 140
Nuzi, 73, 74, 75, 80
Oholiab, 91, 93
oil lamps (as indicative), 37
Old Babylonian period, 79
olympics (see athletics)
Operation Scroll, 221, 226
ossuary, 250, 256, 292
ostraca, 134
Ottoman Empire, 19, 307
Palestine, Palestinian, 18–19
Patriarchs, 21, 24, 29, 38, 39, 45, 74, 75,
    76, 78
Pelagian heresy, 313
Pergamon, 326–27
Persian Gulf, 65
Persian Period, 39, 143, 144, 287, 295
Persians, 29
Peter, 246–47
Pharaoh, 31, 52, 83, 85, 86, 362n80
Pharisees, 203, 222, 251
Philippi, 314, 316
Philistine, 18, 19
Phoenician, 28, 95, 128, 129, 130, 133
Pilate, 273–75
Pixner, Bargil, 284, 291, 292
Pliny the Elder, 60, 326
polydactylism, 125, 126
postexilic period, 21, 24, 27, 75, 100
Primeval Revolt texts, 85
Proto-Canaanite, 28
pyramid, 28, 87
Quirinius of Syria, 266–67
Qumran, 18, 28, 36, 37, 39, 40, 98, 111,
    203, 204, 233
radiocarbon dating (see also Carbon-14), 37,
    66, 121, 351, 356
Ramsay, William, M., 266, 267
Ramesses IV, 92
Ramses II, 106, 112
Reich, Ronny, 114, 120, 212–213, 216, 288
Relative dating, 35
Red Sea, 85
Rephaim, 125
Ritmeyer, Leen (and Kathleen), 133–34,
    256, 294
Rosetta Stone, 29–30
Sadducees, 203, 222
Samaria, 18, 31, 52, 138, 233, 238, 284–87
Samaritan Pentateuch, 28

Samaritans, 284
Sanhedrin, 290
Saqqara, 28, 70, 87
Sargonic Victory Stele, 69
Sargon's Obelisk, 69
scribes, 146, 203, 251
Second Intermediate Period, 90
Second Jewish Revolt, 19, 40
Second Temple Judaism, 18
Second Temple Period, 37, 40, 51, 140,
    249, 251
Seleucids, 203
Semitic Languages, 28
Sennacherib, 136, 137, 138, 143
Septuagint (LXX), 145, 203, 356
Serabit el-Khadim, 91
serpent, 50, 87, 102–03
Shalmaneser III, 135, 136
Shiloh, 115, 116
Shimei, 125
Shukron, Eli, 114, 120, 213, 216, 217, 288
Shuruppak, 71
Sicarii (dagger men), 203
Simmonds Cuneiform Tablet (Ark Tablet),
    58, 65
Sinai, 45
Sinaitic inscriptions as Hebrew, 85
Sixth Dynasty, 90
slaves, 310–11
Smyrna, 323—24
Solomon, 45, 83, 96, 112, 120, 121, 123,
    126–27, 131, 132
Solomon's Temple, 52, 129, 130
Spring Hill, 109
Stele of Merneptah, 90
stratigraphy, 32–33

suzerain-vassal treaty, 104–05
synagogue, 246, 247–48, 249, 251, 264,
    268, 280, 281, 301, 312, 314
Syria, 13, 40, 51, 73, 80, 129, 266, 267, 311
Syro-Palestinian, 18
tabernacle, 52, 92–93, 95, 115–17, 287
Tales of the Magician, 75
Talmud, 40, 51, 145
Taylor Prism, 137, 138
tel
    description of, 31–32
    et-Tel, 278
Tell al-Kharrar, 277
Tell Abrag, 78
Tell as-Sufuh, 78
Tell Brak, 68, 70
Tell ed-Dab'a, 84, 91, 187
Tell el-Amarna, 363n101
Tell el-Ful, 190
Tell el-Hesi, 123
Tell er-Ras, 285, 287
Tell er-Rataba, 83
Tell es-Safi, 114
Tell es-Sultan, 84
Tell Fara, 357
Tell Fekheriyeh, 122
Tell Leilan, 68, 73, 75
Tell Maedikh, 49, 148
Tell Mozan, 68
Tell en-Nasbeh, 39
Tell Qasile, 113
Tell Ta'yinat, 127
temple, 21, 32, 51, 52, 58, 60, 70, 71, 76, 94,
    102, 113–14, 127, 128, 131, 236, 244–45,
    253–56, 266, 280, 284, 285, 287, 294,
    295, 296, 297, 298, 307, 311, 312, 313

Temple Mount, 37, 120, 132, 134, 143–44,
    244, 245, 253–56, 290, 297, 307
Temple of Ay, 92
Ten Commandments, 84, 96–97, 364n117
tetragrammaton, 90
Thebes (see Luxor)
thermoluminescence, 37
Thirteenth Dynasty, 125
Thutmose II, 112
Torah, 21, 80, 97, 100, 249
Tower of Babel, 70–73
Turkmenistan, 79
Tutankhamun, 93
Tzaferis, Vassilios, 270
Ugaritic, 28, 98
Ur, 70, 75, 76
Ur III, 79
Urartu, 61, 65, 65
Uruk, 55, 67, 68, 70, 71
Utnapishtim, 59
Valley of the Kings, 92, 95
weapons, 110, 111
West Bank, 18
Wiseman, Donald J., 183, 184,
Wood, Bryant G., 108
Xsayarsan, 145
Zagros, 65
Zealots, 203
Zechariah, 139–40, 252
Zertal, Adam, 112
Zerubbabel, 205–06
Zeus, 312, 236
Zias, Joe, 228, 252, 253, 257
Ziusudra Epic, 140